Government and Public Health in America

Government and Public Health in America

Ronald Hamowy

Professor Emeritus of History, University of Alberta, Canada and Affiliate Professor of Economics, George Mason University, USA

Edward Elgar
Cheltenham, UK • Northampton, MA, USA

Published by
Edward Elgar Publishing Limited
Glensanda House
Montpellier Parade
Cheltenham
Glos GL50 1UA
UK

Edward Elgar Publishing, Inc.
William Pratt House
9 Dewey Court
Northampton
Massachusetts 01060
USA

A catalogue record for this book
is available from the British Library

Library of Congress Control Number: 2006934138

ISBN 978 1 84542 911 9 (cased)

Typeset by Cambrian Typesetters, Camberley, Surrey
Printed and bound in Great Britain by MPG Books Ltd, Bodmin, Cornwall

To Clement:

ἀλλ᾽ ἓν γὰρ μόνον
τὰ πάντα λύει ταυτ᾽ ἔπος μοχθήματα.
τὸ γὰρ φιλεῖν

One word frees us from all the weight
and pain of life: that word is love.

Sophocles, *Oedipus at Colonus*

Contents

Acknowledgments   viii

Introduction   1
1   The Public Health Service   23
2   The Food and Drug Administration   103
3   The Veterans Administration   271
4   The National Institutes of Health   340
5   Medicare   444

Index   503

Acknowledgments

This project would not have been undertaken had it not been for the moral and financial support of the Social Philosophy and Policy Center at Bowling Green State University in Bowling Green, Ohio. I am especially indebted to Ellen and Geoffrey Paul and to Fred Miller, who were confident that a project of this nature could be completed despite the fact that its writer was notorious for his customary inertness and his unhurried deliberateness. The staff of the Policy Center were unstinting in their help and deserve my deep gratitude. I should also like to thank David Theroux of the Independent Institute in Oakland, California, who originally suggested that I undertake a study of this sort. Finally, and above all, my thanks go to Clement Ho, without whom no undertaking would be possible and whose unstinting help, encouragement, and confidence in me has made this project truly gratifying. I need hardly add that all errors and omissions are solely my own.

Introduction

Most Americans operate under the assumption that, unlike most other first-world countries, the supply and distribution of health care in the United States is in private hands and that market forces play the principal role in determining the quantity and price of medical services. However, while this might have been true at the beginning of the twentieth century it is far from the case today. Indeed, even if one puts aside the sizeable number of laws and regulations governing the structure, qualifications, and powers of the medical profession, the sale and distribution of pharmaceuticals, and the conduct of hospitals, and considers only the proportion of dollar expenditures, more than 45 percent of all such disbursements were made by some political entity and of that amount over 70 percent were made by the federal government in 2001.[1]

The extent of federal involvement in the American health care system is truly massive. Besides annual expenditures of over half a trillion dollars,[2] federal agencies provide some form of hospital and medical insurance to more than 83 000 000 Americans,[3] operate a system of hospitals staffed by physicians, nurses, and technicians that treat a veteran population of almost half-a-million inpatients and 4.5 million outpatients, provide medical and hospital services for 1.6 million American Indians and Alaska natives, over 8 000 000 military personnel and mobilized reservists, together with their families and survivors, and over 166 000 federal prisoners. Indeed, despite its reputation as a center of free-market medicine, the United States has one of the largest socialized medical establishments in the world.

Of course this has not always been the case. Barely more than a hundred years ago the federal government played almost no role whatever in the nation's health care. The only agency charged with responsibility for some medical aspect of Americans was the Public Health Service. Founded in 1798 as the Marine Hospital Service (MHS) during the administration of John Adams, it was originally charged with the care of sick and disabled merchant seamen and for this purpose it established several facilities along the eastern seaboard. The expenses of these hospitals were originally defrayed by a 20 cent-per-month deduction, later raised to 40 cents-per-month, from the wages of American seamen. In 1878 the Service's responsibilities were expanded to include administering quarantines, previously exclusively in the hands of the various states, and in 1891 the MHS was given authority over the medical processing of immigrants. However, its primary function throughout the century remained the care of sick and infirm seamen. It is perhaps worth noting that the costs of this service continued to be borne by either seamen themselves or by ship owners until 1906 and that general tax revenues were not used to underwrite the costs of government-administered medical care.

To the extent that government at some level was involved in the nation's medical institutions during the nineteenth century, these activities took place at the state level and were quite modest. Indeed, there was barely any intrusion whatever into medical practice until the last decades of the century. It was not until the last few years of the century that states began enacting legislation that effectively prevented physicians from practicing without a state license.[4] While a formal medical education was not required to offer oneself as a medical practitioner, the nation possessed a substantial number of medical schools at which the prospective doctor could enroll. These were privately owned for-profit institutions whose course of study customarily extended to two terms of three or four months each. While this might appear inadequate to prepare a student for general practice, the fact is that the state of medical knowledge was, for a good part of the century, extremely primitive and had not yet been placed on a scientific foundation.

It was not until 1864 that Louis Pasteur formulated the germ theory of disease after having conducted a series of experiments showing that diseases were caused by micro-organisms that were not spontaneously generated from non-living matter.[5] It was partially on the basis of Pasteur's work that in the following year Joseph Lister introduced the use of carbolic acid as an antiseptic in the treatment of wounds. Prior to this, physicians had no compunction about ministering to the wounded or performing operations immediately after having dealt with patients with infections. Both Pasteur and Lister were originally treated with hostility and resentment by most physicians, Pasteur, because he himself was not a physician but a chemist and microscopist and Lister, because it was thought inconceivable that doctors could actually contribute to the illness and death of patients. In particular, French medical practitioners totally neglected Lister's recommendations, with the result that during the Franco-Prussian War (1870–71) thousands of wounded French soldiers died for no reason other than having been infected by filthy doctors.

The derision with which physicians greeted Pasteur and Lister's discoveries was nothing new. Throughout the nineteenth century doctors had stubbornly resisted almost every breakthrough in the development of their discipline. Orthodox medicine for the first half of the century had adopted a course of treatment which they themselves dubbed 'heroic therapy', whose therapeutic arsenal was so toxic that it killed far more than it cured. Operating on the principle that symptomatic treatment was all that was required to bring about a cure, physicians engaged in aggressive bloodletting to reduce fevers, blistering to encourage the emission of harmful pus, and to administrating massive doses of emetics and purgatives to 'cleanse the stomach and bowels'. The most popular of these was calomel (mercury chloride), used to purge the intestines, and tartar emetic (tartrate of antimony), to produce intense vomiting. Both were lethal poisons, the effects of which were cumulative, and led to a substantial number of deaths.[6] Those who survived this treatment were then given large quantities of arsenic, which was thought to act as a tonic and improve appetite!

In response to such appalling treatment, several different approaches predicated on radically differing theories regarding the cause and treatment of disease developed. The earliest of these was known as eclecticism, developed by Samuel Thomson, a New England farmer and amateur botanist who, in 1813, patented a system of treatment that relied exclusively on botanical remedies, steam baths, and rest. Thomson repudiated heroic therapy in its entirety, referring to its medications as 'instruments of death' and provided an alternative therapy, although equally flawed in its theoretical analysis of the nature of disease, that was easily understood and that was far less harmful in its effects.[7] His favorite botanicals were lobelia, which was employed as an expectorant and emetic and which is still administered by practitioners today, cayenne, which served as a stimulant and tonic, and bayberry, employed as an astringent and stimulant. None was nearly as dangerous in moderate doses as were the mineral poisons associated with heroic therapy and all three still hold places in the modern medical armamentarium. Probably the most significant contribution eclecticism was to make to general practice was the benefit of rest to the patient's recovery, which had been effectively neglected by most orthodox practitioners. Because of its comparatively benign therapy, eclecticism became extremely popular and made serious inroads into orthodox practice.

A far greater threat to medical orthodoxy was homeopathy, the creation of Samuel Hahnemann, a German physician who had undergone a formal, rigorous medical education. Hahnemann's researches had led him to conclude that the most efficacious remedy for an ailment consisted in the administration of a drug that, when tested in a healthy person, most closely replicated the symptoms of the disease. This law, *similia similibus curantur*, formed the foundation of homeopathic therapeutics. Hahnemann had also developed a somewhat bizarre theory of optimal dosage which called for the administration of as attenuated an amount of medication as was possible, the more diluted, the better. Indeed, Hahnemann had recommended dilutions up to one-decillionth of a drop. While homeopathic medications might not have done much good, they certainly could have done no harm, a vast improvement over heroic therapy, or allopathic medicine as Hahnemann called it, which operated on the assumption that if it were shown that ten grains of some mineral poison were thought to improve the patient's health, than 100 grains was likely to be ten times as effective.[8] Equally important in Hahnemann's theory of disease was the prominent place given to the natural healing powers of the organism itself. Homeopathic physicians recommended fresh air, sunshine, bed rest, proper diet, and personal hygiene in an era when regular medicine regarded these as of little or no value. Certainly this aspect of homeopathy's therapeutic regimen accounted for its immediate and increasing popularity after its introduction in the United States in 1825.

Regular physicians reacted with alarm and hostility to the inroads made by eclectic and homeopathic doctors, both because their approach to illness was predicated on medical theories at radical variance from accepted practice and because of the competitive forces represented by physicians who had embraced them. Indeed, the American Medical Association (AMA), founded in 1847, had among its primary aims the introduction of effective licensing laws in the various states to reduce competition, especially the extremely effective competition posed by these heterodox sects. Yet despite the animus with which orthodox medicine regarded eclecticism and homeopathy, orthodox therapeutics was forced to abandon many of the more extreme recommendations of heroic therapy. By the 1870s homeopathy, emphasizing minute doses of medication and the recuperative energies of nature, and eclecticism, which relied on botanical and herbal remedies, had substantially altered regular medical therapeutics in the United States, lessening its dependence on huge doses of metallic medicines and bloodletting and adding to its *materia medica* a host of new botanical drugs. The two sects had firmly established themselves as competing systems of medicine, with homeopathy especially popular in the large urban areas of the east and eclecticism concentrated in the midwest and south. Of the 62 000 physicians practicing in 1870, estimates place the number of irregular practitioners at approximately 8000, with homeopaths accounting for two-thirds of this number.[9] Despite a string of denunciations in regular medical journals and by regular medical societies that these irregular practitioners were quacks, pure and simple, both homeopathy and eclecticism continued to attract patients at the expense of orthodox medicine.

In the absence of constraining regulations, medical schools abounded. While most medical education at the beginning of the century was via apprenticeship with a practicing physician, the demand for larger numbers of graduates than could be thus accommodated led to the creation of a more formal educational structure, with classrooms, lectures, and degrees, to which was ostensibly added an apprenticeship period of a year or so. Medical schools, of course, reflected the appallingly low level of medical knowledge that marked most of the century. All were proprietary, requiring attendance at, at most, a brief two-year program for graduation. Entrants were not required to have a high school degree and were permitted to take whatever courses were required in any order they chose. A pass grade in a majority of them was sufficient to receive a diploma. In 1871, when Harvard, under then President Charles Eliot, extended the academic year of its medical school from four months to nine, the length of training from two years to three, and compelled students to pass all their courses to graduate, they were the first school in the nation to impose such requirements. They were soon followed by some of the more academically oriented medical colleges, who in 1890 formed the Association of American Medical Colleges.[10]

It was not until 1910 that medical education was given its contemporary form with release of the Flexner Report, the name given a study sponsored by the Carnegie Foundation for the Advancement of Teaching entitled 'Medical Education in the United States and Canada'. The study's chairman was Abraham Flexner, a secondary school teacher and principal from Louisville, Kentucky, and the brother of Simon Flexner, onetime professor of pathology at the University of Pennsylvania and, from 1903, director of the Rockefeller Institute of Medical Research. Simon Flexner had been a firm adherent of stricter educational standards and was crucially influential in shaping his brother's views. Indeed, while Flexner's survey was ostensibly disinterested it was in fact undertaken at the behest of the AMA's Council on Medical Education, which, in 1908, had approached a receptive Carnegie Foundation to conduct the study on its behalf for the purpose of raising educational standards in medicine. The members of the Council, and particularly N. P. Colwell, Secretary of the AMA's Council, acted as advisors throughout and made substantial contributions to the Report's conclusions regarding each medical school and to the Report's general recommendations.

During his ten-month tour of inspection Flexner claimed to have visited and evaluated 156 graduate and twelve postgraduate medical schools in the United States and Canada. The Report was scathing in its indictment of the state of medical education in America.[11] Not only were the standards of admission and the education offered substantially below acceptable levels, but, Flexner insisted, all proprietary schools by virtue of being proprietary were totally unacceptable. By 1910 most states had introduced licensing laws that not only required that applicants sit an examination but that they also present evidence of having graduated from a medical school whose standards were at least those set by the licensing board.[12] Prior to the turn of the century the AMA had sought to raise educational standards by appealing to the medical schools themselves, but it soon became evident that this was hopeless inasmuch as the schools themselves were profit-making and therefore in competition with each other. It was only through legislative intervention and then only through the introduction of effective licensing laws in the various states that major reforms in the minimal educational level for practice were possible. Once licensing laws were established as the only portal of entry to the profession, it then became practicable to enforce whatever standards the state licensing board wished by setting as a prerequisite of all applicants for licensure that they had graduated from an institution satisfying certain criteria.

The effect of the Report on medical education was no less than cataclysmic. Where, in 1906, the AMA reported that there were 162 medical schools from which 5214 students graduated, by 1920 this number had been reduced to 85 schools with 3047 graduates.[13] It is true that this process had begun prior to release of the Report in 1910 but it was accelerated by the publicity the Carnegie study received and by the high costs associated with meeting Flexner's demands for clinical facilities, laboratories, and extensive libraries. The result was that a large number of schools were forced to merge and consolidate, and others to close. Particularly hard-hit were medical schools training heterodox practitioners, which tended to operate on tight budgets and whose students found it far more difficult to forego the opportunities to work that a shorter school-term allowed them. Indeed, one of the explicit goals of increasing the educational requirements for practice was to reduce competition from irregular physicians. Not only had allopathic doctors had to compete with homeopaths and eclectics throughout most of the nineteenth century, but they now found themselves having to contend with osteopaths and chiropractors as well.[14] Structuring the requirements of a medical education so that it reflected orthodox theories of health and disease in order to meet licensing requirements gave regular practitioners a substantial competitive advantage.[15]

From the perspective of the twenty-first century, raising the educational requirements for medical practitioners appears perfectly reasonable. Following the Flexner Report all Class A medical schools[16] instituted a year of college work as a prerequisite for admission and by 1918 this had been extended to two years. Medical schools were required to provide substantial laboratory facilities, whose use formed the core of a two or three-year curriculum comprising extensive clinical research. One effect of these reforms was that as the number of proprietary schools dwindled, more and more schools affiliated with universities, which in turn drew medical education away from private practice and more to medical research, at the cost, of course, of drastically reducing the number of schools and students.

While these reforms in medical education might strike the modern reader as consistent with improvements in the medical care offered the public, the facts proved otherwise. Under the comparatively free market in medical care that had prevailed in the United States during most of the nineteenth century, the quality of medical practice had gradually increased, both as a result of the emergence of competing sects and advances in medical therapeutics. The overall result was that by 1910 a good many physicians were actually in a position to be of some help to their patients, at the least by directing them to the effective painkillers then available. Unfortunately, it was just at this point that the AMA was able to severely curtail the number of practitioners. The reduction in the number of physicians was substantial, with the ratio of physicians to population dropping from one to 630 in 1906 to about one to 800 in 1929. More important, the transformation of the nation's medical colleges into institutions that emphasized laboratory work served little purpose inasmuch as the level of medical knowledge was so limited. At the turn of the century medical treatment, in the main, consisted of administering one of several palliatives, all of which were available to the patient directly at any of dozens of shops. Indeed, were it not for alcohol, morphine, and cocaine, the most commonly prescribed medications and the effective ingredients of most proprietary remedies, doctors could offer little help to their patients. One physician, writing of his practice prior to World War I, described it in this way:

> The usual procedure for a doctor when he reached the patient's house was to greet the grandmother and aunts effusively and pat all the kids on the head before approaching the bedside. He greeted the patient with a grave look and a pleasant joke. He felt the pulse and inspected the tongue, and asked where it hurt. This done, he was ready to deliver an opinion and prescribe his pet remedy.[17]

Even as late as the turn of the century most practitioners still distrusted the findings of the new science of bacteriology, refusing to accept the fact that invisible micro-organisms could bring about such massive, horrifying effects. The major cause of adult deaths during the late nineteenth century was tuberculosis,[18] which also struck a large number of those dying from other causes. In 1882 Robert Koch succeeded in isolating the bacillus that was responsible for the disease. Most physicians, however, dismissed Koch's discovery of the tubercle bacillus, preferring to hold that tuberculosis was an hereditary ailment. Nor did they support public health measures that would have substantially reduced the disease's transmission. Fortunately the situation with respect to diphtheria was somewhat different. The bacillus responsible for this virulent disease had been uncovered in the 1880s and a serviceable antitoxin was developed by Emil von Behring and Shibasaburo Kitasato, working in Koch's laboratory, in 1894.[19] While there was some professional resistance to use of the antitoxin, public interest was so great that the cities' public health departments became strong supporters of its use. As a result, physicians in almost all the nation's larger cities were compelled to administer the serum, with excellent results.[20]

Other than diphtheria antitoxin, however, the physician's arsenal of effective medications at the turn of the century was extremely limited. The most important of these were digitalis, quinine, morphine, and aspirin. The medical uses of digitalis (foxglove) had been discovered in the eighteenth century but its use as a drug for strengthening the heart was not common until the mid-nineteenth century when it became an important part of the *materia medica* of eclectic physicians and when it came into general use by orthodox practitioners. Quinine, from cinchona bark, had been known since the seventeenth century and was in common use, especially in cases of malaria. Certainly the most impressive addition to the list of medications available to the physician in the nineteenth century was aspirin, which made its appearance in the last days of the century. A nonnarcotic, aspirin was found to have wide-ranging analgesic properties and soon was regularly prescribed for fevers, pains, and inflammations. Its properties were discovered by Felix Hoffmann, a chemist with Bayer AG in 1897 and patented by the firm in March 1899.

The area of medicine that experienced the most dramatic change over the course of the nineteenth century was surgery. One historian notes that 'thanks to bold individuals and some epochal innovations, surgery changed more in the nineteenth century than in the previous two thousand years'.[21] Despite this the modern reader would be shocked at how primitive in most other respects surgery remained. However, two important advances took place between 1840 and 1880 that revolutionized surgical interventions. The first of these was the introduction of anesthesia, which occurred in the 1840s when the anesthetic properties of nitrous oxide and ether were discovered in the United States. However, ether's side-effects, irritation of the lungs and nausea, encouraged the search for a substitute and led to chloroform being employed to relieve labor pains in a pregnant woman in Edinburgh in 1847.[22] While the use of anesthetics was an enormous boon to patients, who were now spared the excruciating agony of being operated on while fully conscious, surgery was still extremely dangerous and fatality rates were staggeringly high.[23]

These death rates were largely a result of septicaemia, which was not eliminated until the introduction of antisepsis by Joseph Lister, who used carbolic acid to wash his hands and to bathe the wound. In 1867 he reported his procedure in the *Lancet*, Britain's leading medical publication, but most of the surgical profession were incredulous and it was not until the first decades of the twentieth century that asepsis became universal. Even after physicians began to adopt carbolic washes prior to surgery, operating rooms remained quite dangerous places. One physician, writing of the last decade of the century, described them in this way:

> The surgeon arrived and threw off his jacket to avoid getting blood or pus on it. He rolled up his shirt-sleeves and in the corridor to the operating room, took an ancient frock from a cupboard; it bore signs of a chequered past and was utterly stiff with old blood. One of these coats was worn with special pride, indeed joy, as it had belonged to a retired member of the staff. The cuffs were rolled up to only just above the wrists, and the hands were washed in a sink. Once clean (by conventional standards), they were rinsed in carbolic-acid solution.[24]

Anesthesia and asepsis radically altered surgery but their full benefits did not emerge until the twentieth century, when the modern sterile and gleaming operating rooms became standard. Prior to that surgeons would penetrate the major body cavities only as a last resort. Indeed, septicaemia was so common that being sent to the hospital often constituted a sentence of death. However, by the start of the new century doctors began exploring the abdomen, chest, and skull, and obstetricians were prepared to perform caesarian sections, which earlier had been undertaken only in the direst emergencies.

While some of these surgical interventions took place in hospitals, most did not. Prior to the twentieth century there were few special advantages to performing surgery in a hospital rather than at home. Indeed, during most of the century the incidence of iatrogenic, that is, medically induced, infections in hospital wards was so high that a substantial proportion of physicians refused to send their patients there.[25] Instead, the kitchen in private homes served as a temporary operating room and continued to do so until the older charitable hospitals, most of which were filthy, squalid structures with inadequate ventilation, were replaced by more modern structures.[26] So long as the surgeon did not require a wide range of specialized equipment and so long as the household kitchen supplied most of what the physician needed, operations continued to be performed at home. However, this changed by the beginning of the twentieth century when small urban apartments became more common and more modern hospitals were constructed.

Hospitals had their origin in homes for those patients, mostly indigent, whose circumstances ruled out family care. Their costs were underwritten by the wealthy and whatever medical care was available was donated by local physicians. It appears that a good deal of prestige attached to those practitioners who were associated with a hospital, largely because hospitals were used as educational centers for future doctors. The result was that physicians vied for the privilege of associating their name with these institutions.[27] However, the establishment of more hospitals, despite their charitable nature, did not win universal support since, in the minds of many, they were for so many decades associated with pain and death. Towards the end of the century public attitudes changed as hospitals took on a more modern appearance and reflected a concern for cleanliness and good ventilation. Not only did the introduction of antiseptic surgery play a crucial role in this change but so did the emergence of a dedicated, trained nursing profession. At the same time, a series of technological innovations placed at the disposal of the diagnostician and surgeon equipment that permitted them to monitor the body. In 1895 X-rays were discovered and in 1900 the electrocardiograph was first employed.

Anesthesia, antisepsis, the introduction of specialized diagnostic and surgical equipment, the presence of a trained nursing staff, all contributed to the transformation of the hospital from the charitable almshouse for the indigent sick of the nineteenth century to its twentieth-century counterpart. Unlike the other changes that were to revolutionize medical services, almost all these modifications were in place by the last decade of the nineteenth century. The number of hospitals is indicative of their reception by the public. In 1874 there were only 149 hospitals operating in the United States, each averaging 25 beds, or a total of approximately 3725 beds By 1906 the number of hospitals had increased to 2411 and by 1927 had reached 6807, with a total of over 895 000 beds.[28] Over the next 50 years the number of hospitals remained fairly constant, reaching 6955 in 1980, and then declined to 5900, with 987 000 beds, in 2001.

The sophistication of modern biotechnology is reflected in the staggering increase in hospital costs between 1940, when a private hospital room averaged $7.00 per day[29] (about $88.00 in current dollars), to the present, when it varies between $1200.00 and $1800.00 a day. In addition, patients were, and continue to be, charged for the use of specialized diagnostic and intensive care equipment. While in 1940 a simple appendicectomy cost $188.00 ($2367.00 in 2001 dollars), today hospitals charge about $20 000.00 for a similar operation. However, a good percentage of the procedures currently undertaken did not exist 65 years ago, the most spectacular of which are the transplantation of organs. The charges for these procedures are equally dramatic. The average heart transplant costs $150 000.00, while the price for an average liver transplant averages approximately $250 000.00!

While the hospitals were undergoing transformation into the shape they take today, medical care in most other respects remained quite rudimentary. The chemotherapeutic revolution in medicine was not to occur until the 1920s. We would do well to remember that, prior to the turn of the century, beside immunization against rabies and smallpox[30] there were really only a handful of pharmaceuticals that could be said to be medically efficacious: digitalis, diphtheria antitoxin, aspirin, ether, morphine, and quinine. This is true despite the fact that mortality rates had been steadily dropping throughout the nineteenth and first quarter of the twentieth century. The reduction in the death rate, however, was a function – not of advances in medicine – but of improvements in nutrition and sanitation.[31] Thomas McKeown, the pre-eminent historian of social medicine, has noted that:

> With the exception of vaccination against smallpox, whose contribution was small, the influence of immunization and therapy on the death-rate was delayed until the twentieth century, and had little effect on national mortality trends before the introduction of sulphonamides in 1935. Since that time it has not been the only, or, probably, the most important influence.[32]

The state of medicine at the turn of the twentieth century was thus one where the therapeutic abilities of physicians were extremely limited and where the medical armamentarium available to practitioners was confined to a few effective medications. These were all available to the general population, whether prescribed by a physician or not, at a host of general stores and the few specialized pharmacies that were beginning to appear, both in unadulterated form or as constituent elements in a wide range of proprietary products. Pharmacists, like physicians, were for the most part unlicensed until state legislatures, under intense pressure from the state pharmaceutical societies, began enacting legislation licensing druggists in the last 15 years of the nineteenth century.[33] The sale and distribution of drugs, on the other hand, remained unregulated until after the turn of the century. There were no effective legal impediments to purchasing either cocaine or opiates – or their derivatives – throughout the country before the twentieth century.[34]

The Progressive Era is the name given to the period that witnessed the enormous transformation that occurred in American social and economic life. Between 1885 and 1914 governments at all levels undertook the most extensive intrusion into the private affairs of citizens that has ever been attempted in the history of the nation. During this period both the states and the federal government enacted legislation touching on every facet of social behavior and created administrative agencies to direct, often in minute detail, how we were to act in particular situations. It was during this period that states passed laws licensing physicians and pharmacists, began to regulate the sale of certain drugs, and instituted a wide range of social hygiene measures aimed at eliminating physically or psychologically unhealthy behavior.[35] At the federal level this philosophy of government was wedded to the personal ambitions of President Theodore Roosevelt. Roosevelt and his supporters envisioned an America in which the government, acting in the public interest, would direct a wide range of our actions.

In the area of public health, this ideological shift from the primacy of individual rights to an aggressive concern for social justice through government regulation led to the creation and enlargement at the federal level of several bureaus empowered with supervising various aspects of the nation's health. In 1902 the Marine Hospital Service changed its name to the Public Health and Marine Hospital Service to reflect the agency's greater role in overseeing federal health programs and ten years later it was shortened to the all-inclusive Public Health Service. Four years following the renaming of the Marine Hospital Service, in 1906, the administration of Theodore Roosevelt achieved one of its greatest legislative victories with passage of the Meat Inspection Act and the Pure Food and Drugs Act, which fixed certain standards for the purity of food and drugs, prohibited their distribution or sale if they were either adulterated or misbranded, and mandated that certain ingredients be shown on their labels. Responsibility for enforcing the Pure Food and Drugs Act was originally placed in the Bureau of Chemistry of the Department of Agriculture, which in the 1930s became the Food and Drug Administration with plenary authority over which drugs could be sold and for which purposes.

The proliferation of federal programs dealing with the nation's health was interrupted by World War I but resumed in 1921 with the establishment of the Veterans' Bureau, which was empowered – among other benefits – to extend medical and hospital services to veterans who had been injured or incapacitated during the conflict. Some nine years later a division of the Public Health Service that had devoted itself to bacteriological research was elevated to the National Institute of Health (NIH). The NIH was authorized to conduct its own inquiries into biomedicine and to underwrite extramural research through fellowships and grants. The Institute's funding in its first year of operation as the NIH was $43 000. This marked the advent of public funding of medical research and led to the truly phenomenal growth of the NIH, whose fiscal year (FY) 2004 budget is slightly less than $28 billion.

The most recent extension of the national government into the area of health care occurred in 1965 and was some half a century in the making. In the decade and a half prior to the outbreak of World War I a number of European countries had enacted mandatory national health-insurance schemes. Their seeming success encouraged American reformers to agitate for similar legislation in Washington, with the aid of a number of high-ranking politicians, among them Theodore Roosevelt, who lent his support to the proposal in 1912. Despite repeated attempts over the next 50 years to enact a health-insurance bill, however, Congress was unsuccessful until the first session of the 89th Congress. After successes in both the House and Senate, President Lyndon Johnson, on 30 July 1965 was able to sign a measure extending health-care insurance to all Americans over the age of 65 and to the indigent.

What follows is an account of these five agencies – the Public Health Service, the Food and Drug Administration, the Veterans Administration, the National Institutes of Health, and the Medicare program – which make up the overwhelming proportion of federal efforts in the area of health care. The discussion touches on the efforts that were made to initiate these programs, the forces that opposed them, and the dynamics that account for their spectacular growth. We would do well to keep in mind that we are here dealing with administrative structures that are political in nature and are therefore subject to political forces which often bear no relation to the underlying realities. Thus, the actual demand for a specific medical service need not, and most probably does not, reflect the expenditures Congress was prepared to allocate for that purpose. Nor, one need hardly add, do these expenditures reflect the efforts invested in enforcing specific regulations, which were often counterproductive.

Table 1   National Health Care Expenditures: Aggregates and Per Capita Amounts by Type of Expenditure and Source of Funds, Selected Calendar Years 1929–1965

Type of Expenditure	1929	1940	1950	1955	1960	1965
National Health Expenditures ($ billions)	3.6	4.0	12.7	17.7	26.9	41.7
As a percentage of GNP	3.5%	4.0%	4.4%	4.4%	5.3%	6.0%
Source of Funds						
Private Expenditures ($ billions)	3.2	3.2	9.2	13.2	20.3	30.9
Public Expenditures ($ billions)	.5	.8	3.4	4.6	6.6	10.8
Federal Expenditures ($ billions)	–	–	1.6	2.0	3.0	5.5
State/Local Expenditures ($ billions)	–	–	1.8	2.6	3.6	5.2
Per Capita Expenditures ($)	29.49	29.62	81.86	105.38	146.30	210.89
Source of Funds						
Private Expenditures	25.49	23.61	59.62	78.33	110.20	156.32
Public Expenditures	4.00	6.03	22.24	27.05	36.10	54.57
Federal Expenditures	–	–	10.49	11.90	16.42	27.97
State/Local Expenditures	–	–	11.75	15.15	19.69	26.60
Percentage Distribution of Funds	100.0%	100.0%	100.0%	100.0%	100.0%	100.0%
Private Funds	86.4	79.7	72.8	74.3	75.3	74.1
Public Funds	13.6	20.3	27.2	25.7	24.7	25.9
Federal Funds	–	–	12.8	11.3	11.2	13.3
State/Local Funds	–	–	14.4	14.4	13.5	12.6
Annualized Percentage Change from previous year shown						
National Health Care Expenditures	–	.8%	12.2%	7.0%	8.7%	9.2%
Private Expenditures	–	.1%	11.2%	7.4%	9.0%	8.8%
Public Expenditures	–	4.6%	15.5%	5.8%	7.8%	10.2%
Federal Expenditures	–	–	–	4.3%	8.5%	12.9%
State/Local Expenditures	–	–	–	7.0%	7.2%	7

Table 2   National Health Care Expenditures: Aggregates and Per Capita Amounts by Type of Expenditure and Source of Funds, Calendar Years 1966–1973

Type of Expenditure	1966	1967	1968	1969	1970	1971	1972	1973
National Health Expenditures ($ billions)	45.1	51.3	58.2	65.7	74.7	83.3	93.5	103.2
As a percentage of GNP	6.1%	6.4%	6.7%	7.0%	7.5%	7.0%	7.9%	7.8%
Source of Funds								
Private Expenditures ($ billions)	32.5	32.4	36.1	40.8	46.9	61.6	58.1	63.9
Public Expenditures ($ billions)	13.6	19.0	22.1	24.9	27.8	31.7	35.4	39.3
Federal Expenditures ($ billions)	7.4	11.9	14.1	16.1	17.7	20.3	22.9	25.2
State/Local Expenditures ($ billions)	6.1	7.0	8.0	8.8	10.1	11.3	12.5	14.1
Per Capita Expenditures ($)	230.29	253.73	284.97	318.50	357.90	394.23	437.77	478.34
Source of Funds								
Private Expenditures	162.47	159.98	176.82	197.78	224.68	244.36	271.89	296.19
Public Expenditures	67.82	93.75	108.15	120.72	133.22	149.87	165.88	182.15
Federal Expenditures	37.19	58.90	69.05	77.95	84.69	96.18	107.13	116.75
State/Local Expenditures	30.63	34.84	39.10	42.77	48.54	53.68	58.75	65.40
Percentage Distribution of Funds	100.0%	100.0%	100.0%	100.0%	100.0%	100.0%	100.0%	100.0%
Private Funds	70.6	63.1	62.0	62.1	62.8	62.0	62.1	61.9
Public Funds	29.4	36.9	38.0	37.9	37.2	38.0	37.9	38.1
Federal Funds	16.1	23.2	24.3	24.5	23.7	24.4	24.5	24.5
State/Local Funds	13.3	13.7	13.7	13.4	13.6	13.6	13.4	13.7
Annualized Percentage Change from previous year shown								
National Health Care Expenditures	10.5%	11.4%	13.4%	12.9%	13.6%	11.5%	12.3%	10.3%
Private Expenditures	5.1%	[-.5%]	11.6%	13.0%	14.8%	10.1%	12.5%	10.0%
Public Expenditures	25.7%	39.7%	16.5%	12.7%	11.6%	13.9%	11.9%	10.9%
Federal Expenditures	34.5%	60.1%	18.4%	14.0%	9.8%	15.0%	12.6%	10.0%
State/Local Expenditures	16.5%	15.0%	13.3%	10.5%	14.7%	12.0%	10.6%	12.4%

14

Table 3 National Health Care Expenditures: Aggregates and Per Capita Amounts by Type of Expenditure and Source of Funds, Calendar Years 1974–1981

Type of Expenditure	1974	1975	1976	1977	1978	1979	1980	1981
National Health Expenditures ($ billions)	116.4	132.7	149.7	169.2	189.3	214.6	248.1	287.0
As a percentage of GNP	8.1%	8.6%	8.7%	8.8%	8.8%	8.9%	9.1%	9.4%
Source of Funds								
Private Expenditures ($ billions)	69.3	76.5	86.7	99.1	110.0	124.5	142.9	165.8
Public Expenditures ($ billions)	47.1	56.2	62.9	70.1	79.4	90.1	105.2	121.2
Federal Expenditures ($ billions)	30.4	37.1	42.6	47.4	53.7	60.8	71.0	83.3
State/Local Expenditures ($ billions)	16.6	19.1	20.3	22.7	25.7	29.3	34.2	37.9
Per Capita Expenditures ($)	534.63	603.57	574.14	754.81	835.57	936.92	1054.0	1207.0
Source of Funds								
Private Expenditures	318.18	348.08	390.63	442.14	485.29	543.61	607.0	697.0
Public Expenditures	216.44	255.49	283.51	312.67	350.27	393.31	447.0	510.0
Federal Expenditures	139.86	168.61	191.73	211.39	236.84	265.41	302.0	350.0
State/Local Expenditures	76.58	86.88	91.78	101.28	113.44	127.70	145.0	159.0
Percentage Distribution of Funds	100.0%	100.0%	100.0%	100.0%	100.0%	100.0%	100.0%	100.0%
Private Funds	59.5	57.7	57.9	58.6	58.1	58.0	57.6	57.8
Public Funds	40.5	42.3	42.1	41.4	41.9	42.0	42.4	42.2
Federal Funds	26.2	27.9	28.5	28.0	28.3	28.4	28.6	29.0
State/Local Funds	14.3	14.4	13.6	13.4	13.6	13.7	13.8	13.2
Annualized Percentage Change from previous year shown								
National Health Care Expenditures	12.8%	14.0%	12.8%	13.1%	11.9%	13.4%	15.6%	15.7%
Private Expenditures	8.4%	10.5%	13.3%	14.3%	10.9%	13.2%	15.1%	16.0%
Public Expenditures	19.9%	19.2%	12.0%	11.4%	13.2%	13.5%	16.2%	15.2%
Federal Expenditures	20.9%	21.8%	14.8%	11.4%	13.2%	13.3%	16.4%	17.3%
State/Local Expenditures	18.2%	14.6%	6.6%	11.5%	13.2%	14.0%	15.8%	10.9%

15

Table 4   National Health Care Expenditures: Aggregates and Per Capita Amounts by Type of Expenditure and Source of Funds, Calendar Years 1982–1989

Type of Expenditure	1982	1983	1984	1985	1986	1987	1988	1989
National Health Expenditures ($ billions)	323.6	357.2	390.2	420.1	452.3	492.5	544.0	604.1
As a percentage of GNP	10.2%	10.5%	10.3%	10.5%	10.7%	10.9%	11.2%	11.6%
Source of Funds								
Private Expenditures ($ billions)	188.4	209.7	230.7	245.7	260.9	282.9	315.8	350.9
Public Expenditures ($ billions)	135.3	147.5	159.5	175.1	191.3	209.6.	228.2	253.3
Federal Expenditures ($ billions)	93.2	102.7	111.7	123.6	132.6	143.5	156.7	174.4
State/Local Expenditures ($ billions)	42.1	44.8	47.8	51.5	58.8	66.2	71.5	78.8
Per Capita Expenditures ($)	1348	1473	1595	1700	1813	1955	2139	2354
Source of Funds								
Private Expenditures	784	865	943	992	1046	1123	1242	1367
Public Expenditures	563	608	652	709	767	832	898	987
Federal Expenditures	388	424	456	500	532	570	616	680
State/Local Expenditures	175	185	195	208	236	263	281	307
Percentage Distribution of Funds	100.0%	100.0%	100.0%	100.0%	100.0%	100.0%	100.0%	100.0%
Private Funds	58.2	58.7	59.1	58.3	57.7	57.4	58.0	58.1
Public Funds	41.8	41.3	40.9	41.7	42.3	42.6	42.0	41.9
Federal Funds	28.8	28.8	28.6	29.4	29.3	29.1	28.8	28.9
State/Local Funds	13.0	12.5	12.3	12.3	13.0	13.4	13.1	13.0
Annualized Percentage Change from previous year shown								
National Health Care Expenditures	12.8%	10.4%	9.2%	8.9%	7.7%	8.9%	10.5%	11.1%
Private Expenditures	13.6%	11.3%	10.0%	8.5%	6.5%	8.4%	11.6%	11.1%
Public Expenditures	11.6%	9.1%	8.1%	9.6%	9.3%	9.6%	8.9%	11.0%
Federal Expenditures	11.9%	10.2%	8.7%	11.4%	7.3%	8.2%	9.2%	11.3%
State/Local Expenditures	11.1%	6.4%	6.8%	5.3%	14.2%	12.6%	8.1%	10.2%

Table 5   National Health Care Expenditures: Aggregates and Per Capita Amounts by Type of Expenditure and Source of Funds, Calendar Years 1990–1997

Type of Expenditure	1990	1991	1992	1993	1994	1995	1996	1997
National Health Expenditures ($ billions)	697.5	761.3	833.6	892.3	949.4	993.7	1042.5	1092.4
As a percentage of GNP	12.6%	12.9%	13.3%	13.6%	13.7%	13.7%	13.6%	13.5%
Source of Funds								
Private Expenditures ($ billions)	413.1	441.0	477.0	505.1	528.6	536.5	561.1	585.3
Public Expenditures ($ billions)	284.3	320.3	356.5	387.2	420.8	455.2	481.4	507.1
Federal Expenditures ($ billions)	195.8	224.4	254.8	278.5	303.6	326.0	348.0	367.0
State/Local Expenditures ($ billions)	88.5	95.8	101.8	108.6	117.2	129.2	133.4	140.0
Per Capita Expenditures ($)	2688	2902	3144	3331	3510	3637	3781	3925
Source of Funds								
Private Expenditures	1592	1681	1799	1886	1954	1970.7	2034.9	2103.1
Public Expenditures	1096	1221	1345	1445	1556	1665.9	1745.5	1822.0
Federal Expenditures	754	856	961	1040	1122	1193.0	1262.0	1318.9
State/Local Expenditures	341	365	384	406	433	472.9	483.7	503.1
Percentage Distribution of Funds	100.0%	100.0%	100.0%	100.0%	100.0%	100.0%	100.0%	100.0%
Private Funds	59.2	57.9	57.2	56.6	55.7	54.2	53.8	53.6
Public Funds	40.8	42.1	42.8	43.4	44.3	45.8	46.2	46.4
Federal Funds	28.1	29.5	30.6	31.2	32.0	32.8	33.4	33.6
State/Local Funds	12.7	12.6	12.2	12.2	12.3	13.0	12.8	12.8
Annualized Percentage Change from previous year shown								
National Health Care Expenditures	11.6%	9.1%	9.5%	7.0%	6.4%	4.9%	4.9%	4.8%
Private Expenditures	10.6%	6.7%	8.2%	5.9%	4.7%	2.6%	4.2%	4.3%
Public Expenditures	13.2%	12.7%	11.3%	8.6%	8.7%	7.7%	5.7%	5.3%
Federal Expenditures	11.9%	14.6%	13.5%	9.3%	9.0%	8.2%	6.8%	5.5%
State/Local Expenditures	16.0%	8.3%	6.2%	6.7%	7.9%	6.2%	3.2%	5.0%

Table 6   *National Health Care Expenditures: Aggregates and Per Capita Amounts by Type of Expenditure and Source of Funds, Calendar Years 1998–2003*

Type of Expenditure	1998	1999	2000	2001	2002	2003
National Health Expenditures ($ billions)	1149.8	1215.6	1309.9	1426.4	1559.0	1678.9
As a percentage of GNP	13.1%	13.1%	13.3%	14.1%	14.9%	15.3%
Source of Funds						
Private Expenditures ($ billions)	628.8	666.5	717.5	771.8	841.0	913.2
Public Expenditures ($ billions)	520.9	549.0	592.4	654.6	718.0	765.7
Federal Expenditures ($ billions)	366.9	386.2	416.0	463.8	508.6	541.7
State/Local Expenditures ($ billions)	154.0	162.8	176.4	190.8	209.4	224.0
Per Capita Expenditures ($)	4177	4377	4560	4914	5317	5671
Source of Funds						
Private Expenditures	2285	2400	2498	2659	2869	3084
Public Expenditures	1893	1977	2062	2255	2449	2586
Federal Expenditures	1306	1359	1448	1598	1735	1830
State/Local Expenditures	544	578	614	657	714	756
Percentage Distribution of Funds	100.0%	100.0%	100.0%	100.0%	100.0%	100.0%
Private Funds	54.7%	54.8%	54.8%	54.1%	53.9%	54.4%
Public Funds	45.3%	45.2%	45.2%	45.9%	46.1%	45.6%
Federal Funds	31.9%	31.6%	31.8%	32.5%	32.6%	32.4%
State/Local Funds	13.4%	13.8%	13.4%	13.4%	13.4%	13.3%

Annualized Percentage Change from previous year shown

National Health Care Expenditures	5.4%	5.7%	5.8%	8.9%	9.3%	7.7%
Private Expenditures	6.8%	6.0%	6.1%	7.6%	9.0%	8.6%
Public Expenditures	3.7%	5.4%	5.3%	10.5%	9.7%	6.6%
Federal Expenditures	2.5%	4.7%	5.2%	11.5%	9.7%	6.5%
State/Local Expenditures	6.8%	7.1%	5.6%	8.2%	9.7%	7.0%

Note: *National Health Expenditures* are defined as comprising all spending for individual health care, including the administrative costs of non-profit and government health programs, the net cost to consumers of private health insurance, non-profit health research, and construction of medical facilities.

Sources: Data for 1929 through 1979: Robert M. Gibson and Daniel R. Waldo, 'National Health Care Expenditures, 1980', *Health Care Financing Review,* III (September 1981): 1–54.

Data for 1980 through 1984: Daniel R. Waldo, Katharine R. Levit, and Helen Lazenby, 'National Health Expenditures, 1985', *Health Care Financing Review,* VIII (Fall 1986): 1–21.

Data for 1985 through 1989: Helen Lazenby and Suzanne W. Letsch, 'National Health Expenditures, 1989', *Health Care Financing Review,* XII (Winter 1990): 1–26.

Data for 1990 through 1994: Katharine R. Levit, Helen C. Lazenby, *et al.*, 'National Health Expenditures, 1994', *Health Care Financing Review,* XVII (Spring, 1996): 205–242.

Data for 1995 through 1997: Health Care Financing Administration, Office of the Actuary, National Health Statistics Group, 'National Health Care Expenditures, 1960–1997' (cited 7 October 1999), available from the World Wide Web @ http://medicare.hcfa.gov/stats/nhe-oact/tables/nhegdp97.txt

Data for 1998 and 1999: National Center for Health Statistics, Centers for Disease Control and Prevention, US Department of Health and Human Services, *Health, United States, 2002* (Hyattsville, Maryland: Health and Human Services, 2005): 288 (Table 113).

Data for 2000 and 2003: National Center for Health Statistics, Centers for Disease Control and Prevention, US Department of Health and Human Services, *Health, United States, 2005* (Hyattsville, Maryland: Health and Human Services, 2005): 360 (Table 119).

NOTES

1. Aggregate health expenditures in fiscal year 2001 were $1424.5 billion, of which $454.8 billion were federal disbursements and $191.8 billion were state and local disbursements. See Center for Medicare and Medicaid Services, National Center for Health Statistics, Centers for Disease Control and Prevention, Department of Health and Human Services, *Health, United States, 2003* (Hyattsville, Maryland: National Center for Health Statistics, 2003): Table 112, 306. The Bureau of Management and Budget calculates federal medical outlays in fiscal year 2004 as $559 billion.
2. We live in an age where government expenditures are so far beyond what we are accustomed to dealing with in our day-to-day lives that they have lost all meaning. A half trillion dollars per year is equivalent to slightly less than $1 million per minute, every minute of every day.
3. In 2001 approximately 40 400 000 million Americans were enrolled in medicare programs and an additional 42 800 000 had received some form of medicaid.
4. See Ronald Hamowy, 'The Development of Medical Licensing Laws in the United States, 1875–1900', *Journal of Libertarian Studies*, 3 (Winter 1979): 73–119. While a number of jurisdictions had some form of 'licensing' law prior to the Civil War, they were poorly enforced or short-lived. In most cases no penalty attached other than precluding unlicensed doctors from using the courts to sue for the recovery of fees. See William G. Rothstein, *American Physicians in the Nineteenth Century: From Sect to Science* (Baltimore: Johns Hopkins University Press, 1972): 332–9.
5. His work was carried forward by Robert Koch who, in 1876, established an experimental protocol, known as Koch's postulates, that permitted him to conclusively link anthrax with a specific bacillus. Koch later discovered the bacillae that produced tuberculosis (1882) and cholera (1883).
6. One physician, writing in 1879, estimated that the mortality from this regimen ranged from 10 to 50 percent. J. M. Scudder, 'A Brief History of Eclectic Medicine', *Eclectic Medical Journal*, 39 (1879): 298, quoted in Rothstein, *American Physicians in the Nineteenth Century*, 54. These figures are probably too conservative; while the immediate mortality rate might have been within the range suggested, heroic therapy almost certainly contributed to the deaths of a far greater percentage of patients.
7. For a contemporary account of Thomson's life and system of medicine, see John Uri Lloyd, 'Life and Medical Discoveries of Samuel Thomson', *Bulletin of the Lloyd Library of Botany, Pharmacy and Materia Medica*, Bulletin No. 11, Reproduction Series 7, 1909. The author himself was a well-known proponent of herbal medicine, founder of the Lloyds Brothers Pharmacy, and was twice president of the American Pharmaceutical Association.
8. Hahnemann himself argued that this benefit alone should encourage orthodox physicians to embrace homeopathic therapeutics. 'A dose that appears to [the regular physician] like nothing, could have no worse results', he writes, 'than that of producing no effect at all, which is at least far more innocent than the effects resulting from the strong doses of allopathic medicines'. Samuel Hahnemann, *Organon of Homoeopathic Medicine* (3rd American edn; New York: William Radde, 1849): 222.
9. Stanford E. Chaillé, 'The Medical Colleges, the Medical Profession, and the Public', *New Orleans Medical and Surgical Reporter*, n.s. 1 (May 1874): 818–19. American Medical Association statistics on medical schools and graduates for 1880 show that of the 100 medical schools in operation in that year, fourteen of them taught homeopathic medicine, graduating 12 percent of all new physicians, while nine schools taught eclecticism, from which close to 6 percent of all graduates issued. 'Medical Education in the United States', *Journal of the American Medical Association* 75 (7 August 1920): 382–3.
10. See Paul Starr, *The Social Transformation of American Medicine* (New York: Basic Books, Inc., 1982): 113–15. When the medical school at Johns Hopkins University opened in 1893, it was the first to impose a requirement that all entrants possess a college degree.
11. For those interested in reading the Report, the Carnegie Foundation has made it available online at http://www.carnegiefoundation.org/eLibrary/docs/flexner_report.pdf
12. See Hamowy, 'Development of Medical Licensing Laws', 113–17.

13. 'Medical Education in the United States', *Journal of the American Medical Association*, 79 (1922): 629–33, quoted in Rothstein, *American Physicians*, 287. It has been estimated that the Report was responsible for anywhere between 7 and 22 percent of all school closures and mergers. Mark D. Hiatt and Christopher G. Stockton, 'The Impact of the Flexner Report on the Fate of Medical Schools in North America After 1909', *Journal of American Physicians and Surgeons*, 8(2) (Summer 2003): 39.

14. Osteopathy was the brainchild of Dr Andrew T. Still, who formulated the underlying theories associated with the movement in 1874, soon after having taken courses at the Kansas City School of Physicians and Surgeons. He held that disease was primarily the result, not of germs, but of 'anatomical abnormalities followed by physiological discord'. He opposed the use of drugs, vaccines, and serums, regarded surgery only as a last resort, and believed the cures could be effected by 'correcting the mechanical imbalances within and between the structures of the body'. In 1892 Still founded the American School of Osteopathy at Kirksville, Missouri.

    In 1895 D. D. Palmer, a grocer from Davenport, Iowa, propounded the notion that most disease was the product of misalignments of the spine, known as 'subluxations', which interfered with nerve signals from the brain. Chiropractic provided the theoretical blueprint that allowed practitioners to adjust these misalignments and thereby restore the nerve signals. As with osteopathy, drugs and surgery play almost no role in chiropractic's therapeutic arsenal.

15. An additional benefit that followed from more rigorous standards and hence an increase in the costs of training was that fewer 'undesirable elements', recent immigrants – among them Catholics and Jews – and blacks and other minorities entered the profession. See Martin Kaufman, *American Medical Education: The Formative Years: 1765–1910* (Westport, Conn.: Greenwood Press, 1976): 172–3. The Report explicitly supported the closure of all three medical schools devoted to the education of women, arguing that 'it is clear that women show a decreasing inclination' to become physicians inasmuch as 'any strong demand for women physicians or any strong ungratified desire on the part of women to enter the profession . . . is lacking'. In addition, he urged that the seven medical schools for negroes be reduced to two, and that hygiene rather than surgery be emphasized in their curricula!

16. With release of the Flexner Report, the AMA's Council on Medical Education, which had been rating all medical schools in the nation, effectively became an accrediting agency to which the various state licensing boards conformed.

17. Arthur Hertzler, *The Horse and Buggy Doctor*, quoted in Roy Porter, *Blood and Guts: A Short History of Medicine* (New York: W. W. Norton, 2002): 41.

18. One authority on the disease noted in 1894 that 'one-seventh of the total mortality of the civilized world is due to tuberculosis, and one-fourth of the deaths occurring during the working period of life is caused by it. Over 30,000 deaths were reported to the New York City Health Department as having been caused by the tubercular diseases during the five years ending January 1, 1893. Of these more than 26,000 were caused by pulmonary tuberculosis. . . . As compared with this, the total number of deaths caused by the other infectious diseases, including small-pox, typhus fever, typhoid fever, scarlet fever, diphtheria, measles, and whooping-cough, was only a little over 21,000, or about two-thirds of the number produced by tuberculosis alone.' Hermann M. Biggs, 'To Rob Consumption of its Terrors', *Forum* (February 1894): 763.

19. Both Behring (1854–1917) and Kitasato (1852–1931) are giants of the bacteriological revolution. Among their numerous achievements, both were instrumental in the development not only of the first serum against diphtheria but also of the first therapeutic tetanus serum. In the same year that Behring and Kitasato developed their diphtheria antitoxin, Kitasato uncovered the infectious agent for bubonic plague.

20. For an extended discussion of the reception given to the findings of bacteriology by the American profession toward the end of the century, see Rothstein, *American Physicians*, 261–81.

21. Roy Porter, *The Greatest Benefit to Mankind: A Medical History of Humanity* (New York: W. W. Norton, 1997): 360. Sherwin B. Nuland offers an excellent brief treatment of the development of anesthesia. See chapter 10, 'Surgery without Pain: The Origins of General

Anesthesia', in *Doctors: The Biography of Medicine* (New York: Alfred A. Knopf, 1988): 263–303.

22. It appears that large numbers of fundamentalists opposed the use of any anesthetic in childbirth since Scripture had pronounced that women would bring forth children 'in sorrow'.

23. One historian of medicine notes that before the introduction of antiseptic techniques the mortality rate for amputations was approximately 40 percent. Darlene Berger, 'A Brief History of Medical Diagnosis and the Birth of the Clinical Laboratory', *Medical Laboratory Observer*, 31 (July 1999): 33.

24. Berkeley Moynihan, Baron Moynihan, quoted in Porter, *Greatest Benefit to Mankind*, 373.

25. The number of preventable deaths due to medical error in America's hospitals remains substantial, amounting to approximately 98 000 deaths per year. See the study by HealthGrades, entitled *Patient Safety in American Hospitals*, released in July 2004. The American Iatrogenic Association estimates the number of deaths at more than twice this figure.

26. Similarly, childbirth took place in the home, with a midwife rather than a physician commonly assisting in delivery. The advent of the modern hospital in the twentieth century spelled the end of birth and death as an integral part of the life cycle that was observable to the whole family. These events are now sequestered in cold, streamlined buildings that are foreign to our daily lives, thus shrouding birth and death in fearsome mystery.

27. Starr, *Social Transformation of American Medicine*, 152.

28. Cleon C. Mason, 'Are Hospital Costs Too High?' *North American Review*, 228 (July 1929): 57–8.

29. Anonymous, 'I Can't Afford to Be Sick', *Forum and Century*, 8 (March 1940): 109.

30. In 1885 a rabies vaccine was developed at the Pasteur laboratories and Pasteur administered the vaccine for the first time to a nine-year-old boy who had been bitten numerous times several days prior by a rabid dog. Smallpox inoculation originated in China around 1000 AD and was imported to Europe through Turkey. It consisted of administering a small dose of live smallpox virus to patients, who then contracted a mild form of the disease. In England, variolation was popularized through the efforts of Lady Mary Wortley Montagu, wife of the British ambassador to the Ottoman Empire. In 1796 Edward Jenner, having discovered the connection between cowpox (a mild but related disease) and smallpox, demonstrated that the administration of cowpox virus brought about immunity to smallpox. It might be noted that Jenner's findings were received with ridicule by the medical profession and Jenner was originally labeled a charlatan. In 1979 the World Health Organization noted that smallpox had been eradicated from the planet.

31. Thomas McKeown, *The Role of Medicine: Dream, Mirage or Nemesis* (Princeton: Princeton University Press, 1979): 78.

32. McKeown, *Role of Medicine*, 78.

33. See Ronald Hamowy, 'Introduction: Illicit Drugs and Government Control', in Ronald Hamowy, ed., *Dealing With Drugs: Consequences of Government Control* (San Francisco: Pacific Research Institute for Public Policy, 1987): 10–11.

34. A history of the various states' attempts to regulate the distribution and sale of opiates and cocaine can be found in Hamowy, 'Introduction: Illicit Drugs and Government Control'.

35. The literature on the Progressive Era is immense. One of the best overviews remains that offered by Robert H. Wiebe, *The Search for Order, 1877–1920* (New York: Hill and Wang, 1967).

1. The Public Health Service

The Public Health Service is the successor agency of the United States Marine Hospital Service, which was established in 1798[1] by act of Congress for the purpose of caring for sick and injured merchant seamen.[2] Seamen were required to contribute 20 cents per month to cover the costs of this medical care.[3] In 1800 the first marine hospital was opened at Washington Point, near Norfolk, Virginia, and by 1802 hospitals were also established at Boston, Newport, and Charleston. As the nation expanded, the number of marine hospitals multiplied as more seamen, including those manning boats and rafts on the Mississippi and the Ohio and on the Great Lakes, were brought under the law's provisions. Indeed, by 1861 Salmon P. Chase, at the time Secretary of the Treasury in President Lincoln's cabinet, was compelled to observe that the number of marine hospitals, over which the Department of the Treasury had jurisdiction, 'has been increased far beyond necessity or utility'.[4]

While the tax on seamen was collected without interruption between the genesis of the program and 1870,[5] Congress was compelled to augment these proceeds out of the general revenue during 49 of those years. In addition, appropriations were made for land and construction costs. Twenty-seven marine hospitals were operating at American ports at the start of the Civil War. By 1870, however, this number had been greatly reduced and the Service operated only seven hospitals, while it leased two others to private parties. Of the 31 hospital projects undertaken by the Marine Hospital Service since its inception 72 years earlier,[6] 14 had been sold, one transferred to the War Department, one abandoned, one burned, and three destroyed by flood, hurricane, and earthquake. The remaining two were left unfinished. The amount of waste, in both the construction and operation of these facilities, seems to have been substantial. Hospitals were built in areas where there were no patients[7] or on land to which the title was faulty,[8] or in areas physically unsuited to the construction of a medical facility. The regional Collectors of Customs, who acted as the supervisory authorities for the various marine hospitals with the power to appoint the supervising surgeon and to fix the rules governing these establishments, traditionally took a 1 percent commission on all procurements, which invited graft. A Treasury Department report from 1855 noted that 'in some towns there appears a desire . . . [to act as the site of a Marine Hospital solely so] that additional sums of public money may there be expended. . . . If this feeling not be checked, we shall have sinecure surgeons, sinecure stewards, sinecure matrons, sinecure nurses, without number. We have too many such already.'[9]

Complaints regarding the conditions that prevailed at the nation's marine hospitals were so numerous, especially following the Civil War, that in 1870 the Secretary of the Treasury appointed a team to inspect them and, as a consequence, new legislation was enacted reorganizing the Marine Hospital Service with the aim of bringing to it some level of efficiency and uniformity. The position of Supervising Surgeon of the Marine Hospital Service was created with the authority to direct all matters connected with the disbursement of funds for the relief of sick and disabled seamen throughout the system. To the new office of Supervising Surgeon, Secretary of the Treasury George Bothell appointed Dr John Maynard Woodworth, who had previously acted as chief medical officer attached to the command of General William Tecumseh Sherman and who had accompanied Sherman on his March to the Sea. Immediately upon his appointment in April 1871 Woodworth set about reorganizing the Service along military lines, centralizing its administration and selecting new applicants by examination. These physicians were appointed to the general service, as opposed to a specific hospital, were required to wear uniforms, and given ranks.[10] In 1873 Woodworth was successful in getting his title altered to Supervising Surgeon General.

By the end of the nineteenth century, more and more physicians began joining the movement for the establishment of a national department of public health, with cabinet status, to oversee and regulate all aspects of the public health. The move toward greater government intrusion into health care was substantially accelerated by the shift in the political ideology of the American middle class that was to become known as progressivism.[11] The Progressive Era, which began at the start of the last quarter of the nineteenth century, was marked by a distrust of solutions to social problems that relied on individual initiative and action. Instead, progressive rhetoric reflected an attachment to social planning and bureaucratic control. Progressive ideology held that it was only through extensive and vigorous government action that the social ills of modern society could be effectively addressed and that held true not only of the economic and political problems that beset both urban and rural Americans but also for the vast array of traditionally private problems that had previously been considered as falling within the sphere of autonomous action. This repudiation of individualism and its replacement with ever wider government control over the private lives of citizens applied as much to matters of health as to the economy. The ideal of progressive health reformers was the creation of an army of bureaucratic physicians directing the community in the interests of public health.

The creation of a massive public health bureaucracy was partially brought about by the professionalization of the medical profession, itself in part a consequence of the great discoveries that were made in bacteriology and parasitology in the last quarter of the nineteenth century. The amazing advances made by researchers in these fields encouraged physicians to cartelize their profession and provided the rationale for a vast array of public health legislation.[12] At the local and state levels, public health departments, which had previously done little, were re-energized with the power to inspect and condemn and to regulate in a host of areas touching on the public's health.[13] Equally important, the federal government began taking a far more active part in health issues. This was spurred on by sensationalistic articles in the public press on the dangers of patent medicines and the unsanitary conditions prevailing in the meat packing industry, which led to the passage of the Food and Drugs Act of 1906.[14] The 'capstone to the great edifice of preventive medicine',[15] however, was to be the federal Public Health Service, which became Washington's principal instrument for the investigation and prevention of disease.[16]

While the movement to create a national department of health, under whatever name, did not become a central concern of the American Medical Association until the first years of the twentieth century,[17] many physicians' organizations at the state level began intensive lobbying for more government intervention in health care as early as the 1870s.[18] In 1872, the American Public Health Association (APHA) was established with the aim of advancing the cause of state medicine. Among the APHA's officers was Dr Woodworth, the Supervising Surgeon of the Marine Hospital Service, who was elected to the Association's first executive committee. At the first annual meeting of the Association, held in 1873, one of its speakers issued a call for the establishment of a 'National Sanitary Bureau': to supervise the health of the nation's citizens and to institute the various reforms that the new discoveries in sanitary science dictated.[19] Almost immediately after being formed, it petitioned Congress for the establishment of a national 'sanitary bureau' within the Department of the Interior. In the same year, a sizeable number of members of the AMA recommended that that organization endorse an appeal to the federal government to create a department of health, under the supervision of the AMA.[20] While the AMA rejected the recommendation, its Section on State Medicine passed a similar resolution in 1874 and appointed a committee to draft a bill for a National Department of Public Health.[21]

Prior to 1879, Congress had proved reluctant to intervene in what they regarded as local health concerns. In that year, however, a calamitous yellow fever epidemic struck New Orleans and raged up the Mississippi Valley and this goaded the legislature into establishing a National Board of Health, with responsibility for formulating quarantine regulations between the states.[22] The Board no sooner met than its executive committee proposed that its appropriations be increased tenfold and that certain functions previously in the hands of the Marine Hospital Service be transferred to the Board. Nor were the Board's attempts to increase its authority limited to a request for an increase in funding. It made research grants to university faculty members for the purpose of studying yellow fever, the first instance of government grants for medical research,[23] and, in 1880, it suggested that Congress enact legislation granting it the power to prevent the adulteration of food and drugs, effectively granting to it regulatory authority over the drug trade. The Marine Hospital Service was, of course, strongly opposed to all such measures as threats to its own authority. The new Supervising Surgeon General, Dr John B. Hamilton, who had been appointed to the position exactly one month after the creation of the National Board of Health, made every effort to thwart the authority of the National Board[24] and in the end was successful in convincing Congress that the Treasury Department, under whom the Marine Hospital Service operated, was more effective in preventing the entry and spread of contagious and infectious diseases than was the Board.[25] Indeed, the National Board of Health proved so contentious among the various states with which it dealt that Congress elected to disband it in 1883, at which time its quarantine powers were transferred to the Marine Hospital Service. While no national department of health of the sort contemplated by the APHA was established, the Marine Hospital Service did extend its activities to regulate all internal quarantines and assumed responsibility for the pollution of lakes and rivers. In addition, the number of medical services rendered sailors increased substantially, from 10 560 inpatient and outpatient visits in 1870, to 24 860 in 1880, to 50 671 in 1890.[26]

It was not until 1878 that the federal government's Marine Hospital Service was granted the power to assist state and local officials in enforcing quarantine regulations. Fifteen years later, in 1893, the Service was finally granted the authority to enforce such regulations without first having to obtain local approval. In 1902, the Service's name was changed to the United States Public Health and Marine Hospital Service although by far the greater proportion of its activities were still devoted to tending to seamen, to supervising quarantines, and to carrying out the medical inspections of immigrants.[27] In 1912, however, Congress voted to extend the locus of concern of the Service to a broad range of issues touching on public health and once again changed the bureau's name to the United States Public Health Service.

It was the hope of many physicians whose interests and expertise lay in administration, and particularly the membership of the American Public Health Association, that legislation creating a national Public Health Service would prove to be only the first step in the eventual establishment of a cabinet-level Department of Health, empowered to direct all matters relating to the health and safety of Americans. Nor were physicians alone in supporting this extension of the federal government. Leading Progressives, bent on creating a more efficient, rational society, joined medical practitioners in their call for more regulation in the area of health care. Among the leaders of this movement were two Yale University economists, J. Pease Norton and Irving Fisher.[28] In 1906 Norton addressed the Association for the Advancement of Science (AAAS), in which he called for the creation of a national department of health which would 'take all measures calculated, in the judgment of experts, to decrease deaths, to decrease sickness, and to increase physical and mental efficiency of citizens'.[29] Norton's comments led the AAAS to establish a Committee of One Hundred on National Health to study the issues and to lobby Congress for a cabinet-level Health Department.

A bill whose intent was to meet the Committee's goals was considered by Congress at the same time as the measure to expand the powers of the United States Public Health and Marine Hospital Service and to its change of name.[30] In March 1910 Senate bill 6049, providing for a Department of Public Health under the supervision of a Secretary of Public Health, was introduced into the Senate, whose purpose was to 'supervise all matters within the control of the federal government relating to public health and to diseases of animal life'. The new Department was to have authority over all federal bureaus excepting those of the Departments of War and of the Navy 'affecting the medical, surgical, biological or sanitary service', including the Public Health and Marine Hospital Service, the Bureaus of Entomology, Chemistry, and Animal Industry of the Department of Agriculture, the emergency relief service of the Government Printing Office, and the medical officers of the Revenue Cutter Service, the Pension Office, the Indian Service, and all Soldiers' Homes.[31]

The Committee of One Hundred, as well as other supporters of a Department of Health, viewed the need for adequate administrative and regulatory machinery touching on health matters as pressing, especially in light of recent advances that had been made in uncovering the cause of certain infectious and contagious diseases and in the field of epidemiology. It was argued that the pollution of natural resources, the haphazard enforcement of national health and quarantine regulations, and the impurity of the nation's food and drugs strongly pointed to the urgent necessity for such a Department.[32] Proposals for the establishment of a Department of Health did not go unopposed, however. Immediately prior to Congressional hearings on the creation of a national health department in 1911, opposition groups, comprised in the main of heterodox medical practitioners including osteopaths, homeopaths, eclectic physicians, and Christian Scientists, formed the National League for Medical Freedom to thwart passage of the bill.[33] They argued that the creation of a health bureaucracy of the sort envisioned would, in the end, lead to the destruction of all but the most orthodox medical practices. More important, a

Department of Health exceeded the constitutional powers of the federal government and would constitute a serious threat to personal privacy.

As a consequence of this opposition and in view of the fact that President William Howard Taft regarded expansion of his cabinet to include a Secretary of Health as unacceptable,[34] Congress did not proceed with the bill. However, it did enact a somewhat scaled-down version originally suggested by the Surgeon General, Walter Wyman, whose sudden death in November 1911 prompted some members of Congress to attempt to placate members of the health reform movement.[35] The Public Health Service Act changed the Service's name to its current one and empowered it to disseminate information to the public on health matters and to investigate the causes of diseases and the factors at work in their propagation, including the pollution of the nation's lakes and streams.

With this change the officially authorized functions of the Public Health Service were considerably broadened and were to become substantially larger with America's entry into World War I. The provision granting the PHS authority to 'study and investigate the diseases of man and conditions influencing the propagation and spread thereof' was in later years to prove significant since it conferred explicit legislative authority for what was to become a massive research establishment, the National Institutes of Health. In point of fact, Congress had previously granted the PHS a mandate to conduct research. The Service had been engaged in biological research at its one-room bacteriological laboratory in the Staten Island Marine Hospital since 1887. In 1901, its research activities were transferred to Washington, DC and at that time $35 000 had been appropriated by Congress for the erection of 'necessary buildings and quarters for a laboratory for the investigation of infectious and contagious diseases'.[36] And in the following year, a definite organization for the Laboratory was set down in legislation that authorized the Surgeon General to appoint heads of the Divisions of Chemistry, Zoology, and Pharmacology under a Director, who was to be a member of the Commissioned Officers Corps.

On 3 April 1917, three days prior to Congress declaring war on Germany, President Woodrow Wilson invoked a provision of the 1902 Act that had restructured the Public Health and Marine Hospital Service, making the Public Health Service a part of the military forces of the United States. Fearful that American military effectiveness might be seriously handicapped by the spread of disease among American troops, the federal government instituted an intensive system of supervision in zones surrounding each military camp and around the major industrial centers engaged in war work. By the summer of 1917, the Public Health Service was conducting sanitary work in 26 extra-cantonment zones.[37] In an effort to increase the number of professional personnel serving in the PHS, the Surgeon General drafted a bill whose goal was creation of a Reserve Officer Corps for the Public Health Service along the lines of those that existed for the branches of the military. The bill passed the Senate in June 1917 but, because of delays in the House of Representatives, did not become law until October 1918, too late to benefit the Service during the war. But despite this handicap, the number of professional personnel in the PHS increased from 538 in June 1917 to 1472 in June 1918.[38]

While the objectives of the Service included the supervision of local sewage and water supplies and vaccinating the public against typhoid and smallpox, one of its primary missions appears to have been to educate American troops against the dangers of sexually transmitted diseases. Fears occasioned by the rapid increase in the incidence of venereal diseases among American troops, both overseas and at camps within the United States, led Congress in 1918 to enact the Chamberlain-Kahn Act, which created an Interdepartmental Social Hygiene Board[39] to investigate the problem and to recommend methods to control their spread.[40] At the same time a Division of Venereal Diseases was established in the Public Health Service with an initial appropriation of $20 000.[41] The Service did not limit itself to setting up clinics for the diagnosis and treatment of venereal diseases[42] but lobbied the various state legislatures to enact laws against prostitution. 'In order that the spread of venereal diseases through prostitution may be controlled', the Service contended, 'adequate laws for the suppression of vice must be passed'.[43] Partly in consequence of this kind of lobbying which was undertaken by the federal government and social hygiene and physicians' groups throughout the country, 40 states passed 96 laws relating to the control of venereal diseases and no less than 222 city ordinances were enacted with a similar purpose.[44]

The Chamberlain-Kahn Act also provided that the Public Health Service administer a system of grants-in-aid to the states for the purpose of controlling the spread of venereal diseases. What is particularly significant about these grants is that they constitute the first application of federal aid to the states for health purposes.[45] While Congress appropriated these grants over a period of seven years only, and then only on condition that the states met certain requirements respecting the expenditure of these and state matching funds, substantial sums were disbursed in a national propaganda campaign for social hygiene. It is difficult to understand what the government hoped to accomplish by these expenditures. The educational efforts of the Service were severely hampered by the fact that discussions of prophylaxis were frowned upon and even mention of specific sexually transmitted diseases could not be made in most official documents. The act provided that all instances of venereal disease had to be reported to the local health authorities and all physicians who failed to do so were subject to criminal penalties. Additionally, travel by the victims of venereal infections was to be controlled by state boards.[46] It is no

Table 1.1   Federal Appropriations for Civil Venereal Disease Programs
1918–1925

Year	Congressional appropriation ($)	Actual allotment by the PHS ($)
1918–19	1 000 000	912 168
1919–20	1 087 831	901 486
1920–21	546 340	274 213
1921–22	(unexpended balance)	272 132
1922–23	225 000	209 309
1923–24	100 000	92 842
1924–25	25 000	25 000

Source: Robert D. Leigh, *Federal Health Administration in the United States* (New York: Harper & Brothers Publishers, 1927): 410.

wonder that no one was anxious to be diagnosed with a sexually transmitted ailment. Federal appropriations under the terms of the Chamberlain-Kahn Act are shown in Table 1.1.

With the end of the World War Congress seemed to have lost interest in the sexual health of Americans but the Public Health Service continued to maintain its Division of Venereal Disease. Lack of federal funding had made research into the various venereal diseases impossible and for a few years the Service was reduced to conducting sex education campaigns. However, this situation was altered in 1930 when a private philanthropy, the Rosenwald Fund, approached the Service regarding a joint study of the epidemiology and methods of treatment for syphilis among blacks in the south. The PHS's work seems to have reawakened Congressional interest in sexually transmitted diseases and it enacted legislation in 1935 greatly augmenting the research funds at the disposal of the Public Health Service. Among the projects conducted by the PHS for which these federal funds were used was the notorious study of syphilis conducted at Tuskegee, Alabama.[47] Begun in 1932 and not completed until 1972, approximately 400 black sharecroppers in Macon County, Alabama were given the impression that they were being treated for syphilis, 'bad blood', as the PHS physicians called it, while they were given a placebo. Every effort was made to deny these subjects effective therapy since this would interfere with the purpose of the study, which was to investigate the natural history of the disease.[48] In 1997 President Bill Clinton issued a formal apology for this repellent chapter in the history of American medical research.[49]

The period between 1917 and 1921 witnessed a significant expansion in the size and functions of the Public Health Service as it assumed the role of provider of medical and hospital services for disabled servicemen. When hostilities were suddenly terminated in November 1918 Congress had not as yet developed any demobilization plans. While the federal government had established an elaborate system of pensions for disabled veterans in preceding wars, Congress had determined to reward disabled veterans of the World War differently. Not only were veterans with service-related disabilities to receive compensation but the government undertook to provide all necessary medical care and treatment and to furnish whatever vocational re-education was needed for gainful employment. These commitments were contained in the legislation relating to veterans enacted by Congress in early 1919.[50] Under its terms no new agency with a mandate to discharge all of these functions was created; rather, the Public Health Service was assigned the job of providing for the medical care and treatment of veterans. The result of this legislation was that over the first six months of 1919 the Public Health Service's hospital work expanded at a faster rate than ever in its history. Between 1 April and 30 June, 1919, the Service opened ten new hospitals with a capacity of almost 6000 beds. Although it continued to operate the various marine hospitals, the administration of which constituted the Service's original purpose, this function quickly declined in importance as it took on newer tasks. By mid-1921, the Public Health Service was operating 62 hospitals, treating over 110 000 patients, mostly disabled World War I veterans.[51] Not only did Congress appropriate larger budgets to carry out its functions but the Service was further authorized to appoint reserve officers to augment its ranks. It quickly became apparent that the Public Health Service was unequal to such a massive expansion of its duties. Complaints about waste, mismanagement, and incompetent medical service in the new hospitals set up to treat discharged soldiers were rampant. Indeed, many of these hospitals were obsolete facilities that were foisted on the Federal Government for purely political reasons.[52] In response to the large number of complaints of mistreatment of patients, the Public Health Service found it politic to create a separate administrative bureau to investigate charges made against the Service. In February 1920 an inspection section was established, headed by a commissioned officer with the rank of Assistant Surgeon General.[53] This, however, did not dampen criticism of the Service, whose budget requests kept growing. Indeed, the projected costs of the Public Health Service's program of hospital care for veterans given to the House and Senate in 1920 were so astronomical that some members of Congress regarded them as no less than ridiculous.[54] Table 1.2 gives some notion of the growth in hospital and dispensary treatments provided by the Public Health Service between 1917 and 1921.

Despite the problems it faced in trying to cope with the influx of discharged veterans seeking medical care, the Public Health Service soon found itself

Table 1.2   Hospital and Dispensary Treatments, Public Health Service, 1917 to 1921

Class of service	1917	1918	1919	1920	1921
Patients Treated					
In service hospitals	11 325	12 797	26 991	68 791	111 496
In contract hospitals	6 666	7 812	11 364	50 266	69 520
In dispensaries at service hospitals	23 836	23 197	30 928	76 088	155 431
In other dispensaries	22 194	30 402	74 436	124 808	473 729
Total	64 021	74 208	93 719	389 953	812 176
Hospital Days					
In service hospitals	391 172	415 465	622 827	2 387 884	4 921 314
In contract hospitals	109 406	119 526	134 191	1 763 454	2 850 357
Total	500 578	534 991	757 018	4 151 338	7 771 671
Dispensary Treatments					
At service hospitals	42 919	36 789	57 848	181 873	352 894
At other dispensaries	59 309	59 275	46 915	467 355	1 120 168
Total	102 228	96 064	104 763	649 228	1 473 063
Persons Physically Treated	28 356	30 055	41 185	513 293	1 004 55

Source: Laurence F. Schneckebier, *The Public Health Service: Its History, Activities and Organization*, Institute for Government Research (Baltimore: Johns Hopkins Press, 1923): 64.

having to contend with the worst outbreak of influenza in history. In 1918 Congress appropriated $1 000 000 to the Service to attempt to combat a particularly virulent strain of influenza that had reached the United States from Europe. The 'Spanish flu', as it was then known, surfaced in Europe in the summer of 1918,[55] appeared in New England that September, and rapidly spread down the coast to Virginia and westward across the continent. The medical resources of a number of states were quickly overwhelmed by the epidemic and the Public Health Service was called upon to assist in furnishing doctors and nurses; it was in response to this request for federal help that Congress appropriated funds for combating the epidemic. The Service set up an emergency hospital of some 500 beds in Washington, DC, one of the places hardest hit, to treat government employees and it dispatched physicians and nurses to the areas in most need, but, because of the nature of the illness, its efforts were to prove futile. The Bureau of the Census was later to estimate that, during 1918 and 1919, over a half million Americans died in the pandemic,[56] almost 200 000 in October 1918 alone. Worldwide, anywhere between 20 million and 40 million people perished from the disease.[57]

The substantial growth of the Public Health Service between the outbreak of war in 1917 and 1921 encouraged its officials to believe that Congress and the President would now be prepared to view the Service's transformation into a Department of Health with greater favor. The Surgeon General, Rupert Blue, was so excited by the prospect of heading a national health agency that he drafted an 11-page paper entitled 'Memorandum Relative to the Development of a National and International Program of Public Health'. In it Blue proposed the establishment of a Department of Health at Cabinet level and the creation of an international health body, implicitly led by the United States, to supervise the disparate national health programs of foreign nations.[58] However, Blue and his supporters were once again thwarted in their attempts to raise the PHS to cabinet status by Warren Harding's appointment of Colonel Charles R. Forbes as Director of the Bureau of War Risk Insurance.[59]

The Service's mandate to take charge of the medical examinations of veterans to determine if they were disabled and to provide the necessary care and treatment for disabled veterans in hospitals and dispensaries was originally delegated to it by the Bureau of War Risk Insurance, the agency statutorily charged with these responsibilities. In August 1921, however, under pressure from veterans' groups who sought a greater role in determining the conduct of veterans' affairs, and with Colonel Forbes as their spokesman, Congress established the Veterans' Bureau as an independent agency reporting directly to the President. Led by the American Legion, veterans' organizations had publicized a number of instances of incompetent medical treatment, delays in obtaining needed hospitalization, and poor accommodation, and both President Harding and influential members of the House and Senate were moved to support extensive reforms.

The Public Health Service, of course, denied these charges and strongly opposed the transfer of authority over medical care to a new bureau. The Hospital Division of the Public Health Service, through its 14 district supervisors, had been responsible for providing medical and hospital care to veterans and in fact was at the time furnishing over 80 percent of such care.[60] It was the argument of the PHS that most of the problems brought to the attention of the public occurred at private hospitals which were under contract to the PHS and not at those run by the Hospital Division itself. However, Forbes was a particularly astute lobbyist and was able to convince Representative Burton Erwin Sweet, chairman of the subcommittee of the Interstate and Foreign Commerce Committee, the committee charged with conducting House hearings on establishing a Veterans' Bureau, that the amount of red tape would be minimized were all these functions turned over to a new agency over which he had control. As a consequence, in August 1921 the Sweet Act, creating the Veterans' Bureau, was passed and in April of the following year, President Harding, at Forbes' urging, transferred all veterans' hospitals and outpatient clinics to the new Bureau. Transferred to the Veterans' Bureau were 57 hospitals, 13 000 patients, 17 000 beds, 900 physicians and dentists, and 1400 nurses. Nine additional hospitals under construction were to be transferred when completed. The Public Health Service, with 24 Marine Hospitals with approximately 3000 beds, thus reverted to the programs that it was authorized to undertake prior to 1917, although on a somewhat grander scale.[61]

Since the Public Health Service was no longer responsible for the huge task of providing medical and hospital care to the veterans of World War I, it concentrated its resources on scientific research and on its epidemiological studies. The Service made the most of its work in these areas and was successful in winning Congressional support for a substantial expansion. In 1928, six years after surrendering its responsibilities for the care of veterans and with the support of a group of influential Congressmen and Senators, a bill to expand the Service's Corps of Commissioned Officers passed both the House of Representatives and the Senate. However, Herbert M. Lord, the Director of the Budget under President Calvin Coolidge regarded the expansion as unnecessary and a waste of taxpayer resources and was able to prevail upon the President to veto the bill in May of that year.[62]

Not all legislation whose goal was the expansion of the Public Health Service failed during this period, however. In 1914, at the urging of Secretary of State William Jennings Bryan and of Dr William C. Woodward, Director of the American Medical Association's Committee on Medical Legislation, Congress had enacted the Harrison Narcotic Act restricting the production and distribution of, among other drugs, cocaine, opium, morphine, and heroin. The act provided that medical practitioners were permitted to dispense these drugs to their patients but this was quickly interpreted by the courts to prohibit physicians from prescribing narcotics to addicts 'solely for the purpose of gratifying addiction'. The courts had thus transformed all addicts into criminals.[63] As a consequence, in January 1929 President Coolidge signed into law a bill creating the Narcotics Division of the Public Health Service and authorizing the Service to construct and operate two hospitals for the confinement and treatment of Federal prisoners who were addicted to narcotics and those who voluntarily presented themselves for treatment.

In the following year, the Narcotics Division, having altered its name to the Division of Mental Hygiene, began to conduct extensive research into the effects of narcotics and, more broadly, into the causes, prevalence, and treatment of mental and nervous diseases, of which drug addiction was thought to be an instance. In addition, by a separate measure enacted by Congress in 1930, the Mental Hygiene Division was empowered to provide medical services in federal prisons. The Service had thus added to its other functions that of superintending the medical facilities in prison hospitals. It was therefore perfectly compatible with this role that Congress, when it later in the same year instructed the Attorney General to establish a hospital for defective delinquents, appointed the Surgeon General as the person responsible for designating its administrator.

Of the two 'narcotics hospitals' the PHS had been ordered to establish, the first was opened at Lexington, Kentucky, in 1935 and a second facility was inaugurated at Fort Worth, Texas, in 1938. As Director of the Lexington facility, Surgeon General Cumming selected Dr Lawrence Kolb. Dr Kolb had previously been attached to the Hygienic Laboratory, the Public Health Service's research arm, and had conducted some of the first full-scale studies in narcotics. Kolb's interest in drug addiction dated from his period of service at Ellis Island, New York, where he was assigned to examining immigrants and sifting out those who were in some way mentally defective. Indeed, Kolb was the author of the first Public Health Service instruction manual on the mental examination of immigrants. He continued his studies of alcohol and narcotic addiction at the Hygienic Laboratory in Washington, DC and produced a series of studies on the social and physiological effects of narcotics that were regarded by fellow physicians as definitive. He was the first to point out that withdrawal from drugs such as morphine and heroin was not the chief medical hazard confronting physicians but that the tendency for the user to relapse was a far greater problem. Kolb practically designed the facilities at Lexington, which were large enough to accommodate 1000 inmates. The main buildings were surrounded by a thousand acres of farmland and Kolb expected those incarcerated there to get plenty of outdoor exercise by engaging in farm work. Indeed, the facilities were originally given the title 'United States

Narcotic Farm'. In addition, provision was made for the usual vocational education. The Lexington facilities were dedicated in May 1935, with great ceremony. The Surgeon General himself was in attendance as were 3500 guests, and the facility was thrown open to the public during its first four days of operation. Approximately 280 inmates had been transferred there from the Federal prison system and this group was augmented by several ordinary citizens voluntarily seeking treatment.[64]

There were frequent attempts during this period to restructure the Public Health Service, many of which originated in the offices of Reed Smoot, the Republican senior Senator from Utah. Smoot, an ardent promoter of high tariffs, with which his name is associated, and of conscription, had a particular animus for the Public Health Service, which he thought was 'abusing the prerogatives of states and communities' and which, he maintained, intended to 'Russianize' the United States.[65] Early in 1921, during debate in the Senate on an appropriations bill that provided for additional PHS personnel, Smoot attacked the Service, charging that the Surgeon General, 'while himself an honest and capable man, was surrounded by men with no respect for Congress and no mercy on the Treasury'.[66] Smoot put forward several proposals to permanently consolidate the Public Health Service with other federal departments, including the newly created Veterans' Bureau. While he was unsuccessful in these attempts, a more serious challenge to the existing organizational structure came from the National Health Council, an alliance of voluntary organizations.[67] The Council's analysis showed that no less than 40 government agencies, located in five cabinet departments and employing 5000 workers, were charged with aspects of the public health.[68] What the Council proposed was a consolidation of these disparate but related activities under the direction of an assistant secretary for public health. Fearful that the Public Health Service and his own authority would be weakened by such a reorganization, the Surgeon General, Hugh S. Cumming, opposed the measure and offered as a substitute proposal that the Public Health Service be empowered to detail its officers to work with other agencies for the purpose of coordinating their efforts with those of the PHS. A bill to this effect was introduced in the House of Representatives in 1926 by James S. Parker of New York, Chairman of the Committee on Interstate and Foreign Commerce, but failed to pass that year. The bill was reintroduced, amended, combined with other bills relating to the Public Health Service, separated, passed by Congress and vetoed by the President, until finally, in 1930, it passed both the House and Senate and was signed by President Herbert Hoover. The law provided for regular corps commissions for dentists, pharmacists, sanitary engineers, and Hygienic Laboratory scientists, tying the pay scales of the Service's Commissioned Corps to those of the Army,[69] and empowered the Surgeon General to assign personnel to other agencies.

While there was considerable debate during the 1920s on restructuring the Public Health Service, its Hygienic Laboratory was also receiving Congressional attention. A million copies of a report prepared under the direction of the Chemical Foundation entitled *The Future Independence and Progress of American Medicine in the Age of Chemistry* had been published and distributed in 1921.[70] Established in 1919, the Chemical Foundation was a corporation that had been formed by the major American chemical companies to take over German-owned patents at the close of the World War. The report proposed the creation of a national research institute whose function would be to systematically apply advances made in chemistry and physics to the problems of disease and health.[71] The idea of a research center was extremely popular and was regarded with favor by a number of influential politicians, who saw in such an institute the source of an unending supply of antidotes, vaccines, and other miracle drugs. The Chemical Foundation's report had made reference to the Hygienic Laboratory of the Public Health Service as 'the best adapted for development into a medium of cooperative research' but was wary lest government red tape and public service pay scales inhibit the highest quality research.[72] An editorial in the *Journal of the American Medical Association*, on the other hand, supported the notion of placing a medical research institute within the Public Health Service.[73] While scientists, pharmacologists, and physicians all agreed on the value and importance of establishing a research institute, each feared control by one of the other groups.[74] This rivalry contributed in part to the difficulties supporters had in finding private funding for a research center and served to make the idea of an institute supported by public funds less offensive.

In early 1926 Charles Holmes Herty, chairman of the American Chemical Society's Institute for Chemo-Medical Research and one of the originators of the idea of establishing a national medical research center, met with Senator Joseph E. Ransdell of Louisiana, the chairman of the Committee on Public Health and Quarantine. Ransdell was 'deeply interested' in Herty's scheme, having read *The Future Independence and Progress of American Medicine*, and offered his help. The result of this collaboration was that Ransdell introduced legislation that July to create a National Institute of Health by expanding the Public Health Service's Hygienic Laboratory. Opinion on the bill was divided. The Parker bill expanding the Commissioned Corps and regularizing Corps salaries was being considered at the same time and legislators appeared divided into a multiplicity of camps, some supporting one bill, some the other, some both, and some neither. In addition, President Coolidge had made his position on an expansion of federal authority clear; he was unfavorably disposed toward new programs and greater federal expenditures.[75] In this he was joined by the chief of the Budget Bureau, Herbert M. Lord, who found Ransdell's bill extravagant. However, with the advent of the Hoover administration, which was more agreeable to enlarging the scope of government activity, the bill was reintro-duced and passed in the House and Senate and signed by President Herbert Hoover on 26 May 1930.[76]

The Ransdell Act, by which the National Institute of Health (NIH) came into being, allocated $750 000 for the construction of a new building as the Institute's headquarters and also empowered it to create a system of fellow-ships for those undertaking research and granted authority to the facility to accept private donations.[77] This division of the Public Health Service was to grow to truly colossal proportions, to the point where, in 1968, the year in which the NIH was raised to the status of its own operating agency within the Department of Health, Education, and Welfare (HEW), its staff numbered over 13 000, its operating budget was almost $300 million, and it was charged with distributing over $800 million in grants.[78]

With passage of the Social Security Act in 1935, the role of the Public Health Service was once again expanded and it, together with the Children's Bureau of the Department of Labor, was put in charge of distributing federal grants-in-aid to the various states for health purposes. The Children's Bureau had been established in 1912 with authority to investigate and report 'upon all matters pertaining to the welfare of children and child life'.[79] The Bureau's primary duty was to investigate all questions relating to infant mortality, the birth rate, and diseases of children.[80] In 1921, under pressure from the Bureau and from the National League of Women Voters, Congress enacted the Sheppard-Towner Act,[81] 'for the promotion [and] the welfare and hygiene of maternity and infancy'. Congressional opposition was meager and the bill passed the House by a vote of 279 to 39 and the Senate by 63 to 7. The Act provided for the allocation of appropriated monies to the states for maternal and child care. The formula fixed for the distribution of funds was somewhat complex. Each state was awarded a constant sum to which no conditions were attached. To that amount were added other funds, a portion of which was dependent on the state's population, which had to be matched by the state. The Act created a Federal Board of Maternity and Infant Hygiene, comprising the Chief of the Children's Bureau, the Commissioner of Education, and the Surgeon General, who were empowered to approve state plans for the use of funds. Appropriations for the first year of operation (1922) were $10 000 for each state accepting the Act's provisions and an additional sum of $1 000 000.[82] Over the next few years, as a consequence of the Act, approxi-mately 3000 child and maternal health care centers were established across the country to provide pre- and postnatal care to low-income mothers. A further provision of the Act created the notion of 'registration' of infant births, from which 'birth certificates' are derived.[83]

Surgeon General Walter Wyman had been approached prior to passage of the act establishing the Children's Bureau about the possibility of lodging it in what seemed to be its natural home, the Public Health Service.[84] However, neither Wyman nor his successors, including Hugh Cumming who served on the Federal Board of Maternity, approved of federal grants to state health programs, insisting that all federal monies be dispensed directly by the Public Health Service. And even should Congress insist on legislating a system of state grants it was felt that they should be administered by the Service, under as much central direction as possible. It was, therefore, highly disappointing when Congress, in the face of Wyman's adamant refusal to receive the Children's Bureau into the Public Health Service, proceeded to enact legislation establishing the Bureau within the Department of Labor. The Public Health Service was particularly chagrined because the disbursement of these funds had been placed in the hands of social workers rather than professional public health officials.[85] The Children's Bureau, especially after passage of the Sheppard-Towner Act, remained a constant sore spot for the Public Health Service and its higher-ranking staff. This had apparently become such a thorn in the side of the Service that by 1929, when Congress was considering extending the Act, the Surgeon General applied enormous pressure on Congress to refuse further appropriations. The Service was joined in opposing Sheppard-Towner by the American Medical Association, who viewed all grants for medical care as a threat to the economic well-being of physicians and who regarded the Act as the opening wedge in what might prove to be a more far-reaching system of government-financed health care. They, together with other conservative groups, were successful in prevailing and in 1929 Congress allowed the Act to lapse.[86]

President Hoover was a firm believer in government-by-experts[87] and as such was far less antagonistic toward enlarging the scope of the federal government than was his predecessor, Calvin Coolidge. Indeed, the current historiography of the period suggests that many of the more sweeping economic reforms instituted by Franklin D. Roosevelt were in fact legislated in miniature by Hoover. Hoover's fondness for experts doubtless encouraged him to heed the suggestion of the Chief of the Children's Bureau, Ms Grace Abbott, who urged that a conference be called to study the well-being and health of American children. In November 1930 1200 experts assembled in Washington for the White House Conference on Child Health and Protection.

Overshadowing the various papers and discussions were the protracted and bitter exchanges between Surgeon General Hugh Cumming and Ms Abbott over children's health services. The Public Health Service fiercely resented the fact that the Children's Bureau had been given authority under the Sheppard-Towner Act to administer state grants and was fearful that this 'mistake' would be repeated in future legislation dealing with infant and maternal care. Cumming was successful in lobbying the Conference's subsection on governmental administration of child health laws to support the transfer of all maternal and child health services from the Children's Bureau to the Public Health Service, by a vote of 32 to one.[88] The one opposing vote was that of Ms Abbott, who had administered the provisions of the now defunct Sheppard-Towner Act. The vote was particularly surprising since most child care specialists had been favorably impressed with the administration of the Act and supported its being revived. Indeed, so popular was the Children's Bureau among most of the delegates to the Conference that had they voted on the recommendation at the closing plenary session, it seems clear that the Children's Bureau would have won. In addition, the issue took on the overtones of a feminist struggle since almost all the women delegates supported Ms Abbott. So contentious was the suggested transfer that when it appeared that the issue would result in a fierce public quarrel at the closing meeting, the top Conference leaders settled the issue by simply dropping the subsection's recommendation.[89]

In the event, when Sheppard-Towner was revived as Title V (Section 1) of the Social Security Act in 1935, grants-in-aid to the states for maternal and child health care were once again placed in the hands of the Children's Bureau for disbursement. In addition, Title V provided for grants to the states for locating crippled children and for their medical care and for the care and protection of homeless and neglected children.[90] These grants too were to be administrated by the Children's Bureau. Between fiscal years 1936 and 1966 the amounts allocated under this provision of the Social Security Act, while comparatively small, had increased substantially, from $1.9 million to $87.3 million.[91] Table 1.3 gives some indication of the amounts authorized and appropriated by the Bureau between the mid-1930s and 1962.

Title VI of the Social Security Act called for grants to the states for the purpose of extending state and local health departments. Distribution of these funds was to be administrated by the Public Health Service, which continued to disburse them after 1944 when the provisions of Title VI were transferred from the Social Security Act to the newly legislated Public Health Service Act. The original allocation in 1935 authorized $2 million directly to the PHS for the extension of its staff and $8 million per year for the years 1936 to 1940.[92] Predictably, by 1965 this amount had increased to $65 million.[93] One of the conditions imposed by the Surgeon General on those states applying for grants under Title VI was that they file a plan detailing exactly how the grant would be used and that annual reports be submitted indicating exactly how the monies had been spent. This requirement, which supposedly attempted to impose some quality control on expenditures, also served the far more important purpose of allowing the Public Health Service to determine the scope and functions of the various state health departments and thus allowed the federal government to determine the direction taken by health services throughout the country.

1930 was a banner year for the Public Health Service. Not only were the Parker Act, expanding the Commissioned Corps, and the Ransdell Act, creating the National Institute of Health, passed, but Congress enacted yet a third statute creating the Federal Bureau of Prisons in the Department of Justice and assigning Public Health Service officers to the various prisons to supervise and provide for medical care.[94] Among the officers assigned were physicians, dentists, psychiatrists, and nurses who were charged with the health care of 12 000 inmates. PHS personnel quickly staffed the hospitals and dispensaries at the seven existing prisons and, following its opening in 1933, the Medical Center for Federal Prisoners located at Springfield, Missouri. The Medical Center was especially designed as a prison hospital and had the capacity to serve 1200 patients. Increases in the prison population made the Springfield facility inadequate and a second prison hospital was opened at Rochester, Minnesota, in 1965. A third facility, affiliated with Duke University Medical Center, that will include psychiatric beds, acute care beds, diagnostic and treatment facilities, and ambulatory clinics is due to be opened at Butner, North Carolina. There are currently over 123 000 federal prisoners[95] incarcerated in 95 Federal Bureau of Prisons facilities.

The provisions of Title VI of the Social Security Act, authorizing $2 000 000 annually for the 'investigation of disease and the problems of sanitation' allowed for even greater expansion of the Public Health Service during the Depression.[96] In addition, the Service was charged with undertaking several make-work projects, part of Roosevelt's strategy for combating the nation's economic slump. The most significant of these was the 'Health Inventory', a study covering 865 000 families in 90 cities and 23 rural areas, financed in part by a $3 450 000 grant from the Emergency Relief Fund. At its peak, the project employed more than 5000 people. Field work was completed in February 1936. Among the other projects undertaken by the Public Health Service during this period: (1) a survey of rats in areas where typhus had previously broken out, financed by a $1 000 000 grant from the federal government; (2) a drainage program in 14 states whose purpose was malaria control, at a cost of $4 500 000 for labor; (3) a massive privy-building program in 24 states employing almost 35 000 people, at a cost of $5 000 000 for labor; and (4) the sealing of abandoned coal mines in order to reduce the discharge of acid wastes, which employed some 3000 people.[97]

More importantly, Title VI had placed in the hands of the Public Health Service a device whereby it could shape state and local departments of health through the grants-in-aid over which it had control. Surgeon General Thomas Parran,[98] successor to Hugh Cumming, was keenly aware of this power. In October 1936, just six months after taking office, Parran noted that 'under the public health provisions of the Social Security Act, a national health program has been made possible for the first time in the history of the Public Health

Table 1.3 Children's Bureau: Federal Grants to the States, 1936–1962 (amounts authorized and appropriated) (dollars)

Year	Maternal and Child Care		Crippled Children		Child Welfare	
	Authorized	Appropriated	Authorized	Appropriated	Authorized	Appropriated
1936	3 800 000	1 550 000	2 850 000	1 187 000	1 500 000	625 000
1937	3 800 000	3 624 406	2 850 000	2 849 061	1 500 000	1 376 457
1938	3 800 000	3 799 534	2 850 000	2 849 939	1 500 000	1 499 543
1939	3 800 000	3 800 000	2 850 000	2 850 000	1 500 000	1 500 000
1940	5 820 000	4 800 000	3 870 000	3 350 000	1 510 000	1 505 000
1941	5 820 000	5 820 000	3 870 000	3 870 000	1 510 000	1 510 000
1942	5 820 000	5 820 000	3 870 000	3 870 000	1 510 000	1 510 000
1943	5 820 000	5 820 000	3 870 000	3 870 000	1 510 000	1 510 000
1944	5 820 000	5 820 000	3 870 000	3 870 000	1 510 000	1 510 000
1945	5 820 000	5 820 000	3 870 000	3 870 000	1 510 000	1 510 000
1946	5 820 000	5 820 000	3 870 000	3 870 000	1 510 000	1 510 000
1947	11 000 000	11 000 000	7 500 000	7 500 000	3 500 000	3 500 000
1948	11 000 000	11 000 000	7 500 000	7 500 000	3 500 000	3 500 000
1949	11 000 000	11 000 000	7 500 000	8 250 000[1]	3 500 000	3 500 000
1950	11 000 000	11 000 000	7 500 000	7 500 000	3 500 000	3 500 000
1951	15 000 000	13 200 000	12 000 000	9 975 000	10 000 000	7 075 000
1952	16 500 000	12 524 100	15 000 000	11 385 500	10 000 000	7 590 400

1953	16 500 000	12 746 579	15 000 000	11 482 498	10 000 000	4 370 923
1954	16 500 000	11 927 700	15 000 000	10 843 400	10 000 000	7 228 900
1955	16 500 000	11 927 700	15 000 000	10 843 400	10 000 000	7 228 900
1956	16 500 000	11 927 700	15 000 000	15 000 000	10 000 000	7 228 900
1957	16 500 000	16 000 000	15 000 000	15 000 000	10 000 000	8 361 000
1958	16 500 000	16 500 000	15 000 000	15 000 000	12 000 000	10 000 000
1959	21 500 000	16 500 000	20 000 000	16 500 000[2]	17 000 000	12 000 000
1960	21 500 000	17 500 000	20 000 000	16 000 000	17 000 000	13 000 000
1961	25 000 000	18 167 000	25 000 000	20 000 000	25 000 000	13 666 000
1962	25 000 000	25 000 000	25 000 000	25 000 000	25 000 000	18 750 000

Notes:
[1] Includes a supplemental appropriation of $750 000.
[2] Includes a supplemental appropriation of $1 500 000 for congenital heart disease.

Source: Dorothy E. Bradbury, *Five Decades of Action for Children: A History of the Children's Bureau* (Washington, DC: Department of Health, Education, and Welfare [Children's Bureau, Social Security Administration], 1962): 136.

Service'.[99] Over the course of the next 30 years (1935–65) much of the legislation touching on health matters was explicitly designed to encourage state and local departments to initiate or expand programs that the federal health bureaucracy regarded as particularly important, including programs aimed at altering 'unhealthy' living habits and dealing with environmental threats to health. Toward this end, the Public Health Service tended to rely more and more on narrowly targeted categorical-formula and project grants, rather than on general purpose grants. 'After 1935, and more intensively after 1945,' notes one commentator, 'the cornerstone of [federal] policy had been to exercise assertive federal leadership to create a more uniform, accessible, and comprehensive national health services system. In the public health area the main mechanism had been the federal grant structure, which distributed nationally collected taxes, mainly the income tax, to the states, localities, and nonprofit organizations to promote the federal objectives.'[100]

Dr Parran's particular interest was sexually transmitted diseases, which, together with tuberculosis, he regarded as the two main causes of preventable disease and death in the United States.[101] Under his direction, the Public Health Service earmarked its grants-in-aid to the states for the control of venereal disease. In December 1936 a National Conference on Venereal Disease Control was held in Washington, DC, attended by almost a thousand health officials and clinicians. Predictably, delegates found the allocation of federal funds earmarked for anti-venereal work insufficient and called upon the federal government to commit itself to greater involvement in the struggle against this scourge. Parran's concern was reflected in the distribution of funds under Title VI of the Social Security Act. Approximately 10 percent of these funds were channeled to the battle against syphilis and as a consequence the states were financially able to establish clinics and diagnostic facilities throughout the country.[102] By May 1938 Parran had generated sufficient public interest in his war against sexually transmitted diseases to secure passage of the National Venereal Disease Control Act.[103] The Act provided funds to state boards of health to develop anti-venereal programs. The Public Health Service was authorized to supervise the various state plans for improving their anti-venereal services[104] and to distribute funds, $3 000 000 in the first year, $5 000 000 in the second, $7 000 000 in the third, and 'thereafter such amounts as may be necessary to carry out the provisions of the Act'.[105]

Parran's tenure as Surgeon General, from 1936 to 1948, coincided with a substantial expansion of the Public Health Service. The National Institute of Health had grown considerably[106] and programs such as Title VI of the Social Security Act and the Venereal Disease Control Act had placed in the hands of the Service considerable power to shape the states' responses to public health issues. In addition, the notion of what constituted public health was being pushed to encompass the provision of personal medical care. As one historian has noted of the PHS during this period:

> It was ... the Social Security Act of 1935 that would provide the PHS with the mandate to become an important, independent participant in the reconstruction of the country. That Act and, indeed, the New Deal as a whole invited PHS involvement in the medical and social fabric of the country in a more intense way than ever before.[107]

Parran was a dedicated supporter of compulsory government health insurance, especially for low-income Americans, and regarded the extension of the federal authority into this area as long overdue. Among the recommendations made at the National Health Conference held in Washington, DC, in July 1938 were that public health and maternal and child health services be expanded, that more hospitals be built, and that public medical care be extended to all the 'medically needy', 'including those not on relief yet unable to pay medical bills'. In addition, the Conference called for consideration 'of a comprehensive program designed to increase and improve medical service for the entire population' underwritten by either taxed funds or compulsory premiums.[108] These proposals were translated into political reality when on 23 January 1939 President Roosevelt sent a message to Congress entitled 'Health Security', which called on Congress to give serious consideration to the recommendations of the Conference. One month later, in February, Senator Robert Wagner of New York introduced a bill calling for a system of universal compulsory government health insurance. It was not until 1965, however, that such a scheme, limited to the elderly, was enacted.

When the Public Health Service was originally created as the United States Marine Hospital Service 1798, it was located within the Treasury Department,[109] an anomaly that continued throughout the long history of the Service until the reorganization of executive branch agencies by President Roosevelt.[110] The President had been given authority by Congress to rearrange and consolidate these agencies provided the restructuring did not meet explicit Congressional disapproval. In 1939 Roosevelt created a new agency, the Federal Security Agency (FSA), bringing together the social welfare agencies created in the New Deal and the other federal bureaus concerned with health, education, and welfare. Placed within the FSA was the Public Health Service, the Civilian Conservation Corps, the National Youth Administration, the Office of Education, the United States Employment Service, and the Social Security Board,[111] The Food and Drug Administration, St Elizabeth's Hospital, the Freedmen's Hospital,[112] the Children's Bureau, and the National Office of Vital Statistics were added subsequently.

With the outbreak of war in Europe, it was thought wise to place certain agencies of the federal government on a war footing. In January 1940 the

Secretary of War, who was especially concerned with the spread of venereal infections among American troops, requested the Public Health Service to supervise the 'environmental sanitation' of the municipalities surrounding areas used for military maneuvers on the same basis as had occurred during World War I.[113] And five months later, in July, President Roosevelt appointed a Council of National Defense, to which was appended an advisory council, the Emergency Medical Service, to deal with health and medical activities in which Dr Parran played a crucial role. One year later, in May 1941, the Office of Civilian Defense was established with the Mayor of New York, Fiorello LaGuardia, as its director. The medical component of the Office, which was staffed by PHS reserve corps appointments, was lodged in the Public Health Service, whose officers were in charge of coordinating the various state emergency medical plans. PHS officers were also to serve in positions that put them under enemy fire. When in November 1941 the Coast Guard was militarized, medical, dental, engineer, and nurse officers of the Public Health Service were seconded to serve with the Coast Guard both on land and on its ships, including those in the North Atlantic where losses were high.[114]

Nor was the Public Health Service spared from involvement with the detention[115] of Japanese-Americans by order of President Roosevelt under Executive Order 9066, dated 19 February 1942.[116] More than 120 000 Japanese-Americans who had at least one grandparent with Japanese blood, most of whom were American citizens, were rounded up and shipped to concentration camps. The Western Defense Command of the United States Army, who directed the detentions, was commanded by Lieutenant General John L. DeWitt who, in turn, called upon Medical Director Walter T. Harrison of the San Francisco Public Health Service Headquarters to take charge of all medical and public health services for detainees until their arrival at the permanent camps that were being set up. The PHS oversaw the establishment of hospitals, staffed by Japanese physicians, dentists, and nurses, who themselves had been detained, at the four largest assembly centers, Manzanar, Santa Anita, and Pomona, California, and Puyallup, Washington,[117] and furnished physicians and nurses for each of the 225 trains required to transfer the detainees from the various assembly centers to the concentration camps.[118]

The period from 1940 to 1945 was to have a profound impact on the Public Health Service. Its programs and personnel had been expanded to meet the demands of a nation at war. In the space of those five years the Commissioned Corps quadrupled in size (from 625 officers to 2600), the overall number of staff more than doubled to 16 000, and the Service's budget grew almost fivefold.[119]

A particularly pressing problem that emerged with the outbreak of war was a shortage of trained nurses. This chronic national shortage became more severe as the war progressed and as women were being recruited for fairly

Table 1.4 Public Health Service Appropriations, 1933–1944 (dollars)

Fiscal Year	Amount	Fiscal Year	Amount
1933	11 021 413	1939	24 783 550[2]
1934	10 386 328	1940	29 094 329[3]
1935	9 969 164	1941	33 379 340[4]
1936	11 303 567[1]	1942	42 476 939[5]
1937	20 151 075	1943	52 366 245[6]
1938	21 146 980	1944	55 638 000[7]

Notes:
[1] Includes $8 000 000 for grants.
[2] Includes $3 000 000 for venereal diseases.
[3] Includes $9 500 000 for grants and $5 000 000 for venereal diseases.
[4] Includes $11 000 000 for grants and $6 200 000 for venereal diseases
[5] Includes $3 200 000 for nurses' training, $4 470 000 for emergency health and sanitation activities, and $8 750 000 for venereal diseases.
[6] Includes $8 984 000 for emergency health and sanitation activities and $12 500 000 for venereal diseases.
[7] 1944 Budget.

Source: House Subcommittee of the Committee on Interstate and Foreign Commerce, *Public Health Service: Organization and Functions: Hearings on H.R. 649*, 68th Cong., 1st Sess. 1943, 5.

well-paying civilian jobs. Fearing an even more serious dearth, Congress had included an additional $1 200 000 in its appropriations to the PHS in July 1941 for nurse training and a further appropriation for the program in the following year. All together, approximately $4 500 000 was spent on nurse education over the first two years.[120] The PHS had determined in 1943 that 65 000 women, approximately 10 percent of all high school graduates that year, would need to be recruited into nursing and that it was essential to reduce the nurse training period in order to accelerate entry into the profession. Predictably, nursing leaders originally opposed compromising the requirements for entry but by late 1942 the shortages were so great that they relented. Doubtless the threat to draft nurses into the military played a role in their decision.

Dr George Baehr of the Office of Civilian Defense had conceived a plan, later known as the US Cadet Nurse Corps, whereby students who joined the Corps would undergo professional training over either a 24-month or 30-month period in return for free tuition, maintenance, uniforms, and a monthly stipend financed by the federal government. The costs were estimated at about $65 000 000 per year for some 65 000 entrants per year.[121] This program quickly gained congressional backing and the result was the passage of the Nurse Training Act of 1943, creating the US Cadet Nurse Corps. Cadet nurses enrolled in approved programs throughout the country and committed themselves to two years of assigned service once they graduated. To administer this program, Surgeon General Parran created the Division of Nurse Education, which underwrote nursing schools through an array of tuition and support payments and building grants. The program proved a success and over the course of the next three years, the recruitment target was easily met.[122] The US Cadet Nurses Corps was terminated at the close of World War II and the last student enrolled under its terms graduated in 1949.[123] Eighty-five percent of the nursing schools had participated and 125 000 nurses had graduated through the Corps. The nurse-training program, at its height, accounted for more than half of the wartime increase in the PHS budget.

The expansion of the Public Health Service and the substantial increase in its budget led Surgeon General Parran to petition for legislation that would create a new structure for the PHS and would regularize the anomalous position of the Commissioned Corps. As things stood, officers were neither covered by civil service disability and death benefits nor by the benefits given to members of the Armed Forces. In the spring of 1943 Parran had prepared a bill that would provide military benefits to members of the Commissioned Corps, reorganize the PHS into four Bureaus, and expand the discretionary authority of the Surgeon General to engage in new activities dealing with the nation's health. Congress was at the time considering a bill that would establish a compulsory health insurance scheme covering all Americans, with the Surgeon General acting as national coordinator for the provision of medical care.[124] However, this expansion in the functions of the Public Health Service beyond its missions of quarantine, scientific research, advice to the states, and providing medical service to certain federal beneficiaries would have required legislative redefinition. As a consequence, Congress acted quickly on Parran's request, enacting two bills in successive sessions. The first, signed in November 1943, structured the Commissioned Corps along military lines[125] and gathered the disparate functions of the Service into four subdivisions: the National Institute of Health, the Office of the Surgeon General, a new Bureau of Medical Services, and a new Bureau of State Services. The second, signed in July of the following year, codified the responsibilities of the Service and strengthened the role of the Surgeon General in policymaking, broadening his discretion over programs and budgets.[126]

One of the less publicized provisions of the 1944 Act which was to prove of great importance empowered the Surgeon General to 'make grants to universities, hospitals, laboratories, and other public or private institutions and individuals', thus providing legislative authorization for PHS grants in any area of medicine. Prior to passage of the Act, grants had been limited to cancer research but this provision extended the Public Health Service's grant-making authority to any area of the life sciences. During the war grants-in-aid to universities had been made by the Committee on Medical Research of the

Office of Scientific Research and Development (OSRD) under Dr Vannevar Bush. These grants underwrote research in a wide range of areas. With the end of the war, the OSRD was ordered to wind down its activities preparatory to being abolished. One of its problems, however, was to secure the continuance of 44 of its most important research projects. Dr Eugene Dyer, Director of the National Institute of Health, which was still under the authority of the PHS, suggested that these projects be turned over to the NIH and this was in fact done.[127] Thus began what was later to become one of the largest areas of expenditure for the PHS.

In November 1944 Surgeon General Parran announced the Public Health Service's postwar aims. Rejoicing in contemplation of a nation in which the federal government had successfully intruded into every aspect of health,[128] Parran noted in the PHS's *Annual Report* of that year:

> The upheaval of the present war has cast into plain view the inadequacies of health and medical services in the United States. The people increasingly recognize that health is a paramount public concern; they insistently demand equal recognition and action by their government. Responsible political and professional leaders also recognize that the Nation must have sound and healthy citizens to meet the tasks of peace no less than the tasks of war. Plans are being shaped for international collaboration in peace after victory. World health will undoubtedly be a major field in the permanent organization of nations. It would seem that the United States should now consider the means by which its health resources may be reorganized and developed so as to implement ultimately a comprehensive project for the national health.[129]
>
> . . . .
>
> The United States possesses the potential resources with which to insure to every citizen the maximum benefit from all that the life-saving sciences have to offer. Public Health means the sum total of individual health. Only by considering the needs of the individual, the local community, and the State can we arrive at a program adequate in scope and extent for the Nation as a whole.
>
> A National Health Program such as is envisaged here contemplates the full utilization of all resources – the participation of private institutions, local, State and Federal governments – in a cooperative enterprise for the national welfare.[130]

In keeping with this statement of principles, Parran set out a six-point program for the Public Health Service:

1. A sanitary environment for everyone;
2. a hospital system adequate for the provision of complete medical services for all;
3. expanded public health services in every part of the country;
4. augmented research in health and medical science;
5. training of health and medical personnel in adequate numbers;
6. a national medical care program.[131]

Parran appears to have been fairly certain that the Public Health Service under his direction was on the eve of an immense expansion in its authority and duties, to the point where the agency, under the direction of the Surgeon General, would be placed in charge of all matters pertaining to health. Indeed, if the growth of just one of the Public Health Service's components, the National Institute of Health, was any indication – its budget had ballooned from $464 000 in 1939 to $2 835 000 in 1945 – and if a Democratic President and the more liberal members of Congress had had their way and a national compulsory health insurance scheme were enacted,[132] Parran's predictions might well have been realized.

During the course of the war, Dr Vane M. Hoge had been charged with directing the construction of emergency hospitals in areas of the country swollen by war-industry personnel. Both he and Surgeon General Parran worked closely with the Commission on Hospital Care, which had been created by the American Hospital Association in 1944 to assess the need for hospitals in postwar America.[133] At its 1943 convention, the AHA's House of Delegates had passed a resolution, known as the Bishop resolution, calling on the federal government to institute a system of government aid to cover the costs of hospital care for those who were unable to pay for hospital treatment and to enter on a massive program of hospital construction. As a consequence, the Commission was established to evaluate existing hospital facilities and to make projections about future needs. It was headed by Dr Arthur C. Bachmeyer, dean of the Cincinnati General Hospital, and undertook an extensive study during the period 1944–46 on the number of hospital beds required in each locality, based in part on the concept of requisite bed supply per population, itself a function of population density.[134] Although the Commission Report, 'Hospital Care in the United States', was not officially published until 1947, its contents were made available earlier to those concerned with the issue.[135] The report recommended an elaborate system of regional hospitals offering primary and secondary care based on a national planned program of medical facilities and in this recommendation it was joined by Surgeon General Parran, who was a staunch advocate of a large-scale federal program of hospital construction. Parran envisaged a huge system of medical facilities in which central university hospitals would act as the hub for a ring of lesser hospitals and medical facilities, all coordinated by the Public Health Service. 'Hospitals of the future', Parran noted,

> should form the nucleus around which integrated services are developed. The largest centers should be associated with schools of medicine and would carry on extensive research programs. Patients requiring more complicated services than are available in their communities would have access to the center – or perhaps to a district hospital serving a number of communities. In small towns there would be smaller rural hospitals or health centers – linked administratively with the district hospital and the large medical center.[136]

These pressures, in addition to the almost certain increase in demand for medical services that would follow in the wake of a national health insurance program – should it be enacted by Congress – led the Truman Administration to encourage passage of a bill establishing a program to inventory the country's existing hospitals and public health centers and to support new hospital construction.[137] The bill itself[138] was introduced into Congress by Senators Lister Hill of Alabama and Harold H. Burton of Ohio and was extracted whole from a section of the Murray-Wagner-Dingell bill (originally drafted by the Public Health Service)[139] that provided for a national system of compulsory health insurance. It was enacted as an amendment (Title VI) to the Public Health Service Act in August 1946.[140]

While the American Medical Association adamantly opposed any national health insurance scheme, it strongly supported the Hill-Burton bill since the provision of new hospitals and other medical facilities at public expense constituted a direct subsidy to patients purchasing medical care, who would otherwise have to bear the increased costs associated with the modernization of the country's medical plant.[141] Senator Hill, the son of a physician who named the future Senator after Joseph Lister, the originator of antisepsis, was a fairly reliable supporter of the AMA's political program and not only introduced the hospital construction bill but, in 1962, voted against a national health insurance program. Hill is also credited with having persuaded his colleague from Alabama, John Sparkman, to vote against the health insurance bill, thereby providing the margin of victory for those who sought its defeat.[142]

Under the terms of the Act, the Surgeon General was charged with prescribing the number of hospital beds needed in each state in order for that state to provide adequate hospital service, the upper limit of which, in most cases, was 4.5 acute care beds per 1000 population. As the Act was actually administered, however, the Surgeon General accepted the recommendations of the state as presented in its plan which he felt consistent with the objectives of the law.[143] The requirement that each state meet the standards set down by the legislation before it could receive funding soon led to state licensing of hospitals as a method of certifying that the hospital met federal standards. Construction grants were allocated to each state using a formula that provided funds inversely proportional to the state's per capita income. On any approved project, the Public Health Service would provide one-third of the cost, the state, one-third, and the final one-third would be provided by the local group sponsoring the project. In 1949, this formula was altered when the federal contribution was made variable, ranging from one-third to two-thirds of total costs, depending on need. Another amendment to the Act, in 1954, appropriated an additional $2 million for inventorying diagnostic and treatment centers, chronic disease hospitals, rehabilitation facilities, and nursing homes. Funds were also made available for the construction of these facilities.

While the original act authorized a modest $75 million in grants to the states and to nonprofit groups for the purpose of hospital construction for each of the first five years of the program, this amount soon swelled to $200 million in 1965 and to more than $400 million in 1972. Indeed, from its inception in July 1947 through June 1971, a total of no less than $3.7 billion in Hill-Burton funds was spent on building and equipping inpatient and outpatient facilities. Almost 11 000 projects for the construction of health facilities, particularly hospitals and nursing homes, were approved during this period, providing more than 470 000 beds.[144] So far-reaching were the effects of this program on the American health care system that one author has noted that

> for almost thirty years, until about 1975, the Hill-Burton legislation (the original act and many subsequent amendments) was the major instrument used by the federal government to shape the contours as well as determine the size of the United States system of health facilities.[145]

Table 1.5 conveys some notion of the extent of Hill-Burton effects on the stock of the nation's medical facilities.

Over the course of the 25 years between 1946 and 1971 the program was expanded as the Public Health Service became increasingly active in shaping the health care of Americans. Probably the most important of the various amendments made to the Hill-Burton Act were those enacted in 1964. Known as the Hill-Harris Amendments after Senator Hill and Congressman Oren Harris of Arkansas, the new bill provided funds for hospital modernization and replacement over a four-year period. By virtue of these amendments funds were made available to refurbish obsolete and shoddy equipment, particularly prevalent in the inner cities and slums. At the same time, the formulas for calculating needed hospital beds were altered to reflect differences between areas and states. It is worth noting that the federal government has made a number of attempts to construct a coordinated, regionalized system of hospitals and other health-care facilities, but without much success. The Hill-Harris Amendments appear to be one of the earliest such attempts.

The Hill-Burton program was effectively allowed to lapse with passage of the national Health Planning and Resources Development Act of 1974 which incorporated a revised version of Hill-Burton on a severely reduced scale and limited to underserved areas and primary-care facilities. By the mid-1970s, according to one commentator, the prevailing sentiment in health-care circles was that, rather than too few, there were too many hospital beds.[146] To this one might add the fact that the Nixon Administration was not particularly sympathetic to large-scale public expenses on health care. Indeed, in 1972 President Nixon had vetoed the extension of Hill-Burton but his veto was overturned by Congress. However, during the years when Hill-Burton operated, between 1946 and 1974, it had provided $4 billion in grants to nearly 4000 hospitals

Table 1.5   Hill-Burton Construction (1 July 1946 to 30 June 1971)

Type of Facility		Inpatient Care Beds		Hill-Burton Funds (in millions)
General Hospitals		344 453		$ 2635.5
Units of hospitals	51 983		$312.5	
Nursing homes	37 884		171.6	
Chronic Disease Hospitals	7 491		39.0	
Long-term Care Facilities		97 358[1]		523.1
Mental Hospitals		21 034		78.5
Tuberculosis Hospitals		7 484		27.7
Inpatient Care facilities		470 329		$ 3264.8
Outpatient and Other Health Care Facility Projects				
1078 Outpatient Facilities[2]				204.1
552 Rehabilitation Facilities				135.0
1281 Public Health Centers[3]				99.7
41 State Health Laboratories				14.4
Total				453.2

Notes:
[1]   Excludes 7209 long-term care beds built in conjunction with general and other hospital projects, for which funds cannot be separated from the total project costs. These beds are reported in the following categories of facilities: general hospitals: 7113 beds; mental hospitals: 60 beds; tuberculosis hospitals: 36 beds.
[2]   Previously designated 'diagnostic or treatment centers'.
[3]   Excludes 131 public health centers built in combination with general hospitals.

Source: Hill-Burton Hospital Survey and Construction Act: History of the Program and Current Problems and Issues (Washington, DC: 1973).

and an additional $1.9 billion in loans and loan guarantees to another 300 hospitals.[147]

Not only did passage of the Hill-Burton Act contribute to the spectacular increase in the size and prestige of the Public Health Service, but 1946 also saw the birth of what was to become the Centers for Disease Control. One of the many functions assigned to the PHS during the war was the eradication of the mosquito responsible for spreading malaria (the *Anopheles* mosquito) from the areas surrounding military bases and war industry sites. Toward this end the PHS employed more than 3000 laborers engaged in malaria control work, supervised by teams of physicians, engineers, and entomologists.[148] To its credit, the Service was able to accomplish this gargantuan task, with the aid of huge quantities of larvicide (Paris green) and with sufficient labor to drain the swamps located near certain critical areas in the South and the Caribbean. The Malaria Control in War Areas program, known as MCWA, was headquartered in Atlanta and directed first by Dr Louis L. Williams, Jr and then by Mark D. Hollis; it proved so successful that in 1945 the MCWA was assigned the job of combating typhus as well. Both Dr Hollis and Dr Joseph Mountin, the Director of the Bureau of State Services of the PHS (the arm of the PHS charged with collaborative efforts with states and localities), appear to have arrived at the notion of preserving the infrastructure of the MCWA after the war ended by establishing a permanent agency to monitor infectious diseases and undertake epidemiological and other research into their nature. After having obtained the consent of the National Institute of Health to creating a new research arm of the Public Health Service,[149] Hollis and Mountin proposed that the MCWA be designated the Communicable Disease Center.[150] In describing how he conceived of the new institution, Dr Parran asserted:

> The Institution I have in mind would carry on the training of technical and health education personnel in this particular field. It would serve the States through specialized epidemiological service and laboratory and field studies on communicable disease problems and control. With State health departments, it would conduct demonstrations in the control of communicable diseases – particularly those of tropical origin. However, the first responsibility of such an institution would be to conduct basic research into all the tropical and other diseases which are spread by insects and other intermediate hosts, and which can be checked or eliminated through proper environmental controls.[151]

On 1 July 1946, after Congress had consented to its creation, the Communicable Disease Center was established under the direction of Dr Mark Hollis.

Yet another crucial Congressional bill contributing to the enlargement of the Public Health Service was enacted in 1946. Dr Robert Felix, the Director of the PHS's Mental Hygiene Division, had lobbied for the creation of a national mental health program and for more extensive research into mental disorders. Felix, a psychiatrist who had worked under Dr Lawrence Kolb, the founder of the Lexington narcotics facility and Dr Walter L. Treadway, the first director of the Mental Hygiene Division, was able to prevail on Congress to enact the National Mental Health Act,[152] which authorized the Surgeon General to undertake research into the causes, diagnosis, and treatment of psychiatric disorders and to provide for aid to the states for mental health services.[153] Despite the fact that the bill did not carry with it any appropriations, President Truman signed it on 3 July and a preliminary meeting of the

National Advisory Mental Health Council was held the following month, financed by a $15 000 grant from the Greentree Foundation.[154] Funds were first appropriated in 1948 and in April 1949 the National Institute of Mental Health (NIMH) was formally established with Robert Felix as its director. The Congressional appropriation for the agency was $1 119 000 in 1948, $369 000 of which was for operating expenses. By 1999, the operating expenses of the Institute had risen to almost $148 000 000 and it awarded $712 000 000 in grants.

Yet a fourth expansion of the activities of the Public Health Service – beyond the passage of Hill-Burton and the creation of the Communicable Disease Center and the National Institute of Mental Health – occurred in 1946. On 16 July, as a consequence of President Roosevelt's Reorganization Plan No. 2, the Vital Statistics Division of the Bureau of the Census, located in the Department of Commerce, was transferred to the PHS. The Service's prestige seems to have reached a high point in that year. On 19 June an International Health Conference was convened in New York to draft a constitution for a World Health Organization. Not only did Surgeon General Parran chair the Conference but the constitution of the WHO was modeled on that of the Public Health Service.[155]

Parran's term as Surgeon General expired in 1948 and, somewhat to his surprise, President Harry Truman refused to appoint him for a fourth term. In early 1947 Oscar R. Ewing had replaced Watson B. Miller as Administrator of the Federal Security Agency, of which the Public Health Service was a component. Ewing had been vice-chairman of the Democratic National Committee and one of the leading members of the group responsible for convincing President Roosevelt to choose Senator Truman as his running-mate in the 1944 elections. Ewing did not like Parran and prevailed on Truman to appoint a new Surgeon General, Dr Leonard Scheele, the director of the National Cancer Institute, whose primary interest was medical research rather than public health practice.[156] With the appointment of Scheele, it was hardly surprising that the National Institute of Health prospered. Within a year of his appointment, Congress enacted the National Heart Act creating the National Heart Institute and altered the name of the National Institute of Health to the National Institutes of Health. In the following week, it established yet a fourth institute, the National Institute of Dental Research.[157]

Yet, despite the expansion undergone by the Public Health Service during the quarter century prior to the Presidency of Dwight Eisenhower, its medical services, particularly the Marine Hospitals, continued as the largest employer within the Service, with 7800 employees. In 1952 the personnel of the Division of Hospitals included 50 percent of all the PHS's physicians, 60 percent of its dentists, and 65 percent of its nurses, and was providing complete medical and dental care and hospitalization to merchant seamen,

Coast Guard officers and enlisted personnel and dependents, Federal prisoners and those with leprosy (Hansen's disease).[158] The division operated 18 hospitals, two tuberculosis hospitals, and the National Leprosarium.

The administration of Dwight D. Eisenhower opened somewhat dramatically. The Hoover Commission[159] had recommended the creation of a new cabinet-level department responsible for health and welfare, and Eisenhower, with this in mind, appointed Oveta Culp Hobby as Administrator of the Federal Security Agency to prepare plans for the Agency's reorganization. With the help of White House and Bureau of the Budget staff, the Federal Security Agency was able to develop a reorganization plan for the Agency's elevation to a new Department.[160] In order to insure Congressional approval of the change it was decided to transfer the whole of the existing organizational structure of the Federal Security Agency into a new Department without alteration, to elevate the Administrator to Secretary, and to create an undersecretary, three new assistant secretaries, and a general counsel.[161] In deference to the American Medical Association who insisted that a high-ranking officer within the Department be a physician, one of the assistant secretaries was given the designation 'Special Assistant to the Secretary for Health and Medical Affairs'. The bill creating the new Department, as predicted, met with little Congressional opposition and on 11 April 1953 the Department of Health, Education, and Welfare came into being. At its inception it had 34 000 employees and expenditures of $5.4 billion, of which $3.4 billion was in Social Security trust funds.[162]

A test of the new Department's capabilities in dealing with public health issues came quickly. In 1953 Dr Jonas Salk was commissioned by the National Foundation for Infantile Paralysis (the March of Dimes) to develop an inactivated vaccine for poliomyelitis.[163] By late 1954 Salk had developed a vaccine and had begun massive clinical trials. These trials were closely followed by the media and proved successful. The Federal Laboratory of Biological Safety, a component of the National Institutes of Health, declared the vaccine safe and on 12 April 1955 the Secretary of Health, Education, and Welfare issued licenses to six pharmaceutical firms to produce and distribute the vaccine. These licenses were granted in spite of the fact that one of the Laboratory's researchers, Dr Bernice Eddy, had notified her supervisors that several monkeys had developed paralysis from the vaccine manufactured at Cutter Laboratories. Both the Surgeon General and the National Institutes of Health endorsed the vaccine and millions of children were swiftly inoculated. Two weeks after the vaccine was released to the public, cases of polio were reported in newly vaccinated children. Within a short period 192 cases of paralytic polio and ten deaths had occurred. Most of the deaths were traced to the vaccine manufactured by Cutter Laboratories. Vaccines from Park Davis and Eli Lilly were also discovered to contain live virus, indicating that the method that had been used for killing the virus was inadequate.[164]

On 27 April the vaccine program was temporarily halted and resumed one month later. By November new production safeguards were put in place, including an additional step in the filtering process. The political fallout from the Cutter incident was substantial. The new Department was severely criticized by the press and by members of Congress. The Laboratory of Biological Safety, which had certified that the vaccine was safe, was thoroughly reorganized and placed under the Food and Drug Administration (FDA) as the Division of Biological Standards.[165] Finally, two months after the incident, both Ms Hobby and the Special Assistant for Health and Medical Affairs resigned their positions.

In 1955 the Public Health Service once again acquired a new assignment, the provision of medical, dental, and hospital care for American Indians and Alaskan natives. The Bureau of Indian Affairs of the Department of the Interior had traditionally dealt with all matters pertaining to Indians, including their health care.[166] However, the Bureau faced continuing difficulties in staffing and administering the medical and hospital system. Indeed, the level of medical and hospital care accorded American Indians was so low that a number of organizations, among them the American Medical Association, the American Public Health Association, and the Association of State and Territorial Health Officials, all recommended a transfer of medical services from the Bureau of Indian Affairs to the Public Health Service. In 1949 the Bureau of Indian Affairs employed only 96 full-time physicians to staff 81 hospitals serving 500 000 people.[167] As a result, in 1954 both President Eisenhower and Congress, in the face of opposition from the Bureau of the Budget, determined that the Public Health Service should assume these duties.[168] Transferred to the PHS's new division, the Indian Health Service, were 48 hospitals, most of which had fewer than 100 beds, and about 2500 employees.[169] The PHS Commissioned Corps was particularly useful in carrying out the mandate of the Transfer Act, which was to improve the quality of care available to Indians.[170] Inasmuch as doctors who served in the Commissioned Corps were exempt from the draft and since almost all physicians who met the physical requirements of the military were drafted, those who wished to avoid serving in the armed forces found the PHS an attractive alternative.[171]

The Public Health Service inherited a population in which tuberculosis was rampant[172] and in which the infant mortality rate was almost three times that for American whites.[173] By 1972, the staff of the Indian Health Service was approximately 6500, nearly double the number that was transferred to it in 1955, and a number of hospitals had been modernized. Today, the IHS's network of inpatient and ambulatory care facilities is extensive and covers most of the areas where there are concentrations of American Indians and Alaska natives.[174] The cost for such coverage, however, is quite high inasmuch as large numbers of these populations live in sparsely settled areas. Indeed, in spite of the number of facilities available to them, there are a not inconsiderable number of Indians and Alaska natives who continue to live at vast distances from an IHS facility.[175] In 1975 Congress enacted the Indian Self-Determination Act[176] which extended to the various Indian tribes the option of manning and managing medical and hospital programs in their own communities. As a result of this legislation, Indian tribes and Inuit communities currently manage eleven of the IHS's 49 hospitals and 372 of the IHS's ambulatory facilities.[177]

A further addition to the Public Health Service took place at almost the same time as the Service absorbed the health program of the Bureau of Indian Affairs. Beginning in 1836 the Surgeon General of the Army began collecting medical publications and purchased a number of medical works with a view towards building a medical library.[178] The collection had reached 2000 volumes by the close of the Civil War and at that point it was placed in the hands of John Shaw Billings, an Army physician who was particularly interested in the bibliography of medicine.[179] Billings had joined the Army's Medical Department in 1862 and stayed on after the termination of hostilities to organize the library and museum of the Office of the Surgeon General of the Army and other army records. Billings, who was granted the title of Director of the Library, a post he was to hold until 1895, had early in his tenure determined that the library's collections should be as complete as possible and he began to acquire both new and old biomedical publications as expeditiously as possible.

Following the death of President Abraham Lincoln in 1865, the site of his assassination, Ford's Theater, was closed and became the site of the Army Medical Museum and the Library of the Army's Surgeon General. By 1875 Billings could boast that he had acquired about 75 percent of the medical journals that had been previously published.[180] In the following year Dr Robert Fletcher joined the Library as Assistant Librarian and assisted Billings in issuing his periodical catalog of current medical literature, the *Index-Medicus*, and in cataloguing the Library's own holdings, the *Index-Catalogue*. Fletcher served as co-editor of the *Index-Medicus* from 1879 to 1899 and between 1903 until 1911 as editor-in-chief of the *Index-Medicus*. The *Index-Medicus*, which continues to the present as the pre-eminent listing of current biomedical articles,[181] was first issued in 1879, one year before the first appearance of the *Index-Catalogue*. By the mid-1880s the Library's collections had reached such proportions that new quarters were essential. Billings was able to convince Congress that there was a pressing need for a new home and in 1887 a new building to house the collections was opened on the Mall.[182] By the time of his retirement from the Librarianship, the Library had become the foremost medical library in the world, boasting the largest collection of medical literature to be found anywhere.

The various Librarians who followed upon the retirement of Billings were men of mediocre talent and under their directorship the Library languished. With the end of World War II, however, there appears to have been a revival of interest in medical information.[183] In 1949 Dr Frank Bradway Rogers assumed the Librarianship and it was during his tenure that Congress enacted legislation transforming the Armed Forces Medical Library into the National Library of Medicine (NLM) and transferring it to the Public Health Service.[184] The National Library of Medicine Act of 1956 also authorized the necessary funds for the construction of a new facility, which was begun immediately. It was completed in 1962 and Rogers presided at its opening in that year. Not only was Rogers responsible for promoting the Library to international preeminence but, more importantly, he oversaw the Library's entry into the electronic age. Under Rogers' directorship, the NLM contracted with the General Electric Corporation to devise the necessary hard- and software to sort and arrange the Library's holdings. The result was the Library's Medical Literature Analysis and Retrieval System, MEDLARS.

In 1963 Rogers resigned and was replaced as Librarian and Director by Dr Martin Cummings who, in January 1964, inaugurated MEDLARS, a complex system that cross-references abstracts across the whole range of biomedical subjects using keywords. In October 1965, Congress passed the Medical Library Assistance Act which authorized the Library to award grants to American medical libraries to expand and update their services and to individuals seeking to do research in medical communications. Senator Lister Hill, who had been one of the most fervent advocates of extensive government involvement in health care,[185] declined to stand for re-election to the Senate in 1968. As his final term drew to its close Congress judged it fitting to name a new facility that would house the Library's burgeoning biomedical communications network, the Lister Hill National Center for Biomedical Communications.[186] In 1971 MEDLARS became operational online (there known as MEDLINE) and deliverable through the Internet as Grateful Med and PubMed, and in this guise became the world's most heavily used bibliographic database in biomedical research, covering the fields of medicine, nursing, dentistry, veterinary medicine, and the health care system and providing bibliographical information and author abstracts from over 3800 biomedical journals. In addition, MEDLARS was eventually to spawn a wide array of other databases pertinent to the health sciences, all accessible through the Internet.[187] Predictably, the current budget of the National Library of Medicine is huge; the Library's fiscal year 2000 budget was $214 million.

The National Library of Medicine was not alone in growing substantially through the 1950s and 1960s. In 1951 the Centers for Disease Control expanded its epidemiological work by establishing an Epidemic Intelligence Service (EIS). Dr Alexander Langmuir, who had been trained in epidemiology at Johns Hopkins, was able to prevail on the senior staff at the CDC that a division able to deal with infectious disease emergencies was necessary and his views won support in Congress because of the growing concern with biological warfare, especially after the United States had committed its troops to the conflict in the Korean peninsula.[188] As a consequence, the EIS was created and its epidemiologists assigned to public health units of the PHS and to state and local governments to monitor outbreaks of infectious diseases and to prevent their spread. Not only was the EIS added to the Centers for Disease Control during this period but in 1957 the Public Health Service's Venereal Disease Division was transferred to the Center, as was the Tuberculosis Division three years later. The Center's head offices in Atlanta had by this point outgrown the space available and new quarters were made available to it adjacent to the campus of Emory University.

Ironically, it was the expansion of these various subdivisions, nominally within the Public Health Service, that contributed to the undoing of the PHS. The National Institutes of Health particularly had become so large during the 1950s and 1960s that it could easily stand on its own. Table 1.6 provides some idea of its truly remarkable growth between its inception and 1968, the year in which Senator Lister Hill – the NIH's greatest champion – retired from Congress.

In contrast, in 1967 approximately $71 million was appropriated by Congress to the PHS for inpatient and outpatient medical and dental care furnished to American seamen and coastguardsmen and their dependents.[189]

Not only were the purposes for which the Public Health Service was originally organized just a small part of the PHS's total budget, but during the 1960s the public debate surrounding government involvement in health care centered on the possibility of a government-directed health insurance plan for the elderly, a scheme in which the Social Security Administration rather than the Public Health Service would most likely play the leading role. As a consequence, the PHS was not an important party to the debate on Medicare. At the same time that it was thus relegated to the sidelines, the Public Health Service found itself facing a concerted attack from the Bureau of the Budget and a number of economy-minded Congressmen who wished to follow the recommendations of the second Hoover Commission Report on Organization of the Executive Branch and close the hospitals staffed by the PHS, the Service's original *raison d'être*. The Report, released in 1955, had recommended that all medical and hospital care furnished by the Public Health Service to statutory beneficiaries, that is, merchant seamen, Coast Guard personnel, and federal employees injured in the line of duty, could be better and more economically provided by community hospitals at the port cities and elsewhere.[190] Indeed, the recommendation that the Public Health Service hospitals be permanently closed appeared even earlier, in the first Hoover Commission Report issued in

Table 1.6   National Institutes of Health: Appropriations and Amounts
Obligated for Grants and Direct Operations, Fiscal Years
1938–1968 (thousands of dollars)

Fiscal Year	Total Grants[1]	Direct Operations[2]	Total Appropriations[3]
1938	140	324	464
1939	171	293	464
1940	277	430	707
1941	237	474	711
1942	230	470	700
1943	181	1 097	1 278
1944	182	2 373	2 555
1945	142	2 693	2 835
1946	850	2 565	3 415
1947	4 004	4 072	8 076
1948	8 225	16 401	24 626
1949	15 525	13 015	28 540
1950	28 068	15 412	43 480
1951	34 620	15 923	50 555
1952	29 968	17 147	47 115
1953	30 144	18 022	48 136
1954	37 810	21 248	59 058
1955	40 372	26 749	67 121
1956	45 601	34 856	80 457
1957	101 066	46 744	147 810
1958	108 892	63 074	171 966
1959	165 161	76 803	241 964
1960	243 503	88 407	331 910
1961	355 143	103 957	459 100
1962	509 625	119 834	629 459
1963	592 896	144 305	737 201
1964	568 562	161 817	730 379
1965	589 344	183 747	773 091
1966	662 291	211 640	873 931
1967	751 596	262 658	1 014 254
1968	797 830	278 631	1 076 461

Notes:
[1]   Includes grants for research, fellowships, training, health research facilities and community mental health centers construction, regional medical programs, state control programs, community demonstration projects, and student loans, scholarships, control programs, etc.
[2]   Includes funds for research and development contracts, intramural research, the National Library of Medicine (NLM), and funds necessary for administrative and program management of NIH.
[3]   Includes NLM, Office of the Director (OD), and direct construction. The totals here shown are in some cases significantly lower than the appropriations shown in Miles, *Department of Health, Education, and Welfare*, 189–90.

Source: National Institutes of Health, Office of the Director, *NIH Almanac, 1999* (Bethesda, Md.: National Institutes of Health, 1999).

1949, which proposed that all government-run hospitals, including those of the Veterans Administration, be folded into a 'United Medical Administration'.[191] While the Commission proposal was never acted upon, it did mark the start of a long-term battle between the PHS and the Bureau of the Budget (and its successor, the Office of Management and Budget) about the viability of PHS hospitals.

Concerned about the future of the Public Health Service, Surgeon General Leroy E. Burney, who had been appointed to that position in 1956, established a Study Group on the Mission and Organization of the Public Health Service, which released its report (the Hundley Report) in June 1960. The Report noted that:

> The next great nationwide health efforts may be expected in two broad areas: the physical environment and comprehensive health care. During the present decade, 1961–1970, major national efforts, comparable with the great expansions of medical research and hospitals in the 1950s, will be required in each of these areas.[192]

In keeping with this conclusion, the Hundley Committee recommended that the PHS discontinue its original functions of providing medical care to American seamen and supervising the federal government's quarantine activities while reorganizing itself to concentrate on problems associated with civilian health. As a consequence, Surgeon General Burney divided the PHS's Bureau of State Services in two, one part devoted to dealing with issues relating to service delivery and the other to concentrate on questions relating to environmental health. At the same time the Service's environmental programs were consolidated and upgraded and division-level units created for radiological health (1957) and air pollution (1960).

During his tenure as Surgeon General, Burney refashioned the role of Surgeon General to underscore his function as an advocate of healthy living. His office henceforth became a propaganda mill for all manner of issues affecting one's health.[193] Not surprisingly, the first of these revolved around the dangers of cigarette smoke. In July 1957 Burney released the findings of his Joint Report of the Study Group on Smoking and Health, which found that 'prolonged cigarette smoking was a causative factor in the etiology of lung cancer'. By way of reinforcement, Burney directed that a 'Public Health Statement' be published in the *Journal of the American Medical Association* linking lung cancer to smoking.[194] This was the first of numberless times that the Public Health Service has taken a position on the subject. Since that time, the Surgeon General's office has been in the forefront of efforts to curb smoking in one way or another, either by imposing prohibitively high taxes on cigarettes, by limiting the areas where one may smoke, or by advertising its pernicious effects.

In January 1961, shortly after John F. Kennedy's inauguration, Burney resigned his office and was replaced by Luther L. Terry, who was then Assistant Director of the National Heart Institute.[195] At the time that Terry took over the PHS, the Service had about 24 000 civil service employees and an additional 4000 commissioned officers staffing three divisions, the Bureau of State Services, the Bureau of Medical Services, and the huge National Institutes of Health, whose budget at this point had reached almost a half billion dollars. Terry soon took up the crusade against smoking initiated by his predecessor. In June 1962 the Surgeon General announced the appointment of an expert ten-person Advisory Committee on Smoking and Health whose task was to undertake a comprehensive review of the existing literature on smoking and health. Using the National Library of Medicine as its base, the Committee critically analyzed all available basic, clinical, and epidemiological studies on the effects of smoking. The result was the first Surgeon General's report on *Smoking and Health*, the conclusions of which were made known to a packed crowd of reporters in January 1964. The Report concluded that 'cigarette smoking is causally related to lung cancer in men' and that 'the magnitude of the effect of cigarette smoking far outweighs all other factors'.[196]

The publicity accorded the Surgeon General as a consequence of this announcement propelled the office into public consciousness. At the same time, the Surgeon General, who was nominally 'the top professional administrator within the government concerned with public health',[197] was increasingly bypassed when health policy was being formulated. The Public Health Service, over the course of the 1950s and 1960s, gradually lost influence to other groups within the federal bureaucracy and to members of Congress who were more aggressive in calling for direct federal involvement in matters relating to preventive health programs, environmental hazards to health, and, most importantly, health insurance. An eminent writer on public health has summed up the status of the Public Health Service by the early 1960s in these words:

The leaders and members of the Commissioned Corps of the United States Public Health Service did not create a strong public perception of their being wholeheartedly in the forefront of the drive for increased federal involvement in furthering publicly sponsored medical care services to at least the underserved poor. The perennial battles over the introduction of national health insurance were being waged with other troops in the front lines – largely medical care administrators, publicists, and scholars rather than leading federal public health professionals – so that when many of the new federal programs for improving access to medical care were passed, agencies other than the Public Health Service were assigned to administer them. The administration of Medicare was assigned to the Social Security Administration, the social insurance agency; Medicaid was assigned to Social and Rehabilitation Services, the welfare agency; and when federal attempts to provide greater access to ambulatory care were made by establishing community health centers, the program was placed under an independent agency in the office of the President, Office of Economic Opportunity.[198]

Despite the fact that no less than five major pieces of legislation relating to health were enacted between August and October 1965, the involvement of the Public Health Service was only peripheral.[199] Even more disappointing to the Service was the fact that legislation dealing with water pollution control, which had become particularly fashionable, was likely to bypass the PHS inasmuch as the environmental lobby viewed the Service, whose concerns were primarily medical, as insufficiently interested in environmental issues. In 1961, the authority that had previously been lodged in the Public Health Service was transferred to the Secretary of the Department of Health, Education, and Welfare and in 1965 Congress established the Federal Water Pollution Control Administration, which it promptly moved from HEW to the Department of the Interior. Finally, in 1970, the Environmental Protection Agency was created and assumed responsibility for almost all environmental issues.

The debate over Medicare and Medicaid[200] was a particularly partisan one, pitting those who supported a state-administered system of compulsory, universal health insurance on the one hand against those who favored the provision of medical and hospital services by market forces, as imperfect as they then might have been. The senior staff of the Public Health Service, and especially the Surgeon General, played almost no role in these debates, regarding themselves as above partisan politics. That the public pronouncements of the Surgeon General on smoking and other lifestyle choices were, at bottom, equally ideological rather than purely value-free scientific statements does not seem to have occurred to PHS officials. There is little doubt that the refusal of the Surgeon General to actively participate in the politics of health care in the 1960s contributed to the Service's decline in importance. As one analyst has observed:

> Surgeons general, appointed for a 4-year term, were supposed to be chosen for their professional competence, not their ideological views. Inescapably, the policy issues made it awkward for a surgeon general to occupy so powerful a position unless he was able to make a positive contribution to the development of health policies that coincided with the basic philosophy of the administration in power. Inevitably, health policy moved into the hands of the Secretary of HEW and his politically appointed subordinates.[201]

By March 1968 the Secretary of HEW, Wilbur Cohen, had concluded that, for political purposes, it was imperative to transfer the financial resources and staff positions then in the hands of the Surgeon General, who was required by law to be chosen from the Public Health Service's Commissioned Corps,[202] to a more politically responsive appointee, the Assistant Secretary for Health and Scientific Affairs (later renamed the Assistant Secretary for Health). As a result, on 13 March Cohen ordered that all the functions of the Public Health Service and the Food and Drug Administration[203] be transferred to the supervision of the Assistant Secretary of Health and Scientific Affairs.[204] This marked the first time in its history that the nation's top health officer was not a career official. Additionally, the Assistant Secretary was given responsibility for coordinating and determining policy for the other health programs in the Department, including Medicare, Medicaid, and the Children's Bureau. The functions that had been lodged in the Office of the Surgeon General were transferred to the operating components of the Public Health Service itself and to the Office of the Assistant Secretary. While the title of Surgeon General was not abolished, the position was deprived of all administrative authority except over the Commissioned Corps; it was otherwise reduced to a purely staff advisory role.

Soon after this change in the status of the Surgeon General, Cohen decided to reorganize the PHS itself.[205] A newly created Health Services and Mental Health Administration (HSMHA) was given authority over all the components of what had been the Public Health Service with the exception of the National Institutes of Health, the Bureau of Health Manpower, and the National Library of Medicine. In addition, the new agency was given control over the various mental health functions that had earlier been vested in the NIH.[206] To the NIH, which had experienced dramatic growth over the past few years, were added the Bureau of Health Manpower and the National Library of Medicine – which was physically located on the NIH campus in Bethesda, Maryland. With yet a further reorganization order, which shortly followed, Cohen created yet another new agency, the Consumer Protection and Environmental Health Service (CPEHS), to include all PHS activities having to do with air pollution, urban and industrial health, and radiological health. Also included in CPEHS was HSMHA's National Communicable Disease Center and the Food and Drug Administration.[207] The reorganization appears to have done little except to undermine the morale of the Commissioned Corps. Only eight PHS hospitals remained and even those were under constant attack from the Bureau of the Budget.[208] One commentator notes of the effects of this restructuring:

> However logical this reorganization may have seemed to Secretary Cohen and his advisers, it seemed more like a disaster to many career officers of the Public Health Service who had spent their professional lives with the organization. Although the name Public Health Service was legally retained, nobody quite knew what it meant any more. It could have been used to refer generally to the three main organizations: the Food and Drug Administration, the Health Services and Mental Health Administration, and the National Institutes of Health, but it was almost never used that way. It did not describe a cohesive organization, and it was no longer a

title to conjure up a proud tradition extending back to 1798. The least the Secretary could have done, thought many, was to preserve the name in a meaningful way by assigning it to the organization that now had the awkward and easily forgettable name of Health Services and Mental Health Administration.[209]

The election of Richard Nixon to the presidency did not halt the frequent attempts to reorganize the health functions of the Department of Health, Education, and Welfare. In January 1970 HEW Secretary Robert Finch abolished the Consumer Protection and Environmental Health Service and divided its functions into two operating agencies, the Food and Drug Administration (which reverted to its status prior to the creation of CPEHS two years earlier) and a new bureau, the Environmental Health Service (EHS). By virtue of this change, the nominal Public Health Service now consisted of four operating agencies: HSMHA,[210] NIH, FDA, and the new EHS. However, this was to last no more than a few months. In late 1970 President Nixon created the Environmental Protection Agency and to the EPA were transferred the programs of the Environmental Health Service. Finally, in the summer of 1973 the new Secretary of Health, Education, and Welfare, Casper Weinberger, abolished the HSMHA (established in 1968 by Secretary Cohen) and in its place created four separate agencies: the Center for Disease Control, the Alcohol, Drug Abuse, and Mental Health Administration, the Health Resources Administration, and the Health Services Administration. Thus, after these reforms – to the extent that there can be said to have been a Public Health Service at all – it consisted of the Office of the Assistant Secretary for Health and six line agencies: (1) the Center for Disease Control; (2) the Health Resources Administration; (3) the Health Services Administration; (4) the Food and Drug Administration; (5) the Alcohol, Drug Abuse, and Mental Health Administration, and (6) the National Institutes of Health.[211] But, as one commentator observed of the earlier Health Services and Mental Health Administration, while the Public Health Service continued its nominal existence, it no longer described a cohesive organization.[212] The Assistant Secretary for Health was now the chief administrator of all health programs except for the Medicare functions of the Social Security Administration and the medical assistance (Medicaid) programs of the Social and Rehabilitation Service.

With the election of Richard Nixon, the Secretary of Health, Education, and Welfare, Robert Finch,[213] chose Dr John Knowles, General Director of the Massachusetts General Hospital, to serve as Assistant Secretary of Health. Knowles, who was a strong advocate of compulsory universal health insurance,[214] was blocked by a coalition of conservatives in the Senate in the wake of intense pressure from the American Medical Association.[215] In his place, Finch chose Dr Roger Egeberg, dean of the University of Southern California School of Medicine, who was no less liberal in his views than was Knowles. However, Egeberg was able to pass muster in the Senate and he, in turn, encouraged Finch to select Jesse Steinfeld of the National Institutes of Health Clinical Center as the new Surgeon General.[216] While Egeberg was nominally in charge of almost all health matters in the Department, the reorganization of 1968 had left him with far too small a staff to deal with the various agencies over which he had authority. As a consequence, these agencies (collectively, the 'Public Health Service') began working directly with the Secretary. The Surgeon General, although the traditional head of the Public Health Service, had almost no power at all.

Finch did not stay long as Secretary of HEW and was replaced in 1970 by Elliot Richardson. Responding to pressures from the White House and from his own staff calling for the elimination of the Commissioned Corps, Richardson appointed a committee on the future of the Corps chaired by a former Undersecretary of the Department, John A. Perkins. Perkins' report was issued in 1971 and recommended that the Corps be disbanded.[217] The report pointed out that the staffing of the Commissioned Corps was far too heavily dependent on the existence of the military draft; inasmuch as the Corps, since 1930, had parity with the military, members of the Commissioned Corps could discharge their military obligations by joining the PHS. Once conscription was abolished, however, it was unlikely that the Corps could continue to attract a sufficiently large number of doctors, dentists, and other professionals. In its place the report proposed that all personnel be hired within a 'civil service framework'. In addition the committee recommended that the position of Surgeon General be abolished. Apparently most personnel thought the report would be quickly implemented. One week after the report's appearance, the PHS newsletter *Health and Medicine* noted that there remained 'very little doubt' about the future of the Corps, especially in light of the recent fate of the Surgeon General's office and the PHS hospital system. 'The report', it predicted, 'is expected to be implemented'.[218]

In the event, the report was not acted upon. Surgeon General Steinfeld strongly opposed its recommendations and was able to marshal support for the Corps from a variety of quarters, including some key members of Congress, among them Congressman Paul Rogers of Florida, the Chairman of the House Subcommittee on Health.[219] As a result, Richardson backed down. However, when Steinfeld resigned as Surgeon General on the day President Nixon took office for his second term, Casper Weinberger, who had succeeded Richardson as Secretary, refused to fill the position.[220] However, the demise of the office was short-lived. In 1977, President Jimmy Carter reinstated the position with the appointment of Dr Julius Richmond as Surgeon General and Assistant Secretary for Health of HEW. With Dr Richmond's appointment, the role of the Surgeon General once again carried some administrative weight but only by virtue of the fact that Dr Richmond held a second post, that of Assistant Secretary for Health.

The Commissioned Corps was able to survive this and more recent threats to their continued existence by underscoring the fact that they constitute a corps of highly trained professionals who are organized on military lines and who therefore are on duty 24 hours a day and are obligated to meet any assignment given them.[221] Officers are employed at the Centers for Disease Control, the Food and Drug Administration, and the National Institutes of Health and continue to supply medical care through the Indian Health Service, the National Health Service Corps, the Coast Guard, the Bureau of Prisons, the Immigration and Naturalization Service, and the US Marshals Service.[222]

While a few members of the Commissioned Corps continue to work with the National Health Service Corps the number has been declining since the decision was made to reduce federal involvement in the program. The National Health Service Corps was established in 1970 as a division of the newly created Health Resources Administration (HRA). Its purpose was to supply physicians to 'underserved'[223] communities in the United States in the hope that when these physicians, commissioned in the PHS,[224] separated from the HRA, they would continue to practice in the communities to which they had been assigned. The scheme seems to have been the brainchild of a PHS physician, Dr Laurence Platt, and was brought to fruition by the staff of Senator Warren Magnuson of Washington who, at the time, was Chairman of the Senate Appropriations Subcommittee for the Departments of Labor and Health, Education, and Welfare.[225] Of course, the viability of a physicians' corps serving in areas to which they were directed by a medical bureaucracy depended on the continuation of conscription, which ended in 1973. In light of that possibility, Congress in 1972 added further incentives, including reimbursing the tuition costs of medical and nursing students. However, budget constraints and predictions of physician surpluses[226] led to reductions in the program in the 1980s. Between 1978 and 1981 more than 6700 scholarships were awarded, compared to 40 awards in 1988.[227] As a result in 1987 Congress introduced its current loan repayment program whereby if a medical or nursing student agreed to work in an area designated by the Health Corps for at least two years, the program would repay the student's education loans or, in the absence of any loans, to grant the student a scholarship covering the costs of tuition in addition to a monthly stipend.[228]

At this point in its history, the Commissioned Corps numbers some 5500 personnel out of a total of 37 000 who currently staff the agencies falling under the rubric of the Public Health Service. Table 1.7 shows the number of Officers of the Commissioned Corps and the number of civil servants in the Public Health Service (or, after 1973, in the agencies nominally aggregated as the Public Health Service).

While President Nixon had a reputation for economies in government, the truth was that federal spending increased sharply during his administration,

Table 1.7   Commissioned Officers and Civil Servants in the Public Health Service, Selected Years, 1900–1997

Year	Officers	Civilians
1900	107	988
1910	128	1295
1920	683	13 772
1930	289	5004
1940	627	8895
1945	2342	15 135
1950	2222	15 529
1960	3816	22 614
1970	5501	37 094
1975	5510	43 771
1982	5840	41 474
1987	5441	40 672
1992	6544	46 729
1997	6036	44 891

Source: Department of Health and Human Services, Public Health Service Commissioned Corps, *Report to the Senate Appropriations Committee Responding to a Request in the Committee Report on the FY 1998 HAS Appropriations Bill* (Washington, DC, 1998): 9.

from $183.6 billion in fiscal year 1969 to $332.2 billion in fiscal year 1975, an increase of 80 percent in six years.[229] Among the new, costly programs initiated during Nixon's presidency were those aimed at ostensibly 'safeguarding the environment', the Environmental Protection Agency, and 'protecting the health and preventing injuries to American workers', the Occupational Safety and Health Administration. Bills creating both agencies were passed by Congress in 1970 and greatly expanded the existing operations in these areas that were previously undertaken by units of the Public Health Service. President Nixon was impressed by the popularity of the first 'Earth Day' celebrations that took place in April 1970 and determined to capitalize on the enthusiasm accorded environmental issues. The result was creation of the Environmental Protection Agency (EPA), which consolidated most federal environmental activities. The EPA was charged with 'protecting the nation's public health and environment' by 'finding ways to clean up and prevent pollution, ensuring compliance and enforcement of environmental laws, assisting states in environmental protection efforts, and engaging in scientific research and education to advance the nation's understanding of environmental issues'.[230] Most of the Commissioned Officers of the PHS who had been working in the area of pollution control moved to the new agency, on what amounted to a permanent loan from the PHS.

1970 also witnessed the passage of legislation creating the National Institute of Occupational Safety and Health (NOSH), lodged in the Public Health Service, and the Occupational Safety and Health Administration (OSHA) in the Department of Labor. The traditional manner of dealing with worker safety prior to the creation of OSHA was through state workers' compensation legislation or through the court system, where damage awards would, it was thought, prove a sufficient deterrent to companies maintaining unsafe working environments. However, in the minds of many the court system was too slow and its judgments too uncertain while, with respect to workers' compensation, inflation was continually eating away at the value of legislated payments. As a consequence, by 1970 there was some pressure to institute a federal regulatory board to set safety standards for the nation's workplaces, despite the fact that worker safety had been improving and worker deaths had been dramatically declining for almost half a century.[231] The federal government's involvement in industrial hygiene had been quite modest before 1970. In 1910, Surgeon General Walter Wyman had assigned a medical officer to the newly created federal Bureau of Mines with the object of studying the diseases and injuries of miners[232] and in 1914 the PHS established an Office of Industrial Hygiene and Sanitation, which, under one name or another, had grown steadily. It was the states, however, that assumed the responsibility for occupational safety and health. In this task they were assisted by the PHS, who helped shape the states' programs. Lack of standardization and concern about the wide variation in state laws prompted labor unions to campaign for national standards, which eventuated in the passage of the 1970 Act creating the NOSH and OSHA.[233] To NOSH, which was made a subdivision of the Centers for Disease Control, was assigned the task of research and training in the area of job health and safety, while OSHA was to formulate health and safety standards which it had the power to enforce.

The introduction of Medicare and Medicaid in 1965 almost immediately led to massive increases in the costs of medical care, to which the federal government responded with 'cost containment' schemes. The most popular of these propounded by the Nixon administration was the health maintenance organization (HMO), which was lauded by President Nixon in a speech delivered in 1971,[234] where he announced that he would seek legislation whose goal was the encouragement of health maintenance organizations. HMOs, it was thought, did away with the incentives most doctors had to order tests and other services paid for by a third party. Instead, HMOs rewarded physicians for ordering fewer services. Physicians, who had an economic interest in the HMO to which they belonged, would be paid a flat fee per patient; there would thus be no incentive to order. In 1973 Congress passed the Health Maintenance

Organization Act, which subsidized the creation of HMOs and required employers with more than 25 employees and who provided medical insurance as one of its benefits to offer HMO coverage. As a consequence of this new policy regarding HMOs, the Health Maintenance Organization Service was established within the office of the Administrator of the Health Services and Mental Health Administration in October 1971. Following the 1973 reorganization of the Department, the HMO Service became part of the Health Resources Administration, along with several other agencies whose functions involved supervising the distribution of professional and paraprofessional manpower and facilities.[235]

The 1970s were not particularly good years for the Center for Disease Control (CDC). In 1972 the details of the Tuskegee experiment were made public by one of the employees of the CDC venereal disease program. Rather than admit the PHS's culpability in failing to adequately treat syphilitic patients in the Tuskegee control group, the CDC had the temerity to defend the decision and continued to withhold effective medication on the grounds that adverse reactions had been reported among some patients suffering from advanced syphilis who were treated with penicillin. This defense was quickly shown to be absurd and the survivors and families of deceased participants settled out of court for $10 million. Four years later, in 1976, the CDC once again found itself embarrassed by its ineptitude. In January of that year four Army recruits at Fort Dix, New Jersey, were found to be suffering from an illness identified as 'swine flu', the result of a virus thought to be similar to the organism that caused the 1918 influenza pandemic. In March the CDC and other high-ranking officials of the Public Health Service urged President Gerald Ford to recommend a universal program of vaccination against this flu strain. In a televised address Ford called on Congress to appropriate $135 million for the purpose of preparing a vaccine, under CDC supervision, that would be ready for mass distribution by the autumn. To 'prove' its harmlessness, Ford himself was vaccinated while being televised. General inoculation began at the beginning of October and in the following two months almost 50 million people were vaccinated. By late November several cases of an extremely rare paralytic ailment, known as Gillian-Barer Syndrome (GBS) were reported from Minnesota and Alabama and eventually from the rest of the country. By mid-December it had been determined that there was a causal link between the swine flu vaccine that had been distributed and the cases of GBS that had emerged. To add to the CDC's embarrassment no cases whatever of swine flu occurred other than the four at Fort Dix, which originally gave rise to the CDC's recommendations.

In 1977 Joseph Califano, who was reputed to be an activist administrator, was appointed to the position of Secretary of Health, Education, and Welfare by President Carter. Califano, in turn, chose Dr Julius Richmond to serve as both Assistant Secretary for Health and Surgeon General, an appointment that appeared to mark a change in the fortunes of the Public Health Service.[236] Richmond, a professor of child psychiatry and human development at the Harvard Medical School and who, in 1965, became the first national director of Project Head Start, had thought it possible to revitalize the PHS by once again assuming the role as the nation's chief health officer and the uniformed head of the PHS Commissioned Corps. Richmond was especially interested in the Neighborhood Health Centers, a project of the Office of Economic Opportunity[237] which had been transferred to the Public Health Service in the early 1970s. These medical facilities were renamed Community Health Centers and housed in the Health Services Administration. By 1980 there were almost 900 such centers, specializing in preventive and primary care.[238] At the same time the National Health Service Corps was responsible for dispatching more than 2000 physicians, all members of the Commissioned Corps, into communities thought to be underserved. The Community Health Centers, together with the National Health Service Corps, brought the Public Health Service and its staff in direct contact with the public for the first time and seemed to mark the beginning of a revival in the fortunes of the PHS.

While it is true that Richmond tried to resurrect the Surgeon General's office as a vital part of the Department of Health, Education, and Welfare, he did not neglect his role as propagandist for whatever lifestyle was then officially approved. In 1979 the Public Health Service released a report setting out specific goals for a reduction in the mortality and disability rates among Americans. Entitled *Healthy People: The Surgeon General's Report on Health Promotion and Disease Prevention*, Richmond pointed out the dangers of smoking and consuming alcohol, disregarding good nutritional practices, and not engaging in regular exercise. However, his recommendations did not stop at pointing out the damage to our bodies that might be caused by engaging in unhealthy lifestyles. He went on to advise that, in the interests of public health, laws be enacted controlling the use of guns and requiring that motorcyclists use helmets. Richmond then went on to specify goals which could be met by 1990 if people in fact were to engage in 'risk reduction and health promotion behaviors', including (1) an overall 35 percent reduction in the rate of infant mortality; (2) a 20 percent reduction in the numbers of deaths of children aged one to 14 years to fewer than 34 per 100 000; (3) a 20 percent reduction in the numbers of deaths among adolescents and young adults up to age 24 to fewer than 93 per 100 000; (4) a 25 percent reduction in the number of deaths among adults ages 25 to 65; and (5) a 20 percent reduction in the average number of days of illness among those over 65 years of age.

Richmond appointed Dr J. Michael McGinnis to head an Office of Disease Prevention and Health Promotion to carry through on the recommendations made in the Report and to monitor the mortality and disability status of

Americans. In addition, Richmond's Report set in train a whole series of reports by subsequent Surgeons General condemning certain 'unhealthy' lifestyles and prescribing needed changes. It was the contention of McGinnis' Office of Disease Prevention and Health Promotion that a half of all deaths could be attributed to nine causes and could be reasonably considered 'premature': tobacco, 400 000; diet and activity level, 300 000; alcohol; 100 000; infectious agents, 90 000; toxic agents, 60 000; firearms, 35 000; sexual behavior, 30 000; motor vehicles, 25 000; and illicit drug use, 20 000, a total of 1.6 million deaths per year. As a consequence of this new emphasis on preventive medicine, the Public Health Service established a new program which they hoped would improve the delivery of clinical preventive services. Entitled 'Put Prevention Into Practice', PPIP is a pure propaganda program that distributes posters, booklets, reminder postcards, prescription pads, and alert stickers to physicians and clinics, all aimed at reducing mortality and morbidity rates. The program is quite open about the fact that its goal is to alter the lifestyles of Americans so that they are more compatible with PHS recommendations.[239]

With the election of Ronald Reagan as President, the Public Health Service once again found itself at odds with the Office of Management and Budget (OMB). Reagan had campaigned on a platform of budget cuts and capping or cutting back federal programs.[240] And among the Administration's recommendations regarding health were reforming Medicare and Medicaid and closing down the Public Health Service hospitals. As Secretary of Health and Human Resources[241] Reagan appointed Richard Schweiker, who decided once again to separate the office of Assistant Secretary of Health from that of Surgeon General. Schweiker chose Dr Edward Brandt, dean of the University of Texas Medical Branch, at Galveston, Texas, as his Assistant Secretary for Health and Dr C. Everett Koop, surgeon-in-chief at the Children's Hospital in Philadelphia and professor of pediatric surgery at the University of Pennsylvania Medical School. Koop's appointment was somewhat controversial since he was a strong opponent of abortion. Indeed, so strong did the opposition to his appointment seem that, in March 1981, he was given the temporary post of Deputy Assistant Secretary of Health while awaiting Senate confirmation as Surgeon General. Finally, in November 1981 the Senate voted 68 to 24 to confirm his nomination.

Aware that his role was effectively limited to one of a propagandist for the official view of what constituted healthy living,[242] Koop seems to have thrown himself into his new position with gusto. Indeed, during his eight-year term as Surgeon General there is hardly an area of social life that escaped Koop's pronouncements. Predictably, tobacco was his primary target. Over the course of his eight years as Surgeon General his office issued a report each year but one on the baleful health consequences of smoking, each report underscoring a different aspect of the problem.[243] Additionally, while warning labels on cigarettes were first required by legislation enacted in 1965, Koop lobbied for far stronger wording and for additional restrictions on the sale of tobacco products. The strengthening of legislation was particularly important since tobacco smoke, the Surgeon General concluded, had adverse consequences not only for smokers but on those who were forced to breathe in second-hand smoke.[244] Finally, in what can only be regarded as an attempt to frighten the public into giving serious consideration to criminalizing tobacco use the Surgeon General's *Report* published in 1988 went so far as to assert that cigarettes and other tobacco products were 'addicting in the same sense as are drugs such as heroin and cocaine'.[245] Indeed, in response to the *Report*, anti-smoking groups predictably called for far more extensive regulation of tobacco.

The Surgeon General did not limit his concerns to the harmful effects of tobacco. His office also pointed out the damage her unborn child faced should a pregnant mother consume any alcohol, a warning that has led thousands of women to avoid even so much as a glass of wine while pregnant. Koop also conducted campaigns against sedentary living and extolled the benefits of exercise. 'Look forward to exercising; it's a great time for unwinding and relaxing', he was later to point out, when launching his campaign against obesity. Having enjoyed the position of pronouncing on how unhealthy were the lifestyles of most Americans, Dr Koop continued to rebuke the public after leaving office. In 1994 he started *Shape Up America*, which he describes as 'the only privately funded, national program committed solely to education about the importance of healthy weight, an improved diet, and increased activity'. So dreadful was obesity in Koop's eyes that in 1996, when his organization issued new medical guidelines, he urged doctors 'to treat obesity as a dangerous and chronic disease to be treated with diet, exercise, drugs and even surgery'.[246]

Koop's tenure as Surgeon General coincided with the identification of the AIDS virus. The earliest cases that had come to the attention of the Centers for Disease Control suggested that the disease was restricted to homosexual men, although why remained a mystery.[247] However, in 1982 the disease was diagnosed in a patient with hemophilia and again in a child who had been transfused. These cases suggested that the condition was transmitted through blood or blood products. As a consequence, the first federal funds, $6.5 million, were allocated to study the condition. Epidemiological studies soon suggested that AIDS was a transmissible ailment and that a change in behavior might reduce the risk of suffering from the condition. In 1983 two women whose sexual partners had AIDS contracted the disease, pointing to the fact that AIDS could be transmitted by heterosexual intercourse. By 1985, American scientists had isolated the infectious agent that they believed caused AIDS, which they called

HTLV-III, and had found that condoms appeared to prevent the sexual transmission of the virus. In response to these findings and to comply with a directive from President Reagan, Dr Koop issued his report on AIDS in October 1986. In it he called for those people who had a high risk of acquiring the disease to refrain from donating blood and to adjust their sexual behavior and rejected the notion of using a quarantine to isolate those who were HIV-positive.

Dr Koop's approach to the position of Surgeon General, which carried the suggestion that every personal health problem was in fact a public health problem and the legitimate concern of the public health authorities, seems to have found an echo among some of Reagan's top advisors. However, Dr Koop's style was not sufficient to save the programs of the Public Health Service, which remained under threat of being cut. In 1981, the same year in which Reagan took office, Congress passed the Omnibus Budget Reconciliation Act (OBRA), which reorganized a number of agencies in the executive branch and which called for budget cuts in a number of areas. The Act folded a number of PHS programs into block grants to the states, among them (1) alcohol, drug abuse, and mental health; (2) preventive health services; (3) maternal and child care services; and (4) primary health care services. The amounts authorized by the Act reflected a 25 percent cut from the amounts that had been budgeted in the previous year. These grants were automatically allocated to the states under a new statutory formula created by the Act, which permitted the states broad latitude in how the money was expended. The Public Health Service was thus deprived of the power to shape the structure and content of state health programs, which reversed a long-standing historical trend toward greater federal control over the states in health matters.[248]

Another provision of OBRA finally closed the Public Health Service hospitals. The PHS, which had, after all, been originally founded as the Marine Hospital Service at the end of the eighteenth century, continued to provide hospital services to merchant seamen throughout. By 1943 eligibility was extended to include the personnel of the Coast Guard, the Coast and Geodetic Survey, and the Public Health Service itself, together with their dependents. In addition, members of the Army, Navy, and Marine Corps and a number of other government employees were allowed the use of these hospitals. There were at the time 26 Marine Hospitals with more than 6000 beds and these facilities provided 2.5 million patient-days of care. Even as late as 1970, there were still 37 000 hospital admissions and eligibility was further extended to include all federal employees who either became ill or were injured while on work assignments. However, by 1976, the number of Public Health Service hospitals had been reduced to nine, one of which was designated for the treatment of leprosy.

The primary reason for the decline in Marine Hospital facilities was that almost all merchant seamen possessed comprehensive private medical insurance that permitted a far wider choice of superior facilities. This drop in utilization finally led to calls for the federal divestment of these hospitals that were so insistent that they had to be heeded. Under the terms of OBRA, the federal government was able to transfer the remaining facilities to local or nonprofit auspices or to close them. Five of the eight general hospitals were transferred to community corporations, two to the Department of Defense, and one to the State of Louisiana.[249] With the closure of these hospitals, and the various medical clinics that the PHS also operated, the Service lost all continuity with its original mission.

Despite the fact that the PHS no longer provided either medical or hospital care to merchant seamen, and in the face of calls for its elimination, the Commissioned Corps was able to survive. Its numbers dropped from 7300 in 1980 to 5800 in 1983 but it continued to provide clinical health services in the Indian Health Service, the Coast Guard, and the Bureau of Prisons. The Service's budget also declined, dropping by 20 percent between 1980 and 1982. Finally, the number of civil service employees in the PHS went from 56 000 in 1980 to 48 000 two years later. The agencies responsible for providing health care and health professional training were especially hard-hit. As a consequence, the Health Services Administration and the Health Resources Administration were consolidated into the Health Resources and Services Administration.[250]

Although it had survived OBRA, the Commissioned Corps was not free of detractors, even among the officials of the Department of Health and Human Resources. In April 1987 Surgeon General Koop, determined to save the Corps, took formal command of its 5500 officers with a view to 'revitalizing' the Corps. In this he apparently had the blessing of the Secretary of Health and Human Services, Otis Bowen. One of his first orders was to increase the occasions under which Corps members were required to wear their uniform and to provide 'coordination' between the Corps and the military.[251] It appears that Koop's efforts were successful since the Office of Management and Budget reversed itself and began supporting the Corps' continuation. One can only conclude that the officials at the OMB and other Washington administrators were impressed with the notion of a militarized team of physicians and other professionals wearing formal military dress and insignia and bearing signs of rank who theoretically could be dispatched to any part of the nation at a moment's notice. From a budgetary perspective, however, there is no reason whatever to keep the Commissioned Corps. Were its members civil servants, there would be substantial savings in salaries, of the order of between $10 000 and $30 000 per Corps member per year, according to the General Accounting Office.[252] In addition, inasmuch as they are commissioned officers, members of the Corps qualify for the full range of military benefits including special pay, bonuses, and miscellaneous perquisites, among them housing and subsistence allowances.[253] Finally, PHS commissioned officers are entitled to a generous retirement allowance; after 30 years they may retire at 75 percent of their base pay.[254]

Upon Koop's retirement as Surgeon General in 1989, the new President, George Bush, appointed Antonia Novello to the post in March of the following year. Dr Novello, who had been Deputy Director of the National Institute of Child Health and Human Development, one of the NIH institutes, was the first woman to occupy that position and decided to focus her attention on issues having to do with women and children. Following the lead of her predecessor, Dr Novello issued a series of warnings against habits that she felt compromised one's health. She was particularly concerned with illegal underage drinking, that is, alcohol consumption by those under the age of 21, and was the first person to point out the pernicious effects of 'Joe Camel' advertisements, which she concluded were deliberately aimed at young smokers. Having done what she could to make Americans healthier, she resigned her position in 1993.

Dr Novello was succeeded by Dr Jocelin Elders who, like her predecessor, was Deputy Director of the National Institute of Child Health and Human Development. She was appointed to the position in September 1993 by President Clinton and immediately began lobbying for Clinton's efforts at health care reform. Dr Elders had long been a supporter of government-administered universal health insurance and was pressed into service as one of the leading spokespersons for Clinton's reforms. Indeed, it is not surprising to find that Surgeons General, who tend to view government as a benign weapon to insure the health of otherwise foolhardy citizens, would support an extension of Medicare. In fact, President Clinton also enlisted Dr Koop, who supported the Clinton plan, to moderate discussions between Hilary Rodham Clinton and health care professionals. Not only did Dr Elders support a universal healthcare program, but she also was a firm adherent of sex education, which was to prove her downfall. While extolling the value of sex education in the public schools, Dr Elders commented that masturbation could prove very effective in preventing sexually transmitted diseases and might well be a good substitute for teen sex. Of course this was not what a vocal and politically influential segment of the American population wanted to hear. These comments came on top of her earlier remarks suggesting that the war on drugs was really not winnable and that perhaps it would be useful to study whether the legalization of currently illicit drugs would reduce crime. Dr Elders' observations on masturbation and drugs are, of course, unexceptionable[255] but the President was not prepared to support the Surgeon General if she veered too far from the platitudinous comments normally associated with her office. As a result, Dr Elders was forced to resign her position in December 1994, some 15 months after her appointment.

Doubtless because the Elders appointment proved such a fiasco, President Clinton left the position of Surgeon General vacant for the next three years. Finally, in February 1998 he chose Dr David Satcher, whom he had earlier appointed to head the Centers for Disease Control and Prevention, to serve both as Surgeon General and as Assistant Secretary for Health. Inasmuch as the role of the Surgeon General is to act as chief propagandist for whatever lifestyle happens to be fashionable, the nominee's position on any number of issues touching on matters of health is pertinent to whether he offends the public. This is especially true with regard to the prospective Surgeon General's stand on abortion. There is simply no way to avoid antagonizing some constituency or another and Dr Satcher has in fact managed to do exactly that by supporting a woman's right to abortion. However, he has wisely kept silent on most other issues since assuming his post.

The one notable exception has been mental illness. In 1999 the Center for Mental Health Services of the Substance Abuse and Mental Health Services Administration, the National Institute of Mental Health, and the Office of the Surgeon General released a joint report entitled *Mental Health: A Report of the Surgeon General*, which sought to offer a fairly complete analysis of mental illness in the United States. In some 450 pages the *Report* 'captures the breadth, depth, and vibrancy of the mental health field',[256] and seeks to lay bare the nature of mental illness, the forms it takes, its etiology and treatment, and its extent in the population. We are informed that the social costs of mental illness amounted to approximately $79 billion in 1990, most of which is accounted for by the loss of productivity, and an additional $66 billion in direct medical costs.[257] These direct costs are borne by public and private medical insurers and individuals, despite the fact that 'nearly two-third of all people with diagnosable mental disorders do not seek treatment'.[258] The *Report* makes fascinating reading; it categorizes all feelings of distress as symptomatic of a mental disorder and urges us to seek treatment if we think we might have such a disorder.

In 1996 the agencies of the Department of Health and Human Services once again underwent an extensive reorganization. A new division, the Office of Public Health and Science (OPHS), directly under the Assistant Secretary of Health, was established and the Surgeon General's office was placed in this new division. At the same time, each of the eight[259] former Public Health Service agencies[260] were made full operating divisions directly answerable to the Secretary of Health and Human Services while nominally remaining under the umbrella of the Public Health Service.[261] In effect, however, the PHS had been attenuated to the point where its functions did not extend beyond the Office of the Surgeon General and the Commissioned Corps.

Changes in the UPS Commissioned Corps in the last few years have been primarily cosmetic, doubtless in an attempt to ward off its dissolution. In July 2003 the Secretary of Health and Human Services, Tommy Thompson, recommended a series of changes to the last remnant of the Public Health Service, the Commissioned Corps, which at this point had grown to about 7000 officers. The ostensible purpose of these changes was to improve deployment readiness and to insure that the Corps' officers were ready to deal with what amounted to combat emergencies. The recommendations included more stringent physical fitness standards, including those for height and weight, and the ability to perform certain exercises (among them sit-ups and push-ups), training in a whole range of emergency care, among them basic life support, and an emphasis on emergency deployment. In addition, the Secretary put forward proposals that would have seriously altered existing policies regarding promotion, again emphasizing emergency deployment as a key criterion for advancement in the Corps. In these recommendations the Secretary was joined by the Surgeon General, Richard Carmona. Apparently the Secretary and the Surgeon General were inspired by the thought that the further militarization of the Commissioned Corps following 9/11 would improve the agency in a period of national crisis, despite the fact that a substantial number of its members were physicians, dentists, nurses, and scientists assigned to public health agencies as researchers. However, opposition from members of the Corps was widespread and at hearings on the proposal before the House Committee on Government Reform, former Surgeons General C. Everett Koop and Julius Richmond both voiced their serious reservations. The result was that the proposal was temporarily shelved.

Despite resistance from members of the Corps, however, the Department was determined to go ahead with transforming the Corps into a paramilitary organization, including basic training and extensive plans for deployment in a large number of contingencies. These plans were implemented under Secretary Michael Leavitt and the Corps is currently in the process of undergoing the necessary changes to structure the Commissioned Corps into a 'critical emergency response team'. These changes, once effected, will transform the Corps into the military arm of the Department of Health and Human Services.

The Public Health Service, in one form or another, has lasted for 200 years. In that time it has undergone enormous changes, to the point where it is now difficult to conclude that the PHS, outside of its Commissioned Corps, still exists, on the one hand, as a separate agency within the Department of Health and Human Services or whether, on the other, it has grown so large that it has swallowed almost all of the Department's agencies and its more than 300 programs. Indeed, the 'Public Health Service' agencies now nominally consist of eight of the 11 agencies that make up the Department of Health and Human Services.[262] What follows is a listing of the agencies that now comprises the

Public Health Service, coupled with the dates they were originally established and their recent budgets.

1. *Agency for Healthcare Research and Quality (AHRQ)*   This agency was established in 1989 as the Agency for Health Care Policy and Research. In November 1999, legislation renamed the bureau the AHRQ and charged it with supporting research designed to improve the quality of health care, reduce its cost, and broaden access to health services. Approximately 80 percent of its budget is disbursed in the form of grants and contracts. It defines its mission as 'both the evaluation of the effectiveness and quality of clinical services and the most effective and efficient ways to organize, manage, and safely deliver those services'.

What follows is the agency's budget since FY 1995 and estimates of its budget for FY 2006 and FY 2007.[263]

Year	$	Year	$
1995	168 000 000	2002	323 000 000
1996	134 000 000	2003	327 000 000
1997	154 000 000	2004	331 000 000
1998	158 000 000	2005	342 000 000
1999	182 000 000	2006e	341 000 000
2000	213 000 000	2007e	341 000 000
2001	290 000 000		

2. *Centers for Disease Control and Prevention (CDC)*   The Communicable Disease Center of the Public Health Service was established in 1946 at Atlanta, Georgia, with the aim of controlling malaria in the Southern states during World War II. It soon expanded its role to investigate all infectious diseases and, in 1967, the quarantine powers of the federal government were transferred to the agency. In 1970 its name was changed to the Center for Disease Control, thus preserving the same initials, and in 1992 to the Centers for Disease Control and Prevention. In 2005, the then seven existing centers were consolidated into four coordinating centers. It currently comprises nine centers, including its original bureau devoted to infectious diseases. They are:

> Coordinating Center for Environmental Health:
> > the National Center for Environmental Health;
> > the National Center for Injury Prevention and Control;
> Coordinating Center for Health Information and Services:
> > the National Center for Health Statistics;
> > the National Center for Public Health Informatics;
> > the National Center for Health Marketing;

Coordinating Center for Health Promotion:
   the National Center for Birth Defects and Developmental Disabilities;
   the National Center for Chronic Disease Prevention and Health
   Promotion;
   the Office of Genomics and Disease Prevention
Coordinating Center for Infectious Diseases:
   the National Center for Infectious Diseases;
   the National Center for HIV, STD, and TB Prevention.
   the National Immunization Program,

In addition, the CDC's subsidiary organizations include the National
Institute for Occupational Safety and Health, the Coordinating Office of
Global Health, and the Coordinating Office for Terrorism Preparedness and
Emergency Response.

Indeed, the mandate of the CDC is currently so broad that it effectively
includes anything having to do with the study of disease, injury, or disability.
What follows is the agency's budget since FY 1995 and estimates of its budget
for FY 2006 and FY 2007.

Year	$	Year	$
1995	2 220 000 000	2002	4 535 000 000
1996	2 259 000 000	2003	4 894 000 000
1997	2 461 000 000	2004	4 893 000 000
1998	2 574 000 000	2005	5 053 000 000
1999	2 814 000 000	2006e	6 453 000 000
2000	3 199 000 000	2007e	6 488 000 000
2001	4 104 000 000		

3. *Agency for Toxic Substances and Disease Registry (ATSDR)* Created
by the Superfund Law in 1980, the ATSDR is charged with preventing or
reducing the harmful effects of exposure to hazardous substances from waste
sites, unplanned releases, and other sources of pollution on human health.
Since the Centers for Disease Control perform many of the administrative
functions for the ATSDR, the Director of the CDC is *ex officio* Administrator
of the ATSDR.

Prior to FY 2002 the ATSDR was funded through the Environmental
Protection Agency and its personnel allocation through the CDC. As a consequence of the recommendations of the relevant Congressional committees
responsible for appropriations, a separate account was established for ATSDR
in 2001. What follows is the agency's budget since FY 2002 and estimates of
its budget for FY 2006 and FY 2007.

Year	$	Year	$
2002	78 000 000	2005	73 000 000
2003	78 000 000	2006e	75 000 000
2004	73 000 000	2007e	75 000 000

4. *Food and Drug Administration (FDA)* Created in 1927 as the Food, Drug, and Insecticide Administration, its name was changed to the FDA three years later. The FDA's function is to oversee the safety of food products (other than meat or poultry) and cosmetics, and the safety and efficacy of drugs, therapeutic agents, and medical devices.

The agency is dealt with in detail in Chapter 2. Its budget since FY 1995 and estimates of its budget for FY 2006 and FY 2007 are as follows:

Year	$	Year	$
1995	961 000 000	2002	$ 1 569 000 000
1996	996 000 000	2003	1 747 000 000
1997	992 000 000	2004	1 715 000 000
1998	1 063 000 000	2005	1 827 000 000
1999	1 142 000 000	2006e	1 907 000 000
2000	1 235 000 000	2007e	1 979 000 000
2001	1 356 000 000		

5. *Health Resources and Services Administration (HRSA)* The Health Resources Administration and the Health Services Administration were both established in 1973 and were responsible for, on the one hand, the training, supply, and distribution of health professionals and, on the other, for programs dealing with health care delivery and personnel. The two agencies were consolidated in 1982. It defines its function as 'improving access to health care services for people who are uninsured, isolated or medically vulnerable'. HRSA's expenditures are dominated by its activities in connection with HIV/AIDS, which consume about 35 percent of its current budget.

The agency's budget since FY 1995 and estimates of its budget for FY 2006 and FY 2007 are as follows:

Year	$	Year	$
1995	3 159 000 000	2002	5 753 000 000
1996	3 215 000 000	2003	6 103 000 000

Year	$	Year	$
1997	3 459 000 000	2004	6 853 000 000
1998	3 729 000 000	2005	6 908 000 000
1999	4 254 000 000	2006e	6 701 000 000
2000	4 746 000 000	2007e	6 447 000 000
2001	5 803 000 000		

6. *Indian Health Service (IHS)* In 1954 Congress transferred responsibility for the medical and hospital care accorded Indians and Alaskan Natives to the IHS from the medical division of the Bureau of Indian Affairs of the Department of the Interior. It regards its mandate as no less than 'improving the mental, physical, social and spiritual health' of the approximately 1.8 million Indians and Alaskan Natives who remain members of federally recognized tribes.

The agency's budget since FY 1995 and estimates of its budget for FY 2006 and FY2007 are as follows:

Year	$	Year	$
1995	1 919 000 000	2002	3 214 000 000
1996	1 994 000 000	2003	3 335 000 000
1997	2 134 000 000	2004	3 445 000 000
1998	2 273 000 000	2005	3 636 000 000
1999	2 524 000 000	2006e	3 721 000 000
2000	2 743 000 000	2007e	3 852 000 000
2001	3 129 000 000		

7. *National Institutes of Health (NIH)* Successor to the Hygienic Laboratory of the Public Health Service, which was recognized by Congress in 1901. The NIH was created in 1930 as the research arm of the PHS and currently comprises some 27 institutes and centers. It is by far the largest of the component agencies of the PHS and its numerous institutes tend to reflect the particular medical concerns of one legislator or another. About 80 percent of its expenditures are distributed in the form of grants to individuals and organizations not directly associated with the NIH, while the remaining 20 percent is used for in-house research.

The agency's budget since FY 1995 and estimates of its budget for FY 2006 and FY2007 are as follows:

Year	$	Year	$
1995	11 681 000 000	2002	24 853 000 000
1996	12 230 000 000	2003	28 836 000 000
1997	13 869 000 000	2004	30 401 000 000
1998	14 844 000 000	2005	31 181 000 000
1999	16 741 000 000	2006e	31 273 000 000
2000	19 000 000 000	2007e	31 391 000 000
2001	21 960 000 000		

8. *Substance Abuse and Mental Health Services Administration (SAMHA)*
In 1949 Congress established the second of the NIH's numerous institutes. However, over the next 18 years it had added a variety of programs that had nothing to do with research and as a result was moved out of the NIH and became its own Public Health Service agency in 1967. Two years later it was merged with a number of other programs and became part of the Health Services and Mental Health Administration. In 1973 it was again reorganized as the Alcohol, Drug Abuse, and Mental Health Administration and since then altered its name to its present form.

The agency's budget since FY 1995 and estimates of its budget for FY 2006 and FY2007 are as follows:

Year	$	Year	$
1995	2 214 000 000	2002	3 206 000 000
1996	1 905 000 000	2003	3 155 000 000
1997	2 217 000 000	2004	3 409 000 000
1998	2 214 000 000	2005	3 505 000 000
1999	2 519 000 000	2006e	3 412 000 000
2000	2 682 000 000	2007e	3 341 000 000
2001	2 985 000 000		

In addition, the Office of Public Health and Science, headed by the Assistant Secretary of Health, comprises a number of offices that oversee health programs, including the following:

Office of the Surgeon General
Office of Disease Prevention and Health Promotion
Office of HIV/AIDS Policy
Office of Military Liaison and Veterans' Affairs
Office of Minority Health

Office of Population Affairs
Office of Research Integrity
Office on Women's Health
President's Council on Physical Fitness and Sports
Office of Global Health Affairs
Office of Human Research Protections
National Vaccine Program Office
The PHS Commissioned Corps

The growth of the Public Health Service and its successor agencies is truly remarkable, even for those students of bureaucracy who are inured to such enormous growth rates. In the first year of peace following World War II the budget of the Public Health Service constituted, with the exception of medical care for veterans, almost the whole of the federal government's expenditures on health care. In that year it was $142 million. In 2006, the Department of Health and Human Services, the successor organization responsible for public health, spent that amount every two hours![264]

NOTES

1. It is interesting to note that the Marine Hospital Service was among the earliest government activities at the federal level that was totally unrelated to the day-to-day operation of the federal government.
2. For an overview of the early history of the Marine Hospital Service, see Richard H. Thurm, 'Early History of the U.S. Public Health Service (Marine) Hospitals: The First Federal Prepaid Medical Care Plan', *Mt. Sinai Journal of Medicine*, 37 (July–August 1937): 568–76.
3. The Act for the Relief of Sick and Disabled Seamen was passed on 16 July 1798 and provided that the master of every American ship arriving from a foreign port or engaged in coastal trade should pay to the Collector of Customs 20 cents per month for each seaman, which the captain could in turn deduct from the seaman's wages. This amount was earmarked for the temporary relief and maintenance of sick and disabled seamen. While the original Act had reference solely to members of the merchant marine, its scope was expanded in the following year when the Secretary of the Navy was authorized to deduct 20 cents per month from the pay of naval officers, seamen, and marines, who were made eligible for marine hospital benefits. However, In 1811 naval hospitals were placed under the jurisdiction of the Secretary of the Navy and the pertinent funds were paid into a separate account.

    The tax on seamen for the purpose of maintaining the Marine Hospital Service was abolished in 1884, when the cost of maintaining marine hospitals was paid for out of the proceeds of a tonnage tax placed on vessels entering the United States. From 1906 to 1981, when the marine hospitals were finally closed, their maintenance costs were covered by direct appropriations from Congress. Thurm, 'Early History of the U.S. Public Health Service', 576.
4. Secretary of the Treasury, *Annual Report, 1861* (Washington, DC: 1861): 27.
5. For some reason, there was a one-year hiatus, between April 1837 and April 1838.
6. According to the report of the first Surgeon General, Dr John Maynard Woodworth, at an aggregate cost of $3 214 518.95. See Bess Furman, *A Profile of the United States Public*

Health Service, 1798–1948 (United States Department of Health, Education, and Welfare. Washington, DC: Government Printing Office, 1973): 69.

7. Laurence F. Schmeckebier, *The Public Health Service: Its History, Activities and Organization* (Baltimore, Md.: Johns Hopkins Press, 1923): 6.

8. Furman, *A Profile of the United States Public Health Service*, 69.

9. Quoted in Fitzhugh Mullan, MD, *Plagues and Politics: The Story of the United States Public Health Service* (New York: Basic Books, Inc., 1989): 19. One need hardly add that graft was not peculiar to the Marine Hospital system and was endemic throughout the federal government. One physician, writing in the *Boston Medical and Surgical Journal* in 1847 observed that the surgeon of the Naval Hospital in Boston received a salary of $2000 per year, that his assistant was paid $950 per year, and that they rarely had more than ten patients a day. Quoted in Furman, *Profile of the United States Public Health Service*, 72–3.

10. While physicians with the Public Health Service held ranks and wore military-style dress, it was not until 1889 that Congress officially established the PHS's Commissioned Corps along military lines, with titles and pay corresponding to Army and Navy grades.

11. These developments are recounted in Robert H. Wiebe, *The Search for Order* (New York: Hill and Wang, 1967).

12. By the 1890s, public health had become a recognized medical specialty and in 1912, the first professional school devoted to this branch of medicine was established jointly by the Massachusetts Institute of Technology and Harvard University. See Wiebe, *Search for Order*, 115. It appears that Bess Furman has erred twice when she states that the first School of Hygiene and Public Health was established at Johns Hopkins University in 1919. It was in fact established in 1916 and followed the founding of a similar program at MIT. See Furman, *Profile of the United States Public Health Service*, 339.

13. As one historian notes, medical advances encouraged local boards of health to diversify their activities almost without limit. 'War was declared in many communities upon the mosquito, and as it was proved that the common house fly might be the carrier of typhoid, infantile diarrhea and many other diseases, there started about 1908 a crusade against this pest . . . . Medical inspection of school children brought better control of disease, while the new laboratory science made it possible to inspect milk, to diagnose diseases and to manufacture, distribute and administer antitoxins. To solve the problems of pure water and sewage disposal, which were always acute in the overgrown cities, bacteriology and chemistry continued to lend aid. An important advance was achieved with the chlorination of water, first introduced in America in 1908 and rapidly adopted after 1913. This method proved superior to water filtration as a protection against water-borne diseases.' Harold U. Faulkner, *The Quest for Social Justice, 1898–1914* (New York: Macmillan Company, 1931): 239.

14. The Act and its antecedents are discussed at greater length in the section devoted to the history of the Food and Drug Administration.

15. The description is Faulkner's, *The Quest for Social Justice*, 240.

16. One of the most comprehensive statements regarding the goals of the increasingly ambitious public health movement was made by the Commissioner of Health of Pennsylvania in an address before the American Medical Association annual meeting in Philadelphia in 1907. Speaking of the need for new public health ordinances, the speaker noted: 'These laws must reach into all the relations of human life. As their basis they must start with the prompt and accurate registration of births, deaths and marriages, and of the presence of transmissible and communicable diseases, and they must embrace the control of epidemics by domiciliary quarantine; the employment of prophylactics and disinfectants; the supervision of the transportation both of the quick and the dead; the construction, heating and ventilation of our homes and public buildings; the protection of water supplies and the restoration to purity of our polluted streams and lakes; the manifold occupations and industries of the people; the protection of food stuffs, including milk and other beverages; and of drugs, from adulteration and impurity; the education of physicians, dentists and veterinarians, and the barring of our doors against the introduction of communicable diseases and pestilences from foreign countries.'

  To those who might complain that such invasive laws have no place in a free society, the

Commissioner remarked that 'it is idle to prate of the enforcement of sanitary laws as an infringement of personal liberty. Submission to reasonable personal restrictions intended for the welfare of all is the very foundation stone of civilized liberty. The individual who insists on what he is pleased to call his own rights in defiance of law and to the detriment of the common weal is "an undesirable citizen of the republic." If we are to aim ... to render growth more perfect, decay less rapid, and life more vigorous, in civilized life we must give up many primitive or individual liberties to insure advanced civilized liberties and to permit a free social and commercial intercourse'. Samuel G. Dixon, 'Law, the Foundation of State Medicine', *Journal of the American Medical Association*, 48 (8 June 1907): 1926–8.

17.   See James G. Burrow, *Organized Medicine in the Progressive Era: The Move Toward Monopoly* (Baltimore: Johns Hopkins University Press, 1977): 88–102. 'Many physicians who espoused the creation of health boards assumed that these agencies could be used to license and limit the supply of physicians'. John Duffy, 'The American Medical Profession and Public Health: From Support to Ambivalence', *Bulletin of the History of Medicine*, 53 (Spring 1979): 6.

18.   One historian has noted that physician support for state boards of health was in part due to the belief that these boards were the most effective method of controlling the practice of medicine. Duffy, 'American Medical Profession', 6.

19.   Christopher C. Cox, 'A Report Upon the Necessity of a National Sanitary Bureau', *Public Health: Reports and Papers Presented at the Meetings of the American Public Health Association in the Year 1873*, vol. 1 (New York: American Public Health Association, 1875): 522–32.

20.   Furman, *Profile of the United States Public Health Service*, 129.

21.   Ibid., 129.

22.   Elizabeth Fee, 'Public Health and the State: The United States', in Dorothy Porter, ed., *The History of Public Health and the Modern State* (Clio Medica 26/The Wellcome Institute Series in the History of Medicine; Amsterdam: Editions Rodopi, 1994): 233.

23.   This has been pointed out by Victoria A. Harden, *Inventing the NIH: Federal Biomedical Research Policy, 1887–1937* (Baltimore: Johns Hopkins University Press, 1986): 12.

24.   Dr Hamilton was, at this point, locked in a long and acrimonious battle with Dr John Shaw Billings, who had been the Army's expert on hospitals and one of the strongest advocates for greater federal involvement in health care. Billings had been appointed by Secretary of the Treasury Boutwell to serve as one of the inspectors of the hospitals of the Marine Hospital Service in 1869 and it was his report that ultimately led to the reorganization of the MHS under Woodworth. Indeed, Billings himself would almost certainly have been appointed as the first Supervising Surgeon of the Marine Hospital Service had the legislation creating the position not explicitly excluded those holding military rank. When the National Board of Health was created in 1879 Billings was appointed vice-president of the Board and it was under Billings' direction that the Board sought greater authority, often at the expense of the Marine Hospital Service. While Woodworth, Hamilton, and Billings all supported the creation of a National Department of Health with far-reaching powers, their sectarian interests led to their opposing each other's proposals.

25.   Furman, *Profile of the United States Public Health Service*, 184.

26.   Mullan, *Plagues and Politics*, 26.

27.   The medical inspection of immigrants was begun in the early part of 1890 at New York City. The Public Health Service had started to inspect immigrants at foreign ports in 1889 and this was later extended to aliens entering the United States. Under the terms of an act passed in 1917, admission to the United States was denied to all 'idiots, imbeciles, feeble-minded persons, epileptics, insane persons, persons who have one or more attacks of insanity at any time previously, persons of constitutional psychopathic inferiority, persons with chronic alcoholism . . . [and] persons afflicted with tuberculosis in any form or with a loathsome or dangerous contagious disease'. Schmeckebier, *The Public Health Service*, 105–6.

28.   Harden, *Inventing the NIH*, 32.

29.   J. Pease Norton, 'The Economic Advisability of Inaugurating a National Department of Health', *Journal of the American Medical Association*, 47 (1906): 1005, quoted in Harden, *Inventing the NIH*, 32.

30. Victoria Harden reports that in 1910 some 13 different measures relating to health, the Public Health and Marine Hospital Service, and a proposed cabinet-level Department of Health, were before Congress. The House Committee on Interstate and Foreign Commerce held hearings on all these bills in June 1910 and January 1911. *Inventing the NIH*, 36.

31. Schmeckebier, *The Public Health Service*, 35.

32. See George Rosen, 'The Committee of One Hundred on National Health and the Campaign for a National Health Department, 1906–1912', *American Journal of Public Health*, 62 (February 1972): 261–3. The Committee was appointed by the American Association for the Advancement of Science in 1906 to investigate the need for the creation of a health bureaucracy and to promote the necessary enabling legislation.

33. The economist Irving Fisher, an ardent supporter of the proposed Department of Health and a member of the Committee of One Hundred, charged that the League received financial support from the patent medicine interests, who, already suffering under the regulatory burdens of the Pure Food and Drugs Act of 1906, saw in the creation of a cabinet-level Department of Health yet a further threat to their business interests. See Harden, *Inventing the NIH*, 37.

34. Taft in fact supported creation of a single bureau to deal with health activities but was opposed to its having Cabinet status. Indeed, he found the issue sufficiently important to include it in his second annual message to Congress in December 1910. Schmeckebier, *The Public Health Service*, 36.

35. Harden, *Inventing the NIH*, 38.

36. Quoted in Schmeckebier, *The Public Health Service*, 24.

37. Schmeckebier, *The Public Health Service*, 44. The number of areas supervised had increased to 47 by the end of 1918. In July 1918 the Public Health Service was further empowered to supervise the sanitary conditions at 170 shipyards and at all industrial plants having contracts with the Ordinance Department.

38. Ralph Chester Williams, *The United States Public Health Service, 1798–1950* (2 vols: Washington, DC: Commissioned Officers Association of the United States Public Health Service, 1951): 562–3.

39. Comprising the Secretaries of War, Navy, and Treasury, as *ex-officio* members, and the Surgeons General of the Army, Navy, and Public Health Service.

40. One year prior, in 1917, Congress had conferred upon the Secretaries of War and of the Navy police powers for the suppression of prostitution in the vicinity of any military or naval station. Schmeckebier, *The Public Health Service*, 47. Under urging from the American Social Hygiene Association, itself an alliance of physicians, social workers, and clergymen, it had been decided that, rather than instituting medical inspection of prostitutes and making chemical prophylaxis readily available, the government should stamp out illicit intercourse with all the powers at its disposal. Thus, despite the fact that the Navy had for some time pursued a policy of venereal disease control by the distribution of prophylactic packets, Secretary of the Navy Josephus Daniels, who possessed strong moral scruples in the matter, abandoned the Navy's earlier experiments in favor of the attempted suppression of prostitution. Robert D. Leigh, *Federal Health Administration in the United States* (New York: Harper & Brothers Publishers, 1927): 135. For extended discussions of the social purity movement, see David J. Pivar, *Purity Crusade: Sexual Morality and Social Control, 1868–1900* (Westport, Conn.: Greenwood Press, 1973); Charles Walter Clarke, *Taboo: The Story of the Pioneers of Social Hygiene* (Washington, DC: Public Affairs Press, 1961); and Ronald Hamowy, 'Preventive Medicine and the Criminalization of Sexual Immorality in 19th Century America', in Randy E. Barnett and John Hagel III, eds, *Assessing the Criminal: Restitution, Retribution, and the Legal Process* (Cambridge, Mass.: Ballinger, 1977): 35–97.

41. The Act also provided $100 000 for each of the years 1919 and 1920 to be awarded by the Intergovernmental Social Hygiene Board as grants to university and other scientists for research on venereal diseases and an additional $300 000 for sociological and psychological research on 'more effective educational measures' to prevent their spread. With one small exception, these grants constituted the first allocation of funds by the federal government for biomedical research. Harden, *Inventing the NIH*, 42.

42. Indeed, the venereal disease clinics that were established near military bases, while conducted by the Public Health Service, were, at their inception, financed by the American Red Cross. It was not until Congress appropriated funds for these clinics in July 1918 that the Public Health Service underwrote these expenditures (Schmeckebier, *The Public Health Service*, 48).

43. Quoted in Bess Furman, *A Profile of the United States Public Health Service*, 321. The attempts of the Public Health Service to reduce the incidence of venereal disease by warning American troops of the danger of sexual intercourse were regarded by some as too 'liberal'. Among the PHS's efforts was the production of a film entitled *Fit to Fight* (changed at the close of the war to *Fit to Win*) that followed the experiences of five draftees, two of whom contracted syphilis after engaging in unprotected sex. The central idea of the film, that if abstinence were impossible then one should at least employ chemical prophylaxis, was thought to convey too libertine a message and the New York State Board of Censors declared the film obscene in 1919. John Parascandola, 'VD at the Movies: PHS Films of the 1930s and 1940s', *Public Health Reports*, III (March–April 1996): 173.

44. Public health officials and social hygienists believed it possible to effect a fundamental shift in public attitudes toward sexual behavior and to effectively stamp out prostitution. See Allan M. Brandt, *No Magic Bullet: A Social History of Venereal Disease in the United States Since 1880* (New York: Oxford University Press, 1985): 79.

45. Federal aid to the states appears to have had its genesis with the Morrell Act in 1862 which granted federal lands to the states, provided that profit from the sale of such lands was used for the support of public institutions of higher learning. Jennie Jacobs Knonenfeld, *The Changing Federal Role in U.S. Health Care Policy* (Westport, Conn.: Praeger, 1997): 69.

46. Schmeckebier, *The Public Health Service*, 92.

47. The Tuskegee Syphilis Study was in fact conducted jointly by the PHS, the Tuskegee Institute, and the Macon County Health Department.

48. James H. Jones, *Bad Blood: The Tuskegee Syphilis Experiment* (New York: Free Press, 1981).

49. One historian of the Public Health Service, whose sympathies lie completely with the Public Health Service, writes of its syphilis studies that 'the attack on syphilis launched by the PHS in this period, dependent as it was on the cumbersome and minimally effective therapies of the pre-antibiotic era, was determined and conscientious'. Mullan, *Plagues and Politics*, 86.

50. Act of 3 March 1919.

51. The data appear in Schmeckebier, *The Public Health Service*, 62–3.

52. Furman, *Profile of the United States Public Health Service*, 331. For example, the Mount Alto Hospital in Washington, DC had been built as a girls' school and the Army base hospital at Jacksonville, Florida, had to be abandoned only months after it was leased.

53. Schmeckebier, *The Public Health Service*, 51–2.

54. Furman, *Profile of the United States Public Health Service*, 338.

55. More recent scholarship suggests that this strain of influenza was born in early March 1918 when soldiers at Fort Riley, Kansas, burned tons of manure which led to a choking dust storm over the area. Some 45 soldiers died within a few days of what was thought to be pneumonia. American troops embarking for Europe appear to have transmitted the plague overseas.

56. See Furman, *A Profile of the United States Public Health Service*, 327.

57. While around 20 million is the more common mortality figure, Jeffrey Taubenerger of the Armed Forces Institute of Pathology, in his paper on 'The Search for the 1918 Spanish Influenza Virus', suggests that the number is closer to 40 million. Taubenerger's paper was presented at a scientific colloquium delivered before the Goddard Space Flight Center in October 1999 and is available on the World Wide Web at http://scicolloq.gsfc.nasa.gov/ Taubenberger.htm (accessed 12 January 2000).

58. Furman, *A Profile of the United States Public Health Service*, 326–7.

59. Forbes, who was a close friend of President Harding, was later charged with receiving kickbacks from the contractors chosen to build new veterans' medical facilities. In addition, Forbes appears to have looted large amounts of 'surplus supplies' from the Army and to

have sold them. After Harding's death, Forbes was prosecuted and was sent to prison. Furman, *A Profile of the United States Public Health Service*, 346–7.

60. Furman, *A Profile of the United States Public Health Service*, 344.

61. Ibid., 346.

62. Ibid., 359.

63. Dr Lawrence Kolb of the Public Health Service and an early investigator into the effects of narcotics estimated in 1924 that there were somewhere between 110 000 and 150 000 addicts in the United States, down from its highest point, in 1900, when there were close to 270 000. Lawrence Kolb and A. G. Du Mez, 'The Prevalence and Trend of Drug Addiction in the United States and Factors Influencing It', *Public Health Reports*, 39 (23 May 1924): 1179–204.

64. Furman, *A Profile of the United States Public Health Service*, 354, 264, 386.

65. Mullan, *Plagues and Politics*, 89. Smoot was a rabid anti-Communist who saw the ideology's tentacles everywhere in American society. 'Propagandists who take orders direct from Moscow', he charged in 1931, 'are busy in this country trying to poison the minds of our youth, while in Russia the entire population has been mobilized in one prodigious effort to undermine the economic structure on which our civilization rests'. Quoted in Milton R. Merrill, *Reed Smoot: Apostle in Politics* (Logan, Utah: Utah State University Press, 1990): 280.

66. James A. Tobey, 'State Health Notes – Legislation', *American Journal of Public Health*, 11 (April 1921): 383, quoted in Harden, *Inventing the NIH*, 53.

67. The National Health Council had been founded in 1920 as an umbrella organization and central clearinghouse for voluntary health agencies and was active in lobbying Congress on health-related issues. The Council was an outgrowth of the Committee of One Hundred and had a similar object, the creation of a department of health that would consolidate the federal government's various health agencies. The Council began operations at the beginning of 1921 with Livingston Farrand of the American Red Cross as chairman. Membership included representatives of the American Heart Association, the American Public Health Association, the National Organization for Public Health Nursing, and the American Society for the Control of Cancer. In addition, the Metropolitan Life Insurance Company played a prominent role in the Council. For an extended discussion of the Council, see Harden, *Inventing the NIH*, 56–60.

68. Mullan, *Plagues and Politics*, 89.

69. By 1962 The Commissioned Corps had grown to 5000 officers. Public Health Service, US Department of Health, Education, and Welfare, *The Public Health Service: Background Material Concerning the Mission and Organization of the Public Health Service*, Prepared for the Interstate and Foreign Commerce Committee, US House of Representatives (Washington, DC: Government Printing Office, 1963): 5.

70. Copies of the report were sent to every physician and to educators, heads of women's organizations, financiers, lawyers, businessmen, Boy Scout leaders, editors, agricultural agents, heads of commercial organizations, authors, legislators, public officials, and librarians. Harden, *Inventing the NIH*, 89.

71. Mullan, *Plagues and Politics*, 89.

72. Harden, *Inventing the NIH*, 89.

73. 'The Future Independence and Progress of American Medicine in the Age of Chemistry', *Journal of the American Medical Association*, 78 (18 March 1922): 807.

74. Most academic scientists, including university pharmacologists, supported an institute that would operate under the general guidance of the American Chemical Society while physicians demanded that the American Medical Association play a prominent role in the organization and management of any research establishment. Industrial pharmacologists and members of the drug industry, on the other hand, feared that a facility engaged in the creation of new chemotherapeutic agents would undercut the industry's patents. For an extended discussion of the rivalry between these groups, see Harden, *Inventing the NIH*, 73–91.

75. In light of this, it is a curiosity of Coolidge's presidency that he did in fact come to support the creation of the National Institute of Health toward the end of his administration.

Apparently the influenza epidemic that broke out in the winter of 1928–29 was critical in changing Coolidge's mind. In January 1929 Coolidge decided to support the bill establishing the Institute and so informed Ransdell. Harden, *Inventing the NIH*, 144.

76. Victoria Harden's monograph covers the legislative history of the Ransdell bill in great detail. See *Inventing the NIH*, 92–159.

77. The National Institutes of Health are dealt with in greater detail in Chapter 4.

78. National Institutes of Health, Office of the Director, *NIH Almanac, 1992* (Bethesda, Md.: Editorial Operations Branch, Division of Public Information, National Institutes of Health, 1992): 111, 117.

79. 9 April 1912 (37 Stat. L. 79). The Bureau appears to have been the brainchild of Ms Lillian Wald, the founder of the Henry Street Settlement in New York City who had suggested its creation in 1903. 'If the Government can have a department to look out after the Nation's farm crops,' she is reputed to have asked, 'why can't it have a bureau to look out after the Nation's child crop?' President Theodore Roosevelt supported creation of the bureau and it was one of the recommendations that emerged from the first White House Conference on the Care of Dependent Children in 1909. Dorothy E. Bradbury, *Five Decades of Action for Children: A History of the Children's Bureau* (Washington, DC: US Department of Health, Education, and Welfare (Children's Bureau, Social Security Administration), 1962): 1–3.

80. The first year's budget of the Children's Bureau was slightly over $25 000, with a staff of 15. By its third year of operation, however, Congress had increased its budget to almost $165 000 and the Bureau employed 76 people! See Theda Skocpol, *Protecting Soldiers and Mothers: The Political Origins of Social Policy in the United States* (Cambridge, MA: The Belknap Press of Harvard University Press, 1992): 480–86.

81. The National League of Women Voters was joined by a large number of women's organizations in supporting the Act. Sheppard-Towner was signed into law only a year after passage of the Nineteenth Amendment granting the vote to women. That it passed Congress and was signed into law by President Harding strongly suggests that it was designed to draw these new voters to the Republican Party. See Skocpol, *Protecting Soldiers and Mothers*, 497–506.

82. During the seven years of its existence, $1 240 000 was granted annually as a subvention to the states for maternal and infant care.

83. The rationale put forward for registering births and for birth certificates was the need for more accurate statistics relating to infants. See Skocpol, *Protecting Soldiers and Mothers*, 488–90. The constitutionality of the Act was upheld in *Massachusetts v. Mellon* (262 US 447).

84. When the Children's Bureau was originally established in 1912, Surgeon General Wyman believed that Congress was on the verge of enacting a major reform of the administrative agencies in charge of health care that would result in the creation of a cabinet-level Department of Health.

85. The attitude of the Public Health Service to the Children's Bureau is discussed at length in Robyn Muncy, *Creating a Female Dominion in American Reform, 1890–1935* (New York: Oxford University Press, 1991): 142–5.

86. See Furman, *Profile of the United States Public Health Service*, 329, 350, 378–9.

87. One historian notes of the relationship between government and social engineering in the 1920s and 1930s that 'government reliance upon social scientists certainly did not originate in the 1920s. But under Herbert Hoover's tutelage, professionals did come to believe more confidently in the possibility that scientific research could be transformed into comprehensive social and economic reforms, without undue interference from politicians or popular sentiment. Like Hoover, they wanted to combine progressive humanitarianism, statistical data, and scientific management to insure that socio-economic and political institutions did not fall too far behind technological development.' Joan Hoff Wilson, *Herbert Hoover, Forgotten Progressive* (Boston: Little, Brown and Company, 1975): 138.

88. The rift between the two bureaucracies was discussed at length in the press. See 'Child Parley Split Over Bureau Shift', *The New York Times*, 21 November 1930; 3, col. 1. Both President Hoover and a majority of the conferees attending the Conference supported passage of a slightly altered maternal and infant care act if it were administered by the

Public Health Service, but women's groups were able to forestall passage of such a bill. See Muncy, *Creating a Female Dominion in American Reform*, 147–8.

89. See '19-Point Program of Child Aid Carried', *The New York Times*, 23 November 1930; 20, col. 1.

90. The 'aid to dependent children' provisions of the Social Security Act, also known as 'mother's pensions', were enacted despite the existence of such laws at the state level. Indeed, by 1935, all the states excepting Georgia and South Carolina had such provisions in place. They were originally enacted in order to prevent homes from being broken up by the death, disability, or removal of the primary breadwinner. At the time of passage of the Social Security Act 29 of the states placed the entire financial burden on local governments for such aid; while in only 17 was the state itself a direct financial participant. Added to that, in only 20 states was participation mandatory. Paul H. Douglas, *Social Security in the United States: An Analysis and Appraisal of the Federal Social Security Act* (New York: Whittlesey House, McGraw-Hill Book Company, Inc., 1936): 186–7. See also the historical discussion that appears in Skocpol, *Protecting Soldiers and Mothers*, 424–79.

91. William Shonick, *Government and Health Services: Government's Role in the Development of U.S. Health Services, 1930–1980* (New York: Oxford University Press, 1995): 92.

92. This is the broadest grant of discretion that appeared in any part of the bill. See Edwin E. Witte, *The Development of the Social Security Act* (Madison, Wisc.: University of Wisconsin Press, 1963): 173.

93. Shonick, *Government and Health Services*, 93.

94. Between 1925 and 1935 the PHS workforce expanded from 4700 to 6300 and the Commissioned Corps from 250 officers to 400. Mullan, *Plagues and Politics*, 100.

95. It is of some interest that almost 60 percent of this total are incarcerated for drug offenses. In 1970, federal facilities held approximately 20 600 inmates, of whom slightly more than 16 percent were drug offenders.

96. The drafters of the social security bill had originally hoped to include a provision establishing a system of compulsory health insurance but this was thought politically ill-advised in the face of bitter opposition from the American Medical Association. Instead, Dr Michael Davis, director of the medical activities of the Julius Rosenwald Fund, suggested that the bill include an expansion of the activities of the Public Health Service. See Witte, *The Development of the Social Security Act*, 172–5.

97. Furman, *A Profile of the United States Public Health Service*, 382.

98. Parran had been State Commissioner of Health of New York under Governor Franklin Roosevelt and was an avid adherent of government-managed health care. In a speech in 1934 before the Joint Conference of the American Academy of Political and Social Science and the College of Physicians of Philadelphia, Parran had declared that 'the care of the public health is a primary responsibility of government'. And in a 1937 speech Parran maintained that 'there are sound scientific, social and economic reasons for more aggressive attention to the public health. I think we have reached a stage in our civilization when we must accept as a major premise that citizens have an equal opportunity for health as an inherent right with the right to liberty and the pursuit of happiness.' Quoted in Furman, *A Profile of the United States Public Health Service*, 394, 397.

99. Quoted in ibid., 395.

100. Shonick, *Government and Health Services*, 99.

101. Parran believed that venereal diseases were the most pressing of all public health problems. Brandt, *No Magic Bullet*, 142.

102. Ibid., 143.

103. In July 1936 Parran had published an article, 'The Next Great Plague To Go', in the *Survey Graphic*, which was reprinted in the *Reader's Digest*, and in the following year Parran's book, *Shadow On the Land*, appeared. Both article and book dealt with the problem of venereal disease. See Brandt, *No Magic Bullet*, 138–47.

104. State requirements that couples get blood tests before being married originate from PHS demands during this period.

105. As originally written the bill called for expenditures of no less than $271 million over a 13-year period, but this staggering amount was quickly revised. Brandt, *No Magic Bullet*, 144.
106. In 1937 the National Cancer Institute, the first of the constituent institutes of the National Institutes of Health, was established by federal legislation.
107. Mullan, *Plagues and Politics*, 102.
108. Furman, *Profile of the United States Public Health Service*, 405–6.
109. At the time there were only five Cabinet posts: the Secretaries of State, Treasury, War, and the Navy, and the Attorney-General.
110. The covering legislation was the Reorganization Act of 1939.
111. The most important of the agencies comprising the Federal Security Agency was the Public Health Service which, by 1939, was performing the following functions:

    1. Extensive research into the causes, means of propagation, and spread of disease;
    2. Maritime quarantines and inspection of passengers and crews of vessels arriving from foreign ports;
    3. Interstate quarantines for the prevention or spread of diseases from state to state;
    4. Dissemination of public health information;
    5. Grants-in-aid to the states and to counties, cities and health districts for a variety of purposes touching on public health;
    6. Supervisory control and licensing of manufacturers of biological products (vaccines, serums, toxins, antitoxins, arsenicals, etc.) used in the prevention of disease;
    7. Study of mental diseases and drug addiction;
    8. Provision of hospitalization and medical and dental care for American merchant seamen and members of the Coast Guard;
    9. Operation of the National Leprosarium and the two prison hospitals for drug addiction;
    10. Participation with other Federal agencies in discharging their health functions; and,
    11. Collection and publication of vital statistics.

    See J. W. Mountin and Evelyn Flook, 'State Health Organization', in *Public Health Reports*, 58 (2 April 1943): 551–56.
112. St Elizabeths Hospital was a Federal mental hospital and was reserved for federal beneficiaries who were designated as having mental disorders. The Freedmen's hospital provided treatment for Blacks in the District of Columbia.
113. Williams, *The United States Public Health Service*, 613–14.
114. One of the original functions of the Marine Hospital Service was tending to the medical and hospital needs of the Coast Guard. In 1798, when the MHS was created, the Coast Guard's antecedent, the Revenue Marine Division, was lodged in the Treasury Department, as was the MHS. The Revenue Marine Service was renamed the Revenue-Cutter Service in 1863 and merged with the Life Saving Service in 1915 to become the Coast Guard. In 1938, Light-House Service personnel were merged with the Coast Guard. Mullan, *Plagues and Politics*, 118.
115. Official government documents refer to the wholesale arrest and detention of these Americans as an 'evacuation', to those arrested as 'evacuees', to the temporary detention centers where they were kept as 'assembly centers', and to the concentration camps where they were finally taken as 'relocation centers'.
116. A few days later, Congress enacted Public Law 77-503 on 21 March which made it a federal offense for a civilian to disobey a military order issued under authority of Executive Order 9066.
117. These hospitals were plagued by problems; there were substantial delays in constructing and equipping them and they experienced a chronic shortages of supplies. Furman, *Profile of the United States Public Health Service*, 423.
118. Ibid., 421–4. In what must be one of the most brazen pieces of propaganda written in connection with the internment of Japanese-Americans, one official history of the Public Health Service notes with pride that 'all medical and institutional care required by the Japanese after an area had been posted [that is, after they were expelled from their homes] was provided at Government expense'. Williams, *United States Public Health Service*, 639.

119. Lynne Page Snyder, 'Passage and Significance of the 1944 Public Health Service Act', *Public Health Reports*, 109 (November–December 1994): 721.
120. Philip A. Kalisch and Beatrice J. Kalisch, *Nurturer of Nurses: A History of the Division of Nursing of the U.S. Public Health Service and Its Antecedents, 1798–1977*. Summary Review of the Study (Division of Nursing, Bureau of Health Manpower, Health Resources Administration, US Public Health Service: March 1977): 6.
121. Kalish and Kalish, *Nurturer of Nurses*, 7.
122. Mullan, *Plagues and Politics*, 120.
123. It appears to be a rule among bureaucracies that once established, a bureau or program will never close, regardless of whether or not the purposes for which it was created remain unmet. In 1946, as the Cadet Nurses Corps was winding down, the Public Health Service established a Division of Nursing whose functions included studying the nursing needs of the PHS, suggesting new nurse programs, and devising and implementing nursing research studies. See *Fifty Years at the Division of Nursing, United States Public Health Service* (Washington, DC: Public Health Service, April 1997).
124. The Wagner-Murray-Dingell bill.
125. In the summer of 1944 President Harry Truman issued an Executive Order declaring the Commissioned Corps to be a military force. This measure lasted through 1952.
126. For the details of the two acts, see Snyder, 'Passage and Significance of the 1944 Public Health Service Act', 721–4.
127. Furman, *Profile of the United States Public Health Service* 430–31.
128. Parran's plans went substantially beyond a government-administered national health insurance plan. He noted that 'social insurance, no matter how complete, does not constitute a national health program. It is only part of it and contributory to it just as a national policy for the improvement of housing and a national nutrition program is obviously in the interests of the Nation's health.' United States Public Health Service, *Annual Report for the Fiscal Year 1944* (Washington, DC: Government Printing Office, 1944): xiii.
129. Public Health Service, *Annual Report, 1944*, v.
130. Public Health Service, *Annual Report, 1944*, xiii.
131. Public Health Service, *Annual Report, 1944*, x. Public Health Service expenditures in fiscal year 1944 were approximately $103 million, of which about $54 million were devoted to the training of nurses. The Service would have had to undergo a massive expansion in manpower and in the funds accorded it if Parran's recommendations had been instituted.
132. The Murray-Wagner-Dingell bill was still under consideration by Congress.
133. The Commission was financed by, among others, the Ford Foundation, the National Foundation for Infantile Paralysis, and the Commonwealth Fund. In addition, the Public Health Service contributed money and personnel. Furman, *Profile of the United States Public Health Service*, 437.
134. Shonick, *Government and Health Services*, 358.
135. Indeed, even before its official publication, Dr Hoge drafted a lengthy essay based on the findings of the Commission which was read before the Pennsylvania Hospital Association and for which, we are assured, he was awarded a Master's Degree! Furman, *Profile of the United States Public Health Service*, 437.
136. Quoted in Furman, *Profile of the United States Public Health Service*, 447.
137. With the onset of the Depression almost all new hospital construction ceased except for the construction and remodeling of hospitals by the Federal Government that were part of the make-work projects of the Roosevelt Administration. During the war the only hospitals built were those constructed under the Lanham Act, a war emergency program designed to locate medical facilities in areas newly populated by defense workers. *Hill-Burton Program, 1946–1966: Two Decades of Partnership for Better Patient Care* (Washington, DC: Department of Health, Education, and Welfare, Public Health Service, Division of Hospital and Medical Facilities, 1966): 6.
138. A brief history of the original legislation and subsequent amendments to 1973 can be found in United States Senate, Committee on Labor and Public Welfare, Subcommittee on Health, *Hill-Burton Hospital Survey and Construction Act: History of the Program and Current Problems and Issues* (Washington, DC: 1973).

139. See the account of George Bugbee, Executive Director of the American Hospital Association at the time, in Lewis E. Weeks and Howard J. Berman, eds, *Shapers of American Health Care Policy: An Oral History* (Ann Arbor: Health Administration Press, 1985).

140. Officially, the Hospital Survey and Construction Act of 1946 (P.L. 79–725).

141. See Richard Harris, *A Sacred Trust* (Baltimore, Md.: Penguin Books Inc., 1966): 150–151.

142. Harris, *A Sacred Trust*, 151.

143. Shonick, *Government and Health Services*, 359.

144. *Hill-Burton Hospital Survey*, 11.

145. Shonick, *Government and Health Services*, 359.

146. Ibid., 364.

147. Weeks and Berman, eds, *Shapers of American Health Care Policy*, 45.

148. The funds used for this massive project, it appears, were made available by the Lanham Act, passed in 1940, which authorized the use of federal funds to build public housing for defense industry workers.

149. The Director of the National Institute of Health, Rolla E. Dyer, appears to have accepted the argument put forward by Hollis that the new agency would confine itself to undertaking field research into communicable diseases and not attempt to duplicate the basic science and laboratory research of the NIH. See Mullan, *Plagues and Politics*, 125.

150. In 1970 the Communicable Disease Center's name was altered to the Center for Disease Control.

151. Quoted in Furman, *Profile of the United States Public Health Service*, 440.

152. The bill's chief sponsor in the House was J. Percy Priest, Democrat, of Tennessee, who was consistently favorably disposed to the public health bureaucracy. He was joined by Clarence C. Brown, Republican, of Ohio. In the Senate, the bill's primary sponsor was Claude Pepper, Democrat, of Florida, who was joined by, among others, Lester Hill, Democrat, of Alabama, and Republicans Robert A. Taft, of Ohio, and George Ailken of Vermont. Apparently Pepper was shocked to learn that the Selective Service System had rejected 900 000 men between the ages of 16 and 37 for neuropsychiatric disorders and that an additional 700 000 men were discharged from the Armed Forces for the same reason. Furman, *Profile of the United States Public Health Service*, 449–50. It might be worth noting that during World War II the Selective Service System examined approximately 45 million men, of whom only 31 million were found either physically or mentally qualified. Further, over 16 million Americans served in the military during World War II. Finally, among the 'disorders' that warranted rejection or discharge were a number of 'neuropsychiatric disorders' which are at best questionable, including homosexuality.

153. Dr Kolb had tried to establish a national neuropsychiatric research center in 1938 but had failed.

154. Mullan, *Plagues and Politics*, 126.

155. Furman, *Profile of the United States Public Health Service*, 450–54.

156. Scheele, who was not a political activist, was later to badly disappoint Ewing on the issue of compulsory government-directed health insurance. Truman made a major effort to see the Murray-Wagner-Dingell bill pass Congress in 1948 in the face of strong AMA opposition and assumed the support of both Ewing and Scheele. However, when Ewing approached Scheele about joining him in a debate with the AMA on the issue, Scheele refused, stating 'The minute I do that I'm finished as a professional officer for you, and you want the Surgeon General's job to stay a professional officer's job'. Mullan, *Plagues and Politics*, 131.

157. Two more institutes were established in 1950, the National Institute of Arthritis and Metabolic Diseases and the National Institute of Neurological Diseases and Blindness.

158. Federal Security Agency, Public Health Service, *The Public Health Service Today* (Washington, DC: Federal Security Agency, 1952): 10.

159. In July 1947 Congress had established a Commission on Organization of the Executive Branch, under the chairmanship of Herbert Hoover, to recommend ways to reduce waste and streamline the federal government. The Commission's reports appeared in 24 parts between January and June 1949.

160. A number of names were suggested, only to be rejected for one reason or another. Among them, the Department of Welfare, the Department of General Welfare, the Department of Human Resources, and the Department of Health, Education, and Social Security. Apparently the last suggestion was rejected because its acronym spelled HESS, the name of Hitler's deputy! Rufus E. Miles, Jr, *The Department of Health, Education, and Welfare* (New York: Praeger Publishers, 1974): 26–7.
161. Miles, *Department of Health, Education, and Welfare*, 26.
162. Miles, *Department of Health, Education, and Welfare*, 29.
163. In 1948 Dr John Enders was able to culture intestinal cells on which the polio virus retained its cytopathic effects and could be propagated.
164. Dr Salk had grown virulent polio viruses on Rhesus monkey kidney cells and had inactivated them using a 1:4000 dilution of formaldehyde. The various manufacturers of the vaccine had also used formaldehyde, which in the event proved inadequate. See Center for Complex Infectious Diseases, 'Stealth Virus Research', presented before the Twentieth Century Plague Symposium held in Los Angeles, 1–2 March 1996, available on the World Wide Web at http://ccid.org/stealth/presentations/handout.htm (accessed 23 February 2000). It has since been determined that a particularly tenacious virus, designated SV40, that causes tumors and appears to have contributed to causing lung, bone, and brain cancers, had concealed itself within the renal cells of the Rhesus and Cynomolgus monkeys with which the vaccine was made and had survived all the filtering processes used. A detailed account of SV40 appears in Pat Wechsler, 'A Shot in the Dark', *New York* (11 November 1996).
165. As would be expected from large bureaucracies, Dr Eddy was removed from the task of polio vaccine testing.
166. The Bureau of Indian Affairs was first lodged in the War Department and there were no formal provisions regarding health care. However, in 1849, when the Bureau was transferred to the Department of the Interior, the government adopted a policy of providing medical care on a regular basis.
167. Mullan, *Plagues and Politics*, 134.
168. The Transfer Act (P.L. 83–568).
169. Mullan, *Plagues and Politics*, 139. Miles' study of the Department of Health, Education, and Welfare writes that 57 hospitals and 3400 staff were transferred from the BIA to the new Indian Health Service. Miles, *The Department of Health, Education, and Welfare*, 206.
170. The history of federal medical care to the American Indian community is dealt with in greater detail in Chapter 5.
171. Miles, *The Department of Health, Education, and Welfare*, 206.
172. Ten percent of Alaska natives examined by the Selective Service System during World War II had active cases of tuberculosis. Mullan, *Plagues and Politics*, 134.
173. Tuberculosis was more than nine times as common among American Indians as among the white population in 1955. Indian Health Service, Department of Health and Human Services, *Trends in Indian Health – 1996* (Washington, DC: Indian Health Service, 1996): 80, 40.
174. There are three huge medical centers, at Phoenix, Arizona, Gallup, New Mexico, and Anchorage, Alaska.
175. Peter J. Cunningham, 'Healthcare Utilization, Expenditures, and Insurance Coverage for American Indians and Alaska Natives Eligible for the Indian Health Service', in Gary D. Sandefur, Ronald R. Rindfuss, and Barney Cohen, eds, *Changing Numbers, Changing Needs: American Indian Demography and Public Health* (Washington, DC: National Academy Press, 1996): 289–90.
176. P.L. 93-638.
177. Indian Health Service, *Trends in Indian Health*, 21.
178. The history of the National Library of Medicine can be found in: Wyndham D. Miles, *A History of the National Library of Medicine: The Nation's Treasury of Medical Knowledge* (Bethesda, Md.: National Library of Medicine, National Institutes of Health, Public Health Service, Department of Health and Human Services, 1982).
179. This is the same Billings who, in 1869, was appointed by the Secretary of the Treasury to inspect the hospitals of the Marine Hospital Service and whose report led to the

reorganization of the MHS. Details of Billings' contribution to the history of the Public Health Service and the National Library of Medicine can be found in Carleton B. Chapman, *Order Out of Chaos: John Shaw Billings and America's Coming of Age* (Boston, MA: The Boston Medical Library, 1994).

180. Mullan, *Plagues and Politics*, 136.

181. The *Index-Medicus* is published monthly and indexes, by both subject and author, articles from 3400 journals.

182. The building, at Seventh and Independence Avenue, was designed by Billings and housed the Library's collections until 1961. Billings apparently was an extremely accomplished man. Not only did he plan the facilities for the National Library of Medicine but he is also credited with designing the Johns Hopkins Hospital in Baltimore and the New York Public Library.

183. Mullan, *Plagues and Politics*, 136.

184. In 1922 the Library's name was changed from 'the Library of the Surgeon General's Office', its title since 1836, to 'the Army Medical Library'. Thirty years later, its name was again altered to 'the Armed Forces Library'. The Library's history is chronicled in Michael E. DeBakey, 'The National Library of Medicine: Evolution of a Premier Information Center', *Journal of the American Medical Association*, 266 (4 September 1991): 1252–8.

185. Hill served as Chairman of the Senate Committee on Labor and Public Welfare and regularly awarded the National Institutes of Health substantially more than amounts requested by the agency. Indeed, it appears that most of the increases in the amounts appropriated to the Institutes were made on the initiative of Congress and particularly of Congressman John Fogarty of Rhode Island and Senator Hill. See Miles, *The Department of Health, Education, and Welfare*, 189.

186. In 1956 Hill had worked tirelessly to get the Armed Forces Library transferred from the Department of Defense to the Public Health Service.

187. The evolution of the various computerized bibliographies of the National Library of Medicine can be found in Miles, *History of the National Library of Medicine*, 365–91.

188. Mullan, *Plagues and Politics*, 139. International politics seems to have played a role in the programs and operations of the CDC on a number of occasions. Currently the CDC has requested and been awarded funds for activities related to chemical and biological terrorism.

189. *Budget of the United States Government, Fiscal Year 1967*, Appendix to the Budget (Washington, DC: Government Printing Office, 1967): 461. In the same year the expenditures for activities related to the Indian Health Service amounted to $76 million. *Budget of the United States Government, 1967*, Appendix, 264.

190. Neil MacNeil and Harold W. Metz, *The Hoover Report, 1953–1955: What It Means to You as Citizen and Taxpayer* (New York: The Macmillan Co., 1956): 178. Between 1948 and 1956 the Public Health Service closed five of its 21 hospitals. Mullan, *Plagues and Politics*, 145.

191. Details of the proposed UMA can be found in Frank Gervasi, *Big Government: The Meaning and Purpose of the Hoover Commission Report* (Westport, Conn.: Greenwood Press, 1949): 176–90.

192. United States Public Health Service, Study Group on Mission and Organization of the Public Health Service, *Final Report* (Washington, DC: Government Printing Office, 1960): 7.

193. Interestingly enough, the role of the Surgeon General in the new millennium has, for practical purposes, been reduced to publishing statements and warnings about deviations from the medically acceptable lifestyles.

194. 171 (28 November 1959): 1829–37.

195. Terry's father was a close friend and colleague of Dr Luther Leonidas Hill of Alabama, the father of Senator Lister Hill. Doubtless this connection served Terry well during his tenure as Surgeon General.

196. United States Department of Health, Education, and Welfare. *Smoking and Health. Report of the Advisory Committee to the Surgeon General of the Public Health Service*, PHS Pub. No. 1103 (Washington, DC: Government Printing Office, 1964).

197. The description appears in Miles, *Department of Health, Education, and Welfare*, 199.

198. Shonick, *Government and Health Services*, 99.
199. Legislation passed in 1965 included an act to expand the care extended to migrant work-
      ers, legislation extending the scope of federal vaccine assistance, and funding for a major
      campaign against measles. In addition, the Health Research Facilities Amendments
      provided the NIH with an additional $280 million for construction purposes and the Heart
      Disease, Cancer, and Stroke Amendments, enacted as a result of the recommendations of
      the DeBakey Commission on these diseases, established the Regional Medical Program, a
      network of medical centers linking medical research, education, and care. Mullan, *Plagues
      and Politics*, 153.
200. See Chapter 5.
201. Miles, *Department of Health, Education, and Welfare*, 200.
202. In spite of the fact that over 80 percent of the employees of the PHS were not in the
      Commissioned Corps, no member of the civil service had ever run a bureau. Mullan,
      Plagues and Politics, 158.
203. The history of the Food and Drug Administration is dealt with in greater detail in Chapter
      2.
204. Dr Philip Lee, at the time the Assistant Secretary of Health and Scientific Affairs, was an
      active participant in designing the new organizational structure. See Miles, *Department of
      Health, Education, and Welfare*, 53.
205. The Public Health Service had undergone an internal reorganization in the mid-1960s. In
      1966 President Lyndon Johnson was able to obtain Congress's consent to his
      Reorganization Plan Number 3, which empowered the Secretary of Health, Education, and
      Welfare, John Gardner, to reorganize the Public Health Service without formal approval
      from Congress. There followed a detailed study of the DHEW's health functions made by
      an ad hoc committee chaired by Dr John Corson of Princeton. As a consequence, Gardner
      restructured the PHS, effective in January 1967, into five operating divisions, all under the
      Office of the Surgeon General: the National Institutes of Health; the Bureau of Disease
      Prevention and Environmental Control; the National Institute of Mental Health; the Bureau
      of Health Manpower; and, the Bureau of Health Services. In addition, the Service had
      authority over the National Center for Health Statistics and the National Library of
      Medicine.
206. The National Institute of Mental Health, which had been a component Institute of the
      National Institutes of Medicine, had become responsible for such a mixture of functions,
      research, service, and professional training programs, that it was thought best to remove it
      from the NIH, whose primary focus was on research.
207. According to a Public Health Service publication, the rationale behind CPEHS was that
      'man's environmental milieu consisted of the products he consumed and used, as well as
      the elements of nature; therefore, it was felt that the FDA and the environmental health
      aspects of DHEW should be brought together'. Office of Administrative Management,
      Public Health Service, *History, Mission, and Organization of the Public Health Service*
      (Washington, DC: Government Printing Office, 1976): 3.
208. The Foreign Quarantine Division of the Service, which employed 600 officers prior to the
      reorganization was transferred to the Centers for Disease Control in 1967 and was reduced
      to a staff of 60 several years later. Mullan, *Plagues and Politics*, 162.
209. Miles, *Department of Health, Education, and Welfare*, 54.
210. Among the components of this huge agency were the Indian Health Service, the National
      Center for Health Statistics, the Center for Disease Control, the Regional Medical Program,
      the Public Health Service hospitals, and the health planning functions of the PHS.
211. Weinberger also removed the extensive health manpower functions of the National
      Institutes of Health and lodged them in the newly created Health Resources Administration.
      The Bureau of Health Manpower Education, a half-billion dollar program, was created in
      1967 and made part of the Public Health Service. In the reorganization of 1968 the Bureau
      was transferred to the National Institutes of Health.
212. While it is true that the constituent agencies of the Public Health Service, particularly the
      National Institutes of Health, the Food and Drug Administration, the Center for Disease
      Control, and the National Institute for Mental Health were all rapidly expanding, it would

be misleading to claim, as does one historian, that the PHS was expanding in scale and scope. The core functions of the PHS and of the Commissioned Corps, providing medical and hospital care for seamen and coastguardsmen and handling the nation's quarantines and sanitation projects, were fast disappearing and its other functions were carried on by agencies that were effectively independent of the PHS. See Mullan, *Plagues and Politics*, 168.

213. Finch had been lieutenant governor of California and one of Nixon's closest political advisers. It appears that he was offered a choice of cabinet positions and decided on the Department of Health, Education, and Welfare.

214. He is reputed to have observed that inasmuch as Americans are required by law to arrange insurance for their cars it made little sense to object to a requirement that they arrange health insurance for themselves.

215. Eric Redman, *The Dance of Legislation* (New York: Simon and Schuster, 1973): 42.

216. At this point, a number of higher echelon medical bureaucrats supported the idea of leaving the post of Surgeon General vacant.

217. Department of Health, Education, and Welfare, *Report of the Secretary's Committee to Study the Public Health Service Commissioned Corps* (Washington, DC: Government Printing Office, 1971).

218. *Washington Report on Health and Medicine*, 1252 (28 June 1971): 2, quoted in Mullan, *Plagues and Politics*, 173.

219. Mullan, *Plagues and Politics*, 173.

220. The Deputy Surgeon General, Dr Paul Ehrlich, was given the task of carrying out any required ceremonial functions.

221. See Department of Health and Human Services, Public Health Service Commissioned Corps, *Report to the Senate Appropriations Committee Responding to a Request in the Committee Report on the FY 1998 HHS Appropriations Bill* (Washington, DC, February 1998): 4. In reality, the overwhelming number of Commissioned Corps officers work in US government agencies alongside civil servants and are not called on to any greater degree than are civilian employees.

222. Of the approximately 6000 Commissioned Officers of the Public Health Service, about 2250 are currently assigned to the Indian Health Service, 163 are serving with the Coast Guard, and 530 are with the US Bureau of Prisons. In addition, Commissioned Officers provide needed medical care for aliens held in the detention facilities of the Immigration and Naturalization Service and detainees in the custody of the US Marshals Service. Commissioned Corps, *FY1998 Report to the Senate Appropriations Committee*, 15.

223. The Department of Health, Education, and Welfare had determined that approximately 22 million Americans lacked adequate access to medical care and that even more lacked access to dental and/or mental health care.

224. This is the first instance when members of the Commissioned Corps of the PHS were authorized to offer medical treatment to members of the general public.

225. The history of the Act creating the National Health Service Corps is presented in great detail in Redman, *The Dance of Legislation*.

226. Throughout its history the American Medical Association has advanced the view that the country contained far too many physicians.

227. Office of the Inspector General, Department of Health and Human Services, *National Health Service Corps: A Survey of Providers, Facilities, and Staff* (Executive Summary) (Bethesda, Md., May 1997): i.

228. Currently the stipend is $915.00 per month.

229. During the same period, discretionary outlays increased from $117.3 billion to $157.9 billion, or 34 percent. All figures are from the Congressional Budget Office..

230. Statement of the Environmental Protection Agency History Office, 'A Look at EPA Accomplishments'. available at http://www.epa.gov/history/faq/milestones/htm (accessed 29 March 2000).

231. Thomas J. Kniesner and John D. Leeth, 'Abolishing OSHA', *Regulation* (The Cato Review of Business and Government), 18 (Fall 1995): 48.

232. Mullan, *Plagues and Politics*, 174.

233. Ibid., 174–5.
234. Nixon had declared 'a massive crisis in our medical system' in 1969 and ordered his aides to recommend some method of slowing the increase in health-care costs without introducing price controls.
235. The other components of the Health Resources Administration were the National Center for Health Statistics, the National Center for Health Services Research and Development, the Comprehensive Health Planning Service, the National Health Service Corps, the Health Care Facilities Service, the Regional Medicine Programs Service, the Emergency Medical Services Program, and the Bureau of Health Manpower Education.
236. Richmond was the first Surgeon General not to have served in the Commissioned Corps.
237. The Office of Economic Opportunity, created by the Economic Opportunity Act of 1964, was the product of President Lyndon Johnson's War on Poverty, declared in his State of the Union address in January of that year. Lodged in the White House, the OEO acted as the coordinating bureau of the various agencies and projects created to combat poverty in America, including Operation Head Start, Follow-Through, Upward Bound, Volunteers in Service to America (VISTA), the Model Cities Program, the Neighborhood Youth Corps, the Job Corps, the Legal Services Program, and countless others. To insure maximum bureaucratization of the program, recipients were encouraged to establish their own agencies and to apply to the OEO for grant money to underwrite their goals.
238. Mullan, *Plagues and Politics*, 185.
239. In keeping with the new, fashionable mission of the Department of Health and Human Services to emphasize preventive health measures, the Centers for Disease Control established the Center for Chronic Disease Prevention and Health Promotion in 1988. Four years later the CDC added the words 'and Prevention' to its title.
240. As was the case with the Nixon Presidency, the Reagan Administration in actuality increased government spending. During his eight years in office federal expenditures climbed from $745.8 million in 1982 to $1143.7 million in 1989, or 53 percent. Discretionary spending increased from $325.9 million to $488.8 million, or 50 percent. It is true that a portion of each year's budget, about 2.4 percent, was appropriated by Congress despite Reagan's having requested a smaller amount but these excess amounts do not affect the budget's rate of growth.
241. In September 1979 Congress divided the Department of Health, Education, and Welfare into two, a Department of Education and a Department of Health and Human Services.
242. Some years later, when asked if the positions of Assistant Secretary of Health and of Surgeon General should be held by the same person, Koop replied that 'the person that holds both jobs can't give adequate attention to both at the same time. In the political world, the problems of the assistant secretary come first. That means that the bully pulpit, which is the best weapon the surgeon general has, must be neglected. I think that's unfortunate.' 'Chat With C. Everett Koop', *Living* section of *ABC News*, available on the World Wide Web at http://204.202.137.113/sections/living/DailyNews/drkoop_chat.html (accessed 2 April 2000).
243. (1981): *The Health Consequences of Smoking – The Changing Cigarette: A Report of the Surgeon General*; (1982): *The Health Consequences of Smoking – Cancer: A Report of the Surgeon General*; (1983): *The Health Consequences of Smoking – Cardiovascular Disease: A Report of the Surgeon General*; (1984): *The Health Consequences of Smoking – Chronic Obstructive Lung Disease: A Report of the Surgeon General*; (1985): *The Health Consequences of Smoking – Cancer and Chronic Lung Disease in the Workplace: A Report of the Surgeon General*; (1986): *The Health Consequences of Involuntary Smoking: A Report of the Advisory Committee to the Surgeon General* and *Smoking and Health: A National Status Report to Congress*; (1988): *The Health Consequences of Smoking – Nicotine Addiction: A Report of the Surgeon General*. Dr Koop's crusade did not end when he left government service. He continued to attack smoking in his writings, speeches, and television appearances and on his Website, www.drkoop.com. In 1998, Dr Koop testified before the Senate Commerce Committee on a bill that would have limited the amount of liability of the tobacco companies to $6.5 billion per year in state and local suits in return for some measure of immunity from further legal action. Koop was outspo-

ken in his criticism of the bill. 'There is no reason', he testified, 'why we of the public health community should agree to, or this Congress should facilitate, anything which grants this rogue industry immunity or limited liability'. (The quotation appears in the testimony of Dr Koop before the Senate Commerce Committee Hearings on S.1415 on 20 April 1998.)

244. In reporting on the Surgeon General's report on *The Health Consequences of Involuntary Smoking: Chronic Obstructive Lung Disease. Facts on File* noted that the report maintained that 'children whose parents smoked had a greater susceptibility at an early age to respiratory problems, including bronchitis and pneumonia. Children of smoking parents were also reported to show a "measurable but small" reduction in breathing ability compared with children of nonsmokers. The report noted that "high levels of involuntary smoke exposure" might cause reduced breathing ability in the general population.' 'Warning Issued on Passive Smoking', *Facts on File* (22 June 1984).

245. In light of Koop's attitude towards tobacco, it is no surprise that he advocated the continued criminalization of marijuana even when used for the relief of pain by terminally ill patients. During the 1996 campaign to allow its use for this purpose in Arizona, Koop acted as spokesman for those opposing the proposition.

246. As reported by CNN: 'Former Surgeon General Wages War on Obesity', 26 October 1996. (Posted on CNN's Website at http://www.cnn.com/HEALTH/9610/29/nfm/obesity/index.html (accessed 2 April 2000).)

247. AIDS, Acquired Immunodeficiency Syndrome, was originally assigned the name GRID, or gay-related Immunodeficiency, until it was discovered that the disease was not peculiar to homosexuals. The CDC had begun reporting cases of *Pneumocystis carinii* pneumonia and Kaposi's sarcoma in gay men living in Los Angeles and New York in 1981 and the first article on AIDS appeared in *The New York Times* on 3 July 1981.

248. Mullan, *Plagues and Politics*, 201.

249. Ibid., 201

250. These data appear in ibid., 203.

251. Ibid., 207. Just *what* coordination between the Corps and the military or why it would be necessary remains a mystery.

252. Jessica Gavora, 'Doctor, Can I Have This Agency Removed?' *Policy Review* (No. 81) January–February 1997.

253. Housing and subsistence allowances amounted to approximately $80.5 million in 1994.

254. The retirement system in place for Commissioned officers is a 'pay-as-you-go' system rather than being accrual-based, as in the case with federal civilian and Department of Defense personnel. When a member of the Corps is employed in some agency of the federal government, the salary for that officer is paid for out of agency funds. However, the retirement benefits are not. As a consequence, there is a strong incentive for agencies to hire members of the Commissioned Corps. Carrie Gavora, 'Public Health Service Commissioned Corps', in Scott A. Hodge, *Balancing America's Budget: Ending the Era of Big Government* (Washington, DC: Heritage Foundation, 1997).

255. Admittedly, Dr Elders is occasionally given to making somewhat bizarre statements. In January 1994, while delivering a sermon at a Methodist Church in Austin, Texas, she chided ministers for being concerned with the ethical behavior of their parishioners: 'It is time for ministers to stop moralizing from the pulpit', she said, 'and get out here and help me save the children'.

256. US Department of Health and Human Services, *Mental Health: A Report of the Surgeon General* (Rockville, Md.: Department of Health and Human Services, Substance Abuse and Mental Health Services Administration, Center for Mental Health Services, National Institutes of Health, National Institute of Mental Health, 1999): 12.

257. Surgeon General, *Report on Mental Health*, 411, 417.

258. Surgeon General, *Report on Mental Health*, 8.

259. The eight separate agencies include the Agency for Toxic Substances and Disease Registry. However, for administrative purposes, it was in fact an arm of the Centers for Disease Control and Prevention.

260. The Health Resources and Services Administration; the Indian Health Service; the Centers

for Disease Control; the National Institutes of Health; the Food and Drug Administration; the Substance Abuse and Mental Health Administration; and the Agency for Health Care Policy and Research.

261. Indeed, the only agency concerned with medical matters not nominally a part of the Public Health Service is the Center for Medicare and Medicaid Services (CMS), which was created in 1977 by the Secretary of Health, Education and Welfare, Joseph Califano, to oversee both the Medicare and Medicaid programs. Its original title, the Health Care Financing Administration, was altered to its current form in 2001 by the then Secretary of Health and Human Services, Tommy Thompson. Prior to 1977 Medicare was administered by the Bureau of Health Insurance of the Social Security Administration, while Medicaid was the responsibility of the Social and Rehabilitation Service of the DHEW. The administrative budget of the agency since FY 1995 and estimates of its budget for FY 2006 and FY 2007 are as follows:

1995	$ 2 189 000 000	2002	$ 2 505 000 000
1996	2 111 000 000	2003	2.497 000 000
1997	1 745 000 000	2004	3 066 000 000
1998	1 891 000 000	2005	3 429 000 000
1999	2 063 000 000	2006e	3 268 000 000
2000	2 132 000 000	2007e	3 293 000 000
2001	2 335 000 000		

262. The Department has among its agencies only two which are not concerned with health issues, the Administration for Children and Families (established in 1991 as a successor to the Family Support Administration) and the Administration on Aging (established in 1965 with passage of the Older Americans Act). Both administer a multiplicity of grants and programs dealing with children, families, and the elderly. Among the constituent bureaus of the Administration for Children and Families are: (1) The Administration on Developmental Disabilities; (2) the Administration for Native Americans; the Office of Family Assistance; the Office of Child Support Enforcement; the Office of Refugee Resettlement; the Administration on Children, Youth, and Families; and the Office of Community Services.

263. Budget figures for each of the subdivisions of the OPHS that follow are taken from the relevant issues of the *Budget of the United States*.

264. The Department of Health and Human Services, *Budget in Brief, Fiscal Year 2007* (Washington, DC, 2006). This document indicates that the total HHS budget, less allocations to the two non-medical agencies, was $627 135 000 000.

2. The Food and Drug Administration

The Food and Drug Administration is charged by the federal government with responsibility to oversee the purity of most of the nation's food and cosmetic products and the purity and effectiveness of the whole range of therapeutic agents sold in the United States. Its 2003 fiscal year budget is somewhat more than $1.7 billion but the agency's potential effect on the country's economy and welfare is far greater than might be assumed from this figure. Products accounting for no less than 25 cents of every dollar spent by American consumers are under the jurisdiction of the FDA, approximately $1 trillion annually, including all foodstuffs excepting meat and poultry and all human and animal drugs and therapeutic devices. The FDA's mandate is immense inasmuch as it is empowered to determine which drugs are available to American consumers; it thus ultimately has the power of life and death over hundreds of thousands of people suffering from fatal illnesses. We must all, at one point or another, rely on the FDA's permission to obtain and ingest what might prove a live-saving medication prescribed by our physician without which we might well die. Indeed, there can be no doubt that over the years the delays involved in FDA approval of therapeutic agents that have been shown to be life-saving have cost the lives of hundreds of thousands of Americans.[1]

Prior to the twentieth century, the federal government was involved in overseeing the nation's food and drug supply in only the most marginal way. In 1848, largely through intensive lobbying by Dr M.J. Bailey, the Special Examiner of Drugs at the Port of New York Customs Office and a passionate crusader for federal regulation, Congress passed legislation empowering the United States Customs Service to prevent adulterated drugs from entering the country.[2] Dr Bailey was one of the first in a long line of pharmacists who regularly attacked patent and ready-made medications as poisons and who pressed for passage of legislation eliminating the sale of all patent drugs in groceries, general stores, and other 'nonprofessional' establishments. The 1848 law, however, limited itself to prohibiting the importation of drugs that were shown to be adulterated. The House select committee charged with holding hearings on the bill, chaired by Dr Thomas Owen Edwards of Ohio and comprising a majority of physicians, occurred at a time when America was in the midst of a war with Mexico. Convinced that the condition of the American drug supply was so poor as to constitute a serious threat to the nation's war effort, Congress quickly passed the bill despite reservations that the federal government lacked the authority to limit commerce. Congressman Edwards' response to this criticism is worth noting inasmuch as it must constitute one of the broadest arguments ever put forward in support of government involvement in private life. Edwards called attention to a section of the Tariff Act passed by Congress six years earlier and noted that it provided that 'all indecent and immoral books and pictures' imported into the country were subject to confiscation and destruction. He then went on to argue that just as 'the paternal supervision of all good governments is not only needed to protect the morals of the people', so it 'is justly demanded in all that pertains to their health and physical well being'.[3] Edwards was joined in this sentiment, which could serve to allow passage of almost any invasion into what would ordinarily be regarded as a matter of individual choice, by the Secretary of the Treasury, Robert J. Walker.

Despite hopes for this measure by domestic druggists, however, the Act had little effect on curtailing the supply of imported drugs since it did not apply to patent medicines and was further emasculated by the fact that inspectors could choose from no less than five different standards for other drugs.[4] Pressure for passage of the law came largely from the few professional druggists who sought to distinguish themselves from the large number of lesser trained dispensers of medications and from the nation's grocers and general-store owners who freely competed with apothecaries in selling medications. These druggists, then known as pharmaceutists, had established 'Colleges of Pharmacy', in, among other cities, Philadelphia in 1821 and New York in 1829, with the aim of limiting the right to sell drugs solely to those whom they regarded as equipped with the credentials to prepare and dispense medicines. This attempt to establish a druggists' guild resulted in the creation of the American Pharmaceutical Association (APhA) in 1852.

American druggists were clearly more concerned with the competition of substandard imported drugs than those compounded in their own shops. It was not that the amount and level of adulteration in domestically produced medications was less but that limiting the supply of these therapeutic agents from overseas insured that a larger proportion of American medicines, adulterated or not, were sold than would otherwise have been the case in the absence of a law prohibiting their importation. Clearly it was in the interests of local pharmaceutists to keep out foreign products. Indeed, one of the principal goals of the APhA was 'to improve and regulate the drug market, by preventing the importation of inferior, adulterated or deteriorated drugs, and by detecting and exposing home adulteration'.[5]

During the last half of the nineteenth century it was commonly believed that a substantial portion of food and drugs were adulterated, much of it to the point of being poisonous. In fact, there was no evidence that warranted arriving at this grave conclusion, yet a substantial number of people in positions of influence believed this to be the case.[6] Concern for the purity of the nation's food and drug supply had developed over the course of the nineteenth century, especially as families relied more and more on store-bought foods and medicines. Canning, which had been pioneered in Europe at the beginning of the nineteenth century, had become a commonplace by the 1850s.[7] In addition, the development of railroads permitted the manufacturers of foodstuffs to transport their products throughout the country so that by the close of the Civil War the average American family relied on groceries and general stores for almost all their foods. Indeed, the only families that continued to rely on home-grown staples were pioneers and homesteaders.

While adulteration was not uncommon, in fact had always been practiced if only on a limited and local scale, it was rarely seriously harmful or lifethreatening. Prior to the middle of the nineteenth century store owners were primarily concerned with the weight of foodstuffs and as a consequence adulteration took the form of cheap additives.[8] Thus, pepper was traditionally diluted with mustard seed and linseed, or bean meal with chillies, all serving to restore the pungency of the original and all more or less innocuous.[9] So too was milk often diluted with water by less reputable vendors and bread made from a mix that contained less expensive potato flour.

Another commodity commonly subjected to adulteration was tea, which was extremely popular throughout the eighteenth and nineteenth centuries. When Catherine da Braganza of Portugal married Charles II in 1662 she had introduced the continental custom of drinking tea to the English court and this quickly became fashionable among Englishmen. The importation of tea soon became a significant source of revenue for the English government,[10] which quickly placed a 5 shilling-per-pound duty on tea that was retailing on the Continent for 1 shilling a pound. The effect of this prohibitively high tariff in both Great Britain and British North America was massive smuggling and adulteration, which persisted even after duties had been substantially lowered. Tea merchants found that the cheapest and most effective method of adulterating tea was to buy up used tea leaves from hotels, coffee houses, and from servants employed by the wealthy, to stiffen these leaves with a gum solution, and to then retint them.[11] The result was an infusion only mildly less potent than the original tea but that could be sold at a substantially lower price.

By the 1860s manufacturers of foodstuffs found that the application of certain additives could enhance the flavor, texture, and appearance of their products and, more important, could deter spoilage. These additives, in most cases harmless, were also regarded, as is the case today, as adulterants and impurities that compromised the nutritional value and efficacy of the product.[12] Even starch, without which, for most of the nineteenth century, chocolate could not be made[13] was held by some to be an adulterant. Perhaps one of the most curious accusations was made regarding coffee, the largest single adulterant of which was chicory, which was viewed as severely diminishing the healthful and nutritive value of the product.[14] Indeed coffee appears to have been singled out throughout the century as the object of particularly unusual or noxious adulterants, which included baked horse liver, chalk, and ground date-stones.[15]

Concern for the purity and cleanliness of the foods and drugs manufactured and sold domestically was significantly heightened by advances in analytical chemistry, which placed in the hands of scientists the ability to detect and measure the degree to which foods and drugs were adulterated. The first significant study of adulteration which appears to have roused the imagination of the public on both sides of the Atlantic was published in London in 1820 by a German chemist, Fredrick Accum, then living in England.[16] The work rapidly went through four editions and there appears to have been a pirated edition almost immediately published in the United States.[17] Suitably illustrated with a skull and crossbones on the cover, the book was written in a somewhat hysterical style and heavily exaggerated the amount of adulteration to which the average British consumer was subject. Among the author's more sensational claims, for which there appears to have been only the most meager evidence, was the fact that British wine merchants were poisoning their table wines with bitter almonds, a virulent poison, to give them a nutty flavor. Accum also made much of the fact that annatto, a vegetable agent, was employed by dairies in the winter months to color cheese. Changes in cattle feed during the winter led butter and cheese to lose their color, which dairymen replaced with annatto. The problem, Accum maintained, was not with annatto itself, but with the fact that it was occasionally contaminated with small quantities of red lead, at the time a common coloring agent.[18]

As lurid as were Accum's descriptions they were moderate compared to the claims made in a monograph published in London anonymously some ten years later. The book's full title alone is sufficient evidence of its sensationalistic nature. Entitled *Deadly Adulteration and Slow Poisoning Unmasked, or Disease and Death in the Pot and the Bottle, In Which the Blood-Empoisoning and Life-Destroying Adulterations of Wines, Spirits, Beer, Bread, Flour, Tea, Sugar, Spices, Cheesemongery, Pastry, Confectionery, Medicines, &c, &c are Laid Open to the Public*, the publication was written by 'an enemy to fraud and villany' [sic]. The author's list of poisons and loathsome substances to which all Englishmen (and Americans, for those reading the book on the other side of the Atlantic) were subjected was huge and included such colorful items as sheep's brains and ground human bones in the milk supply. Nor did the book limit itself to food and drugs but included fabrics, dyes, and a host of other commodities. *Deadly Adulteration* was aimed at a general audience, which was clearly undeterred from accepting the author's conclusions by the fact that he provided no evidence whatever for his claims. The book, known by its abbreviated title of 'Death in the Pot', was immensely popular in both Britain and the United States and contributed much to the paranoia over adulterated food and drugs that periodically swept both nations. It is true that conditions surrounding the preparation and sale of food in both Britain and the United States throughout most of the century were unsanitary, especially by today's standards, and, in rare instances, no less than filthy and that a number of foodstuffs were adulterated with cheap additives which served as fillers. However, it must be borne in mind that this was largely a function of the fact that sanitation and purity entailed costs for which most of the consuming public were unable or unwilling to pay. Indeed, Accum and other sanitarians who wrote on the topic maintained that cheapness alone was prima-facie evidence of adulteration. As might be expected, these reformers were soon joined by the more established grocers whose goods were being sold at higher prices in warning against cheaper foodstuffs and in calling for regulations to stop their sale.[19]

Unfortunately claims regarding food and drug adulteration were accepted and spread by men of good will and high repute without the least confirming evidence. Thus in 1850 Arthur Hill Hassall, the eminent physician and microscopist, was approached by Thomas Wakley, editor of the leading British medical journal, the *Lancet*, to investigate Britain's food and drug supply.[20] His findings[21] had a profound effect in Great Britain and the United States and led directly to passage of the British Adulteration of Food Act in 1860.[22] While Hassall appears to have investigated a large number of substances and uncovered extensive adulteration, in most cases these instances were far less dramatic than were reported. One historian notes that Hassall 'reached conclusions about the vast extent of adulteration that – while they may have been true – he could not really establish, never having conducted a systematic investigation of the scope of adulteration, merely of its nature' and goes on to observe that Haskall 'seems to have made it a practice to name even the most doubtful adulterant, then indicate that its use "is but little probable" '.[23] The same commentator, one of the leading authorities on the history of pure food and drug legislation, notes of Haskall's testimony before the House of Commons committee investigating the need for a statute prohibiting adulteration:

> For all his unquestionable skill with the microscope, and despite the fact that the parliamentary committee found him more than credible, Hassall was an unreliable witness. Yet, for a generation, Hassall's assertions continued to be the authoritative source upon which American reformers would draw.[24]

In sum, over the course of the century, and more commonly during its second half, the evidence seems to suggest that adulterated foods competed in the marketplace side by side with pure foods produced under comparatively clean conditions. For those who were ready to bear the costs it was always possible to obtain unadulterated food prepared in a sanitary environment and this became true of greater numbers of people as average incomes rose. The greed of food suppliers alone simply cannot account for the poor conditions that marked food-processing, as is often suggested. That both lack of sanitation and impure ingredients were far more common in mid-century than was the case by the time the Pure Food and Drugs Act was passed in 1906 attests to the fact that these improvements were a reflection of market conditions. By 1906 food processing had reached fairly high standards, to the point where most food was prepared and sold in comparatively sanitary conditions. This improvement cannot be credited to government officials who were to analyze foodstuffs and to institute serious inspections of food-processing facilities long after conditions had begun to improve.

While also subject to occasional adulteration, the production and distribution of drugs during the nineteenth century differed in several important respects from that of foodstuffs. It is difficult to appreciate just how primitive the practice of medicine was 200 years ago. Throughout the early part of the century orthodox medical practitioners relied on symptomatic treatment, consisting, in the main, of bloodletting and blistering, augmented by a number of therapeutic agents comprising mercury, antimony, lead, and other mineral poisons that were administered in massive doses as purgatives and emetics. This regimen was often followed by treatment with arsenical compounds, which were thought to act as tonics. In reaction to what became known as 'heroic therapy' two sects – eclecticism and homeopathy – emerged between 1830 and 1850 as successful competitors to regular medicine.

Eclecticism's principal theoretician was a New Hampshire farmer named Samuel Thomson, who in 1813 developed and patented a system of medicine that relied exclusively on botanical remedies, steam baths, and bed rest. The introduction of herbal, or galenical, medications did much to advance the condition of American medicine and doubtless saved numerous lives. An even greater threat to orthodox medical practice was homeopathy, the creation of Samuel Hahnemann, a German physician possessed of formal and rigorous medical training. Homeopathy's most significant contribution, and that which contributed most heavily to its popularity among Americans after it was introduced into the United States in 1825, was its stress on the natural healing powers of the organism itself. Homeopathic physicians were strong proponents of fresh air, sunshine, bed rest, proper diet, and personal hygiene in an age when regular medicine regarded these as of little or no value. With respect to its *materia medica*, Hahnemann's researches led him to conclude that the most efficacious remedy for any ailment consisted in the administration of a drug which, when tested in a healthy person, induced those symptoms most closely approximating the symptomology of the disease. Equally revolutionary was the homeopathic theory of optimal dosage. Regular physicians had prided themselves on the strength and quantity of medication administered, many believing that if ten grains of a substance were thought beneficial, then 100 would prove ten times as effective. Hahnemann, on the other hand, argued that the more attenuated and minute the dose of a medication was, the more effective it was. He went so far as to recommend dilutions to the one-decil-lionth of a drop of the original medication.

The rigors of heroic therapy, which killed in far larger numbers than it cured, and the relatively benign nature of eclectic and homeopathic treatment led to a decline in the use of bloodletting and the administration of calomel (mercurous oxide) and other mineral compounds in the second half of the nineteenth century.[25] In their place orthodox practitioners, who continued to operate on the assumption that reducing the temperature of fevered patients was the most important therapeutic priority, had recourse to several vegetable poisons, the most common of which were aconite and veratrum. Both aconite and veratrum were so dangerous, however, that the introduction of quinine as an antipyretic constituted a major advance in the physician's therapeutic arsenal, especially after the cost of isolating it from the cinchona bark was appreciably reduced in the 1860s. While practitioners regarded reducing their patients' fevers as their highest priority, they were also concerned with the symptomatic treatment of pain. For this reason analgesics were essential elements in the physician's armamentarium. Certainly the most important of these, in terms of both the degree to which physicians relied on them and their frequency of use, were opium and its alkaloid, morphine.

Opium and morphine were employed in the treatment of every possible illness and were routinely prescribed for all kinds of pain. Interestingly, physicians do not seem to have been at all concerned with their addictive properties, not even after it became routine for practitioners to administer morphine by hypodermic syringe after the Civil War.[26] In the second half of the century, concerns about the rising consumption of opium led to the increased popularity of cocaine as an analgesic, especially for ailments involving the nose, among them the common cold. In addition, several hypnotics, milder in their effects than was opium and its derivatives, were developed in the late nineteenth century and were regularly prescribed, among them chloral hydrate and sulphonal. Finally, doctors had constant recourse to beverage alcohol which, alongside cocaine, was employed as a tonic and stimulant for both the mildest ailments and the most acute and chronic diseases. In addition, alcohol was a highly recommended specific for, among others, cases of typhoid and pneumonia and was administered in such large doses that, as one historian has noted, 'continual inebriation must have been the state of many patients'.[27]

Throughout the nineteenth century there existed no law regulating the sale of cocaine and opium or any of their derivatives in any of the states and territories of the Union. There were a few exceptions to this generalization in the last few years of the century – the Territory of Montana, for example, enacted legislation in 1889 that limited the sale or disposition of cocaine, opium, morphine, and any of their compounds solely through the prescription of a physician – but enforcement of these early statutes was sporadic and the penalties imposed for violation were usually limited to a small fine.[28] As a result, those medications that were most efficacious in reducing pain, alcohol, opium, morphine, and cocaine, were readily available to the consumer not only at pharmacies, groceries, and general stores, but in the form of a host of patent medicines. Patent medicines were exactly as described, medications developed by individuals, often medical practitioners, that were patented and sold over the counter at all sorts of stores.[29] There were an enormous number of them. In 1857 a Boston catalog listed some 500 to 600 national labels while a year later a local newspaper advertised no less than 1500 different brands.[30] Finally, beginning in the 1870s, reputable pharmaceutical manufacturers began distributing unpatented packaged products, known as 'ethical' drugs, that reproduced the formulas of medications as they were listed in the US Pharmacopoeia. Despite the fact that these ethical drugs occasionally bore copyrighted names, they were in fact made in factories in keeping with accepted formularies.

Not only did the American *materia medica* reflect the therapeutic arsenal of all three medical approaches, but this was true as well of the patent medicines that were sold through thousands of retail outlets. Many of these nostrums were endorsed or manufactured by physicians themselves who saw in their sale a lucrative source of income to supplement their consultation fees. Even though in many cases physicians themselves had developed and patented these remedies, medical practitioners were in the forefront of the group calling for legislation to restrict their sale. Each practitioner-owner, with his competitors in mind, demanded an end to the 'patent medicine fraud' and called for legislation that would limit the public's access to medications, demanding that they be dispensed exclusively through licensed pharmacists and physicians.

Few if any of these nostrums were effective in providing any relief for those in pain except medications that contained alcohol, opium, morphine, or cocaine, the very substances in the physicians' armamentarium that proved most efficacious. Additionally, there is ample evidence that a number of users consumed narcotics as they did alcohol, as a recreational drug. Indeed, the consumption of opium in the United States prior to 1914 was prodigious, although apparently with little ill effect. There seem to have been few social problems caused by its use despite the large number of Americans who consumed opium and morphine, either occasionally or on a regular basis. The amount of opium imported into the United States in 1910 was more than 20 times as much per capita as was imported into Germany, Italy, or Austria-Hungary. In fact, in the 50 years following the beginning of the Civil War the quantity of opium brought into the country increased at a rate three times as fast as the population.[31]

The agitation against drug adulteration was essentially a demand that patent medicines cease including these components in their formulas, the very components used by physicians in treating their patients, at which point most nostrums would become totally ineffective and lose most of their sales. The struggle for legislation regulating the purity of drugs called for two distinct provisions. The first was that manufacturers of patent medicines be required to reveal the contents of their secret formulas on their labels, a requirement that would certainly have had the effect of significantly reducing sales of these remedies, especially given the nature of the ingredients and the growing popularity of the temperance movement. Secondly, and more important, physicians and pharmacists sought passage of legislation at both the state and national levels that would prohibit the sale of medicines containing alcohol or narcotics through any outlet other than those operated by a licensed pharmacist.[32] Pharmacists had succeeded in establishing themselves as a licensed profession in most of the states in the last quarter of the century[33] and had immediately put most of their efforts into agitating for legislation that would limit sales of most drugs through outlets directly controlled by licensed pharmacists, thus removing once and for all the destructive competition of countless other retail outlets.[34]

The efforts to gain passage of pure food and drug legislation were greatly facilitated by the women's temperance movement, which was particularly appalled by the alcohol and narcotic content of most medicines and who saw in these 'impure' medications a dire threat to the puritan values they had embraced with such fervor. The result was that the organizations comprising this popular national movement, the most important of which was the Woman's Christian Temperance Union (WCTU), campaigned as much against drugs as they did against alcohol. They held that 'adulterated food predisposed individuals to alcoholism and vice; doctored soft drinks and proprietary medications addicted individuals to alcohol and opium, and all addictive "narcotics and stimulants" – opium and its alkaloids, tobacco, chloral hydrate, cocaine, and cannabis – belonged in the same category with alcohol'.[35] In fact, prior to 1898 the Departments of Hygiene and Heredity, Scientific Instruction, and Narcotics, which agitated for pure food and drug laws, were among the most active of the WCTU's auxiliaries.[36]

It is difficult to overemphasize the singular importance played by the temperance movement in agitating for and in gaining passage of the first federal pure food and drug act in 1906. Despite the fact that the conditions connected with the manufacture and distribution of food and drugs continued to improve throughout the second half of the nineteenth century, the crusade against adulterated food and drugs gained momentum largely through the work of woman crusaders who associated impurities in these substances with alcohol and narcotic addiction and with fundamental threats to the maternal function and to the home. While the temperance movement, at its inception, concentrated on alcohol abuse, it quickly expanded its concerns to include anything that might prove a danger to the Victorian family.[37] It was claimed that adulterated foods predisposed individuals to alcoholism and to the vices that followed in its wake while proprietary medications led inexorably to addiction to narcotics.[38] In the last two decades of the century, reformers and sanitarians mounted nothing less than a fanatical crusade against the food and drug industry, whom they accused of poisoning Americans. Consumers, who were not yet completely accustomed to the many new products produced by new methods and marketed in novel ways, were subjected to an unceasing campaign in which they were assured that they and their families were being poisoned by filthy foodstuffs and tainted drugs and that they were being slowly addicted to alcohol and narcotics.

The temperance movement itself was strongly influenced by late nineteenth-century evangelical Protestantism with its emphasis on a particularly strict form of the well-ordered life involving individual restraint and virtue. To this was added the belief that true social improvement could come only through extensive legal regulation. What most of these reformers sought to accomplish was to impose by law nothing less than the whole system of Victorian values on Americans and thus to keep in check the proclivities of the dissolute, degenerate immigrants from eastern and southern Europe who were in the process of flooding the country. Both the first two presidents of the WCTU were devout evangelical Methodists while Harvey W. Wiley, the chief chemist with the Department of Agriculture and the principal lobbyist for a pure food and drug act, came from a fundamentalist Christian home.

The WCTU was founded in 1874, having developed out of the Women's Temperance Crusade, which was founded the year before and continued to operate alongside the WCTU. Both organizations were untiring in their ongoing pursuit of prohibition.[39] Under the guise of 'protection of the home', the WCTU urged enactment at the state and federal level of laws to severely restrict the distribution and sale of alcohol, tobacco, and all 'harmful' narcotic substances, including those that formed part of the medication either sold directly to patients or prescribed by a physician. It chose as its first president Annie Wittenmyer, editor of two Methodist magazines, *The Christian Woman* and *The Christian Child*, and one of the principal organizers of the Methodist Home Missionary Society. Wittenmyer was in effect responsible for transforming the women's auxiliaries of the various Protestant churches into temperance societies which banded together into an extremely effective organization for social reform. The goal of both the WTC and the WCTU since their creation had been not only to close down saloons but to pressure town druggists to remove all medications containing alcohol and narcotics from their shelves. Wittenmyer's approach to social reform, however, proved to be too moderate and too limited for the WCTU's membership. Her support for prohibition was the product of the view that alcoholism was almost exclusively a male problem and that its victims were invariably women and children. Her response was a species of temperance known as gospel temperance, whose goal was to reform drunkards and liquor drummers through mass meetings and prayer.[40]

It quickly became apparent that the executive and a substantial portion of the WCTU membership wanted to extend the demand for reform to encompass a whole range of social issues whose aim was 'protection of the home'. These included age-of-consent legislation, censorship of putatively obscene material, child labor laws, equal pay for equal work, the eight-hour day, prostitution, women's suffrage, strict limits on immigration, and pure food and drug legislation.[41] Pressures to expand the organization's concerns and to put more effort into lobbying for political change led to Wittenmyer's resignation in 1879 and her replacement by Frances Willard, who had been chosen as the WCTU's first secretary. Willard was a woman of extreme views and a devout Methodist. A college graduate, Willard held several teaching positions before becoming the first Dean of Women at Northwestern University, a post she resigned on being appointed secretary of the WCTU in 1874. In 1879 Willard succeeded Wittenmyer as president and determined to place all the efforts of the WCTU into seeking legislation to achieve the social ends she sought, including women's suffrage and a host of other social issues from raising the age of consent to mandating an eight-hour working day.[42] Willard's program of broad social reform gave direction to the WCTU and led to a substantial increase in the organization's membership so that by the turn of the century it had become the largest and most influential women's group in the nation.

Equally active in seeking a broad array of progressive reforms, among them a pure food and drug act, was the General Federation of Women's Clubs (GFWC), founded in 1890. While membership often overlapped with the WCTU, members of the constituent organizations comprising the GFWC were not bound to commit themselves to prohibition. However, they did seek legislation that would purify the nation of its unclean and unfit elements, whether in its food or in its population. As a result many of the member organizations supported the same spectrum of legislation, limitations on immigration, laws raising the age of consent, the prohibition of obscene material and prostitution, and child labor laws. Beyond that, the GFWC appears to have called for the elimination of all marks of 'privilege' as inimical to the notion of American democracy, including large businesses, private schools, and 'lack of worker independence'. Were it not for the government, their leadership maintained, commerce and the values associated with commerce threatened to create 'a triple aristocracy of birth, wealth and intellect that counterbalanced character and public service'. The GFWC's activities on behalf of a pure food law were concentrated in their Standing Committee of Domestic Science and of Civic Improvement, which energetically pursued federal regulation over almost every aspect of domestic life. The populist sentiments of its members and their efforts on behalf of the reforms they sought proved extremely valuable when the pure food and drug bill was finally enacted.[43] Indeed, a massive letter writing campaign conducted by the GFWC was acknowledged as decisive in securing passage of the measure in 1906.[44]

The 'progressive reform' movement, in which women played such a crucial part, was largely a movement to impose Protestant middle-class values on the millions of working class immigrants whose customs and habits could not be reconciled with those of evangelical Protestantism. The claim that nineteenth-century agitators for temperance who supported the whole string of reforms from pure food and drug legislation to sexual purity organized 'out of a sense of necessity and responsibility' and were motivated by altruism has no historical warrant.[45] This view, however, is shared by a number of historians who are sympathetic to the disabilities under which women during the last century were compelled to live and whose own political biases coincide with the legislative aims of women's organizations such as the WCTU. The facts, however, show that the leaders of the temperance movement lobbied vigorously for sanitary legislation at both the state and federal level because they were obsessed with notions of purity and viewed with disgust those Americans who embraced different values. To these crusaders the impurities Americans were forced to consume in their food, drink, and drugs destroyed their bodies and weakened their minds; they were nothing less than the work of Satan himself, evils that had to be stamped out if the nation were to survive and prosper.

A novel notion of government seems to have emerged during the period between the end of the Civil War and the outbreak of the World War, that it was the duty of democratic governments to undertake the task of protecting the general public from decisions that were judged by bureaucratic experts as contrary to their long-term interests. Consumers, it was felt, were at the mercy of avaricious businessmen driven by competitive forces who had to be held in check by a beneficent government motivated by a deep concern for the welfare of its citizens. Like kindly mothers, governments, local, state, and national, would employ their substantial powers to see to it that we all would live healthy, safe, and comfortable lives as free from the anxieties brought on by our own ignorance or poor judgment as was possible. Toward this end, using the legal apparatus to insure that the food and drink that we bought in no way defiled our bodies and that the medicines we were administered contained no sinful substances was perfectly sensible to sanitarians and supporters of the temperance movement. As one recent sympathizer approvingly maintains: 'This concept seemed elementary and fundamental to democracy's principles. People's rights should take precedence over property rights.'[46]

The movement in support of pure food and drug legislation was given substantial impetus by the national debate over the sale of purely artificial foods that emerged in the 1880s. This was particularly true of glucose and oleomargarine. Like all 'artificial' foods, glucose and oleomargarine were creations of chemical science, created and manufactured in the laboratory and chemically so closely resembling their 'natural' counterparts, 'natural sugar' and 'natural butter', that it was beyond the abilities of most consumers to detect the difference. This, it was thought by many, constituted the rankest swindle, both deceiving the public and debasing the food supply. As Robert M. LaFollette observed on the Senate floor in 1886:

> We face a new situation in history. Ingenuity, striking hands with cunning trickery, compounds a substance to counterfeit an article of food. It is made to look like something it is not; to taste and smell like something it is not; to sell like something it is not, and so deceive the purchaser.[47]

Glucose,[48] whose chemistry had been uncovered almost a hundred years earlier, was nothing more than a complex mixture of carbohydrates obtained by boiling starch with dilute mineral acids, the effect of which was a form of sugar different from that which came from cane. This starch sugar was, in Europe, almost always made from potatoes, while in the United States it was produced from Indian corn.[49] In the 1880s significant quantities of glucose were being manufactured in the United States since – even though its sweetening power was only about two-thirds that of cane sugar – it was cheaper to produce. It was employed in the manufacture of candies, jellies, canned fruit, and bakery goods and replaced the use of barley malt in brewing beer.[50] It also appears that granulated glucose was used fairly frequently as an adulterant of cane sugar. Ordinarily this revelation would not have occasioned the kind of hysteria that it did were it not for the fact that the leading sanitarian of the day, George Thorndike Angell, pronounced glucose 'a rank poison'.[51]

Angell was a dedicated and extremely effective opponent of the ill treatment of animals and the founder of several state and local organizations committed to halting their abuse, including one of the nation's first such associations, the Massachusetts Society for the Prevention of Cruelty to Animals. So successful was Angell in lobbying for passage of legislation mandating the humane treatment of animals that Massachusetts enacted its law only two months after Angell had begun his campaign. Within three years the movement had achieved immense popularity and states from Connecticut to California had passed similar statutes. During the course of his investigations into the mistreatment of cattle, Angell had noted the connection between dead and dying cattle and unsanitary beef, which in turn led him to take up the cause of pure food and drugs in the 1870s. In 1879 Angell presented a paper before the annual meeting of the American Social Science Association (ASSA), then meeting in Boston, in which he launched a passionate attack on the adulteration of food. Angell began his remarks with a demand that all physicians and pharmacists be required to obtain state licenses before entering practice but most of his paper was devoted to the problem of adulterated foods and poisonous fabrics.[52] He was unequivocal in emphasizing 'the need for laws prohibiting the manufacture and sale of these poisonous and dangerous articles under severe penalties, and compelling the manufacturers and sellers of adulterated articles to tell buyers the precise character of the adulteration'.[53] Glucose particularly constituted a danger to the public since, Angell contended, it was commonly made from rags and sawdust and the sulphuric acid employed in converting starch commonly left a deadly residue.[54]

While there existed no evidence whatever to confirm any of Angell's claims they soon gained national attention thanks to the enormous publicity they received and this in turn led to a string of articles of a similar nature in the daily and periodical press.[55] Angell's charges were repeated at the September 1879 meeting of the ASSA, at which most of the leading reputable scientists of the day were invited to assess Angell's claims, with particular reference to glucose and oleomargarine. Yet despite the fact that almost all these experts dismissed Angell's conclusions as capricious and without merit[56] they remained immensely popular and were regularly reproduced in the press. In the spring of 1879, spurred on by Angell's call for Congressional action against adulterated foods and especially his accusation that glucose was a serious hazard to human health, Richard Lee Beale of Virginia introduced a bill in the 46th Congress to forbid the transportation in interstate commerce of any article of food or drink mixed with a substance of less commercial value or harmful to the consumer unless the package bore a label indicating the name and extent of the adulterant.[57]

Among the groups most opposed to the manufacture and use of glucose, as one might suspect, were the manufacturers of cane sugar. Several of the nation's largest refineries charged that newer entrants into the industry were adulterating their sugar with glucose and thus compromising the health of the American public. They and Angell were able to prevail upon one of the more gullible Congressmen, Hiram Casey Young of Tennessee, Chairman of the Committee on Epidemic Diseases, to introduce a bill into the 47th Congress calling for a special levy on the manufacturers of and dealers in glucose and imposing a tax of a dollar a gallon on glucose in its liquid form and 10 cents a pound on grape sugar, the name given to glucose in its solid form.[58] Young's proposal was not acted upon by Congress, but both it and Angell's charges induced the commissioner of internal revenue to request a committee of the National Academy of Sciences to investigate glucose with a view, among other things, to determining whether it might be harmful when used as an ingredient in food. In one of those rare instances where an investigatory commission acting on an issue put before it by a government agency actually determines that prohibitory legislation is unnecessary, the committee concluded that glucose was in fact harmless.

The history of the government's treatment of oleomargarine was quite different. Oleomargarine had been patented by a French food chemist, Hippolyte Mège-Mouriés, in 1869 in response to a call by Napoleon III for an economical butter substitute. Mège had pressed digested beef suet and the chopped-up stomachs of cattle to obtain a mass of solidified animal fats; the resulting oil was at that point mixed with yeast during constant whisking to become margarine. While almost all margarine is today manufactured from vegetable oils that have been hydrogenated, earlier forms of margarine were made from animal fats. Mège was able to sell his patent rights to a number of different firms,[59] among them the United States Dairy Company, which initiated the production of oleomargarine in New York City in early 1876. The introduction of oleomargarine outraged the farming industry, which was suffering the effects of an extended agricultural depression that had started in the early 1870s. What particularly alarmed the dairy industry was that it was virtually impossible to distinguish butter from margarine without extensive chemical tests. Indeed, as one historian has pointed out, in this era a mixture of oleomargarine and butter could defy any microscopic or chemical test then known.[60]

Loud and prolonged agitation from dairy farmers that something be done soon aroused the New York legislature to enact legislation in 1877 that sought to 'prevent deception in sales of butter'.[61] Under the terms of the act manufacturers of margarine were required to 'distinctly and durably stamp, brand or mark upon every tub' some identifying mark, and retailers were to submit to every customer buying margarine a slip of paper on which the word 'margarine' was printed. It appears that the law was never enforced nor, indeed, could it have been effective without a massive army of inspectors.[62] In response to the industry's demand for some relief from the competition posed by increased margarine sales, the New York legislature passed a series of anti-margarine bills over the next half dozen years, most of which proved ineffective until finally, in 1884, it prohibited the manufacture and sale of butter substitutes entirely. The law, however, was quickly struck down by the state courts.[63]

A new threat to the dairy industry emerged in the 1880s when America's giant meat packers began producing margarine according to the Mège method. Both Gustavus Swift and Philip Armour, in their search to make use of all parts of the slaughtered pig, had developed a method by which leaf lard[64] could be converted into tasteless pork fat to form the basis of a butter substitute.[65] At the same time increased demand for beef encouraged producers to breed fatter cattle which, in turn, led to larger quantities of margarine manufactured from beef. Packers named the substance 'butterine' and it was aggressively marketed throughout the country, both in competition with margarine produced by the Mège method and butter. Not a small proportion of 'butterine' margarine was sold as butter, especially in the export market, even in the face of a series of statutes passed at the state level to mandate explicit labeling.

Despite the predicament in which the dairy industry found itself, the impetus for passage of federal legislation came not solely from the complaints of butter producers but also from the fear that oleomargarine was an unsafe food. Almost immediately after the appearance of margarine in the United States, lobbyists for the dairy industry had been joined in their demand for a vigorous statute that required demarking margarine from butter by a number of sanitarians, the most outspoken of whom was George Thorndike Angell. In 1882 John R. Thomas, Republican Congressman from Illinois, had introduced a bill placing a 10 cents-per-pound tax on oleomargarine. Thomas' bill was ignored in the 46th Congress but was reintroduced in the 47th, at which time hearings were held before the House Ways and Means Committee.[66] Thomas himself testified that the sale of margarine was in fact a swindle and that 'Americans delight in being defrauded and . . . they go yawping around with their mouths open, seeking to be taken in'.[67] While the bill passed in Committee it failed to gain a hearing in the House, nor did similar bills in that and the following session of Congress ever make it beyond committee. Finally in 1886 the 49th Congress, unable to withstand the political pressures brought to bear by the nation's agricultural interests and bombarded by claims that margarine, manufactured in filthy and diseased environments, caused a wide variety of illnesses and national dyspepsia,[68] enacted a law levying an annual fee on every manufacturer, wholesaler, and retailer of margarine and placed a tax of 2 cents a pound on all oleomargarine sold.[69]

Debate on the Oleomargarine Tax Law was the first instance in which either house of Congress considered a pure food issue and its passage constituted a substantial broadening of the powers of the federal government. Senator Matthew C. Butler of South Carolina referred to its provisions as reflecting 'the most flagrant, unblushing disregard of the principles of the Constitution that has ever been introduced into the Congress'.[70] President Grover Cleveland appears to have had some reservations when signing the bill when he suggested that this might well constitute a misuse of the government's powers to tax but, he added, 'I do not feel called upon to interpret the motives of Congress'. The bill's chief legacy, however, was not simply that the federal government had greatly expanded its role in supervising the private lives of its citizens but that oleomargarine, like other artificial foods, was singled out as less 'pure' than were their natural counterparts and, as such, believed to be the cause of a host of illnesses.[71]

The pressure for passage of a pure food and drug act continued unabated over the course of the next two decades. This ongoing campaign was spearheaded by the leaders of the temperance movement and by sanitarians, who argued that a large proportion of our food was impure and a danger to health and that our medications, consisting in the main of alcohol and narcotics, were poisoning us. These social reformers and an array of alarmists who were convinced that the American food supply was being poisoned by unscrupulous manufacturers and distributors were joined in demanding legislative reform by a large number of businessmen and farmers, who, although claiming an unselfish concern for the nation's health, agitated for pure food and drug legislation solely to limit or eliminate competition. Commercial and agricultural interests were responsible both for much of the publicity given to the dangers of 'adulterated' foods and drugs and for the several pure food conventions that met in Washington, DC in the late 1880s to draft legislation prohibiting the sale of such products. A prominent historian of the intersection of science and government, himself a strong proponent of extensive government regulation of food and drugs, has noted that the motive behind business support was a desire to restrict the sale of competing products. 'The commercial pressure for a national food and drug law', he writes,

> was in large part an effort, particularly by the grocery trade, to protect the honest businessman from the competition of the adulterator and to build public confidence. But it was also an attempt to capture the initiative to the end that any legislation enacted would in objectives and details conform to the business point of view. . . . [In particular,] pressure for food legislation came from agricultural interests. Producers of dairy products sought protection from fraud, especially oleomargarine, their bête noire. Growers of corn and hogs clamored for defense against the adulteration of lard and for inspection of all slaughtered animals destined for export so that the nations of Europe might be stripped of any excuse for discriminating against American exports on sanitary grounds. . . . Most of the demand for legislation from the agricultural sections was inspired by the belief of producers that adulteration restricted their markets.[72]

These special interests had a substantial stake in limiting the production of some competing product, among the most vocal of whom were sugar refiners, dairy farmers, hog raisers, tea distributors, and canned fish producers. Between the introduction into Congress in 1879 of the first bill aimed at regulating the adulteration of food and passage of the Pure Food and Drugs Act 27 years later, no fewer than 190 measures dealing with the quality of the nation's food and drugs were brought before Congress.[73] Of these only eight became law and of the eight all were extremely limited in scope, either relevant to only one product or, in two instances, solely to the District of Columbia.[74] Perhaps the most important of these numerous attempts occurred in the second session of the 51st Congress (December 1890 to March 1891), when Senator Algernon Sidney Paddock, Republican of Nebraska, having been deluged by petitions from temperance and women's groups and trade associations representing the nation's agricultural interests, introduced a pure food and drug bill in the Senate. The bill assigned responsibility for enforcing its provisions against mislabeling and adulteration to the Department of Agriculture's Bureau of Chemistry and was vigorously supported by its director, Harvey Wiley. No action was taken on the measure, however, and Paddock proposed the same bill in the following session. This time he was able to prevail in the Senate, but the measure died in the House.

While a stalemated Congress was unable to pass a national pure food bill, it did enact legislation regulating the sale of serums and toxins that came into interstate or foreign commerce. The law, which placed in the hands of the US Public Health Service supervision over the production of all biological products applicable to human disease, was passed by Congress in June 1902. Like so much regulatory legislation it was moved to act by a deplorable occurrence that took place immediately before the issue was taken up by Congress, a tragedy, also like so much regulatory legislation, that would have been avoided had the new law already existed. On 26 October 1901 a five-year-old girl died in the St Louis city hospital from tetanus. The child had been admitted several days earlier and administered two shots of diphtheria antitoxin, an antitoxin whose source was the City Health Department. Despite attempts to cleanse the city's supply of diphtheria antitoxin of any that might be contaminated with tetanus, four more children were reported to have died of the same cause on 1 November. At this point the St Louis Board of Health launched an inquiry into the city's method of preparing and testing serum which showed it to be completely inadequate. It appeared that almost no serum was in fact tested, that laboratory bottles were improperly identified and mislabeled, and that those in charge of serum production were aware of having distributed diphtheria antitoxin that was contaminated. While the investigation was proceeding, another eight children died as a result of being administered contaminated serum.

The effect of these revelations was that people throughout the country became distrustful of all biologic agents and many refused to allow physicians to administer these products to their children. Desperate to restore the reputation of the nation's medical practitioners and especially the various state and city boards of health, the Medical Society of the District of Columbia, in the spring of 1902, proposed legislation along the lines eventually passed by

Congress. The bill was drafted by the Commissioners of the District of Columbia and was treated as a routine District measure handled by the committees of the House and Senate responsible for District affairs. It called for the creation of a board, comprising the Surgeon General of the Army, the Surgeon General of the Navy, and the Supervising Surgeon General of the Marine Hospital Service, which was empowered to issue regulations for licensing establishments that were engaged in the preparation and sale of biologic substances destined for interstate or foreign commerce. The Public Health Service was authorized to inspect all establishments that had been licensed and all substances covered by the act were required to carry an expiry date. The bill was signed into law on 1 July 1902 by President Theodore Roosevelt and represented the most significant legislation having to do with federal regulation of drugs prior to passage of the Pure Food and Drugs Act.[75]

When the Pure Food and Drugs Act was finally enacted in 1906, its passage through Congress could in large measure be credited to one man, Harvey Washington Wiley who, between 1883 and 1912, held the post of chief chemist at the Bureau of Chemistry at the Department of Agriculture, the division of the federal government charged with certifying the purity of the nation's food supply and the forerunner of the Food and Drug Administration. Wiley was a graduate of Hanover College in Indiana and the Indiana Medical College, where he took his degree in 1871.[76] In 1874 he was appointed professor of chemistry at the newly opened Purdue University and while associated with the University spent a good deal of time in Germany studying the principles of food analysis. In 1882 Wiley was offered the position of chief chemist by George Loring, who was then the US Commissioner of Agriculture[77] in the administration of Chester Arthur. Wiley's major interest when first arriving in Washington appears to have centered on the domestic sugar industry.[78] Wiley was a strong supporter of bounties on the production of sugar and of high tariffs on imported sugar. However, he soon added to this concern for America's inefficient sugar producers fears that America's food supply contained adulterants[79] that were poisoning the public.

Toward this end he began a series of experiments on certain foods to test their purity, the first of which was on commercial maple syrup, which he found was commonly 'adulterated' by the admixture of glucose and sugar syrup! Over the course of the next few years the Bureau of Chemistry issued a series of bulletins dedicated to specific foods, each of which contained a detailed study on how they were adulterated and with what other substances. These technical studies were rewritten in 1890 in a report aimed at a lay audience and published under the title *A Popular Treatise on the Extent and Character of Food Adulteration*, which concluded that almost every article of food was in some way or another impure and that this fact deprived the farmer of his livelihood, damaged our export market, and compromised the morals of the

American public.[80] At no point was it claimed that these investigations uncovered any adulteration that seriously compromised the health of consumers. Despite this the report noted that the American food supply contained 'to an alarming extent, poisonous adulterations that have, in many cases, not only impaired the health of the consumer, but frequently caused death' and urged that pressure for both state and federal pure food and drug laws should continue with even greater vigor.[81]

Efforts to enact a pure food and drug law were substantially lessened between 1893 and 1897 during the presidency of Grover Cleveland. However, with the election of William McKinley in November 1896, Wiley's Bureau of Chemistry underwent a massive expansion and efforts to gain passage of a comprehensive bill were revived. In the spring of 1897 the Bureau numbered 20 employees; by 1902 it had increased to 50 and by 1906 to 110.[82] These workers, it appears, felt a personal loyalty to Wiley and all enthusiastically supported passage of a sweeping pure food and drug law that called for the strictest standards of what could be sold to the public. Needless to say, the effect of such a law would be to consolidate and increase Wiley's authority within the Department of Agriculture and to extend his administrative control.

In December 1897 a bill was introduced in the House of Representatives by Marriott Brosius of Pennsylvania, the provisions of which were similar to those that had been considered by the Senate in 1890, to which authority over cosmetics and an expanded definition of drugs were added. The draft itself had been prepared by the Association of Official Agricultural Chemists (AOAC), an organization of state and federal government chemists founded in 1884 with the original purpose of adopting uniform methods for analysing fertilizers. Wiley played a crucial role in its founding and became the organization's second president. The AOAC was soon given semi-official status by the federal government with the Department of Agriculture as its sponsor and its members regularly served as advisors to the Department. The AOAC quickly extended its concerns to include support for pure food legislation and struck a committee chaired by Wiley for the purpose of preparing a draft measure. It was this bill that was put before the House by Brosius in December and was the centerpiece of a National Pure Food and Drug Congress that was held in Washington in the spring of 1898.

The congress was convened by Alexander J. Wedderburn, an agricultural journalist and enthusiastic agitator for a pure food act. Wedderburn, the editor of *National Farm and Fireside* and master of the Virginia Grange, had hoped to supplant Wiley as the principal spokesman for pure food legislation but despite the success of the national congress his efforts proved unsuccessful. The 1898 meeting was attended by some 150 delegates, including representatives of most relevant federal departments, state and local public health agencies, farm groups, national professional societies, food and drug manufacturers, the AOAC, and, of course, the Woman's Christian Temperance Union. A reception was held in the delegates' honor by President McKinley at the White House and the pure food congress then proceeded to spend the next several days debating just how urgent the need for a stringent pure food and drug act was. After much self-congratulatory oratory, the congress voted to support a somewhat modified version of the Brosius bill.[83] Additionally, what emerged from the Congress was an ongoing working relationship between the Department of Health of the WCTU and Wiley's Bureau of Chemistry. The real success of the Congress was measured by the fact that Wiley was able to strengthen the Brosius bill by providing that the authority to determine standards which would have to be met if a product were to legally be sold would be placed in the hands of the Secretary of Agriculture. Despite what were clearly favorable conditions for passage, however, the bill remained in committee in the House by the time the Fifty-fifth Congress adjourned in March 1899.

The National Pure Food and Drug Congress had met in March, less than three weeks after the US Battleship *Maine* exploded in Havana harbor. Despite the fact that the explosion was caused by the combustion of coal dust in the ship's bunker next to the magazine, a Naval Board of Inquiry determined that the ship was destroyed by a mine. However, the fact that there existed not one whit of evidence that the Spanish authorities were culpable in the ship's destruction, did not stop the McKinley administration from seizing on these events as an excuse for war with Spain. The result was that American troops were dispatched to Cuba in June under the command of Major General Nelson A. Miles, whose reputation as a soldier had been made some years earlier by slaughtering Indians. Soon after arriving in Cuba Miles alleged that the beef that had been furnished American soldiers in Cuba and Puerto Rico by the Swift and Armour companies was rotten.[84] Both meat packers, whose shipments of beef to the military forces in the field were either refrigerated or canned, insisted that the meat was perfectly wholesome[85] and tests conducted by Wiley and others supported this conclusion, despite the fact that beef that had been canned had a decidedly unpleasant taste. The charges, however, had focused the attention of the public on the problem of impure meat and increased interest in pure food legislation.

While Brosius reintroduced his bill in December 1899, he found that he was competing with several other measures of a similar sort brought independently by Senator William V. Allen of Nebraska, who had been elected as a Populist, and Senator Henry Clay Hansbrough of North Dakota, a Republican.[86] The result of these competing measures was that revisions were made to Brosius' bill and in amended form it was introduced into the House and Senate on 15 January 1900, by Brosius and by Senator William E. Mason. Mason, a Republican from Illinois and Chairman of the Senate Committee on

Manufactures, had, pursuant to a Senate resolution, recently conducted hearings on the American food industry. The committee's investigations were extensive and lasted almost two months. Testimony was taken from some 200 witnesses and the committee's staff inspected a large number of processing plants, warehouses, and retail stores in the east and midwest. Mason, who supported far-reaching legislation, appointed Wiley as his scientific advisor, which, at the least, insured a dispute over the relative safety of preservatives. Yet despite the intense examination that the food industry underwent, the committee could describe very little food and drink as impure or unsanitary. The primary objection to certain foods, Wiley noted, was not that they were injurious to the health of the consumer but that they injured his pocketbook.[87] However, as was the case with complaints regarding rotten meat during the Spanish-American War, the Mason committee's conclusions served only to increase concern that America's food supply was tainted and that legislation was badly needed.

Between 1900 and 1905 several dozen pure food and drug bills were introduced either in the House or the Senate, each differing in some particular: which agency of the government would be charged with monitoring the food and drug industries, which articles would be subject to the law's purview, and what powers the enforcing agency would possess. Several called for the creation of a new 'food bureau' and were, accordingly, opposed by Wiley, who wished to see the enforcement provisions of any new statute lodged in the Bureau of Chemistry, which he headed. It was for this reason that Wiley made every effort to undermine support for a bill introduced by Congressman Joseph W. Babcock of Wisconsin, which called for the creation of a new enforcement bureau within the Department of Agriculture headed by a presidential appointee. Apparently the bill was the brainchild of William D. Hoard, the former governor of Wisconsin, who had hopes of heading the new agency himself and who saw it as an opportunity to advance the state's dairy interests.[88]

Despite increasing public interest in a pure food bill Congress was unable to agree on the provisions of a new law and competing interests were successful in preventing majorities in both houses from reaching an accord. In March 1902 the House Committee on Interstate and Foreign Commerce, chaired by William P. Hepburn of Iowa, and the Senate Committee on Manufactures, now chaired by Porter J. McCumber of North Dakota, held joint hearings on a pure food bill.[89] The food interests that testified before the joint committee, aware that a law of some sort was inevitable and strongly opposed to the measure put forward by Hepburn and McCumber, supported a bill sponsored by Representatives James R. Mann of Illinois and John B. Corliss of Michigan and Senator Shelby M. Cullom of Illinois. Among supporters of this substitute measure was the Association of Manufacturers and Distributors of Food Products, a trade association representing manufacturers of pickles, preserves, and other condiments, who objected to any labeling requirement, which, it was felt, would discourage people from buying their products despite their being wholesome and palatable.[90] Under the bill's terms, no food could contain any ingredient deleterious to health in quantities large enough to be harmful but labeling of any safe ingredient was not required. In gist, what the bill prohibited was interstate traffic in foods containing unsafe ingredients in sufficient doses to harm those who consumed them. In the event, the Mann-Corliss-Cullom bill was able to garner barely any support. Far more popular was the bill introduced by William Hepburn, who had taken over leadership of the pure food forces in the House on the death of Marriott Brosius in March 1901. The Hepburn bill was similar to the measure introduced by Brosius in the previous year and was introduced in the Senate by Henry Hansbrough of North Dakota in January 1902. The Hepburn-Hansbrough bill contained a concession to the alum interests, namely, that baking powder residues be labeled and that the standards that would be set by the administrative agency responsible for enforcing the law should not be considered in determining adulteration until they had been approved by the courts. Wiley was hopeful that this measure might pass both the House and Senate but in the end no action was taken as a consequence of the opposition of several influential groups, the association representing the manufacturers of food products, the National Association of Retail Grocers, and the baking powder interests.

As the leading historian of the Pure Food and Drugs Act has noted, while the pure-food issue received far more discussion during the Fifty-seventh and Fifty-eighth Congresses than it had earlier, by 1905 it appeared no nearer enactment than it had been in 1900.[91] However, the publication of two separate 'exposés', the first, a series of articles that appeared in *Collier's Weekly* on patent drugs, the second, a novel, *The Jungle* by Upton Sinclair, ostensibly describing the filthy conditions prevailing in the Chicago stockyards, caused a sensation and catapulted the issue of preventive legislation to one of pressing importance.

Wiley's interest was in the adulteration of food rather than with drugs, about which he knew almost nothing. The result was that propaganda for a new law had centered on the dangers of impure foodstuffs and little attention had been paid to drugs. This changed in the fall of 1905 with the publication of a series of eleven articles in *Collier's* entitled 'The Great American Fraud' by Samuel Hopkins Adams on patent medicines. Adams was a freelance journalist, a socialist, and muckraker.[92] The series had a profound impact on the literate public; it was read and discussed extensively and reprinted as a pamphlet by the American Medical Association, which did its utmost to popularize the issue. Even before its publication in October, *Collier's*, starting with its 1 April issue, had devoted its pages to advertising the series in editorials, jingles, and cartoons.[93] The AMA reprint sold no less than half-a-million copies at 50 cents each and led to the creation of the AMA's Propaganda Department to combat the sale of patent nostrums. Even before the publication of Adams' first article, the *Ladies' Home Journal*, under the editorship of Edward William Bok, had begun its own campaign against proprietary medicines and this was accelerated with the appearance of Adams' series.

The opening paragraph of Adams' 'Introduction' well reflects the gravamen of his charges against the patent medicine industry:

> Gullible America will spend this year some seventy-five millions of dollars in the purchase of patent medicines. In consideration of this sum it will swallow huge quantities of alcohol, an appalling amount of opiates and narcotics, a wide assortment of varied drugs ranging from powerful and dangerous heart depressants to insidious liver stimulants; and, in excess of all other ingredients, undiluted fraud. For fraud, exploited by the skilfulest of advertising bunco men, is the basis of the trade. Should the newspapers, the magazines and the medical journals refuse their pages to this class of advertisement, the patent medicine business in five years would be as scandalously historic as the South Sea Bubble, and the nation would be the richer not only in lives and money, but in drunkards and drug-fiends saved.[94]

In sum, what Adams charged of the patent medicine manufacturers is that they included alcohol and narcotics in their products and that they claimed that these nostrums were effective in treating a whole range of ailments. This was, of course, exactly what almost every physician in the nation was regularly doing at the time. What so distressed the medical association was that patent medicines proved extremely effective in competing with the services of a physician. The slogan created by Adams was now invoked whenever opponents of patent medicines wrote or assembled. It was adopted by the American Medical Association as the title of countless editorials and was popularized by the Woman's Christian Temperance Union, who were active in distributing copies of Adams' series.[95] So popular did Adams' articles become that they were successful in bringing the issue of 'impure' drugs to a level equal to that earlier occupied by adulterated foods and insured that pending legislation would include both food and drugs.

Adams' final article appeared in the *Collier's* issue dated 17 February 1906. On the following day Doubleday, Page & Company published Sinclair's *The Jungle*, whose first chapters had earlier been serialized as *An Appeal to Reason* at Sinclair's own expense. The reaction to Sinclair's charges was immense and immediate, such that it was clear that Congress would have to act immediately. Indeed, the effect of Sinclair's book was to galvanize the Congress into passing two major bills within four months of its publication.

In 1890 Senator Algernon S. Paddock of Nebraska, chairman of the Senate Committee on Agriculture and Forestry, who was in the process of sponsoring a pure food and drug measure, had submitted a draft of his bill to Jeremiah Rusk, recently appointed Secretary of Agriculture by President Benjamin

Harrison, for his comments. The Department had just been raised to cabinet rank and Rusk for some reason felt that the provisions of Paddock's draft that concerned meat inspection should be separated and dealt with in its own bill. This recommendation was accepted by Congress when, in August 1890, it enacted a measure calling for the inspection of meat for export and prohibiting the importation of any adulterated article of food or drink. The 1890 act was clearly retaliatory, a result of the fact that between 1879 and 1881 seven European countries, among them France, Germany, Italy, and Austria-Hungary, had stopped importing American pork bellies because of concerns about trichinosis.[96] At the same time the smaller, less efficient meat packers were agitating for a meat inspection law which they thought would fall more heavily on the larger companies.[97] When the value of American exports of meat fell by almost 40 percent, Congress was moved to act and the Meat Inspection Act of 1890 passed both the House and the Senate with minimal opposition. In 1906, when efforts to enact legislation mandating meat inspection were again undertaken, meat and meat products were once more treated separately from other provisions concerned with the adulteration of food and drugs.

The Department of Agriculture, through its Bureau of Animal Industry, had consistently supported legislation that would grant it powers over the meat-packing industry greater than those supplied it by the Meat Inspection Act of 1890, which authorized the Department to make ante-mortem inspections of cattle, hogs, and sheep whose meat was intended for interstate or foreign commerce. The Department's efforts, however, met with no success until publication of Sinclair's *The Jungle* in February 1906. Sinclair's book purported to recount the appalling practices that prevailed in the meat-packing industry and so alarmed the public, already predisposed to distrust the meat-packing companies because of a steady increase in beef prices, that support for more extensive federal regulation of the industry became a popular issue. President Theodore Roosevelt, a consistent enemy of unfettered markets and especially of large companies and ever ready to align his political agenda with demands for greater government involvement in the economy, quickly responded by calling for a more far-reaching meat inspection bill and was prepared to use his political authority with Congress to insure its passage.[98]

Like so much regulatory legislation, a new law was hardly needed to prevent the foul and unhealthy conditions that Sinclair supposedly witnessed in the Chicago abattoirs he visited.[99] The Meat Inspection Act of 1890 had already provided sufficient authority to the Department of Agriculture to prevent these conditions from occurring or to punish the companies that allowed them to occur. Indeed, there is every reason to believe that Sinclair's more lurid descriptions were manufactured by the author. Although he claimed that he had explored every inch of the packing plants about which he wrote, he admitted at one point that he had made only three visits to the stock-yards.[100] Sinclair was a committed socialist who was deeply sympathetic to stockyard workers when they went on strike in 1904. He immediately moved to Chicago where he spent some time among them collecting their most sensationalistic stories and weaving them into a fictional account of life in the stock-yards which purported to recount the onerous working conditions under which the laborers were required to work and the noisome environment of the packing plants.[101]

Among Sinclair's more revolting charges were that packing houses were infested with thousands of rats whose dung was regularly included in packaged meat products. When attempts were made to kill the rats with poisoned bread, the poisoned bread itself together with the dead rat carcasses and other leavings were ground up and packaged. Hogs that had died of cholera were often used in the production of lard and sausages, and canned meat frequently contained parts of cattle that had died of tuberculosis and other diseases. Factories were filthy beyond belief, the floors slippery from the spit of workers ill with consumption. Animal leavings, refuse, and the gangrenous parts of cattle and hogs that had been cut away from dressed meat were ground up and used in the manufacture of sausages, potted ham, and other ground meat products. Occasionally, when workers fell into the large vats used to prepare lard, they too became part of the packages sold to consumers![102] It was, of course, absurd to suggest that the government was without any effective remedy to curtail these abuses, had they in fact occurred, since all of these conditions fell within the purview of federal legislation that had been enacted in 1890. However, the public were deliberately left with the impression that the government could do nothing unless sweeping legislation were enacted.

Despite the fact that Sinclair intended *The Jungle* primarily as a metaphor for the corruption and venality of capitalism, Roosevelt saw the book as an invaluable propaganda tool to gain passage of a bill that would greatly enlarge the federal meat inspection service and bring down the 'beef trust', towards which he had a particular animus.[103] Sinclair's charges appear to have confirmed a series of articles written by Adolphe Smith which had appeared in the *Lancet* in the year prior to the publication of *The Jungle*. These articles had referred to the Chicago packing houses as 'truly Augean stables' and observed that Americans were regularly consuming trichinae and tuberculosis germs. It was Smith who first maintained that workers who had fallen into vats in the packing plants were incorporated into lard sold to the public.[104] Inasmuch as the Department of Agriculture had possessed sufficient authority to prevent most of the practices Sinclair and Smith had alleged and since Sinclair had also charged the Department with negligence and corruption, the Secretary of Agriculture, James Wilson, immediately dispatched a group of investigators to Chicago. The team, consisting of his three highest-ranking aides – the

Department's chief lawyer and the chiefs of inspection and of pathology from the Bureau of Animal Industry – reported back that most of Sinclair's claims were without merit and that *The Jungle* had taken a few isolated instances of uncleanliness and offered them as endemic.

Roosevelt found Wilson's report unsatisfactory and unlikely to encourage Congress to enact more stringent legislation. To overcome the resistance that many Congressmen felt at further expanding federal authority in this area the President undertook to conduct his own study of conditions in the meat-packing industry. As a result, he appointed his own investigatory committee comprising Charles P. Neill, the US Commissioner of Labor, and James B. Reynolds, Assistant Secretary of the Treasury,[105] whose report appeared to confirm some of Sinclair's less extreme claims.[106] The meat packers' cause was not helped by the preposterous claim made by Ogden Armour, the chief of Armour & Co., in the *Saturday Evening Post* that 'not one atom of any condemned animal carcass finds its way, directly or indirectly, from any source, into any food product or food ingredient'.[107] Such extravagant exaggeration only served to lend credence to Sinclair's and Smith's equally exaggerated charges.

Roosevelt had decided to place the authority of the White House behind a meat inspection bill introduced by Senator Albert J. Beveridge, Republican from Indiana.[108] Beveridge had introduced a far-reaching measure in the Senate as an amendment to the agriculture appropriations bill and it was duly passed without dissent by that body. The House, however, was far more hesitant. Representative James W. Wadsworth, Republican from New York and chairman of the House Committee on Agriculture, had grave reservations about Beveridge's bill, which included two particularly offensive provisions: that meat packers were required to underwrite the costs of all inspections carried out by the Department and that any 'unsanitary' plant could be shut down by order of the Secretary of Agriculture, without appeal to the courts on substantive grounds. Consequently, Wadsworth and Representative William Lorimer of Chicago, a loyal friend of the meat-packing industry, rewrote Beveridge's bill to eliminate its most offensive features.

Roosevelt was outraged by these actions in the Agriculture Committee and immediately released the Neill-Reynolds Report corroborating some of Sinclair's charges, hoping to gain sufficient support for the Beveridge bill in the House. However, the meat packers and their allies in Congress were fully aware of what really was at issue. As one historian of the period has pointed out, those who opposed Roosevelt realized that passage of the Beveridge bill would constitute an unprecedented expansion of government powers and of public interference in what had hitherto been regarded as an area of life subject only to market forces.[109] They therefore made every effort to moderate the bill's provisions. In the end, however, Congress was unable to resist the pressures that the White House had brought to bear. After much wrangling, including a series of bitter disputes in conference committee, a compromise was finally reached between Wadsworth and Beveridge. The provisions of the new law, which were attached to an agricultural appropriations bill, called for the ante-mortem inspection of all cattle, hogs, goats, and sheep whose meat was destined for interstate commerce or for shipment overseas and the postmortem inspection of each carcass. All canned meat and meat products were to be inspected and dated and, if crossing state lines, were required to carry a stamp marked 'inspected and passed'. No meat products were permitted to contain any dye or 'deleterious chemical'. Finally, the Department was given author-ity to inspect the sanitary conditions of all packing houses. Of the two most offensive provisions, those referring to the cost of inspections and to the inability of companies injured by a ruling to appeal to the federal courts regarding the constitutionality of the ruling, the first was eliminated while the second was restored in the final bill. Finally, fearing that the bill would result in a bitter division among House Republicans and at the urging of the Speaker, Joseph Cannon, the Agriculture Committee raised the annual appropriation for inspection from $1 000 000 to $3 000 000.[110]

What is particularly interesting is that none of the sensationalist accusations brought by Sinclair, Smith, or the other journalists who joined in condemning the meat-packing industry appear to have made an appreciable difference to the buying habits of the public, who continued to purchase dressed and canned meats in the same quantities as previously. Nor, after a brief period of anxiety, did Americans appear agitated by the charges leveled at these firms. This was in sharp contrast to the Congress, which was moved to enact not only a meat inspection bill but was finally prevailed upon to pass a pure food and drug act.

Spurred on by President Roosevelt's state of the union speech supporting a pure food and drug act Senator Weldon Heyburn of Idaho introduced a pure food and drug bill in December.[111] The bill was similar to that brought before the Senate by Porter McCumber in the previous Congress. However, he was unsuccessful in bringing the measure to a vote until mid-February when thanks to the intercession of the Republican leader in the Senate, Nelson W. Aldrich of Rhode Island, who had led the opposition forces, resistance to voting on the bill was withdrawn on orders from the President. Opponents of the Heyburn measure, among them various trade associations, were particu-larly incensed at a new provision whereby officers of offending companies would be held personally responsible for any violation of the act. In addition, Heyburn had modified one of the most objectionable features of the McCumber bill by providing that wholesalers and retailers who sold any prod-uct that contravened the act could be charged only if they were aware of the illegality of the offending article. In addition the bill contained a new clause regarding liquor which required that liquor be labeled to indicate whether it was blended or rectified, and provided that no poisonous or deleterious ingredient be added. The Heyburn bill was vigorously opposed by the National Wholesale Liquor Dealers' Association, who were joined by a host of groups, including the National Food Manufacturers' Association and the Proprietary Association of America, in trying to prevent its passage.

The dissenting associations and the senators sympathetic to them supported another bill that had been introduced by Senator Hernando DeSoto Money of Mississippi. Money was vehemently opposed to the Heyburn bill as an unwarranted encroachment on the power of the states that would subject a vast industry to the arbitrary authority of a federal bureaucracy. Indeed, he was outraged that the Bureau of Chemistry would be charged with determining what was misbranded or adulterated, whether or not a substance was injurious, which medications would cure disease, and just when a manufacturer would be compelled to disclose the contents of his product.[112] In consequence, one of the provisions of Money's bill was that it placed enforcement of the new measure in the hands of the Department of Commerce and Labor and empowered Congress, rather than the enforcing agency, to set standards. In addition, the bill limited itself to dealing with foodstuffs and drugs only while in the process of being moved in interstate commerce. Once these items had reached their destination the laws of that state alone would apply. The bill permitted food manufacturers to add chemical preservatives to their products and exempted all proprietary medications from the provisions of the act. While the measure's supporters were aware that the Money bill stood no chance of passing the Senate, it was thought that it would at least serve to force compromises in the Heyburn bill.[113]

Wiley worked unceasingly in favor of the Heyburn bill, giving advice to its Senate supporters behind the scenes, taking on a host of speaking engagements, and making it clear that the Bureau of Chemistry possessed the best equipment to undertake the task of determining whether a food was adulterated or misbranded. He continued his unreasonable and stubborn campaign against the use of artificial coloring and preservatives, insisting that preservatives deceived the public into thinking that a product was sterilized. Wiley was not alone in trying to muster support for the Heyburn bill. The WCTU and the American Medical Association actively endorsed the measure and petitioned for its passage. On 21 February the bill came to a vote and while 22 Senators did not participate in the voting, the final tally was 63 to four in favor. Wiley, who watched the proceedings from the Senate gallery and who had orchestrated a national movement of sanitarians, physicians, and prohibitionists favoring the measure, was elated.

While the Senate was considering the Heyburn bill, the House Committee on Interstate and Foreign Commerce had begun hearings on the bill earlier introduced by Representative William Heyburn of Iowa and reintroduced in each subsequent session of Congress. The Hepburn measure differed from that passed in the Senate in several particulars, among them, that the authority to set standards and to determine the safety of all food additives including preservatives was vested solely in the Secretary of Agriculture which the courts were obligated to follow, and that all foods were required to label all their components. One particularly significant clause newly added to the bill concerned proprietary medicines, which were required to indicate on their labels the quantity of alcohol, opium, cocaine, 'or other poisonous substances' they contained. As chairman of the committee Hepburn had arranged that Wiley should testify last and he was thus given the opportunity to respond to the witnesses who had opposed the measure. Again he took the occasion to attack preservatives as poisons, maintaining that benzoate-of-soda, contrary to the claims of several eminent bacteriologists who had testified in its favor, brought on stomach cramps and nausea. And faced with the fact that when Brooklyn had banned preservatives in 1886 the death rate had immediately soared, Wiley countered that the whole increase in deaths could be attributed to other causes, none having anything to do with preservatives in food.

Following passage of the bill in committee Wiley was consulted about reworking its provisions to bring them more into line with the measure the Senate had earlier passed. After a number of changes, the bill was finally reported out of committee to the full House on 7 March, but it was thought expedient to delay consideration for another three months. In the meanwhile both Adams' series on patent medicines and Upton Sinclair's *The Jungle* appeared and had been seized upon by pure food and drug enthusiasts and by many of the nation's newspapers and commentators as evidence that a strict law was needed. By this point it was apparent that there was no way to stop those favoring the bill. On 20 June the House resolved itself into a Committee of the Whole to consider the measure. The leader of the meager forces antagonistic to the Hepburn bill was William C. Adamson of Georgia who was outspoken in his criticism, noting that such a law offended the traditional rights of Americans and would bring with it a vast bureaucracy and 'the attendant evils of spies and informers and pestiferous agents running around meddling with the business of the people'.[114] In spite of Adamson's comments, the House voted overwhelmingly in favor of the measure by a roll-call vote of 241 to 17, with six representatives voting 'present' and 112 not voting.

The work of the conference committee apparently went smoothly. The final bill as reported out of committee was closer to the Senate bill than to that passed by the House, although the Senate bill conceded more in the face of objections from the trade associations. The changes, however, did not seem to weaken the measure and Wiley regarded its final form as 'stronger in its provisions' than was either the Senate or House version.[115] On 29 June both the

House and the Senate passed the bill in its final form and on the following day President Roosevelt, in a ceremony at the Capitol, signed a number of measures including the Meat Inspection Amendment to the Agricultural Appropriations Act and the Pure Food and Drugs Act into law.

The Pure Food and Drugs Act prohibited the manufacture and sale of adulterated and misbranded foods, drugs, and liquors and regulated traffic in such products. They forbade introducing them into interstate or foreign commerce or buying them for resale. The Secretaries of the Treasury, of Agriculture, and of Commerce and Labor were empowered to devise the rules and regulations for enforcing the Act while the authority to police the industry was given to Wiley's Bureau of Chemistry. The Bureau was empowered to examine specimens of foods and drugs and to determine which had been misbranded or adulterated. Proprietary medicines were required to 'bear a statement on the label of the quantity or proportion of any alcohol, morphine, opium, cocaine, heroin, alpha or beta eucaine, chloroform, cannabis indica, chloral hydrate, or acetanilide, or any derivative or preparation of any such substances'.[116] Violators were subject to fines not exceeding $200 for the first offense; subsequent offenses could result in a $300 fine or imprisonment for up to one year or both. The law also provided that adulterated goods could be seized and destroyed by the government. The Act, quickly dubbed the Wiley law by the press, was warmly received by all the groups that had worked with such effort for its passage. The American Pharmaceutical Association and the American Medical Association were especially delighted with the labeling provisions as they related to over-the-counter medications.

Wiley regretted that the Act did not contain a provision allowing the Bureau of Chemistry to establish standards to which products would have to conform in order to be legally sold. However, the statute did provide that a food was adulterated if anything were 'mixed or packed with it so as to reduce or lower or injuriously affect its quality or strength'. This clause appeared to provide Wiley with the authority to specify which additives would be prohibited and in which quantities. He therefore proceeded to declare that almost all preservatives were in contravention of the Act.[117] Apparently Wiley was concerned more with the possibility that preservatives were harmful – despite their having proven themselves effective in retarding spoilage – than he was with the illnesses and deaths caused by ptomaine poisoning. As others studying the question have pointed out, however, Wiley's objections to preservatives were very much of a piece with his insistence that a vigorously enforced pure food law was essential to insure the public health. If in fact preservatives accomplished what those who supported their use claimed for them, then there would be far less need for any legislation to protect consumers from rotten food.[118]

A good indication of the kinds of questions which most concerned Wiley in the years immediately following passage of the Act involved whether foods whose safety was never at issue should be permitted to carry their conventional designations. For example, Wiley used his position as the head of the Bureau of Chemistry to prosecute his ongoing crusade against glucose, which dated back to his first arrival at the Bureau of Chemistry in 1883. In 1902 the Corn Products Refining Company was formed and began selling Karo Corn Syrup to the public. Prior to that, glucose was sold only to food manufacturers, including confectionary makers, looking for an inexpensive substitute for sugar. Corn syrup appeared to have quickly become popular with consumers. Advertised as 'the great spread for daily bread', Karo sales steadily increased and cook books began including recipes that called for it. In briefs filed with the Bureau of Chemistry soon after passage of the Pure Food and Drugs Act the Company petitioned to keep its name, claiming that corn syrup was simply a trade name.[119] Nor was it deceptive to label the product as such inasmuch as its corn syrup came from corn and was indeed a syrup. Wiley, however, was unmoved by Karo's petition, claiming that the term corn syrup could properly be employed solely to describe 'juice expressed from the stalk of the maize plant and concentrated'.[120] Wiley's hare-brained position was to have wide ramifications. The Corn Products Company called for a second hearing while the Iowa Grain Dealers' Association, which was particularly outraged, began a massive campaign involving letters to Congress and the President that attacked the decision. In the meanwhile the Department of Agriculture's solicitor and the Bureau's associate chemist had reversed their position and now found 'corn syrup' an acceptable appellation. In addition, the Company was able to find a large number of prominent chemists who supported their position. Finally, in February 1908 the Secretaries of the Treasury, of Agriculture, and of Commerce and Labor, empowered by the Pure Food Act with final authority, found for the Company.

Wiley's next major battle surrounded whiskey. He was determined that rectified whiskey no longer be permitted to label itself 'blended'. The conflict over whether this was deceptive dated back to at least 1903 when the first pure food bills that included provisions referring to liquor were introduced in Congress. Wiley had insisted that labeling a mix of bourbon and neutral spirits a 'blended' whiskey constituted a clear example of misbranding, a conclusion embraced by the straight whiskey manufacturers who provided financial support to the campaign for a pure food act. In opposition stood the National Wholesale Liquor Dealers' Association which, while in principle not opposed to pure food legislation, was fearful that any provisions respecting whiskey would work to its disadvantage. The association's fears were justified.

Once the 1906 law was enacted, Wiley issued a food inspection decision that whiskeys containing such mixes were not really 'blended', inasmuch as a blend could have reference only to a mixture of like substances. That these whiskeys had traditionally been referred to as 'blended' for decades appears to have made no difference whatever. Wiley determined that only straight whiskeys or mixes of straight whiskeys were entitled to label their products as either straight or blended 'whiskey'. Rectified whiskeys would henceforth have to be identified as 'imitation whiskey'. Once again Wiley's decision vibrated throughout the federal bureaucracy, in this instance eventually involving the Secretary of Agriculture, the Speaker of the House, and the President himself. Distilleries throughout the east and midwest were inspected and Congressional hearings were held. Wiley's biographer reports that when Wiley, while testifying before the House Committee on Agriculture, was asked for a definition of blended whiskey he responded that 'crooked' was what was meant. 'If one is straight,' he maintained

> the other is crooked. Crooked whisky is not whisky at all, but is made of neutral spirits, and flavored and colored. It is an imitation. It has none of the aromatic and flavoring congeneric products which are volatile at the ordinary temperature of distillation. I think that pure spirits is a poison, pure and simple. It coagulates the protoplasm in the cells.[121]

Wiley was so wedded to this decision that he was quite prepared to defend it in a series of court cases. Finally it required the intercession of President William Howard Taft to overrule the Bureau of Chemistry's determination. In December 1909 he ruled that it was a perversion of the pure food act to limit the term 'whiskey' in the manner suggested, and thus to deny products that had traditionally been designated 'whiskey' the right to label themselves as such.

As Jack High and Clayton A. Coppin have argued, Wiley's position on rectified whiskey had proved of great help in winning the support of the temperance movement for passage of a pure food act.[122] The liquor industry had been under siege from the WCTU, the Anti-Saloon League, and a number of women's groups who were particularly disturbed at the ready availability of cheaper whiskeys, which tended to be those that were rectified. Although they supported complete prohibition, they welcomed any measure that might lessen consumption of these products and seized upon Wiley's insistence that rectified whiskeys were not really whiskeys as a first step in decreasing sales. More important, Wiley's relation with the straight whiskey manufacturers appears to be consistent with the theory that regulation is sought by both bureaucrats and businessmen.[123] Bureaucrats wished to secure their positions within the bureaucratic hierarchy and expand their locus of control while businessmen sought to extract monopoly rents from consumers.[124] Nor was Wiley underpaid for his efforts. As early as 1898 his salary had been raised to $5000.00 a year, the equivalent of $110 000 in 2003 dollars.[125]

There is strong evidence to suggest that Wiley's eager support for a pure food and drug bill was motivated by considerably more than a simple desire to purify the nation's food and drug supply. As chief chemist of the Department of Agriculture, the task of monitoring compliance with the act would fall to the Bureau of Chemistry, which in turn entailed a sizeable expansion of the department over which he presided. During his three decades at the Department of Agriculture, Wiley made every effort to consolidate and increase his authority within the bureaucracy, to the point where his maneuvering was a continual source of friction with James Wilson, who served as Secretary of Agriculture from 1897 to 1913, a period that coincided with the last 16 years of Wiley's tenure in the Department. One historian describes Wiley's efforts to gain greater administrative control in this way:

> Wiley the entrepreneur was as interested in building his organization as Wiley the crusader was in reforming the food industry. During the struggle to pass the [1906] law, he expended as much effort maintaining administrative control in the Bureau of Chemistry as he did securing provisions to regulate food and drugs. Therefore, the coalition that he established to secure passage of the law also supported specific administrative features that placed him in control.[126]

Wiley, it appears, was prepared to accept any organization or group as an ally in his unceasing efforts to gain passage of the Pure Food and Drugs Act, even if the reasons behind their support were purely self-interested and had little to do with the ostensible goals of the act. Thus, Wiley made common cause with straight whiskey producers, sugar refiners, baking powder producers, and the Heinz Company of Pittsburgh, all of whom favored a pure food bill because its effect would be to give them a competitive advantage.[127]

Wiley retired from his position in 1912 after a series of increasingly bitter disagreements with the Secretary of Agriculture, James Wilson. In fact so highhanded had Wiley's decisions become that in 1910 the Secretary transferred to the Department's solicitor most of the authority to determine what constituted a violation of the Act. The Bureau of Chemistry was henceforth required to submit the results of its tests to the solicitor's office, who would then determine whether a hearing would or would not be held and whether the government would proceed with a prosecution. Finally, on 15 March 1912, Wiley, unable to reclaim his earlier authority in the Department, resigned to take up the position as head of the laboratories at *Good Housekeeping* magazine at a salary of $10 000.00 a year. From his vantage point as director of *Good Housekeeping*'s Bureau of Foods, Sanitation, and Health, Wiley was able to occasionally call into question the decisions of his former superiors. Finally, in 1929 he wrote and published a bitter and totally self-serving volume entitled *The History of a Crime Against the Food Law*.[128] Running to more than 400 pages, the book contained a series of attacks on all those who had disagreed with him regarding his conduct at the Bureau of Chemistry, accusing them of conniving with manufacturers and industry associations to pervert and weaken the law.

While it is true that Wiley worked tirelessly to gain passage of a pure food and drug law that entrusted its administration to the agency he directed, even a cursory examination of his career shows him to have been primarily concerned with his own power within the federal bureaucracy. In this he succeeded. The Bureau of Chemistry which had a staff of 110 and a budget of $155 000 when the Pure Food and Drugs Act was passed had grown to 546 employees and a budget of almost $1 million at the time of his resignation six years later.[129] But other than being a successful negotiator and political manipulator he seems to have done little to protect the nation's foods and drugs. Despite the orthodox view that prior to 1906 Americans were being incapacitated and killed by a steady diet of rotting foods, harmful additives, and poisoned medications, there was in fact very little wrong with the nation's food and drug supply.

Even when Wiley was empowered to carry out the provisions of the Act, he consistently opposed the inclusion of preservatives in prepared foods and seemed to devote an inordinate amount of attention to the 'mislabeling' of foodstuffs that Americans had been consuming without any damage.[130] In light of this record it is amazing that so many historians have praised Wiley as one of the truly great figures of the Progressive Era whose efforts on behalf of the public's health were colossal and decisive. Consider the following:

> On June 30, 1906, President Theodore Roosevelt signed the original Pure Food and Drugs Act (often referred to as the Wiley Act). No single event has had greater significance in the history of consumer protection laws or the industries they regulate. It signaled the beginning of an era of progress in these areas which has no precedent. A large book could be written on the subject. And its central figure certainly would be the towering one of Dr Harvey Washington Wiley, one of the truly great personalities of his time, and the one individual most responsible for the development of food and drug laws in this country.[131]

While it is true that this sycophantic tribute was written by the FDA's official historian, it is far closer to reflecting the views of most historians than is a description of Wiley's years in government warranted by the facts.[132]

Between 1906 and Wiley's resignation in 1912, the Bureau's main concern, which naturally reflected Wiley's interests, was the adulteration and misbranding of foods.[133] Drugs, however, were not totally overlooked, especially when employed as preservatives added to foods. He nicknamed his team the 'Poison Squad' and among the additives for which a wide range of foods were tested were boric acid, salicylic acid, and benzoic acid. It has already been observed that Wiley's understanding of what constituted a poison was no less than bizarre. Despite the fact that preservatives in the quantities used had been shown to be harmless and were clearly effective in preventing wholesome foods from rotting, Wiley appears to have shared the obstinate closemindedness of so many other sanitarians bent on stamping out 'impurities' in all foods sold to the American consumer. One manufacturer of catsup pointed out to a congressional committee before which he was testifying that raw cranberries contained a higher proportion of benzoic acid than his firm planned to add to their brand of catsup. 'If the Almighty put it there,' he is reported as saying, '[then] it seems to me that the manufacturer ought to be allowed to use it'. To this Wiley responded that cranberries would have been more wholesome had the Almighty left benzoic acid out.[134]

Some years after joining the Bureau of Chemistry and in response to the demands of certain groups that Congress enact a drug law Wiley embraced their goals and began to make anti-nostrum speeches. He called not only for a law that would apply to every kind of medicine for external and internal use, especially proprietary medicines, but also provided that no remedy containing alcohol or cocaine should be sold except on the prescription of a physician.[135] Had this provision been included in the law it would have effectively made illegal the sale of a substantial proportion of the patent medicines then available. In the event the Pure Food and Drugs Act contained no such provision. However, the dangers from patent medicines were perceived by reformers to pose a far greater threat to the health of Americans than was tainted food. The American Medical Association was particularly exercised by the exorbitant therapeutic claims many of these medicines made on their labels while pharmacists were disturbed by the competition these remedies, which were readily available from most general stores and by mail order, posed to their business. In 1903 Wiley set up a division devoted to examining drugs to determine whether they were mislabeled and the division was expanded upon passage of the Act in 1906.

While only 135 of the Bureau's first 1000 Notices of Judgment had reference to drugs,[136] the first criminal prosecution under the Act involved a patent medicine, a headache remedy with the colorful name of Cuforhedake Brane-Fude (Cure-for-Headache-Brain-Food). The medication had been concocted and first offered for sale to the public in 1888 by Robert N. Harper, a pharmacist of some repute who, at various points in his career, had served as President of the Retail Drug Association and Commissioner of Pharmacy of the District of Columbia. Cuforhedake Brane-Fude comprised a mixture of acetanilid (an extremely effective antipyretic), antipyrine, caffeine, sodium and potassium bromide, and alcohol. It appears that Harper's medicine became extremely popular and some 2 000 000 bottles were sold by 1908. After passage of the Pure Food Law Harper changed the labels on his medicine to indicate that each bottle contained 30 percent alcohol and 16 grains of acetanilid. However, Wiley and the chief of the Bureau's drug division, Dr Lyman Kebler, found these changes in labeling insufficient and misleading inasmuch as their tests showed an alcohol content of 24 percent and the information pamphlet packed with each bottle declared Cuforhedake Brane-Fude 'a most wonderful, certain and harmless relief' containing 'no poisonous ingredients of any kind'. In actual fact, Wiley contended, large doses of acetanilid could indeed prove dangerous. In addition, the medication neither cured headaches nor was it brain food!

Harper contested the Bureau's findings, noting that he made several additional modifications to his labels and that there was ample evidence for the therapeutic value of his medicine, including the testimony of two Senators. This response had no effect on the Bureau and it was decided that not only would civil action be taken against the patent medicine, which permitted the federal authorities to seize it, but that criminal charges would be leveled against Harper himself. Among the issues raised at trial was whether Harper's medicine could be considered food for the brain, whether acetanilid was indeed a poison, and whether it was misleading to claim that a medication that 'relieved' headaches 'cured' them. The prosecution case, it appears, was quite sloppy despite the fact that among those who took the stand was Harvey Wiley himself, who testified that alcohol 'tends to harden all the cells with which it comes into contact and to coagulate their contents'. In his defense, Harper's attorneys called a number of experts who effectively destroyed most of the Bureau's case. To the charge that Harper had mislabeled the amount of alcohol in his medicine, one authority pointed out that the Bureau was apparently unaware of the difference between absolute alcohol and commercial alcohol – the standard alcohol used in patent medications – which is 94.9 percent pure. The professor of pharmacy from Columbia University, a recognized expert on acetanilid and a one-time student of its discoverer, testified that doses as large as 437 grains of acetanilid had proved not to be lethal and that the quantity contained in a bottle of Harper's Cuforhedake Brane-Fude was extremely moderate.

Despite what gave every indication of being a sufficient defense the jury found Harper guilty. Before sentencing, in what must surely be a violation of his oath to protect the Constitution, including its provisions respecting the separation of powers, President Roosevelt summoned the prosecuting attorney to the White House and ordered him to seek a jail term for Harper. 'It is your duty', he is reported to have said,

> to make an example of this man, and show to the people of the country that the pure food and drug law was enacted to protect them. He has been convicted after a fair and impartial trial, and you should use every argument in your power to convince the judge to impose a jail sentence. To a man of wealth, a fine as the penalty . . . would be little less than ridiculous.[137]

Despite this unprecedented interference in the judicial process the judge in the case spared Harper a jail term and instead fined him the maximum the law permitted.

Fresh from his partial victory in the Cuforhedake-Brane Fude case, Wiley decided to take on the Coca-Cola Company and was finally permitted to do so by his superiors in the Department of Agriculture in 1909.[138] Coca-Cola had been invented in 1886 by John Styth Pemberton, a pharmacist in Atlanta, who two years later sold the rights to the soft drink to Asa Griggs Candler, another Atlanta pharmacist. By 1909 Candler had transformed Pemberton's tonic from a drink that was available only locally into the largest selling soft drink in the nation with annual sales of 5 million barrels of syrup and revenues of over $6 000 000.[139] The syrup had originally contained extracts of the kola nut and a minute quantity of cocaine, largely because coca and its derivative were then regarded as miracle ingredients for pain and fatigue. As a result, Coca-Cola's label was decorated with a coca leaf and a kola nut. By 1903 some controversy had begun to surround the use of cocaine and Coca-Cola made the decision to substitute 'spent coca leaves'. At the same time it was determined to stop advertising the drink as a cure for headaches. Neither of these changes was sufficient to satisfy Wiley once the Pure Food and Drugs Act was passed.

Soon after the Act went into effect at the beginning of 1907 Wiley dispatched the head of the Bureau's drug division, Lyman Kebler, to the South to collect data on Coca-Cola. Apparently Kebler, while visiting a number of Southern cities and army posts, reported that use of the product was creating thousands of 'Coca-Cola fiends' and was appalled by the fact that the beverage was consumed by children as young as four or five years of age.[140] While Kebler was shocked that so many innocents were unknowingly ingesting traces of spent coca leaves, Wiley's main concern was that Coca-Cola, and the hundreds of soft drinks that attempted to copy its formula, contained small quantities of caffeine. Caffeine, like the chemical preservatives commonly used in foods, was another of Wiley's *bêtes noires*. In fact, he had earlier testified before a Senate committee on food adulteration that caffeine was a poison 'exactly similar in its chemical relations to strychnine and morphia' and described Coca-Cola, because of the caffeine it contained, as resembling opium, chloral hydrate, and cannabis indica.[141] Its presence in Coca-Cola seems to have especially outraged Wiley, who might possibly have had a particular animus for Candler because of his policy of conducting extensive advertising campaigns for the soft drink.[142]

In 1909 the Bureau of Chemistry had 40 barrels and 20 kegs of Coca-Cola syrup seized in Chattanooga with the intention of condemning them. In addition to claiming that the syrup contained a poisonous additive, caffeine, the beverage was further charged with being misbranded inasmuch as it contained no coca and only a minuscule amount of cola, as its name would suggest. This violation was compounded by the fact that Coca-Cola's label depicted images of a coca leaf and a kola nut, implying that these two substances were present in significant quantities. The label, therefore, was false and misleading and thus contravened the Pure Food and Drugs Act. This simple-minded accusation is indicative of the lengths to which Wiley was prepared to go to establish his authority as a national figure and to punish those whom he regarded as his opponents.

Both prosecution and defense called an impressive array of expert witnesses to adjudicate the issue of whether caffeine was indeed 'a poisonous and deleterious ingredient injurious to health' and as such violated the Act. The trial lasted some three weeks but this crucial question was never decided. Late in the trial the attorneys for Coca-Cola submitted a motion to dismiss the case on the grounds that the law did not apply to Coca-Cola since all of its ingre-dients were 'inherent'. Had Coca-Cola violated the law with respect to its caffeine content, it would have had to have been shown that the caffeine was an added ingredient but Coca-Cola now argued that the small amount of caffeine present in the drink was inherent to the product. The judge in the case affirmed Coca-Cola's motion, ruling that 'the entire proof unquestionably shows that the caffeine . . . in . . . Coca-Cola is one of its regular, habitual and essential constituents and that without its presence . . . the product would lack one of its essential elements and fail to produce upon the consumers a characteristic if not the most characteristic effect which is obtained from its use. In short Coca-Cola without caffeine would not be Coca-Cola.'[143]

The government appealed and three years after the trial the Sixth Circuit Court in Cincinnati affirmed the trial judge's ruling. So appalled was the Bureau by the decision, however, that it was decided to again appeal, on the grounds that the lower court's opinion would undermine the very purpose behind passage of the 1906 law. In 1916 the Supreme Court handed down a decision[144] in which it held that component parts of compound foods, of which caffeine in Coca-Cola was an example, were not excluded from the purview of the Pure Food and Drugs Act's ban on injurious substances. It went on to remand the case to the district court for retrial to determine whether caffeine was in fact an injurious poison. Meanwhile, Coca-Cola had, on its own initiative, altered its formula and reduced the amount of caffeine in the beverage, making further litigation irrelevant. It offered to forfeit all claims to the Coca-Cola syrup that had been seized seven years earlier and to pay the court costs of the earlier district court trial if the government agreed not to proceed. In December 1917, several months after the United States entered the World War, both the district attorney and the judge in the first case accepted Coca-Cola's offer and the case came to a close. By that point, of course, Wiley had left the enforcing agency and the zeal with which the action against Coca-Cola had been prosecuted had considerably lessened.

Even before the Supreme Court ruling in *United States v. Coca-Cola*, pure food and drug reformers were disappointed by a decision of the High Court which construed the Pure Food and Drugs Act as not applying to the curative claims made by manufacturers of proprietary medications. The case involved Dr Johnson's Mild Combination Treatment for Cancer, which was sold in tablet and bottled form by a Dr Johnson who had taken care to accurately label the contents of his preparations.[145] It was solely on the basis of its therapeutic claims that action was taken by the Bureau. The defendant moved for a quashing of the indictment on the grounds that the prohibition against misbranding within the meaning of the Act applied solely to a patent remedy's contents and did not refer to any accompanying statements regarding its remedial powers. The district court in Kansas City, where the trial was held, found for the defendant and dismissed the charges. The government appealed. Finally in May 1911 the case reached the Supreme Court. To the surprise of many, most especially the government, the Court, in a split decision, affirmed the decision of the lower court, agreeing that the term 'misbranded' was 'aimed at false statements as to identity of the article, possibly including strength, quality and purity . . . and not at statements as to curative effect'.[146]

The reaction to the decision was immediate. President William Howard Taft was appalled, noting that a large number of similar cases were pending in the courts. He pressed Congress to amend the law to eliminate this loophole but insisted that new legislation should proscribe only 'knowingly' making false claims of fact regarding the therapeutic effects of proprietary medicines. As a result, Representative J. Swagar Sherley, Democrat of Kentucky, introduced an amendment to the Pure Food and Drugs Act that prohibited false and fraudulent curative or therapeutic claims on the label or packaging of any medicine. In fact, the wording of the new amendment imposed an even greater burden on any prosecution since the new requirement compelled a showing that claims were both false and fraudulent. However, it is extremely difficult to establish an intent to deceive. When it was pointed out that the amendment burdened the prosecution with the almost impossible task of having to prove intent, Representative James Covington, Democrat of Maryland, responded that proof of intention in the criminal law was not beyond the abilities of the prosecution since 'a false statement on a label regarding a drug is one from which fraudulent intent may be implied. Conviction in all proper cases will be consequently comparatively sure.'[147] In the event there were few 'proper' cases brought before the statute was again changed.

While the setback to the enforcement powers of the Bureau of Chemistry as a result of the Supreme Court's opinion in *United States v. Johnson* appeared to have been corrected by the Sherley Amendment, another challenge to the Bureau had come two years earlier, also in the form of a Supreme Court decision, this one concerning food additives. In April 1910 the Lexington Mill and Elevator Company shipped a number of sacks of bleached flour from Lexington, Nebraska, to Castle, Missouri. The sacks were seized by the government and action taken against the company on the grounds that the flour contained nitrite residues. These substances, the Bureau contended, were injurious to health and the flour was therefore adulterated within the meaning of the Pure Food and Drugs Act. The company admitted the presence of very small amounts of nitrites but pointed out that these were residues left after bleaching, or whitening, the flour using what was then the standard process for this purpose, the Alsop Process. Not only were the quantities present minute enough to be harmless, it was claimed, but even these amounts were lessened or entirely eliminated during the course of baking bread. While admitting these claims, the prosecution argued that nitrites in even small doses were harmful and that they constituted an additive to natural flour; therefore the Lexington Mill and Elevator Company had violated the Act.

The jury in the trial court found for the prosecution. The company appealed and the verdict was reversed by the Court of Appeals for the Eighth Circuit which held that, while the additive in question might indeed be harmful, if it were present in such minute quantities as to be non-injurious, then, contrary to the instructions of the trial judge, it did not fall under the provisions of the Act. The case was then remanded for a new trial. The government once again appealed and the Supreme Court, in *United States v. Lexington Mill and Elevator Company*[148] unanimously affirmed the decision of the Appeals Court, holding that it was incumbent on the government to prove an additive in the quantities used caused the final product to be injurious to health.

While the Pure Food and Drugs Act had provided that all proprietary medicines be labeled with the quantity of alcohol or narcotic they contained, no ceiling was set on the proportion present in any medication. However, in response to pressure from the Bureau and from a public who had been led to believe that narcotics, in any quantity, were poisonous, a number of manufacturers had voluntarily reduced the amount of these substances in their preparations. Limits on the proportion of narcotics these medicines could contain were finally made a matter of statute in 1914 with passage of the Harrison Narcotic Act. The statute was passed by Congress at the urging of Secretary of State William Jennings Bryan, a man of deep fundamentalist beliefs and possessed of a missionary ardor for purifying America. He pressed for enactment of the bill on the grounds, he claimed, that the United States was obligated by the terms of the Hague Convention of 1912 to control the distribution of opium and its derivatives.[149] The Act's ostensible purpose was to register all users, sellers, distributors, and manufacturers of opium, coca, or their derivatives and to impose a tax on them. Patent medicine manufacturers were exempt from the licensing and taxing provisions if their preparations contained less than two grains of opium or less than one-fourth of a grain of morphine, or less than one-eighth of a grain of heroin in each ounce. Manufacturers of medications whose narcotic content exceeded these amounts were guilty of violating the Act and were subject to substantial penalties.[150]

In January 1919 Nebraska became the 36th state to ratify the Eighteenth Amendment and in October Congress passed the Volstead Act, implementing nationwide Prohibition, to take effect on 1 January 1920. While the alcoholic content of proprietary medicines was not affected by the Act,[151] manufacturers were aware that the amount of alcohol their medications contained had to be limited to the medicine's ostensible therapeutic function and they were encouraged in this by the Commissioner of Internal Revenue, who threatened to tax manufacturers whose medicines seemed aimed primarily at those who enjoyed a drink.[152] Even before passage of the Pure Food and Drugs Act, they had begun to reduce the alcohol present in their remedies and this reduction was accelerated in response to passage of prohibition statutes in a number of states. In 1918 and 1919 the Proprietary Association, representing some 80 percent of all patent medications sold, issued a series of guidelines regarding the content of these medicines that conformed to the anti-alcohol sentiments that were sweeping the nation, among them that the amount of alcohol should be kept to a minimum and should not exceed the amount needed to keep the active ingredients in solution or to prevent freezing.

The Harrison Narcotic Act and the Volstead Act had established standards for the amount of alcohol and narcotics that could be present in patent medicines, thus removing from the Bureau of Chemistry the authority to set standards in these areas. However, it soon became apparent to those responsible for enforcing the Pure Food and Drugs Act that there were a number of other areas touching on foods and drugs in which their authority was limited and that corrective legislation was needed. They therefore pressured Congress to pass a number of amendments to strengthen their powers. For example, while the Act required that all drugs and prepared foods be labeled to show their contents, there was no requirement that they indicate their weight or measure. A number of food manufacturers supported federal legislation in this area as a way of pre-empting conflicting state laws. The result was that in 1913 Congress enacted the Gould amendment, which placed on manufacturers an affirmative requirement that their labels indicate the quantity of contents 'in terms of weight, measure, or numerical count'.[153]

A number of other amendments were considered by Congress during the next decade but none was enacted. An amendment to prohibit slack-filled packaging was introduced in the House by Representative Gilbert Nelson Haugen, Republican of Iowa and Chairman of the Committee on Agriculture from 1919 to 1930. No fewer than four House hearings were held on the amendment and it was the subject of two Senate hearings, in 1921 and 1928.[154] The measure passed in the House on each of these occasions but the bill was defeated in the Senate in both 1921 and 1928. In 1926 both the House and Senate held hearings on a bill, which was passed by both Houses of Congress, to permit the use of corn sugar in food without having to carry a special designation. However, the bill was never enacted. Labeling to reflect the origin of foreign-grown food products was the subject of yet another bill on which House hearings were held in 1926 but the measure was never reported out of committee. Finally, in 1930 both the House and Senate held hearings on a bill that called for standards of identity for fruit preserves. The measure passed the Senate but was never reported out of committee in the House.[155]

While these amendments failed, the Supreme Court handed the Bureau of Chemistry a substantial victory in 1924. In that year, overruling the Sixth Circuit Court of Appeals, the High Court held that the Pure Food and Drugs Act made illegal every statement, design, or device that might mislead or deceive the public, even if technically true. The case involved the Douglas Packing Company of Rochester, New York, which was marketing their Excelsior brand vinegar as 'apple cider vinegar'. The Bureau had seized a quantity of the vinegar and charged the Company with misbranding, inasmuch as it was found not to have been made from fresh apples, but from dried, or evaporated, apples. The Company argued that during the apple season, from about 25 September to 15 December, its vinegar was indeed made from fresh apples but during the remainder of the year it was compelled to use dehydrated apples. The approved process of dehydration required the employment of small quantities of sulphur fumes to prevent rot, fermentation, and discoloration. The principal effect of dehydration was to remove 80 percent of the water in the apples. The apples were then reconstituted with pure water and the liquid then subjected to the same alcoholic and acetic fermentation as was the case with the liquid from fresh apples. During fermentation small amounts of barium carbonate were added which, in turn, when precipitated eliminated itself and any sulphur residue. The result was a product chemically similar and similar in taste to apple cider made from unevaporated apples. The Court ruled that the two products, one made from fresh, the other from dried, apples were clearly different products since the juice of an apple, which had been removed during dehydration, was not the same as the pure water which replaced it, despite the similarities in chemical composition and taste of the final product. The Circuit Court had therefore erred in reversing the decision of the trial court in finding the Company in violation of the Act.[156]

While the 1906 Act did not authorize the Bureau of Chemistry to set standards for foods, it continued to do so. In 1903, well before passage of the Pure Food and Drugs Act, the Bureau had begun to establish informal standards for unadulterated food products and this continued after the new law became effective. By 1906 more than 200 food standards had been published in Department of Agriculture circulars. When appropriations for its Food Standards Committee were not renewed in 1906, however, the Department abolished it and its functions were taken up by the United States Commission on the Purity of Foods, under state auspices. In 1914, however, the Department restored the Committee, which continued in operation until superseded by changes in legislation in 1938.

Congress itself had set specific standards for a few foods – for example, apples in 1912 and milk in 1923 – and in 1930 passed the McNary-Mapes Amendment, which empowered the Secretary of Agriculture to establish standards for canned foods. Senator Charles L. McNary, Republican from Oregon and Chairman of the Senate Committee on Agriculture and Forestry and Representative Carl E. Mapes, Republican from Michigan, introduced an amendment to the Pure Foods and Drugs Act that sought to address one of the inadequacies brought to their attention by the Department of Agriculture. It was pointed out that, while consumers might be able to see differences in the quality and quantity of a food when bottled, this was not the case with canned items. The result was that there existed significant variation in the quality and amount of a product from brand to brand. The McNary-Mapes Amendment dealt with this variation by empowering the Secretary to set 'a reasonable standard of quality, condition, and/or fill of container' for each class of canned food. If a manufacturer should proceed to market any canned food that fell below the standard that had been set, the product's label was required to carry 'a plain and conspicuous statement prescribed by the Secretary of Agriculture' to that effect.[157]

It had long been suggested that the regulatory functions of the Bureau of Chemistry be separated from its research activities, largely because of the problems caused by Harvey Wiley's tenure as director. Finally, in 1927 Congress decided to act and proceeded to separate the two. Research remained the concern of the Bureau of Chemistry, which became the Bureau of Chemistry and Soils, but the regulatory functions were invested in a new Food, Drug, and Insecticide Administration under the immediate supervision of the Secretary of Agriculture. In 1910, following complaints about the adulteration of insecticides, Congress had enacted the Federal Insecticide Act giving the Department of Agriculture authority to regulate insecticides in much the same way it had been regulating the adulteration and mislabeling of foods and drugs. In order to take advantage of what were thought to be similarities in the enforcement of the two laws and to avoid duplication of function, Congress decided to establish one agency that brought together food and drugs on the one hand and insecticides on the other. It therefore created the FDIA by amendment to the 1927–28 agricultural appropriations bill. The name of the new agency was clearly infelicitous. This appears to have finally occurred to Congress who, three years later, shortened the agency's name to the Food and Drug Administration.

The budget of the Bureau of Chemistry remained fairly constant from passage of the Pure Food and Drugs Act, more accurately from 1909, at which

Table 2.1   *Appropriations for the Bureau of Chemistry (the Food, Drug, and Insecticide Administration), 1909–1931 (dollars)*

Year	Amount
1909	685 460
1910	702 340
1911	610 110
1912	625 000
1913	675 000
1914	644 301
1915	635 161
1916	632 951
1917	623 521
1918	589 801
1919	620 221
1920	579 361
1921	671 401
1922	671 402
1923	704 401
1924	716 260
1925	788 860
1926	785 408
1927	918 780
1928	938 000
1929	1 030 000
1930	1 125 000
1931	1 315 865

Source: Lauffer T. Hayes and Frank J. Ruff, 'The Administration of the Federal Food and Drugs Act', *Law and Contemporary Problems*, 1 (December 1933): 24–5.

point Congress began explicitly legislating appropriations to enforce the Act, to 1927, when the Bureau became the Food, Drug, and Insecticide Administration. At that point enforcement expenditures began to increase at a significant rate, to the point where its budget was twice the size it had been ten years earlier. Table 2.1 shows the amounts granted by Congress to the Bureau from 1909 to 1931.

Soon after Carl L. Alsberg, Wiley's successor, resigned as director of the Bureau in 1921 and was replaced by Walter G. Campbell, the Bureau had also begun addressing the question of insecticide residues in food. The agency had clear authority to take action against foods that contained ingredients injurious to health but there was some question whether that authority extended to sub-lethal residues of insecticides. The use of arsenicals in insect control had begun around 1870 and rapidly spread throughout the country after the intro-duction of lead arsenate in 1890.[158] The Bureau was reluctant to take legal action against spray residues in foods if the amounts detected were smaller than those established as lethal, especially since there was no hard evidence that these sub-lethal doses were actually harmful. Indeed, during the early part of the century pests were regarded as a far more serious threat to health than were the insecticides used to kill them and several states, such as Washington state, had enacted laws to force apple growers to use more, not fewer, pesti-cides.[159] Even in the absence of evidence respecting the detrimental effects of sub-lethal doses of pesticides, the Bureau in 1925, with some reluctance, seized four carloads of apples and one of pears in Chicago that were shipped from the Suncrest Orchards in Oregon. The grower, Llewellan Banks, had publicized the fact that the shipment comprised unwashed fruit and the Bureau determined to make a test case of his produce. During the course of the trial the government presented testimony on the harmful effects of sub-lethal amounts of arsenic and was able to win the case. However, they were disin-clined to prosecute other offenders, especially in jurisdictions more favorably disposed to growers until the statute was changed to allow for the fixing of standards.[160]

Restraints on the regulation of pesticide residues were by no means the only limitations the FDA faced prior to the New Deal. During the Depression, food manufacturers, in an effort to provide prepared foods to the public at lower prices, began marketing cheaper but equally wholesome substitutes for a number of products, among them 'Salad Bouquet', which could be used 'like vinegar', 'Peanut Spred', a replacement for peanut butter, and 'Bred Spred', a jam substitute which came in a variety of flavors. These new, less expensive foods made every attempt to meet the FDA's labeling requirements and were careful not to carry descriptive names that suggested they were simply varia-tions of their more expensive counterparts. The FDA, however, urged on by the preserves industry, regarded the sale of these products as attempts to swin-dle the public. 'Consumers', they argued, 'had no way of knowing that the products were of low quality'.[161] Rather than viewing the new products as offering poorer consumers a choice of dressings and spreads that were not earlier available to them, the FDA was infuriated that these manufacturers were attempting to sell inferior merchandise. Once again the manufacturers of more expensive commodities joined with FDA bureaucrats in attempting to prohibit the sale of cheaper competitive products.

In 1931 the federal Court of Appeals for the Eighth Circuit affirmed the verdict of the trial court in a case involving the seizure of ten cases of Bred Spred. The FDA had contended that the spread was an imitation jam and, as such, was misbranded, and that the product was adulterated in order to conceal its inferiority. The Court, however, concluded that these charges were without merit. It is true, the Court conceded, that Bred Spred was inferior to jam in that it had less fruit but Bred Spred's manufacturer, the Crandell Company, had at no point compared itself to jam and none of the product's ingredients was unwholesome, damaged, or of inferior quality. The FDA's claims were therefore dismissed.[162] The decision was an important victory against bureaucratic highhandedness but it proved to be short-lived. In 1938 Congress was prevailed upon to enact the Federal Food, Drug, and Cosmetic Act, which completely revised the Pure Food and Drugs Act and granted the FDA unprecedented powers over the nation's food and drug supply.

Almost immediately following passage of the 1906 Act the Bureau of Chemistry initiated attempts to strengthen its enforcement powers.[163] For example the 1917 Annual Report of the Bureau identified a number of areas where its powers were severely limited and would need to be augmented: among them, the absence of legal standards to which all foods were required to conform; the lack of authority to inspect food establishments; and the absence of any jurisdiction over advertising claims.[164] Over the next few years the enforcement agency, under its several names, discovered additional shortcomings. The law as it stood did not cover cosmetics[165] nor were the provisions dealing with patent medicines effective, especially after passage of the Sherley amendment. Nor did the FDA find the powers vested in it by the McNary-Mapes Amendment adequate since they did not allow for multiple standards but limited the agency to setting *minimum* standards for canned products only. The FDA insisted that it could not properly perform its functions unless it were authorized to grade all foodstuffs and determine to which, of a number of standards of quality, each canned product conformed.

Over the course of the first three decades of the twentieth century it was the Republicans who had been in the forefront of calling for wider government powers to regulate commerce and to structure the personal lives of Americans. However, in 1932 the Democratic party underwent a radical shift in political philosophy with the election of Franklin Delano Roosevelt. With the New Deal, the Democrats replaced the Republicans as the principal party embracing massive government intervention in the economy. Walter Campbell, who had become director of the FDA (under its earlier designation) in 1921,[166] was one of the first to try to capitalize on Roosevelt's election by lobbying to expand the powers of the FDA and in this he was encouraged by the new Assistant Secretary of Agriculture, Rexford Tugwell. Indeed, it is Tugwell, one historian notes, who must be awarded the credit for initiating the movement to revise the 1906 Act.[167] Tugwell was an enthusiastic proponent of economic planning. One-time professor of economics at Columbia University and a member of Roosevelt's Brain Trust, he had spent two months in the Soviet Union in 1927 and was enthusiastic about what he had seen there.[168] Early in his career as a high-ranking member of the Roosevelt Administration, he is reputed to have maintained that 'property rights and financial rights will be subordinated to human rights'.[169] Tugwell sympathized with the need to broaden the agency's authority and quickly obtained approval for a revision of the 1906 Act from President Roosevelt.

Campbell was hopeful that he could quickly prevail on Congress to increase his agency's authority. He was particularly sensitive to accusations that the FDA was remiss in taking action against offenders under the 1906 Act at a time when public support for expanding its powers was essential. In 1927 Howard K. Ambruster had managed to purchase a substantial amount of Spanish ergot[170] and charged that ergot that had been imported from Russia, with which he found he had to compete, was substandard. Soon Ambruster's charges were enlarged to apply to a variety of imported medicines, including ether and digitalis. The implication was that the FDA had been negligent in allowing adulterated material into the country. Ambruster was joined by Dr Henry Hurd Rusby, Dean of the Columbia University College of Pharmacy, and by none other than Dr Harvey Wiley, one-time director of the Bureau of Chemistry. At the same time the American Association of Obstetricians, Gynecologists, and Abdominal Surgeons had launched an official investigation into Ambruster's allegations and found them legitimate. Finally, the case was taken up by the newly created Consumers' Research Organization and accusations of neglect and failure to act were again repeated by Senator Burton K. Wheeler, Democrat from Montana, in the pages of *Plain Talk* magazine.

The upshot of Ambruster's charges was a lengthy hearing on the FDA before the Senate Committee on Agriculture and Forestry, chaired by Senator Charles McNary, Republican from Oregon. While a number of embarrassing questions were asked of the agency, especially by Senator Wheeler, the FDA invariably fell back on the same explanation for any deficiencies of which they were accused, that it was the law itself that was inadequate. All problems were blamed on the existing law's weaknesses, especially its lack of effective deterrents and the absence of any control over advertising. No formal report issued from the hearings but it was the feeling of the FDA and its friends that it had been vindicated and that the groundwork had been effectively laid for supplementary legislation to increase the agency's authority. Indeed, at least in one respect the hearings had worked to the advantage of the FDA in that the agency had cemented its relationship with Senator Royal Copeland, Democrat of New York, who had shown sympathy with the FDA's battle for stronger powers. Copeland, a physician and one-time commissioner of health of New York City, had been invited to sit with the Committee during its hearings and did much to deflect any questions that might have put the agency in a bad light. Indeed, during the hearings the press had begun referring to him as 'counsel for the defense'.[171]

The FDA's campaign was appreciably aided by the publication in late 1932 of *100,000,000 Guinea Pigs* by F.J. Schlink and Arthur Kallet.[172] Both Schlink and Kallet were engineers and executives of the newly created Consumers' Research, which Schlink had founded in 1928. Schlink immediately hired Kallet as the organization's director and both launched a crusade to restructure the nation's economic system so that competitive forces could no longer exploit the American public. *100,000,000 Guinea Pigs* ostensibly laid bare the evils of advertising, which was responsible for brainwashing Americans into purchasing a huge number of worthless products. More important, many of these items, they claimed, were extremely dangerous to our health. Among the accusations were that *All-Bran* could cause irreparable intestinal damage, that *Pebeco* toothpaste contained enough lead so that if a whole tube were eaten it could be lethal, and that one of the ingredients of *Bromo-Seltzer* was a poisonous drug that could cause sexual impotence. Hiding behind a weak and ineffective pure food and drug law which was used as a smokescreen, they argued, advertisers had been making huge profits at the expense of our health and well-being. Food and drug manufacturers were not even required to prove beyond doubt that their products did not cause harm. Rather, the burden of proof fell on the FDA. Despite these limitations, the real culprit, according to Schlink – as he had made clear as early as 1925 in an article jointly authored with the socialist economist Stuart Chase – was competition, which would be eliminated were the government to set exact specifications for each food and drug. This would have the benefit of setting quality, as scientifically defined by a government agency, and would do away with unnecessary variations. Under such a system 'the buyer knows exactly what he is getting, the manufacturer knows exactly what he has to produce'.[173]

100,000,000 Guinea Pigs was a tremendous success. It remained on the bestseller lists for more than two years and went through 31 editions by 1936. It spawned a large number of similar works, all pointing to the evils of advertising and to the greed and rapaciousness of businessmen who were prepared to enrich themselves even at the cost of endangering the lives of millions of gullible food and drug consumers. The authors of these volumes were almost uniformly in favor of replacing the market economy with a *dirigiste* regime. These sentiments, while not explicitly arguing for an amended Pure Food and Drugs Act that was purged of its existing weaknesses, could clearly be marshaled to support new and stronger legislation. This was not lost on the FDA bureaucracy. In 1932 Paul Dunbar, then assistant chief of the FDA, wrote its director that 'certainly Schlink had no intention of posing as an ally of the Food and Drug Administration but unconsciously he may be a very valuable one' and Dr Walter Alvarez of the Mayo Clinic, in a letter to T. Swann Harding of the Department of Agriculture, noted: 'I think the value of [*100,000,000 Guinea Pigs*] lies in its calling attention to the rottenness and inadequacy of our laws'.[174]

FDA bureaucrats were encouraged by these new muckrakers who hammered at the manufacturers of prepared foods, and especially of proprietary medicines, as purveyors of poisons. As the Depression deepened, more and more Americans were turning to self-medication as a way of avoiding physicians' fees, and advertising claims were becoming more extravagant. According to Schlink and Kallet, more than $350 000 000 was spent annually on patent medications, enough for three or four bottles for every man, woman, and child in the nation.[175] These increased sales were paralleled by the growth in the membership of Schlink's Consumers' Research organization, which had increased from 1000 in 1929 to 45 000 in 1933.[176] The governing officials of the FDA determined to take advantage of this public discontent with the 1906 Act to prevail on Congress to scrap the Pure Food and Drugs Act and substitute a new statute. When news reached the nation's food and drug manufacturers that the FDA would seek a completely new law, many manufacturers became convinced that it would contain so many restrictions that anything even vaguely resembling a free market would disappear. This was especially true of drug manufacturers, a good number of whom feared that they would be forced out of business by the new Act's provisions. In the event, their fears proved justified.

In late May 1933 a draft measure, S. 1400, known as the Tugwell bill, was introduced in the Senate by Royal Copeland of New York, who had now become the FDA's greatest champion. The bill was intended to replace the 1906 Act and was crafted in Tugwell's offices in the Department of Agriculture.[177] Under its terms the FDA would no longer have to prove fraudulent intent in order to take legal action against a proprietary remedy. A medication could be held to be misbranded if its labeling made any therapeutic claim whatever, even if the claim were only implied, that was contrary to the general agreement of medical opinion. Additionally labels were required to specify that their contents were palliatives and not cures, unless evidence existed that proved that the medication could indeed cure. Finally, all ingredients, not solely a group of specified narcotics, must be disclosed and medicines containing certain narcotic or hypnotic substances were required to carry the following notice: 'Warning – May be habit forming'. For the first time medical devices were brought under the purview of the bill and were subject to provisions similar to those applied to drugs. With respect to foods, manufacturers were compelled to disclose all ingredients on their labels, in order of predominance by weight. The government was empowered to establish standards regarding the quality and fill of all food in containers. Adulteration was redefined to include substances that the FDA regarded as poisonous when used in excess of tolerance levels set by the Department of Agriculture. Inspectors were authorized to inspect any establishment in which food, drugs, or cosmetics were either manufactured or held. 'Voluntary' inspections were permitted, but at the owner's expense. To refuse such inspections, however, would prove so onerous that manufacturers would have had no option but to invite inspectors in. Cosmetics were, for the first time, brought under the terms of the bill,[178] as was advertising. All advertising of foods, drugs, and cosmetics was required to adhere to the standards established for labeling. Should the FDA determine that self-treatment was either dangerous or futile, advertising was totally prohibited. Finally, the bill contained a provision which empowered the Secretary of Agriculture to make regulations based on the FDA's interpretation of the statute that would have the force of law.[179]

Copeland's bill, as it stood, lodged an extraordinary degree of discretionary authority in the FDA. Despite this, the food industry was not particularly distressed by its provisions since most of the changes were aimed at the drug industry. This was immediately apparent and was greeted with grave concern by the makers of proprietary medications. It was clear that the measure reflected the FDA's dislike of self-medication, which it regarded as unsafe and which it sought to reduce as much as politically possible.[180] Were the agency successful, home remedies would disappear and the proprietary medicine industry along with it. The industry made their intense opposition clear during subcommittee hearings on S. 1400 held by Senator Copeland in December 1933. So outspoken were they that the *New Republic* asserted that the proprietary manufacturers became 'the first group of industrialists openly to declare war on the Roosevelt administration'.[181] As a result, the suggestions of Frank Blair, President of the Proprietary Association, and other representatives of the patent medicine industry were subject to contemptuous dismissal. Charles Dunn, the counsel of the Associated Grocery Manufacturers of America, on the other hand, was treated with great courtesy and his advice was given serious consideration.[182]

A large number of trade groups joined in opposition to the bill, primarily because of the negative economic effects the measure would likely have on their businesses. These included the National Drug Trade Conference, the American Newspaper Publishers Association, the National Association of Retail Druggists, and the National Publishers Association, who all engaged in sponsoring public protests and radio programs attacking the bill. In addition, several ad hoc groups were formed in an attempt to get the measure defeated, among them the Minute Men, who were founded with the specific intent of opposing the bill's drug provisions, the Joint Committee for Sound and Democratic Consumer Legislation, the National Advisory Council of Consumers and Producers, and the Drug Institute of America, founded by Charles Walgreen of the Walgreen Drugstore chain.[183]

The first few months of Roosevelt's administration witnessed a revolutionary change in politics as the role assigned to the federal government by
Congress was expanded beyond all expectations. Against this backdrop, newspapers and radio stations apparently did not regard the Tugwell bill as important enough to occupy a prominent place in their reports. In addition, some
were fearful of losing advertising from food, drug, and cosmetic companies,
many of whom were likely to be put out of business by the measure's sweeping provisions and were therefore reluctant to publicize the FDA's propaganda
supporting the bill. The resulting absence of a press that favored the new
measure, unlike the situation prior to passage of the Pure Food and Drugs Act
in 1906, was deeply disturbing to the FDA, who determined to launch a
publicity campaign to drum up support for the measure. The FDA's information officer, Ruth deForest Lamb, was instructed to make every effort to
encourage newspapers to carry editorials favorable to the agency and to reprint
the agency's more sensational horror stories concerning adulterated and
misbranded foods and patent medicines. As one historian has recounted:

> Through radio spots, mimeographed material circulated from field offices, and
> direct mailing of reprinted articles by FDA staff members, the agency began a care-
> fully coordinated effort to build support for the new bill. . . . By late November
> [1933] field office reports indicated that many offices were providing four to five
> speakers a week. FDA discovered also that radio could be an effective weapon.
> Using such vehicles as the National Farm and Home Hour, Copeland, Campbell,
> and other agency officials pleaded their case over the airways several times in the
> fall of 1933.[184]

The most effective of its propaganda tools was a series of posters pointing out
the inadequacies of the 1906 law. Dubbed 'the American Chamber of Horrors'
by the press,[185] it was exhibited at the Century of Progress Exposition in
Chicago, loaned out to groups, and taken on a road tour of FDA field offices.
Depicting a number of products of questionable value or effectiveness that the
FDA and its predecessor agencies were unable to deal with because of the
limitations of the Pure Food and Drugs Act of 1906, the exhibit suggested that
most of the food and drugs with which the American consumer were
confronted were of a similar nature, a situation that would continue unchanged
if a new food and drug law were not enacted. Examples of the food 'horrors'
included (1) bottles of 'Bred Spred', 'Peanut Spred', and 'Salad Bouquet',
each a cheaper substitute containing fewer natural ingredients than their more
expensive counterparts; (2) two brands of malted milk, one mixed dry, the
other wet. The wet mix allowed the mixture to evaporate into a uniform
consistency, while the dry did not; (3) three brands of noodles: one brand
contained some egg so that the package appeared to contain egg noodles,
another contained no egg but was wrapped in yellow cellophane, the third was

wrapped in plain cellophane. All three packages were clearly labeled 'plain noodles'! (4) bottles and cans of peaches, tomatoes, and peas, with the notation that when packed in bottles consumers were able to determine the quality of the produce, while, when packed in cans, they could not; (5) bottles of stringless beans of clearly differing quality but all meeting minimum Department of Agriculture standards. Under the existing law no further government grading was permitted; (6) bottled chicken, with the white meat prominently shown, while the dark meat was 'hidden' behind the label; (7) a can of 'maple flavored' syrup which contained only a small amount of actual maple syrup; (8) a variety of bottles in different shapes and sizes, which suggested that some contained more material than others. The actual amount contained in each bottle was shown on the label; (9) an array of ice creams, each containing differing amounts of cream and air.[186]

In addition, a portion of the exhibit was devoted to medicines which were of little or no help either as palliatives or remedies and whose use had, in some instance or another, caused serious injury or death.[187] However, most of the 'horrors'[188] that the FDA had managed to come up with were foods. In light of the examples on display by the agency, it is somewhat surprising that the exhibit did not become the laughing-stock of the nation. Indeed, it is hard to imagine any housewife who was unaware of these 'deceptive practices'. Yet so impressed was Eleanor Roosevelt with the FDA exhibition that she had it mounted in the White House and invited the wives of members of Congress to view it! Not to be outdone, Representative William Sorovich, Democrat of New York, a physician and one-time commissioner of child welfare of New York, had portions of the exhibit shown on the floor of the House so that his colleagues could see it first-hand. The exhibit makes clear how woefully ignorant the officials of the FDA were of how free markets operate. There is no appreciation whatever that private institutions can act as effective sources of information about products that are available in the marketplace: retailers who insure that the goods they stock are of a certain quantity, radio stations and newspapers that carry advertisements only from manufacturers of goods whose quality meets a minimum standard, consumer organizations whose function it is to rate and compare products and prices, manufacturers who have reputations to uphold, and so on.[189] The idea that a government agency alone was able to warrant the quality of goods sold is, at best, naïve yet FDA propaganda appears to have been predicated on the belief that the public shared this view.

Whether or not its campaign was particularly effective, the FDA did find allies in the national women's organizations, whose support once again was to prove crucial in the eventual passage of a new law. The American Association of University Women, the American Home Economics Association, the National Congress of Parents and Teachers, the National Women's Trade Union League, and the National Board of the YWCA, among others, together with the same constellation of groups that had worked so tirelessly for the 1906 law, all endorsed the Copeland bill in much the same terms as women's groups had supported passage of the earlier Act. As had been the case prior to enactment of the 1906 law, a substantial proportion of the women who sought passage of the Copeland bill welcomed a greater role for government in private life and looked on massive social engineering as the only effective method for social betterment. The American Home Economics Association, for example, was identified with the whole range of Progressive Era legislation, very much along the lines of the General Federation of Women's Clubs, including labor legislation limiting hours of work and minimum pay, child-labor laws, women's suffrage, tighter controls on pornography, prostitution, and drug use, and a host of government programs to 'improve American health and hygiene practices'. They were joined by the other women's groups in enthusiastically endorsing similar reforms.

Opposition to the 1933 Copeland bill was so intense, however, that in February 1934 the Senator introduced a revision of his earlier bill, S. 2800. In response to criticism, Copeland had modified the bill in several ways: proprietary drug labels would no longer have to carry a list of all their ingredients but only of a group of specified components. Publishers could no longer be held liable for false advertising. In its place, the bill required that publishers turn over the names of the manufacturers who had prepared the offending copy. The Agriculture Department was no longer empowered to establish multiple grades for specific foods but only a minimum grade. Finally, the bill called for the creation of two advisory boards to which appeals could be made respecting regulations promulgated by the FDA. These revisions, however, were not sufficient to mollify the manufacturers of proprietary medicines who remained bitterly opposed to the bill, and especially to its provisions regarding the advertising of therapeutic claims. At a special meeting of the Proprietary Association held in the fall of 1933, one advertising executive gave a sample of the kinds of statements he thought would be permissible under the proposed Act:

> We think our medicine is good. There may be other better brands, but at least ours is as good as the average. – Thousands of physicians have prescribed it . . . for certain disorders, but we dare not tell you what the disorders are. – If your doctor should prescribe it for a headache . . . you will still have the headache long after you think it is gone. – In spite of all this, we must urge you to buy our medicine anyhow, as we need the money to push our sales of impure food for the purpose of poisoning your children.[190]

While S. 2800 does not appear to have diminished the opposition to a revised food and drug law, it did lose the support of a number of groups that had endorsed Copeland's earlier draft. The Consumers' Research organization, headed by Schlink and Kallet, accused Copeland of caving in to lobbyists for the drug industry.[191] They were joined by the *Nation* and other supporters of a strong measure, including none other than Rexford Tugwell, who is reported to have labeled Copeland's revision 'very disappointing' and threatened to withdraw his personal support for the new bill.[192] Tugwell's dissatisfaction appears to have contributed to the measure's low priority in the administration's list of desired legislation and the bill died after having been reported out of committee.

It had occurred to many opponents of S. 2800 that some reform of the Pure Food and Drugs Act was inevitable. They therefore encouraged the introduction of several substitute measures that would revise the weakest aspects of the 1906 Act while eliminating the most offensive provisions of the Copeland bill. The first of these, H.R. 6376, was put forward by Representative Loring M. Black, Democrat of New York, and had the endorsement of several patent medicine manufacturers. Black's measure provided that the FDA enforce its rulings by cease and desist orders rather than through criminal prosecutions and that substantial latitude for the therapeutic claims of proprietary medications be permitted inasmuch as these claims were as much opinion as fact. The measure had little chance of passing but a second substitute represented a more serious threat to S. 2800. Senator Pat McCarren, Democrat from Nevada, and Representative Virginia Jenckes, Democrat from Indiana, introduced a pure food and drug bill (S. 2858; H.R. 7964) written by Charles Dunn, counsel for the Associated Grocery Manufacturers of America, which was strongly supported not only by the Grocery Manufacturers but also by the American Pharmaceutical Manufacturers and the National Drug Trade Conference. It was much like Copeland's bill with the significant exception that its enforcement provisions were complex and permitted a very large number of appeals.

In addition to these two substitute measures, the Consumers' Research group had drafted its own bill, which pushed the discretionary powers of government far beyond its prior limits. Sponsored by Representative Patrick J. Boland, Democrat of Pennsylvania, the labeling and advertising provisions of the bill (H.R. 8316) were unprecedented. It called for the creation of a Board of Labeling, Packaging, and Advertising Control with final authority to determine how a product should be labeled and advertised. With respect to the manufacture and sale of drugs, processed foods, and cosmetics, every person who participated in any way in 'the manufacture, processing, preparation, or treatment' of the product prior to its shipment in interstate commerce was required to be licensed by one of three newly established Bureaus of Control. These Bureaus were armed with broad discretionary powers to inspect all manufacturing and processing facilities and to determine who would receive a license. The measure contained no provision for appeal from the decisions reached under the bill.[193] It is a reflection on how far the nation had moved from the principles on which it was founded that a measure such as this could have been introduced into the national legislature and that there was even some speculation that it might be passed into law. Not only was this bill not treated with the contempt it deserved but soon after its introduction Schlink was asked to address the American Academy of Political and Social Science where he received a warm reception[194] and in the following year Boland became House Majority Whip.

In the event, no pure food and drug measure was passed in 1934, the Copeland bill having died in committee at the close of the 1934 Congressional session. When Congress reassembled in January of the following year, Copeland, whose efforts on behalf of a new measure were tireless, introduced yet another bill, S. 5, which he had written without having consulted with the Food and Drug Administration. In an attempt to blunt the opposition of the proprietary medicine manufacturers Copeland had altered the more objectionable provisions of his earlier measure. Among them, labels no longer had to indicate whether the medication was a palliative or a cure and some illnesses for which advertising claims were prohibited were removed. Finally, provision for the multiple grading of foodstuffs, which had been removed from Copeland's first bill, was not restored. Copeland was hopeful that yet another set of hearings could be avoided. However, this proved impossible and his subcommittee once again was forced to hear testimony on the measure.

Aware that it was only a matter of time before a new law would be enacted, several groups who had opposed Copeland's earlier drafts, among them the Associated Manufacturers of Toilet Articles, were prepared to accept S. 5 for fear that Congress would approve even more restrictive legislation. Among the bill's other supporters, as expected, were the manufacturers of prescription drugs, who saw in the Copeland bill's restrictions on the labeling and sale of proprietary medicines an opportunity to increase their sales at the expense of over-the-counter medications. While the ethical drug industry originally had some reservations about supporting Copeland's revised bill, Copeland ordered that several changes be made to win their support. As a result S. 5, which originally contained a provision requiring that manufacturers of ethical drugs detail every variation in the content of their medications should these differ in any particular from the formulas shown in the US Pharmacopeia or the National Formulary, was altered to remove this requirement. The effect was that the American Pharmaceutical Manufacturers Association and the American Drug Manufacturers Association abandoned their opposition. The professional organizations representing the nation's pharmacies also viewed the bill with favor. The American Pharmaceutical Association, which called for quick passage of the measure, even recommended that the labeling requirements on proprietary medicines, which had been eased, should be again strengthened to require that all ingredients be shown and, more significantly, urged that all drug manufacturers be licensed. 'This is in the interest of the decent manufacturer of medicines', the President of the American Pharmaceutical Association testified, 'as well as the public interest, because there has been a multiplicity of fly-by-night concerns which have flooded the market with various types of remedies of questionable value'.[195]

The two sections of the bill to which the patent medicine interests most objected remained. They were the restrictions on advertising and the provision that permitted the FDA to make multiple seizures of a product before a hearing was held. Armed with such authority the FDA could institute legal action against a product at a number of sites at the same time, thus placing in the agency's hands the power 'to paralyze and destroy a business, no matter how reputable, no matter how old, no matter how great the investment, no matter how meritorious the preparation'.[196] Extensive efforts were made to amend Copeland's bill to remove the two offending provisions. Senator Josiah Bailey, Democrat of North Carolina and an outspoken critic of the New Deal, had tried to remove the FDA's powers over advertising but failed. He was, however, successful in weakening the agency's multiple seizure authority. After the vote, 44 to 29, Copeland became completely dispirited and is reported as having remarked that, as far as he was concerned, the bill was dead.[197] However, his spirits apparently revived when the President ended his long silence and urged that a food and drug bill be passed. The result was that Copeland's bill, somewhat revised, passed the Senate on 28 May 1935.

The bill was to have less success in the House of Representatives. Its sponsors once again hoped that it would proceed through committee without the need to hold hearings on the measure but, once again, they were disappointed. Sam Rayburn, Democrat of Texas and Chairman of the House Committee on Interstate and Foreign Commerce, insisted that hearings be held and chose Representative Virgil Chapman, Democrat of Kentucky, to head the subcommittee before which testimony would be heard. Hearings began on 22 July and lasted three weeks. Most of what was presented had already been heard numerous times before the various Senate subcommittees, although there were a few surprises. The American Medical Association, traditionally vigorous supporters of any effort to hobble the patent medicine industry, regarded certain provisions of the Copeland bill with some misgiving, particularly its requirement that physicians' prescriptions meet the bill's labeling requirements. Equally annoying was the fact that the Homeopathic Pharmacopeia was recognized as a legal standard[198] and that drug manufacturers should be represented on the committee on health that the bill called for.[199]

One effect of the hearings was that it made of Chapman an energetic champion of the new food and drug bill, to the point where he was prepared to go on the radio and appear in newsreels in an effort to alert the public to the pressing need for a new law. Chapman had determined that the bill, including its controversial provisions regarding advertising, was unlikely to pass the House in its present form. He therefore decided that the bill should remain in committee until he had successfully 'educated' his colleagues in the House. In fact, it was not reported out of committee until May 1936. Over the course of the nine months that the bill remained locked in committee, Rexford Tugwell, who had been appointed head of the Resettlement Administration in 1935,[200] had made clear that he had little sympathy with the current measure, which he found far too weak. There is some evidence that he was prepared to publicly announce his displeasure with S. 5 and demand that Copeland's original bill be reintroduced until Walter Campbell threatened to resign should Tugwell undermine the new measure. The result was that Tugwell kept his reservations private.

In the absence of Congressional action to enact a new law, Campbell determined to reactivate the FDA's propaganda campaign and its 'Chamber of Horrors' display was again exhibited at conventions and professional meetings. At the same time a number of books were released by a new generation of muckrakers pointing out the dangers faced by the public from impurities and poisons in their food, drugs, and cosmetics. In 1934 M.C. Philips and Consumers' Research, which had remained as zealously dedicated to a new law as they had earlier been, published *Skin Deep: The Truth about Beauty Aids* and in the same year James Rorty issued *Our Master's Voice: Advertising*.[201] Rorty's essay was nothing less than a plea for socialism and looked forward to the day when the nation would be free of the incubus of competitive capitalism. In the following year Consumers' Research renewed their attacks in no less than three books: *Eat, Drink and Be Wary* by F.J. Schlink, *Counterfeit: Not Your Money but What It Buys*, by Arthur Kallet, and *Paying through the Teeth* by Bissell Palmer.[202] The parade of books purporting to document the evils perpetrated by the food, drug, and cosmetic industries and the need to put an end to the competitive forces that gave rise to these dangers continued into 1936.[203]

None of these books was as important in gaining support for the new bill as that written by the FDA's information officer, Ruth deForest Lamb, who published a 418-page work with the same title as the FDA's traveling exhibit, the *American Chamber of Horrors*.[204] The book was distributed throughout the country and purported to present documentary evidence of how the American public had been gulled by unscrupulous vendors into buying worthless nostrums, rotten foods, and dangerous cosmetics. Not only did Ms Lamb's book reproduce the examples that appeared in the FDA's exhibit but it also detailed many more of like nature. Among the outrages recounted were butter made in unspeakably filthy conditions, diet formulas that did not work, cosmetics which, when employed by people suffering certain medical conditions, could exacerbate those conditions, proprietary medicines that advertised themselves as effective treatments for certain illnesses but weren't or if taken in massive doses constituted a danger to health, and a host of packaged foods that simply were not what consumers thought they were. These included Kraft's Miracle Whip, 'masquerading as mayonnaise', Kraft's Old English Cheddar, 'made without chemical emulsifying agents', Vermont Maid Syrup, 'containing only 25 percent maple syrup', Del Monte and Libby canned fruits, which had varying qualities of ingredients, and the usual accusations of margarine posing as butter and glucose masquerading as sugar. The book detailed how Copeland's original bill had been progressively weakened in an attempt to gain sufficient support for passage through Congress and how desperately the nation needed a strong act to protect itself from similar unprincipled profiteers.

The train of muckraking books continued through 1937 and 1938. Indeed there appeared to be no limit to their number, all of which repeated the same charges. What is particularly striking is that all, for some reason, were well received by the public. One of the effects of these books was a demand that Congress investigate the food, drug, and cosmetic lobby to uncover who was behind the efforts to prevent passage of such a vital law and what tactics were employed. The fact was that by 1936 most manufacturers affected by the bill except for the proprietary medicine industry had reconciled themselves to its enactment. Their opposition was directed by the United Medicine Manufacturers of America and the Institute of Medicine Manufacturers, who, in late 1935, had merged their efforts to concentrate on three aspects of the bill, the elimination of the FDA's control over advertising, and both its multiple seizure provisions and its label disclosure requirements, which members of the Administration and numerous organizations wished to see strengthened. Time, however, was against the patent medicine industry. Between January 1935 and October 1936, 39 states had passed no fewer than 92 laws that dealt with the manufacture and sale of drugs[205] and it appeared that comprehensive legislation similar to the Copeland bill would be enacted in each of the states if a national measure were not soon passed.

One possible solution to the advertising problem which the proprietary manufacturers were prepared to accept was to place control over the advertising of foods, drugs, and cosmetics in the hands of the Federal Trade Commission, which already was entrusted with the regulation of certain instances of false advertising. The Federal Trade Commission (FTC) was another product of the Progressive Era,[206] established during the Wilson Administration to combat the various trusts that Theodore Roosevelt, Wilson's predecessor, claimed were dominating the nation's economy.[207] It was established in 1914 ostensibly to insure free and fair competition and originally hoped to accomplish these ends by economic planning. Wilson, it appears, envisaged the Commission as a critical instrument in regulating all of the nation's commercial enterprises and overseeing their conduct. Its earliest commissioners were prepared to act boldly against the many instances where its staff determined that companies were acting in restraint of trade. However, the Commission's grandiose plans were soon thwarted by the fact that the Supreme Court limited its authority[208] and Congress refused to appropriate the funds needed for a robust regulatory program. President Franklin Roosevelt attempted to breathe new life into the agency with passage of the National Industrial Recovery Act (NIRA), under which the FTC began to file complaints against firms that violated the NIRA's production codes. Despite the fact that in May 1935 the Supreme Court invalidated the NIRA, the FTC continued to regain some of its lost authority and its appropriations grew substantially under a Democratic Congress.

By 1934 a series of court decisions had finally shaped the agency's authority. It was empowered to define unfair methods of competition and draft regulations for the purpose of carrying out the various statutory prohibitions. Among its powers was jurisdiction over false advertising, an authority, according to the High Court in the *Raladam* case,[209] that was limited to taking legal action against false advertising only when the advertising affected the firm's competitors. Deceiving the public, the Court ruled, was not sufficient warrant. In light of this decision, it is no wonder that the proprietary medicine manufacturers made every effort to place control over deceptive advertising in the hands of the Federal Trade Commission rather than the FDA. Additionally, the FTC proceeded against deceptive claims through the use of cease and desist orders rather than relying on criminal prosecutions. Nor was the FTC averse to the proposal. With Roosevelt's acquiescence the agency had become a creature of Senator Kenneth D. McKellar, Democrat of Tennessee and chairman of the Senate appropriations subcommittee responsible for regulatory agencies. McKellar, together with Edward Hull Crump, who had been mayor of Memphis and was the political boss of Tennessee, treated the FTC as a private fiefdom. One of their first appointments was of Ewin L. Davis, a former congressman, who served as chairman of the agency from 1933 until his death in 1945.

Davis was one of those who testified at the 1935 House hearings and maintained that his agency alone had jurisdiction over false and misleading advertising and that such authority had never rested in the Food and Drug Administration nor in its predecessor agency, the Bureau of Chemistry. He went on to underscore the fact that in the overwhelming majority of cases in which false or misleading advertising is charged, even with respect to foods, drugs, and cosmetics, the central issue is commercial and not medical. 'It is not a question involving public health in the vast majority of cases', Davis argued:

> It is a question of filching the public out of some of their earnings by inducing them to buy something that, while not dangerous, is worthless or partially so. That is purely a commercial matter. So far as the protection of public health is concerned, the Food and Drug Association does not need jurisdiction over advertising, because it can stop it under even its present authority.[210]

Davis, who had served as a congressman from Tennessee from 1919 to 1932, had a number of friends in the House who were sympathetic to expanding the role of the FTC by giving the agency jurisdiction over the advertising of food, drugs, and cosmetics. The President appeared to a number of observers to have lost interest in the Copeland bill, especially since Copeland had effectively disassociated himself from most of the President's New Deal program by the summer of 1935. By the close of the session in 1936 the House and Senate versions had undergone so many changes since they were originally introduced that there now existed serious divergences in the two bills. To the dismay of those in favor of aggressive legislation in this area, the Senate version had undergone several changes that weakened the measure considerably. With respect to multiple seizures, the Senate measure permitted them only when a product was 'imminently dangerous to health'. The House bill, on the other hand, had added the words 'or in a material respect, false, misleading or fraudulent'. And, unlike the Senate version, the House measure authorized the Secretary of Agriculture to establish standards for multiple grades of foodstuffs. In one respect, the proprietary medicine interests did prevail in the House, which had placed in the hands of the FTC authority to regulate advertising. Walter Campbell was so disappointed with this provision that he wrote the Secretary of Agriculture, Henry Wallace, that 'every effort should be made to kill the measure'.[211]

Its weaknesses notwithstanding, Senator Copeland was hopeful that his bill would finally be passed into law, as was Sam Rayburn, the Chairman of the House Commerce Committee. Rayburn tried to bring the measure to the House floor but was thwarted by the Speaker, J.W. Byrns, who was reluctant to bring the measure forward out of sequence without a specific request from President Roosevelt. In June the President did indeed intercede and the bill was brought to the floor. House rules were suspended and the House quickly voted on the measure, which passed overwhelmingly. The differences in the Senate and House versions, however, required that they be reconsidered in conference. The sticking point, predictably, surrounded which agency should be accorded authority to deal with false or misleading advertising. The Senate conferees suggested that advertising that related to health should be regulated by the FDA while those touching on commercial matters or having to do with food and cosmetics would fall under the jurisdiction of the FTC. While the change was acceptable to the conference committee's House members, it was bitterly attacked in the House itself, especially by the Representatives from Tennessee. In the end they proved successful and the motion to enact the bill as amended by the conference committee was defeated by the lopsided vote of 190 to 70.

Once again Congress had failed to enact a new pure food and drug law that was regarded as adequate by the FDA, despite an administration that was amenable to legislation that placed broad discretionary powers in the hands of regulatory agencies and a Congress that, on the whole, was prepared to do the President's bidding. By 1937 it became apparent to the pure food and drug bureaucracy and their allies that the only effective opposition to an acceptable bill, one that included FDA authority over advertising, was centered on the proprietary medicine manufacturers, whose dogged resistance they would have to overcome. From this point forward almost all their efforts were directed at attacking the patent medicine industry, its worthless and harmful products, its dishonest advertising, and its unscrupulous efforts to block badly needed legislation. Pleased with the results of its earlier exhibit, the FDA prepared a new display, showing the most egregious examples of false or misleading advertising, among them: *Blakeley's Acid Iron Material* and *4-44*, both insuring a sound stomach; *Frog Pond*, 'a sure cure for Chill-Fever-Cold'; *Casey's Compound*, for sufferers from rheumatism, neuritis, and arthritis, *Dr Young's Rectal Dilators*, which strengthened the rectal muscles, assuring regular bowel movements; and, *Persenico,* to combat 'neurasthenic impotence, pre-senility, low vitality' and other ailments 'of sexual origin'.

Copeland, ever-optimistic, once again drafted a new bill, which was again, confusingly, designated S. 5 and introduced it in the Senate in January 1937. At the same time Representative Virgil Chapman introduced a companion bill, H.R. 300, in the House. The bills dealt with advertising differently. Both measures[212] placed control over advertising in the FDA but under the Copeland measure enforcement of the agency's findings were by injunction while the Chapman bill provided for civil and criminal penalties. A further difference concerned multiple seizures, permitted under the Chapman bill in instances where products were determined to be 'imminently dangerous to health', as opposed to the Copeland bill, which dropped the word 'imminently'. Other than these distinctions, the two measures were much alike and closely paralleled the Tugwell bill that had been introduced into Congress in 1933.

As had been the case with Copeland's earlier bills, this version of S. 5 had the backing of the American Drug Manufacturers Association and the Toilet Goods Association. However, several traditional supporters were less than enthusiastic. The American Medical Association was prepared to support the measure but found several of its provisions objectionable. The AMA was particularly unhappy with the bill's provision that allowed proprietary medicines to vary the strengths of its components from those that had been officially set, provided they conformed to a standard shown on the label.[213] Nor were the women's organizations, customarily the FDA's most devoted supporters and the most vocal lobbyists for a sweeping new law, especially pleased that the only weapon Copeland had allowed the FDA to deal with false or misleading advertising was the injunction. In addition, women's groups wanted a bill that authorized multiple seizures, even if the effect might be to force a manufacturer out of business.

That these groups had reservations regarding the new bill was not nearly as important an obstacle to passage as were the attempts by the Federal Trade Commission to assume control over the advertising of food, drugs, and cosmetics. Copeland was intent on getting the bill past the Senate as soon as possible and he reported it out of committee on 15 February 1937. However, Senator Bailey had once again been successful in amending the measure to weaken its most objectionable provisions. Multiple seizures of misbranded products were limited to those that were 'imminently dangerous to health', and Copeland's phrase 'or [are], in a material respect, false, grossly misleading or fraudulent' was excised. The bill's definition of misbranding was altered so that what had earlier been 'false or misleading' now read 'false or misleading in any material particular'.[214] All the organizations who had lobbied for a vigorous bill were appalled by these changes, as was the FDA, who immediately submitted a critique of the amended measure to the President. Most outraged were the many women's groups who had worked tirelessly for a law that would place the patent medicine industry at the mercy of a federal bureaucracy. As soon as these organizations had been apprised of the details of the bill they contacted Eleanor Roosevelt, the President's wife, who was as eager to enlarge federal authority in this area as were they. She in turn, it appears, complained to the President.[215] These objections did not go unheeded. On 23 February Roosevelt held a press conference in which he charged that S. 5 was weaker than the current law and that if it were to reach his desk in its current form he might possibly veto it. The following day Copeland requested that the Senate postpone a vote on the bill and invited new amendments. In Committee the bill was yet again subject to a series of changes and the labeling and misbranding clauses, which had caused so much trouble, were rewritten to restore wide discretionary authority to the FDA.[216] In this form it passed the Senate on 9 March and was sent to the House for consideration.

Forces favorable to the Federal Trade Commission were far more powerful in the House than in the Senate. In addition, a number of Representatives opposed enacting a bill that would carry the name of a politician who was now regarded as unfriendly to the Administration. Copeland and Roosevelt had been drifting apart for several months, to the point where, by March of 1937, they had become political enemies. Copeland had refused to embrace Roosevelt's far-reaching legislative program and, despite his support for a strong food and drug law, had misgivings about restructuring the American economy by placing such extensive authority in the hands of the federal bureaucracy. Copeland had refused to attend the Democratic National Convention in Philadelphia in June 1936 and chose the occasion of the 150th Anniversary of Tammany Hall, held on 4 July, to attack the Administration.

Rather than participate in the 1936 elections, Copeland sailed for the Holy Land while his wife, whom he left behind, spoke glowingly of Roosevelt's presidential opponent, Alf Landon. Finally, Copeland was one of several Democratic members of the Senate who had the backbone to object to Roosevelt's attempt to subvert the Constitution by packing the Supreme Court and thus won the President's enduring enmity.[217] Roosevelt's flunkeys in the House were concerned that an act as significant as was the one introduced by Copeland would carry his name, thus honoring one of Roosevelt's opponents, 'bestowing kudos on a White House foe', as one of them put it.[218] There were even rumors that a completely new bill, with provisions similar to those in the Copeland bill, would be put forward in the House simply to circumvent this result.

In the event, a new bill was in fact introduced in the House on 23 March 1937 by Clarence Lea, Democrat from California and the new Chairman of the House Committee on Interstate and Foreign Commerce.[219] Lea was somewhat hostile to the FDA's ambition to regulate the advertising of food, drugs, and cosmetics, possibly a legacy of the agency's attempts to declare as adulterated certain shipments of dried fruit from a firm in Lea's constituency. His bill was designed to place control over all advertising in the Federal Trade Commission, thus depriving the FDA of any authority whatever in this area. It was based on a measure, S. 1077, earlier introduced in the Senate by Burton K. Wheeler of Montana, whose purpose was to extend the regulatory powers of the FTC, without specific reference to the products over which the FDA had jurisdiction. Lea made every effort to insure passage of his bill and to prevent Copeland's measure, whose advertising provisions conflicted with those of the Lea bill, from coming before the House. As Chairman of the Commerce Committee he took over chairmanship of the subcommittee that held hearings on his bill, rather than allow Virgil Chapman to act as chairman. He than stacked the subcommittee with Representatives sympathetic to the FTC. In addition, he saw to it that Copeland's bill would not reach the floor of the House until the House had acted on his own measure.

S. 1077 had passed the Senate on 29 March 1937 and in May Lea's subcommittee began closed-door hearings on both the Wheeler-Lea and Copeland-Chapman bills. It early became clear that the subcommittee supported authorizing the FTC, rather than the FDA, to regulate the advertising of food, drugs, and cosmetics. However, there was some disagreement over the harshness of the penalties for violation of the bill's provisions, some arguing for severe criminal sanctions as opposed to simple cease and desist orders. It was predictable that Chapman would favor the more extreme option, while Lea supported a milder approach. In the end the subcommittee authorized the FTC to prohibit false and misleading advertising through the use of cease and desist orders. Under certain circumstances they were empowered to bring suit in any District Court to restrain the advertisement's dissemination or, in those instances where advertisers could be proved guilty of fraud or who advertised commodities that were inherently dangerous, to institute criminal proceedings.[220] In August 1937 the Wheeler-Lea bill was reported to the House. The Copeland-Chapman forces had won a small victory by having their bill remain in committee until the following year, thus preventing a weakened draft of the bill from going to the House in 1937. Chapman was hopeful that if the bill remained in committee for another year he could again strengthen it before it was reported out. This delay proved decisive although no one could have predicted the events that occurred in September and October of 1937.

In the mid-1930s German and French bacteriologists had discovered the truly dramatic effects of sulfanilamide, which was an extremely powerful antibacterial. The drug soon became enormously popular and by 1937 was routinely used to combat streptococcal infections, the majority of which occurred in children. It was marketed in powder and tablet form but these proved difficult to administer to the very young. As a result, in 1937 the S.E. Massengill Company of Bristol, Tennessee, introduced the medication in liquid form in response to growing demand, especially from the firm's Southern customers.[221] The company, which had been founded in 1897, was directed by Dr Samuel Evans. Massengill had an excellent reputation for producing only the highest quality pharmaceuticals. The firm's chief chemist was Harold Cole Watkins, who, in attempting to prepare a liquid form of sulfanilamide, had discovered that the drug would dissolve in diethylene glycol. When the mixture was tested for taste, appearance, and fragrance, it was found to be acceptable. Amazingly, Watkins did not bother to test for toxicity. Over 600 cases, some 240 gallons, of the elixir were compounded and shipped throughout the country from the company's plant in Bristol and from its branch plant in Kansas City in early September.

On 11 October American Medical Association officials in Chicago were informed that six deaths had occurred in Tulsa, Oklahoma, following the administration of Elixir Sulfanilamide-Massengill.[222] The AMA's Council on Pharmacy and Chemistry had not received a sample of the product for testing nor had it been informed by Massengill of its composition. The organization requested a sample of the medicine from Tulsa and proceeded to contact Massengill for more information on the product. It then began a series of tests. Meanwhile the number of deaths mounted and a number of fatalities were reported from East St Louis, Illinois. At the same time, the national press and radio were informed and made every effort to alert the public to the danger of the medicine. When the Company learned of the poisonous effects of the medication, it immediately telegraphed more than 1000 salesmen, druggists, and doctors. Rather than admit culpability for the deaths that had occurred, however, the telegrams simply requested that any preparations of Elixir Sulfanilamide be returned to the Massengill offices immediately.

It was only at this point, on 14 October, that the FDA heard about the incident, from a physician in New York who was associated with another pharmaceutical company. As a result, FDA inspectors were dispatched from Kansas City to Tulsa to investigate. On 16 October, five days after the AMA had been notified of the deaths and their probable cause, an FDA investigator telegraphed the agency from Tulsa that nine persons had died after having taken the preparation. This was the first date on which official notice of the problem occurred. Having been informed of the Company's attempts to recall all the Elixir Sulfanilamide still outstanding, the FDA urged that Massengill send a follow-up telegram warning of the immediate dangers that might follow from ingesting the drug and insisted that the telegram contain the caution 'Product may be dangerous to life'. The fact was that diethylene glycol, a chemical customarily employed as an anti-freeze, was a deadly poison and known to be such by the FDA.[223] However no pre-sale examination of the drug's safety was made by the Company nor was it customary for the FDA to conduct such tests. It is true that once informed of its toxicity FDA, along with state and local officials made every effort to track down the shipments and were eventually successful, but not before 107 people, many of them children, had died as a result of ingesting the drug. Since passage of the 1906 Act, the Massengill Company had had an excellent record with the FDA. Only three cases had been brought against the company, all three during the 1930s. The first involved Fluidextract of Colchicum, which was found to be slightly over strength when compared with the standard shown in the National Formulary. The second, Tincture of Aconite, was found to be somewhat under strength. Finally, in reference to a shipment of Elixir Terpin Hydrate and Codeine, it was held that there existed a disparity in the quantities of both ingredients between what was stated on its label and its actual contents. These violations resulted in two small fines, $250.00 and $150.00.

Estimates that had all of the 240 gallons of Elixir Sulfanilamide that had been manufactured been consumed, it would have resulted in some 4000 deaths and that the nation was thus indebted to the FDA for having saved almost 3900 lives is absurd. Much has been made of the fact that it was only because of a minor technicality that the FDA was able to involve itself in the incident. Elixir Sulfanilamide was, technically, mislabeled. Inasmuch as it contained no alcohol, it could not properly be called an 'elixir'. Had it been labeled a 'solution' instead, it is argued, the agency could have done nothing to track down and confiscate what medication remained in the hands of the public. This is simply not true. The FDA, had it so chosen, could have used the same rationale to enter the case as it later employed to bring criminal charges against the owner of the Massengill Company, a rationale more than adequate to support its attempts to ferret out what medication remained unaccounted for. Indeed, the Company strongly supported a total recall of all the remaining Elixir and both state and local authorities actively participated in the search for the portion unaccounted for.[224] But even if the FDA had chosen not to participate in the search and seizure, to imply that the public would have been helpless while this lethal material continued to circulate and that no authority or organization would have attempted to locate and confiscate the outstanding Elixir is preposterous. Nor was it the case that, in the absence of an FDA prosecution, the public would have been helpless to punish the offenders. At common law the sale of a medication was regarded as a contract that, in the case of medicines and foods, contained an implied warranty of quality. Should that warranty not be met, the seller could be judged to have engaged in fraud and was subject to an action of tort.[225]

In the end, the Massengill Company is reputed to have paid out over half a million dollars in wrongful death suits. In addition, the FDA brought criminal charges against S.E. Massengill. The rationale for FDA action was that Elixir Sulfanilamide was adulterated. It was the agency's contention that the drug 'fell below the professed standard under which it was sold' inasmuch as the medication professed to offer the same therapeutic results as did sulfanilamide whereas 'its principal action was that of an acute poison'.[226] In September 1938 Dr Massengill's attorneys filed a demurrer but his plea was overruled. Inasmuch as the FDA did not seek imprisonment,[227] Massengill pled guilty to most of the charges and he was fined $150.00 on each of 164 counts, a total of $26 100.00, the largest fine ever assessed under the Pure Food and Drugs Act. Watkins, the chemist whose criminal incompetence was directly responsible for having determined the ingredients of the poisoned medication, committed suicide before Dr Massengill's trial began.

The Food and Drug Administration, as expected, capitalized on the event to link the disaster to the absence of a new food and drug bill, and this view soon became the orthodox one, constantly repeated in the press. Walter Campbell, in the very first public statement the agency made, suggested that it was catastrophes of this nature that pointed to the need for passage of a reinvigorated version of the Copeland bill and for the future licensing of all drug manufacturers. That the FDA had assumed jurisdiction over the events connected with Elixir Sulfanilamide under the provisions of the 1906 Act does not seem to have occurred to most supporters of a new measure nor did it strike anyone as odd that, were the FDA's comments taken at face value, even the Copeland bill, then stalled in Congress, would have proved inadequate in dealing with the crisis. Indeed, the FDA, with a field force of 239 inspectors and chemists, did not even learn about the incident until three days after the AMA was made aware of the problem and more than five weeks after Massengill had made its first shipments to its customers, and then only by virtue of the fact that a physician associated with another drug manufacturer telephoned the FDA offices.

The demand for passage of the Copeland bill soon became enormous. The AMA, women's groups, and the American Pharmaceutical Association were joined by the national press in calling for action and the FDA, again in violation of the Deficiency Appropriations Act, publicized the disaster and its own heroic efforts in its literature and its bulletins. The FDA was even able to get two motion pictures about the events surrounding Elixir Sulfanilamide produced in which the agency's inspectors were depicted as heroes. In both *Permit to Kill* and *G-Men of Science* Walter Campbell appeared and, as had J. Edgar Hoover in any number of G-man movies, spoke of the need for an ever-vigilant food and drug police – the very last thing the FDA had proved itself to be – and for strict new legislation.[228] Despite the tragic deaths of so many people, the agency viewed the incident as somewhat of a victory and were particularly pleased, the word used by one historian is 'jubilant', that the offending medicine had been produced in the Tennessee constituency of Representative Carroll Reece, who was a fierce opponent of the Copeland bill.[229] All this favorable publicity for the Copeland measure was not lost on Congress. On 16 November Copeland brought up the Massengill incident in the Senate and was followed the next day by Virgil Chapman in the House.

Both legislators introduced resolutions in their respective chambers calling on the Department of Agriculture to report on the tragedy. The resolutions were passed unanimously and a 34-page summary of the events was duly presented to Congress on 20 November.[230] It immediately became obvious that the Copeland bill in its most recent form would have had no effect on the events leading up to the tragedy and as a result on 1 December 1937 Copeland introduced a supplementary bill, S. 3073, not meant to replace S. 5 but to be acted on independently.[231] The bill had reference to all new drugs and provided that manufacturers were required to furnish the Secretary of Agriculture with records of all the tests regarding the drug's safety that had been conducted, a complete list of the drug's ingredients, a description of how the drug was to be manufactured, processed, and packaged, and specimens of all projected labels the drug would carry. In addition, if requested, the manufacturer would be obligated to supply samples of the drug to the FDA. The Secretary would then either certify the drug as safe for sale to the public or, if no certificate were issued, provide the reasons detailing why it was refused. A similar bill, H.R. 9341, was introduced in the House by Virgil Chapman on 4 February.[232] The bills resembled each other but apparently the Chapman version was regarded as clearer and, as a result, was eventually incorporated into S. 5.

S. 3073 was brought to the Senate floor in May 1938 and, despite some grumbling on the part of a handful of senators, was passed unanimously.

Things went a little less smoothly in the House, however, inasmuch as Chapman's equivalent, H.R. 9341, was caught up in the debate over passage of the Wheeler-Lea bill, designated S. 1077. While a majority of the Commerce Committee favored placing regulation of all advertising in the hands of the FTC, a minority continued to argue that the Food and Drug Administration was far better equipped to deal with the advertising of these products and that cease and desist orders were simply not sufficient deterrents to false claims. Amendments to strike those sections of S. 1077 that had reference to food, drugs, and cosmetics, and to increase the civil penalties for first offenses to $5000.00 were put forward but both failed. On 12 January 1938 the Wheeler-Lea bill passed the House by a large majority. The FDA bureaucracy was appalled that the House had passed the bill and made every effort to prevent its enactment into law. J.J. Durrett, the chief of the agency's drug division, attempted to use a personal connection with James Roosevelt, the President's son, in the hope of getting the President to veto the bill and Henry Wallace, the Secretary of Agriculture, urged Roosevelt not to sign it. Behind the FDA were a large number of organizations, led by women's and consumer groups, who joined in the chorus calling for the President's veto. On 14 March S. 1077 reached the Senate floor. Again, attempts were made to increase the civil penalties for fraudulent advertising but they failed. The same day the bill was passed by the Senate and it was signed into law on 21 March.

The Copeland-Chapman bill had still to pass the House but Clarence Lea, as Chairman of the Commerce Committee, continued to temporize and the measure did not go forward until mid-April. Not only were its supporters fearful that it might not pass in that session of Congress, thus requiring that the process begin anew yet again in 1939, but the manufacturers of proprietary medicines also sought federal legislation in the area, thus forestalling enactment of a mass of conflicting state laws. Indeed, three states had already passed such laws and bills were pending in 12 other states.[233] Following the Elixir Sulfanilamide disaster the nation's press had become slavish supporters of a strong food and drug bill and began reporting every incident involving a food, cosmetic, or proprietary medication that resulted in illness or death. In March a Kentucky woman was rendered blind by a certain eyelash dye and in the same month six women in Florida died after having been injected with a 'cancer cure' sold in drugstores under the name *Ensol*.[234] Reports of this sort could not help but force Lea to bring Copeland's bill forward and on 14 April it was reported out of committee.

The new bill contained most of the stronger provisions that had at one point or another been removed in the four years since Copeland originally introduced the measure, excepting FDA control over advertising. There was one further provision that the bill's supporters would have preferred to see removed. Section 701 permitted appeals to the federal district courts to enjoin the Secretary of Agriculture from enforcing any new regulation that had been promulgated. The courts were given the authority to hear evidence bearing on the regulation and to determine its validity.

Both sides regarded this provision as of vital importance. Supporters of the Copeland bill viewed it as the bill's Achilles' heel, which could undo the work of the FDA by tying up the agency's resources in attempting to defend its decisions. On the other hand, to those who were affected by the Secretary's regulations on the identity, quality, and labeling of their products, the provision was essential, especially in light of other sections of the bill. The measure defined as adulterated any food containing poisonous ingredients, subject, however, to the determination of the Secretary of Agriculture as to what levels would be tolerated when a poison could not be entirely eliminated. This proviso allowed the use of certain poisonous insecticides in non-lethal doses. What alarmed many fresh fruit and vegetable producers was that the Agriculture Department would set these tolerances at levels below what was regarded as necessary to growing their produce. The provision to which the Copeland bill's supporters so strenuously objected would have required that the Secretary of Agriculture prove not only that the amount of insecticide that had been employed was above tolerance levels but that the levels used were in fact dangerous to health.

Apparently the fruit and vegetable growers had good reason to fear the arbitrary decisions of the Department. In 1933, armed with the power to promulgate regulations respecting tolerance levels, Assistant Secretary Tugwell reduced the tolerance level for lead arsenic from 0.02 to 0.014 grains. After loud protests from apple growers the Secretary of Agriculture, Henry Wallace, was forced to re-establish the old level.[235] But this lesson of just how arbitrary the Department could be was not lost on producers, who insisted that judicial review of Department of Agriculture regulations be written into the 1938 law. Many supporters of a bill were categorical in their refusal to accept the provision. Secretary Wallace went so far as to announce that 'if section 701(f) [the judicial provision] remains in the bill its effect will be to hamstring its administration so as to amount to a practical nullification of the substantial provisions of the bill. . . . It is the department's considered judgment it would be better to continue the old law in effect than to enact S. 5 with this provision.'[236] Despite the fierceness with which proponents of the Copeland bill fought judicial review, however, the House passed the measure with the section intact and at that point the Senate requested a conference on the bill.

The food growers were not alone in preferring the House version of the Copeland-Chapman bill. The Proprietary Association supported it as well, especially since the House version of S. 5 allowed sales of new drugs to proceed unless the manufacturer's application for certification to the Secretary of Agriculture was rejected within 60 days. On the other side were the

Department of Agriculture bureaucracy, consumer groups, and women's organizations led by the National League of Women Voters. Its president, Marguerite Wells, wrote President Roosevelt that she had been assured by Mrs Roosevelt, who had taken personal responsibility for interceding with the President regarding the bill, that he would bring pressure to bear to remove the House judicial provisions before the final bill was enacted by Congress. The entreaties of his wife and those of the Secretary of Agriculture appear to have been sufficient to induce Roosevelt to act. He is reputed to have informed members of the House Commerce Committee that he would veto the bill if the offending provisions remained part of the measure. The result was that the conference committee compromised on the section of the bill relating to judicial review. Aggrieved parties were permitted to lodge an appeal with any one of the ten federal circuit courts of appeal, rather than in any of the 85 federal district courts. Additionally, the revised bill limited the circumstances under which new evidence could be introduced or when rehearings could be ordered. Several other minor revisions were made in the bill regarding labeling and multiple seizures which had the effect of strengthening the authority of the FDA, but no change was as significant as was that relating to judicial review of the regulations promulgated by the Secretary of Agriculture.

The conference report was issued on 11 June and was quickly ratified by both the House and Senate. The bill was signed in law by President Roosevelt on 25 June. In sum, the act prohibited the introduction into interstate commerce of 'any food, drug, device, or cosmetic, that is adulterated or misbranded'.[237] The overwhelming portion of the bill then proceeded to deal with what constituted a misbranded or adulterated product, with a chapter of the Act devoted to each category. For the first time the government extended its regulatory control to cosmetics and therapeutic devices and required that new drugs be shown to be safe before they could be marketed. It empowered the Secretary of Agriculture to fix tolerance levels for poisonous substances whose use was unavoidable. In addition it authorized factory inspections and authorized the Secretary of Agriculture to set standards of identity, quality, and fill-of-container for foods. It permitted multiple seizures in misbranding cases where the Secretary, 'without hearings by him or any other officer or employee of the Department', determined that an article was 'dangerous to health' or where the label was 'fraudulent or, in a material respect misleading'. Finally, to the existing penalties of seizure and prosecution, the Act added the use of court injunctions.

The FDA's expansion in regulatory authority was matched by a substantial increase in its budget in fiscal year 1940[238] and there is every reason to believe that this would have continued had it not been for World War II and the need to divert expenditures to the war effort. As soon as the war ended, however, appropriations once again returned to pre-war levels and began to again increase. Table 2.2 shows appropriations for fiscal years 1930 and 1935 to 1946.

Table 2.2   FDA Appropriations, Fiscal Years 1930 and 1935–1946

Fiscal Year[1]	Appropriations
	$
1930	1 849 000
1935	1 167 000
1936	1 540 879
1937	1 600 000
1938	1 750 000
1939	1 748 000
1940	2 741 138
1941	2 544 156[2]
1942	2 415 600
1943	2 484 295
1944	2 520 000
1945	3 278 000
1946	2 858 000

Notes:
[1]   The government fiscal year until 1976 ran from 1 July to 30 June.
[2]   The decrease in appropriations between 1940 and 1941 reflected the transfer of the FDA from the Department of Agriculture to the Federal Security Agency. Upon being transferred, the FDA lost responsibility for the administration of the Insecticide Act of 1910 and the Naval Stores Act.

Source: James Robert Dean, Jr, 'FDA At War: Securing the Food That Secured Victory', in *Food and Drug Law Journal*, 53 (1998): 458.

Despite the fact that the Act broadened the powers of the federal government far beyond its previous limits the FDA bureaucracy was disappointed that its regulatory decisions would be subject to appeal to the courts. Equally frustrating was the fact that the agency had been denied control over the advertising of the products that it otherwise regulated. The FDA continued to argue that the public would be better protected if an agency composed of experts in the area to be regulated were empowered to determine whether advertisements were false or misleading and to deny it this authority was to seriously compromise its status as the guardian of the nation's foods and drugs. If, however, one were to put these 'weaknesses' aside, the Food and Drug Administration was pleased that the Act had granted the agency a truly unprecedented and sweeping control over drugs. All drug labels had to carry a vast amount of information; they were required to show all ingredients and the quantity of each, together with directions for the use of the product and warnings regarding its dangers. Drugs that the agency determined dangerous to health if taken in the dosages recommended on the label were deemed mislabeled. Of far greatest significance was the Act's treatment of new drugs. As one analyst of the Act notes:

> There had never before been a distinction between new and old drugs, and never before had a producer needed to get government permission to start marketing a drug. In one sense, he still did not. He needed to file an application, but the government did not have to respond. Silence by the government left the producer free to act. Nevertheless, the requirement of filing a new drug application represents a chipping away at the ideal of competition. In some cases *not* involving fraud or misrepresentation, the government – not the market – would decide what would be sold.[239]

The 1938 Act had far more extensive implications for the market in drugs than what one might have at first supposed. As Peter Temin points out, despite the fact that the Act restricted the number of drugs that manufacturers were permitted to offer for sale to the consumer and required that their labels provide information on their contents and use, it appeared to leave the ultimate choice of which drug to use to the consumer. Certainly this was the intention of Congress and the Food and Drug Administration claimed that it shared this goal. The purpose of the new Act, Walter Campbell declared, was to improve and facilitate self-medication, not to limit it. As early as December 1933, at a Senate Commerce Committee hearing on Copeland's proposed new food and drug law, Campbell, in response to a question as to whether the FDA sought to curtail self-medication, testified:

> This bill does not contemplate its [self-medication] prevention at all. If it did a single short section in the measure could have been drawn up to that effect. But what is desired by the particular paragraph [requiring a listing of ingredients and their quantities] and by others which impose restrictions on statements made about the remedial properties of drugs is to make self-medication safe. There will always be self-medication to some extent. As I have said, from our law enforcement standpoint we do not object to it, but it should be intelligent; it should not be based on a faith created by a supposition, usually an erroneous supposition.[240]

The same sentiment appears in the House Report that accompanied House passage of S. 5 in 1938, where it was noted that 'the bill is not intended to restrict in any way the availability of drugs for self-medication. On the contrary, it is intended to make self-medication safer and more effective.'[241]

However, Congress and the public appear not to have appreciated the fact that if it were possible to limit self-medication, the FDA would make every effort to do just that. As Temin reports, despite the agency's assurances, within six months of passage of the 1938 Act the FDA moved to place strict limits on self-medication and over the next few years devoted an increasing proportion of their resources to enforcing these limits.[242] Temin outlines how the agency was able to accomplish this. Among the duties imposed by the law on drug manufacturers was that each drug demonstrate that it was 'safe for use under the conditions prescribed, recommended or suggested in the proposed labeling thereof'. The effect of this requirement was to impose on manufacturers the duty of labeling their products with a wealth of detailed information, including the medication's contraindications, all of which would have to meet the FDA's scrutiny once the product was offered to the public. Manufacturers were thus placed in an almost impossible position, especially since the cost of having to recall a medication because the FDA did not approve the label would be prohibitive. As James F. Hoge of the Proprietary Association testified in requesting that the agency set definitive labeling requirements: 'Many of these products sell 8, 10, 20 million packages and more a year. They have to be bought months in advance, and go into production months in advance. Millions of dollars are involved not only in discarding stocks of goods on hand, mind you, but in the purchase of these tens of millions of new labels.'[243] The problem was further compounded in the case of manufacturers of drugs whose physiological effects were complex. One manufacturer of drugs whose products were in the main marketed to physicians but whose concerns were shared by many manufacturers of over-the-counter medicines, complained:

> Under the proposed regulation the labeling must include a full and complete description of the conditions, with their symptoms, for which the preparation is indicated, and a statement of the treatment thereof in such detail that every consumer may determine the proper course of self-medication. In effect, a correspondence course in medicine is to be afforded to laymen.[244]

Together with these onerous labeling requirements, the Food, Drug, and Cosmetic Act had authorized the FDA to promulgate regulations stipulating what conditions had to be met to exempt a drug's label from having to carry all required information. These regulations were issued in December 1938 and provided that 'if the label of such drug or device bears the statement "*Caution: To be used only by or on the prescription of a [Physician, Dentist, or Veterinarian]*" ' and if the instructions for its use 'appear only in such medical terms as are *not* [my italics] likely to be understood by the ordinary individual' then the drug or device was exempt from the law's labeling provisions.[245] If a drug did not meet these conditions, then the manufacturer was required to comply with all aspects of the labeling requirement, under penalty of being charged with misbranding. These provisions did nothing less than allow the drug manufacturers to create a category of drugs that could be sold only by prescription through the simple expedient of attaching a label that read '*Caution: To be used only by or on the prescription of, etc.*'. Temin further notes that to ensure that drugs that carried the 'Caution – Prescription only' designation would be sold *only* by prescription the FDA ordered that they be shipped from the manufacturer for that exclusive purpose and that the instructions attached to the drug be unintelligible to laymen. With respect to new drugs, the FDA, which now was in a position to dictate what they regarded as an acceptable label, that is, one meeting the requirements of the law, could order manufacturers to designate the medication 'Prescription only'.[246]

Henceforth almost all new drugs would be available to consumers only through the mediation of a physician.[247] The FDA itself was fully aware of this transformation. In the agency's *Annual Report* for 1939, the first following full operation of the new law, the FDA admitted that it had reached 'an administrative conclusion of some moment'. In attempting to comply with the law's requirement that all drugs be adequately labeled, the agency admitted that there was no way to label certain drugs such that they did not constitute a danger to health except to allow their use only by prescription. 'Many drugs of great value to the physician are dangerous in the hands of those unskilled in the use of drugs. The statute obviously was not intended to deprive the medical profession of potent but valuable medicaments'.[248] The category of drugs judged dangerous to health except by prescription grew at an enormous rate. Indeed, the 20 years following passage of the 1938 Act witnessed a therapeutic revolution that saw the emergence of a host of new and efficacious drugs.[249] Needless to say, these were available to the consumer only via prescription. Immediately after the Food, Drug, and Cosmetics Act was passed, the industry journal *Proprietary Drugs* cautioned that the law was 'based upon an entirely new conception of regulatory control' and provided the federal government with 'absolute dictatorial power' over the industry.[250] Events were to prove them correct.

No sooner had the 1938 Act been signed into law than the FDA ruled that sulfanilamide, in whatever form, could not be sold without a prescription. Using the Elixir Sulfanilamide incident as the excuse, the FDA ruled that the drug was clearly far too dangerous to permit its uncontrolled use by laymen.[251] Several days later it made similar rulings regarding aminopyrine and cinchophen. After having established its 'prescription only' requirements in December, the FDA had determined that its regulations were still loose enough to permit some over-the-counter sales.[252] Indeed, it soon became aware that announcing a drug that was ostensibly available only through the prescription of a physician was a sure method of encouraging its general sale. As a result, in February 1939 Commissioner Campbell circulated another letter to drug manufacturers urging a more conspicuous and stronger warning. In the fall of 1940 the agency hit upon the idea of instructing firms selling prescription-only drugs to remove from their labels any information whatever that might guide lay users. Instructions regarding a drug's use were limited to leaflets targeted at physicians only. Far from making all medications safer for the public, the FDA had now managed to make some as unsafe as was possible. Instructions for the use of prescription medications that passed from one user, who had perhaps obtained the medicine through a physician, to another were henceforth limited to what the first user could recall respecting the drug's purpose. And drugs that remained in patients' medicine chests, unused for months or perhaps years, would now be employed at the direction of the original user's memory alone.

While its primary struggle was against a free market in drugs, the FDA had not totally abandoned its responsibility to regulate the nation's food supply. Rather than bring legal action against companies for adulteration, however, the agency chose to concentrate on the misbranding sections of the 1938 Act by setting food standards to which foods were required to comply. The authority granted it by the Act was virtually unlimited in this respect.[253] Armed with its new powers, the FDA, in the 1940s, began defining these standards in such a way as to require food manufacturers to add discrete nutrients to their products. The American Medical Association had long advocated a program of this kind in the interests of public health and in 1942 the FDA initiated this policy with respect to flour. Following the war, enrichment levels were introduced for a variety of staples, among them bread, dairy products, macaroni and noodles, and margarine. The agency, however, was not prepared to allow any private determination of what nutrients might be added. The food standards that were set specified each food's exact ingredients, by chemical name, with which each product carrying that specific designation had to comply. No deviation was permitted. A considerable proportion of the resources of the agency was devoted to the task of setting food standards, to the point where by the 1960s it was estimated that roughly half the food sold in the United States was subject to such standards.[254] This situation was somewhat eased in 1951 when the Supreme Court determined that, in certain instances, the FDA requirements were too strict. In 1949 the FDA seized 62 cases of Delicious Brand Imitation Jam on the grounds that it did not meet the prescribed standards set by the agency. It was conceded that the food was perfectly wholesome and did not differ from standardized jam in taste and appearance. Its only differences appeared to have been that its ingredients were not the same as the FDA standard for jam and that it sold for substantially less than jam. The defendant company chose to fight the seizure and in a seven to two decision won its case.[255] The effect of this decision was that, for the next 20 years, the FDA permitted deviations from a standardized food, but only if the product was clearly marked as an imitation.

There appears to have been no limit to the FDA's meddling. In 1962 it set regulations limiting the number of vitamins that could be added to any food, their levels, and the foods to which they could be added.[256] So detailed did the regulatory control over foodstuffs become that the agency was forced to respond to pressures to loosen its controls. In December 1969, the White

House Conference on Food, Nutrition, and Health, called by President Richard Nixon, recommended that all restrictions on fortifying new foods with vitamin additives be removed. The FDA had no alternative but to comply. In 1972 there was a fundamental shift in agency policy on food standards in light of the substantial resources that were being devoted to enforcing them. The FDA eased all existing food standards so that foods could contain any 'safe and suitable' functional ingredient, provided that the food's label fully disclosed its contents. And it further decided that it would not issue food standards in the future where appropriate labeling would be sufficient to protect consumers.

The agency's regulatory supervision of the purity and safety of foodstuffs did not interfere with what it had begun to regard as its primary area of interest. By the time of America's entry into World War II, the FDA viewed the regulation of the nation's drug supply as its most important task. There were several reasons for this. First, the safety and purity of foods sold in the United States were, for the most part, fairly high. Certainly by the end of World War II economic adulteration, that is, adulteration to conceal an inferior product, such as watering milk, had practically disappeared. Early attempts by the FDA to prosecute food manufacturers for selling adulterated products by using functional additives such as preservatives, thickeners, or stabilizers, or for artificially coloring or flavoring their food, while sustained by the courts,[257] were fortunately abandoned. Had this policy continued, it is doubtful whether most modern packaged foods would have met FDA requirements. By the close of the war, the FDA's intrusions into the market for food tended to be limited to insuring that the foods sold met the detailed standards set by the agency. Possibly the most important reason why the FDA decided to emphasize the regulation of drugs was their increasing impact on the health and well-being of Americans. The chemotherapeutic revolution that marked the 1940s and 1950s was without precedent in the history of medicine. One historian notes: 'So vast was it in scope, so significant in repercussions, this revolution ranks as one of the major events in medical history'.[258]

The far-reaching change in medical therapeutics was adumbrated in the preceding 15 years by the development of commercially available insulin. Discovered by Frederick Banting and Charles Best in 1922, insulin began to be produced commercially by the Eli Lilly Company by the end of 1923. This form of insulin was short-acting and was superseded by a longer acting insulin which was developed in 1936. Until 1941 insulin was manufactured under license from the University of Toronto, which owned the patent to the drug. Because exact dosages were essential in the treatment of diabetes, the University set standards for the product and established a testing laboratory whose function it was to insure that all insulin sold to the public was of uniform strength and quality. When the University's patent expired on 23 December 1941 a committee comprising the University's Insulin Committee, the American Medical Association, and the governing board of the United States Pharmacopeia recommended that responsibility for the quality of future production be lodged in the Food and Drug Administration. As a result, Congress enacted an amendment to the 1938 Act[259] expanding the authority of the FDA to include the batch-certifying of all insulin manufactured in the country. The amendment authorized the FDA to test each batch of insulin for compliance with identity standards and for strength, quality, and purity. Temin reports that the insulin manufacturers collaborated in drafting the FDA regulations and that there appears to be no record of opposition to the FDA assuming this new authority.[260]

In 1942 the War Production Board requested that the Food and Drug Administration assay batches of penicillin, which was then being produced almost exclusively for use by the armed forces. At the close of the war, when penicillin once became available for civilian use, the 1938 Act was again amended to provide for the batch-testing of all penicillin products manufactured in the United States. This same section was later amended three more times. In 1947 batch-certification requirements were extended to include streptomycin and two years later, to apply to bacitracin, chloramphenicol, aureomycin, and their derivatives. Finally, in 1962, Congress amended the section to cover the batch certification of all antibiotics intended for use in man.[261]

The increasing importance of drugs was reflected in an organizational change which the FDA underwent in 1940. In June of that year the FDA was taken out of the Department of Agriculture and moved into the Federal Security Agency, created in 1939 to consolidate the public health and welfare functions of the federal government. Its transfer put an end to the agency's long-standing conflicts with other divisions within the Department of Agriculture and removed the FDA's primary association with the nation's food supply. Additionally, the Department of Agriculture had increasingly become associated with the welfare of farmers, which conflicted with the FDA's mandate as a consumer protection agency. Henceforth the agency's principal function, in the minds of most Americans, was to guard the nation's drug supply and only secondarily was it associated with the safety and purity of foods.

The FDA's campaign against self-medication continued unabated throughout the 1940s. To plug the leak through which prescription medicines were being sold directly to the public, the FDA undertook to prosecute pharmacists for violating the Act. Not only were druggists charged with selling restricted items without a prescription but also for the unauthorized refilling of prescriptions. The agency was reluctant to devote its resources to taking legal action against pharmacists during the war but once hostilities ended the FDA's efforts accelerated, especially in 1949 and 1950. There was one prosecution in 1943, two in 1945, 12 in 1946, three in 1947, six in 1948, 22 in 1949, and 71 in 1950.[262] Temin has noted that in these prosecutions two classes of drugs continually reappear, sulfa drugs (chiefly sulfathiazole)[263] and barbiturates (Nembutal and Seconal), two drugs whose dangers, according to the FDA, are the mirror image of each other. The FDA claimed that the reason why sulfa drugs were too dangerous for over-the-counter use was that consumers would likely use less of the medication than was required to adequately deal with their infection, while they would use too much of the barbiturates and thus would be unable to avoid addiction. Of course, inasmuch as these drugs were marketed for sale via prescription only it was illegal for their labels to include information on proper dosages.

In 1943 the FDA was handed a substantial victory by the Supreme Court. In October 1939 the Buffalo Pharmacal Company shipped several items to physicians through the mail, one of which was alleged to have been misbranded, the other two, adulterated. The items were manufactured by another company and were repackaged and relabeled by Buffalo Pharmacal. While the general manager did not supervise this particular shipment, he had given instructions that orders from physicians were to be filled as received. The trial court, while finding the corporation innocent of the charges, did hold the manager, Dotterweich, criminally guilty. The Alice in Wonderland reasoning behind this finding of guilt led the Second Circuit Court of Appeals to reverse the judgment. However, the agency decided to appeal to the High Court. In a five to four decision written by Felix Frankfurter, the Court ruled that Dotterweich, as a responsible official of the corporation, could be prosecuted for violations of the Food, Drug, and Cosmetics Act even though the corporation was found innocent of any wrongdoing and even though he was not aware that any violation had taken place. It need not be proven, the Court held, that the official intended, or even knew of, the violation.[264] As a result of the Dotterweich decision, the executives of the many companies engaged in the packaging of foods and drugs could be held criminally liable for acts in which they did not participate and of which they had no knowledge. As Justice Murphy in his dissent noted, the decision violates a fundamental principle of Anglo-Saxon jurisprudence and places the stigma of criminal conviction upon those without evil intention or consciousness of wrongdoing.[265]

Several years after the Dotterweich decision, the Supreme Court again enlarged the authority of the FDA in *United States v. Sullivan*[266] by extending to intrastate sales the labeling requirements mandated by the 1938 Act for interstate sales. Sullivan's Pharmacy in Columbus, Georgia, had received a shipment of sulfathiazole tablets in bottles of 1000, each of which was correctly labeled 'Caution. – To be used only by or on the prescription of a physician'. The wholesaler had bought the tablets from the manufacturer, who had shipped them from Chicago, Illinois. Sullivan, in turn, bought one of these bottles from the wholesaler in Atlanta, Georgia, and transferred it to his Columbia, Georgia, pharmacy. The pharmacy then resold the tablets, in two instances removing 12 tablets from the properly labeled bottle and placing them in pill boxes. The boxes were simply labeled 'sulfathiazole' and the tablets were sold without prescription. The trial court held Sullivan guilty but his conviction was overturned by the Fifth Circuit Court of Appeals on the grounds that Sullivan's actions were not covered by the Act since the product in question was no longer in interstate commerce. However, in 1948, the Supreme Court found that 'interstate commerce' was to be understood as covering all steps between the producer in one state and the consumer in another. The High Court reversed the decision of the Circuit Court, holding that the 1938 Act covered drugs even though bought for resale within a state since it had previously passed from one state to another. In overruling the Circuit Court the High Court explicitly denied the legal validity of the following argument put forward by the Court of Appeals:

> the retail sales here involved were made in Columbus nine months after this sulfathiazole had been shipped from Chicago to Atlanta. . . . [I]f the statutory language 'while such article is held for sale after shipment in interstate commerce' should be given its literal meaning, the criminal provisions relied on would 'apply to all intrastate sales of imported drugs after any number of intermediate sales within the State and after any lapse of time; and not only to such sales of drugs, but also to similar retail sales of foods, devices and cosmetics, for all these are equally covered by these provisions of the Act.' . . . [S]uch consequences would result in farreaching inroads upon customary control by local authorities of traditionally local activities, . . . [T]o afford local retail purchasers federal protection from harmful foods, drugs and cosmetics should not be ascribed to Congress in the absence of an exceptionally clear mandate, . . .[267]

Lest there be any confusion regarding the intent of Congress to pre-empt the traditional authority of states and localities and to supply the 'exceptionally clear mandate' of which the Court of Appeals wrote, Congress, in June 1948, enacted an amendment to the 1938 Act, known as the Miller amendment after its sponsor, Representative William Jennings Miller, Republican from Connecticut. Indeed, the amendment had been introduced in July 1947 largely as a response to the difficulty the courts were having in attempting to answer the question, at what point does interstate commerce begin and where does it end.[268] The decision of the High Court in Sullivan, which was to have the same effect as the Miller amendment, in fact, intervened before it could be enacted. The value of the amendment served to clarify once and for all what Congress understood by the term interstate commerce. The amendment explicitly provided the FDA with authority over the interstate shipment of food, drugs, and cosmetics 'when introduced into or while in interstate commerce or while held for sale (whether or not the first sale) after shipment in interstate commerce'. It further expanded the definition of misbranding to include changing a label in any way at any point after its shipment in interstate commerce.[269]

In a period when the federal government's regulatory authority over food and drugs seemed to increase with each new development, Congress finally was forced to reconsider its earlier treatment of oleomargarine, which had been subject to a special tax since 1886. The rationale for the statute had been supplied by sanitarians who had concluded that margarine, an 'artificial' substitute for more natural butter, was a serious danger to health, clearly caused dyspepsia in most of its users, and occasionally killed when ingested. In hearings held prior to passage of the 1886 bill, the Department of Agriculture's 'experts' reported that, in addition to its intrinsic dangers, margarine was produced in such unsanitary conditions that hogs dead from cholera or from a diet of distillery swill found their way into the manufacturing process.[270] There was no truth whatever to these charges. There is no question that the real purpose of the legislation was to protect the dairy industry from the competition butter producers faced from margarine by placing a tax on the lower-priced product. The dairy industry, which had recently undergone a major technological change by processing milk and cheese in factories, had sought such legislation at both the state and federal level.[271] Congress responded in 1886 by enacting a law that licensed all manufacturers, wholesalers, and retailers of oleomargarine and subjected each to an annual tax of $600.00, $480.00, and $48.00 respectively. In addition, margarine itself was subject to a tax of 2 cents a pound.[272] In 1902 the Act was amended so that margarine that was artificially colored any shade of yellow was taxed at a rate of 10 cents a pound while if it were left uncolored or given a different color it was taxed at 1/4 of a cent.[273] The Food and Drug Administration had set identity standards for oleomargarine, as it had for countless other foods and oversaw the product's purity, quality, and color.

Some of the legal disabilities under which margarine was forced to compete in the market were finally removed in 1950, with passage of a new Act that repealed the taxes earlier levied on the product.[274] Shortages of butter during World War II, exacerbated by price controls on dairy products, had led to substantially increased use of margarine without the dire consequences for health that margarine's opponents had earlier warned of. In 1941 annual per capita consumption of butter was 15.9 pounds, while for margarine it was 2.7 pounds. By 1945 these amounts had changed to 10.5 for butter and 4.3 pounds for margarine. The average retail price for butter in 1941 was 41.1 cents a pound and 17.1 cents a pound for margarine. In 1943 costs had increased to 52.7 cents a pound for butter and 23.6 cents a pound for margarine.[275] The increased popularity of margarine and its cheaper price led a number of consumer groups after the war to lobby for removal of federal taxes. They were soon joined by organized labor, at which point the Democratic Party was forced to act. During the 1948 Presidential campaign, the party promised to repeal both the licensing fees and taxes on the product.

On 31 January 1949 Representative Walter P. Granger, Democrat of Utah, introduced a bill in the House that repealed all licensing fees and taxes. The bill, however, made clear that margarine, once dyed yellow, constituted one of the most destructive substances ever created. The bill was prefaced with this statement:

> Yellow oleomargarine resembles butter so closely that it lends itself to substitution for or confusion with butter and in many cases cannot be distinguished from butter by the ordinary consumer. The manufacture, sale, or serving of yellow oleomargarine creates a condition conducive to substitution, confusion, fraud, and deception, and one which if permitted to exist tends to interfere with the orderly and fair marketing of essential foods in commerce.

While it allowed the use of yellow margarine in private homes, it provided that

> the manufacture, transportation, handling, possession, sale, use, or serving of yellow oleomargarine in commerce, or after shipment in commerce, or in connection with the production of goods for commerce, or which affects, obstructs, or burdens commerce or the free flow of goods in commerce, is declared unlawful.[276]

The bill underwent a series of hearings both in the House and Senate and was amended numerous times before it finally passed both chambers on 9 March 1950. All licensing fees and taxes connected with margarine were repealed. In addition, the Act required that all colored margarine sold be packaged and that each package identify itself as margarine 'in type or lettering at least as large as any other type or lettering on such label'. If colored margarine were to be served at a public eating place, the establishment was required to display a notice 'prominently and conspicuously' that its customers were being served margarine. In addition, each serving of margarine must be in triangular packages and must be labeled as such. Enforcement of the Act's provisions were placed in the hands of the Food and Drug Administration. The Act was signed by President Truman on 16 March 1950.[277] It is worth noting that the tax on margarine was not repealed, in the words of one analyst, 'because the federal government suddenly came to its senses and decided it had overstepped its constitutional authority. Rather, the shortages of the war years helped alter the balance of political power and, as a result, competing interest, along with "public opinion," could no longer be ignored'.[278]

Concerned that a large number of chemical compounds employed as food additives were of unknown safety, the FDA, soon after the end of World War II, approached Congress once again for authority to declare such substances a danger to health when used at whatever level the agency determined. Under the terms of the 1938 statute growers and the manufacturers of packaged foods were not obligated to supply advance notification of the introduction of a new additive nor were they required to prove the substance's safety. This burden of proof was shouldered by the FDA. However, despite the fact that food processors did not have to test these compounds for toxicity, the incentive to do so was strong and most of them in fact did so. Should an additive have proved unsafe, chemical manufacturers and food manufacturers would have been faced with the FDA's enforcement sanctions under the adulteration provisions of the 1938 Act. Nor could these companies risk the adverse publicity that would be associated with discovering that their product contained a hazardous substance. Finally, the tort liability that these firms could face were anyone injured was substantial.

These safeguards, however, were not sufficient for the FDA and in 1949 the agency's commissioner, Paul B. Dunbar, approached Representative Frank B. Keefe, Republican from Wisconsin, one of several Congressmen who were particularly friendly toward FDA requests. Keefe introduced a resolution in the House calling for an investigation of chemicals in food and, later, in cosmetics, that resulted, in June 1950, in House Resolution 323 that provided for the creation of a Select Committee to Investigate the Use of Chemicals in Food Products. The Committee was chaired by James T. Delaney, Democrat from New York, and hearings ran from September 1950 to March 1952. No fewer than 217 witnesses were heard over the course of nine months and from this issued three reports; the first, submitted in May 1952 dealt with 'Fertilizers', the second and third, issued in June 1952, concerned 'Cosmetics', and 'Food'. The Committee acknowledged that chemicals were used at some stage in the production or storage of almost every food sold and that currently some 704 different substances were in use. Having said that, however, it noted that, according to the FDA, only 428 of these were 'definitely known to be safe'.[279] It then urged Congress to amend the Food, Drug, and Cosmetic Act to empower the FDA 'to require that chemicals employed in or on foods be subjected to substantially the same safety requirements as now exist for new drugs'.[280]

Not confronted with any crisis that called for radical legislative reform, Congress chose to 'correct' this problem by acting incrementally, through a series of three separate statutes passed over several years. The first of these was the Pesticide Residues Amendment,[281] enacted in 1954, which dispensed with formal hearings prior to establishing tolerances for pesticide chemicals. The amendment was introduced in the House in March 1953 by Representative A.L. Miller, Republican of Nebraska and a member of Delaney's Committee. Hearings were held on the amendment before a subcommittee of the Committee on Interstate and Foreign Commerce[282] in July. The amendment provided that any food bearing or containing a pesticide chemical, unless a tolerance had first been prescribed or unless the pesticide was explicitly exempt, would be deemed adulterated. The onus for proving a pesticide safe was now placed on the manufacturer, which had the effect of effectively placing in the hands of the FDA final authority respecting which pesticides would be permitted, regardless of the quantity of residue.

A number of bills were introduced in the 83rd, 84th, and 85th Congresses whose purpose was to implement the recommendations of the Delaney Committee with respect to food additives. Prior to the Food Additives Amendment[283] the development and use of compounds whose toxicity was unknown was beyond the reach of the statute until the FDA was able to prove to a court that the substance was poisonous or deleterious. The new Act attempted to address this problem by placing in the hands of the FDA the authority to prevent the use of any additive whatever unless the food additive manufacturer or food processor had first demonstrated to the satisfaction of the FDA that the compound was safe.[284] The 1958 Amendment divided what is commonly understood as food additives into two groups: those generally recognized as safe, designated GRAS, and (2) those that are not known to be harmless under the conditions of their intended use. The definition was understood to include any food-contact material that might migrate into food, without regard to its level of migration.[285]

GRAS compounds constituted a new category of substance, those that had already received administrative approval, thus vesting a right in these compounds by exempting them from the requirements imposed on newer additives. This was particularly significant with respect to what became known as the Delaney clause, a truly remarkable provision that held that:

> no additive shall be deemed to be safe if it is found to induce cancer when ingested by man or animal, or if it is found, after tests which are appropriate for the evaluation of the safety of food additives, to induce cancer in man or animal.[286]

The clause barred any residue, at whatever measurable level, that was regarded as carcinogenic from being approved for use. Requirements such as these did nothing but display a woeful ignorance not only of the natural world but of the world of science. The clause was a particularly apt example of the harm that could be caused by well-meaning politicians who know nothing about the subject-matter being legislated. Delaney added the clause on 28 May 1957, some months after having introduced the original bill.[287] The Congressman was shocked at a recent decision of the Food and Drug Administration to allow small quantities of a pesticide chemical, Aramite, to be used when it was found that minute quantities of the substance had been associated with tumors in animals. Dr William Smith, who had solid credentials in cancer research, testified that he was shocked that the FDA would have approved Aramite, a carcinogen which 'citizens of this country are being obliged to eat . . . without their consent'.[288] Delaney's reaction was outrage and led directly to his urging that a clause be added to the bill prohibiting approval of any carcinogen no matter the risk level. The bill had originally been approved by the House Commerce Committee without an anti-cancer clause but the provisions was added at Delaney's insistence before the measure reached the House floor. In altering his original bill, Delaney informed the Committee that the clause had the support of the International Union Against Cancer in Rome and noted:

> The part that chemical additives play in the cancer picture may not yet be completely understood, but enough is known to put us on our guard. The safety of the public health demands that chemical additives should be specifically pretested for carcinogenicity, and this should be spelled out in the law. The precedent established by the Aramite decision has opened the door, even if only a little, to the use of carcinogens in our foods. That door should be slammed shut and locked. That is the purpose of my anticarcinogen provision.[289]

The requirement that no compound could be approved that was found to contribute to cancer in either man or animal was not limited by the amount of carcinogenic residue detected. When the Delaney clause was originally enacted in 1958 scientists were able to measure residues in parts per thousand, at best, several parts per million. In the succeeding 40 years, however, the ability to measure had improved sufficiently to detect carcinogens when present in parts per trillion and even parts per quadrillion, the equivalent, according to Ronald Hart of the National Center for Toxicological Research, of one tablespoon of a substance dropped into a body of water as large as the entire Great Lakes![290] These minuscule amounts were sufficient to prohibit the use of approximately half of all chemicals, natural and synthetic, all of which, in large enough doses, have produced tumors. It has often been pointed out that had the Delaney clause been taken literally, hundreds of ordinary products would be banned. Coffee, for example, is known to contain at least 10 milligrams of rodent carcinogens[291] while an endless list of foods that are commonly consumed fall outside the Delaney standard.[292]

The absurdity of this requirement cannot be appreciated until one considers that a number of additives awarded a GRAS rating, which were exempt from the Delaney clause, were more carcinogenic than were newer chemicals but could not be replaced because of the amendment's requirements. Nor did the law recognize natural carcinogens, which were far more prevalent in American diets than were those contained in additives. Finally, there are serious methodological problems with regard to animal testing for carcinogens.[293] Dosages given to test animals, say laboratory mice, are enormously high, as high as is possible without killing the animal, known as the maximum tolerated dose (MTD). It is clear why this is necessary. If a compound were to cause 20 cancers in a population of 300 000 000, the results, as low as they are, would be regarded as significant. Since laboratories cannot experiment on populations that size, they operate on the principle that if you increase the dosage by a factor of, say, 100 000 you can reduce the population on which tests are performed by a similar factor. The theory, that the relationship between dose level and bodily response is linear, is questionable at best. This, however, constitutes the methodological underpinning of most FDA-approved toxicity studies: that the appearance of tumors in 60 laboratory mice given the higher dosage, in a population of 1000 mice tested, translates to cancers in 20 human beings who will have consumed 1/100 000 the amount of the substance that was fed to a test animal.[294] There are a number of problems with this kind of simple extrapolation, not the least of which is that it is predicated on the assumption that there exist no thresholds below which a substance might well be harmless.[295] Secondly, it does not follow that because a compound is carcinogenic in laboratory mice it will act in the same way in other animals and in humans. Finally, it does not take into consideration the fact that other physiological attributes, such as weight, might contribute to the number of tumors displayed.

Even the FDA occasionally found the Delaney clause a hindrance to its regulatory functions. In 1986 it approved Drug and Cosmetic Dye Orange No. 17, despite the fact that it had been tested to show one additional cancer in 19 billion (approximately three times the world population), over a 70-year lifetime. However, the United States Court of Appeals for the District of Columbia ruled that the Delaney cause was clear in permitting no exemption.[296] Similarly, in 1990 Red Dye No. 3, one of the oldest food and cosmetic dyes, which had been in use since the beginning of food processing, was banned for a variety of uses by the FDA in light of tests that had shown it to cause thyroid cancer in rats when extremely large doses were consumed. The risk to humans was estimated at between 1 in 100 000 to 1 in 1 000 000. Saccharin, which was discovered at Johns Hopkins University in 1879, came close to sharing the fate of Orange No. 17 when a Canadian study indicated that the substance was responsible for bladder cancers in laboratory mice who had been fed sodium saccharin. Yet another test, on rats who were fed the equivalent of 800 cans of diet soda per day, also suggested that the compound was linked to cancer. Under the terms of the Delaney clause the FDA, in 1977, proposed to ban the substance but because of its long history, substantial public pressure, and the fact that the ban would have a direct effect on a number of Congressmen and their families, Congress imposed a moratorium pending further research but required that the substance carry a warning label. Both Public Citizen and the Center for Science in the Public Interest[297] objected to the decision but without result. Finally in 1991 the Food and Drug Administration formally withdrew its 1977 proposal to ban the use of saccharin and in 2000 President Bill Clinton ordered that the compound need no longer carry its warning label.

The third of the three amendments enacted as a result of Delaney Committee hearings was not passed until two years after the Food Additives Amendment and some ten years after the Committee itself had ceased operating. In June 1959 Representative Oren Harris, Democrat from Arkansas, introduced a bill drafted by the FDA to amend the Food, Drug, and Cosmetic Act regarding the regulation of color additives in foods.[298] As was the case with food additives, the bill empowered the Food and Drug Administration to regulate the conditions for safe use and imposed on manufacturers and food processors the burden of proof that a color additive was safe for its intended use. Color additives already on the market were allowed up to two-and-a-half years to obtain FDA approval. While prior to the amendment's enactment only coal tar dyes had to be batch-certified, the measure called for all compounds to be batch-certified unless exempted by the Secretary of Health, Education, and Welfare. The bill, as introduced, contained Delaney provisions similar to those that had been inserted in the Food Additives bill. Several days later, Senators Lister Hill, Democrat from Alabama, and Barry Goldwater, Republican from Arizona, put forward a similar bill (S. 2197) in the Senate. However the Delaney clause was not present in the Senate version and as a result Arthur S. Flemming, Secretary of Health, Education, and Welfare, testified that the Department and the FDA strongly supported the measure introduced by Representative Harris inasmuch as it contained the 'anticancer' provision. 'The preponderance of scientific evidence', Flemming testified,

clearly dictates our position. Our advocacy of the anticancer proviso in the proposed color additives amendment is based on the simple fact that no one knows how to set a safe tolerance for substances in human foods when those substances are known to cause cancer when added to the diet of animals.[299]

The Administration's support for the Delaney clause insured that it would be included in the amendment as finally enacted by Congress. It was signed into law by President Eisenhower on 5 July 1960.[300]

In light of the problems posed by a literal reading of the Delaney clause, the Food and Drug Administration occasionally interpreted the law's reference to a zero-risk standard for carcinogenicity to mean negligible risk.[301] In 1970 Congress established the Environmental Protection Agency (EPA), to which the FDA's program for setting pesticide tolerances was transferred. The EPA was thus bound by the same provisions relating to residues on foods as had limited the FDA. It too felt compelled to interpret the Delaney provision requiring no measurable risk whatsoever to one allowing negligible risk, on the assumption that *de minimis* risks could be disregarded. However, the Natural Resources Defense Council, the AFL-CIO, and Public Citizen[302] sued to overturn this standard and in 1992, in a case involving four pesticides used as food additives, the United States Court of Appeals for the Ninth Circuit ruled that

> the Delaney Clause leaves the FDA room for scientific judgment in deciding whether its conditions are met by a food additive. But the clause affords no flexibility once FDA scientists determine that these conditions are satisfied. A food additive that has been found in an appropriate test to induce cancer in laboratory animals may not be approved for use in food for any purpose, at any level, regardless of any 'benefits' that it might provide.[303]

The Delaney clause proved so unworkable that in 1987 the National Research Council (NRC), having studied the 'negligible risk' standard as it applied to food safety, determined that a uniform negligible risk standard applied consistently could in fact reduce, rather than increase, the risks following exposure to potentially carcinogenic food additives, whatever form these additives might take. The NRC recommended that both agricultural commodities and processed foods should be subject to the new standard. For some time the FDA kept silent on the NRC's report but in early 1995 the FDA Commissioner, David Kessler,[304] declared that he was strongly opposed to changing the law. 'These proposals', among them repeal of the Delaney clause, he asserted, 'are an assault on forty years of consumer protection'.[305]

Despite Kessler's obscurantist sentiments, the Congress eventually considered a bill to relax the Delaney standards. In large measure as a consequence of the National Research Council's report, Representative Tom Bliley, Republican from Virginia, introduced a measure, H.R. 1627, in the House that effectively implemented the NRC's recommendations. A similar measure was put forward by Richard Lugar, Republican from Indiana, in the Senate. The bill was passed overwhelmingly in both chambers (the measure had no fewer than 243 co-sponsors in the House and passed on a roll-call vote of 417–0) and was signed into law as the Food Quality Protection Act by President Clinton on 3 August 1996.[306] While the law did not affect food additives other than pesticide residues, at least henceforth federal regulators were freed from having to apply this unworkable criterion to chemical compounds used as pesticides.

There are innumerable examples of the destructive nature of FDA rulings from every area over which the agency has had regulatory control. The 1938 Act extended the authority of the Food and Drug Administration to therapeutic devices, about which, the agency had complained, fraudulent health claims were made no less often than they were about drugs. There were indeed a large number of mechanical and electrical contrivances that were promoted for their abilities to improve one's health or to cure disease and they continued to flourish following the end of hostilities in 1945. These devices promised an amazingly wide range of physical improvements, including the ability to arrest age and disease. While it is true that most of these were of no medical benefit except as placebos, these devices were, with rare exceptions, quite harmless and posed no threat to the health and safety of Americans other than in very exceptional instances where those who used them did not also take advantage of orthodox treatment. It was while enforcing its regulations regarding these devices immediately following World War II that the FDA most clearly displayed its malicious parochialism.

Wilhelm Reich was a psychiatrist of some importance, a friend of Sigmund Freud's, a member of the faculty of the Vienna Psychoanalytic Society from 1924 to 1930, and the author of numerous books and articles that contributed significantly to the development of psychoanalysis.[307] During this period he developed his theory of the role of sexuality in shaping a healthy psyche. Reich had concluded that a satisfactory sexual life, that is, gratification in the sexual act, what he called 'orgastic potency', was absolutely essential to discharging excess energy and to maintaining a stable energy level in the organism. This libidinal energy, Reich reasoned, was not simply a psychic concept but real energy. It also followed for Reich that, inasmuch as neuroses existed only on repressed excess energy, someone capable of true sexual release cannot maintain a neurosis. These views eventually led to his break with Freud.

Having turned his attention to the social causes of neurosis, Reich soon became involved in a host of socialist groups. In 1930 he left Vienna for Berlin where he joined the Communist Party. Being Jewish he was forced to flee Germany in 1933 and took up a position with the Institute of Psychology at the University of Oslo. His researches had convinced him that the energy that he had earlier discovered was associated with pleasure, which could be measured at the skin's surface. Neuroses resulted from the presence of 'muscular armor', the rigidity that comes through muscular contraction and prevents the regulation of energy, inhibits its discharge, and thus prevents relaxation. The natural flow of life energy in the body is thus blocked, leading to mental disease. During a satisfactory sexual experience this 'bioelectric energy' was discharged, thus relieving stasis in the organism. Reich maintained that this biological energy was capable of charging tissue and had the ability to repel germs and cancer cells. On the basis of his experiments Reich concluded that this was the ultimate life energy that was involved not only in sexuality but in all other life processes. The energy itself he called 'orgone energy', which it was possible to accumulate and concentrate by means of an orgone energy accumulator whose function was to charge living tissue and blood, thus strengthening resistance to disease. In 1939 Reich accepted an invitation to lecture on medical psychology at the New School for Social Research. He continued to live in the United States, even after he stopped teaching. He bought a home in Forest Hills, New York, where he established his Orgone Institute and continued his experiments on orgone energy and human psychological and physical health.

In 1947 he was approached by Mildred Edy Brady, a writer and wife of the founder of the Consumers Union, who was to write several articles 'exposing' Reich. Ms Brady had worked as an officer of the Consumers Union until the outbreak of World War II, when both she and her husband, who had previously been an economics professor at the University of California, joined the Office of Price Administration. Brady is one of the ugliest figures to play a role in the FDA's persecution of Reich. A malevolent liar, she had strong sympathies with the Soviet Union and was likely outraged by Reich's virulent anti-Stalinism and his belief that Moscow-style communism and psychic health were totally incompatible. It appears that Brady had discovered from a concerned friend of someone suffering from cancer that the patient was interested in Reich's orgone boxes and this piqued her interest in Reich's work. Determined to bring Reich's confidence game to the attention of the authorities, Brady gained access to Reich's home by claiming friends in common. She learned nothing to her advantage during her visit but went ahead with her articles. The primary focus of the first of these[308] was only partially about Reich's views on sexuality and authoritarianism. It focused on the new 'bohemianism' that was becoming increasingly popular and attempted to place Reich in the context of this larger movement. In itself it would not have warranted FDA interest in Reich's work. The second article,[309] however, was a vicious, dishonest attack on Reich's orgone theory, including the claim attributed to Reich that orgone accumulators would automatically increase orgastic potency for its users. At most Reich had contended that these accumulators would help depleted tissue until a therapist had the opportunity to work on the 'character armor' to release the psyche's rigidities. However, Brady's charge, that Reich maintained that his orgone accumulators increased one's libido, so disturbed the FDA that they soon began an investigation.

Two months after Brady's articles appeared, the FDA dispatched an agent to Rangeley, Maine, where Reich had established a laboratory and research center which he called Orgonon. The agent, a somewhat dull-witted man named Charles Wood, had had great difficulty in understanding the theoretical foundations of Reich's work and had, in fact, made up his mind before arriving in Maine that Reich's orgone boxes were in violation of the Food, Drug, and Cosmetic Act of 1938. While at Rangeley, Wood and Clista Templeton, the daughter of the man who was responsible for building Reich's accumulators, fell in love and three months later they married. Convinced that Reich was perpetrating a fraud of major proportions, Wood and his supervisor began collecting evidence against Reich.[310] They were helped in this task by Clista Templeton Wood, who had taken over the building of accumulators following the death of her father from prostate cancer. In addition, the American Psychoanalytic Association, who sent a stream of representatives to Rangeley to ferret out Reich's illegal transactions, reported to Wood about Reich's alleged violations of the 1938 Act. It was suspected that the accumulators that were rented out and the publications of the Orgone Institute Press were both aimed at the sex market but the FDA was unable to garner any evidence to support this finding. However, this hardly prevented the agency from going forward. On 20 February 1954, in a complaint issued through the United States District Court at Portland, Maine, the FDA charged that the orgone energy accumulator was a fraud, that orgone energy did not exist, and that all the literature relating to orgonomy was merely labeling for the sale of the accumulator.

Rather than appear in court to defend himself, Reich sent a letter to the judge in the case arguing that the proper function of the legal system was to protect the work of sincere scientists and that a court of law was no place to determine the scientific merit of his conclusions. The result was that an all-inclusive injunction was issued against Reich on 19 March. All accumulators were to be destroyed and all literature referring to them burnt. The FDA had managed to obtain a court order to destroy all of Reich's work without so much as having to offer any proof whatever of any fraud. The agency made no attempt to investigate the merits of Reich's work nor to question any of his associates or followers. Reich himself moved to Arizona but his work was continued at Orgonon by Dr Michael Silvert, who, having been assured that the injunction that the court had issued was directed solely at Reich, assumed direction of the Orgone Institute Press and the distribution of accumulators. Reich returned to Maine in 1955 and in the fall moved to Washington, DC. In July the FDA, having tapped Reich's telephone and harassed him in a number of other ways, was successful in seeing to it that he and Silvert were cited for contempt. Both men were found guilty; Silvert was sentenced to a jail term of a year and a day, Reich to two years. The Wilhelm Reich Foundation was fined $10 000.[311] One final indignity remained. Admitted to Danbury Prison in Connecticut, Reich was diagnosed as paranoid by the prison physicians and transferred to Lewisburg Penitentiary in Pennsylvania, which possessed psychiatric facilities. On 3 November 1957 Reich was found dead in his cell, his death attributed to heart failure. Silvert served his one-year sentence and committed suicide soon after being released. Following Reich's contempt verdict, the FDA undertook to burn all of Reich's books and notes, none of which survives. No harm whatever issued from Reich's work nor from his relationship with his patients nor was any ever proven by the FDA, who determined to use the full weight and authority of the United States government to punish him for defying orthodox medicine. In this struggle the FDA expended no less than $2 000 000!

Despite the substantial costs involved in persecuting Reich, whose heretical theory of disease had thrown the FDA into a frenzy, its goal of reducing the availability of drugs to consumers except through the mediation of a physician continued to be its primary interest. Although it appeared that the FDA had effectively established its authority to determine which drugs were to be immediately available to the public and which would require the mediation of a physician as early as the end of World War II,[312] a desire to regularize the agency's ability to prosecute offenders led them to approach Congress for definitive legislation. In testifying before the House Committee on Interstate and Foreign Commerce in May 1951, Oscar Ewing, the Administrator of the Federal Security Agency, noted further that the American Pharmaceutical Association was particularly unhappy that drugs sold solely by prescription could not be renewed once filled.[313] The FDA was outraged that patients were refilling prescriptions without first getting the permission of their physician and, to their dismay, found that state laws in some jurisdictions did not prohibit this practice. In October 1948, at a meeting of the National Association of Retail Druggists, the Commissioner of the FDA, Paul B. Dunbar, announced that henceforth the agency would regard all prescription refills as illegal unless they were explicitly authorized by a physician. Pharmacists viewed this decision with alarm, arguing that most refills were for perfectly safe drugs and that refilling amounted to 40 percent of their prescription business.[314] The antagonism of pharmacists to the FDA ruling made it imperative that the rule receive the imprimatur of Congress. The hearings at which Ewing testified were being held in connection with an amendment to the Food, Drug and Cosmetic Act, H.R. 8904,[315] introduced by Representative Carl Durham, Democrat from North Carolina, which legally exempted prescription medications from the Act's labeling requirements and which specified in what ways prescription drugs were to be distinguished from over-the-counter medicines. A somewhat more restrictive measure was put forward in the Senate as S. 1186[316] by Hubert H. Humphrey, Democrat from Minnesota. Humphrey, like Durham, had been a pharmacist before turning to politics and was far more sympathetic to the position taken by the FDA than was Durham. The amendments themselves were amended and debated at some length and a bill, closer to the original measure put forward in the Senate, finally passed both chambers on 18 October 1951.[317]

The statute amended the 1938 Act by making it unlawful to dispense a drug bearing the R̸ legend without a prescription from 'a practitioner licensed by law to administer such drugs'.[318] Nor could prescriptions be refilled without authorization of the prescriber, on the theory that the physician alone should have complete control over the medication the patient received.[319] Prescriptions could be authorized by telephone but physicians were required to promptly reduce them to writing. Narcotic drugs could be dispensed only on written order of a medical practitioner. All prescription drugs were required to carry the R legend while the same legend was prohibited on any over-the-counter medication. The amendment defined three categories of prescription drugs: (1) hypnotics or habit-forming drugs; (2) 'new drugs' which have not been shown to be safe for use in self-medication, and (3) drugs that the FDA had determined were not safe for self-medication 'because of [their] toxicity or other potentiality for harmful effect, or the method of use, or collateral measures necessary to [their] use'. This third category was not nearly broad enough to satisfy the demands of the FDA. The agency maintained that toxicity should not constitute the only criterion that makes a drug unsuitable for self-medication. The agency had originally requested that the bill before Congress authorize the agency to determine whether a prescription was needed for drugs that, while in themselves not toxic, were ineffective for the purposes for which they might be used or that, if taken for a certain condition, masked an underlying medical problem. As George Larrick, the Associate Commissioner of the FDA, testified: 'It is just as important that a drug be effective in the hands of the person who acts as his own physician as that it be safe in the sense that it will not poison him'.[320] However, protests from drug manufacturers and pharmacists at such enormous discretionary power were so intense that the authority to make such decisions was removed.

Beyond stipulating the requirements for classifying a drug as available only by prescription, the amendment also mandated that all other drugs had to carry adequate directions for safe and effective use and warnings against misuse. The distributor of any over-the-counter drug was responsible for seeing to it that each over-the-counter drug bore a seven-point label, showing (1) the name of the product; (2) the name and address of the manufacturer; (3) the net contents of the package; (4) the established name of all ingredients, whether active or not; (5) the name of any habit-forming drug contained in the preparation; (6) cautions and warnings needed for protection of the user;[321] and (7) adequate directions for safe and effective use.

Not all concerned groups supported this extension of FDA authority. The General Counsel of the American Pharmaceutical Association, Mr Charles Wesley Dunn, was clearly aware of the nature of discretionary authority of this sort. Dunn noted that

> experience in this country and abroad has amply proved that when the government is given an important control of private affairs, it will be increasingly and largely used, and it will be seriously abused in the long view. Moreover, once this control over drugs is vested in the government, it will be a strong precedent for its infinite extension in the course of time.[322]

The Humphrey-Durham Amendment altered the scope of drug legislation and broadened its purpose far beyond what was intended even as late as 1938. As Peter Temin has observed:

Before 1938 the function of drug legislation was to prevent fraud – to ensure that the labels informing consumers about the chemical and known therapeutic properties of drugs were adequate and correct. The government did not undertake to limit consumers' drug choices, other than for narcotics, an exception that shows by its restricted scope how broad the domain of consumer choice was to be. The 1938 act added the function of assuring safety – of assuring the public that any drug on the market could be taken in reasonable quantities without harm. . . . By the end of 1938, the FDA had announced that the government would sharply curtail this freedom of choice. . . . This change in the underlying assumptions of drug legislation came about through internal FDA processes. The shift from assuming a capable consumer to assuming an incompetent one occurred in the FDA within six months of the Federal Food, Drug, and Cosmetic Act's passage.[323]

With passage of the Humphrey-Durham Amendment the FDA determined to crush public access to most medications without a prescription. In 1954 it devoted no less than one-third of the total appropriation earmarked for drug regulation to ensure control over restricted drugs.[324] Over the course of slightly more than a decade the FDA had moved from preventing fraud in the drugs sold to competent Americans to guaranteeing their safety, to supervising the sale of medicines to consumers blind to their own welfare and incapable of making decisions regarding their own health. The next step was not only to insure the safety of medicines consumed by ignorant consumers but also to guarantee their efficacy.

In 1960 the FDA found itself confronted with another drug disaster as horrendous as had occurred in 1937 when Elixir Sulfanilamide had been responsible for the deaths of over 100 people and, just as in 1937, the agency was able to capitalize on the tragedy to obtain legislation expanding its authority. In 1953 Ciba, the Swiss drug company initially synthesized a new drug, thalidomide, which, after extensive testing, appeared to possess no pharmacological effects. At that point Ciba decided to abandon it and in 1954 turned it over to a German drug manufacturer, Chemie Grünenthal, which showed interest in the substance. Chemie Grünenthal first marketed thalidomide as an anticonvulsant for the treatment of epilepsy but continued to test the product more extensively, in particular in trials for a new allergy treatment. While the drug proved of no value in this regard it did seem extremely effective as a sedative which was especially efficacious for those experiencing nausea and morning sickness. It therefore seemed an ideal medication for pregnant women suffering nausea and insomnia. Testing appeared to show it completely safe and having no side-effects. Indeed, it was suggested that no lethal dose could be established. It is now known that the first thalidomide baby was born in 1956; however, the causes of the birth defects that were exhibited had not yet been traced to thalidomide and the drug was still regarded as quite safe for the purposes for which it was prescribed. As a result, in 1957 Chemie Grünenthal began general marketing of the drug, which quickly became extremely popular with pregnant women and was widely prescribed in Germany, Britain, Australia, and Canada.

Chemie Grünenthal attempted to expand to the United States during 1960 and applied to the Food and Drug Administration for approval to sell thalidomide through its US distributor, William S. Merrill Company. It appears that approval was considered, both by the distributor and by the FDA, as routine and as a result the application was turned over to one of the agency's most junior people, Dr Frances Oldham Kelsey. Concern over some of the routine tests that Chemie Grünenthal had originally conducted on thalidomide and earlier scattered reports that thalidomide might cause neuropathy in some of its users led Dr Kelsey to delay approval of the application for about a year. It is worth underscoring that neither of these concerns was in any way fatal to thalidomide's application and had reports that the drug was extremely dangerous when used by pregnant women not intervened, there is no question that the drug would have been approved in the United States as it had been in Europe, Britain, and Canada. The reasons for Dr Kelsey's delay had nothing whatever to do with birth defects nor with the drug's effect on the human embryo and the later claim by the FDA that her prior work in animal toxicity, including toxic effects in pregnancy, suggested that a delay was warranted is without any foundation whatever.[325]

In mid-1960 an Australian gynecologist in Sydney reported his suspicions that thalidomide was responsible for severe limb and bowel malformations in three children he was treating. By the end of the year a number of observations were reported in Great Britain and in other areas and evidence began to accumulate that thalidomide was the responsible agent in the increasing number of severe birth defects that were occurring. These reports soon reached the press and Chemie Grünenthal felt obligated to withdraw the drug from distribution, as did Distillers, its manufacturer in Britain. It was quickly established that thalidomide was teratogenic when ingested by pregnant women in the first trimester but not before it had caused many thousands of stillbirths and miscarriages and was responsible for severe birth defects in thousands of others. That its application was withdrawn in the United States,[326] however, has nothing to do with the fact that the FDA was more vigilant than were the agency's counterparts in other parts of the world. The truth is that thalidomide was not distributed throughout the United States[327] because the agency's approval process was mired in red tape and because a bureaucrat had determined that it really didn't matter how long it took her to approve a drug that might have relieved hundreds of thousands of pregnant women from serious discomfort. The nation is indeed lucky that Dr Kelsey decided to temporize but we can only be thankful that it was not a vaccine for polio that was under consideration. Thalidomide had not undergone reproductive tests before 1961 nor were such tests required by the FDA. Indeed, it appears that if such tests had been performed in rats it would not have resulted in any malformed births. At most tests on rats have shown that litter size was decreased after ingestion of thalidomide.

Once again, however, the FDA was able to turn this tragedy into a victory for itself. Thalidomide, we are told, was halted at our borders by an alert pharmacologist dedicated to seeing to it that all Americans were safe from the dangers that might beset them from untested or inadequately tested drugs. Indeed, Dr Kelsey, whose delays in approving thalidomide were in fact a function of her own foot-dragging, appears not to have been in the least embarrassed by the myth that it was through her efforts alone that the nation was spared a tragedy of the sort that befell Germany and Britain. The historian of drug regulation in America whose work is regarded as definitive has referred to the thalidomide episode as 'one of the agency's great triumphs' and notes that 'the shrewdness and firmness of an FDA woman physician had kept the United States from sharing in a terrible medical disaster'.[328] For her efforts, Dr Kelsey received from President John F. Kennedy the highest civilian award her nation could bestow, the President's Award for Distinguished Federal Civilian Service, in August 1962.[329]

The events surrounding thalidomide were crucial not only in making of the FDA an agency of government that had spared Americans a major disaster but also in deflecting a series of negative reactions to the FDA's attempts to tighten restrictions on access to drugs. This was a pure power play in which the agency, allied with the American Medical Association (AMA), sought to further restrict what they regarded as quack medicines available to the consumer, thus deflecting him from consulting a trained professional who alone had the power to dispense effective therapeutic agents. This cooperation was sealed at the Congress on Medical Quackery held in Washington in 1961 under the joint sponsorship of both the FDA and the AMA. Of particular concern were medications aimed at conditions that orthodox medicine was then helpless to treat, particularly cancer and arthritis.[330] These medications, in fact, did no harm. Nor, in most cases, could it be argued that they prevented patients from taking advantage of more efficacious drugs, since none existed. Still, both the FDA and the AMA were infuriated that individuals were allowed to choose their own medications despite the fact that they might not have had therapeutic value.

The move to prohibit the distribution and sale of drugs and medical devices that the FDA had decided were without therapeutic merit had begun in 1910, when Wiley's Bureau of Chemistry attempted to prosecute packages of medicine that bore labels stating that they could cure cancer. The Supreme Court then ruled that therapeutic effectiveness was not covered by the 1906 Act.[331] The issue, however, remained uppermost in the minds of FDA bureaucrats who were exasperated that they were unable to deal with the large number of remedies that they regarded as of no value. In 1955 Oveta Culp, the Secretary of Health, Education, and Welfare,[332] appointed a Citizens' Advisory Committee to investigate quackery in America. As was expected, the Committee recommended that the FDA's 'educational' efforts be considerably strengthened, both about the hazards of quack medicines and therapeutic devices and about the role of the FDA as protector of the nation's drug supply. Partly in response to these recommendations, the FDA organized a Division of Public Information in 1958 which issued a stream of press releases and in the same year the new Secretary, Arthur Flemming, held a number of press conferences on the dangers of questionable nutritional and dietary products.[333]

The 1961 Congress on Medical Quackery did not confine itself to the issue of drugs and devices that were felt to be without value but also addressed the fact that the chemotherapeutic revolution that had been under way for a decade had produced drugs of such potency that were prescription drugs misused or were they prescribed to certain patients despite their contraindications dire consequences could result. In addition, a certain number of drugs, while effective, had cumulative toxic effects. While such information could not appear on the label of medications resold to the public by prescription, new prescription drugs were required to enclose with each package accompanying material that described the drug's proper purpose and dosage, together with any relevant warnings and contraindications. However, it was sometimes the case that only pharmacists saw this information since it was not routinely distributed to physicians. The FDA was also concerned about drug advertising aimed at physicians, which, the agency argued, did not present 'a balanced picture' of the benefits and liabilities of a particular drug. Finally, accusations were made that the price of prescription medications was substantially higher than one would have expected in a competitive environment.

The Kefauver Commission, whose first meeting on prescription drugs occurred at the end of 1959, was especially interested in the prices of drugs and whether the drug industry was in fact competitive. Senator Estes Kefauver from Tennessee had run for the Democratic nomination for President in 1952. He lost the nomination to Adlai Stevenson but in 1956 was chosen as Stevenson's running-mate in a hopeless campaign against President Dwight Eisenhower. In 1959, as chairman of the Senate's Subcommittee on Antitrust and Monopoly of the Committee on the Judiciary, he began hearings to investigate the drug industry, which the committee believed was responsible for charging exorbitant price for drugs of dubious value.[334] As Kefauver himself remarked: 'Ethical drug prices are generally unreasonable and excessive. They are unreasonable whether compared to costs, to profits, or to prices in foreign countries.'[335] The meetings of the Kefauver committee seemed endless, its hearings filling volume after volume, in the main directed at the competitive position of firms that comprised the pharmaceutical industry. In April 1961

Kefauver submitted his drug bill to the Senate.[336] S. 1552[337] was introduced primarily to amend and supplement the antitrust laws with respect to the manufacture and distribution of drugs. The bill limited the conditions under which a new drug could be patented and included a provision that patent holders were compelled, after three years, to award licenses to all manufacturers who sought them. The measure further required that all producers of prescription drugs be licensed, that all advertising and promotional material fully disclose all negative information associated with the drug, called for the inspection of all manufacturing facilities, empowered the Food and Drug Administration to determine the generic name of any drug, and required manufacturers to present evidence not only of the safety but of the efficacy of all medications.[338]

On 15 March 1962 President John F. Kennedy submitted a message to Congress on consumer protection, calling for a huge number of new regulations relating to everything from automobile safety to all-channel television sets. That portion of his remarks that was devoted to drugs, while similar in most particulars to Kefauver's bill, neither mentioned the issue of drug prices, which was of particular concern to Kefauver, nor explicitly endorsed S. 1552, as the Senator had requested. 'I recommend', Kennedy announced,

> legislation to strengthen and broaden existing laws in the food-and-drug field to provide consumers with better, safer, and less expensive drugs by authorizing the Department of Health, Education, and Welfare to –
> (a) Require a showing that new drugs and therapeutic devices are effective for their intended use – as well as safe – before they are placed on the market;
> (b) Withdraw approval of any such drug or device when there is substantial doubt as to its safety or efficacy and require manufacturers to report any information bearing on its safety or efficacy;
> (c) Require drug and therapeutic device manufacturers to maintain facilities and controls that will assure the reliability of their product;
> (d) Require batch-by-batch testing and certification of all antibiotics;
> (e) Assign simple common names to drugs;
> (f) Establish an enforceable system of preventing the illicit distribution of habit-forming barbiturates and amphetamines;
> (g) Require cosmetics to be tested and proved safe before they are marketed; and
> (h) Institute more effective inspection to determine whether food, drug, cosmetics, and therapeutic devices are being manufactured and marketed in accordance with the law.[339]

While the Kefauver bill had passed his own subcommittee, the full Committee on the Judiciary referred the measure for consideration to another of its subcommittees, the Subcommittee on Patents and Trademarks, chaired by John McClellan, Democrat of Arkansas. Kefauver was convinced that this would have the effect of killing his bill but instead the McClellan Committee excised the measure's Sherman Act amendments and its provisions for compulsory licensing and, in that form, reported it to the Committee on the Judiciary. Coincidentally, reports of the thalidomide disaster focused the attention of the nation and of Congress on the issue of drug safety and greatly increased the likelihood that some drug bill would be enacted during that session of Congress. Indeed, the administration, apparently fearful that its poor record on health care legislation would work against the President in light of the failure of his Medicare proposals, endorsed Kefauver's measure in a letter to the Chairman of the Senate Judiciary Committee, James Eastland from Mississippi.

In addition to having indicated support for the Kefauver bill in the Senate, on 23 April Kennedy sent his own drug bill to the House. It was introduced by Representative Oren Harris, Chairman of the House Committee on Interstate and Foreign Commerce on 2 May 1962 and covered the various specifics raised in the President's message.[340] Several weeks later Harris' committee conducted hearings on the bill and in September the measure passed the House. Both the Kefauver and the Harris bills, which closely reflected the wishes of the Food and Drug Administration and the President, cemented the approach embraced by the agency to food, drugs, cosmetics, and medical devices, that the function of government, and not each consumer, was to specify exactly what level of safety each of us should demand in these products, regardless of the disparate circumstances in which each of us might find ourselves. To this was now added the notion that the federal bureaucracy should determine for us the amount of risk we each should take that a particular product was efficacious or that, indeed, its efficacy might vary from person to person. It had been determined that a panel of functionaries was more competent than were adults to make these decisions. In this respect, 280 000 000 Americans were no more able to care for their own welfare than were their pets. It was therefore especially appropriate that, in testifying in support of the Harris bill, Abraham Ribicoff, the Secretary of Health, Education, and Welfare, noted that the new law 'will, for the first time, give men, women, and children the same safeguards against worthless drugs that Congress has been giving hogs, sheep, and cattle since 1913'.

While a series of amendments incorporating the objectives of the FDA were pending before Congress prior to the thalidomide incident, the events associated with the tragedy increased the confidence of the agency that a stronger bill with a more complex approval process would pass even though it likely meant that fewer new drugs would be developed. Senator Kefauver must have struck the agency as a perfect sponsor for such legislation since he had often voiced the belief that a good deal of drug innovation was socially wasteful. As one economist characterized Kefauver's view:

> The waste was said to arise from product differentiation expenditures in an imperfectly competitive market permeated by physician ignorance; product differentiation expenditures were incorporated in prices which therefore did not reflect the

'true value' of the drug to the consumer. It was argued that only in hindsight would doctors or patients discover that claims for new drugs were exaggerated; consumers would have been better off if they had used lower-priced old drugs (especially unpatented old drugs and most especially non-branded unpatented old drugs) instead of the new drugs.[341]

The Kefauver bill in its final form differed substantially from the measure as it was introduced 16 months earlier.[342] It had undergone a number of changes, both at the hands of the McClellan subcommittee and in the Eastland Committee on the Judiciary, many of which were crafted by the Food and Drug Administration. It had passed the Senate several weeks before the Harris bill passed the House and the two measures were then sent to a conference committee. Finally, the Kefauver-Harris amendments were signed into law on 10 October 1962.[343] The changes in the 1938 law made by Congress in 1962 contained several significant provisions that extended the power of the FDA. All drug manufacturers were required to register their establishments with the agency and to undergo a thorough inspection at least once every two years. In addition, the new act required that all pertinent records be kept and made available for inspection. More important, all reports on drugs that suggested any adverse effects were to be promptly transmitted to the FDA. In what must have been a particularly sweet victory for the agency, all authority over the advertising of prescription drugs was transferred from the Federal Trade Commission to the FDA. All advertising copy henceforth had to contain a full disclosure of adverse effects and contraindications. Trials on human subjects could not be undertaken without informed patient consent. Finally, and of greatest import, manufacturers were required to prove, by substantial evidence, not only the safety but the effectiveness of all new drugs, and all time constraints associated with the approval process were removed. The FDA thus became the only agency of government with the power to determine whether the public should have access to a new product despite its having proved harmless. None of these provisions had anything whatever to do with the thalidomide incident nor would these provisions have contributed one whit to preventing it. However, they would assure that the approval of new drugs would slow considerably.

Some two years following passage of the Kefauver-Harris Amendments the FDA contracted with the National Academy of Sciences/National Research Institute to evaluate the effectiveness of several thousand prescription drugs that had been approved between 1938 and 1962 on the basis of safety alone. The Drug Efficacy Study Implementation (DESI) tested more than 3400 drugs and more than 16 000 therapeutic claims.[344] The last evaluative report, according to the FDA, was finally submitted in 1969 and one of its earliest effects was the introduction of the ANDA (Abbreviated New Drug Application). ANDA status was extended to all products whose labels the agency ordered changed in order to comply with its new requirements. Thirty panels of experts, each consisting of six members, were authorized to determine whether a drug was or was not effective. The FDA completed its review process of 3443 prescription drugs in 1984, having found 2225 to be effective, 1051 not effective, and 167 pending. In sum, the effect of the efficacy study was to prohibit the sale of more than 30 percent of all prescription drugs on the basis of the opinion of six 'experts', despite the fact that both doctor and patient might wish to continue their use.[345]

The Kefauver-Harris efficacy requirement applied not only to prescription drugs but to over-the-counter remedies as well. As a result, in May 1972 the FDA decided to undertake a retrospective review of the efficacy of all over-the-counter drugs that had been approved between passage of the 1938 Act and enactment of the new amendments. Because of the truly huge number of such preparations, somewhere in the order of several hundred thousand, however, the review had by necessity to take a different form. Rather than analyze each medication, the FDA concentrated on approximately 1000 active ingredients which were evaluated by panels of experts. Each active component was assigned to one of three categories: (1) safe and effective; (2) unsafe and/or ineffective; and (3) probably safe and effective but needing further treatment. All drugs falling in the last two categories were taken off the market. The review is ongoing but has resulted in the prohibition of thousands of medications.

In its zeal to deal with medical heretics whose preparations were based on theoretical foundations at odds with orthodox medicine, The FDA was at its most energetic in grappling with medications aimed at treating cancer. One of the first actions taken by the agency under the Kefauver-Harris Amendments was against Mucorhicin. Mucorhicin was extracted from a mold that had been grown on a mix of wheat, salt, yeast, and water. At trial the defendant insisted that it was meant as a food supplement and not a drug and therefore was not subject to the provisions of the Food, Drug, and Cosmetic Act. However, a wealth of evidence was presented that Mucorhicin was sold for the treatment and mitigation of cancer.[346] As a result, the drug was held in violation of the 1962 amendments and its sale prohibited.

Of far greater import was the FDA's action against Krebiozen, a drug which many patients were convinced helped them in dealing with cancer. Krebiozen was originally developed in Argentina by Stevan Durovic, a Yugoslav physician, who, with his brother, brought the drug to the United States in 1949. There it caught the attention of Dr Andrew Ivy, Professor of Physiology and Chairman of the Department of Clinical Sciences at the University of Illinois. It was claimed that the drug was an extract of blood from horses that had been inoculated with *Actinomyces bovis*, a micro-organism responsible for a condition called 'lumpy jaw' in cattle. Tests performed by Dr Ivy convinced him and

a number of others, including Senator Paul Douglas of Illinois, that the preparation was effective in reducing or eliminating tumors and he announced this
at a press conference held in Chicago in 1951. Despite Ivy's claims, however,
a number of research centers were unsuccessful in replicating his findings. In
1962 the Krebiozen Research Foundation reported that some 3300 physicians
had treated over 4200 patients, with substantial reductions in tumor size. There
appears to be no confirmation of these reports although a number of users were
enthusiastic about the effects of the medication. When samples of Krebiozen
were turned over to the FDA, however, the substances submitted, when in
powdered form, were found to be composed solely of creatine monohydrate, a
normal constituent of muscle. The liquid was tested as plain mineral oil. The
Krebiozen Foundation argued that the active element had been contaminated
but was still present in minute amounts.

The FDA's campaign against Krebiozen was fiercely resisted by a vocal
group of supporters who insisted that they had benefited from the drug but the
agency persisted in its attempts to prohibit its use and sale, armed with the
requirements imposed on medications by the Kefauver-Harris Amendments.
The Krebiozen Foundation was now obligated to present a program of clinical
trials acceptable to the FDA. However, a committee of the National Cancer
Institute, having examined a number of patients that had been treated with
Krebiozen, declared the medicine worthless and determined that no clinical
trials were warranted. Distribution and use of the medication were now illegal.
This appears not to have been sufficient for the government. Krebiozen had
never been shown to have done any harm whatever. Additionally a large
number of people, fully aware of the heterodox nature of the preparation, were
devoted to it and were hoping to proceed with their treatments. It is possible
that Krebiozen did nothing more for them than improve their state of mind.[347]
Ordinarily this would be sufficient grounds for them to continue their course
of treatments without the intervention of a government that was prepared to
put their suppliers in jail. However, in the last century the ingestion of
substances of which the government disapproves has been dealt with differently. In 1964, Dr Ivy, Dr Durovic, and Marko Durovic, his brother, were
indicted on 49 criminal counts for violations of the Food, Drug, and Cosmetic
Act and mail fraud. The trial was held in Chicago and lasted from April 1965
to January 1966. The cost of the trial was between $3 and $5 million, yet
despite its length and cost the defendants were acquitted of all charges.

While the 1962 Amendments were still in Congressional committee, a
second bill, H.R. 11582, was also under consideration by Congress. Modeled
on the Kefauver-Harris Amendments, it required that medical devices meet
pre-market conditions similar to those that applied to drugs.[348] It was eventually deleted from the final bill but there were numerous attempts to enact legislation tightening the regulations regarding medical devices. President

Kennedy urged passage of a new law insuring the safety and efficacy of medical devices and in 1966 President Johnson recommended enactment of a Medical Device Safety Act[349] that would empower the FDA to pre-clear certain therapeutic materials, including organ transplants, and establish standards for the safety and performance of a number of commonly used devices, among them bone pins, catheters, x-ray equipment, and diathermy machines. Again Congress failed to act nor were two bills introduced during the Nixon Administration[350] reported out of committee.

Meanwhile, two important court decisions were handed down regarding what constituted a medical device. In the absence of explicit legislation, the FDA had decided to regulate devices by simply classifying them, when possible, as drugs. In 1968 this tactic was sanctioned by the Court of Appeals for the Second Circuit, which held that a suture product used to stitch blood vessels, consisting of a disposable applicator, a nylon ligature loop, and a nylon locking disc, was a drug. The court found that inasmuch as the product was a suture and since sutures were classified as drugs in medical compendia, this entailed that the product could properly be regarded as a drug.[351] In the following year the Supreme Court in an eight to one decision ruled similarly in *United States v. An Article of Drug . . . Bacto-Unidisk* [352] that an antibiotic sensitivity disc used as a laboratory screening test to help determine the proper antibiotic drug to administer to patients was a drug and not a device. The Court's rationale for this decision was purely political. It held that the term 'drug' as used in the 1938 Act was clearly a term of art and that

> the legislative history, read in light of the statute's remedial purpose, directs us to read the classification 'drug' broadly, and to confine the device exception as nearly as possible to the types of items Congress suggested in the debates, such as electric belts, quack diagnostic scales, and therapeutic lamps, as well as bathroom weight scales, shoulder braces, air conditioning units, and crutches.[353]

The Court's decision underscored the need for a legislative resolution to the question of what in fact constituted a device and, as a result in 1969 Robert Finch, the Secretary of Health, Education and Welfare, appointed a study group on medical devices chaired by Theodore Cooper, MD, at the time Director of the National Heart and Lung Institute. The Cooper Committee comprised ten officials, two from the FDA, five from various agencies of the NIH, and three from other sections of HEW. The report, issued in September 1970, recommended that all medical devices currently on the market be inventoried and that they be classified to determine (1) those that should be subject to premarket approval by the FDA, (2) those for which performance standards should be set, and (3) those for which neither premarket approval nor performance standards were necessary. As a result of the report, bills were introduced in 1973 and 1975[354] by Representative Paul Rogers, Democrat from

Florida, which formed the basis of the Medical Device Amendments of 1976. Even before passage of enabling legislation, however, the FDA began to establish performance standards and to create a comprehensive system of labeling.[355] The Congress was finally impelled to action by the FDA's order that the Dalkon Shield, an interuterine device implicated in the deaths of several women, be recalled.[356] Hearings on medical device legislation were held in the Senate in September 1973 and a bill, S. 2368, was favorably reported out of the Senate Committee on Labor and Public Welfare in January 1974. While the measure passed the Senate in the following month, it failed in the House and was again considered by the Senate in the following session. Once again, following hearings in January 1975 the Senate enacted similar legislation, S. 510, in April 1975. The House also held hearings on IUDs in May and June 1973 and again in October 1973 but no further action was taken. Finally, in a series of drafting sessions that included representatives from the FDA, the device industry, the House subcommittee and the House Office of Legislative Counsel, a new bill was drafted in December 1974 and January 1975. The measure was introduced as H.R. 5545 and hearings were held on the bill in July 1975. It passed the House in March 1976, was reported out of Conference committee in May, and signed into law later that month by President Gerald Ford.

The provisions of the 1976 Amendments were similar to the recommendations earlier made by the Cooper Committee. All medical devices were divided into three classes, those that required general controls[357] (class I), those for which performance standards had been set (class II), and those needing premarket approval (class III). The amendments called for manufacturers to notify the FDA of all medical devices prior to their being marketed. Subject to any existing or future requirements set by the agency, new devices that were substantially the same as those marketed prior to 1976 could be offered for sale immediately. All other devices developed after passage of the Amendments were subject to premarket clearance requirements and could not be marketed before the submission of preclinical and clinical data and FDA approval. In addition, the Amendments contained the usual bureaucratic provisions regarding registering all devices and maintaining records and filing reports. The FDA was empowered to ban all devices it had determined were deceptive in some way or another or presented an unreasonable risk of injury or illness. In addition, the agency was given authority to make regulations regarding the repair, replacement, and refund of defective devices.

Subjecting all new devices that represented a significant departure from anything on the market prior to 1976 as class III devices mandating preclinical and clinical trials and approval by the FDA has stifled innovation and added greatly to the cost of new devices. Those familiar with the difficulties encountered by Inventive Products in gaining approval of their Sensor Pad, which aids in detecting breast lumps and consequently reduces the mortality rate from breast cancer, can testify to the infuriating red tape to which these products are subject before they may be sold to the public. The Sensor Pad, comprising two latex-like sheets between which is a layer of silicon lubricant, took 11 years to approve and cost its manufacturer millions of dollars in legal fees. The Pad reduces friction between the hand and the breast during self-examination, thus permitting the fingers to glide more smoothly over the surface of the breast. Despite the simplicity of the device the FDA eventually granted approval on condition that it be available to users only via prescription!

A particularly distressing aspect of FDA policy respecting devices is the decision to classify all medical software as medical devices over which the agency has jurisdiction. It may and does exempt certain types of software from class III requirements but these exemptions are determined through a case-by-case assessment. The agency's software policy was first stated in 1987 and reiterated in 1989 in its 'FDA Policy for the Regulation of Computer Products'. All software whose purpose is to aid in the diagnosis, cure, mitigation, or treatment of disease meets the FDA's definition of a medical device and this has been determined to include analysis of potential therapeutic interventions and hospital information systems. The FDA has ruled that it will not subject to class III requirements software intended for the storage and retrieval of medical information or designed for general accounting functions – although it may if it so wishes – and this software continues to be subject to the adulteration and misbranding provisions of the 1938 Act. Software that is developed as either a component of or accessory to a medical device, however, is obliged to meet all FDA class III requirements, as are patient record systems or software designed to remind physicians to order certain tests. Indeed, under the FDA's reasoning, there is no reason why all medical textbooks and journals should not be classified as medical devices.

Among the most profound effects of the Medical Device Amendments of 1976 was the time it took manufacturers to get a new device to market. But the costs, in terms of the effect on patients who would benefit from the new technology but were required to wait, were not nearly as onerous as was the case with new drugs and the delays brought about as a result of the Kefauver-Harris Amendments. The 1962 Amendments provided that no drug could be marketed without first receiving FDA approval. Prior to their enactment firms were required to submit evidence of the safety of their products but could then begin marketing them if the FDA lodged no objection within 60 days. A study done a decade after passage of the new requirements has shown that removing any time constraints on the FDA's treatment of new drug applications

Table 2.3 *FDA Processing Time for NDA Submission to Approval, 1962–1978 (months)*

Year	Processing Time
1962	17
1963	18
1964	22
1965	25
1966	31
1967	36
1968	31
1969	44
1970	29
1971	19
1972	17
1973	29
1974	21
1975	26
1976	23
1977	27
1978	20

Source: Peter Temin, *Taking Your Medicine: Drug Regulation in the United States* (Cambridge, MA: Harvard University Press, 1980): 141.

significantly extended the time necessary to get a new drug approved. Table 2.3 shows the amount of time it took the Food and Drug Administration to process a new drug application (NDA) from the time it was originally submitted to the time it was approved. The table reflects the fact that FDA approval standards rose steadily during the 1960s, which, in turn, extended the period for which these submissions were under consideration by the agency. By the beginning of the 1970s, the approval process appears to have settled to between one-and-a-half and two-and-a-half years.

In addition, the 1962 Amendments required pharmaceutical manufacturers to offer evidence regarding not only the safety but the efficacy of any drug. The burden on manufacturers was thus substantially increased, in terms of both cost and time. In 1973 William M. Wardell published an analysis of the availability of new pharmaceuticals approved in Great Britain and the United States for the ten years ending in 1971 in which he found that, not only were a greater variety of drugs available in Britain, but for those drugs eventually available in both countries, on average they were able to reach the market two years earlier in Great Britain than in the United States.[358] Evidence shows a similar lag in drug approval for the period 1977 to 1987.[359] These lags, of course, cost lives, in some cases tens of thousands of lives. They are, however, the sort of costs that the FDA is more than willing to bear inasmuch as they are invisible.

Substantially longer approval times were not the only legacy of the Kefauver-Harris Amendments. They also were to have an appreciable effect on the number of new drugs introduced. The process of bringing a new drug to market is a complex and tedious one.[360] Once a substance has been identified as possibly having a new therapeutic use, the identifying firm almost invariably applies for a 'use' patent, thus laying claim to the substance as a therapeutic agent, and then begins animal testing. These early tests allow the manufacturer to determine safe dosage levels in the clinical trials to follow. Human clinical trials require that the firm file an investigational new drug (IND) application with the FDA. At that point the firm may begin clinical trials unless the FDA intervenes within 30 days. There follow three phases. In the first phase firms are required to test for safety, usually using between 20 to 80 healthy volunteers. The second phase is more extensive, involving somewhere between 100 and 300 patients, the purpose of which is to test for efficacy under differing doses. The final phase, involving anywhere between 1000 and 3000 patients, is directed at testing for efficacy and side-effects. Should the drug continue to show promise, the firm then applies for a new drug application (NDA). These applications, according to one analyst, are typically 100 000 pages long! The final stage involves FDA approval of the medication. This approval is extended to the treatment for a specific condition. If the firm later determines that the drug is effective in treating another condition, the firm must file another NDA.

According to Michael Ward, data for the period 1964 to 1989 show that approximately 5000 compounds were awarded drug patents annually. Of these between 800 and 2200 investigational new drugs (IND) were filed with the FDA. Of those not previously tested on humans for some other condition, the probability of entering the second stage was between 70 and 75 percent, of which about half entered the third stage (between 80 and 250 compounds). Of these new drug applications (NDA) the FDA approved about 20 to 60 per year, many of which were reformulations of existing products. Approximately one out of every 100 products for which patents were awarded was eventually marketed as a new drug.[361] More current estimates by the Office of Research and Development of the Pharmaceutical Research and Manufacturers Association are considerably starker. The Association maintains that of the 10 000 to 15 000 compounds tested in the laboratory, only one manages to get to market. The times involved in each stage of drug development are approximately:

Preclinical Testing	6.5 years
Phase 1	1.0 year
Phase 2	2.0 years
Phase 3	3.0 years
FDA Approval	3.5 years
Total	15.0 years[362]

The enormously long lead time before a new product can be marketed reflects the substantial costs of research and testing. In February 1993 the Office of Technology Assessment estimated that the full after-tax cost of developing a new drug that reaches the market was $194 million 1990 dollars.[363] The Tufts Center for the Study of Drug Development currently estimates the cost of bringing a new medication to market at about $802

Table 2.4   Number of New Single Drugs Introduced in the United States, 1941–1979

Year	New Drugs	Year	New Drugs
1941	20	1961	48
1942	14	1962	29
1943	10	1963	16
1944	14	1964	18
1945	14	1965	23
1946	20	1966	12
1947	24	1967	25
1948	27	1968	11
1949	42	1969	9
1950	33	1970	16
1951	39	1971	14
1952	40	1972	13
1953	54	1973	19
1954	43	1974	18
1955	40	1975	16
1956	47	1976	15
1957	54	1977	18
1958	49	1978	23
1959	66	1979	16
1960	51		

Source: Peter Temin, *Taking Your Medicine: Drug Regulation in the United States* (Cambridge, MA: Harvard University Press, 1980): 6. (Taken, in turn, from *Nonproprietary Name Index* (New York: Paul de Haen, 1974); *New Product Survey* (New York: Paul de Haen, 1977–79)).

million.[364] With such massive costs confronting pharmaceutical firms, the number of new medications introduced in the American market dropped precipitously following passage of the 1962 Amendments. In 1974 Sam Peltzman of the University of Chicago undertook a thorough study of the effects of the Kefauver-Harris Amendments on the introduction of new drugs. He found that the number of new pharmaceuticals dropped from an average of 43 per year prior to the 1962 amendments to 16 annually in the ten years following. Peltzman also discovered that new FDA regulations made it extremely difficult for pharmaceutical manufacturers to introduce new drugs aimed at competing with existing drugs, thus substantially reducing competition in the industry.[365]

Much has been made, and rightly so, of the fact that the 1962 Amendments greatly increased both the amount of time necessary to satisfy the FDA that a new drug was safe and efficacious and the costs of getting a new drug to market. And it is certainly of great importance that the agency is in large part responsible for the hundreds of millions of dollars needed before a new drug can legally be sold. Even more significant is the fact that the delays brought about by the FDA's demands for proof of efficacy have led to hundreds of thousands of deaths that would have been avoidable had certain drugs been available earlier.[366] But, as important as these facts are, there is yet another dimension of the Kefauver-Harris Amendments that deserves mentioning. Peter Temin has called attention to the fact that these amendments further divorced medications from their ultimate consumers by requiring that a small group of government-nominated experts determine when a medicine was effective. The law's definition of 'efficacy' is not a definition at all but the description of a process by which 'experts qualified by scientific training and experience' have evaluated a drug. This is reflected on the drug's label. It follows from this, as Temin notes, that

> if a drug has any desirable effects at all, the process of getting FDA approval will be centered on the label. The experts, through their manipulation of drug labels, will affect not only which drugs are marketed, but also what they are used for.[367]

The patient, no matter how well informed, no longer plays a role in determining his medicine, nor indeed, does the patient's physician, except marginally. The official reason for this, Wallace Janssen, the FDA's court historian, informs us, is that 'drug labeling is different from the labeling of other products in the marketplace. It is an adjunct of medical care, not mere identification or salesmanship.'[368] It is doubtful that Congress would have agreed to enact legislation transmuting the FDA into a super-physician which all Americans were required to consult before they could gain access to medication. Certainly it is hard to imagine, even if a majority of politicians approved of a medical bureaucracy armed with such powers, that most of the public would have concurred. Indeed, there is strong evidence pointing to the fact that most people, physicians and patients alike, have no sympathy with the FDA's self-appointed task of determining what medication will be used in what context.

Medications customarily can be used in the treatment of several disorders, including those untested for efficacy by the FDA. The agency does not permit a drug used in a variety of contexts from bearing a label that indicates its utility in the treatment of a medical condition other than that for which clinical trials for efficacy were undertaken and approved. Yet these off-label uses abound. One analyst has noted that most hospital patients are given drugs that are not FDA approved for the condition for which they're administered.[369] Nor are they likely to be approved for these conditions given the prohibitively high costs of FDA-mandated trials. Despite the absence of such clinical testing, however, off-label usage is an integral part of medical treatment. In fact, for physicians not to prescribe certain off-label medications to treat certain conditions would almost certainly constitute a cause of medical malpractice. These include, among a host of others, the use of antibiotics in the treatment of stomach ulcers, the treatment of lung, bladder, breast, and cervical cancers with mitomycin, and the management of cardiac conditions with aspirin.[370] In sum, the off-label use of drugs is an accepted part of medical practice and is ubiquitous, in large part because medical knowledge increases at a far faster rate than the testing and approval process mandated by the FDA. As one analyst has observed: 'The FDA, even with cooperation from drug manufacturers, could not review drugs in its lengthy testing process at a pace equal to that at which physicians discover beneficial off-label uses'.[371]

That the FDA refuses to allow drug labels to indicate these additional uses and that they prohibit, under penalty of criminal sanctions, advertising the benefits these pharmaceuticals could have in the treatment of other conditions speaks to the fact that the agency's primary interest is in preserving its bureaucratic control over medications, even should it compromise the health of thousands of Americans. Despite the FDA's explicit denials,[372] the agency has even attempted to regulate the practice of medicine throughout the country by throwing obstacles in the path of off-label prescribing. It is important to keep in mind that a medication's 'label' legally includes the informational inserts and other literature supplied by manufacturers to physicians. In 1992 the FDA initiated an informal policy of warning drug manufacturers against disseminating articles in peer-reviewed journals or medical texts authored by independent scientists that discussed the specific benefits that could follow from non-label use of a medication. In addition, firms were cautioned that any Continuing Medical Education (CME) programs which they sponsored were to avoid focusing on off-label uses of medications. The agency claimed that the circulation of this information amounted to distributing addenda to a drug's label and therefore violated the labeling provisions of the 1962 Amendments. In October 1996 two federal regulations formalized this policy and led the Washington Legal Foundation to bring a suit against the agency on First Amendment grounds.[373] The United States District Court for the District of Columbia found against the FDA but the agency appealed.[374] The appeal was heard in the Court of Appeals for the District of Columbia in January 2000. By that point, however, Congress had pre-empted both the agency and the Court by enacting the Food and Drug Administration Modernization Act,[375] which explicitly permitted the distribution of peer-reviewed journal articles that referred to non-label uses of drugs and medical devices, provided that the manufacturer had filed a supplemental application 'based on appropriate research to establish the safety and effectiveness of the unapproved use'. It is clear that the FDA was compelled to accommodate off-label use not so much by the nation's medical needs as by the intervention of Congress.[376]

Viewed in terms of its consequences for the health of Americans, the Kefauver-Harris Amendments were uniformly profound and calamitous. They did, however, contribute to the remarkable growth of the FDA. In the five years between 1961 and 1966, the agency's budget almost tripled, from just over $19 million to $53 million, and its personnel more than doubled, from 2199 to 4710. Indeed, the 1960s was a decade of unceasing expansion for the FDA as Congress broadened the agency's regulatory authority. Table 2.5 reflects this growth.

In 1959, some three weeks before Thanksgiving, the FDA announced that the nation's cranberry crop had been sprayed with aminotriazole, a USDA-approved herbicide that had been shown to be carcinogenic in laboratory animals. The recently enacted Food Additives Amendment, which contained the Delaney proviso, prompted the agency to issue a nationwide recall and sales of the uncontaminated cranberries dropped precipitously. In actuality only about 1 percent of the total crop, two batches from the Pacific Northwest, had been contaminated. However, the Secretary of Health, Education, and Welfare, Arthur Flemming, had managed to convey the erroneous impression that all cranberries were unsafe. Flemming's recommendation that the public refrain from purchasing cranberries for Thanksgiving proved disastrous for the industry. Cranberries were removed from grocery shelves, restaurants stopped serving them, and health officials in a number of jurisdictions banned their sale. Despite assurances from the Department of Agriculture that the remaining crop was safe, cranberry sales declined to one-third their normal levels. Both party presidential candidates, Richard Nixon and John Kennedy, were photographed feasting on cranberries and the industry undertook a massive advertising campaign, but these efforts were to no avail. Despite the substantial damage done to the cranberry industry,[377] the

Table 2.5   Annual Appropriations and Personnel, Food and Drug Administration, 1960 to 1970 (millions of dollars)

Year	Appropriation	Personnel
1960	13.8	1678
1961	18.8	2199
1962	23.0	2412
1963	29.1	3012
1964	35.8	3864
1965	40.4	4039
1966	53.1	4710
1967	60.0	4692
1968	66.0	4603
1969	67.3	4247
1970	72.7	4252

Source: National Commission on Product Safety, *Federal Consumer Safety Legislation* (A Study of the Scope and Adequacy of the Automobile Safety, Flammable Fabrics, Toys, and Hazardous Substances Programs) (June 1970): 210; reprinted in *Consumer Product Safety Act* (Hearings Before the Subcommittee on Commerce and Finance of the Committee on Interstate and Foreign Commerce, House of Representatives, 92nd Congress, 1st and 2nd Sessions, H.R. 8110, H.R. 8157, etc., Serial No. 92-59) (Washington, DC: Government Printing Office, 1972): Part 2, 748.

action once again placed the FDA in the nation's headlines as the watchdog of the nation's well-being.

One result of the cranberry recall was that when Congress enacted a law requiring that hazardous household chemical products be labeled as such, they decided that the Food and Drug Administration should assume authority over its enforcement. The effect was to substantially enlarge the agency's mandate and to point it in an entirely new direction. The Federal Hazardous Substances Labeling Act[378] was passed in 1960 and was prompted by FDA claims that 'thousands of children were being poisoned, burned, overcome by fumes, and otherwise accidentally injured annually through contact with household or inadequately labeled hazardous household chemical products'.[379] The Act was intended to provide a uniform standard for 'adequate precautionary warning labels' on hazardous substances intended for household use. It required manufacturers to label all active ingredients in household products regarded as 'proximate' hazards and empowered the FDA to pass on such labels. Exempt from the labeling requirement were inert ingredients whose effects were regarded as being chronic or long term. Hazardous substances were defined as all substances that might cause substantial personal injury or illness when reasonably handled. The Act divided these substances into six categories (1) toxic, (2) corrosive, (3) an irritant, (4) a strong sensitizer, (5) flammable or combustible, or (6) pressure-generating that is, a substance that 'generates pressure through decomposition, heat, or other means'. The FDA attempted to enforce this law with the same vigor that attended its control over food and drug labeling. Indeed, there seems to have been no limit to how extensive the FDA's authority might become.

In 1966 new legislation was enacted that enlarged the scope of the Act to include any hazardous household product, whether chemical or not. At hearings that led to passage of the Child Protection Act[380] the FDA testified that precautionary labeling alone was insufficient to adequately protect the public from a number of 'extremely hazardous products ... particularly products intended for use by children'.[381] The agency requested legislation that empowered it to 'rule a product off the market for household use when the substance is so dangerous that no amount of reasonable cautionary labeling would serve the purpose of this act'.[382] Congress not only complied with the wishes of the FDA in this regard but also authorized the Secretary of HEW, that is, the FDA bureaucracy, to ban all toys and other articles intended for the use of children that contained any hazardous substance. Finally, the Act was broadened to include unpackaged, as well as packaged, products that contained hazardous material. Three years later, in 1969, the FDA's authority over product safety was again broadened to include 'any toy or other article intended for use by children' that the agency determined 'presents an electrical, mechanical, or thermal hazard'. The Child Protection and Toy Safety Act[383] was passed because of testimony from the FDA that a wide range of hazardous toys and other products intended for children were not covered by existing legislation. These hazards were 'associated with sharp or protruding edges, fragmentation, explosion, strangulation, suffocation, asphyxiation, electric shock and electrocution, heated surfaces and unextinguishable flames'.[384] The House Committee hearing testimony on the proposed Act was informed that 'of the nearly 56 million children under 15 in the United States, more than 15,000 die each year from accidents – a rate of 28 per 100,000 population'.[385] The series of hazardous substances laws enacted in the 1960s gave ample proof that Congress had determined to intervene in regulating the risks to which we are subject and that their chosen method was to legislate product safety. It appeared for a time that the FDA was on the verge of enlarging its administrative control to embrace all consumer goods of whatever sort, thus placing the agency in the position of ultimately determining what each American would be permitted to buy. Indeed, the Nixon Administration had decided to support the creation of a new super-agency within the Health, Education, and Welfare Department to oversee both food and drugs and product safety. Had that occurred, it would have elevated the FDA to one of the most powerful bureaucracies in the federal government.

In 1970 the FDA, anxious to take on these added tasks, created a Bureau of Foods, Pesticides, and Product Safety, to which the agency's new functions were assigned. The following year, in preparation for even further expansion overseeing product safety, the FDA established a Bureau of Product Safety. Product safety was then regarded with particular favor and was politically popular with both parties. The National Commission on Product Safety, established in November 1967, had submitted its final report in June 1970 which strongly urged legislation creating a Consumer Product Safety Commission to administer a new law regulating the safety of consumer products and setting safety standards for those regarded as 'unreasonably' hazardous. Its recommendations were contained in a bill, H.R. 8157,[386] introduced by Representative John E. Moss, Democrat of California, on 6 May 1971. Not to be outdone, the Administration had prepared its own measure along similar lines but placing regulatory authority not in an independent commission but in the Department of Health, Education, and Welfare, where it would be lodged in the Food and Drug Administration, renamed the Consumer Safety Commission and restructured to include an Office of Drug Regulation, an Office of Food Regulation, and an Office of Product Safety Regulation.[387] Had the Administration version been enacted, the FDA would have been transmuted into a super-agency with authority to regulate almost every product used in or around the home, from food and drugs to household appliances, bedding, bleach, and toys. Representatives Harley Staggers, Democrat of West Virginia, and William Springer, Republican of Illinois, jointly introduced the Administration measure on 5 May as H.R. 8110.[388] Hearings were held by the Subcommittee on Commerce and Finance of the House Committee on Interstate and Foreign Commerce. While Staggers chaired the Commerce Committee and Springer was its senior Republican member, Moss had the benefit of chairing the subcommittee charged with taking testimony.

In light of what was at stake, both the Department of Health, Education, and Welfare and the Food and Drug Administration made every effort to see to it that the Administration bill was enacted. Every argument was put before the subcommittee in support of attaching the regulation of product safety to that of food and drugs: that it was cost effective to combine field offices and laboratories; that both regulatory areas dealt with the public health; that centralizing the responsibilities of both would consolidate consumer protection efforts; and so on. However, it was not so much the Moss bill that concerned HEW. What was somewhat worrisome was a bill introduced by Senator Warren Magnuson, Democrat from Washington, that would have created an independent commission with responsibility for consumer product safety, to which the regulation of food, drugs, cosmetics, and meats would be transferred. Had the bill passed, it would almost certainly have been the case that the FDA bureaucracy would have staffed most of the positions of the new commission. However, it was unlikely that many of the FDA's executive officials would have been appointed as the commission's senior officers and, as a result, the agency actively worked to defeat Magnuson's bill. In fact, the measure had little chance of passage, to a large extent because of the opposition of several powerful entrenched bureaucracies with a substantial amount to lose. In the event, the Moss bill easily passed both chambers and was signed into law in October 1972. The Consumer Product Safety Act[389] created the Consumer Product Safety Commission, which was charged with protecting consumers from 'unreasonable risk of injury from hazardous products'. It thus has one of the most extensive mandates of any agency within the government, exercising responsibility over a huge and varied assortment of health and safety risks. Under the terms of the Act, the CPSC was given responsibility for implementing the Federal Hazardous Substances Labeling Act of 1960 and its amendments, thus consolidating these functions and removing the FDA's authority over consumer product safety.

For a time, in the mid-1960s, it appeared as if the FDA would assume control not only over a wide range of hazardous products but that it would also be given the authority to deal with illicit drugs, including efforts to suppress the drug trade. Perhaps in compensation for the loss of its product safety functions, in 1965 Congress supplemented the authority of the FDA in this area by transferring to it authority to deal with problems caused by the abuse of depressants, stimulants, and hallucinogens. In 1942 the Food and Drug Administration initiated a program to deal with the illegal distribution of prescription drugs.[390] Its agents began a campaign to curb the use of nonnarcotic drugs[391] by those not holding a prescription by, in the main, prosecuting pharmacists for selling barbiturates and amphetamines to those not authorized to buy them. By the end of World War II, barbiturate and amphetamine use[392] was becoming increasingly common and they were joined by hallucinogens in the early 1960s. Congress was particularly alarmed by reports that these substances were illegally ingested by literally millions of Americans and made several attempts to bring them under the Harrison Narcotics Act. However, the Bureau of Narcotics, the agency charged with enforcing the government's narcotics laws, strongly opposed the suggestion on the grounds that the problems the Bureau would confront in attempting to enforce the law against substances legally manufactured and distributed in such quantity were qualitatively different from those it faced in dealing with narcotics. The FDA, on the other hand, continued to publicize the dangers of barbiturate and amphetamine use and their association with crime. In testifying before a special subcommittee[393] of the Senate Judiciary Committee chaired by Senator Price Daniel, Democrat of Texas, in 1955 George Larrick, Commissioner of the FDA, had reiterated the FDA's position on these substances:

Addiction produces a general dissolution of character. We know of men who have
held responsible positions but gradually became derelicts through the use of these
drugs. Whole families may become relief problems when the breadwinner becomes
addicted. Oftentime housewives begin to use the drug on a doctor's prescription for
a nervous condition; they gradually increase the dosage as tolerance and emotional
and physical dependence develop. They no longer take an interest in the home or
children, get dirty and slovenly; steal money and sell furniture to get the drug.
Again, because the drug is odorless, the victim may be far along before his family
recognizes the real trouble.[394]

Larrick then went on to offer estimates, without the least basis in fact, of the
sizeable abuse of these drugs, of their link to juvenile delinquency, and of the
huge number of highway fatalities that occurred as a result of amphetamine
use.[395]

Both Congress and the federal bureaucracy were incensed at the fact that
the recreational use of psychoactive drugs appeared to have become fashionable among a broad spectrum of the population, especially among Americans
of college age and that this 'drug culture' was strongly linked to opposition to
the Vietnam War. As a result, the government made every effort to stamp out
the illicit use of drugs which, it was argued, was undermining America's moral
will. The public were made a party to this effort, having been frightened by the
Bureau of Narcotics and the Food and Drug Administration into believing that
millions of young men and women were becoming enslaved to narcotics and
hallucinogens. The result was that in 1962 President Kennedy held a White
House Conference on Drug Abuse, which led in January 1963 to the creation
of an Advisory Commission on Narcotic and Drug Abuse (the Prettyman
Commission). The Commission was charged with recommending additional
legislation aimed at stopping the spread of illegal use. While it confessed to
having no reliable data to assess its actual prevalence it was clear, the
Commission concluded, that usage had increased substantially during the
1960s. Among its recommendations were (1) that the functions of the Federal
Bureau of Narcotics be transferred from the Department of the Treasury to the
Department of Justice; (2) that the number of federal agents that were assigned
to investigating the trafficking in illicit drugs be substantially increased; (3)
that non-narcotic drugs that had the capacity to produce psychotoxic effects be
placed under stricter control; (4) that any responsibility for investigating the
traffic in illicit drugs that was currently in the hands of the Department of
Health, Education, and Welfare (that is, lodged in the Food and Drug
Administration) be moved to the Department of Justice; and (5) that all regulation of the legitimate traffic in narcotic drugs and marijuana be moved from
the Department of the Treasury, where it had been since passage of the
Harrison Narcotic Act, to the Department of Health, Education, and Welfare
(i.e., the Food and Drug Administration).[396]

As a result of the Prettyman Commission's recommendations, Congress, in 1965, enacted the Drug Abuse Control Amendments,[397] augmenting the power of the FDA to deal with drugs of considerable 'abuse potential'. In order to eliminate the illegal traffic in amphetamines, barbiturates, and hallucinogens the agency established a Bureau of Drug Abuse Control with several hundred inspectors assigned to some nine field offices to track down illegal sales. The agency enthusiastically took on its new role and was overjoyed to share the glamor traditionally accorded government agents tracking down criminals and racketeers. Many of its agents went undercover disguised as peddlers and street bums in the agency's attempts to infiltrate the distribution system through which these drugs reached the public.[398] For a while the FDA hoped that its new crime-busting functions would lead to a period of substantial growth but, like its earlier product safety functions, President Lyndon Johnson soon disappointed the agency by consolidating the policing of all illicit drugs in a new agency, the Bureau of Narcotics and Dangerous Drugs (BNDD), located in the Department of Justice. Both the FDA's Bureau of Drug Abuse Control and the Treasury Department's Bureau of Narcotics were transferred to this new bureau in 1968, a bare three years after passage of the Drug Abuse Control Amendments. The transfer was a product of the President's Reorganization Plan No. 1[399] and turned over to the Attorney General full responsibility for the control of all dangerous drugs, of whatever kind. In 1970 Congress passed the Comprehensive Drug Abuse and Control Act,[400] Title II of which was the Controlled Substances Act. The Act established a single system of control for both narcotic and psychotropic drugs and created a classification system for controlled substances comprising five schedules. A drug's classification was determined by its 'potential for abuse', how dangerous the drug was thought to be, and whether the drug was conceded to have any legitimate medical use.

The transfer of responsibility for the enforcement of illicit drug use did not mean that the FDA surrendered all responsibility for illegal drug traffic. In 1988 Congress enacted the Prescription Drug Marketing Act (PDMA), which dealt with prescription-drug-marketing practices. It was feared that large quantities of drugs were being diverted into a gray market. The Act addressed the distribution of free samples, the use of coupons that could be redeemed for no cost or at a discount, and the sale of deeply discounted drugs to hospitals and health care facilities. Many of the drugs distributed in this way, it was claimed, fueled a massive drug diversion market. These diverted drugs, a good number of which were mislabeled or expired, entered the legitimate drug distribution system.

The penalties associated with violation of some of the provisions of the Act were truly ludicrous. For example, knowingly selling, trading, or buying or offering to sell, trade, or buy, a prescription drug sample is punishable by up to ten years' imprisonment! Nor could hospitals or health care facilities resell any drugs that they purchased. Wholesalers, who henceforth had to be licensed by the state in which they operated, were required to provide buyers with a statement of origin, including all prior sales, thus providing a paper trail for each shipment of drugs. Among the other prohibitions listed in the Act were the sale, purchase, or counterfeiting of prescription drug coupons (that is, coupons redeemable for free or low-cost prescription drugs), the wholesale distribution of prescription drugs without a license, and the reimportation of exported prescription drugs by anyone other than the drug's manufacturer.

The rationale for the Act was to protect the public from substandard, ineffective, and counterfeit drugs which, the FDA claimed, were a product of the fact that buyers possessed no knowledge about the source of the drugs they purchased. Despite the agency's concern that some prescription medications were making their way into a gray market, however, the agency, to its credit, did not feel that additional legislation was needed to deal with the problem. The PDMA had its origins in the 1984 discovery by G.D. Searle and Company that its Ovulan 21, a birth control medication, had been counterfeited. The result was that the staff of the House Oversight and Investigations Subcommittee of the Committee on Energy and Commerce issued a report about drug diversion.[401] Representative John Dingell, Democrat from Michigan, who chaired both the Committee and the Subcommittee, sensing an opportunity to increase his popularity by linking his name to the war on drugs, decided to hold hearings on what he termed 'a serious potential problem relating to the effectiveness and accountability of prescription pharmaceuticals sold to American consumers'.[402]

The result of these hearings was that Representative Dingell introduced a bill in January 1987 whose provisions were close to those of the final Act. The measure, H.R. 1207, predictably, had the support of those groups who stood to gain from its provisions while those who were likely to lose opposed the bill. The Pharmaceutical Manufacturers Associations supported the prohibition against the buying or selling of drug samples but was opposed to the bill's provisions regarding reimportation; the National Association of Retail Druggists and the National Association of Chain Drug Stores maintained that one of the primary causes of a flourishing gray market was the fact that manufacturers were allowed to price-discriminate by selling drugs at lower prices to charitable institutions; health care institutions opposed any attempt to control drug prices to hospitals and other health care facilities; and physicians strongly supported the practice of receiving drug samples.[403] Despite lukewarm support the bill passed the House in May and in March of the following year was passed by the Senate. It was reluctantly signed into law by President Ronald Reagan on 22 April 1988.[404]

The effect of the law seems to have been minimal except to add another layer of bureaucracy for the already overburdened pharmaceutical industry to deal with. The Act served no purpose except to increase the size and regulatory authority of the FDA, which set up an Office of Criminal Investigations to investigate drug diversion cases. In fact, the agency had already possessed ample authority to deal with instances of counterfeiting, adulterating, and misbranding and had successfully prosecuted several offenders before the PDMA was passed.[405] As evidence that it was not idle, however, the FDA, in 1992, conducted a sting operation in conjunction with an army of other federal and state agencies.[406] Known as 'Operation Goldpill', it was aimed at 'pill mills', which were responsible for counterfeiting and drug tampering. The operation resulted in 107 arrests and the seizure of 11 pharmacies. In the decade and a half since passage of the Act few violators have been prosecuted and those who have would have been subject to other prohibitory provisions of the Food, Drug, and Cosmetic Act. In sum, the PDMA appears to have served no purpose except to enlarge the FDA bureaucracy. As one analysis concludes: 'Many of the provisions of the PDMA are superfluous, of minimal benefit, and costly. Some of the problems that Congress hoped to solve could have been resolved by stricter enforcement of existing laws or by amending others. . . . The limited benefits of the PDMA simply do not justify its substantial burden imposed on many American entities and individuals.'[407]

Having lost the battle to expand its operations into the area of illicit drug use, the FDA set its sights on taking on the dietary supplement industry. The effects of the incursion into this relatively unregulated area would prove substantial. In the late 1960s there were approximately 600 supplement manufacturers in the United States with sales of more than $4 billion annually and it was estimated that about half of all Americans consumed dietary supplements of one kind or another, either vitamins, minerals, or herbs, to improve their nutrition.[408] During this period the FDA initiated a process that was to end in its attempt to treat dietary supplements, which it regarded as having no nutritional value, as drugs. Between May 1968 and May 1970 the agency held a series of public hearings on the regulation of these substances. The attending administering law judge showed little sympathy with those opposing the FDA's proposals and effectively suppressed evidence that called into question the basis of the agency's conclusions. In August 1973 the judge ruled in the FDA's favor with the result that a series of rules respecting dietary supplements, including definitional standards, labeling, and maximum potencies were adopted.[409]

The FDA announced that it would henceforth prohibit such supplements from making any health claims and require them to carry a warning label to the effect that an abundant supply of vitamins and minerals could be found in foods that were commonly available. Additionally, a limitation was placed on the potency of vitamins and minerals to 150 percent of their FDA-determined recommended daily allowance (RDA) while higher potencies would hence-forth be treated as drugs. The effect of classifying these supplements as drugs, of course, was to make their sale illegal inasmuch as they would be sold in dosages that exceeded their RDA and therefore would have been judged as therapeutically ineffective. Finally, dosages of vitamin A exceeding 10 000 IU and of vitamin D in excess of 400 IU, which the FDA had concluded were potentially toxic, could be sold only by prescription. These regulations were immediately challenged by 15 separate petitions, which were consolidated for consideration by the Court of Appeals. In *National Nutritional Foods Association v. Food and Drug Administration*[410] the Court of Appeals for the Second Circuit struck down most of the FDA regulations and remanded the case for rehearing. At the same time, in a separate action also heard by the Court of Appeals for the Second Circuit, the Court categorized the agency's decision to require prescriptions in order to purchase vitamin A and vitamin D in high potencies as 'arbitrary and capricious'.[411]

This attempt by the agency to arrogate to itself the same authority over dietary supplements as it had over prescription drugs alarmed a vast number of supplement users. Congress was bombarded with more than a million letters from constituents protesting the actions of the FDA and a number of Congressmen were determined to take action to formally limit the agency's power in this area. Senator William Proxmire, Democrat from Wisconsin, introduced a bill to this effect in 1974 which passed the Senate but was defeated in the House by another measure sponsored by Representative Peter Kyros, Democrat of Maine. Kyros' bill, had it passed, would have been disas-trous for the dietary supplement industry. The bill allowed any vitamin that was regarded as toxic at a certain dose to be regulated in the same way as were drugs and classified all vitamins, minerals, or other food ingredients as food additives, subject to premarket safety trials. Proxmire was eventually able to convince Kyros to rework his bill to bring it into line with Proxmire's own, and in 1976 the measure passed both Houses as an amendment to the Heart and Lung Act. The Act prevented the FDA from imposing potency limits on vitamin and mineral supplements or on regulating these dietary supplements as drugs. It further classified these supplements as foods and, as such, required only that their ingredients be accurately listed.[412]

In the meanwhile the FDA had lost its battle against foods making health claims in their advertising. The Federal Trade Commission had altered its position on the question in the late 1970s in light of a series of medical stud-ies linking health to diet. In 1984 the Kellogg Company, at the urging of the National Cancer Institute, called the public's attention to the link between fiber consumption and a reduced risk of colon cancer in its advertisements for its All-Bran cereal. The mention of a specific disease was unprecedented and in fact violated FTC regulations but that agency did not protest Kellogg's actions.

Indeed, in the following year the Trade Commission formally changed its policy to permit publication of this kind of information. The proliferation of claims respecting health, nutrition, and disease led Congress to enact the Nutrition Labeling and Education Act (NLEA) in late 1990[413] which called on the FDA to develop regulations regarding these claims.

In January 1990 the FDA reported a link between the consumption of a dietary supplement known as L-tryptophan and a cluster of symptoms known as Eosinophilia-Myalgia Syndrome (EMS). L-tryptophan, an amino acid crucial in balancing mood and sleep patterns, was commonly used to relieve depression, anxiety, and PMS, to control pain, and as an aid to natural sleep. More than 1000 cases of EMS were reported by state health authorities to the Centers for Disease Control, some resulting in death. The CDC had concluded that a 'virtually unequivocal link' existed between the supplement and the illness and consequently the FDA instituted a nationwide recall of L-tryptophan.[414] Once again the FDA determined to capitalize on the incident to lobby for legislation that would extend its own authority despite the fact that it had been responsible for the safety and purity of L-tryptophan when the incident occurred. In response to the mishap, Representatives Henry Waxman, Democrat from California, introduced a bill, H.R. 2597, that would have greatly augmented the enforcement powers of the FDA, including its authority to embargo or recall any drug, food, cosmetic, or device over which it had jurisdiction. Under its terms, the agency could order a recall on any substance, food, or device should it be determined that there exists 'a significant risk to human or animal health'.[415] At the same time a second bill called for amending the Federal Trade Commission Act to make it illegal to advertise any nutritional or therapeutic claim made by a dietary supplement other than what might have been allowed by the FDA on the supplement's label. The bill, H.R. 1662, was introduced by Representative John Moakley, Democrat from Massachusetts, and had the full support of the FDA and the medical lobby.[416] However, the public's mood and the disgust of many members of Congress at the continual arrogance of the FDA was sufficient to kill both measures.

Indeed, public outrage at the FDA's attempts to constrain the dietary supplement market following the L-tryptophan incident had led to inclusion of an amendment referring specifically to dietary supplements in the Nutrition Labeling and Education Act (NLEA) which was enacted in November 1990. While the NLEA was directed primarily at the health claims made for foods, it also contained a section bearing on supplements. During debate on the bill Senators Orrin Hatch, Republican from Utah, and Howard Metzenbaum, Democrat of Ohio, had added an amendment to establish a standard separate from that which applied to foods for the pre-approval of health claims made by dietary supplements, which were understood to include seed oils, nutritional drink mixes, enzymes, amino acids, pollens, orotates, glandulars, antioxidants, and herbal tinctures. The Act directed the FDA to develop regulations governing nutritional claims made by foods and required that they be supported by 'significant scientific agreement'. The measure further authorized the FDA to promulgate rules governing the health claims of dietary supplements as well but the clear intent of Congress was that these would be less strict than for other foods.

In spite of Hatch's amendment, one of the first acts of the new Commissioner of the FDA, David Kessler, who had replaced James Benson in November 1990 and who had vowed to 'restore credibility and integrity' to the agency, was to strike a Dietary Supplements Task Force[417] to recommend how nutritional supplements should be regulated. In the meanwhile, Kessler decided that the agency would apply the same regulations to supplements as it did to foods.[418] In November 1991, even before its Task Force had reported, the FDA issued regulations covering nutritional supplements, which opened with the following statement:

> The Agency recognizes that proposing the same standard for conventional food and dietary supplements is contrary to the view expressed by some members of Congress. . . . However, FDA has reviewed the legislative history . . . and has tentatively concluded that Congress did not intend that the agency be forced to adopt a different standard for the products.

The supplement industry was infuriated by the FDA's decision, which was a clear violation of the intent of those provisions of the Act that had reference to nutritional supplements. However, Congress and the public had no recourse from the agency's deliberate contravention of Congress's wishes except to enact a new law. In *United States v. Rutherford*[419] the Supreme Court had ruled that should an administrative agency misread the intentions of Congress in interpreting the provisions of an Act, the public have no standing to sue for redress. Congress alone possesses a remedy and that solely through enacting another law.

The actions of the FDA appear to have precipitated an avalanche of mail protesting its decision concerning nutritional supplements. As a result, Congress, once again at the urging of Senator Hatch, quickly passed the Dietary Supplement Act of 1992, which was appended as Title II of the Prescription Drug User Fee Act.[420] The Act established a one-year moratorium on implementing the NLEA with regard to dietary supplements, although it did allow the FDA to approve or disapprove health claims for these products. Soon after its passage, Senator Hatch introduced a measure, S. 784, to more permanently limit the authority of the FDA over dietary supplements and was successful in pushing the bill through the Senate Committee on Labor and Human Resources by a vote of 12 to five, over the objection of its Chairman, Senator Edward Kennedy, Democrat of Massachusetts. Events in the Senate reflected those that were to occur in the House, where a similar bill was put forward by Bill Richardson of New Mexico, H.R. 1709, and was under consideration by the House Subcommittee on Health and Environment of the Committee on Energy and Commerce, chaired by Representative Henry Waxman, a strong opponent of the measure. Despite these early divisions, efforts to bring the two opposing factions together proved successful and a compromise bill passed both chambers unanimously.

In October 1994 President William Clinton signed into law the Dietary Supplement Health and Education Act[421] limiting the authority of the FDA with respect to dietary supplements. The Act created a new regulatory class for these substances and thus put an end to the FDA's requirement that nutritional supplements meet the same regulatory requirements as foods. The Act defined dietary supplements as vitamins and minerals taken by mouth that contain a 'dietary ingredient' intended to supplement one's diet. In addition, the Act encompassed other supplements such as amino acids, glandular extracts, herbs and other botanicals, and glandular extracts, about which the agency claimed to have serious safety concerns.[422] Despite the agency's wishes, however, the Act explicitly exempted supplement manufacturers from having to register with the agency before producing or selling their products. Under the terms of the Act, FDA authority was limited to insuring that these substances were free from impurities and that the information accompanying their sale, including their labels, was not misleading. Before demanding the recall of any nutritional supplement the agency was required to first show that there was an 'imminent and substantial public health hazard'. While Senator Hatch expressed his elation at the bill's passage, the Center for Science in the Public Interest viewed the Act as marking the start of 'America's Second Age of Quackery'.[423]

In 1980 Representative Henry Waxman was approached by a constituent who was unable to obtain medication for her son, who was suffering from Tourette's syndrome. The boy's medicine had been seized at the Canadian border and was not available in the United States, not having been approved by the FDA. As a result, Waxman decided to hold hearings on the problem of rare diseases. The events surrounding the boy suffering from Tourette's syndrome eventuated in an episode of *Quincy*, a weekly TV series starring the actor Jack Klugman, which features a medical examiner who solves a new mystery each week. The episode that centered on Tourette's syndrome, which was aired in March 1981, has been credited with calling public attention to the problem of orphan diseases and, ultimately, to the need for an Orphan Drug Act. What was not made clear in the *Quincy* episode was that the FDA was directly responsible for the oppressively high costs of developing new pharmaceutical products and that the dearth of drugs for the treatment of orphan diseases was a function of the allocation of resources brought about by these costs.

In part because of public interest in the proposal, Representative Waxman introduced H.R. 5238 in December 1981. Congress enacted the Orphan Drug Act and it was signed into law in January 1983.[424] A large number of diseases, many severely debilitating, affected only a relatively small number of Americans, among them Huntington's disease, amyotropic lateral sclerosis, Tourette's syndrome, cystic fibrosis, Gaucher's disease, and muscular dystrophy. Because of the costs of research and testing associated with a new drug, it simply would not have proved economical to devote substantial resources to the development of new drugs useful in treating illnesses the incidence of which was comparatively low. The expenses involved in meeting FDA requirements were so large, approximately $802 million according to the Tufts Center for the Study of Drug Development,[425] that manufacturers would be very unlikely to undertake the development of new medications with such modest markets.

The purpose of the law was to address this problem by providing incentives for drug manufacturers which would compensate them for the prohibitively high expenses involved in developing new drugs for orphan diseases and conditions. According to the National Organization of Rare Disorders (NORD), approximately 25 million Americans suffer from some 6000 comparatively rare disorders. While the number of people affected by an orphan disease is definitionally set at 200 000, 47 percent of these affect fewer than 25 000 people. Prior to passage of the Act not only were the costs of development an insuperable obstacle to bringing new drugs to market but pharmaceutical firms had great difficulty in recruiting suitable subjects for mandatory clinical trials. The Orphan Drug Act was passed to help in overcoming these obstacles. The original statute, passed in 1983, required that firms present evidence, in the form of market data and detailed financial reports, that there existed no reasonable expectation that sales of a new drug would be sufficient to recover the costs of development. However, this proved to be so onerous a task in some cases[426] that Congress amended the law in the following year to allow firms to qualify if they could show that the disease affected fewer than 200 000 people in the United States. A successful applicant was granted market exclusivity for a period of seven years following approval of the application, in addition to tax incentives and research grants. Manufacturers may claim a tax credit for up to 50 percent of the costs of clinical research and may apply for research grants to help cover the costs of conducting trials.

The law appears to have been a success. In the two decades prior to passage of the law, only 40 therapies were developed for the treatment of orphan diseases,[427] compared to almost 240 drugs, foods, and devices since 1983. These are employed in the treatment of over 11 million patients in the United States. Eighty-five percent are used to treat life-threatening diseases, 31 percent, rare forms of cancer, and about 50 percent in pediatric cases. Although the Act benefited victims of orphan diseases by reducing the costs of development of orphan drugs, it also necessitated an expansion of the FDA bureaucracy. In 1982 the agency created a new bureau, the Office of Orphan Products Development, to administer the major provisions of the Act, including the determination of which products would receive funding for clinical research. In typical bureaucratic fashion, the government had increased the costs of producing new drugs and then enacted supplementary legislation to partially correct the problem, adding yet another layer of bureaucracy.

In 1984 Congress enacted Title II of the Drug Price Competition and Patent Term Restoration Act,[428] which sought to balance two competing goals: on the one hand, to maintain and extend the incentives firms had in developing new drugs and, on the other, to encourage competition from generic drugs. The Act, also known as the Hatch-Waxman Act, extended the life of patents on drugs to compensate holders for the extensive wait they were forced to undergo during the FDA approval process. The Act established a program that allowed patent holders of human drug products, medical devices, or food or color additives to recoup some of the lost time during which they were prevented from marketing their product. The measure set a maximum patent life of 14 years from the product's approval date and a maximum extension time of five years. The FDA was empowered to assist the Patent Trademark Office in determining whether a product were eligible for patent restoration. In addition to an extension of the patent life of a drug, the Act ostensibly abbreviated the approval process.

At the same time, the Act also made it easier and less expensive to enter the generic drug market. Under its provisions, the approval process for generic drugs was greatly simplified and shortened. At the time substantial public pressure was brought to bear to reduce pharmacy costs. As a result many health care plans, including Medicaid, promoted the substitution of generic drugs for brand names, and many states that had enacted drug-substitution laws, permitted pharmacists to dispense a generic drug when a prescription called for a specific brand. These factors played a crucial role in reducing the proportion of brand name drugs that were sold. In 1984 19 percent of all prescription drugs sold were generic. By 1994 this had climbed to 43 percent. In effect the Act shortened the time between expiration of a drug's patent and the marketing of new generic copies from three years to three months.[429] Possibly the most important change contributing to shorter approval times was that generic drug manufacturers were permitted to conduct clinical tests for bioequivalence[430] before the brand-name drug patent expired. Since clinical tests can begin that much earlier, approval of generic applications could theoretically be extended immediately after the patent on a drug expired. The law did a great deal to advance sales of generic drugs and became necessary after the United States Court of Appeals had ruled in 1984 that clinical tests using patented drugs before the patent had expired constituted patent infringement.[431] Following approval of the Act, prescription drug sales rose rapidly. Between 1985 and 1995, sales, valued at manufacturer prices, increased from $21.6 billion to $60.7 billion, going from 5.7 to 6.9 percent of all health care expenditures.[432]

In terms of its effect on the Food and Drug Administration, certainly the most significant event of the past two decades has been the AIDS epidemic. In 1987 the FDA introduced an expanded access program, permitting limited access to experimental pharmaceuticals for AIDS sufferers who had exhausted the benefits of currently marketed therapies. The regulations bearing on this permitted prescription of a treatment investigational new drug ('treatment IND') during the third phase of human testing. Under this program, for example, AZT, the first medication that showed any promise for AIDS patients, was distributed to about 5000 people after completion of a single controlled clinical trial that pointed to its efficacy. Patients other than those few who had access to drugs prior to their full approval would be forced to wait for the completion of clinical trials before being able to try a new medication. With respect to AIDS, these clinical trials were quite macabre since there were only two ways to determine whether a drug was in fact efficacious: determining when the onset of some opportunistic infection had occurred and measuring the time it took for a patient to die.

In the following year, under intense pressure from AIDS activists, particularly those directed by ACT UP,[433] the FDA established a new program that allowed AIDS sufferers access to medications that were in the process of undergoing clinical trials. In order to make new therapies available sooner to a larger number of patients suffering from life-threatening diseases, the agency allowed creation of a parallel track alongside those patients enrolled in controlled tests of a medication. This 'parallel track' program was supported by Dr Anthony Fauci, the Director of the National Institute of Allergy and Infectious Diseases, a division of the National Institutes of Health, who announced at a meeting in San Francisco that he supported the procedures before having consulted the FDA. The Department of Health and Human Services was forced to create a task force to develop a set of procedures, and the FDA, infuriated that it had been taken unawares, now had no option but to agree to implementing the plan. Medications were made available to patients not through pharmacies but through participant physicians who received them directly from the manufacturer. Bristol-Meyers-Squibb dispensed a new drug, didanosine (Videx), to 19 000 AIDS patients without charge in this way before the drug was formally approved in October 1991. It was found, however, that those who took advantage of the program tended to be well-educated while most sufferers were not even aware that they were eligible for the drug.

Additionally, smaller drug companies were reluctant to underwrite the costs of a program that, according to some estimates, cost $2 million a month.

In order to expand access to these medications the FDA next instituted an accelerated approval program which permitted manufacturers to market certain drugs provided they agreed to continue conducting clinical trials after approval. Drugs used in the treatment of diseases classified as life-threatening or severely debilitating were eligible to receive accelerated approval status after only two, rather than three, phases of human testing. This fast-track approval procedure, unlike the expanded access program, actually reduced the amount of time needed for a drug to enter the market. The program had the further advantage that these drugs could no longer be regarded as experimental and therefore would be covered by both public and private health-care insurers, including Medicaid. The evidence suggests that fast-track approvals have reduced the time for drugs to reach the market by several years. Even in such cases, however, the approval process took as long as eight years.[434]

This three-to-five-year waiting time for FDA approval of a drug was unquestionably responsible for thousands of deaths from AIDS. As a result, a number of AIDS patients and their physicians, having concluded that the risk was worth taking if an experimental drug proved fatal, chose to use experimental drugs from underground laboratories. As one sufferer noted: 'People are dying of AIDS anyway. I'm tired of being protected.'[435] In 1991 Representative Tom Campbell, Republican from California, introduced a bill, known as the Access to Life-Saving Therapies Act.[436] The measure authorized the FDA to change its standards for drugs used in the treatment of AIDS, cancer, Alzheimer's disease, and Parkinsonism and to permit patient access far earlier than had been the case. In addition, health insurers would be required to reimburse patients who were prescribed drugs approved under the new law. Despite the fact that the bill had 110 co-sponsors in the House, it failed to reach the House floor and died in committee.

In its place Congressional efforts, in the fall of 1992, were centered on a bill introduced by Representative John Dingell that authorized the FDA to levy user fees on drug manufacturers to help defray the costs involved in the FDA approval process. Inasmuch as Dingell chaired the House Energy and Commerce Committee, the committee to which health measures were referred, any bill he sponsored had a substantial advantage over competing measures. In 1992 Congress enacted the measure which permitted the FDA to charge drug manufacturers for the costs of reviewing new drug applications. The Prescription Drug User Fee Act (PDUFA)[437] was introduced in the House in early October and became law within several weeks, having passed both chambers without objection. The drug companies supported the measure in return for the FDA's commitment to expand and computerize its drug review process, thus permitting new drugs to be marketed sooner. Despite its seeming popularity in Congress, the initiating and driving force behind this reform were AIDS patients and their physicians, who hoped that the legislation would accelerate FDA approval of new drugs.[438] In the event, the measure proved less effective than was expected. The agency, of course, testified that it was a great success because review times had in fact been shortened. Indeed, the Tufts University Center for the Study of Drug Development found that in the 1990–93 period the average review time for new drugs was 2.7 years, compared to 1.7 years for the period 1994–95.[439] Yet despite faster approval times, the total time required for a new drug to reach the marketplace remained fairly constant between the late 1980s and the year 2000.[440]

In addition, there seems to have been some question whether all fees collected from drug manufacturers were in fact used to reduce approval times. More important, a portion of this improvement can be credited to the FDA's introduction of a new policy, known as 'refusal to file', whereby the FDA rejects an application if it determines that it is either incomplete or in some way deficient. Since these applications are culled out of the total number, the mean review time of the applications remaining is, of course, significantly shorter than would otherwise have been the case. In any case approval times represent only a fraction of the time between discovery and approval of a new drug. Overall development approval times have risen substantially since passage of the Kefauver-Harris Amendments, from 8.1 years in the early 1960s to 15 years in the mid-1990s.[441] While this has since declined, it remains fairly significant.

Despite these concerns, when the PDUFA came up for reauthorization in 1997, Congress renewed the FDA's authority to charge such fees but included more rigorous performance goals, imposing on the agency the obligation to meet substantially tighter review times.[442] In 2002 Congress once again reauthorized the program for a further five years.[443] At the time the 1997 Act was passed it included a provision that permitted the FDA to impose higher fees to cover the program's costs. These fees are now considerably higher than they were when the program was initiated. The application fee in 1993, the first year user fees were imposed, was $100 000; a similar fee today, 12 years later, is $573 000! At the same time the proportion of drug review funding underwritten by these fees has increased dramatically, from 7 percent in 1993 to almost 50 percent in 2001.[444]

Efforts to reduce overall development times, however, appear to have been mixed. Burrill & Company, a merchant bank specializing in the health industry, reported in 2002 that average drug development during the 1990s was almost exactly the same as it was in the decade before. While approval times during the decade decreased, the time necessary for clinical trials increased. Table 2.6 gives a breakdown of drug development times in the last four decades.

Table 2.6   Drug Development Times, by Decade, 1960s through 1990s (years in development)

	Preclinical	Clinical	Approval	TOTAL
1960s	3.2	2.5	2.4	8.1
1970s	5.1	4.4	2.1	11.6
1980s	5.9	5.5	2.8	14.2
1990s	5.6	6.7	1.8	14.1

Source: Burrill & Company, Presentation by G. Steven Burrill, CEO, Burrill & Company, 9 October 2000 http://www.chi.org/brandomatic/othermedia/chi/PDF_IDPC_SP_Laguna_Niguel-presentations.pdf (accessed 19 August 2003).

None of these changes in FDA regulations were as important, however, as was passage of the Food and Drug Administration Modernization Act of 1997 (FDAMA). The Congressional elections of 1994 returned Republican majorities in both houses of Congress and they determined to make comprehensive reform of the Food and Drug Administration a legislative priority. After a series of hearings in both the House and Senate, several bills were introduced in both chambers but they were not reported out of committee.[445] Following the 1996 elections, however, there was some pressure to act expeditiously on an FDA bill since the Prescription Drug User Act of 1992 contained a sunset clause that required renewal in that session of Congress. The FDA reform bill (S. 830), containing a renewal of drug user fees, was introduced in the Senate in June 1997 (S. 830) by James Jeffords, Republican from Vermont, and passed by the Senate in September by a vote of 98 to two. In the House three separate bills were introduced, covering drugs in April (H.R. 1411), medical devices in May (H.R. 1710), and food in October (H.R. 2469). The three bills were combined and passed without debate in October. After ironing out the substantial differences in the bills enacted by the two chambers, the Conference Committee reported and the measure was passed by both Houses of Congress in November.[446]

Beside renewing the prescription drug user fee, the provisions of the FDAMA included sections covering every aspect of the Food, Drug, and Cosmetic Law. Its provisions included granting the FDA authority, which it might or might not use, to reduce the number of clinical trials necessary before a drug was approved, expediting the approval of drugs used in the treatment of serious conditions, including authorizing a new mechanism for fast-track approval, allowing manufacturers to distribute information about the 'off-label' uses of approved drugs, and permitting broader access to unapproved drugs in life-threatening situations. The Act also extended market exclusivity for six months on drugs found to have new pediatric indications, permitted qualified practitioners to manufacture, on a limited scale, products not commercially available, eliminated the batch certification requirements for insulin and antibiotics, and reduced the approval time on medical devices.[447]

Earlier fears that the prescription drug user fee program would tempt Congress to reduce the FDA's tax-supported appropriation led the agency's supporters to include a complex formula for a 'water-line' base budget below which appropriations could not fall in the original 1992 Act. This feature was re-enacted in 1997 and again in the FDAMA. In addition, the new Act established a series of performance goals that the agency was required to meet. Among the Act's other novel provisions was that it explicitly permitted pharmaceutical manufacturers to disseminate 'health care economic information', that is, cost-effectiveness claims, if such claims were based on reliable evidence and to promote prescription drugs directly to the public.[448]

The gains in approval times that have occurred since 1992 are not without cost, especially with regard to drugs that are considered breakthroughs, which get a special fast-track approval review of six months. Despite the fact that very few overall savings in time took place during the PDUFA's first decade, there is some evidence that quicker approval times had, as a byproduct, an increase in the number of adverse drug reactions (ADRs)[449] that resulted in hospitalization and, in several cases, death. In December 2000 a writer for the *Los Angeles Times* published an article in which he reported that seven drugs that had undergone shorter approval times were cited 'as suspects' in 1002 deaths and had had to be recalled.[450] While the medications were the subject of adverse drug reports, there is no evidence that the deaths were a product of ADRs. The Public Citizen's Health Research Group[451] has consistently maintained that the faster review process instituted by the FDA is responsible for a large number of ADRs, thousands of which have resulted in death.[452] In addition, since the inception of fast-track approvals, more drug recalls have occurred. But it is important to keep in mind that early drug recalls are exactly what would be hoped for were drugs subject to accelerated approval. A very large number of ADRs, several hundred thousand, occur regularly, and only a minor proportion of these can be attributed to drugs that were subjected to quicker approval than had been the case before 1992. A statement prepared by the Academy of Managed Care Pharmacy dismisses the more sensationalistic claims of groups like Public Citizen and notes:

> FDA approval does not mean that medications are risk-free. First, approved medications are *generally* safe and effective and then only *when used appropriately.* Second, even when used appropriately, there are potential side effects, with health care professionals and the patient making the judgment as to *whether the benefits outweigh the adverse secondary effects.* Third, problems associated with drugs are

sometimes identified either only after a drug has been on the market and available to a broader population than was tested during the approval process or only after the passage of a certain period of time.[453]

In March 2004 the FDA released a report that dealt with the declining number of new drugs approved by the agency. Entitled 'Innovation/ Stagnation: Challenge and Opportunity on the Critical Path to New Medical Products', the analysis suggested that the approval process could be made more predictable and less costly if the FDA were to collaborate to a greater degree with academic researchers and product developers. Known as the Critical Path Initiative, the program appears to have done nothing toward expediting the compliance process. In 2004 only 36 new drugs were approved by the FDA while in 2005 the number had dropped to 20.[454]

Among the reasons for clinical trials taking as long as they do is the inordinate amount of time that must be devoted to complying with FDA demands that certain tests be conducted that serve no scientific purpose. Two examples among many include the fact that drug manufacturers are obligated to run 12-month non-rodent toxicity studies when six-month studies have proven just as accurate, and requiring drug interaction studies when there exists no mechanistic reason to predict interaction between two drugs.[455] These examples are indicative of how risk-averse the agency is. Indeed, it is so risk-averse that it regularly delays the introduction of new drugs that both physicians and patients seek to use, at the cost of the health and lives of thousands of sufferers.[456]

More recently the functions of the FDA were expanded as a result of the Bioterrorism Act of 2002. Title III of the Act, which deals with 'Protecting the Safety and Security of the Food and Drug Supply', provides that the FDA assume responsibility for the registration of all food facilities and for receiving prior notification of and approving all foodstuffs imported into the country. These tasks are substantial inasmuch as there are about 400 000 facilities involved in the preparation of food throughout the nation and that approximately 25 000 separate food shipments enter the United States every day. The overwhelming portion of bioterrorism expenditures earmarked for the FDA are directed at complying with these two programs. However, in addition, the statute called for the FDA to insure the safety and effectiveness of all medical products that might prove necessary in dealing with bioterrorist attacks, including those involving anthrax, smallpox, plague, nerve agents, or radioactive contaminants. By fiscal year 2004 the FDA was spending over $116 million on these functions,[457] despite the fact that state laws and local ordinances, pre-empted by federal statute, appear to have been doing a fully adequate job in protecting the nation's food supply. Nor, of course, do these expenditures take into account the fact that food vendors, warehousers, and

Table 2.7   Dates of First Enactment of State Laws Prohibiting the Sale of Certain Drugs Except by Prescription

	Cocaine	Opium	Morphine	Heroin	Marijuana	Peyote
Alabama	1907	1909	1907	1909		
Arizona	1899	1899	[1899]	[1899]		1923*
Arkansas	1899	1923	1923	1923	1923	
California	1907	1907	1907	1907	1915	
Colorado	1987	1915	[1915]	[1915]	1917	1915*
Connecticut	1905	1913	1913	1913		
Delaware	1913	1913	1913	[1913]		
Dist. of Columbia	1906	1906	1906	[1906]		
Florida	1909	1909	1909	[1915]		
Georgia	1902	1907	1907	[1907]		
Idaho	1909	1909	1909	1909	1927	
Illinois	1897	1915	[1915]	[1915]		
Indiana	1907	1907	1907	1913	1913	
Iowa	1902	1923	1923	1923	1921	1925
Kansas	1901	1921	1901	[1921]	1927*	1920
Kentucky	1902	1912	[1912]	[1912]		
Louisiana	1998	1918	1918	1918	1924*	
Maine	1899	1913	1913	1913	1913	
Maryland	1904	1912	1904	1912		
Massachusetts	1906	1910	1910	1910	1914	
Michigan	1905	1910	1909	[1909]	1929	
Minnesota	1905	1915	1915	1915		
Mississippi	1900	1924	1924	[1924]		
Missouri	1905	1915	1915	1915		
Montana	1889	1889	1889	[1889]	1927	1923*
Nebraska	1905	1915	1915	[1915]	1927	
Nevada	1911	1877	1911	[1911]	1917	1917

New Hampshire	1909		1915	1915	
New Jersey	1904	1908	1908	1915	
New Mexico	[1909]	1909	[1909]	[1909]	1923
New York	1907	1914	[1914]	[1914]	1927
North Carolina	1905	1905	1905	1907	
North Dakota	1905	1885	1917	1915	1923*
Ohio	1902	1913	1902	[1902]	1927
Oklahoma	1910	1910	1910	1910	
Oregon	1913	1913	1913	1913	1923
Pennsylvania	1903	1917	[1917]	[1917]	
Rhode Island	1906	1906	1906	1906	1918
South Carolina	1907		[1915]	[1915]	
South Dakota	[1915]	1885	[1913]	[1913]	1923*
Tennessee	1901	1913	1903	[1903]	1919
Texas	1903	1903	1911	1911	1915
Utah	1907	1911	1915	1915	1915
Vermont	1915	1915	1915	1915	
Virginia	1908	1904	1904	1908	
Washington	1909	1909	1909	[1909]	
West Virginia	1907	1907	1907	1907	
Wisconsin	1907	1907	1907	1907	
Wyoming	1903	1903	[1903]	[1903]	1913

North Dakota 1923* · South Dakota 1923* · Utah 1917 · Wyoming 1929*

Notes: Statutes to 1930 only.

Dates enclosed in brackets indicate that the drug is not explicitly mentioned in the statute referred to but is covered by virtue of such language as 'salt or compound' or 'any alkaloid or derivative' of opium, coca leaves, etc.

* Unavailable even by prescription of a physician.

Source: Ronald Hamowy, 'Introduction', in Ronald Hamowy, ed., *Dealing With Drugs: Consequences of Government Control* (Lexington Books; Lexington, MA, D.C. Heath and Co., 1987): 10–11.

Table 2.8   Earliest Statewide Pharmaceutical Licensing Acts

State	Year	State	Year
Alabama	1887	Nebraska	1887
Arizona	1903	Nevada	1901
Arkansas	1891	New Hampshire	1875
California	1891	New Jersey	1877
Colorado	1897	New Mexico	1889
Connecticut	1881	New York	1900
Delaware	1883	North Carolina	1881
District of Columbia	1878	North Dakota	1890
Florida	1889	Ohio	1884
Georgia	1881	Oklahoma	1890
Idaho	1887	Oregon	1891
Illinois	1881	Pennsylvania	1887
Indiana	1899	Rhode Island	1870
Iowa	1880	South Carolina	1876
Kansas	1885	South Dakota	1890
Kentucky	1874	Tennessee	1893
Louisiana	1888	Texas	1889
Maine	1877	Utah	1892
Maryland	1908	Vermont	1894
Massachusetts	1885	Virginia	1886
Michigan	1885	Washington	1891
Minnesota	1885	West Virginia	1881
Mississippi	1892	Wisconsin	1882
Missouri	1881	Wyoming	1886
Montana	1895		

Source: Ronald Hamowy, 'Introduction', in Ronald Hamowy, ed., *Dealing With Drugs: Consequences of Government Control* (Lexington Books; Lexington, MA: D. C. Heath and Co., 1987): 10–11.

preparers are as eager to insure the purity and safety of their products and devote great effort and expense toward these ends.

In April 1997, testifying before the House Subcommittee on Health and the Environment, Michael A. Friedman, Lead Deputy Commissioner of the Food and Drug Administration, observed that 'FDA's primary mission for ninety years has been to promote and protect the public health'. [458] In fact there is no historical warrant whatever for this claim. The Pure Food and Drugs Act was not intended to 'promote the public health' and only incidentally to protect it.

Table 2.9 FDA Funding in Current and Constant (1996) Dollars, Fiscal Years (FY) 1985–2004 (in thousands of dollars)

Fiscal Year	Current Dollars			FY1996 Constant Dollars	
	President's Request to Congress[a]	Congressional Appropriation	Percent Change from Previous Year	Congressional Appropriation	Percent Change from Previous Year
1985	392 554	409 694	7	550 738	3
1986	417 400	420 306[b]	2	552 961	0.4
1987	453.575[c]	436 430	4	556 245	0.6
1988	488 604	476 116	9	585 413	5.2
1989	507 456	507 456	7	602 393	2.9
1990	582 183[c]	592 691	17	675 508	12.1
1991	680 420[c]	682 131	15	753 986	11.6
1992	763 216[c]	751 574	10	812 073	7.7
1993	782 650[c]	817 647	9	862 588	6.2
1994	915 914[c]	918 698	12	949 657	10.1
1995	974 582[c]	943 398	3	955 050	0.6
1996	1 011 756[c]	963 988	2	963 988	0.9
1997	1 010 472[c]	967 197	0.3	939 939	-2.5
1998	1 034 029[c]	1 008 965	4	955 459	1.7
1999	1 236 125[c]	1 098 140	9	1 043 165	9.2
2000	1 350 000[c]	1 186 072	8	1 101 478	5.6

237

Table 2.9 *(continued)*

Fiscal Year	Current Dollars			FY1996 Constant Dollars	
	President's Request to Congress[a]	Congressional Appropriation	Percent Change from Previous Year	Congressional Appropriation	Percent Change from Previous Year
2001	1 390 000[c]	1 217 787	2	1 109 307	0.7
2002	1 414 000[c]	1 345 386	10	1 209 336	9
2003	1 787 000[c]	1 630 727	21	1 453 800	20.2
2004	2 000 000[c]	1 695.442	4	1 485 476	2.1
2005	1 844 604	1 881 489	11.4	1 628 052	9.6

Notes:

[a] Data are for salaries, expenses, and GSA rent. They do not include funds for buildings and facilities, reimbursable activities or certain collected fees.

[b] After 1986, the numbers indicate amounts available after the Gramm-Rudman-Hollings sequesters. For example, the amounts originally appropriated were $420 306 000 in FY1986 and $585 883 000 in FY1990.

[c] The numbers include the following amounts to be collected through user fees: 1987: $31 425 000; 1990: $100 000 000; 1991: $157 175 000; 1992: $197 500 000; 1993: $200 000 000; 1994: $254 000 000; 1995: $337 923 000; 1996: $141 667 000; 1997: $145 749 000; 1998: $244 272 000; 1999: $293 380 000; 2000:$195 000 000; 2001: $202 600 000; 2002: $204 000 000; 2003: $295 000 000; 2004: $300 000 000; 2005: $350 000 000.

Source: Data from 1985 through 1995 is from the FY1995 Congressional Budget Submission, pp. 31–3. FY1995-FY1999 appropriation levels are from the relevant conference reports. Data for FY1999 through FY2004 are from the relevant Budget Submissions and Appropriations bills.

Its purpose was to insure that the food and drugs sold throughout the country were neither spoiled nor poisonous and that buyers were informed if the commodity contained any of a very limited number of substances. The 1906 Act went no further and if the power of the FDA has now reached the point where it determines what we may eat or how we may medicate ourselves, this authority is largely a function of the agency's own efforts, with the help of a succession of Congressional allies, who have worked unceasingly to expand and consolidate the agency's power even when it clearly contravened the public interest. While the FDA presents itself to the public as a watchdog agency that insures the safety of our medications, its powers are far more sweeping, since it demands a mass of evidence demonstrating the efficacy of the product for the specific purpose for which it is sold. Harmless and ineffective products contravene the law as much as do those that prove harmful.

The FDA refers to itself as 'the nation's premier consumer protection agency', in that it makes it illegal to engage in the buying, selling, or manufacturing of any medical or food product of which it does not approve, despite the fact that some people want to acquire these products and others want to market them. In this sense, it is a 'consumer protection agency' no different from the vice squad, which also prohibits the buying or selling of goods and services it feels are harmful to the public, under penalty of fine or imprisonment. Nor does the FDA limit its far-reaching powers to 'protecting' the public. Were that the case, it would restrict itself to informing Americans of the effects of the possible harmful effects of certain drugs.[459] Instead, it acts as a barrier between the producer of drugs and consumers and their physicians, even in instances where all are fully aware of their possible consequences. In the process the FDA is responsible for severe suffering and often death to untold thousands. It is significant that Robert Kessler, certainly one of the most zealous defenders of bureaucratic medicine, while FDA commissioner at one point noted: 'If members of our society were empowered to make their own decisions about the entire range of products for which the Food and Drug Administration has responsibility, then the whole rationale for the agency would cease to exist'.[460] Surely nothing could be more destructive of the ends of an all-intrusive government than that people would be permitted to make their own decisions.

NOTES

1. In 1974, Prof. Sam Peltzman published an extremely important study of the net effects of the 1962 amendments to the Food, Drug, and Cosmetic Act. These amendments made it mandatory that before drugs be marketed their efficacy had to be proved to the satisfaction of the FDA. Peltzman calculated that the new legislation, by the most conservative of estimates, added an additional two years to the FDA approval process. As a consequence, there

was an annual net loss of over \$300 million in 1962 dollars (\$1800 million in 2002 dollars) in additional morbidity and mortality costs. There is overwhelming evidence that these delays bring about a net loss of many thousands of lives. *Regulation of Pharmaceutical Innovation: The 1962 Amendments* (Evaluative Studies; Washington, DC: American Enterprise Institute for Public Policy Research, 1974). Indeed, it has been estimated that more than 100 000 people died who might have been helped had they had access to new beta blocker medications that regulate hypertension. These, however, were denied FDA approval for eight years on the grounds that they might contribute to causing cancer. See Robert M. Goldberg, 'Breaking Up the FDA Medical Information Monopoly', in *Regulation*, 18(2) (Spring 1995): 40–52.

2. James Harvey Young, *Pure Food: Securing the Federal Food and Drugs Act of 1906* (Princeton, NJ: Princeton University Press, 1989): 11.

3. See Mitchell Okun, *Fair Play in the Marketplace: The First Battle for Pure Food and Drugs* (Dekalb, Ill.: Northern Illinois University Press, 1986): 13, and Young, *Pure Food*, 13.

4. Glenn Sonnedecker, 'Controlling Drugs in the Nineteenth Century', in John B. Blake, ed., *Safeguarding the Public: Historical Aspects of Medicinal Drug Control* (Baltimore and London: Johns Hopkins Press, 1970): 102. Not only was the *Pharmacopoeia of the United States*, established in 1820, used as a standard, but the pharmacopoeias and dispensatories of Edinburgh, London, France, and Germany were all regarded as definitive.

5. Constitution of the American Pharmaceutical Association, quoted in Sonnedecker, 'Controlling Drugs in the Nineteenth Century', 100.

6. The implication, which the Food and Drug Administration does nothing to rectify, that prior to passage of the Pure Food and Drugs Act of 1906 Americans had no legal protection against foods and drugs that had been corrupted with the most virulent poisons is pure nonsense. The sale of adulterated foods was actionable under English common law and statutes dealing with adulterated food and short weights, especially if life-threatening, were as old as the American colonies. See Wallace F. Janssen, 'America's First Food and Drug Laws', *FDA Consumer* (June 1975): 12–19. An extensive history of government regulation of food adulteration in the United States is contained in Peter Barton Hutt and Peter Barton Hutt II, 'A History of Government Regulation of Adulteration and Misbranding of Food', *Food, Drug and Cosmetic Law Journal*, 39 (1984): 2–73.

7. The notion of preserving food in airtight containers to prevent spoilage was first put forward by Nicholas Appert of France at the end of the eighteenth century. In 1810 the Englishman Peter Durand patented a food-preservation process based on packaging food in airtight tin-plated wrought-iron containers. By the 1860s the time needed to process food in a can had been reduced from six hours to 30 minutes.

8. Reay Tannahill, *Food in History* (new, fully revised, and updated; New York: Crown Publishers, Inc., 1988): 293.

9. Currently the favorite adulterant in pepper in the third world appears to be papaya seeds.

10. In 1720 Parliament enacted legislation prohibiting the importation of textiles from Asia, thus making tea the primary Chinese export.

11. This was especially true after black tea, *Camellia assamica*, from India and Ceylon was introduced into England after the Opium Wars in 1839–42. The tea earlier imported from China was green and lent itself less easily to counterfeiting. It was largely because of the frequency with which black tea was adulterated that John Horniman, an English Quaker, began retailing sealed lead-lined packages of tea in 1826.

12. This of course does not apply to legally mandated adulterants, from which we are not protected and which by law we are required to ingest. The most well-known of these is fluoride, placed in the water supply of the nation's towns and cities. Less well known is the fact that during World War II the British government mandated that chalk, which had been singled out in the nineteenth century as a particularly pernicious example of adulteration, be added to bread to insure that the population consume a sufficient quantity of calcium in their diet. This additive was the brainchild of Dr Elsie Widdowson, the eminent British nutritionist and the inventor of dried eggs.

13. Roasted cocoa, no matter how finely ground, was neither soluble nor miscible in water in the absence of starch due to the substantial amounts of fatty cocoa butter present in cocoa

beans. See David Satran, 'The Chocolate Girl Defiled: Cocoa, Gender, and Food Adulteration in Nineteenth-Century Confections' (accessed 15 August 2002 at http://www. english.udel.edu/satran/cocoagirl.htm).

14. Now sold at a premium and known as 'French' coffee! It is worth emphasizing in relation to the inclusion of chicory in coffee, said to be the foremost example of adulteration by nineteenth-century reformers, that chicory was openly produced as an additive to coffee and that it was in no way found an unhealthy comestible. Yet it consistently took pride of place as an example of the evils of adulteration and the need for stringent regulation. See S. D. Smith, 'Coffee, Microscopy, and the *Lancet*'s Analytical Sanitary Commission', *The Journal of the Society for the History of Medicine*, 14(2) (2001): 197.

15. Okun, *Fair Play in the Marketplace*, 45, 77, 81.

16. Fredrick Accum, *A Treatise on Adulterations of Food and Culinary Poisons* (London: printed by J. Mallett, 1820).

17. Young, *Pure Food*, 42.

18. Okun, *Fair Play in the Marketplace*, 4–5. While lead is indeed a poison, orthodox medicine at the time Accum's book was published regarded lead and its salts as specifics for syphilis and other venereal ailments and it was routinely administered in large doses.

19. 'After the Civil War,' Okun observes, 'both sanitarians and spokesmen for the grocery trade warned that buying the "cheapest" commodity encouraged competition, which induced adulteration'. *Fair Play in the Marketplace*, 6.

20. Wakley was prompted to commission Hassall as a result of Hassall's researches into the composition of ground coffee, which he found, to the horror of the coffee-drinking public, to be heavily adulterated with chicory. Indeed, of 34 samples of coffee tested, Hassall found no fewer than 31 had chicory as a component. *Encyclopedia Britannica*, 11th edition (1910), s.v. 'Adulteration'.

21. Arthur Hill Hassall, *Food and Its Adulterations* (London: Longman, Brown, Green, and Longmans, 1855) and *Adulterations Detected: or, Plain Instructions for the Discovery of Frauds in Food and Medicine* (London: Longman, Brown, Green, Longmans, and Roberts, 1857).

22. The *Lancet*'s campaign to obtain passage of a pure food and drug law through the use of Haskall's researches was regarded by Wakley's biographer as 'the most useful agitation in favour of legislative reform that ever engaged his attention'. S. S. Sprigge, *The Life and Times of Thomas Wakley* (originally published: 1897; New York: R. E. Krieger Pub. Co., 1974): 460; quoted in Smith, 'Coffee, Microscopy, and the *Lancet*'s Analytical Sanitary Commission', 171.

23. Okun, *Fair Play in the Marketplace*, 16, 17.

24. Okun, *Fair Play in the Marketplace*, 17–18. See also S. D. Smith, 'Coffee, Microscopy, and the *Lancet*'s Analytical Sanitary Commission', 171–97, which raises serious questions regarding Hassall's and Wakley's objectivity and which suggests that what passed for scientific fact was in reality polemic.

25. William G. Rothstein, *American Physicians in the Nineteenth Century: From Sects to Science* (Baltimore: The Johns Hopkins University Press, 1972): 181–3.

26. The side-effects of oral administration of opium, gastric and 'cerebral' disturbances, did not follow injection of the drug. See Rothstein, *American Physicians in the Nineteenth Century*, 192.

27. Ibid., 195.

28. See Table 2.7: Dates of First Enactment of State Laws Prohibiting the Sale of Certain Drugs Except by Prescription.

29. It is true that patent medicines regularly carried wildly extravagant claims regarding their curative powers but these were no more absurd than those that appeared on any container of bottled water sold at thousands of establishments throughout a number of European countries only a few years ago.

30. James Harvey Young, *The Medical Messiahs: A Social History of Health Quackery in Twentieth-century America* (Princeton, NJ: Princeton University Press, 1967): 19.

31. Edward M. Brecher, *Licit and Illicit Drugs* (Boston, MA: Little, Brown, 1972).

32. The following sentiment is illustrative of the attitude of an overwhelming proportion of druggists. At the 1893 American Pharmaceutical Association convention one druggist who had taken the floor inquired: 'Do we not recognize that this [patent medicine] industry is one of our greatest enemies, and that there are millions of dollars' worth sold all over the country, thus diverting money which rightly belongs to the retail drug trade, in the way of prescriptions and regular drugs?' Quoted in James Harvey Young, *The Toadstool Millionaires: A Social History of Patent Medicines in America Before Federal Regulation* (Princeton, NJ: Princeton University Press, 1961): 208–9.

33. In the 12 years between 1881 and 1892 no fewer than 32 states enacted laws establishing pharmaceutical licensing boards. See Table 2.8: Earliest Statewide Pharmaceutical Licensing Acts.

34. Opium and morphine not only served as staples in the orthodox *materia medica* and as crucial ingredients in a substantial proportion of patent medicines but were also sold in pharmacies and general stores, and by mail-order houses. A survey of Iowa during the period 1883–85, which then had a population of less than 2 million, uncovered the fact that, besides physicians who dispensed opiates directly, no fewer than 3000 stores in the state sold opiates. Brecher, *Licit and Illicit Drugs*, 3.

35. Lorine Swainston Goodwin, *The Pure Food, Drink, and Drug Crusaders, 1879–1914* (Jefferson, NC: McFarland & Co., 1999): 89.

36. Goodwin, *Pure Food Crusaders*, 90.

37. While the WCTU's primary goal at its founding was to criminalize the manufacture and sale of liquor, it quickly expanded its concerns to a whole spectrum of social causes. Despite the fact that the organization's current membership is today somewhat less than 5000, down from its high of 500 000, it continues to lobby for the legal prohibition of a variety of activities, including marijuana use, pornography, gambling, and homosexuality. See the WCTU's website, http://www.usiap.org/Archives/NewsArticles/NA2000_07_09B.html (accessed 19 November 2002).

38. Goodwin, *Pure Food Crusaders*, 89.

39. The WCTU was originally organized in a Chautauqua Sunday School Assembly in Cleveland, Ohio, attended by members of the temperance crusade, who regarded breaking up saloons as insufficiently effective in achieving their immediate end of limiting the consumption of alcohol.

40. Thomas R. Pegram, *Battling Demon Rum: The Struggle for a Dry America, 1800–1933* (Chicago: Ivan R. Dee, 1998): 67.

41. By 1896, 25 of the 39 departments of the WCTU were dealing with non-temperance issues.

42. Woman's Christian Temperance Union website: 'Early History', http://www.wctu.org/earlyhistory.html (accessed 7 September 2002).

43. See Goodwin, *Pure Food Crusaders*, 131–51.

44. Harvey Wiley later wrote the GFWC member charged with heading the campaign that 'the passage of the bill was due to the woman's clubs of the country. Trust them to put the ball over the goal line every time. The enactment has proven the finest example of political education I have ever seen.' The quotation appears on the official GFWC website and can be accessed at http://www.gfwc.org/about_us.jsp?pageId=gfwc_org_242 (accessed 15 June 2003).

45. See Goodwin, *Pure Food Crusaders*, 39, who makes this claim. Indeed, the many woman leaders of the movement have left ample testimony in their speeches and writings to their meddlesome, mean-spirited dislike of 'foreign values' and differences in social behavior. They abhorred immigrants, especially those from southern and eastern Europe, whom they regarded as, in the main, mentally deficient and whose customs and religions they found indecent and degrading.

46. Goodwin, *Pure Food Crusaders*, 139. It is this same sense that 'bad' choices should be, at best, criminalized and, at a minimum, discouraged by government action that led the temperance movement to successfully agitate state legislatures to enact laws mandating the teaching of STI – 'scientific temperance instruction' – in the public schools. See Jonathan Zimmerman, '"The Queen of the Lobby": Mary Hunt, Scientific Temperance, and the Dilemma of Democratic Education in America, 1879–1906', *History of Education Quarterly* 32 (Spring 1992): 1–30.

47. *Congressional Record*, 49th Congress, 1st Session (1886): Appendix: 223–6, quoted in Young, *Pure Food*, 66.
48. Also known chemically as dextrose.
49. Hence the more popular name, corn sweetener.
50. Young, *Pure Food*, 67–8.
51. Okun, *Fair Play in the Marketplace*, 224.
52. Ibid., 77.
53. George Thorndike Angell, 'Public Health Associations', *Sanitarian*, 7 (1879): 130–131; quoted in Young, *Pure Food*, 50.
54. Okun, *Fair Play in the Marketplace*, 224.
55. Ibid., 77–82.
56. One expert, whose comments were typical, observed that glucose and oleomargarine were perfectly healthful foods and that the most hysterical warnings regarding adulterants were either scientifically absurd or outright lies. See Okun, *Fair Play in the Marketplace*, 129.
57. Young, *Pure Food*, 51. No session of Congress from 1879 until passage of the Pure Food and Drugs Act of 1906 failed to consider one or another bill of this type.
58. H.R. 3170, *Congressional Record*, 47th Congress, 1st Session, p. 430; quoted in Young, *Pure Food*. 66–7.
59. In 1871, Mège sold his European rights to the Dutch firm Jurgens, a predecessor of Unilever, which began the manufacture of margarine in Europe in 1878.
60. Okun, *Fair Play in the Marketplace*, 253.
61. There is little question that legislation against oleomargarine was a reaction to pressures from the dairy industry, which was seeking state and federal protection. See Donna J. Wood, *Strategic Uses of Public Policy: Business and Government in the Progressive Era* (Marshfield, MA: Pittman Publishers, Inc., 1986): 154–64. Similarly, manufacturers of baking powder made from cream of tartar sought to curtail the sale of baking powder based on other acidic chemicals, particularly calcium acid phosphate, tartaric acid, aluminum phosphate, or sodium aluminum phosphate. These 'alum' powders were considerably less expensive to manufacture with the result that the tartar baking powder industry made every effort to have the cheaper substitutes declared poisonous or, at least, to convince the public that they were poisonous. Wood, *Strategic Uses of Public Policy*, 164–5. In this effort they would eventually have the full support of the federal government's Bureau of Chemistry, forerunner of the Food and Drug Administration.
62. The law is discussed in Okun, *Fair Play in the Marketplace*, 254.
63. Okun, *Fair Play in the Marketplace*, 273–6. Some economic analysts have suggested that the primary reason why pressure was brought to bear on governments in the late nineteenth century to regulate the purity of food was that information costs regarding the quality of food became prohibitively high as production and distribution became technologically more complex. Food manufacturers and distributors were therefore in a position to adulterate or misbrand their products with impunity unless overseen by some regulatory agency. (See, for example, Marc T. Law, 'The Origins of State Pure Food Regulation', available at http://economics.wustl.edu/~law/Origins.pdf (accessed 17 January 2003).) This argument has no greater merit than any similar argument that rests on informational asymmetries. It is far more likely that those consumers concerned with obtaining more extensive knowledge regarding the reliability of food products would have relied, as indeed they did, on the reputation of the manufacturer or on the publicity given particular foods in the press. The literature of the period confirms that the public demand that governments act to halt the distribution and sale of adulterated goods was in fact a demand that laws be enacted that banned the sale of foods containing 'impurities' that were in no way harmful to human health. More important, at the state level pure food laws were enacted in those states where lobbying by agricultural interests was most intense.
64. Leaf lard is generally regarded as the best lard produced and is made by clarifying the fat around the animal's kidneys.
65. Young, *Pure Food*, 73.
66. Ibid., 74.

67. Remarks of Hon. James R. Thomas, in Hearings Before the Committee on Ways and Means in Relation to House Bill 142, 25 April (and 9 May) 1882, 47th Congress, 1st Session (Washington, 1882): 1–5; quoted in Young, *Pure Food*, 75.

68. Young, *Pure Food*, 83.

69. Perhaps the best discussion of the legislative treatment of oleomargarine by the federal government is that of Geoffrey P. Miller, 'Public Choice at the Dawn of the Special Interest State: the Story of Butter and Margarine', *California Law Review*, 77 (January 1989): 83–131.

70. Remarks of Matthew Butler in *Congressional Record*, 49th Congress, 1st Session (Washington, DC, 1886): 7149; quoted in Young, *Pure Food*, 77.

71. This view is startlingly similar to that held by certain naturalists and 'environmentalists' today toward genetically engineered foods, their arguments against biotechnology being almost identical to those earlier leveled against chemically altered foods.

72. Oscar E. Anderson, *The Health of a Nation: Harvey W. Wiley and the Fight for Pure Food* (Chicago: University of Chicago Press, 1958): 76.

73. Thomas A. Bailey, 'Congressional Opposition to Pure Food and Drugs Legislation, 1879–1906', *American Journal of Sociology*, 36 (1930): 52.

74. Beside the law placing a tax on oleomargarine enacted in 1886, Congress was prevailed upon two years later to enact a measure prohibiting the sale of adulterated foods in the District of Columbia. In contrast with earlier attempts to pass similar legislation applicable to the nation as a whole, the 1888 law faced negligible opposition and was signed by President Cleveland in October 1888. In 1890 a meat inspection act aimed primarily at meat destined for export was passed. Eight years later legislation regulating the purity of candy sold in the District of Columbia was enacted without debate. Finally in 1902 Congress passed a second measure with specific reference to oleomargarine and enacted legislation requiring that food products be branded in accordance with the requirements of the state where it was made. These measures are discussed in Bailey, 'Congressional Opposition', 52–64.

75. For a detailed history of the Biologic Control Act of 1902, see Kamunas A. Kondratas, 'The Biologic Control Act of 1902', James Harvey Young, chairman of the symposium, *The Early Years of Federal Food and Drug Control* (Madison, Wisconsin: American Institute of the History of Pharmacy, 1982): 8–27.

76. It should be underscored that the academic requirements for physicians at the time that Wiley was preparing himself for the practice of medicine were far from rigorous. Indeed, Wiley's formal medical education at Indiana Medical College in Indianapolis, a reputable medical school sponsored by the local Academy of Medicine, comprised only two four-month terms in 1869–70 and 1870–71. See Anderson, *Health of a Nation*, 11.

77. It was not until 1889 that the Department of Agriculture was raised to cabinet status.

78. According to Wiley sugar consumption was a measure of how civilized a country was. He especially urged children to include a large amount in their diets. 'Childhood without candy', he is quoted as saying, 'would be Heaven without harps'. Clayton A. Coppin and Jack High, 'Entrepreneurship and Competition in Bureaucracy: Harvey Washington Wiley's Bureau of Chemistry, 1883–1903', in Jack High, ed., *Regulation: Economic Theory and History* (Ann Arbor, Mich.: University of Michigan Press, 1991): 100.

79. Wiley defined adulteration as not solely the debasement of a product but 'as any purposeful change that altered its composition or the meaning of the name under which it was sold'. Anderson, *Health of a Nation*, 69. Thus, should a product include any cosmetic or preservative, it would be regarded as adulterated.

80. Anderson, *Health of a Nation*, 75.

81. Quoted in ibid., 75. Compare Wiley's comments before the Franklin Institute in Philadelphia in December 1892, where he noted that only a small proportion of the food Americans consumed was adulterated and even that portion was 'not so dangerous on account of being deleterious to health as because of [its] pretensions to furnish to the poorer part of our people a food ostensibly pure and nutritious, but in reality valueless'. *Journal of the Franklin Institute*, 137 (1893): 266–88; quoted in Anderson, *Health of a Nation*, 80.

82. Ibid., 105.
83. *Journal of the Proceedings of the National Pure Food and Drug Congress* (held in Columbian University Hall, Washington, DC, 2, 3, 4, and 5 March 1898) (Washington, DC: Government Printing Office, 1898). It appears that the delegates from the WCTU were disappointed that too many compromises had been made with 'the commercial interests'. Goodwin, *Pure Food Crusaders*, 114.
84. Miles' charges were made primarily to embarrass his military and political opponents in Washington and to avenge himself for the humiliation he underwent in the Chicago stockyards in 1894 during the Pullman strike. See Louise Carroll Wade, 'Hell Hath No Fury Like a General Scorned: Nelson A. Miles, the Pullman Strike, and the Beef Scandal of 1898', *Illinois Historical Journal*, 79 (1986): 162–84.
85. Apparently Miles preferred the manner traditionally used of supplying the army with beef, 'driven on the hoof and slaughtered as it was required by the troops'. Quoted in Young, *Pure Food*, 136.
86. See table below:

Pure Food Bills Introduced in Congress Between 1889 and 1906

Bill Number	Chamber	Date	Introduced by
H283	House	18 December 1889	Edwin H. Conger (R., Iowa)
S2291	Senate	3 June 1890	Algernon S. Paddock (R., Nebraska)
H11297	House	8 July 1890	Erastus J. Turner (R., Kansas)
S1	Senate	10 December 1891	Algernon S. Paddock (R., Nebraska)
H109	House	5 January 1892	William S. Holman (D., Indiana)
S1488	Senate	11 January 1892	Frank Hiscock (R., New York)
S2984	Senate	22 April 1892	James F. Wilson (R., Iowa)
H8603	House	6 May 1892	Elisha E. Meredith (D., Virginia)
S3796	Senate	30 January 1893	Charles J. Faulkner (D., West Virginia)
S471	Senate	18 March 1897	Jacob H. Gallinger (R., New Hampshire)
H5441	House	18 December 1897	Marriott Brosius (R., Pennsylvania)
S4015	Senate	2 March 1898	Charles J. Faulkner (D., West Virginia)
H9154	House	15 March 1898	Marriott Brosius (R., Pennsylvania)
S4144	Senate	16 March 1898	Charles J. Faulkner (D., West Virginia)
S5375	Senate	27 January 1899	John M. Thurston (R., Nebraska)
H2561	House	7 December 1899	Marriott Brosius (R., Pennsylvania)
H4618	House	18 December 1899	Joseph W. Babcock (R., Wisconsin)
S2048	Senate	3 January 1900	William V. Allen (Populist, Nebraska)
S2049	Senate	3 January 1900	William V. Allen (Populist, Nebraska)
S2050	Senate	3 January 1900	William V. Allen (Populist, Nebraska)
S2222	Senate	8 January 1900	Henry C. Hansborough (R., North Dakota)
H6246	House	15 January 1900	Marriott Brosius (R., Pennsylvania)
S2426	Senate	15 January 1900	William E. Mason (R., Illinois)
H6442	House	16 January 1900	Martin H. Glynn (D., New York)
H7667	House	30 January 1900	James S. Sherman (R., New York)
S3618	Senate	15 March 1900	Redfield Proctor (R., Vermont)
H9677	House	16 March 1900	Marriott Brosius (R., Pennsylvania)
S3796	Senate	26 March 1900	James K. Jones (D., Arkansas)
S4047	Senate	6 April 1900	Addison G. Foster (R., Washington)
S5262	Senate	18 December 1900	William E. Mason (R., Illinois)
H12973	House	19 December 1900	Marriott Brosius (R., Pennsylvania)
H276	House	2 December 1901	James S. Sherman (R., New York)

Pure Food Bills Introduced in Congress Between 1889 and 1906 (continued)

Bill Number	Chamber	Date	Introduced by
H3109	House	6 December 1901	William P. Hepburn (R., Iowa)
S1347	Senate	9 December 1901	William E. Mason (R., Illinois)
H4342	House	10 December 1901	Julius Kahn (R., California)
H9351	House	18 January 1902	Vespasian Warner (R., Illinois)
S2987	Senate	20 January 1902	Shelby M. Cullom (R., Illinois)
S3015	Senate	20 January 1902	William W. Mason (R., Illinois)
H9960	House	23 January 1902	James S. Sherman (R., New York)
S3340	Senate	27 January 1902	Chauncey M. Depew (R., New York)
S3342	Senate	29 January 1902	Henry C. Hansborough (R., North Dakota)
H12348	House	10 March 1902	John B. Corliss (R., Michigan)
S6303	Senate	28 June 1902	Porter J. McCumber (R., North Dakota)
S198	Senate	11 November 1903	Porter J. McCumber (R., North Dakota)
H5077	House	27 November 1903	William P. Hepburn (R., Iowa)
H6295	House	8 December 1903	William P. Hepburn (R., Iowa)
H6295	House	21 January 1904	William P. Hepburn (R., Iowa)
H4527	House	6 December 1905	William P. Hepburn (R., Iowa)
S88	Senate	6 December 1905	Weldon B. Heyburn (R., Idaho)
H12071	House	16 January 1906	William Lorimer (R., Illinois)
S3623	Senate	24 January 1906	Albert J. Hopkins (R., Illinois)
H13859	House	2 February 1906	William A. Rodenberg (R., Illinois)

Source: House Report No. 2118: Pure Food (Washington, DC: Government Printing Office, 1906).

87. Anderson, *Health of a Nation*, 129.
88. Ibid., 132.
89. McCumber was an ardent advocate of a pure food law. He published an article entitled 'The Alarming Adulteration of Food and Drugs' in the 5 January 1905 issue of the *Independent* in which he recounted some of the findings of Professor E. F. Ladd, the Food Commissioner of North Dakota, including the fact that chemical preservatives, which the sanitarians regarded as poisonous, were present in 90 percent of the foods sold locally, with deplorable results. Quoted in C. C. Regier, 'The Struggle for Federal Food and Drugs Legislation', *Law and Contemporary Problems*, 1 (1933): 7–8.
90. The Association of Manufacturers and Distributors of Food Products did not include the more established manufacturers who were fearful of the competition they faced from cheaper products of a similar nature. Indeed several manufacturers, among them the H.J. Heinz Company, were active supporters of a pure food and drug act and Heinz even approached President Roosevelt to offer his support for the measure. Heinz was behind the creation of a group calling itself The National Association of Canned Food Packers which maintained that strong pure food legislation was essential to insure the public safety. See Robert C. Alberts, *The Good Provider: H.J. Heinz and His 57 Varieties* (Boston, MA: Houghton Mifflin Company, 1978): 172–3.
91. Young, *Pure Food*, 157.
92. Adams' efforts are reported in some detail in Stewart H. Holbrook, *The Golden Age of Quackery* (New York: Macmillan, 1959), and Young, *Toadstool Millionaires*, 205–25.
93. Young, *Toadstool Millionaires*, 217.
94. Samuel Hopkins Adams, 'The Great American Fraud', *Collier's Weekly*, 34 (7 October 1905): 29. Adams' series is accessible in electronic form. See http://www.mtn.org/quack/ephemera/overview.htm (accessed 4 June 2003).

95. James H. Cassedy, 'Muckraking and Medicine: Samuel Hopkins Adams', *American Quarterly*, 16 (Spring, 1964): 86.
96. See John L. Gignilliat, 'Pigs, Politics, and Protection: The European Boycott of American Pork, 1879–1891', *Agricultural History*, 35 (1961): 3–12; and Louis L. Snyder, 'The American-German Pork Dispute, 1879–1891', *Journal of Modern History*, 17 (March 1945): 16–28.
97. The smaller slaughterhouses seem to have been particularly active in seeking meat inspection legislation. One economic historian has concluded that 'meat inspection legislation was a consequence of . . . changing competitive conditions, and there is no evidence that a documented consumer information problem or a domestic health threat were the principal factors behind adoption of the 1891 law. Instead, the disease issue was stressed by local slaughterhouses in an effort to limit or redirect the economic effects of the introduction of refrigeration.' Gary D. Libecap, 'The Rise of the Chicago Packers and the Origins of Meat Inspection and Antitrust', *Economic Inquiry*, 30 (April 1992): 259.
98. By 1906 several companies had emerged to dominate an industry that itself had grown huge. The first long-distance shipment of refrigerated meats took place in 1869 and by 1880 had become fairly common. Gustavus Swift, who opened his first plant in 1875, began regular shipments of dressed beef in 1877 and by the early 1880s his firm was joined by Armour & Co., both headquartered in Chicago. By the end of the nineteenth century each accounted for over one-quarter of all the cattle slaughtered in the United States and meat-packing had become the nation's largest industry.
99. To the charge that slaughterhouses were filthy in that the abattoirs stood in close proximity to huge quantities of manure, it can only be noted that this was one of the unavoidable costs of moving cattle on the hoof into a city and penning them there.
100. Young, *Pure Food*, 223.
101. Sinclair was assisted in his 'researches' by Adolphe Smith, who had come to Chicago to prepare an article on conditions in the yards for the British medical journal, the *Lancet*. Smith, also a confirmed socialist who favored nationalization of the meat-packing industry, was not above exaggerating the deplorable conditions that prevailed in privately owned plants. See Young, *Pure Food*, 223.
102. See Upton Sinclair, *The Jungle*, Introduction and notes by James R. Barrett (Urbana, Ill.: University of Illinois Press, 1988). An extensive account of the effect *The Jungle* had on the American public and on the eventual shape of federal legislation can be found in Young, *Pure Food*, 221–52.
103. The President had earlier referred to the meat-packing industry as 'evil'. In 1903 he prevailed on Congress to establish a Bureau of Corporations, located in the Department of Commerce, whose function it was to investigate the ways in which America's large corporations conducted their affairs and to report on their abuses. It was therefore not surprising that the first object of the Bureau's inquiry was the 'beef trust'. See Mary Yeager, *Competition and Regulation: The Development of Oligopoly in the Meat Packing Industry* (Greenwich, Conn.: Jai Press, 1981): 185–8. The meat-packing industry's relations with the Roosevelt administration are dealt with in Francis Walker, 'The "Beef Trust" and the United States Government', *The Economic Journal*, 16 (December 1906): 491–514.
104. Adolphe Smith, 'Chicago, the Stockyards and Packing Town', *Lancet*, 1 (7 January 1905): 122, (28 January 1905): 259–60, quoted in Young, *Pure Food*, 228.
105. Neill was a consistent supporter of more extensive government involvement in the economy. He was a determined supporter of industrial safety and workmen's compensation legislation and was, with Reynolds, instrumental in seeing to it that child labor laws were enacted by Congress. Reynolds had been a long-time social worker in New York, an executive with the University Settlement, and a confirmed progressive. Before he became Assistant Secretary of the Treasury, Roosevelt had appointed him to investigate living conditions and the status of children in the District of Columbia. Neither man was even minimally sympathetic to big business.
106. Despite the fact that there is no evidence to support the conclusion that their report was any more reliable than was that of the Secretary of Agriculture, most historians have assumed

that the conclusions reached by Neill and Reynolds more accurately reflected conditions in the packing plants.

107. Ogden Armour, 'The Packers and the People', *Saturday Evening Post*, 178 (10 March 1906): 8. There seems no doubt, for example, that some of Armour's products contained prohibited adulterants and preservatives for which the Company had at one time pled guilty and paid fines. See Young, *Pure Food*, 230.

108. Beveridge had been instrumental in gaining passage of the legislation creating the Interstate Commerce Commission and was a vigorous proponent of the graduated income tax and child labor laws. He had earlier established a reputation during the Spanish-American War as one of the most extreme imperialists, given to frenzied rhetoric in support of an American empire, and apparently had no particular interest in the issue of wholesome food until he thought it might advance his political fortunes. See Young, *Pure Food*, 236.

109. Louis Filler, 'Progress and Progressivism', *American Journal of Economics and Sociology*, 20 (April 1961): 297. Beveridge had at one point boasted of his bill that it was 'the most pronounced extension of federal power in every direction ever enacted' (quoted in Young, *Pure Food*, 237).

110. G. Wallace Chessman, *Theodore Roosevelt and the Politics of Power* (Boston, MA: Little, Brown and Company, 1969): 137–8.

111. The following account of the passage of the Pure Food and Drugs Act relies heavily on that provided by Young, *Pure Food*, 204–20, 253–72.

112. Anderson, *Health of a Nation*, 177.

113. Young, *Pure Food*, 206–7.

114. *Congressional Record*, 59th Congress, 1st Session, 8955, quoted in Young, *Pure Food*, 255.

115. Wiley's letter to Congressman James R. Mann, 6 July 1906, Letter-books, Bureau of Chemistry, General Correspondence, RG 97, National Archives; quoted in Young, *Pure Food*, 262.

116. 34 US Stats. 768 (1906).

117. Anderson, *Pure Food*, 200, 206.

118. Clayton A. Coppin and Jack High, *The Politics of Purity: Harvey Washington Wiley and the Origins of Federal Food Policy* (Ann Arbor, Mich.: University of Michigan Press, 1999): 118. Wiley concluded, one would suppose based on his eight months of medical education, that preservatives constituted a danger to human health by virtue of the fact that substances that were capable of killing micro-organisms also inhibited digestive ferments. See Young, *Pure Food*, 112.

119. The Company noted that it was not possible to market its product under the name 'glucose' since the public associated glucose with glue! Anderson, *Pure Food*, 205.

120. Anderson, *Pure Food*, 205.

121. House Committee on Agriculture, *Hearings on Appropriations, 1908*, 278–9, quoted in Anderson, *Health of a Nation*, 202. The Department's solicitor, George P. McCabe, objected that Wiley's definition was no less than 'absurd'. McCabe maintained that 'whiskey is any alcoholic beverage made from grain, properly colored and flavored, according to the prevailing custom of the trade'. Quoted in Coppin and High, *The Politics of Purity*, 101.

122. Coppin and High, *Politics of Purity*, 70.

123. Among Wiley's most enthusiastic supporters was Edmund Taylor, the maker of Old Taylor brand straight whiskey. See Jack High and Clayton A. Coppin, 'Wiley and the Whiskey Industry: Strategic Behavior in the Passage of the Pure Food Act', *Business History Review*, 62 (Summer 1988): 287–309.

124. Donna J. Wood's analysis of the genesis of the Pure Food and Drugs Act of 1906 is persuasive in detailing the interests certain businesses had in securing this legislation. Ms Wood notes: 'On the basis of the evidence presented here, it seems that businesses in the food and drug industry were quick to understand that law and regulation could form a crucial part of any competitive strategy. In this case, at least, it seems that the federal government's power to regulate interstate commerce 'in the public interest' was viewed by businesses as both threat and opportunity, and that the direction of the business response depended very much

on the structure of the industry and the positioning of key firms within it" Wood, *Strategic Uses of Public Policy*, 192–3.

125. Alberts, *The Good Provider*, 173. Wiley's biographer refers to his salary as 'modest'. Anderson, *Heath of a Nation*, 249.

126. Clayton Coppin, 'James Wilson and Harvey Wiley: The Dilemma of Bureaucratic Entrepreneurship', *Agricultural History*, 64 (Spring 1990): 173–4.

127. Clayton Coppin, 'James Wilson and Harvey Wiley', 176. See also Wood, *Strategic Uses of Public Policy, passim*, but esp. 23–9; High and Coppin, *Politics of Purity, passim*; and Alberts, *The Good Provider*, 166–80.

128. (Washington, DC: W. H. Wiley, 1929). The whole of this work is available at http://www.soilandhealth.org/03sov/0303critic/030305wylie/030305toc.html (accessed 18 June 2003).

129. Anderson, *Health of a Nation*, 237.

130. Indeed, there is ample evidence to support Gabriel Kolko's claim that Wiley was not even particularly concerned with impurities in foods but in what he regarded as mislabeling. See *The Triumph of Conservatism: A Reinterpretation of American History, 1900–1916* (New York: Free Press of Glencoe, 1963): 108–10.

131. Wallace F. Janssen, 'Outline of the History of U.S. Drug Regulation and Labeling', *Food Drug Cosmetic Law Journal*, 36 (August 1981): 420.

132. While this assessment of Wiley's efforts and his dedication to public service is the norm, it is by no means universal. Lorine Swainston Goodwin, for example, in her zeal to credit the women's movement with a whole range of Progressive Era reforms including the pure food and drug law, writes of Wiley that 'despite [his] expertise and prominence, he limited his influence by placing his primacy emphasis upon food fraud at the expense of adequate attention to consumer health protection and diverted attention away from consumer objectives by becoming involved in relatively insignificant and controversial issues'. *Pure Food Crusaders*, 264.

133. As one high official of the Bureau later recalled: 'The drug work of the Bureau got off to a bad start. It never seemed to interest Dr Wiley as the food work did. It suffered, too, from less-than-competent technical directions.' Paul B. Dunbar, 'Memories of Early Days of Federal Food and Drug Law Enforcement', *Food Drug Cosmetic Law Journal*, 14 (February 1959): 123.

134. Quoted in James Harvey Young, 'Drugs and the 1906 Law', in John B. Blake, ed., *Safeguarding the Public: Historical Aspects of Medicinal Drug Control* (Baltimore: Johns Hopkins Press, 1970): 148.

135. Young, *Toadstool Millionaires*, 226.

136. James C. Munch and James C. Munch, Jr, 'Notices of Judgment: The First Thousand', *Food Drug Cosmetic Law Journal*, 10 (April 1955): 219–42.

137. Washington Herald, 17 May 1908, quoted in Young, *Medical Messiahs*, 10. This account of the Cuforhedake Brane Fude prosecution is taken from *Medical Messiahs*, 3–12.

138. The sources for this account are James Harvey Young, 'Three Southern Food and Drug Cases', *The Journal of Southern History*, 49 (February 1983): 3–36; and Coppin and High, *Politics of Purity*, 142–52.

139. Coca-Cola was first bottled in Vicksburg, Mississippi, in 1894, by the Biedenham Candy Company.

140. Young, 'Southern Food and Drug Cases', 11.

141. *Adulteration of Foods*, Senate Reports, 57th Congress, 1st Session, No. 972 (Washington, DC: Government Printing Office, 1902), 119: quoted in Young, 'Southern Food and Drug Cases', 10. The Drug Division of the Bureau prior to Wiley's resignation appears to have been preoccupied with the presence of caffeine in foods and drugs. Tests for caffeine constituted a fairly large proportion of all examinations undertaken between 1907 and 1912.

142. Coppin and High speculate that Wiley's enmity toward the Coca-Cola Company might have been exacerbated by the Company's decision in 1903 to switch sugar suppliers from the Arbuckle Brothers Company to Henry Havermeyer's American Sugar Refining Company, inasmuch as John Arbuckle was a close friend and supporter of Wiley's. *Politics of Purity*, 146–7.

143. *United States v. Forty Barrels and Twenty Kegs of Coca-Cola*, 191 Fed 431, at 438; quoted in Young, 'Southern Food and Drug Cases', 17.

144. *United States v. Coca Cola Co. of Atlanta*, 241 US 265, 36 S. Ct. 573 (1916). The Court's decision was written by Charles Evans Hughes.

145. The 'treatment' comprised a series of several different medications, each containing different ingredients and each making distinct claims: 'Cancerine tablets', 'Blood purifier', 'Antiseptic tablets', 'Special No. 4', 'Cancerine No. 17', and 'Cancerine No. 1'. 'Blood purifier', it was claimed, removed impurities in the blood while 'Special No. 4' was alleged to remove swelling, arrest development, and restore circulation. *United States v. Johnson*, 221 US 488 (1911).

146. *United States v. Johnson*. The majority opinion was written by Oliver Wendell Holmes. In light of the history and intent of the statute it is difficult to understand how Holmes, usually a friend to any government legislation no matter how obnoxious, could have construed the Act so narrowly.

147. *Congressional Record*, 62nd Congress, 1st Session, Appendix, 676; quoted in Young, *Medical Messiahs, 50.*

148. 232 US 399; 34 S. Ct. 337 (1914).

149. The Hague Convention had grown out of the 1909 International Opium Conference held in Shanghai, called to deal with the problem of opium trafficking, and a second Conference held in The Hague in 1911.

150. The Harrison Narcotic Act was designed as a registration act and was not originally meant to prevent physicians from prescribing drugs to addicts in their care. Indeed, the Act contained a clause that stated that nothing in the Act shall apply 'to the dispensing or distribution of any of the aforesaid drugs to a patient by a physician, dentist, or veterinary surgeon registered under this Act in the course of his professional practice only'. However Congress and the thousands of physicians who supported passage of the measure appear not to have foreseen the duplicity of the Wilson Administration. Soon after the Act was passed law enforcement officers began arresting physicians who had been dispensing opiates to their addict patients on the grounds that this did not constitute acting 'in the course of [one's] professional practice'. This interpretation was sustained by the Supreme Court in a five to four decision in *Webb et al. v. United States*, 249 US 96; 39 S. Ct. 217 (1919).

151. § 4(e) of the Volstead Act exempted 'patented, medicinal, and antiseptic preparations and solutions that are unfit for use for beverage purposes'. 41 US Stats. 305 (1919).

152. Young, *Medical Messiahs*, 44.

153. 37 US Stat. 732 (1913).

154. The House Committee on Agriculture held hearings on the measure in 1919, 1921, 1924, and 1928, while the Senate Committee on Agriculture and Forestry heard testimony on the bill in 1921 and 1928.

155. These defeated amendments are detailed in Hutt and Hutt, 'History of Government Regulation of Food', 58.

156. *United States v. Ninety-five Barrels, More or Less, Alleged Apple Cider Vinegar*, 265 US 438; 44 S. Ct. 529 (1924).

157. 46 US Stats. 1019 (1930)

158. Aaron J. Ihde, 'Food Controls Under the 1906 Act', in Young, chairman of the symposium, *Early Years of Federal Food Control*, 45.

159. Andrew P. Morriss and Roger E. Meiners, 'Property Rights, Pesticides, and Public Health: Explaining the Paradox of Modern Pesticide Policy', *Fordham Environmental Law Journal*, 14 (Fall 2002): 4–5. Morriss and Meiners point out that these laws were enacted because 'farmers who sprayed saw their non-spraying neighbors as getting the benefits of the sprayers' expenditures on pest control, while not contributing to pest control themselves. In economic terms, the non-sprayers were 'free riders' taking advantage of the efforts of others without contributing. Non-sprayers thus gained a competitive advantage (lower costs because they did not have to pay for spraying) over the sprayers. To solve the so-called free-rider problem, the sprayers turned to their state legislatures to force their non-spraying neighbors to contribute to the common good of wiping out the pests that threatened all their apple crops.'

160. The trial and the FDA's fears are discussed in James C. Whorton, *Before Silent Spring: Pesticides and Public Health in Pre-DDT America* (Princeton, NJ: Princeton University Press, 1974): 141–3.

161. See the FDA's website, particularly the pages devoted to the Spring 1999 Conference of the Society for the Social History of Medicine, titled 'The Rise and Fall of Federal Food Standards in the United States: The Case of the Peanut Butter and Jelly Sandwich', http://www.fda.gov/oc/history/slideshow/default.htm (accessed 22 June 2003). Apparently during World War I a method was developed which permitted the production of jelly from sugar and water. The result was that it was possible to make a jam-like substance with considerably less fruit than was the case with most jams, which were 45 parts fruit to 55 parts sugar. Bred Spred had approximately 17 parts fruit, 55 parts sugar, 11½ parts water, 1/4 part pectin, and 0.04 part tartaric acid.

162. *United States v. Ten Cases, More or Less, Bred Spred, Etc., et al.*, 49 F.2d 87 (8th Cir. 1931).

163. This account of the events leading up to passage of the Food, Drug, and Cosmetic Act of 1938 relies heavily on the work of Charles O. Jackson, *Food and Drug Legislation in the New Deal* (Princeton, NJ: Princeton University Press, 1970), and of David F. Cavers, 'The Food, Drug, and Cosmetic Act of 1938: Its Legislative History and Its Substantive Provisions', *Law and Contemporary Problems* 6 (Winter, 1939): 2–42.

164. Bureau of Chemistry, *1917 Report of Bureau of Chemistry* (Washington, DC: Government Printing Office, 1917): 16; reprinted in Food Law Institute, *Federal Food, Drug, and Cosmetic Law: Administrative Reports, 1907–1949* (Chicago: Commerce Clearing House, 1951): 370.

165. The 1897 Brosius bill had included cosmetics under its definition of drugs but the language was altered in response to pressure from the drug industry in return for their support of the bill at the 1898 National Pure Food and Drug Congress.

166. Campbell, whose area of expertise was enforcement, had been appointed to succeed Carl Alsberg as head of the Bureau of Chemistry in 1921. However, there was strong sentiment that a scientist should head the agency and as a result Campbell was replaced as chief of the Bureau by Charles A. Browne, an agricultural chemist, in 1924. At the same time Campbell was given authority over all of the Bureau's enforcement operations. With the creation of the Food, Drug, and Insecticide Administration in 1927, Browne, whose interests were in research, became head of the new Bureau of Chemistry and Soils while Campbell was appointed chief of the new enforcement agency, the FDIA. He retired from the position in 1944.

167. Cavers, 'Food, Drug, and Cosmetic Act of 1938', 5.

168. Tugwell had no patience with an economic system based on competitive market forces. In 1933 he maintained in an address before the Bar Association of Western New York that 'the jig is up. The cat is out of the bag. There is no invisible hand. There never was. . . . Men were taught to believe that they were, paradoxically, advancing co-operation when they were defying it. That was a viciously false paradox.' 'Design for Government', Address before the Eighth Annual Meeting of the Federation of Bar Associations of Western New York, 24 June 1933, quoted in Bernard Sternsher, *Rexford Tugwell and the New Deal* (New Brunswick, NJ: Rutgers University Press, 1964): 13. One historian ably summed up the economic views embraced by Tugwell and the other technocratic progressives, many of whom took an active role in the Roosevelt administration. 'They took part in a campaign to publicize the irrationality of the existing capitalist order and create a demand for a planned society guided by "experts who are not representatives of the capitalists but of the public interest"'. Robert B. Westbrook, 'Tribune of the Technostructure: The Popular Economics of Stuart Chase', *American Quarterly*, 32 (Autumn 1980): 388.

169. Quoted in Young, *Medical Messiahs*, 160. In 1933 Tugwell wrote: 'It is doubtful whether nine-tenths of our sales effort and expense serves any good social purpose'. Rexford G. Tugwell, *The Industrial Discipline and the Governmental Arts* (New York: Columbia University Press, 1933): 180.

170. Ergot is a poisonous fungus that lives on rye and has been a basic component in a number of medicines. Today it is an essential ingredient of, among other chemicals, Dopamine,

crucial to the treatment of Parkinsonism, and ergotamine, used to treat migraine. One of its derivatives is LSD.

171. Jackson, *Food and Drug Legislation*, 15.
172. Its full title was *100,000,000 Guinea Pigs: Dangers in Everyday Foods, Drugs, and Cosmetics* (New York: Vanguard Press, 1932). Prior to the appearance of *100,000,000 Guinea Pigs*, Schlink had cooperated with the economist Stuart Chase in writing *Your Money's Worth: A Study in the Waste of the Consumer Dollar* (New York: Macmillan Company, 1927) which took very much the same position.
173. Stuart Chase and F. L. Schlink, 'A Few Billions for Consumers', *The New Republic*, 30 December 1925: 155. In fact Chase and Schlink proposed that all goods, without exception, be produced according to specifications set by government. The benefits of this were clear. Among them, 'the manufacturing process itself tends to become simplified. It is no longer necessary to make so many styles and variations on the chance of catching the consumer's eye. "Special features," fancy packages, drop out of the picture. One can produce in large units; one has a better chance of "balancing the load" in plant operation.' Additionally, 'the consumer, buying to specification, is in a position to buy for a *specific purpose*. If tests have made it clear that a cheaper product or a lower grade or a different product will adequately meet his need, he can buy the cheaper article and save the difference.' 'A Few Billions', 155.
174. Dubar to Campbell, 8 October 1932, and Alverez to Harding, 29 April 1933; quoted in Jackson, *Food and Drug Legislation*, 19.
175. F. J. Schlink and Arthur Kallet, 'Poison for Profit', *Nation*, 135 (21 December 1932): 610.
176. Jackson, *Food and Drug Legislation*, 20.
177. James Harvey Young reports that Stuart Chase was present at a meeting held by Tugwell with FDA officials to discuss the proposed measure. *Medical Messiahs*, 161, n. 7. Tugwell and Chase were apparently old friends. They were both part of the delegation that had traveled to Russia in 1927 and had co-edited the account of the delegations' findings: *Soviet Russia in the Second Decade: A Joint Survey by the Technical Staff of the First American Trade Union Delegation* (New York: John Day, 1928).
178. During the Depression manufacturers of cosmetics, like the food industry, had begun offering for sale less expensive cosmetics that lacked the quality of their more expensive competitors. The FDA was incensed not only at the fact that poorer quality cosmetics were being sold but that they had no authority whatever over these preparations, which they regarded as falling naturally within their area of authority.
179. The bill is reprinted in Food and Drug Administration, *A Legislative History of the Federal Food, Drug, and Cosmetic Act and Its Amendments* (24 vols plus 10 vols of appendices; Rockville, MD: Department of Health, Education and Welfare, Public Health Service, 1979): 1: 1–32.
180. Walter Campbell, in testifying before the Senate subcommittee, stated that he wished to make self-medication illegal in certain instances. How broad this category was he did not indicate but it was clearly substantially larger than that allowed by some members of the subcommittee. 'There are certain diseases', Campbell maintained, 'where it may be contrary to the interests of society to have a self-diagnosis and self-treatment undertaken'. *Food, Drugs, and Cosmetics* (Hearings Before a Subcommittee of the Committee on Commerce, United States Senate, S. 1944: 73rd Congress, 2nd Session (1933)) (Washington, DC: Government Printing Office, 1934): 72, reprinted in *Legislative History of the Federal Food, Drug, and Cosmetic Act*, 1: 164.
181. The *New Republic*, 77 (December 1933): 119; quoted in Young, *Medical Messiahs*, 166.
182. Jackson, *Food and Drug Legislation*, 30–31.
183. These and the following details are taken from Jackson, *Food and Drug Legislation*, 38–48.
184. Jackson, *Food and Drug Legislation*, 43.
185. The FDA's campaign in support of the Copeland bill was a clear violation of the 1919 Deficiency Appropriations Act, which prohibited lobbying expenditures by federal agencies. Indeed, complaints from Congress eventually forced the agency to curtail its advertising efforts. See Jackson, *Food and Drug Legislation*, 47–8.

186. Substantial portions of the exhibit are available at the FDA website. See http://www.fda.gov/oc/history/slideshow/default.htm (accessed 24 June 2003).
187. There is, of course, no medication, no matter how seemingly innocuous, that will not, in some set of circumstances, cause harm.
188. Charles O. Jackson, who has written the most extensive history of the 1938 Act, refers to this exhibit in the following way: 'Neatly arranged for all to see were the most worthless, the most fraudulent, and the most dangerous products on the market'. *Food and Drug Legislation*, 44.
189. See Michael Krauss, 'Loosening the FDA's Drug Certification Monopoly: Implications for Tort Law and Consumer Welfare', *George Mason Law Review*, 4 (Spring 1996): 457–83.
190. 'Tugwell Bill is Assailed', *Printers Ink*, 165 (19 October 1933): 88; quoted in Jackson, *Food and Drug Legislation*, 54.
191. In fact Schlink and Kallet went so far as to accuse Copeland of having sabotaged his own bill by diluting its most important provisions in response to pressure from several firms with which he had dealings, namely Fleischman's Yeast, Eno Salts, and Phillips' Milk of Magnesia. Jackson, *Food and Drug Legislation*, 59.
192. Quoted in Jackson, *Food and Drug Legislation*, 61.
193. The text of the bill is reprinted in *Legislative History of the Federal Food, Drug, and Cosmetic Act*, 1: 841–89.
194. Jackson, *Food and Drug Legislation*, 69.
195. *Food, Drugs, and Cosmetics* (Hearings Before a Subcommittee of the Committee on Commerce, United States Senate, 74th Congress, 1st Session on S. 5) (Washington, DC: Government Printing Office, 1935): 102; reprinted in *Legislative History of the Federal Food, Drug, and Cosmetic Act*, 3: 192.
196. *Standard Remedies* (May 1927): 22; quoted in Young, *Medical Messiahs*, 97. In the forefront of the firms leading the attack against the provision allowing multiple seizures was the Vicks Chemical Company and the Lambert Pharmacal Company, makers of *Listerine*. Cavers, 'Food, Drug, and Cosmetic Act of 1938', 13.
197. Young, *Medical Messiahs*,175.
198. Copeland himself was a homeopathic physician.
199. Testimony of Dr William C. Woodward, *Food, Drugs, and Cosmetics* (Hearing Before a Subcommittee of the Committee on Interstate and Foreign Commerce, House of Representatives, 74th Congress, 1st Session (H.R. 6906, H.R. 8805, and S. 5)) (Washington, DC: Government Printing Office, 1935): 297–321; reprinted in *Legislative History of the Federal Food, Drug, and Cosmetic Act*, 4: 610–33.
200. The Resettlement Administration was one of the many agencies created by executive order to further Roosevelt's make-work schemes. It replaced the Agricultural Adjustment Administration in 1935 and was empowered to extend low interest loans to farmers, to resettle urban dwellers onto communal farms, and to organize camps for migrant laborers. In 1937 it was renamed the Farm Security Administration.
201. *Skin Deep: The Truth About Beauty Aids – Safe and Harmful* (New York: Vanguard Press, 1934), and *Our Master's Voice: Advertising* (New York: The John Day Co., 1934).
202. *Eat, Drink and be Wary* (New York: Covici, 1935); *Counterfeit: Not Your Money but What It Buys* (New York: Vanguard Press, 1935); *Paying through the Teeth* (New York: Vanguard Press, 1935).
203. Among them Rachel Lynn Palmer and Sarah K. Greenberg, *Facts and Frauds in Woman's Hygiene* (Garden City, NY: Garden City Publishing Co., 1936), and J. B. Matthews, *Guinea Pigs No More* (New York: Covici, Friede, 1936).
204. *American Chamber of Horrors: The Truth About Food and Drugs* (New York: Farrar & Rinehart, 1936). The book is dedicated to a group of women and their organizational affiliations, 'who have been holding the front-line trenches in the consumer war for pure foods, drugs and cosmetics'.
205. Sol Herzog, 'New State Laws Affecting Pharmacy', *American Druggist*, 94 (October 1936): 464–7; in Jackson, *Food and Drug Legislation*, 114.
206. A brief history of the agency appears in Susan Wagner, *The Federal Trade Commission* (New York: Praeger Publishers, 1971): 3–34.

207. It is in fact beyond dispute that, at the point where Roosevelt launched his crusade, large corporations were losing market share to smaller companies in every sector of the economy. See Alan Stone, *Economic Regulation in the Public Interest: The Federal Trade Commission in Theory and Practice* (Ithaca, NY: Cornell University Press, 1977): 28–32.

208. The Court circumscribed the FTC's regulatory authority in a number of cases. The first of these occurred in 1920 where the Court ruled that the Commission was not empowered to proceed against the actions of a firm if these actions were not regarded as illegal either by the terms of the Sherman Act or by common law. *Federal Trade Commission v. Gratz* 253 US, 421; 40 S. Ct. 572 (1920).

209. *Federal Trade Commission v. Raladam Co.*, 283 US 643; 75 L. Ed. 1324 (1931).

210. Testimony of Hon. Ewin L. Davis, *Food, Drugs, and Cosmetics* (Hearing Before a Subcommittee of the Committee on Interstate and Foreign Commerce, House of Representatives, 74th Congress, 1st Session (H.R. 6906, H.R. 8805, and S. 5)) (Washington, DC: Government Printing Office, 1935): 642; reprinted in *Legislative History of the Federal Food, Drug, and Cosmetic Act*, 4: 953.

211. Campbell to Wallace, 25 May 1936, quoted in Jackson, *Food and Drug Legislation*, 120.

212. The texts of the two bills are reprinted in *Legislative History of the Federal Food, Drug, and Cosmetic Act*, 5: 327–69 and 372–413.

213. Jackson, *Food and Drug Legislation*, 137.

214. The bill, with amendments, as reported out of committee is reprinted in *Legislative History of the Federal Food, Drug, and Cosmetic Act*, 5: 432–77.

215. Jackson, *Food and Drug Legislation*, 142.

216. With regard to the conditions under which multiple seizures could be ordered, 'imminently dangerous to health' was altered to read 'actually dangerous to health' and the phrase 'or is, in a material respect false or fraudulent' was restored. The misbranding provisions were reworded and were held to have occurred when a label was 'false or misleading in any particular', the word 'material' having been removed. The bill is reprinted in *Legislative History of the Federal Food, Drug, and Cosmetic Act*, 5: 536–81.

217. See Jackson, *Food and Drug Legislation*, 139–40.

218. Jackson, *Food and Drug Legislation*, 144.

219. With the sudden death of Joseph W. Byrns in June 1936, Sam Rayburn moved up to the position of Speaker of the House, while Lea replaced Rayburn as Chairman of the Commerce Committee.

220. The Act's provisions respecting false advertising are dealt with at some length in Milton Handler, 'The Control of False Advertising Under the Wheeler-Lee Act', *Law and Contemporary Problems*, 6 (1939): 91–110. See also Martin L. Lindahl, 'The Federal Trade Commission Act as Amended in 1938', *Journal of Political Economy*, 47 (August 1939): 497–525.

221. Details of the Elixir Sulfanilamide disaster can be found in 'Taste of Raspberries, Taste of Death: The 1937 Elixir Sulfanilamide Incident', *FDA Consumer* (75th Anniversary Issue) 15 (June 1981): 18–21; James Harvey Young, 'Sulfanilamide and Diethylene Glycol', in John Parascandola and James C. Whorton, eds, *Chemistry and Modern Society: History Essays in Honor of Aaron J. Ihde* (ACS Symposium Series 228; Washington, DC: American Chemical Society, 1983): 105–24; and *Elixir Sulfanilamide: Letter from the Secretary of Agriculture* (in Response to Senate Resolution No. 194, Document No. 124, 75th Congress, 2nd Session) (Washington, DC: Government Printing Office, 1937), reprinted in *Legislative History of the Federal Food, Drug, and Cosmetic Act*, 5: 883–921.

222. The mixture was not invariably fatal. 'Many persons who took it but discontinued use with the onset of the symptoms completely recovered'. Jackson, *Food and Drug Legislation*, 155.

223. 'For some years prior to Watkins' employment of diethylene glycol, the Food and Drug Administration had advised against the use of glycol solvents in foods, declaring that definite, comprehensive conclusions as to the physiological action of these chemicals could not be reached on the basis of existing scanty research. . . . Beginning in 1931 more explicit reports of the poisonous nature of the chemical appeared in medical journals.' Young, 'Sulfanilamide', 109.

224. The official magazine of the Food and Drug Administration, the *FDA Consumer*, in recounting the calamity, noted: 'Through the dogged persistence of Federal, State, and local health agencies and the efforts of the AMA and the news media, most of the elixir was recovered'. 'Taste of Raspberries', 20.

225. See Sir William Holdsworth, *A History of English Law* (17 vols; London: Methuen & Co., Inc., 1903–77) 3: 387 and 8: 69. In fact, a similar case was punished under common law in Massachusetts in 1630! Jannsen, 'America's First Food and Drug Laws', 17.

226. Young, 'Sulfanilamide', 116.

227. Massengill could have received a prison term of 261 years!

228. Ruth deForest Lamb even boasted that 20th Century Fox was planning to make a film out of the *American Chamber of Horrors*. Jackson, *Food and Drug Legislation*, 166.

229. Jackson, *Food and Drug Legislation*, 165.

230. *Elixir Sulfanilamide* in *Legislative History*, 5: 883–921.

231. The bill is reprinted in *Legislative History of the Federal Food, Drug, and Cosmetic Act*, 5: 924–27.

232. The bill is reprinted in *Legislative History of the Federal Food, Drug, and Cosmetic Act*, 6: 1–7.

233. Jackson, *Food and Drug Legislation*, 176.

234. Ibid., 177.

235. Cavers, 'Food, Drug, and Cosmetic Act of 1938', 15.

236. Wallace's letter appears in the *Congressional Record*, 83 (31 May 1938), 7779, reprinted in *Legislative History of the Federal Food, Drug, and Cosmetic Act*, 6: 350.

237. The Federal Food, Drug, and Cosmetic Act, P.L. 75–717, reprinted in *Legislative History of the Federal Food, Drug, and Cosmetic Act*, 6: 453–74.

238. By 30 June 1941 the FDA had 849 employees, of which 298 were based in Washington and the remainder in a number of field offices.

239. Peter Temin, *Taking Your Medicine: Drug Regulation in the United States* (Cambridge, MA: Harvard University Press, 1980): 44.

240. 'Testimony of Walter Campbell', *Food, Drugs, and Cosmetics* (Hearings (1933)); reprinted in *Legislative History of the Federal Food, Drug, and Cosmetic Act*, 1: 59. At hearings held the following year, Campbell reiterated these sentiments: 'And let me stop at this point to comment upon the criticism so extensively voiced by the patent-medicine interests that the purpose of this bill is to stop self-medication. This [section of the 1938 Act requiring complete and explicit directions for use] would certainly be unnecessary if it were not contemplated that self-medication will continue in the future as it has in the past. Physicians do not need such information; . . . All of the provisions dealing with drugs, aside from those recognized in the official compendia, are directed towards safeguarding the consumer who is attempting to administer to himself.' Testimony of Walter Campbell, *Food, Drugs, and Cosmetics* (Hearings Before the Committee on Commerce, Senate, on S. 2800) (Washington, DC: Government Printing Office, 1934): 590; reprinted in *Legislative History of the Federal Food, Drug, and Cosmetic Act*, 2: 593.

241. *House Report on the Food, Drug, and Cosmetic Act* (Report No. 2139, 75th Congress, 3rd Session (1938)): 8; reprinted in *Legislative History of the Federal Food, Drug, and Cosmetic Act*, 6: 307.

242. Temin, *Taking Your Medicine*, 45–6. See also Harry M. Marks, 'Revisiting "The Origins of Contemporary Drug Prescriptions"', *American Journal of Public Health*, 85 (January 1995): 109–15. There appears to be a good deal of evidence to support Marks' contention that the FDA was abetted in its attempt to curtail public access to over-the-counter drugs by certain manufacturers whose products were mainly distributed through physicians' prescriptions. It was to their advantage to limit the number of drugs directly available to the public and thus to force them to consult a doctor.

243. Statement of James F. Hoge, *Hearings on Proposed Regulations, November 17 and 18, 1938*, Book 1, Washington: National Records Center, Suitland, Maryland; quoted in Marks, 'Revisiting "Compulsory Drug Prescriptions"', 110.

244. Memorandum submitted by Winthrop Chemical Company, 25 November 1928, *Hearings*

on Proposed Resolutions, Book 3, quoted in Marks, 'Revisiting "Compulsory Drug Prescriptions"', 110.

245. The FDA interpreted the law in such a way that if a drug were sold solely by prescription it need not meet the usage and danger labels. Temin, *Taking Your Medicine*, 47.

246. Ibid., 46–7.

247. The American Medical Association was, of course, delighted with the development. Its Council on Pharmacy and Chemistry had long lobbied for these limitations on self-medication. See James G. Burrow, 'The Prescription-Drug Policies of the American Medical Association', in Blake, ed., *Safeguarding the Public*, 112–122.

248. The report continued: 'The administrative conclusion was therefore announced that dangerous drugs like aminopyrine, cinchophen, neocinchophen, sulfanilamide, and related products may not be distributed for unrestricted use by the lay public without violating the statute; to insure compliance with the law drugs of this character must be labeled with warnings so conspicuous as certainly to arrest attention and in such informative terms as will unfailingly apprise the user of the danger of irreparable injury if the drug is consumed without adequate and continuous medical supervision'. US Food and Drug Administration, *1939 Report of Food and Drug Administration* (Washington, DC: Government Printing Office, 1939): 5, reprinted in Food Law Institute, *Federal Food, Drug, and Cosmetic Law: Administrative Reports, 1907–1949* (Chicago: Commerce Clearing House, 1951): 929.

249. The Food and Drug Administration's 1956 *Annual Report* notes that no less than 90 percent of the prescriptions then written were for drugs not commercially available when the 1938 law was enacted. This figure at the least suggests that most effective medications developed during that period were available to the pubic solely by prescription.

250. Editorial, *Proprietary Drugs*, 25 (June 1938): 1; quoted in Jackson, *Food and Drug Legislation*, 197.

251. A study made soon after the events by the FDA determined that of the 107 people who had died from having taken Elixir Sulfanilamide, in 100 cases the drug was administered by a physician. Marks, 'Revisiting "Compulsory Drug Prescriptions"', 111.

252. Janssen, 'History of Drug Regulation', 431.

253. Hutt and Hutt, 'History of Government Regulation of Food', 62.

254. Ibid., 66.

255. *Sixty-two Cases of Jam et al. v. United States*, 340 US 593; 71 S. Ct. 515 (1951).

256. Hutt and Hutt, 'History of Government Regulation of Food', 67. Apparently some food manufacturers were fortifying their products with vitamins which the FDA deemed 'unnecessary and inappropriate' and 'which does not increase the dietary value of the food'. Hutt and Hutt, 69.

257. *United States v. Thirty-six Drums of Pop 'n Oil*, 164 F.2d 250 (1947). The FDA was successful in charging that a mineral oil that was artificially flavored and colored to look and taste like butter was adulterated since its intent was to appear like butter to patrons of a movie theater who bought popcorn which appeared to be buttered, even though the popcorn was clearly labeled. The case reflects another example of the agency's crackpot determinations regarding which foods were safe. It had reached the conclusion that mineral oil in any form constituted a danger to humans. With respect to a salad dressing based on mineral oil, the agency had noted in 1943 that it had 'consistently held that a product having the properties of mineral oil can only be regarded as an adulterant in food' and further that 'it is our considered judgment that the proposed labeling or any form of label which advocates food uses of mineral oil would be seriously misleading and therefore contrary to the provisions of the [1938 Act]'. Trade Correspondence 404 (13 July 1943), reprinted in Vincent A. Kleinfeld and Charles Wesley Dunn, *Federal Food, Drug, and Cosmetic Act: Judicial and Administrative Record, 1939–1949* (Chicago: Commerce Clearing House, 1949): 735. This view was made authoritative in April 1946 when the FDA determined salad dressings containing mineral oil were indeed adulterated. James Robert Dean, Jr, 'FDA at War: Securing the Food That Secured Victory', *Food and Drug Journal*, 53 (1998): 467.

258. Young, *Medical Messiahs*, 260. Indeed, as another historian has noted, in 1969 of the 200 prescription drugs most often dispensed in American pharmacies, only five had been introduced prior to 1900, another five in the period 1900 and 1929, nine in the 1930s, 18 in the

1940s, 95 in the 1950s, and 66 in the 1960s. In describing the medical armamentarium of 1974, he continues: 'In place of the relatively few drugs, many of them of natural origin, available to physicians as recently as 1935, there were thousands of products, most of them created synthetically and most of these introduced since World War II'. Milton Silverman and Philip R. Lee, *Pills, Profits, and Politics* (Berkeley, CA: University of California Press, 1974): 5.

259. P.L. 77–66 (1941), reprinted in *Legislative History of the Federal Food, Drug, and Cosmetic Act*, 7: 103.

260. Temin, *Taking Your Medicine*, 56.

261. Penicillin, P.L. 79–139, 6 July 1945, reprinted in *Legislative History of the Federal Food, Drug, and Cosmetic Act*, 7: 490); streptomycin, P.L. 80–16, 10 March 1947, reprinted in *Legislative History of the Federal Food, Drug, and Cosmetic Act*, 7: 522; aureomycin, chloramphenicol, and bacitracin, P.L. 81–164, 13 July 1949, reprinted in *Legislative History of the Federal Food, Drug, and Cosmetic Act*, 8: 153; all other antibiotics for human use, P.L. 87–781 (1962): 6–7, reprinted in *Legislative History of the Federal Food, Drug, and Cosmetic Act*, 23: 233–4.

262. *Federal Food, Drug, and Cosmetic Act* (Hearings Before the Committee on Interstate and Foreign Commerce, House of Representatives, on H.R. 3298) (Washington, DC: Government Printing Office, 1951): 97–105; reprinted in *Legislative History of the Federal Food, Drug, and Cosmetic Act*, 11: 123–31.

263. Both sulfa drugs and penicillin were used in the treatment of VD infections and doubtless accounted for a substantial number of over-the-counter sales.

264. *United States v. Dotterweich*, 320 US 277; 64 S. Ct. 134 (1943).

265. 320 US 277 at 286.

266. *United States v. Sullivan*, 332 US 689; 68 S. Ct. 331 (1948).

267. 332 US 689 at 693.

268. In 1945 the FDA seized 150 cartons of spaghetti and 25 cartons of macaroni from a warehouse in Douglas, Arizona. These goods had originated in Denver, Colorado, and were shipped to the Phelps Dodge Mercantile Company in Douglas in mid-1943, where they remained in their original packaging. The FDA charged that the spaghetti and macaroni were adulterated in that they contained rodent excreta, rodent hairs, and insect fragments. Phelps Dodge did not deny the charge of adulteration but argued that the FDA had no jurisdiction in the matter inasmuch as the goods seized were not in interstate commerce. The Ninth Circuit Court of Appeals held that since the goods had become adulterated after having arrived and been stored in Douglas, action by the FDA was unwarranted. *United States v. Phelps Dodge Mercantile Co.*, 157 F.2d 453 (1946). The FDA appealed to the Supreme Court but the High Court refused to grant certiorari.

269. P.L. 80-749 (1948), reprinted in *Legislative History of the Federal Food, Drug, and Cosmetic Act*, 7: 743.

270. Young, *Pure Food*, 83.

271. Miller, 'Public Choice at the Dawn of the Special Interest State', 90.

272. 24 Stat. 209, ch. 840 (1886).

273. 32 Stat. 193, ch. 784 (1902). While margarine was thus taxed when colored yellow, butter was not. In 1904 the Supreme Court upheld the tax as constitutional, despite admitting that the tax on colored margarine was undoubtedly not an excise for revenue but a prohibition. *McCray v. United States*, 195 U.S. 27; 24 S. Ct. 769 (1904).

274. The legal disabilities to which this discussion refers are those that were imposed by the federal government. In addition, the states had enacted a number of laws against margarine. In 1946 23 states continued to prohibit the sale of yellow margarine; seven states imposed stiff excise taxes on uncolored margarine, 13 states required retailers of margarine to be licensed, while 16 imposed a license fee on wholesalers. See William H. Nicolls, 'Some Economic Aspects of the Margarine Industry', *Journal of Political Economy*, 3 (June 1946): 221–42. New Hampshire required that all margarine be colored pink!

275. These figures are taken from Nicolls, 'Economic Aspects', 223–4.

276. H.R. 2023, reprinted in *Legislative History of the Federal Food, Drug, and Cosmetic Act*, 10: 97–101.

277. P.L. 81-459 (1950), reprinted in *Legislative History of the Federal Food, Drug, and Cosmetic Act,* 10: 1342–4.

278. Adam Gifford, Jr, 'Whiskey, Margarine, and Newspapers: A Tale of Three Taxes', in William F. Shughart, II, *Taxing Choice: The Predatory Politics of Fiscal Discrimination* (New Brunswick, NJ: Transaction Books, 1997). 71.

279. *Report: Investigation of the Use of Chemicals in Foods and Cosmetics* (83rd Congress, 2d Session, House of Representatives, Report No. 2356): 4, reprinted in *Legislative History of the Food, Drug, and Cosmetic Act,* 12: 502.

280. *Use of Chemicals,* 27, reprinted in *Legislative History of the Food, Drug, and Cosmetic Act,* 12: 525.

281. P.L. 83-518 (1954), reprinted in *Legislative History of the Food, Drug, and Cosmetic Act,* 12: 1037–43.

282. *Federal Food, Drug, and Cosmetic Act (Pesticides)* (Hearing Before a Subcommittee of the Committee on Interstate and Foreign Commerce, House of Representatives, H.R. 4277) (Washington, DC: Government Printing Office, 1953), reprinted in *Legislative History of the Food, Drug, and Cosmetic Act,* 12: 577–723.

283. P.L. 85-929 (1958), reprinted in *Legislative History of the Food, Drug, and Cosmetic Act,* 14: 949–54.

284. A detailed discussion of the history of the Food Additives Amendment is contained in Lars Noah and Richard E. Merrill, 'Starting From Scratch: Reinventing the Food Additive Approval Process', *Boston University Law Review,* 78 (April 1998): 330–443.

285. In *Monsanto Co. v. Kennedy,* the Court of Appeals for the District of Columbia Circuit ruled that, while migration of a poisonous substance might in fact have occurred, the Commissioner of the Food and Drug Administration had the discretion to disregard the amount as trivial. 198 US App. D.C. 214; 613 F.2d 947 (1977).

286. 21 P.L. 85-929 §409(c)(3)(A) (1958), reprinted in *Legislative History of the Food, Drug, and Cosmetic Act,* 14: 951.

287. H. R. 7798, reprinted in *Legislative History of the Food, Drug, and Cosmetic Act,* 14: 91.

288. Testimony of William E. Smith, *Food Additives* (Hearings Before a Subcommittee of the Committee on Interstate and Foreign Commerce, House of Representatives, 85th Congress) (Washington, DC: Government Printing Office, 1958): 171; reprinted in *Legislative History of the Food, Drug, and Cosmetic Act,* 14: 336.

289. Statement of James J. Delaney, *Food Additives,* 498; reprinted in *Legislative History of the Food, Drug, and Cosmetic Act,* 14: 660.

290. Quoted in Tom Holt, 'Modernize Our Food Safety Laws: Delete the Delaney Clause', paper prepared for the American Council on Science and Health', 7, available at http://www.acsh.org/publications/booklets/delaney.pdf (accessed 22 July 2003).

291. That is, a carcinogen that, in sufficiently large doses, can cause death in laboratory rats.

292. The American Council on Science and Health prepared a 'holiday dinner menu' in which each course contains known carcinogens. Their 2002 menu (with carcinogens indicated within parentheses) comprised: *cream of mushroom soup* (hydrazines); *relish tray* consisting of: *fresh carrots* (aniline, caffeic acid), *cherry tomatoes* (benzaldehyde, caffeic acid, hydrogen peroxide, quercetin glycosides), and *celery* (caffeic acid, furan derivatives, psoralens); *mixed roasted nuts* (aflatoxin, furfural); *green salad of lettuce and arugula with mustard vinaigrette* (allyl isothiocyanate, caffeic acid, estragole, methyl eugenol); *roast turkey* (heterocyclic amines); *bread stuffing with onions, celery, black pepper, and mushrooms* (acrylamide, ethyl alcohol, benzo(a)pyrene, ethyl carbamate, furan derivatives, furfural, dihydrazines, d-limonene, psoralens, quercetin glycosides, safrole); *cranberry sauce* (furan derivatives); *prime rib of beef with parsley sauce* (benzene, heterocyclic amines, psoralens); *broccoli spears* (allyl isothiocyanate); *baked potato* (ethyl alcohol, caffeic acid); *sweet potato* (ethyl alcohol, furfural); *rolls with butter* (acetaldehyde, benzene, ethyl alcohol, benzo(a)pyrene, ethyl carbamate, furan derivatives, furfural); *pumpkin pie* (benzo(a)pyrene, coumarin, methyl eugenol, safrole); *apple pie* (acetaldehyde, benzaldehyde, caffeic acid, d-limonene, estragole, ethyl acrylate, quercetin glycosides); *red wine, white wine* (ethyl alcohol, ethyl carbamate); *coffee* (benzo(a)pyrene, benzaldehyde, benzene, benzofuran, caffeic acid, catechol, 1,2,5,6-dibenz(a)anthracene, ethyl benzene,

furan, furfural, hydrogen peroxide, hydroquinone, d-limonene, 4-methylcatechol); *tea* (benzo(a)pyrene, quercetin glycosides); *jasmine tea* (benzyl acetate). Available at http://www.acsh.org/publications/booklets/menu02.html (accessed 22 July 2003).

293. While the law specifies 'carcinogens', this has been taken to mean tumor-producing, whether the tumor is malignant or benign.

294. In early 1989 the Environmental Protection Agency proposed to ban the use of Alar (daminozide), a chemical used to prevent apples from falling off trees before they were fully ripe. Tests on mice suggested that the substance decomposed into a carcinogen. The Natural Resources Defense Council claimed that the use of Alar constituted a major threat to the nation's health, especially to the health of children, and these charges were publicized on the television program *60 Minutes*. As a result, schools stopped serving apples and apple juice to their children, supermarkets removed the fruit and juice from their shelves, and Uniroyal, the manufacturer of Alar, halted production of the chemical. In fact, as Uniroyal was eventually to point out, 'a child would have to drink 19,000 quarts of apple juice a day to equal the excessive dosages fed to the mice that developed vascular tumors'. Marion Nestle, *Food Politics: How the Food Industry Influences Nutrition and Health* (Berkeley, CA: University of California Press, 2002): 162.

295. Laboratory experiments have shown that 'in one-third or more of the cases in which the MTD caused tumors in laboratory rodents, one half of the dose – still many times the likely equivalent human exposure – did not result in more tumors than in control subjects'. Tom Holt, 'Modernize Our Food Safety Laws', 13.

296. *Public Citizen v. Young*, 831 F.2d 1108 (1987). The suit was brought by Public Citizen, a consumer advocacy organization founded by Ralph Nader in 1971.

297. The Center for Science in the Public Interest has little to do with science and much to do with regulation. Founded in 1971, it is devoted almost exclusively to lobbying for legislation having to do with nutrition. In 1993 its executive director made the following announcement in connection with pesticides and food additives: 'If we had our way, everyone would be dining on whole grains, beans, vegetables, and fruit, along with low-fat dairy food and maybe a little lean meat or poultry. All the food would be fresh and unprocessed, and grown organically on local farms.' Michael F. Jacobson, 'Memo from MJ', *Nutrition Action Healthletter* July/August 1993, 3; quoted in Tom Holt, 'Modernize Our Food Safety Laws', 25.

298. H.R. 7624, reprinted in *Legislative History of the Food, Drug, and Cosmetic Act*, 15: 460–80.

299. Testimony of Arthur Flemming, *Color Additives* (Hearings Before the Committee on Interstate and Foreign Commerce, House of Representatives, 86th Congress, 2nd Session, H.R. 7624 and S. 2197) (Washington, DC: Government Printing Office, 1960): 61; reprinted in *Legislative History of the Food, Drug, and Cosmetic Act*, 16: 66.

300. P.L. 86-618, reprinted in *Legislative History of the Food, Drug, and Cosmetic Act*, 16: 810–20.

301. 'Negligible risk' was defined by the FDA and the EPA as 'one additional case of cancer per million people by daily exposure to high concentrations of a chemical over a 70-year lifetime'. Tom Holt, 'Modernize Our Food Safety Laws', 11.

302. The National Resources Defense Council is an 'environmental action' organization engaged in environmental lobbying. Among its board members at one time included Robert Redford and Laurence Rockefeller.

303. *Les v. Reilly*, 968 F.2d 985, at 988 (1992).

304. Kessler was FDA Commissioner from 1990 to 1997 and was likely the most aggressive director of the agency since its original establishment as the Bureau of Chemistry in 1906. He is perhaps best known for attempting to classify tobacco as a drug and thus regulating the industry's products under the terms of the Food, Drug, and Cosmetic Act. A review of Kessler's record as Commissioner points to the fact that there is no area touching the health of Americans that he would not have placed under the direction of government bureaucrats, including dictating what Americans might be allowed to eat and drink. The facts are that Kessler's notion of the proper role of government more closely reflects that embraced by German and Italian politicians in the 1930s than by Americans at the turn of the twentieth

century. He has no sympathy whatever for a free and open society and no patience with ideas of individual autonomy. Not only does Kessler have no sympathy with individual choice, but his record as Commissioner is one of unceasing dishonesty and deceit. He went on to become Dean of the Yale University School of Medicine.

305. Quoted in Tom Holt, 'Modernize Our Food Safety Laws', 17.
306. P.L. 104-170 (1996).
307. Details of the FDA's action against Reich are contained in Jerome Greenfield, *Wilhelm Reich v. The U.S.A.* (New York: W. W. Norton & Company, Inc., 1974).
308. Mildred Edy Brady, 'The New Cult of Sex and Authority', *Harper's*, 194 (April 1947): 312–22.
309. 'The Strange Case of Wilhelm Reich', *The New Republic*, 21 (26 May 1947): 20–23; reprinted in *The Bulletin of the Menninger Clinic*, 12 (March 1948): 61–7.
310. Wood, who was the FDA's resident inspector for Maine, later reported of W.R.M. Wharton, Chief of the Eastern Division of the FDA: 'He was crazy about that Reich case and didn't think of anything else during the whole time. He built it way up out of proportion.' Quoted in Greenfield, *Wilhelm Reich*, 62.
311. Reich's conviction was affirmed by the United States Court of Appeals for the First Circuit. See *Wilhelm Reich et al., v. United States*, 239 F.2d 134 (1956).
312. It might prove worthwhile to remind the reader of just how duplicitous the Food and Drug Administration could be. Even while it was actively considering regulations that would prevent the public from having access to a large number of medications unless prescribed by a physician, a Senate Report on the Copeland bill (later the 1938 Food, Drug, and Cosmetic Act) maintained: '*There are no useful products which would be barred from the market under this [the labeling] provision*, since labeling with proper directions for use would remove any worth-while article from this ban. Under the present law [the 1906 Act], which contains no provision of this character, there have come on the market a number of dangerous drugs from the use of which many authenticated cases of death and impairment of health have been reported. So long as their labels bore no false or misleading statements, the public could not be protected.

  'There are certain drugs whose employment is necessary in the treatment of some diseases, which none the less may in very exceptional cases prove harmful to persons to whom they are administered. Their action in such circumstances is comparable to the allergic action of eggs and other common foods, . . . *It is not intended that this provision should ban the sale of useful drugs of this kind when they are appropriately labeled*' (emphasis added). *Foods, Drugs, and Cosmetics* (Report to Accompany S. 5, 74th Congress, 1st Session, Senate, Report No. 646) (Washington, DC: Government Printing Office, 1935): 7–8; reprinted in *Legislative History of the Food, Drug, and Cosmetic Act*, 4: 99–100.
313. Testimony of Oscar Ewing, *Food, Drug, and Cosmetic Act* (Hearings Before the Committee on Interstate and Foreign Commerce, House of Representatives, 82nd Congress, 1st Session, on H.R. 3298) (Washington, DC: Government Printing Office, 1951): 15; reprinted in *Legislative History of the Food, Drug, and Cosmetic Act*, 11: 43.
314. Pharmacists were so horrified with the FDA's ruling that they prevailed upon Carl Durham of North Carolina, himself a pharmacist, to introduce legislation that would have exempted all prescription drugs from the jurisdiction of the FDA. The bill is reprinted in *Legislative History of the Food, Drug, and Cosmetic Act*, 11: 1–2.
315. The bill is reprinted in *Legislative History of the Food, Drug, and Cosmetic Act*, 11: 4–6.
316. The bill is reprinted in *Legislative History of the Food, Drug, and Cosmetic Act*, 11: 20–23.
317. P.L. 82-215 (1951), reprinted in *Legislative History of the Food, Drug, and Cosmetic Act*, 11: 688–9.
318. The question of whether a pharmacist dispensing a prescription drug at retail fell under the rubric of 'interstate commerce' when the transaction was clearly an intrastate one seems to have been definitively settled by the Sullivan case, where the Supreme Court ruled that the coverage of federal statutes extends 'to every article that had gone through interstate commerce until it finally reached the ultimate consumer'. *United States v. Sullivan*, 332 US 689, at 697.

319. It seems clear that his requirement was aimed at patients who received prescriptions for barbiturates.
320. Testimony of George P. Larrick, *House Hearings* (H.R. 3298), 94, reprinted in *Legislative History of the Food, Drug, and Cosmetic Act*, 11: 120. The original wording of the amendment permitted the FDA more discretion on what could not be sold directly to the public than any other provision of the law. The requirement of 'efficacy' added a huge new category to requirements of what drugs were available for over-the-counter sale. Indeed, when asked by one Representative at the House hearings on the amendment whether it might be the case that aspirin would be included on the list of drugs needing a prescription, Oscar Ewing opened the door to this possibility. He replied: 'Well, as of today, I would say 'No,' but I think you have to recognize that under this bill you might have an Administrator who would call a hearing to put aspirin on the list of dangerous drugs. If he held that aspirin was a dangerous drug and that were appealed to the circuit court of appeals and they upheld it, then, you would be in that situation.' Testimony of Oscar R. Ewing, *House Hearings* (H.R. 3298), 38, reprinted in *Legislative History of the Food, Drug, and Cosmetic Act*, 11: 66.
321. Examples include: 'Do not apply to broken skin'. 'Do not drive or operate machinery', 'Discontinue use if rapid pulse, dizziness, or blurring of vision occurs', 'If pain persists for more than ten days or redness is present, consult a physician immediately'.
322. Charles Wesley Dunn, 'The Durham-Humphrey Bill', *Food, Drug, and Cosmetic Law Journal*, 5 (December 1950): 864.
323. Temin, *Taking Your Medicine*, 53–4. Marshall Shapo, a well-known legal commentator, offers a particularly apt example of the disdain towards consumers this kind of legislation reflects. Shapo notes of the color additive amendment: 'Consumers may "want" their oranges to be orange instead of greenish, and their lemon cokes to be yellow instead of white, but these wants are related in large measure to merchandising. Recognizing this reality, it is appropriate for Congress to make the judgment that purely extrinsic changes in the appearance of products, such as those achieved by color additives, command a lower social priority than defense against potential long-term risks.' Marshall S. Shapo, *A Nation of Guinea Pigs* (New York: The Free Press, 1979): 160.
324. Temin, *Taking Your Medicine*, 121.
325. The FDA was fortunate in being able to capitalize on an article in the *Washington Post* by Morton Mintz, who credited Kelsey's 'determined opposition' to thalidomide for the fact that it was not available in the United States. Mintz himself was one of the strongest supporters of legislation to expand the powers of the FDA and had written a book, *The Therapeutic Nightmare* (Boston, MA: Beacon Books, 1965), calling for many of the powers awarded the agency by the Kefauver-Harris Amendments. The second edition of Mintz' book was titled *By Prescription Only: A Report on the Roles of the United States Food and Drug Administration, the American Medical Association, Pharmaceutical Manufacturers, and Others in Connection with the Irrational and Massive Use of Prescription Drugs That May Be Worthless, Injurious, or Even Lethal*.
326. In 1998 thalidomide was approved for the treatment of, among others, the symptoms of leprosy, as an antineoplastic agent, and of AIDS, by reducing inflamation.
327. This is not, strictly speaking, true. At the time the FDA permitted thalidomide's American distributor to issue samples of the drug to doctors for 'clinical trials' while awaiting approval. About 2 500 000 pills were given to over 1000 physicians who, in turn, distributed them to approximately 20 000 patients between 1958 and 1961. It is estimated that 17 victims were born in the United States.
328. Young, *Medical Messiahs*, 415.
329. The Senate's tribute to Dr Kelsey, which contains a summary of the President's remarks, can be found at *Congressional Record: Senate*, vol. 108 (7 August 1962): 15745; reprinted in *Legislative History of the Federal Food, Drug, and Cosmetic Act*, 22: 175. The idea that President Kennedy honor Dr Kelsey with the gold medal originated with Senator Estes Kefauver of Tennessee, who had written the President to that effect and who addressed the Senate on her 'heroism' on 18 July. See Richard Harris, *The Real Voice* (New York: Macmillan, 1964): 187–9.
330. See Young, *Medical Messiahs*, 390–407. Young, in dismissing those elements opposed to

further undermining of the right of choice in medication by the government, writes: 'Waving the banner of 'medical freedom,' these groups spent thousands for propaganda in an appeal to millions of Americans who were in some way disenchanted with life – the sick, the unhappy, the ignorant, the illogical, the fearful, the bored, the lonely'. 392.

331. See *United States v. Johnson*, 221 US 488; 31 S. Ct. 627 (1911).

332. The Department of Health, Education, and Welfare was created in April 1953, having assumed the responsibilities of the Federal Security Agency. President Eisenhower had decided to reorganize certain divisions of the executive branch, particularly the FSA. Besides its infelicitous name, which conjured up images of spies and code breakers, the Agency's budget had at that point exceeded the combined budgets of the Departments of Commerce, Justice, Labor, and Interior.

333. Young, *Medical Messiahs*, 392–4.

334. The subcommittee's examination of the prescription drug industry was part of a larger inquiry into administered prices throughout the economy which was launched in July 1957. By 1961 the subcommittee had issued four reports and had published 26 volumes of hearings. The fourth report is titled *Administered Prices: Drugs* (Report of the Committee on the Judiciary, US Senate, Made by the Subcommittee on Antitrust and Monopoly, 87th Congress, 1st Session, Report No. 448) (Washington, DC: Government Printing Office, 1961), reprinted in *Legislative History of the Food, Drug, and Cosmetic Act*, 17: 178–374. One of the fallouts of Kefauver's investigations was the resignation of Dr Henry Welch, then Director of the FDA's Division of Antibiotics. In 1959 an article in the *Saturday Review* (J. Lear, 'The Certification of Antibiotics,' *Saturday Review* (7 Feburary 1959): 43–48) reported that Dr Welch's objectivity was compromised by improper financial connections with the pharmaceutical industry. Investigations undertaken at the direction of Senator Kefauver later uncovered the fact that Welch had been paid approximately $200 000 over a period of seven years by a medical publishing firm selling advertising space and journal reprints to pharmaceutical firms. As a result of these revelations, Welch was forced to resign his office. See Peter Barton Hutt, 'Investigations and Reports Respecting FDA Regulation of New Drugs', *Clinical Pharmacology and Therapeutics*, 33 (1983): 539.

335. Remarks by Estes Kefauver, Chairman, *Drug Industry Antitrust Act* (Hearings Before the Subcommittee on Antitrust and Monopoly of the Committee on the Judiciary, US Senate, 87th Congress, 1st Session, S. 1552) (Washington, DC: Government Printing Office, 1961): 2, reprinted in *Legislative History of the Food, Drug, and Cosmetic Act*, 17: 566.

336. The legislative history of the Kefauver-Harris Amendments are discussed in some detail in Harris, *Read Voice*.

337. The bill is reprinted in *Legislative History of the Food, Drug, and Cosmetic Act*, 17: 122–43.

338. The FDA had attempted to impose a requirement of efficacy on medications prior to the passage of the Kefauver-Harris Amendments. The FDA's trade correspondence of 27 June 1945 noted that certain glandular preparations possessed no useful therapeutic properties despite the fact that they were in demand by certain medical practitioners. 'If further scientific evidence demonstrates conclusively that the products of this class are therapeutically useless', the correspondence continued, 'the Administration will have no alternative but to regard them as misbranded because among other things, their labelings cannot bear adequate directions for drug use'. As one commentator noted: 'This apparently means that if the Administration concludes that a drug is therapeutically useless it will regard it as contraband of commerce regardless of whether some physicians want to employ it in their practice'. Edward B. Williams, 'Exemption from the Requirement of Adequate Directions for Use in the Labeling of Drugs', *Food, Drug, and Cosmetic Law Journal*, 2 (June 1947): 160. For a history of attempts by the federal government to prohibit the distribution and sale of remedies that were ineffective, attempts that date back to the nineteenth century, see John Swann, 'Sure Cure: Public Policy on Drug Efficacy Before 1962', in Gregory J. Higby and Elaine C. Stroud, eds, *Inside Story of Medicine: A Symposium* (Madison, Wis: American Institute of Pharmacy, 1977): 223–61.

339. *Consumers' Protection and Interest Program* (Message from the President of the United

States, House of Representatives, 87th Congress, 2nd Session, Document No. 364), 7, reprinted in *Legislative History of the Food, Drug, and Cosmetic Act*, 21: 9.

340. H.R. 11581, reprinted in *Legislative History of the Food, Drug, and Cosmetic Act*, 21: 19–51. On the following day Harris introduced a second bill relating to cosmetics and therapeutic devices: H.R. 11582, reprinted in *Legislative History of the Food, Drug, and Cosmetic Act*, 21: 53–80.

341. Sam Peltzman, *Regulation of Pharmaceutical Innovation: The 1962 Amendments* (AEI Evaluative Studies 15; Washington, DC: American Enterprise Institute for Public Policy Research, 1974): 7.

342. The bill is reprinted in *Legislative History of the Food, Drug, and Cosmetic Act*, 22: 351–84.

343. P.L. 87–781 (1962), reprinted in *Legislative History of the Food, Drug, and Cosmetic Act*, 23: 228–44.

344. The Center for Drug Evaluation and Research of the Food and Drug Administration offers a fairly extensive history of the agency's activities respecting drugs, from which this account is taken, at http://www.fda.gov/cder/about/history/ (accessed 27 July 2003).

345. The review process is subject to extensive analysis in Temin, *Taking Your Medicine*, 126–40.

346. *United States v. Nutrition Service, Inc.*, 227 F. Supp. 375 (1964).

347. The temerity of the Food and Drug Administration in having judged states of mind, including fear of death, as insignificant in the treatment and progression of cancer is truly breathtaking.

348. The history of FDA regulation of medical devices in discussed in some detail in Peter Barton Hutt, 'A History of Government Regulation of Adulteration and Misbranding', *Food Drug Cosmetic Law Journal*, 44 (1989): 99–117, and Rodney R. Munsey, 'Trends and Events in FDA Regulation of Medical Devices Over the Last Fifty Years', *Food and Drug Law Journal*, 50 (1995, Special Issue): 163–77.

349. H.R. 10726 (1967).

350. H.R. 12316 (1972) and H.R. 6073 (1973).

351. *AMP Inc. v. Gardner*, 389 F.2d 825 (1968). Even before passage of the Food, Drug, and Cosmetic Act in 1938 the FDA had been able to prevail on the courts to permit use of the fiction that devices were in fact drugs. In 1938 the Court of Appeals for the Second Circuit found that a bandage, clearly a 'medical device', was a drug within the meaning of the 1906 Act. *United States v. Forty-eight Packages . . . of Gauze Bandage*, 94 F.2d 641 (1938). The appeals court ruled that in order to prevent injury to the public health it was necessary to give a fair and reasonable construction to the language of the Act.

352. 394 US 784 (1969).

353. 394 US 784, at 799–800.

354. H.R. 6073 (1973) and H.R. 5545 (1975).

355. In 1970 the FDA established standards for impact-resistant lenses in eyeglasses and in 1972 the agency began regulating *in vitro* diagnostic products as devices rather than drugs. Peter Barton Hutt, 'A History of Government Regulation of Adulteration and Misbranding of Medical Devices', *Food Drug Cosmetic Law Journal*, 44 (1989): 111.

356. The Dalkon Shield, introduced in 1970, was a plastic interuterine contraceptive that, under pressure from the FDA, was recalled in 1975. The device had the shape of a shield, with an eye in its center and five small protruding arms on its sides. More significant, it had a long tail composed of a number of fibers enclosed in a sheath that descended from the uterus to the vagina. This 'wick', it was claimed, acted as a conduit for bacteria, drawing them from the vagina into the uterus and fallopian tubes. Its use was associated with an increase in the number of dangerous pelvic infections. Twelve deaths were ostensibly associated with miscarriage-related infections and the device was withdrawn from the market. Despite the fact that more than 2.8 million women had employed the device without ill effect, the Shield's manufacturer, A.H. Robins Company, was forced to pay out more than $3 billion in claims before the firm eventually declared bankruptcy. It has since been shown that the Shield was blameless in contributing to the infections for which it was held responsible. However, the firm has been regularly taken to task for limiting its tort liabilities by

declaring bankruptcy and the company's officers, who were able to 'escape' any personal liability, have been accused of unbridled greed and complete indifference to the welfare of those harmed by the IUD. One of the reporters active in this vilification of the A. H. Robins Company was Morton Mintz, who was responsible for canonizing Dr Frances Kelsey in connection with the thalidomide incident.

357. Understood to include prohibitions against adulteration and misbranding, adherence to the regulations governing good manufacturing practice, and registering the device with the FDA.

358. William M. Wardell, 'Introduction of New Therapeutic Drugs in the United States and Great Britain: An International Comparison', *Clinical Pharmacology and Therapeutics*, 14 (September–October 1973): 773–90.

359. Kenneth I. Kaitin, Nancy Mattison, Frances K. Northingham, and Louis Lasagna, 'The Drug Lag: An Update of New Drug Introductions in the US and UK, 1977 Through 1987', *Clinical Pharmacology and Therapeutics*, 46 (August 1989): 121–38.

360. See Michael R. Ward, 'Drug Approval Overregulation', *Regulation*, 15 (Fall 1992): 47–53. The approval process is discussed at great length on the FDA website: See http://www.fda.gov/cder/handbook/develop.htm (accessed 29 July 2003).

361. Ward, 'Drug Approval Overregulation', 48.

362. 'The Drug Discovery, Development and Approval Process', at http://www.phrma.org/mediaroom/press/releases/01.07.2002.522.cfm#ii (accessed 30 July 2003).

363. United States Congress, Office of Technology Assessment, *Pharmaceutical R & D: Costs, Risks, and Rewards* (OTA-H-522) (Washington, DC: Government Printing Office, February 1993): 1. Another study puts this amount at $259 million in 1990 dollars. J. A. DiMasi, R. W. Hansen, H. G. Grabowski, et al., 'The Cost of Innovation in the Pharmaceutical Industry', *Journal of Health Economics*, 10 (1991): 107–42.

364. 'Backgrounder: How New Drugs Move Through the Development and Approval Process', Tufts Center for the Study of Drug Development, available at http://csdd.tufts.edu/NewsEvents/RecentNews.asp?newsid=4 (accessed 11 August 2003). The data are reprinted in Merrill Matthews, Jr, 'From Inception to Ingestion: The Cost of Creating New Drugs', *IPI Ideas* (Lewisville, Tex.: Institute for Policy Innovation, 9 September 2002): 1

365. Sam Peltzman, *Regulation of Pharmaceutical Innovation*. See also, Sam Peltzman, 'An Evaluation of Consumer Protection Legislation: The 1962 Drug Amendments', *Journal of Political Economy*, 81 (September–October 1973): 1049–91.

366. In 1985, Dale Gieringer estimated the benefits and costs of the FDA-induced drug-lag as follows: 'The benefits of FDA regulation relative to that in foreign countries could reasonably be put at some 5,000 casualties per decade or 10,000 per decade for worst case scenarios. In comparison, it has been argued . . . that the cost of FDA delay can be estimated at anywhere from 21,000 to 120,000 lives per decade. These figures would seem to support the conclusion that the costs of post-1962 regulation outweigh benefits by a wide margin, similar to Peltzman's results of a 4:1 cost–benefit ratio for the 1962 amendments. Given the uncertainties of the data, these results must be interpreted with caution, although it seems clear that the costs of regulation are substantial when compared to benefits.' D. H. Gieringer, 'The Safety and Efficacy of New Drug Approval', *Cato Journal*, 5 (Spring/Summer 1985): 196.

367. Temin, *Taking Your Medicine*, 127.

368. Janssen, 'History of U.S. Drug Regulation', 440.

369. Alexander T. Tabarrok, 'Assessing the FDA via the Anomaly of Off-Label Drug Prescribing', *Independent Review*, 5 (Summer 2000): 25. Tabarrok quotes several studies that show that 56 percent of cancer patients and 81 percent of AIDS patients have been given non-FDA approved prescriptions. These accounted for 33 percent of all prescriptions administered to patients with cancer and 40 percent of all prescriptions given to those with AIDS (p. 26).

370. Tabarrok, 'Off-Label Prescribing', 27. See also James M. Beck and Elizabeth D. Azari, 'FDA, Off-Label Use, and Informed Consent: Debunking Myths and Misconceptions', *Food and Drug Law Journal*, 53 (1998): 71–103.

371. W. I. Christopher, 'Off-Label Drug Prescription: Filling the Regulatory Vacuum', *Food and Drug Law Journal*, 48 (1993): 261.

372. Beck and Azari, 'Off-Label Use', 77–80.
373. *Washington Legal Foundation v. Friedman*, 13 F. Supp. 2d 51 (1998); 36 F. Supp. 2d 16 (1999).
374. *Washington Legal Foundation v. Henney*, 340 US App. D.C. 108; 202 F.3d 331 (2000).
375. P.L. 105-115 (1997).
376. The Modernization Act was not a total defeat for the FDA. Under its terms the agency was acknowledged as having some role in regulating the off-label uses of prescription drugs beyond determining their safety. Prior to passage of the law, once a drug had met the FDA's safety and efficacy tests, it could be employed in the treatment of any condition to which physician and patient agreed, without any reference whatever to the FDA. Under the Modernization Act, however, pharmaceutical manufacturers are now obligated to compile and submit data from the existing literature that show the benefits of supplemental use. It is true that this procedure is the same as currently employed by the AMA and the various drug formularies in determining whether off-label use is justified. However, it does introduce the FDA into an area where it earlier played no role whatever.
377. In 1960, Congress authorized a $10 million payment to cranberry growers as an 'indemnity payment' for the damage done the industry by the governrment's actions.
378. P.L. 86-613 (1960).
379. H.R. Report No. 2166, 89th Congress, 2nd Session, in 3 US Code Cog. & Adm. News 4095–6 (1966), quoted in National Commission on Product Safety, *Federal Consumer Safety Legislation* (A Study of the Scope and Adequacy of the Automobile Safety, Flammable Fabrics, Toys, and Hazardous Substances Programs) (June 1970): 164; reprinted in *Consumer Product Safety* (Hearings Before the Subcommittee on Commerce and Finance of the Committee on Interstate and Foreign Commerce, House of Representatives, 92nd Congress, 1st and 2nd Sessions, H.R. 8110, H.R. 8157, etc., Serial No. 92-59) (Washington, DC: Government Printing Office, 1972): Part 2, 704.
380. P.L. 89-756 (1966).
381. H.R. Report 2166 at 4096, quoted in *Federal Consumer Safety Legislation*, 166; reprinted in *Consumer Product Safety Act*, Part 2: 706.
382. H.R. Report 2166 at 4103, quoted in *Federal Consumer Safety Legislation*, 167; reprinted in *Consumer Product Safety Act*, Part 2: 707.
383. P.L. 91-113 (1969).
384. National Commission on Product Safety, *Interim Report 3 (1969)*, quoted in *Consumer Product Safety Act*, Part II: 709.
385. The leading causes of accidental deaths among children under 14 in the United States are (1) motor vehicle occupancy, (2) drowning, (3) residential fires, (4) pedestrian injuries, and (5) bicycle accidents. These account for over 85 percent of all accidental deaths.
386. The bill is reprinted in *Consumer Product Safety Act*, Part I: 35–86,
387. *Consumer Product Safety*, Part 3: 1048.
388. The bill is reprinted in *Consumer Product Safety*, Part I: 3–34.
389. P.L. 92-573 (1973).
390. See the Food and Drug Administration, *Annual Report, 1942–1943* (Covering the period 1 July 1941 to 30 June 1943) (Washington, DC: Government Printing Office, 1943): 39–40.
391. Enforcement of the narcotics laws was in the hands of the Treasury Department's Bureau of Narcotics.
392. Barbituric acid was originally synthesized in Germany in the 1860s. The first barbiturate that was marketed was a sedative, sold under the name 'barbital' in 1882. Early medical discussions referred to barbiturates as hypnotics and were commonly prescribed for sleep and as tranquillizers. Amphetamines are considerably newer, having been developed and introduced into medical practice in the early 1930s. During World War II amphetamines were in wide use in the armed forces, especially to counteract symptoms of extreme fatigue, while LSD (lysergic acid diethylamide) was developed in 1938 by two Swiss chemists, Arthur Stoll and Albert Hoffmann. It was originally intended as a headache cure until Hoffman accidentally discovered its hallucinogenic properties.
393. Testimony of George P. Larrick, *Illicit Narcotics Traffic* (Hearings Before the Subcommittee on Improvements in the Federal Criminal Code of the Committee of the Judiciary, Senate,

84th Congress, 1st Session) (10 parts; Government Printing Office, 1955–56): Part 6: 2226. What emerged from these hearings was the Narcotic Control Act of 1956, also known as the Daniel Act, signed into law by President Eisenhower in July 1956 (P.L. 84-728 (1956)). It extended the penalties that had already been substantially increased by the Boggs Act of 1951 for the sale and possession of narcotics to ludicrous proportions. A first offender found guilty of illegal possession could now be imprisoned for two to ten years and fined up to $20 000.00. Second offenses carried a penalty of five to 20 years in prison and a fine of up to $20 000. In the case of second offenses or higher, minimum sentences were mandatory and probation, suspension of sentence, and parole were strictly forbidden.

394. *Illicit Narcotics Traffic*, Part 6: 2217–41, 2246–63. Larrick was at pains to show the Subcommittee that barbiturate use was a greater danger than was the use of morphine and that the task of the Food and Drug Administration in enforcing the prohibitions against the illicit use of drugs was in fact more important than was the Bureau of Narcotics. 'Because barbiturates produce greater mental, emotional and neurological impairment than morphine [i.e., opiates], informed medical experts express the opinion that addiction to them is actually more detrimental to the individual and society than morphine addiction. Like morphine, barbiturates produce physical dependence, but withdrawal of barbiturates is even more serious – in some cases, patients even die during withdrawal.' *Illicit Narcotics Traffic*, Part 6: 2220. Meanwhile, Harry Anslinger, Commissioner of the Bureau of Narcotics, was insisting that the opiates were far more dangerous than were barbiturates. See Alfred K. Lindesmith, *The Addict and the Law* (Bloomington, Ind.: Indiana University Press, 1965): 279–80.

395. One historian writes of the FDA during this period: 'Periodically the Food and Drug Administration put out alarming new estimates, such as 819,000 pounds of barbiturates, worth $40 million, produced in 1959; more deaths from barbiturates than from any other poison, and a 670 per cent increase in such deaths in Los Angeles; 8 million amphetamine tablets a year, with at least 50 per cent going into the illicit market . . . etc.' Rufus King, *The Drug Hang-Up: America's Fifty-Year Folly* (New York: W.W. Norton & Co., Inc., 1972): 274.

396. President's Advisory Commission on Narcotic and Drug Abuse, *Final Report* (Typescript, November, 1963): 48–64.

397. P.L. 89-74 (1965).

398. The illicit supply of barbiturates and amphetamines was radically different from that associated with narcotics and was fed by diversions from the chain of legitimate drug distribution. President's Commission on Law Enforcement and Administration of Justice, *Task Force Report: Narcotics and Drug Abuse* (Annotations and Consultants' Papers) (Washington, DC: Government Printing Office, 1967): 7.

399. P.L. 90-623 (1968).

400. P.L. 91-513 (1970).

401. House Committee on Energy and Commerce, *Report on Prescription Drug Diversion and the American Consumer: What You Think You See May Not Be What You Get* (99th Congress, 1st Session, Committee Print R) (Washington, DC: Government Printing Office, 1985).

402. Letter of Transmittal by Representative John D. Dingell, House Committee on Energy and Commerce, *Report on Uncertain Drugs: The Multimillion Dollar Market in Reimported Pharmaceuticals* (99th Congress, 1st Session, Committee Print GG) (Washington, DC: Government Printing Office, 1986): 1.

403. House Committee on Energy and Commerce, *Dangerous Medicine: The Risk to American Consumers from Prescription Drug Diversion and Counterfeiting* (99th Congress, 1st Session, Committee Print Z) (Washington, DC: Government Printing Office, 1986). The testimony is summarized in Robert T. Angarola and Judith E. Beach, 'The Prescription Drug Marketing Act: A Solution in Search of a Problem?' *Food and Drug Law Journal*, 51 (1996): 25–7.

404. P.L. 100-293 (1988).

405. See *United States v. Midwest Pharmaceuticals, Inc.*, 633 F. Supp. 316 (1986), aff'd in part, rev'd in part, remanded 82 F. 2nd 1238 (8th Cir., 1987), aff'd 890 F. 2nd 1989 (8th Cir.,

1989); *United States v. Jamieson-McKames Pharmaceuticals*, 651 F. 2nd 532 (8th Cir., 1981).

406. Among the other agencies, in addition to the FDA's Office of Criminal Investigation, were the Federal Bureau of Investigation, the Drug Enforcement Administration, the Department of Health and Human Service's Office of the Inspector General, the Postal Inspection Service, state Medicaid fraud control units, state and local police units, state medical licensing boards, state boards of pharmacy, offices of state attorneys general, insurance investigators, and pharmaceutical industry managers. Surely this preposterously huge assemblage of law enforcement personnel could more fittingly be used for the Normandy invasion than to track down a few pill makers!

407. Angarola and Beach, 'The Prescription Drug Marketing Act', 55.

408. Dietary Supplement Health and Education Act of 1994, P.L. 103-417 (1994).

409. 38 Fed. Reg. 20 708, at 20 717 (1973).

410. 504 F.2d 761 (1974).

411. *National Nutritional Foods Association v. F. David Matthews*, 557 F.2d 325 (1977).

412. P.L. 94–278 (1976). The bill explicitly prohibited the FDA from classifying a vitamin or mineral as a drug 'solely because it exceeds the level of potency which the Secretary [of Health, Education, and Welfare, i.e, the FDA] determines is nutritionally rational or useful'.

413. P.L. 101-535 (1990).

414. Analysis by the Mayo Clinic and the Centers for Disease Control has since traced the link to a contaminant present in batches of L-tryptophan manufactured by the Japanese firm Showa Denko. However, the FDA continues to ban sales of the supplement, claiming it is an untested and hazardous drug.

415. The staff of the Subcommittee on Oversight and Investigations of the House Committee on Energy and Commerce, charged with reporting on H.R. 2597, prepared a staff report entitled Filthy Food, Dubious Drugs, and Defective Devices: The Legacy of FDA's Antiquated Statute (102nd Congress, 1st Session, Committee Print No. 102-N) (Washington, DC: Government Printing Office, 1991). The report, as its title indicates, argued that the FDA was devoid of effective weapons to enforce the mandates of Congress and referred to opposition to the unprecedented authority conferred on the agency by the proposed statute as 'incredible'. 'The record shows', it maintained, 'that dangerously adulterated foodstuffs, substandard medical devices and prescription drugs of dubious effectiveness or which are unlicensed are reaching American consumers on a regular basis because the FDA has neither the resources nor the authority required to prevent abuses' (p. 2).

416. H.R. 1662.

417. The report was completed in May 1992 and recommended that the FDA: (1) determine maximum safe intake levels for vitamins and minerals; (2) initiate rules that would categorize many amino acid products as drugs; (3) continue to apply the 'food additive' standard to most dietary supplement products unless drug claims were made; and (4) implement good manufacturing practice standards.

418. In 1995 Alexander Volokh reported that 'since 1990, when David Kessler took over as FDA commissioner, enforcement has been one of the FDA's top priorities. In his first two months, Kessler added 100 new criminal investigators to his enforcement staff, many of them formerly with the Secret Service and the Drug Enforcement Administration. Armed raids on alternative health clinics and dietary supplement dealers followed, as well as increased warning letters, product seizures, and criminal prosecutions in the drug and device industries.' Alexander Volokh, 'Clinical Trials: Beating the FDA in Court', *Reason* (May 1995).

419. 442 US 544 (1979).

420. P.L. 102-571 (1992)

421. P.L. 103-417 (1994).

422. This type of product, the FDA maintained, contains substances about which little is known and which have not been evaluated for safety. For a summary of the efforts to limit the FDA's attempts to control the sale of dietary supplements, written by an advocate of agency regulation, see Nestle, *Food Politics*, 219–93.

423. Christopher Smith, 'Supplements and the Feds', *Salt Lake Tribune*, 21 May 2001,

reproduced at http://www.lef.org/newsarchive/vitamins/2001/05/21/SLTR/0000-3677-KEYWORD.Missing.html?GO.X=8\&GO.Y=7 (accessed 8 August 2003).

424. P.L. 97-414 (1983).

425. In 2001 the FDA claimed that evidence from the IRS's Orphan Tax Credit showed that the actual costs of clinical testing of new drugs, including the cost of failures, was $7.9 million per approved drug before tax, and $3.9 million after the benefits of the tax credit! James Love and Michael Palmedo, 'Cost of Human Use Clinical Trials: Surprising Evidence from the US Orphan Drug Act', available at http://www.cptech.org/ip/health/orphan/irsdata9798.html (accessed 11 August 2003).

426. Only 15 applications for Orphan Drug designation were made during the first year of the program and of these only ten were granted.

427. Prior to passage of the Act, drugs developed to treat orphan diseases were designated 'public service' drugs. A survey conducted by the staff of the House Subcommittee on Health and the Environment in 1981 found that of approved public service drugs only 20 percent had resulted from research that was targeted specifically at a rare disease. The overwhelming majority of the remainder resulted from serendipitous discoveries while researching other illnesses. Peter S. Arno, Karen Bonuck, and Michael Davis, 'Rare Diseases, Drug Development, and AIDS: The Impact of the Orphan Drug Act', *The Milbank Quarterly*, 73 (June 1995): 233.

428. P.L. 98-417 (1984).

429. Congressional Budget Office, *How Increased Competition From Generic Drugs has Affected Prices and Returns in the Pharmaceutical Industry*, July 1998, ix. Available at ftp://ftp.cbo.gov/6xx/doc655/pharm.pdf (accessed 12 August 2003).

430. That is, that the active ingredient in the generic drug is released and absorbed at the same rate as is the case for the corresponding brand-name drug.

431. *Roche Products, Inc. v. Bolar Pharmaceutical Company, Inc.*, 733 F.2d 858 (1984).

432. Congressional Budget Office, *Increased Competition from Generic Drugs*, 4

433. ACT UP, the AIDS Coalition to Unleash Power, the leading AIDS activist organization, describes itself as 'a diverse, non-partisan group of individuals united in anger and committed to direct action to end the AIDS crisis'. The organization appears to specialize in disruptive demonstrations that garner maximum publicity.

434. Steven R. Salbu, 'The FDA and Public Access to New Drugs: Appropriate Levels of Scrutiny in the Wake of HIV, AIDS, and the Diet Debacle Episode', *Boston University Law Review*, 79 (February 1999): 115.

435. Sabin Russell, 'New Campaign on AIDS Testing', *San Francisco Chronicle*, 11 July 1991, reproduced at http://www.aegis.com/news/sc/1991/SC910706.html (accessed 15 August 2003).

436. H.R. 2872 (1991).

437. P.L. 102-571 (1992).

438. 'The FDA pledged to cut by almost half the amount of time it takes to review new drugs and to review so-called breakthrough drugs in no longer than six months if the pharmaceutical industry paid the FDA $300 million in fees over five years. Agency officials said they were able to make this pledge because of their experience with the AIDS drugs DDI and DDC. Both were approved in record time because of pressure by AIDS activists, showing that extra resources could be translated into faster scientific reviews.' 'AIDS Activism Improves Medicine', *Washington Post*, 16 October 1992, p. 3. See also, Eve Nichols, 'Historical Perspective', in *Expanding Access to Investigational Therapies for HIV Infection and AIDS* (Washington, DC: National Academy Press, 1991): 5–18.

439. Joseph A. DiMasi, 'A New Look At United States Drug Development and Approval Times', *American Journal of Therapeutics*, 3 (1996): 1.

440. Kenneth I. Kaitin and Joseph A. DiMasi, 'Measuring the Pace of New Drug Development in the User Fee Era', *Drug Information Journal*, 34 (2000): 673–80.

441. Joseph A DiMasi, Mark A. Seibring, and Louis Lasagna, 'New Drug Development in the United States from 1963 to 1992', *Clinical Pharmacology & Therapeutics*, 55 (June 1994): 609–22.

442. The PDUFA was reauthorized as part of the Food and Drug Administration Modernization Act, P.L.105-115 (1997).

443. The 2002 reauthorization was enacted as Title V of the Public Health Security and Bioterrorism Response Act, P.L. 107-188 (2002).
444. Congress clearly regarded user fees as a great success. In October 2002 a law authorizing the FDA to impose user fees on the manufacturers of medical devices similar to the PDUFA was enacted by Congress and was signed by President George W. Bush. The measure, the Medical Device User Fee and Modernization Act (P.L. 107-250 (2002)), sponsored by Representative James Greenwood, Republican of Pennsylvania, was passed by unanimous consent in both chambers the day following its introduction. The standard fee for a premarket application in FY 2004 is $206 811!
445. Several segments of what would have been a consolidated bill were, however, enacted. The FDA Export Reform and and Enhancement Act (P.L. 104-134 (1996)), reduced the regulatory requirements and in some cases eliminated the obstacles for exporting unapproved human drugs, biologics, devices, and animal drugs; The Food Quality Protection Act (P.L. 104-170 (1996)) mandates a single health-based standard for pesticides in all foods; The Animal Drug Availability Act (P.L. 104-250 (1996)), was aimed at streamlining the efficacy aspects of the regulatory process with respect to animal drugs.
446. P.L. 105-115 (1997).
447. A detailed analysis of all the provisions of this massive statute is available at http://cov.com/publications/DRUGDEV.asp (accessed 21 August 2003).
448. Richard A. Merrill, 'Modernizing the FDA: An Incremental Revolution', *Health Affairs*, 18 (March/April 1999): 96–111.
449. The World Health Organization defines an 'adverse drug reaction' (ADR) as 'an effect which is noxious and unintended, and which occurs at doses used in many for prophylaxis, diagnosis, or therapy'. Quoted in Barbara A. Noah, 'Adverse Drug Reactions: Harnessing Experimental Data to Promote Patient Welfare', *Catholic University Law Review*, 49 (Winter 2000): 455. ADRs, in turn, are a subset of ADEs, adverse drug events, which include unpredictable side-effects, foreseeable side-effects, such as nausea as an adjunct to chemotherapy, and unwelcome effects resulting from errors in prescribing or administering drugs.
450. David Willman, 'How a New Policy Led to Seven Deadly Drugs', *Los Angeles Times* (20 December 2000): 1.
451. An arm of Public Citizen, founded by Ralph Nader in 1971.
452. A study conducted by Dr Bruce Pomeranz of the University of Toronto for Public Citizen claimed that no fewer than 76 000 to 137 000 people died in 1994 from properly prescribed medications. While only a small portion of these fatalities can be attributed to drugs approved after the introduction of fast-track approval, it suggests that, despite substantial approval times, ADRs resulting in death are common. Whether they are appreciably more common among drugs given fast-track approval is questionable. Allthough Pomeranz's study did not specify which drugs were most dangerous, other studies have shown that narcotics, used to kill pain but resulting in halting breathing; aspirin, which occasionally leads to stomach bleeding; antibiotics and anti-viral drugs, which can cause severe diarrhea; and cardiovascular drugs, which can lead to internal bleeding, are mainly responsible for fatal ADEs.
453. Statement of the Academy of Managed Care Pharmacy, 7 December 2001, available at http://www.amcp.org/professional_res/analysis/12701.pdf (accessed 20 August 2003).
454. *Congressional Quarterly*, Hearings Before the Senate Committee on Health, Education, Labor and Pensions, by Dr Sandra Kweder, Deputy Director of the Office of New Drugs, Food and Drug Administration, 1 March 2005.
455. There appear to be a host of unnecessary requirements that add a substantial amount of time to the approval process. See Larry R. Versteegh, 'Symposium: Who Knows Where the Time Goes?: Science and Regulatory Rituals Associated With the Drug Development Process', *Food and Drug Law Journal*, 52 (1997): 155–61.
456. One example out of many is the FDA's late approval of the drug Erbitux, effective in treating patients with colorectal cancer, which was withheld from sale for an additional two years while the agency on numerous occasions requested further information of questionable value from its manufacturer. Ironically, Erbitux was approved under the FDA's accel-

erated-approval program! 'FDA's bungling on Erbitux led to the creation of a group called Abigail Alliance, which argues that there should be wider access to experimental drugs'. Chris Edwards, *Downsizing the Federal Government* (Washington, DC: Cato Institute, 2005): 99–100.

457.   FDA food safety expenditures were $11.5 million in FY 2001, $100 million in FY 2002, $97.8 million in FY 2003, and 11.6 million in FY 2004.

458.   Testimony of Michael A. Friedman, *Reauthorization of the Prescription Drug User Fee Act and FDA Reform* (Hearings before the House Subcommittee on Health and the Environment of the Committee on Energy and Commerce, 23 April 1997, 105th Congress, 1st Session) at http://www.house.gov/commerce/health/hearings/042397/friedman.pdf (accessed 17 August 2003). The phrase is repeatedly employed by the FDA to describe its mandate and constantly reappears in its literature.

459.   Where a product is consistently or commonly dangerous to the life or health of users and this were known to the seller and not the buyer, there already exists criminal legislation prohibiting its sale, not to mention the serious consequences that follow from civil actions brought against the seller.

460.   'David Kessler, ' The Basis of the FDA's Decision on Breast Implants', *New England Journal of Medicine*, 326 (18 June 1992): 1715.

3. The Veterans Administration

Prior to World War I, the federal government provided no hospital or medical care to veterans other than extending domiciliary care, including incidental medical care, to a few disabled veterans.[1] The United States Soldiers' Home in Washington, DC, which began operations in 1851, and the National Home for Disabled Volunteer Soldiers[2] provided domiciliary care to disabled veterans incapable of earning a livelihood because of age or disability.[3] While it had been the policy of the National Home that veterans who had not been disabled in the line of duty were ineligible for domiciliary care, disabled soldiers who had been honorably discharged and who were incapacitated, regardless of cause, were extended such care by federal statute in 1884.[4] Despite the fact that the statute provided that applicants had to prove that they were incapable of earning a living by virtue of their disability, the provisions of the 1884 Act so enlarged the number of veterans eligible for admission to the National Home that Congress was compelled to establish additional branches over the course of the following few years.[5]

Domiciliary care, with its ancillary medical benefits, was, at best, limited to a very small number of American veterans.[6] The traditional method of dealing with those who had served in the military prior to World War I was to award them pensions, although, even then, earlier legislation limited pensions to soldiers who had been disabled or killed in the line of duty and their widows. However, during the Presidential campaign of 1878, Rutherford B. Hayes had pledged to liberalize existing pension legislation if elected.[7] The Republican Party consistently supported a generous pension scheme for political purposes.[8] In 1879, after intense lobbying by, among others, attorneys acting as claims agents, Congress passed the Arrears Act, which permitted veterans with newly discovered war-related injuries to receive the total of all previously due pension payments in a lump sum.[9] Claims agents, who acted on behalf of veterans applying for pension benefits, were entitled to a fee for their services and, while the maximum charges for these services were set by Congress, they were likely to be substantial in the case of veterans awarded sums retroactively and proved a windfall to attorneys specializing in pursuing pension benefits. Indeed, by 1880 more than 85 percent of claims pending before the Pension Bureau were controlled by fewer than 100 attorneys.[10] With passage of the Arrears Act the amount paid out in pensions increased from approximately $27 000 000 in 1878 to $51 000 000 in 1880. More dramatically, the expenditures of the Pension Bureau in 1883 were as great as the entire pre-Civil War budget of the federal government.

Despite these increases, agitation from soldiers' groups, particularly the Grand Army of the Republic,[11] for larger payments and more liberal qualifications continued unabated. In 1888, Benjamin Harrison, a former brevet brigadier general in the Union Army, defeated Grover Cleveland in the Presidential election, largely because of Cleveland's earlier veto of a bill calling for expanded pensions.[12] Harrison quickly appointed James Tanner,[13] at the time a member of the pension committee of the Grand Army of the Republic, as head of the United States Pension Bureau. It is reported that on his appointment Harrison confided to Tanner: 'Be liberal with the boys'.[14] And Tanner himself is reputed to have declared 'God help the surplus revenue'.[15] Tanner's reputation for open-handedness with federal money was so great, however, that demands for his resignation could not be ignored and he was forced to surrender his position as commissioner of the Pension Bureau only three months after being sworn in. He was succeeded by Green B. Raum, who, it appears, was no less profligate than was Tanner. As expected, in 1890, a Republican Congress enacted the Dependent Pension Act, which provided that all honorably discharged Civil War veterans or their widows and minor children were entitled to a pension if the veteran were suffering some disability that incapacitated him from earning a livelihood, whether the disability were war-related or not. The effect of this legislation was dramatic. By 1893, no less than 41.5 percent of the federal government's income was spent on veterans' pensions.[16] It did not take long to transform these pensions, now extended to almost a million veterans, into old-age and survivors' benefits. In 1906, a new statute provided that 'the age of sixty-two years and over shall be considered a permanent specific disability within the meaning of the pension laws'.[17] And, finally, in 1907, the federal government's pension provisions were extended to all Civil War veterans, even if not disabled.[18]

With American entry into the World War, the question of providing medical and hospital care to veterans was once again raised and, in October 1917, Congress enacted legislation providing that injured military personnel were eligible to receive medical, surgical, and hospital services from the United States government. The Democratic Party under President Woodrow Wilson, not wishing to appear less generous to veterans than were Republicans, decided to scrap the pension system then in place and to substitute for it a new system of compensation with a new agency to administer it. The details of the new plan were drafted by a committee chaired by United States Circuit Court Judge Julian W. Mack, under the direction of Secretary of the Treasury William G. McAdoo.[19] After two months of Congressional hearings, the War Risk Insurance Act passed Congress by unanimous vote. Under the Act, five

classes of benefits were established for veterans of the World War, including
(1) support for the dependents of members of the armed forces during service;
(2) low-cost insurance on a voluntary basis; (3) compensation for the war-
disabled and for the dependents of the dead; (4) vocational rehabilitation for
the disabled; and (5) medical and hospital care for those veterans with service-
related illnesses and disabilities.[20] It fell to the Public Health Service to
perform the necessary physical examinations by which disability was determined and to provide the hospital facilities and treatment called for under the
Act.

The effect of these provisions was a spectacular growth in the size of the
Public Health Service. In 1917, Congress had appropriated $3 000 000 for the
Service, but in the following year the appropriation was increased to
$50 000 000 or almost 17-fold! At the same time, its personnel increased from
3000 to 23 000.[21] While the Public Health Service attempted to administer
medical and hospital care to the veterans of the World War, it was not equipped
for this task without an even greater number of hospital beds at its disposal.
While the Service made much use of contract hospitals, especially for
neuropsychiatric patients, the 62 hospitals at its disposal by June 1920 still
proved insufficient and the growing protests about inadequate hospital facilities available to veterans proved a telling issue in the Presidential election of
1920. Despite the fact that in the same year Congress had appropriated
substantial sums for the Public Health Service for the construction of new
hospitals,[22] veterans' groups continued to complain bitterly about the seemingly impenetrable bureaucracy surrounding any application for veterans'
benefits and about the lack of medical facilities available to them.

In response to these criticisms, the new Harding Administration quickly
appointed a commission[23] to investigate the matter, chaired by Charles G.
Dawes, first director of the Bureau of the Budget and later Calvin Coolidge's
vice-president. Among its other members were the labor leader John L. Lewis
and Dr Charles E. Sawyer, a card-playing buddy of the President's, who had
earlier been made a brigadier general in the Medical Corps by President
Harding and provided with a suitably extravagant uniform to accompany his
new 'rank'. The newly created American Legion[24] was also represented on the
committee by five of its executives and used every opportunity to advance the
organization's interests, most importantly in advocating the consolidation of
those sections of the three government agencies then responsible for veterans'
affairs[25] into one grand veterans' bureau. Indeed, the Committee effectively
turned over its investigative powers to the Legion, whose national commander, Frederick Galbraith, was empowered to question witnesses. The result of
the Committee's recommendations was passage of the Sweet Bill in August
1921, by which an independent agency, the Veterans' Bureau, was established,
to which was transferred total responsibility for veterans' benefits.[26] To head

the Bureau, Harding appointed Colonel Charles R. Forbes, his old crony and a loyal campaign worker, who, at the time, was director of the War Risk Insurance Bureau. Forbes had had a checkered past, hardly a liability to the Harding Administration. As a boy of 12 he had enlisted in the Marines as a drummer boy and, as a young man, had some years later joined the army. However, two months after having enlisted in the army he deserted. This appears not to have greatly bothered the military authorities, who reinstated him without trial. Several years later he was posted to Pearl Harbor, Hawaii, where he first met Harding. They soon became close friends, a friendship that was rewarded several years later by his appointment to direct the newly created Veterans' Bureau.[27]

The Bureau quickly became a dumping ground for those seeking jobs who were lucky enough to have had the right political connections. Indeed, it was reported that appointments to some positions had been set a full two months prior to the passage of the bill that created the Veterans' Bureau.[28] With an annual operating budget of more than $450 000 000 and a headquarters staff of some 30 000 bureaucrats,[29] opportunities were rife for corruption.[30] Forbes, it appears, found his $10 000 annual salary as director insufficient for his personal needs. Aware that the hospital construction program that the Public Health Service had undertaken provided abundant opportunity for graft and kickbacks, he was able to prevail on the President to transfer all veterans' hospitals, including those under construction, to the Veterans' Bureau.[31] In addition, he managed to wrest from Congress an additional appropriation of $17 000 000.[32]

Forbes was able to make the most of this change, especially through his dealings with the Thompson-Black Construction Companies. In return for Thompson-Black being chosen as one of the construction contractors, Forbes was paid substantial bribes and, additionally, was given a third of the profits the firm made in the construction of hospitals. The costs of this graft were so high that it was calculated that almost $1000 per bed went to Forbes and his friends. In addition, there appears to have been no supervision of the actual construction so that hospitals were built without laundries or kitchens and with substandard materials.[33] In the 18 months following his appointment, Forbes spent approximately $33 000 000 on new hospital construction, but had added only 200 beds – all located in Memphis, Tennessee.[34] The purchase of supplies for veterans' hospitals was yet another area that permitted substantial kickbacks. It is reported that on one occasion, despite the fact that the Veterans' Bureau had already accumulated thousands of gallons of floor wax, he purchased an additional shipment from the Continental Chemical Company for which the Bureau paid almost $71 000, enough – it was claimed – to last the Bureau for 100 years! And from another supplier, the Bureau purchased 45 045 gallons of soap at 87 cents a gallon, of quality comparable to soap then selling for 1.8 cents per gallon. In addition to getting kickbacks from government contracts to build and supply the various veterans' facilities over which he had charge, Forbes looted the storage facilities under his control, selling their contents for a fraction of their value. He had no difficulty in finding a purchaser for the $5 000 000 worth of morphine, cocaine, and codeine sitting in Bureau warehouses, to whom he also sold, among a number of other items, 67 000 quarts of bourbon, rye, and gin – originally purchased prior to Prohibition for medicinal purposes. These items, all located in the Bureau warehouse at Perryville, Maryland, included bath towels, bedsheets, and almost 100 000 pairs of winter pajamas sewn by American women and donated to the Red Cross. All together, goods sufficient to fill 126 railroad cars were sold to the Thompson-Kelly Company, a sister company of Thompson-Black.[35]

Rumors of massive fraud were so common that Congress was finally forced to act and early in March 1923 the Senate called for an investigation of the Veterans' Bureau. Forbes, having sensed that things were falling apart, had resigned as Director a few days earlier and had sailed for Europe on a 'much-needed' vacation. The results of the Senate investigation were so startling that even Washingtonians inured to the depredations of the Harding Administration were shocked.[36] Forbes was charged with conspiracy to defraud the government, convicted, and sentenced to two years in prison. He served 20 months in Leavenworth, was fined $10 000, and was released in November 1927. It has been estimated the waste and graft that occurred in the Veterans' Bureau over the course of Forbes' 18 months in office amounted to well over $225 000 000 – approximately two-thirds of the federal government's surplus.[37]

In part as a consequence of the investigation of the Veterans' Bureau following Forbes' resignation, the administration of all veterans' affairs was consolidated in 1930 and the Bureau was renamed the Veterans Administration, under an Administrator of Veterans Affairs. The new Veterans Administration was made responsible not only for all medical services extended to veterans but also for the military pension system, previously vested in the Bureau of Pensions. By far the major portion of the Administration's resources, however, was devoted to providing medical and hospital care. A number of Congressmen were reluctant to continue to grant additional funds for hospital construction years after the war had ended, especially after having appropriated $47 000 000 for this purpose between 1919 and 1922. In addition, the Senate committee that had investigated Colonel Forbes' conduct as head of the Veterans' Bureau had uncovered the fact that no less than 40 percent of all men in veterans' hospitals could have been served equally well as outpatients.[38] The effect of these findings was a bitter and seemingly endless contest between the American Legion, whose

Conventions annually recommended the construction of additional hospitals, and Congress, who were disinclined to vote further expenditures for this purpose. Despite their reluctance, however, Congress was to make available $80 000 000 more for hospital construction by 1931. Between 1919 and 1941, Congress appropriated a total of $205 000 000 for the construction of hospital and domiciliary facilities for veterans.[39]

Another contentious issue revolved around the question of whether veterans who required medical care for a non-service connected illness or disability should be accommodated without cost at veterans' facilities. Prior to 1924, medical and hospital care was restricted to those suffering from some service-related problem and, in the main, to veterans of the World War.[40] However, partly in response to pressure from the American Legion,[41] this policy was altered by Congress to provide universal medical care for all veterans, regardless of the source of the problem. This enormous expansion of medical services, provided in government-run medical facilities, was, of course, without precedent. However, the massive corruption that had plagued the Veterans' Bureau under Forbes, for which Congress felt itself in part responsible, led to passage of the World War Veterans' Act of 1924, which sought to make amends for this misfeasance. Under the terms of the Act, the right to hospitalization and medical care was extended to all honorably discharged veterans, without regard to the origin of their disability or illness.

While the law did not make it mandatory that the Veterans' Bureau furnish hospitalization for veterans with non-service-related illnesses, it did encourage the Bureau to extend hospital benefits to all veterans, despite the substantial costs involved. By 1926, no fewer than 17 percent of all patients in veterans' hospitals were receiving treatment for illnesses or injuries that were unrelated to their military service.[42] The American Legion had predictably engaged in an intense lobbying effort to get Congress to enact legislation that would bind the Veterans' Bureau to extend hospital benefits to veterans for all illnesses, whatever the origin or cause, and in 1930 made this demand a focus of its legislative program. By this point the nation had entered the Depression, and there was a good deal of resistance to the extra costs of such legislation. As a consequence, Congress failed to act on the measure. In the following year, however, yet another veterans' hospital bill came before Congress. Frank T. Hines, who had succeeded Forbes as Director, had asked for an additional 2900 beds to accommodate veterans with war-related illnesses and added that if all non-service-connected cases were to be admitted, the Bureau would need 6000 beds. After debate on the issue, Congress appropriated sufficient funds for an additional 6000 beds, thus effectively instituting the policy of providing hospital facilities for all veterans.[43]

The effect of this change in policy was profound. By virtue of this innovation, 5 million veterans were now qualified for publicly funded medical care for life.[44] There followed a huge influx of veterans into government-administered hospitals, whose construction accelerated; over the course of the next decade more than $125 000 000 was spent on hospital construction. By 1941, some four-fifths of admissions to veterans' hospitals were for conditions unrelated to military service. And among general medical and surgical cases, only 4.25 percent were service-connected.[45]

Table 3.1 provides some sense of the escalation in size and cost of the hospital benefits accorded veterans up to World War II.

Table 3.1   Beds Available in Veterans Administration Facilities, Total, Beds Occupied, and Net Hospital Operating Costs, 1922–1941 (in thousands)

Fiscal Year	Beds Available	Beds Occupied	Operating Cost ($)
1922	17 792	26 869	23 531
1923	15 448	23 611	21 658
1924	15 861	21 730	19 188
1925	20 655	26 610	23 354
1926	20 598	24 915	25 322
1927	20 810	25 310	25 282
1928	22 156	25 899	26 091
1929	22 280	27 487	28 178
1930	22 732	30 311	28 520
1931	26 307	34 948	30 414
1932	36 572	43 567	31 996
1933	40 213	33 457	33 391
1934	43 292	39 445	32 620
1935	44 793	42 599	39 859
1936	45 873	41 542	42 386
1937	47 421	46 142	43 252
1938	51 991	50 670	44 204
1939	54 779	53 861	47 988
1940	59 637	56 596	49 921
1941	61 849	58 120	55 444
Total			672 599

Note: Operating costs refer solely to the costs of hospital operations and do not include the costs of outpatient care, prosthetic devices, dental care, and so on. Nor do these figures include the costs of outpatient care, prosthetic devices, dental care, and so on. Nor do these figures include expenditures for new construction, major alterations, nonexpendable equipment, or the diagnostic facilities located at Palo Alto, California, and Hines, Illinois.

Source: William Pyrle Dillingham, *Federal Aid to Veterans, 1917–1941* (Gainesville, Fla.: University of Florida Press, 1952): 65.

Beyond normal medical and hospital expenses, disabled veterans were supplied with all necessary supplies and prosthetic devices at government expense; this policy was extended in 1926 to patients hospitalized for non-service connected disabilities. In addition, beginning in 1921, veterans were entitled to dental care, which was customarily performed by private dentists who then submitted their bills to the Bureau. Finally, with passage of the 1924 Act, necessary traveling expenses to veterans' medical facilities were underwritten by the government.

By 1932 the Depression was in full swing and it was clear to many that such profligate spending had to be curtailed. The federal government was then spending approximately $750 000 000 annually on veterans' benefits of one sort or another, almost 20 percent of its total administrative budget.[46] In June 1932, Congress created a joint congressional committee 'to conduct a thorough investigation of the operation of the laws and regulations relating to the relief of veterans' and 'to report and recommend such economies as will lessen the cost to the United States government of the Veterans Administration'.[47] And in December of that year, President Herbert Hoover, in his budget message for fiscal 1934, recommended a series of cutbacks to the Veterans Administration's budget which would have saved about $125 000 000, but these were ignored by Congress. The joint committee, having spent six months holding hearings, finally reported in May 1933, dodging the whole issue with the statement that 'the question of a definite policy with reference to pensions and emoluments of all kinds for veterans and their dependents is now an Executive function'.[48]

Forced to act independently of any formal recommendation from Congress, Franklin D. Roosevelt, newly elected to the Presidency, submitted for consideration a bill that, for the first time in the nation's history, called for cuts in veterans benefits. The bill, passed on 20 March 1933, laid down principles for granting pensions and other benefits but gave the President the authority to prescribe administrative details by Executive order.[49] Between March 1933 and March 1935, when the power to issue regulations terminated, the President's executive orders implementing the Economy Act confined eligibility for medical and hospital care to veterans suffering from service-connected disabilities and severely limited the size of pensions paid to any veteran receiving hospital treatment. This tightening of eligibility requirements, together with the strong disincentive to potential patients associated with reducing the size of their pensions during hospitalization, served to reduce the hospital load of those under treatment by 23 percent.[50] The extent of savings afforded by these new regulations amounted, in fiscal year 1934, to $34 000 000, out of a total expenditure estimated – prior to factoring in the cuts made – to be $111 000 000, or over 30 percent.[51] In addition to curtailing admissions to veterans' hospitals, all hospital construction, with the exception of that already in progress, was halted.[52] However, Congress did appropriate $21 000 000 for hospital construction in 1935 and two years later the Federal Board of Hospitalization and President Roosevelt agreed on a policy of hospital construction that emphasized neuropsychiatric care. Veterans admitted for more general medical and surgical reasons were to be placed in other government hospitals, if necessary.[53]

The American Legion, needless to say, vehemently opposed these economy measures and its legislative committee was quick to prepare a bill for introduction during the second session of the 73rd Congress in 1934. Its main provision respecting medical care called for extending hospitalization or domiciliary care, including transportation, to all veterans unable to pay these expenses, regardless of whether the disability was the result of service. And, as expected, Congress passed the measure.[54] Public Law 141, enacted in 1934, provided that:

> any veteran of any war who was not dishonorably discharged, suffering from disability, disease or defect, who is in need of hospitalization or domiciliary care, and is unable to defray the necessary expenses therefor (including transportation to and from the Veterans Administration facility) shall be furnished necessary hospitalization or domiciliary care (including transportation) in any Veterans Administration facility, within the limitations existing in such facilities, irrespective of whether the disability, disease or defect was due to service.[55]

As expected, the period of comparative austerity was short-lived.

The priorities for eligibility that were established during this period, the essentials of which continue in place up to the present, are: (1) medical and hospital care arising out of a service-related disability; (2) medical and hospital care not arising out of a service-related disability, provided the patient also had a service-related disability and if a bed were available; and, (3) all other cases of medical and hospital need, provided the veteran could not afford to pay the costs of the service and if a bed were available.[56] The original rationale in granting to veterans with non-service-related medical needs the right to hospital treatment was that there would, from time to time, exist a certain number of vacancies in veterans' hospitals primarily dedicated to the treatment of those having a service-connected injury or disease and that, rather than let these beds go unused, veterans who would not have originally qualified for space in these facilities could be treated there. However, hospital construction has traditionally outpaced the need for beds[57] to house veterans in categories 1 and 2, thus allowing for the admission of large numbers of non-service-connected cases. By 1944 80 percent of all admissions since World War I had been for the treatment of non-service-related disabilities.[58]

As early as 1937, the Veterans Administration (VA) had conceived of a ten-year hospital building program designed to provide 100 000 hospital and domiciliary beds.[59] This program was approved in principle by President Roosevelt in May 1940 and, in keeping with this commitment, Congress appropriated $6 100 000 for hospital construction between mid-1940 and June of 1942. Soon after America's entry into World War II, it became apparent that the VA's medical and hospital program would require massive expansion, especially after Congress extended veterans' benefits to veterans of World War II in 1944. As a consequence, during the fiscal year 1943–44, Congress authorized an additional expenditure of over $49 000 000 and, under the GI Bill, an additional appropriation of $500 000 000 was authorized 'to expedite and complete the construction of additional hospital facilities'.[60]

With America's entry into World War II, the American Legion embarked on a campaign to extend to returning veterans the same benefits earlier accorded to veterans of World War I, a campaign which increased in intensity in late 1943 as German forces were retreating before the Allies in central Italy. The Legion's lobbyists were soon joined by William Randolph Hearst, who was prepared to put all the resources of his publishing empire behind a generous benefit scheme.[61] The Legion's first salvo concerned a bill that would have provided a mustering-out payment of up to $500 to discharged veterans. Hearings on the bill were conducted before the House Military Affairs Committee, chaired by Representative Andrew Jackson May of Kentucky, in late 1943. May had been charged by the House Speaker, Sam Rayburn of Texas, and the Majority Leader, John McCormack of Massachusetts, to write a bonus bill but May refused to report the bill out of committee before he returned to his home in Kentucky for the Christmas holidays. May's actions were a public relations disaster[62] and he was forced to act expeditiously as soon as Congress reconvened in January 1944. May's bill, with the bonus reduced to a maximum of $300, was duly passed by the end of the month. However, enactment of this legislation did not remove the pressure for passage of a far more comprehensive package of benefits, including medical and hospital care. The Legion had crafted an omnibus bill, originally titled 'The Bill of Rights for GI Joe and Jane', that provided an extravagant array of benefits for returning veterans and was successful in getting the bill introduced into the House on 10 January by Congressman John E. Rankin, chairman of the Committee on World War Veterans' Legislation. On the following day, a companion bill was introduced in the Senate by Bennett Champ Clark of Missouri, one of the founders of the American Legion in 1919.

Competing with the Legion bill were a large number of other measures relating to returning veterans, including one that had been prepared by the National Resources Planning Board (NRPB) headed by the President's uncle, Frederic A. Delano. The NRPB had been charged by the President with post-war planning, including veterans' concerns, and had drafted a proposal that would have provided one year of vocational training for all veterans and a college education for a select few who could meet certain strict qualifications.[63] This was hardly a comprehensive measure, but the Administration attempted to create the impression that it had given prolonged thought to the question of returning veterans. In July 1943 Roosevelt, in one of his fireside chats, told the nation:

> While concentrating on military victory, we are not neglecting the planning of things to come, the freedoms which we know will make for more decency and greater democracy in the world. Among many other things we are, today, laying plans for the return to civilian life of our gallant men and women in the armed services. They must not be demobilized into an environment of inflation and unemployment, to a place on the bread line or on a corner selling apples. We must, this time, have plans ready – instead of waiting to do a hasty, insufficient, and ill-considered job at the last minute.[64]

Nothing could have been further from the truth. What Roosevelt did in fact suggest to Congress in June 1943 was that, at the end of hostilities, the government would underwrite the costs of one year's vocational training and would permit servicemen to remain on furlough in the military for up to three months while they sought civilian jobs.[65]

Without serious competition, the American Legion proposal quickly gained headway, aided by the Hearst newspapers and a string of horror stories publicized by the Legion of badly injured servicemen discharged without a penny and denied benefits while the VA adjudicated their disability claims.[66] So popular was the measure in the Senate that no less than 81 Senators sponsored it, thus assuring the bill's passage in that chamber even before it reached the Senate floor. However, things did not go quite as smoothly in the House. Among the bill's more controversial provisions were those relating to education. The bill stipulated that the government would underwrite an educational allowance plus all educational expenses in established colleges and universities for up to four years.[67] While the GI Bill's educational features were strongly supported by the nation's labor unions, who viewed a workforce increased by so many millions of discharged men with alarm and feared for the future of the closed shop, many educators thought the proposals a threat to higher education standards. No less contentious was the large-scale bureaucracy that would be needed to administer a package of veterans' benefits as munificent as those proposed. President Roosevelt, in his State of the Union message of January 1944 had called not only for massive tax increases and for his 'Economic Bill of Rights', but for a national service program that would apply to all adults, in effect conscripting all Americans, with the federal government as the nation's sole employer.[68] Quite a number of Congressmen were understandably appalled by Roosevelt's suggestions, which smacked more of the policies of the fascist regimes with whom Americans were then engaged in battle than of traditional notions of a free society.[69] Against this backdrop, some Representatives were apprehensive lest a bloated VA act as the vanguard of a postwar federal government that intruded into every aspect of social life.

By far the most serious threat to passage, however, was the bill's provisions regarding unemployment compensation. The bill authorized a readjustment allowance to each veteran of $20 per week for up to 52 weeks (the so-called 52-20 Club), while he sought employment. Some critics regarded the program as yet another welfare giveaway that would encourage indolence among able-bodied veterans while at the same time depriving the wounded and disabled of much-needed funds. Thus, an officer of the Disabled Veterans of America wrote of the provision: 'The lazy and "chiseley" types of veterans would get the most benefits, whereas the most resourceful, industrious and conscientious veterans would get the least'.[70] Significantly, John Rankin, Democrat from Mississippi,[71] who chaired the House committee considering the bill, also had grave reservations about its unemployment compensation provisions. Rankin, and a few other Congressmen who were less vocal in their views, had concluded that since the same benefits would be extended to all veterans regardless of race, the effect would be that taxpayers would end up supporting large numbers of shiftless blacks. 'I see the most violent discrimination', Rankin noted,

> against that strong, virile, patriotic, determined man who goes into the Army to fight for his country and comes back and says, 'I don't want anything. I am going back and going to work and that is what the rest of you ought to do.' . . . At the same time, I see a tremendous inducement to certain elements to try to get employment compensation. It is going to be very easy . . . to induce these people to get on federal relief, what we call unemployment compensation, rather than getting back into active employment.[72]

Despite Rankin's reservations, however, he was forced to report the bill out of committee. The American Legion had applied intense pressure on the other members of the committee who compelled Rankin to present the bill to the full House in April. After prolonged debate in the House, the bill finally passed that chamber unanimously in May 1944 and was signed into law as the Servicemen's Readjustment Act of 1944 on 22 June 1944.

The extension of the same medical benefits as had been accorded the veterans of World War I to those of World War II quadrupled the potential eligible population, from 5 million to 20 million veterans. Negotiations while the GI Bill was under consideration by the House had already included provision that $500 000 000 would be appropriated for new hospital construction.[73] The new facilities that had been authorized to accommodate new users as a consequence of this expansion of the VA program required a substantial increase in the number of medical personnel. At the same time, the VA sought to raise the quality and variety of facilities and the quality of care. While the medical care accorded soldiers on the battlefield was generally regarded as commendable, there had been a large number of complaints about the level of care at VA hospitals. Not only was the American Legion vocal in its protests, but a series of articles criticizing the Veterans Administration for shoddy medical treatment in VA facilities appeared in the public press. In March and April of 1945, *Cosmopolitan* magazine ran a series by Albert Q. Maisel, accusing the VA of allowing veterans admitted to VA hospitals to suffer needlessly and, 'all too often', to die needlessly.[74] Overcrowding and overworked doctors were held largely responsible for these conditions but much criticism was directed at the Administrator of the Veterans Administration, Frank T. Hines, who had served in that position since succeeding Charles Forbes in 1923. In August 1945, President Truman accepted Hines' resignation and appointed General Omar N. Bradley as Administrator.

Bradley took charge of an agency that had 65 000 civilian employees, the largest in the federal bureaucracy, that was mandated to extend benefits to 43 percent of the adult male population.[75] Within two years, the VA workforce had increased to over 200 000 and its budget had grown by a factor of ten, from $744 000 000 in 1944 to $7 470 000 000. But despite Bradley's eager attempts to provide veterans with the benefits stipulated in the GI Bill, the American Legion under its national commander, John Stelle, at one time Governor of Illinois, charged the Veterans Administration with an 'unbalanced diet of promises', including the slow pace of new hospital construction and the fact that the VA was contracting out medical care to private hospitals.[76] In addition, a whole series of complaints from Legion officials regarding problems at specific hospitals was forwarded to the Veterans Administration concerning a wide range of issues, among them the availability of army or navy medical records on new claims and the lack of space for Legion representatives at VA stations. Even more aggravating, Bradley was considering a new policy that called for the suspension of the VA hospitalization privileges of all veterans who had not been injured in the war, as long as any beds were still needed by those with combat-related disabilities. Those opposed to this policy argued that it was brutally shortsighted since even soldiers without combat-connected disabilities might later become seriously ill as a result of the stresses of combat and that these veterans were as much entitled to hospitalization as were veterans wounded or disabled in battle.

To the complaints leveled against the VA, the Legion received no reply. As a consequence, in February 1946, Stelle held a press conference in Washington at which he effectively called for Bradley's ouster, arguing that 'what we need in charge of the VA is a seasoned businessman, not a soldier, however good a soldier he may be'.[77] Congressman Rankin, chairman of the House Veterans' Committee, reacted to Stelle's comment with the claim that 'it sounds like communism to me', to which Stelle pointed out that a new VA hospital was being built in Tupelo, Mississippi, Rankin's home. Stelle further charged that between 300 000 and 500 000 veterans who were suffering from war-connected disabilities had received no benefits because their medical records had not been retained by the Veterans Administration. Criticism continued throughout the summer and fall of 1946, until, finally, at the Legion's annual convention in San Francisco late that year, General Bradley was compelled to conclude his speech before the assembled legionnaires with these words: 'What we have been able to accomplish during this year in the Veterans Administration has been achieved not because of, but in spite of, your national commander'.[78] At the same meeting, Paul H. Griffith of Pennsylvania was elected to replace Stelle as national commander.

Despite complaints from veterans' groups that the VA was simply not doing enough for those who had fought for their country, the VA continued to expand. By November 1949 the agency was operating under the authority accorded it by over 300 laws that provided benefits to nearly 19 million living veterans and to dependents of deceased veterans.[79] Among the benefits which it administered were disability compensation, pensions, vocational rehabilitation and education, the guaranty of home and farm loans and loans for businesses, readjustment allowances for unemployed veterans, life insurance, death and burial expenses, adjusted compensation, emergency officers' retirement pay, and, not least, an extensive system of hospital and outpatient treatment and domiciliary care in the United States.[80] By the end of the 1950 fiscal year, it was operating 136 hospitals, comprising 18 dedicated to the care of tuberculosis, 34 specializing in neuropsychiatric problems, and 84 for general medical and surgical needs. Its facilities boasted 106 287 operating beds and over the course of the preceding 12 months, almost 600 000 patients had been admitted for treatment to VA hospitals. The agency's hospital, medical, and domiciliary programs employed approximately 120 000 employees, including almost 4000 full-time physicians, 4375 part-time physicians, about 1000 dentists, and over 13 000 nurses. Approximately 2 000 000 veterans were given treatment in outpatient clinics and a further 500 000 in dental clinics.[81] Not only was the Veterans Administration medical program by far the most extensive in the country, but it was larger and more comprehensive than that of many nations with national health-care schemes.

During the 15 years following World War II, there was a steady expansion in hospital facilities. Table 3.2 indicates the average daily patient load and the average number of operating beds in facilities under Veterans Administration control for the 1930s, 1940s, and 1950s.

The conflict between the American Legion and General Bradley was not the only political struggle the Legion found itself fighting in the years immediately following the end of World War II. While much of the nation's military

Table 3.2   Average Daily Patient Load in VA and non-VA Hospitals, and
Average Number of Operating Beds in VA Hospitals, 1931–1960

| Fiscal Year | Average Daily Patient Load | | | Operating Beds |
	Total	VA Hospitals	Non-VA Hospitals	VA Hospitals
1931	32 949	24 398	8 553	24 255
1932	42 606	32 568	10 038	28 278
1933	42 129	33 649	8 480	31 192
1934	36 583	35 220	1 363	39 456
1935	41 333	39 030	2 303	43 017
1936	43 524	40 972	2 552	44 521
1937	44 879	41 939	2 940	45 905
1938	48 973	45 639	3 334	49 451
1939	52 763	49 147	3 616	53 077
1940	56 251	52 409	3 842	56 429
1941	58 423	54 582	3 841	60 245
1942	57 927	54 636	3 291	60 952
1943	56 147	53 470	2 677	61 103
1944	61 332	58 338	2 994	65 972
1945	68 260	64 317	3 943	73 777
1946	78 586	71 493	7 073	80 927
1947	98 248	85 715	12 533	96 451
1948	105 882	92 891	12 991	102 854
1949	106 985	94 539	12 446	103 854
1950	108 038	96 643	11 395	106 012
1951	104 391	96 305	8 086	107 568
1952	105 110	98 024	7 086	109 790
1953	104 482	97 975	6 507	108 967
1954	108 944	103 491	5 453	114 244
1955	110 733	106 682	4 051	117 643
1956	113 458	111 205	3 253	120 649
1957	114 325	111 265	3 060	121 144
1958	114 581	111 599	2 982	121 201
1959	114 103	111 050	3 053	120 489
1960	114 356	111 408	2 948	120 257

Source: Administrator of Veterans Affairs *Annual Report, 1963* (Washington, DC: Government Printing Office, 1963): 194 (Table 4).

establishment was rapidly dismantled at the end of the war,[82] a substantial portion of the government's civilian arm, grown to massive proportions as a result of the war, remained. In 1940, the last full year of peace, the federal government had just over 1 million employees and spent approximately $9 billion. By 1947, these numbers had grown to 2.1 million employees and to expenditures of more than $39 billion. In that year the executive branch was a bureaucratic labyrinth comprising 1816 components, including nine departments, 104 bureaus, 12 sections, 108 services, 51 branches, 460 offices, 631 divisions, 19 administrations, six agencies, 16 areas, 40 boards, six commands, 20 commissions, 19 corporations, five groups, ten headquarters, 20 units, three authorities, and an additional 263 miscellaneous and functionally designated parts.[83] So complex was the administrative arm of the national government that even Franklin D. Roosevelt, whose policies routinely called for further extensions of the federal bureaucracy, wrote as early as 1937 that

> the Executive structure of the Government is sadly out of date. I am not the first President to report to the Congress that antiquated machinery stands in the way of effective administration and of adequate control by the Congress. ... Neither the President nor Congress can exercise effective supervision and direction over such a chaos of establishments, nor can overlapping, duplication, and contradictory policies be avoided.[84]

In response to such complaints, in July 1947 – in one of its periodic obeisances to efficiency – Congress unanimously voted to establish a blue-ribbon Commission on Organization of the Executive Branch, whose purpose was to recommend ways to economize and streamline the federal government.[85] Herbert Hoover, who was reputed to be a brilliant organizational tactician, was appointed its chairman, while its membership included Dean Acheson, soon to be Secretary of State, Arthur Fleming, formerly Civil Service Commissioner, James Forrestal, former Secretary of Defense, Senators John McClellan of Arkansas and George D. Aiken of Vermont, and Joseph P. Kennedy, formerly Ambassador to Great Britain. The Commission proceeded to hire more than 300 consultants whose area of expertise was government activity and these experts were, in turn, assisted by professional research and management firms. The result of this was a mammoth report issued in 24 parts between January and June 1949. Among its many recommendations was a complete reform of the Veterans Administration. The Report pointed out that VA rules were contained in no fewer that 88 manuals, 665 technical bulletins, and over 400 circulars. The Commission's investigation of the VA uncovered a staggering amount of waste. As examples, the Report cited the fact that, as of June 1948, the VA was handling almost 7 million life-insurance policies with a face value of $40 billion, to which over 15 000 employees were assigned, handling an average rate of 450 policies apiece. The Commission observed that a comparable private insurance company had an average work-load of almost 1800 policies per employee. And while private companies were able to process almost all their death claims within 15 days of notification, it took the Veterans Administration 80 days.[86] Nor did its handling of veterans' educational benefits fare any better. The Commission concluded that the VA often paid the highest possible fees for tuition and equipment, despite the poor quality and usefulness of many schools, and was habitually clumsy in handling subsistence allowances to student-veterans. Despite these inefficiencies, however, the focus of the Commission's complaints centered on the federal government's medical programs, the largest and most comprehensive of which was that administered by the VA.

The Report pointed out that the federal government undertook the medical care of some 24 million people, about one-sixth of the nation's population, of which approximately 18 million were veterans. Other groups included members of the armed forces and their dependents, government employees, and merchant seamen. Medical care was handled by some 40 government agencies, spending about $2 billion in 1949, a figure ten times as large as in 1940. The Report went on to note:

> These agencies obtain funds and build hospitals with little knowledge of, and no regard for, the needs of the others. On June 30, 1948, there were only 155,000 patients in government hospitals having a capacity of 255,000. Yet the agencies, led by the Veterans Administration, are now planning to build over $1 billion worth of new hospitals.
>
> Aside from waste of money and materials, the most serious question is where they will find the doctors to man their hospitals. Already the Veterans Administration has had to close 5,600 beds for lack of medical manpower to service them. And there is talk of a draft to provide enough doctors for the armed forces. Meantime, the competing federal services unnecessarily drain doctors from private practice, and the country is now dreadfully short of doctors.[87]

Among the particulars specified in the Report was the fact that the Army had just completed a $37 000 000 hospital in Honolulu, despite the fact that the Navy had in the same area a comparable hospital adequate to care 'for all military personnel' of all three services; that it would be possible to close four large Army and Air Force hospitals in the New York City area without reducing the level of care given patients, yet, despite this, the VA was in the process of building new hospital facilities with construction costs of more than $100 000 000; that VA facilities for the treatment of tubercular and neuropsychiatric patients, accounting for 60 percent of all VA beds, were inefficient and suffered from a chronic shortage of trained personnel; and that the length of stay of patients suffering from similar diseases was three times as long in VA hospitals as in comparable voluntary hospitals.[88]

The Commission found that construction costs of government hospitals, almost all of which were built by and for the Veterans Administration, ran from $20 000 to over $50 000 per bed, compared to about $16 000 per bed for voluntary hospitals. More importantly, it observed that while the VA was authorized to hospitalize veterans with non-service-connected disabilities only if beds were available, over 100 000 hospital beds had been built or authorized that could serve no purpose other than to provide for non-service-connected cases.[89] Building hospitals far in excess of what was needed to undertake the care of veterans with service-connected diseases or injuries was the method by which the VA was able to extend medical care to other veterans. As a solution to this problem, in what must constitute one of the strangest recommendations of a panel ostensibly opposed to the creation of even larger bureaucratic entities and to the expansion of federal power, the Commission proposed that Congress create a United Medical Administration (UMA) that would take over the Public Health Service, all Veterans Administration hospitals and medical services, and all general hospitals of the armed forces located in the continental United States.[90]

The American Legion, predictably, strongly opposed the Commission's proposals. The organization's reaction to the establishment of any committee whose function was to recommend economies in the Veterans Administration was highly negative inasmuch as this raised the specter of a reduction in veterans' benefits, as had occurred for a brief period in 1933. However, the Legion was especially upset over the suggestion that the VA be dismembered and that a new super-agency take over its medical responsibilities. As one Legion executive put it:

> the major benefit programs for veterans are so dependent upon and integrated with the medical, hospital, and domiciliary care programs as to preclude separation from the VA without disastrous effects on the efficient administration of veterans' benefits.[91]

In May 1949 the Legion's national executive committee went on record as being unalterably opposed to the Commission's recommendations and especially to the creation of a UMA and this was affirmed at the national convention in Philadelphia later that year.[92] The Veterans Administration, since its establishment in 1930 as the successor agency to the Veterans' Bureau, had – for most of its history – been extremely responsive to the wishes of the American Legion, which was instrumental not only in the running of the VA but in shaping the legislation governing it. The proposal that several of the VA's most important functions be hived off constituted a grave threat to this relationship.[93] Not only did the Legion itself attack the notion that the VA should be split up, but it was able to enlist the support of several influential Congressmen in its criticism of portions of the Hoover Report. Thus, in January 1949 House majority leader John W. McCormack of Massachusetts issued a statement opposing any division of authority in administering the affairs of veterans, and maintaining that 'the Hoover Commission had failed to recognize that the VA was already set up on the one basis on which veterans' affairs could be handled with the greatest dispatch and the least cost'.[94]

Additionally, it appeared that the Hoover Commission's recommendations might be used as an 'excuse' to trim expenditures on veterans' benefits. In March 1950 the VA's administrator, General Carl Raymond Gray, Jr, ordered a reduction of 7800 personnel[95] and President Truman, in a series of budget messages, had suggested that only veterans with service-connected disabilities should receive medical treatment at government expense.[96] The position of the American Legion was that military service in time of war conferred on veterans a distinct status that warranted their receiving special benefits not accorded other citizens, among them treatment for all illnesses and disabilities, whether service-connected or not. As the director of the Legion's Rehabilitation Division observed: 'It is our belief that the government created a special class when it selected millions of young Americans for service'.[97] These illnesses, the Legion maintained, were not merely trivial ailments but often serious. A member of the National Executive Committee gave voice to the position of the Legion: 'We feel', he commented, 'that a veteran, even with a non-service-connected disability, is entitled to a little extra treatment from the government he fought to uphold, provided he needs such treatment'.[98] Ongoing medical care for veterans did not fall under the category of 'special interests' – a term that the Legion strongly condemned – but rather a 'special social need', the term the Legion preferred.[99]

Despite the support accorded the Hoover Commission by Americans familiar with its findings,[100] in the end, few of its recommendations were enacted. In late 1949 it appeared that the Legion would be unsuccessful in its attempts to block legislation dismembering the Veterans Administration and creating a United Medical Administration. To encourage Congress to enact the necessary reforms recommended in the Commission Report, a group of prominent citizens launched the Citizens' Committee for the Reorganization of the Executive Branch under the chairmanship of Robert L. Johnson, President of Temple University. Among its members were two former Vice-Presidents, Charles G. Dawes, and John Nance Garner, a former Supreme Court Justice, Owen J. Roberts, and a large number of former Cabinet members, Senators, Congressmen, and Governors. In addition to these political luminaries, the Committee boasted more than 40 college and university presidents, 50 publishers, editors, and writers, and the leaders of farm, professional, business, labor, and women's organizations.[101] Nor was the Citizens' Committee alone in pushing for support of the Hoover Commission reforms. The Tax Foundation, a policy research organization founded in 1937 to monitor government fiscal policy, gave strong support to the implementation of the

Hoover recommendations and, in October 1949, urged that the VA be authorized to investigate the ability of patients to pay for medical treatment for non-service-connected disabilities.[102] Against these organizations, the Legion engaged in a national campaign to inform the public of its concerns and issued a series of papers outlining its reservations. In March 1949 Legion officials testified before the House Committee on Expenditures in the Executive Departments (on H.R. 5182), which was examining the proposal to merge the federal government's medical services. The new United Medical Administration, the Legion contended, would be unworkable since it called for a mix of medical treatments: veteran (civilian), military (highly specialized), and public health (preventative and research). Equally important, under the plan the veteran would not only lose his 'right' to exclusive hospitalization but 'his identity as a veteran', thus disassociating him from his service to his country.[103] The reception accorded Legion executives at both the House hearings and those of the Senate the following month was less than cordial and it appeared that Congress would proceed with the creation of a UMA that year. In addition, President Truman, on the recommendation of the Bureau of the Budget, immediately altered the VA's hospital construction program by canceling earlier authorization for the building of 24 hospitals and ordering a reduction in the size of 14 additional hospitals, with savings in construction costs of approximately $279 000 000.[104]

However, almost providentially, foreign affairs intervened to delay consideration of any executive reorganization. In June 1950 the Korean peninsula erupted into warfare and President Truman, eager to halt the advance of forces hostile to American interests, dispatched American troops to the region. The law then governing veterans' benefits had placed veterans of the Korean conflict in a somewhat anomalous position inasmuch as they were not legally regarded as entitled to wartime benefits.[105] The American Legion engaged in intense lobbying effort to alter this[106] and, as a result, Congress enacted Public Law 28 in May 1951 whereby veterans of the Korean war were granted entitlement to the same benefits, including medical, hospital, and domiciliary care, as were veterans of World War II. Having now expanded the number of veterans entitled to medical care, the Legion once again turned its attention to campaigning against the Hoover Commission recommendations and to agitating for additional beds and physicians at VA facilities. In March 1952 the Legion initiated a new public relations campaign to oppose legislation inspired by the Hoover Report. The Legion was particularly troubled by a Senate bill, S. 1140, then being considered, to create a new cabinet-level position, the Department of Health, which would consolidate the Public Health Service, the Department of Medicine and Surgery of the Veterans Administration (including all VA hospitals and outpatient services) and all general hospitals of the army, navy, and air force in the United States and the Canal Zone. This, of course, simply amounted to establishment of the UMA under another name, which the Legion had so tirelessly fought. Not only was the Legion fighting the dismemberment of the Veterans Administration but it found it had to contend with efforts to cut appropriations to the VA by economizing Congressmen. The Legion's news releases decried the 'senseless cuts [that] would disastrously cripple VA service and add a tremendous load upon American Legion workers . . . [and] would cause much injustice to hospitalized veterans'.[107] Fortunately, the Legion had a friend in Congress in the form of Representative John Rankin, who chaired the Veterans Affairs Committee. Rankin, who was in a position to kill any bill simply by refusing to give it a hearing, allied himself with the Legion against the Hoover recommendations and thus was able to insure the continued integrity of the VA. In addition, in June 1952 the Senate restored most of the VA's 1953 operating funds, earlier cut by the House, thus averting a reduction in medical and hospital personnel and allowing the completion of 21 hospitals then in the process of being built.[108] And, in the following year, the Legion was again successful in getting the House to reverse itself, this time restoring an earlier cut of $279 000 000 in appropriations to the VA that had been recommended by the Bureau of the Budget.[109]

Having succeeded in blocking attempts to reorganize the federal government's bureaucracy responsible for administrating veterans' benefits during the Truman presidency, the Legion found itself faced with similar problems under President Eisenhower. The Republicans who controlled the 83rd Congress, the first, other than a brief period between 1946 and 1948, that the party controlled for two decades, sought to reduce the spectacular amount of waste and inefficiency that had come to light with the first Hoover Commission reports. In this they were joined by a Republican President, who was anxious to reorganize the executive branch to make it more responsive to aggressive management. At the opening of the 83rd Congress, Congressman Clarence Brown, Republican from Ohio, one of the sponsors of the bill creating the first Hoover Commission, and Senator Homer Ferguson, Republican from Michigan, introduced a measure calling for the establishment of a new commission, authorized to identify reductions in spending and the elimination of services in the executive branch.[110] Once again, Herbert Hoover was appointed chairman;[111] among the other members were Herbert Brownell, the Attorney-General, James A. Farley, who had been a close political advisor of Franklin Roosevelt, Senators Homer Ferguson and John McClellan of Arkansas, and Congressman Brown.

Once again, the Commission took aim at the enormous waste in medical and hospital services provided by a variety of federal agencies, particularly the Veterans Administration.[112] It pointed out that a total absence of coordination between the military and civilian medical services of the federal government was responsible for a huge excess of hospital beds and contributed to the chronic shortage of medical personnel. Thus, with reference to the San Francisco Bay Area, the Commission found that four separate agencies operated 16 hospitals. Of the 11 565 beds available in these facilities, 5233, or 45 percent, were unoccupied at the time the Commission made its survey. And with specific reference to VA facilities in the area, the figure was actually 81 percent! Similar problems were discovered in New York City and Norfolk, Virginia. Among the 12 federally operated hospitals in the New York area, 3010 of a total of 12 841 beds, or 25 percent, were found to be unoccupied, with the figure at VA hospitals standing at 86 percent. In Norfolk, 1659 out of 3971 beds, or 42 percent, were unoccupied, with the VA figure once again far surpassing those for the other federal agencies, standing at 85 percent.[113] Despite such excess capacity, the VA's hospital construction program was adding new facilities daily. In mid-1951, the total number of beds in VA hospitals was 115 945, of which 11 554, or 10 percent, were unoccupied. By 1954, the number of unoccupied beds had increased to 14 percent of the total, during which time the VA had spent $375 000 000 on added hospital facilities.[114]

Not only were large numbers of VA hospital beds standing empty, but patients admitted to these facilities were hospitalized for much longer periods than was the case at civilian voluntary hospitals. One small example: the average stay for tonsillectomies at voluntary hospitals was 1.4 days while at VA hospitals it was eight days.[115] The General Accounting Office concluded that these longer periods of hospitalization were in large part accounted for by the absence of cost to patients and a tendency on the part of hospitals with light patient loads to continue care 'beyond necessary limits'.[116] Indeed, the whole VA hospital program was riddled with inefficiencies. Not only were there an inadequate number of patients for the number of hospital beds available, but the size and location of these hospitals made little economic sense, having been determined for political rather than economic reasons.[117]

The major problem with the VA medical and hospital program, the Commission found, centered not so much on the care provided the 3 500 000 veterans with service-connected disabilities, but rather on the 21 000 000 other veterans who were able to receive hospitalization for illnesses or disabilities unconnected with their military service provided they stipulated they were unable to pay for such services. When in 1923 Congress had authorized the extension of medical benefits to veterans with non-service-connected disabilities who were unable to pay for medical services, the Commission observed, they operated on the assumption that this would involve no additional costs. In fact, the construction of new hospital beds for the care of such cases had totaled over $1 000 000 000 by 1954 and the cost of such care was running at $500 000 000 per year.[118] While the provision of medical and hospital care to veterans admitted for non-service-connected disabilities was to be limited to those unable to pay, apparently no effort was made to determine whether prospective patients were in fact indigent. In fact, the VA was prohibited from challenging statements made to that effect and when a bill incorporating a provision for verifying inability to pay was introduced in Congress in 1953, it failed.[119] The Commission found all of the 369 000 such veterans cared for in 1954 were provided care without having to pay for it and quoted a 1952 General Accounting Office study that found that out of a sample of 336 cases of veterans with annual incomes of over $4000 and receiving hospitalization, one had an annual income of $50 000, at least four had assets of between $100 000 and $500 000, and 25 had assets of more than $20 000.[120] The Commission further noted:

> The Veterans' Administration has found it difficult even to collect on the health-insurance policies of veterans treated for non-service-connected disabilities. Frequently these contracts provide that the insurance company need make no payment for treatment received in veterans' hospitals. As a result, these companies refuse to reimburse the Veterans' Administration on the ground that the veteran has had no personal loss. In such circumstances, the Veterans' Administration does not even bill the company. In 1954, the administration billed insurance companies for $15,000,000, but collected only $3,300,000.[121]

The Commission was alarmed that the prevailing situation, whereby responsibility for the medical care of more than 21 000 000 Americans was placed in the hands of the federal government, was a giant first step in undermining the notion of private responsibility for one's medical treatment and thereby paved the way for instituting a national system of socialized medicine.[122] As a result of these findings, the Commission strongly urged that the financial status of veterans admitted to VA facilities with non-service-connected ailments be verified and that they be made to pay for any services if they were found to be financially able to do so. In instances where the veteran was incapable of paying, the Commission proposed that he be made to sign a note of obligation for the costs of service, payable in the future.[123] 'The Commission's recommendations', the Report concluded:

> recognize that the American public is willing to give some preferment to any veteran. However, it would require that veterans take responsibility for their own care when their disabilities are not service-connected. Thus, while the Government is the agent of the people in granting a special privilege for specified causes, there should be no assumption of the right of any group of citizens to receive such care at the expense of all the citizens.[124]

As had been the case with the first Hoover Commission, the American Legion found itself in the forefront of those groups with a vested interest in maintaining the inefficiencies of the government's medical programs. Among the Commission's recommendations was that 20 veterans hospitals be closed immediately and that no new VA hospitals, other than those then under construction, be built. The Legion's response was to label the Commission's findings both 'misinformed and uninformed' and to assail its purely 'dollars and sense' approach to the health of those who fought for their country.[125] In the event, the Legion need not have worried. By the time the Commission had submitted its recommendations, Congress had lost interest in reform, especially in those areas that threatened traditional congressional policy. Indeed, inasmuch as the Democrats had recaptured both houses in the 1956 elections, no incentive existed to undo programs that were regarded as the private preserve of certain powerful congressmen.[126] The effect was that the movement for reform simply wound down to a stop and the Veterans Administration continued to operate in much the same way as it had prior to the convening of the first Hoover Commission seven years earlier.

The Hoover Commission reports notwithstanding, the Veterans Administration medical programs continued their expansion throughout the 1950s. One of the problems the VA sought to address was the poor quality of medical treatment offered at its facilities. A continuing complaint leveled at the Veterans Administration from its inception through World War II was the poor quality of the medical care offered. In an effort to remedy this, General Omar Bradley, who had been appointed the Administrator of the VA in 1945, began affiliating the various Veterans Administration hospitals with the nation's medical resources. Toward this end, in 1946, Congress established the Department of Medicine and Surgery within the VA with the purpose of creating a separate VA medical staff capable of participating in the graduate training of physicians. At the same time, the VA was encouraged to call upon the expertise of the nation's medical faculties in treating its patients. As a consequence, a large number of new VA hospitals were constructed near the nation's medical schools. By 1959, nearly half of the VA's 171 hospitals were associated with teaching institutions.[127]

The organizational structure of these new facilities called for the various medical schools to take a large measure of responsibility for the quality of medical care while supervision of the hospitals' operations would remain in the hands of the VA. This plan required that the VA's physicians, dentists, and nurses cease being subject to the restrictions of the Civil Service, a reform undertaken by Congress concurrent with the establishment of the Department of Medicine and Surgery. At the start of fiscal year 1946, 1700 of the VA's 2300 physicians were on active military duty. At the close of the year, however, of the more than 4000 full-time staff physicians employed by the Veterans Administration, only about 400 were still in active military service[128] and by 1950, all full-time physicians of the VA were civilian employees. The new medical program inaugurated a residency training program at a number of VA hospitals, which allowed medical schools to participate in the treatment of patients and at the same time alleviate the VA's shortage of physicians. The VA's residency program became increasingly important over the following years as larger and larger numbers of the nation's physicians were trained in VA hospitals (see Table 3.3).

Table 3.3   Number of Residents and Interns Working at VA Facilities 1947–1972

Year[1]	Medical Residents	Interns	Dental Residents	Interns
1947	1 914	n/a	–	–
1949	2 200	n/a	–	–
1950	2 418	n/a	–	–
1951	2 127	n/a	–	–
1952	2 014	n/a	3	n/a
1953	2 014	80	13	1
1954	2 255	101	17	2
1955	2 314	102	18	7
1956	2 315	77	20	7
1957	2 542	89	37	12
1958	2 515	83	29	24
1959	2 994	95	44	38
1960	3 089	110	39	38
1961	3 119	116	31	42
1962	3 001	131	43	47
1963	3 023	162	37	58
1964	3 199	172	50	57
1965	3 318	185	52	52
1966	3 704	286	64	53
1967	3 754	353	80	66
1968	4 210	485	99	96
1969	4 375	531	121	98
1970	4 476	585	127	98
1971	4 546	667	136	89
1972	5 366	771	153	91

Note: [1] Statistics refer to number of residents and interns working in VA facilities as of the following dates: 1957: *30 January*; 1952, 1953, 1954, 1955, 1956: *15 April*; 1949, 1950: *15 May*: 1947, 1951: *30 June*; all other years: *31 December*.

Source: *VA Annual Reports*, various years.

Indeed, by 1957, fully 12 percent of all medical residents in the United States were working at VA facilities. In addition, some 61 medical schools had assigned their students as clinical clerks to VA hospitals. These trends were accelerated by passage of Public Law 89-785, in November, 1966, which provided statutory recognition of the VA's program of training and education and authorized the VA to increase its contacts with the country's medical schools. Medical and dental students and graduates were not the only groups to undergo training in VA facilities. Pharmacists, nurses, social workers, dietitians, and a host of other health workers were provided training facilities within the VA's medical program. Over the next few years, the VA entered into affiliations with dental schools, nursing schools, schools of social work, and departments of psychology. In the aftermath of the 1966 legislation the medical manpower training functions of the VA were greatly expanded and intensified and as a result the total number of trainees in VA medical facilities increased sharply, from approximately 23 600 in 1966 to 37 900 in 1969.[129]

In addition to acting as a huge training ground for future medical personnel, the VA attempted to integrate its clinical and research programs with those of the country's medical schools in the hope that an 'environment of academic medicine' would increase the quality of care that veterans were offered. Efforts to provide better medical treatment at veterans' facilities by aligning its standards with those prevailing in civilian hospitals had been made in the past, with little result. As far back as 1925, the Veterans' Bureau had arranged with the American College of Surgeons to undertake a survey of the Bureau's hospitals with the intent of raising their standards to those recommended by the College.[130] However, widespread criticism of the quality of medical care accorded veterans continued through the 1930s and 1940s. Complaints during this period were most often directed at the quality of medical facilities and at the poor qualifications of VA personnel. These concerns were in part addressed in 1946, with the creation of the Department of Medicine and Surgery and the severing of the VA's medical staff from the Civil Service, which had the effect of almost immediately elevating the level of competence in VA facilities. This was especially true as more and more VA hospitals became affiliated with medical schools.[131] At the same time, appropriations for the construction of hospitals and other facilities and the hiring of qualified staff were substantially increased. The long-run effect of these changes was to advance the quality of medical care in many VA hospitals. Despite improvement in the VA's training facilities, however, complaints about poor care continued. Numerous articles in newspapers and magazines reported horror stories about careless and inadequate treatment at VA medical facilities. In 1970 the *Los Angeles Times* carried a series of articles decrying the level of care offered at the nation's VA hospitals[132] and in 1982 and again in 1993, the General Accounting Office complained that the VA was extending inconsistent, and often poor, care to female veterans, who at that time comprised over 4 percent of the veteran population.[133]

A secondary effect of substantially increased budgets, which came in the wake of World War II, was an underutilization of expensive specialized medical facilities in many VA hospitals, leading to a large-scale waste of resources.[134] This misallocation was in part due to the distribution of VA resources between inpatient and outpatient facilities. When the veterans' health care system was originally established, emphasis was placed on inpatient care, and ambulatory services were regarded as a secondary adjunct. The relation between inpatient and outpatient services in the VA is, in fact, the inverse of what it is in civilian medical practice, where the overwhelming proportion of one's medical care occurs in doctors' offices. Since the VA was originally designed to deal almost exclusively with hospitalized patients, little was originally done to develop an extensive network of outpatient clinics to provide ambulatory care. Consequently, when outpatient services began to be extended to veterans on a regular basis, facilities were comparatively scarce. Even as late as 1976 most outpatient clinics were located in existing VA hospitals and there were therefore too few locations at which such care was conveniently available.[135] Indeed, with only 214 clinics in the whole of the United States, most veterans lived too far from a clinic to take advantage of the outpatient care offered by the VA. The effect of this uneconomic distribution between inpatient and outpatient resources was (and continues to be) to hospitalize ailing veterans who should, more properly, be treated as outpatients, especially at hospitals that would otherwise be underutilized.[136]

The situation was exacerbated in August 1973 with passage of legislation that extended outpatient benefits to veterans without service-connected disabilities if such care would obviate the need for hospitalization. Prior to that time, outpatient care, other than that connected with pre- or post-hospitalization, had been confined to veterans under treatment for service-connected disabilities. The effect of this change was to immediately increase the demand for ambulatory care. In fiscal year 1973 the VA reported 10.9 million visits while in the following year the number jumped by 13 percent, to 12.3 million visits.[137]

It is clear from these data that the removal of restrictions on who could be treated at outpatient facilities led to an even greater increase in the already substantial growth of outpatient visits. As a consequence, Congress soon chose to constrain the rate of increase by mandating a queuing system based on a series of priorities and at the same time limited the VA's option to contract with private facilities 'only when the VA or other government facilities are not capable of furnishing economic care because of geographical inaccessibility or cannot furnish the care or services required'.[138]

The National Academy of Sciences, in its study of the medical facilities of the Veterans Administration, conducted a survey of outpatients in 1975 and

Table 3.4 Growth in Outpatient Visits, by Type of Visit, 1969–1976

	Staff Visits		Fee Visits		Total Visits	
	Number (thousands)	% Increase over Prior Year	Number (thousands)	% Increase over Prior Year	Number (thousands)	% Increase over Prior Year
1969	5776	–	1174	–	6948	–
1970	6136	6	1176	0	7312	5
1971	6798	11	1266	8	8064	10
1972	7930	17	1597	26	9527	18
1973	9165	16	1693	6	10 858	14
1974	10 458	14	1809	7	12 267	13
1975	12 596	20	2035	12	14 631	19
1976	14 223	13	2187	7	16 410	12

Source: Committee on Health Care Resources, Assembly of Life Sciences, National Research Council, *Health Care for American Veterans* (Washington, DC: National Academy of Sciences, 1977): 116.

found that no fewer than 67 percent of the sample reported that they considered the VA their usual source of outpatient care. Indeed, only 17 percent claimed to have a private physician.[139] In light of this and inasmuch as the number and geographical distribution of outpatient clinics militated against widespread usage, the authors of the NAS report predicted that the principal consequence of the new law would be a further misallocation of medical resources as more and more patients were hospitalized unnecessarily.[140] This, in fact, appears to have occurred.[141]

A significant adjunct to outpatient medical treatment offered veterans by the VA was oral diagnosis and treatment.[142] The Veterans' Bureau began providing dental services in 1921 to veterans with service-connected disabilities. Such treatment was, for the most part, performed by private dentists on a fee-for-service basis. These dentists performed the necessary examinations and treatments and then submitted their bills to the Bureau. However, while Colonel Forbes served as the Bureau's director, abuses became so common that it was felt necessary to eliminate this method of providing dental services and to place them in the hands of the Bureau's own dentists, who operated on a salaried basis.[143] Among the practices that were widespread during Forbes' tenure were fixing teeth at government expense regardless of need or entitlement, charging the government for gold fillings while substituting copper, nickel, or brass, and charging for dental work that was never in fact performed.[144]

Under the directorship of General Hines, who replaced Forbes in 1924, dental treatment was extended to veterans with non-service-connected disabilities. These services were originally regarded as 'adjunct relief', required to help patients to recover from some other condition. Dental services were conducted both at clinics located in VA hospitals and in regional offices, a good proportion of services being performed as an extension of inpatient care by staff dentists on patients with chronic medical conditions who required prolonged hospitalization or on veterans confined to domiciliaries. Thus, in fiscal 1943, of the 42 300 beneficiaries of dental treatment, 38 300 were either hospital patients or domiciliary members, while an additional 3000 patients were treated in outpatient clinics maintained by the VA. In addition, a further 1000 veterans were treated by private practitioners at fees established by the VA.[145]

As with medical care, the demand for dental treatment ballooned following World War II. In 1948, more than 800 000 veterans applied for outpatient dental care. Of these, 700 000 were determined as eligible, that is, were found to have had service-connected dental problems that required treatment, and 656 000 of these received treatment during the year. About 60 percent of all examinations and 92 percent of all treatments were provided by free-designated dentists, to whom the VA paid over $50 000 000.[146]

Table 3.5   Outpatient Dental Examinations and Treatments Completed by VA Staff and Fee-for-Service Dentists, Fiscal Years 1946–1953

Fiscal Year	Examination Cases Completed				Treatment Cases Completed			
	Total	By VA Staff Dentists	By Fee-basis Dentists	Cost per Case	Total	By VA Staff Dentists	By Fee-basis Dentists	Cost per Case
1946	85 537	78 271	7 266		160 400	141 683	18 717	
1947	554 171	176 864	377 307		259 516	31 570	227 946	
1948	701 187	280 560	420 627	13.17	655 198	53 198	602 617	74.16
1949	578 839	315 689	263 150	13.20	513 742	83 372	430 370	32.12
1950	527 487	322 732	204 755	13.47	430 065	87 088	342 977	86.85
1951	424 807	261 503	163 304	13.21	348 392	76 036	272 356	90.12
1952	440 039	242 322	197 717	13.42	362 236	60 589	301 647	96.66
1953	419 431	258 635	100 796	13.66	260 409	61 745	198 664	96.72

Sources: Annual Reports, various years.

When the Korean War added another 5 million veterans potentially eligible for dental care, the VA requested that Congress review its current policy regarding dental treatment in the hope that more funds would be appropriated to support care at existing levels. Rather than increase funding, however, Congress enacted legislation reducing the scope of the VA's dental program.[147] The Act provided that, with certain specified exceptions, no veteran could receive outpatient dental treatment for noncompensable, service-connected disabilities beyond one year of his discharge unless the dental condition were service-connected due to combat wounds. The effect was immediate. During fiscal year 1955, 57 000 fewer applications for dental care were received by the VA as compared to the previous fiscal year[148] and the number of dental visits continued to decline until the beginning of the 1960s. In August, 1962, however, new legislation was enacted that authorized the VA to provide dental treatments to peacetime veterans with service-connected dental problems[149] and for the next 12 years the VA's dental caseload increased.

The limitation on providing dental care to those having service-connected disabilities did not apply to inpatients, regardless of what condition led to their admission. Pilot studies undertaken in the 1960s had shown that about one-half of the newly hospitalized VA patients had not been treated by any dentist for more than five years.[150] Consequently, the VA had adopted the policy of giving dental examinations to at least 75 percent of the patients admitted to the VA's general hospitals and to 90 percent of those admitted to psychiatric hospitals or long-term-care facilities. However, during the early 1970s staff limitations prevented the VA from examining more than 50 to 60 percent of patients admitted to VA hospitals and led to treatment for only a fraction of those found to need dental work, the majority of whom were long-term patients.[151] Despite staffing and funding constraints, however, the VA's dental program continues to flourish, in part because the VA's in-house dental staff proved able to handle a greater proportion of dental patients than previously, with concomitant savings in payments to fee-basis dentists.[152] Between 1981 and 1997, the number of dental cases completed by VA staff rose by 78 percent while the number of cases treated by fee-basis dentists declined by 79 percent.

The current eligibility requirements for outpatient dental care are similar to what they have been for some time. Veterans with a service-connected compensable dental disability, one-time prisoners of war, and those with dental conditions aggravating service-connected medical conditions are all entitled to treatment, as are veterans whose dental treatment was begun while in a VA medical center. In fiscal year 1997, the VA's dental staff handled over 1 million dental visits.[153] In addition, almost 16 000 treatment cases were completed on a fee basis.

The propensity of the VA to underutilize its facilities, particularly by

Table 3.6 Outpatient Dental Program, Fiscal Years 1979–1997

Year	Total Staff and Fee Cases Completed	Staff Cases Completed			Fee Cases Completed		
		Number	Yrly Change	% Change	Number	Yrly Change	% Change
1979	128 003	60 101	4 492	8	67 902	-21 538	-24
1980	145 881	74 331	14 230	24	71 550	3 648	6
1981	160 564	86 036	11 205	15	74 528	2 978	4
1982	149 700	97 768	11 732	14	51 899	-22 629	-30
1983	138 534	107 653	9 885	10	30 881	-21 018	-40
1984	135 556	111 643	3 990	4	23 913	-6 968	-23
1985	139 455	116 867	5 224	5	22 588	-1 325	-6
1986	141 944	120 792	3 925	3	21 152	-1 436	-6
1987	146 477	126 365	5 573	5	20 112	-1 040	-5
1988	121 582	104 790	-21 789	-17	16 792[1]	-3 320	-17
1989	157 181	142 576	37 786	36	14 605[1]	-2 187	-13
1990	159 085	143 736	1 160	1	15 349[1]	744	5
1991	152 178	136 834	-6 902	-5	15 344	-5	–
1992	166 509	144 431	7 597	5	22 078	6 734	44
1993	161 372	143 031	-1 400	-1	18 341	-3 737	-17
1994	163 109	146 262	3 231	2	16 847	-1 494	-8
1995	166 775	149 535	3 273	2	17 240	393	2
1996	167 522	152 373	2 838	2	15 149	-2 091	-12
1997	168 775	152 955	582	–	15 820	671	4

Note: [1] Net cases authorized by the Veterans Administration.

Source: Annual Reports, various years.

assigning patients in need of long-term care to acute-care facilities,[154] had substantially added to the costs of its medical program. Pressures from Congress to rationalize its program encouraged the VA in 1965 to establish a new category of medical care, nursing-home care. Nursing-home care also served to provide a more intensive level of care than was available in the VA's domiciliary program, where enrollments had been declining. The average daily member load in VA domiciliaries, which had stood at over 26 500 in 1959, had shrunk to just over 20 000 in 1968, although the numbers needing some level of long-term care remained constant. Legislation authorizing the establishment of a nursing-care program was enacted by Congress in 1964[155] and the VA complied with the installation of 1000 nursing beds at 27 of its hospitals.[156] These facilities were designed to accommodate veterans who were diagnosed as too physically disabled for domiciliary living but not ill enough to warrant care in acute medical wards. By the end of fiscal year 1975 the VA was operating almost 27 000 long-term care beds, constituting more than 24 percent of the 112 000 beds operated in VA facilities, but even then the actual number of long-term care patients was substantially greater.[157] The quality of care in the VA nursing-care units does not seem to have been particularly good, although there is some evidence that it has improved somewhat over the course of the last 25 years. The National Academy of Science study undertaken in 1975 found that no less than 69 percent of the patients in nursing-care facilities received less than adequate care.[158] By the late 1990s, nursing-home care had become one of the most important aspects of the VA's medical program. Currently, of a total of 67 371 operating beds throughout the VA system, 15 098 were nursing-home beds.[159]

The shift toward extended care followed demographic changes in the veteran population.[160] By 1965, 20 years after the end of World War II, the average age of veterans was 45.8. As these ex-servicemen grew older, one would have expected that their use of the medical facilities of the Veterans Administration would have immediately increased as their need for medical care grew. However, the introduction of Medicare in 1965 initially led large numbers of veterans entitled to the use of VA facilities to continue in private care. While the average age of veterans treated in VA facilities barely changed in the ten years following the introduction of Medicare, over the next decade there was a fairly constant decline in the proportion of patients aged 65 years and over. In 1965, 33 percent of the patients in VA medical facilities were over the age of 65, while in 1974 the figure had dropped to 23.8 percent. Conversely, the number of patients under 35 increased from 7.1 percent to 11.7 percent. The data shown in Table 3.7 were compiled by the VA from periodic censuses of inpatients in VA hospitals.[161]

Another factor contributing to this reversal in the average age of VA

Table 3.7   VA Inpatient Censuses, 1965–1974

Census Date	Total		Under 35 Years Old		65 Years Old and Over	
	Number	Average Age	Number	Percent	Number	Percent
27 October 1965	107 295	54.3	7 558	7.1	35 408	33.0
30 November 1966	104 870	53.7	8 495	8.1	30 870	29.4
30 November 1967	98 390	53.8	8 085	8.2	27 545	28.0
26 November 1968	90 930	53.9	7 765	8.5	23 940	26.3
15 October 1969	87 545	54.3	7 985	9.1	22 276	25.4
14 October 1970	85 550	53.6	9 018	10.5	20 247	23.7
20 October 1971	81 150	54.3	8 813	10.9	20 196	24.9
18 October 1972	83 425	53.7	9 617	11.5	19 351	23.2
3 October 1973	82 485	54.1	9 679	11.7	19 710	23.9
2 October 1974	80 715	54.5	9 435	11.7	19 216	23.8

Source: Administrator of Veterans Affairs, *Annual Report, 1974* (Washington, DC: Government Printing Office, 1975): 20.

patients was the passage, in March 1966 of the Veterans Readjustment Benefits Act, which extended VA benefits, including non-service connected hospitalization, to veterans serving after 1 January 1955.[162] The post-Korean GI Bill, which became effective in June 1966, had the effect of adding approximately 3 million more veterans to the VA's medical program. In the following year, Congress enacted yet another piece of legislation extending all veterans' benefits to Vietnam veterans serving between 5 August 1964 (later adjusted to 28 February 1961) and, as was later determined, 7 May 1975. A major difference between Vietnam-era veterans and those of earlier wars was the larger percentage of disabled military personnel that emerged from the battlefield,[163] which led to increased usage of VA medical facilities by younger veterans.[164] The trend towards younger patients proved short-lived, however, and in 1974 the average age of veterans discharged from VA hospitals once again began to increase. In 1997, only 3 percent of veterans discharged from the VA's medical facilities were under 35 years of age, while over 43 percent were 65 years old or over.

As a response to the increase in the median age of American veterans, the VA established an Office of Assistant Chief Medical Director for Extended Care in September 1975 and instituted several new medical programs. These included hospital-based home care, which provided chronically ill veterans with hospital-based treatment in their own homes, and residential care, a more ambitious program in which the VA arranged for the provision of room, board, personal care, and general medical treatment to veterans incapable of living independently but who were judged not to require either hospital or nursing-home care. In addition, the Geriatric Research, Education and Clinical Centers (GRECC) program was created to centralize the study of the health care requirements of aging veterans and to undertake original research in gerontology within the VA clinical system. The Personal Care Home Program, under which the veteran paid for his care (usually out of a combination of VA pension, supplemental security income, and Social Security disability payments), appears to have been particularly successful and in June 1978 the General Accounting Office, in a study of the Personal Care Home Program (renamed the Residential Care Program in 1980), concluded that the program was a cost-effective alternative to hospitalization and recommended that it be expanded.[165] Finally, a contract program (titled Community Nursing Home Care) was established whose goal was to help veterans requiring skilled or intermediate nursing care. Toward this end, a large number of community nursing homes were established throughout the United States. Veterans with service-connected disabilities were eligible for indefinite placement in these facilities, while veterans whose disabilities were non-service-connected were limited to a six-month stay.

In addition to these new programs, the VA was forced to completely revise its approach to health care in light of the aging of the veteran population. Despite the fact that they were covered by Medicare, larger and larger numbers of older veterans were turning to the VA to cover the costs of extended care inasmuch as Medicare did not cover long-term nursing home charges.[166] The result was that the demand for nursing home care increased while the demand for VA acute medical and surgical care, obtainable under Medicare, decreased sharply. Between 1971 and 1995, the average daily workload in VA hospitals dropped by 56 percent while demand for nursing-home and outpatient care increased.[167] By the mid-1990s over 90 percent of all veterans had some form of public or private health insurance sufficient to meet their acute-care needs. The 10 percent who were without insurance relied on public hospitals and clinics, particularly VA facilities for medical care, including – when geographically available – outpatient care.[168] The reduction in the VA's hospital workload was not reflected in a decrease in the VA's medical budget, in part because the costs per average patient day and per hospital inpatient increased substantially over this period.

Table 3.8   *Cost Per Average Patient Day and Per Hospital Inpatient,[1] Fiscal Years 1975–1984*

Fiscal Year	Per Diem		Cost Per Hospital Inpatient	
	Amount ($)	Index (1975 = 100)	Amount ($)	(1975 = 100)
1975	75.71	100	1984	100
1976	87.86	116	2135	108
1977	103.27	136	2346	118
1978	119.10	157	2583	130
1979	133.82	177	2772	140
1980	154.00	203	3077	155
1981[2]	166.05	219	3222	162
1982	190.36	251	3629	183
1983	206.89	273	3833	193
1984	220.49	291	3947	199

Notes:
[1]   Includes physicians' fees, medications, and all other direct costs plus administrative costs and assets acquisitions.
[2]   Beginning in 1981, data are calculated on the basis of obligations rather than costs.

Source: Administrator of Veterans Affairs, *Annual Report, 1984* (Washington, DC: Government Printing Office, 1985): 56.

While these changes were occurring, Congress enacted the Veterans' Health Care Expansion Act of 1973,[169] whose provisions included authorization that the VA undertake to furnish medical care to the spouse or child of a veteran who either has a total and permanent service-connected disability or has died as a consequence of a service-connected disability. The law was later amended so that, beginning in 1980, eligibility was extended to the surviving spouse or child of a member of the armed forces who died while on active duty. The program, known as the Civilian Health and Medical Program of the Veterans Administration (CHAMPVA), was designed to offer the same benefits as were extended to families of members of the armed services by the Department of Defense.[170] The program was fully implemented during fiscal year 1975 with somewhat over 80 000 applications representing more than 150 000 persons approved.[171] It is interesting that few of the services, either inpatient or ambulatory, to which the beneficiaries were entitled were performed at VA facilities. Instead, and more sensibly, the VA acted as a health insurer, underwriting the costs of approved medical treatment by private physicians and hospitals. Over $17 000 000 was expended on the program in its first year of operation, with a total of somewhat less than $600 000 000 by 1986, treating approximately 135 000 adults and 80 000 to 90 000 children annually. Studies conducted by the VA itself indicated that contracting out for medical services was more cost-effective than was providing the services directly.

Every attempt to reduce funding for the VA's medical care programs was met by sustained and vigorous opposition by the American Legion and other veterans' groups. The Legion's Medical Affairs Committee was one of the most powerful lobbies in Washington and consistently fought for more generous funding and against all attempts to decrease inefficiencies by putting pressure on the agency's budget.[172] It was therefore in the face of considerable opposition from veterans' groups that the Reagan Administration had, during the early and mid-1980s, several times proposed that a means test be established for certain classes of VA medical care. In 1985, Congress began debating the inclusion of a means test and third-party reimbursement, against which the American Legion strenuously protested. The Legion maintained that inasmuch as the largest number of VA patients were elderly and comparatively poor, the cost of screening claimants would prove more costly than any savings to the VA. With respect to third-party reimbursements, through which the government sought to recoup a portion of health care costs from private insurance companies that insured health care claimants, the Legion argued that the government was morally and legally bound to care for those who had contributed a portion of their lives to their country and that 'cost-sharing' violated this obligation. The Legion was further concerned that any third-party reimbursement scheme would ultimately lead the VA to steering veterans to private sector hospitals, thus eroding the special medical status of accorded veterans.[173]

In the event, the Legion's objections were overruled by Congress, which passed the Veterans' Health Care Amendments in April 1986.[174] The Act granted statutory authority to Veterans Affairs to bill third-party health insurance carriers for medical care provided to veterans for treatment of their non-service-connected disabilities and established a means test for VA medical treatment of non-service-connected disabilities and authorization to charge veterans earning more than $20000 per year. The law established three categories of veteran eligibility for medical care, depending on whether the veteran seeking treatment was suffering from a service-connected disability and, in the case of non-service-connected disabilities, on the applicant's income. All veterans falling under Category A received priority admission to VA facilities, whether for hospital or nursing-home care. These included (1) veterans with service-connected disabilities; (2) those who were in receipt of a VA pension; (3) those eligible for Medicaid; (4) former POWs; and (5) veterans whose incomes were below a certain specified amount. Category B and Category C veterans were those with non-service-connected disabilities, with a means test determining to which category one belonged. Those in Category C were obligated to agree to reimburse the VA for a portion of the expenses incurred in their treatment, either directly or through their medical insurance. This marks the first time the VA established a means test for medical treatment. While those veterans with incomes in excess of the means test levels continued to be eligible for both inpatient and outpatient care if the resources were available, they now had to agree to a co-payment.[175] The Legion complained bitterly that these provisions were 'insulting' and amounted to disenfranchising veterans and immediately called for the establishment of a team to gather data on its operation. 'Project Concern', as this group was known, soon released a series of case histories detailing the 'abuses' of the law by VA personnel and the horrors to which some veterans were subjected as a consequence of these provisions. Finally, in September 1986, the Legion authorized 'litigation to challenge and clarify VA policies on Public Law 99-272'.[176] Notwithstanding the Legion's objections, the existence of a means test for veterans suffering from non-service ailments continued, even after Congress revised the eligibility requirements for VA medical treatment in 1996.

While veterans' groups were unsuccessful in preventing the introduction of a means test, they did finally prevail on Congress to elevate the Veterans Administration to Cabinet status. President Reagan had issued a statement in support of a Department of Veterans Affairs while the House was considering the matter in the fall of 1987. The bill, which had almost 200 sponsors, soon cleared the House Government Operations Committee and was passed by the full House in December by a vote of 399 to 17. Senate hearings before the Committee on Governmental Affairs, under the chairmanship of Senator John Glenn, were held on a similar measure in March of the following year. The motives behind the bill were, predictably, purely political. The Senate bill had 65 co-sponsors and the witnesses appearing before Senator Glenn's Committee gave overwhelming support to the proposal, the arguments favoring the change couched in the most fatuous language. In almost 400 pages of testimony there is not one substantive argument put forward for raising the Veterans Administration to a Cabinet Department other than references to 'the nation's debt' to its veterans. The testimony of Senator Strom Thurmond of South Carolina was typical:

> In recognition of the contributions to freedom and liberty made by servicemen and women, our Government has placed a high priority on the welfare of its veterans. It is the highest obligation of citizenship to defend this Nation in time of need and this obligation creates an equal responsibility on the part of our Nation to care for the men and women who have worn the uniform. It would be more appropriate for the principal Federal agency charged with providing benefits and services to veterans, and their dependents and survivors, to have Cabinet-level status. The honor and respect due our veterans requires no less.[177]

Only Senator Alan Simpson of Wyoming expressed some reservations about the proposed Department of Veterans Affairs, pointing out that American veterans were extremely well-treated and that the proliferation of political appointments that would follow the creation of a Cabinet-level department was unnecessary. At the same time, Simpson urged that the Senate bill be amended to allow judicial review of decisions of the VA's Board of Veterans' Appeals,[178] a provision the American Legion firmly opposed. After much lobbying, the Legion was able to prevail on Senator Glenn to quash the judicial review provisions in Committee where it was approved for action on the Senate floor in April. The bill passed the full Senate in July. The Legion was ecstatic and its National Commander remarked that Congress had at last 'ignored the bankrupt bleatings of a few who would deny veterans their earned place in the executive branch'.[179] In October 1988 President Reagan signed the new Act[180] and on 15 March 1989 the Veterans Administration became the Department of Veterans Affairs with Edward J. Derwinski, at the time VA Administrator, appointed Secretary of Veterans Affairs. Among the three main divisions in which the new Department was divided, the most important was the Veterans Health Administration (VHA), which inherited the functions of the Veterans Health Services and Research Administration.

When the Veterans' Bureau was initially established in 1924, its primary mission had been to treat veterans of World War I, particularly those with service-connected disabilities such as blindness, paralysis, and loss of limbs. Since that time the VA's medical services have become the largest in the nation, with an annual budget of over $17 billion and a vast physical plant, including 172 hospitals, 600 ambulatory and community-based clinics, 132 nursing-care units, 40 domiciliary sites, and 206 readjustment counseling centers. These involved over 40 million patient visits. In fiscal year 1998, over 840 000 patients were admitted to its hospitals.[181] In addition, another 2.6 million unique patients were treated by its staff. One hundred and thirty of its facilities are affiliated with 107 of the nation's medical schools and its training facilities accommodate over 50 percent of the country's medical students and residents.[182]

In spite of its history of treating discharged military personnel for disabilities obtained while in service, the VA's medical facilities have, over the last few years, increasingly become the treatment facility of choice for poorer veterans whose medical problems are unconnected with their military service. In fiscal year 1997 the number of patients remaining in or discharged from VHA hospitals who were receiving treatment for service-connected conditions was slightly over 12 percent while another 22 percent had service-connected disabilities but were treated for conditions unrelated to those problems. The remaining 65 percent of the patients treated had no service-connected disability.[183] It has been estimated that almost a half of all patients treated by the VA are enrolled in Medicare and most have significantly lower incomes than the average Medicare-only user.[184] Their most prevalent disorders are alcohol dependence syndrome (7.8 percent), schizophrenic disorders (3.9 percent), various forms of chronic ischemic heart disease (2.8 percent), drug dependence (2.6 percent), affective psychoses (2.5 percent), heart failure (2.4 percent), adjustment reaction (2.4 percent), respiratory and chest symptoms (1.9 percent), diabetes (1.9 percent), and cardiac arrhythmias (1.8 percent).[185]

Indeed, alcohol and drug dependence play a far more prominent role in the list of disorders presented by veterans seeking medical treatment than these figures suggest. A General Accounting Office study found that in fiscal year 1995 almost 25 percent of all VA patients discharged from impatient settings had been diagnosed as having alcohol or drug abuse problems. The VA then estimated that it spent $2 billion, about 12 percent of its total health-care budget – to treat veterans with substance abuse disorders.[186] That alcohol and drug dependence is so prominent among veterans who make use of the VA's medical facilities is a reflection not only of veteran demographics but of the role played by the Vietnam War. In addition to setting up treatment centers for substance dependence, the VA found it necessary to deal with the large number of homeless veterans throughout the country. In 1987 the Veterans Administration launched a program which sought to offer treatment for these veterans. Current estimates indicate that about one-third of the adult homeless population have served in the military and that up to 250 000 veterans live on the streets or in shelters, while approximately twice that number are homeless at some point during the year.[187] Most of this population are Vietnam-War veterans and while the Department of Veterans Affairs claims that they can discover no link between combat exposure or service in Vietnam, impressionistic evidence seems to suggest that the mental conditions that give rise to homelessness are yet another legacy of that dreadful war. The VA's program for the homeless includes 61 Homeless Chronically Mentally Ill (HCMI) sites that provide physical and psychiatric exams, treatment, referrals, and ongoing case management. This program places those veterans assessed as needing longer-term treatment in one of its 150 contract community-based facilities. About 20 000 veterans are enrolled in such programs each year, with over 3000 receiving residential treatment.[188]

The transformation in the VA's structure in the last five years has been dramatic. In the words of a high-ranking official of the Department of Veterans Affairs, the Veterans Health Administration has, since the mid-1990s sought to transform itself from a disease-oriented, hospital-based health care system to a system that is 'patient oriented, prevention-oriented, community-based, and which has universal primary care at its foundation'.[189] In keeping with this, major changes were made to the VHA's organizational structure in late 1995. Prior to its reorganization, the VHA's numerous medical facilities throughout the United States were under the authority of an Associate Chief Medical Director for Operations, who provided operational direction and supervision of four geographical regions, each of which was headed by a regional director who supervised the operation of the approximately 35 to 45 medical care facilities within his region. In place of this schema, the VHA has restructured its facilities into 22 service delivery networks, called Veterans Integrated Service Networks (VISNs), thus integrating services within and among medical centers. Each VISN was designed to form a fully integrated health care system providing a whole range of health care services to patients residing in a particular geographic area. Emphasis has shifted from inpatient hospital care to primary care in a far greater number of community-based clinics and has expanded evening and weekend hours.[190]

As a consequence of the shift in veteran demographics and the restructuring of the VHA, veterans' medical facilities have undergone a series of changes in the past few years. Among them:

- Between fiscal year 1994 and fiscal year 1998, more than 52 percent of all hospital beds in FHA facilities have been closed;
- The number of bed days of care per 1000 patients has declined by more than 62 percent nationally from October 1995 to September 1998, from 3530 to 1333;
- Inpatient admissions have declined by 31 percent since fiscal year 1994;
- The number of ambulatory care visits has increased by almost ten million, a 35.4 percent increase between fiscal year 1994 and fiscal year 1998;
- Between 1995 and fiscal year 1998, ambulatory surgeries have increased from approximately 35 percent of all surgeries performed to about 92 percent.

In addition to these changes, since September 1995 the management and operation of 48 hospitals and clinic systems have been merged into 23 locally integrated health care systems, and 271 community-based outpatient clinics have been sited.[191]

In October 1996, Congress enacted new legislation providing that the VA institute an annual enrollment system based on seven specified priority categories. After October 1998 treatment by the VA, either inpatient or outpatient, was confined to those enrolled in the system. Highest priority is given (1) to veterans with service-connected disabilities who are rated as at least 50 percent disabled), (2) those with lesser disabilities whose ailments are service-connected, (3) former POWs, and (4) veterans determined to be 'catastrophically disabled' are next in order. These groups are followed by (5) veterans determined to be unable to defray the costs of needed care, that is, veterans with incomes below the means-test threshold (currently $22 351 for single veterans and $26 824 for veterans with one dependent). The final categories include (6) all other veterans not obligated to make co-payments for their treatment,[192] and (7) veterans without service-connected disabilities who agree to make co-payments for their treatment. As is evident from the data shown in Table 3.9, almost 43 percent of VA users fall in category 5 or below, with incomes below the means-test threshold.

Table 3.9   Enrollees, Users, and Associated Costs, by Priority Group, October 1998 through March 1999

Priority Group	Total Number of Enrollees	Number of Users	Cost per User[1] ($)	Total Costs ($)
1	443 134	362 240	4 514	1 635 117 425
2	297 480	205 256	2 394	491 465 728
3	532 913	329 059	2 216	729 292 271
4	120 398	94 786	11 733	1 112 088 333
5	1 378 924	1 047 098	2 679	2 805 336 809
6	58 678	27 095	1 542	41 767 687
7	486 260	243 080	2 629	316 213 510
Unprioritized	685 921	141 253	1 991	281 186 735
Total	**4 003 708**	**2 449 867**	**3 026**	**7 412 468 498**

Note: [1] Total costs divided by number of users.

Source: General Accounting Office, 'VA Health Care: Progress and Challenges in Providing Care to Veterans', Statement of Stephen P. Backhus, Director, Veterans' Affairs and Military Health Care Issues, Testimony before the Subcommittee on Health, Committee on Veterans' Affairs, House of Representatives (15 July 1999), GAO/T-HEHS-99-158: 6.

Table 3.10   Number and Median Age of Veterans, Fiscal Years 1969 to 2005

Year	Total	Under 35		Over 65		Median Age
		Number	Percent	Number	Percent	
1969	26 925	6 224	23.1	2 024	7.5	44.3
1970	27 647	6 666	24.1	1 996	7.2	44.4
1971	28 288	7 110	25.1	1 993	7.0	44.5
1972	28 804	7 455	25.9	2 025	7.0	44.7
1973	29 073	7 505	25.8	2 076	7.1	45.0
1974	29 265	7 510	25.7	2 125	7.3	45.5
1975	29 459	7 520	25.5	2 202	7.5	45.9
1976	29 607	7 463	25.2	2 294	7.7	46.3
1977	29 844	7 487	25.1	2 374	8.0	46.5
1978	29 984	7 283	24.3	2 540	8.5	47.0
1979	30 072	7 054	23.5	2 757	9.1	47.5
1980	30 118	6 750	22.4	3 011	10.0	48.0
1981	30 083	6 239	20.7	3 320	11.0	48.0
1982	28 522	5 312	18.6	3 506	12.3	50.8
1983	28 202	4 370	15.5	4 175	14.8	51.8
1984	28 027	3 906	13.9	4 618	16.5	52.3
1985	27 839	3 569	12.8	5 040	18.1	52.9
1986	27 382	3 400	12.4	5 507	20.1	53.4
1987	27 469	3 205	11.6	5 986	21.8	53.9
1988	27 279	3 061	11.2	6 431	23.6	54.4
1989	27 105	2 899	10.7	6 888	25.4	54.9
1990	26 885	2 759	10.3	7 283	27.1	55.3
1991	26 629	2 590	9.7	7 645	28.7	55.7
1992	26 838	2 641	9.8	8 035	29.9	56.0
1993	26 655	2 689	10.1	8 354	31.3	56.3
1994	26 365	2 555	9.7	8 542	32.4	56.7
1995	26 067	2 400	9.2	8 750	33.6	57.1
1996	25 881	2 309	8.9	8 994	34.8	57.4
1997	25 551	2 193	8.6	9 149	35.8	57.7
1998	26 267	2 064	7.9	9 258	35.2	56.5
1999	25 947	1 914	7.4	9 619	37.1	57.1
2000	25 498	2 212	8.7	9 531	37.4	57.4
2001	25 038	2 105	8.4	9 409	37.6	57.7
2002	24 570	2 213	8.6	9 269	37.7	58.0
2003	24 098	2 116	8.8	9 107	37.8	58.3
2004	23 625	2 007	8.5	8 938	37.8	58.6
2005	23 150			8 761	37.8	59.1

Source: *Annual Reports*. various years.

Table 3.11 *VHA: Medical Care Appropriations and Medical Consumer Price Index (CPI), Fiscal Years 1980–2003*

Fiscal Year	Actual Appropriations ($ 000)	Medical CPI	Unique Individuals[2]	Inpatient Episodes[3]	Outpatient Visits	Total Episodes	Full-time Employees	Hospitals	Nursing Homes	Domiciliaries	Outpatient clinics
1980	5 832 039	10.73%		1 159 028	18 204 000	19 363 028	185 698	172	92	16	227
1981	6 339 396	10.33%		1 159 287	18 165 000	19 324 287	184 865	172	96	16	226
1982	7 101 028	11.39%		1 159 317	18 202 000	19 361 317	186 836	172	98	16	226
1983	7 773 254	9.78%		1 199 434	18 754 000	19 953 434	188 713	172	99	16	226
1984	8 244 414	6.37%		1 207 690	18 836 000	20 043 690	190 463	172	99	16	226
1985	8 971 169	6.11%		1 224 010	19 331 000	21 055 010	193 828	172	105	16	226
1986	9 130 137	7.25%		1 248 010	20 437 000	21 685 010	194 453	172	115	16	229
1987	9 728 303	7.05%		1 247 595	21 890 000	23 137 595	194 459	172	117	17	228
1988	10 151 387	6.34%		1 263 235	23 232 000	24 495 235	193 798	172	119	26	233
1989	10 887 671	7.22%	2 690 194	1 186 840	22 643 000	23 829 840	191 801	172	122	28	339
1990	11 436 306	8.84%	2 654 512	1 148 652	22 602 000	23 750 652	193 821	172	126	32	339
1991	12 335 330	9.11%	2 645 860	1 105 576	23 039 000	24 144 576	196 103	172	127	35	341
1992	13 625 685	7.67%	2 726 899	1 085 126	24 195 000	25 280 126	199 811	171	129	35	362
1993	14 642 723	6.29%	2 764 858	1 075 111	24 406 000	25 481 111	204 527	172	128	37	354
1994	15 640 150	4.95%	2 793 920	1 066 534	25 442 000	26 508 534	203 884	172	128	37	366
1995	16 214 684[1]	5.00%[2]	2 822 584	1 061 741	25 900 000	26 961 741	200 987	173	133	39	376
1996	16 373 000	3.63%	3 337 000	807 000	29 295 000	30 181 000	195 153	173	133	40	398

1997	17 149 000	2.80%	3 375 000	671 000	31 919 000	32 677 000	186 135	172	131	40	439
1998	17 441 000	3.20%	3 615 000	617 000	34 972 000	35 687 000	184 768	172	132	40	551
1999	17 876 000	3.51%	3 847 000	611 000	39 928 000	37 631 000	182 661	172	134	40	519
2000	19 327 000	4.07%	4 074 000	579 000	38 370 000	39 040 000	179 520	172	135	43	601*
2001	21 316 000	4.60%	4 498 000	584 000	42 901 000	43 578 000	182 946	172	137	43	859*
2002	23 003 000	4.69%	4 892 000	590 000	46 058 000	46 735 000	183 720	172	137	43	913*
2003	25 647 000	4.03%	5 715 000	588 000	49 760 000	50 441 000					

Notes:

* Includes hospital clinics.

1 'Total Episodes' includes nursing home stays.

2 Validated data for the period prior to 1989 not available.

3 Includes both acute and long-term care discharges plus those inpatients remaining in the Veterans Administration Medical Center at the end of the fiscal year. Some patients are admitted more than once in the same fiscal year.

Source: Data for 1980 through 1995: Kenneth W. Kizer, *Vision for Change: A Plan to Restructure the Veterans Health Administration* (Washington: Department of Veterans Affairs, 1995): 79.

Data for 1996, 1997, 1998, and 1999: various sources.

1996 to 1998: *Health, United States, 2000*: 356 (Table 138); 1997 to 2003: *Health, United States, 2005*: 402 (Table 144): *Statistical Abstract of the United States, 2006*: 482 (Table 706).

Table 3.12   Gross Expenditures: Medical Expenses and Hospital Construction Costs, 1962–1985 (in thousands of dollars)

Year	Total	Medical and administrative expenses				Hospital and domiciliary construction costs
		General operating expenses	Medical administration and miscellaneous operating expenses	Medical care	Medical and prosthetic research[1]	
1962	1 195 892	161 001	40 854[1]	994 037		53 008
1963	1 246 130	158 933	15 984	1 043 762	27 451	66 170
1964	1 291 692	157 845	14 296	1 087 848	31 704	68 576
1965	1 358 051	162 764	14 137	1 144 011	37 139	76 996
1966	1 406 409	164 339	13 142	1 190 451	38 477	83 464
1967	1 518 199	178 940	14 000	1 281 232	44 027	59 957
1968	1 620 047	189 641	12 762	1 372 301	45 343	47 993
1969	1 735 043	206 239	14 322	1 464 104	50 378	46 103
1970	2 007 783	243 025	17 782	1 687 623	59 355	71 154
1971	2 256 980	260 147	20 186	1 913 509	63 139	80 139
1972	2 650 982	290 516	22 322	2 269 186	68 959	107 336
1973	2 966 238	317 105	25 044	2 545 677	78 412	92 635
1974	3 290 195	343 916	31 034	2 833 622	81 582	106 364
1975	3 919 257	438 660	36 663	3 348 139	95 795	119 580

1976	4 446 766	479 214	34 479	3 831 943	101 130	185 570
T.Q^{276}	1 195 771	123 645	11 249	1 033 503	27 374	49 196
1977	5 072 994	522 061	39 435	4 402 752	108 745	224 546
1978	5 683 811	575 214	42 737	4 948 297	117 563	245 082
1979	6 205 942	625 741	46 372	5 408 252	125 577	240 305
1980	6 646 753	605 217	47 047	5 857 450	137 039	286 095
1981	7 199 254	627 612	51 047	6 378 209	142 385	399 733
1982	8 008 924	660 649	55 099	7 155 117	138 059	439 300
1983	8 722 449	691 690	56 306	7 813 302	161 151	432 233
1984	9 123 371	696 457	65 576	8 171 039	190 300	469 753
1985	9 992 001	765 036	65 798	8 936 261	65 798	517 344

Notes:

[1] Expenditures for medical and prosthetic research prior to 1963 were included in medical administration and miscellaneous operating expenses.

[2] T.Q. refers to the transitional quarter that resulted from the fact that the federal fiscal year was altered in 1976. Fiscal year 1976 began on 1 July 1975 and ended on 30 June 1976. Fiscal year 1977 began on 1 October 1976 and ended on 30 September 1977. The period 1 July 1976 to 30 September 1976 is designated the 'transitional quarter'.

Source: 1962–71: Administrator of Veterans' Affairs, *Annual Report, 1971* (Washington, DC: Government Printing Office, 1972): p. 133. 1976–85: Administrator of Veterans' Affairs, *Annual Report, 1985* (Washington, DC: Government Printing Office, 1986): p. 252.

Table 3.13 Net Outlays: Medical Expenses 1985–2003[1] (in thousands of dollars)

Year	Total	Medical Care			Medical and prosthetic research
		Other[2]	Medical administration and miscellaneous operating expenses	Medical care	
1985	9 014 120	11 735	65 571	8 721 690	215 124
1986	9 351 202	19 870	54 780	9 095 306	181 246
1987	9 758 414	23 276	40 265	9 499 750	195 123
1988	10 292 167	9 064	40 463	10 045 310	197 330
1989	10 800 897	56 325	45 094	10 514 538	184 940
1990	11 612 800	30 604	45 566	11 330 062	206 568
1991	12 545 150	73 084	47 951	12 210 722	213 393
1992	13 944 261	129 627	45 942	13 566 532	202 160
1993	14 760 797	157 845	61 412	14 295 510	246 030
1994	15 578 580	148 176	73 634	15 115 925	240 845

1995	16 430 595	175 461	70 836	15 933 197	251 101
1996	15 910 412	(426 365)[3]	56 697	16 047 971	232 109
1997	17 067 272	(353 503)[3]	63 375	17 122 549	234 851
1998	17 670 000	95 000	57 000	17 271 000	247 000
1999	18 251 000	28 000	61 000	17 846 000	316 000
2000	19 664 000	26 000	59 000	19 250 000	329 000
2001	22 086 000	24 000	79 000	21 631 000	352 000
2002	23 545 000	28 000	81 000	22 052 000	378 000
2003	25 416 000	30 000	84 000	24 899 000	403 000

Notes: Figures from 1998 rounded to nearest million.

[1] In 1986 the data here presented replaced the VA's data on gross expenditures.

[2] Includes grants to the Republic of the Philippines and for the construction of state extended care facilities, the canteen service revolving fund, the special therapeutic and rehabilitative revolving fund, the nursing home revolving fund, the medical care cost recovery fund, the nursing scholarship program, and assistance for health manpower training institutions.

[3] The medical care cost recovery fund showed a credit of $484 837 000 in 1996 and of $397 113 000 in 1997.

Source: Veterans Administration *Annual Reports*, 1986 through 1997. Figures for 1998 through 2003 are taken from the various *Budgets of the United States*.

Table 3.14 *Outpatient Visits to VA Staff and to Private Physicians on a Fee-for-Service Basis, Fiscal Years 1924–2002*

Fiscal Year	Total	To VA Staff	To Private Physicians
1924	2 843 024	2 730 132	112 892
1925	2 261 408	2 183 186	78 222
1926	1 865 830	1 791 447	74 383
1927	1 696 516	1 599 254	97 262
1928	1 597 042	1 480 560	116 482
1929	1 588 933	1 446 096	142 837
1930	1 626 339	1 459 429	166 910
1931	2 637 978	2 162 660	475 318
1932	2 822 569	2 366 244	456 325
1933	2 074 374	1 806 421	267 953
1934	1 088 704	847 823	240 881
1935	1 611 659	1 392 646	219 013
1936	2 156 515	1 985 932	170 583
1937	1 879 703	1 736 283	143 420
1938	2 010 212	1 881 270	128 942
1939	2 088 090	1 964 036	124 054
1940	2 171 230	2 052 602	118 628
1941	2 166 456	2 050 947	115 509
1942	1 829 512	1 729 647	99 865
1943	1 535 674	1 455 409	80 265
1944	1 803 476	1 725 631	77 845
1945	2 502 940	2 370 113	132 827
1946	4 243 302	3 636 137	607 165
1947	11 510 548	7 323 051	4 187 479
1948	3 998 786	2 645 567	1 353 219
1949	3 606 429	2 430 233	1 176 196
1950	3 508 471	2 406 810	1 101 661
1951	3 072 753	2 139 364	933 389
1952	2 492 361	1 700 756	791 605
1953	2 359 453	1 638 564	720 889
1954	2 270 330	1 616 883	653 447
1955	2 267 168	1 647 969	619 199
1956	2 199 667	1 594 915	604 752
1957	2 122 072	1 537 958	584 114
1958	2 148 264	1 591 539	556 725
1959	2 207 301	1 597 222	610 079
1960	2 364 758	1 701 912	662 846
1961	2 367 354	1 706 343	670 011
1962	3 656 104	2 429 229	1 226 875
1963	5 900 554	4 672 952	1 227 602

Fiscal Year	Total	To VA Staff	To Private Physicians
1964	6 178 633	4 945 717	1 232 916
1965	5 987 225	4 770 802	1 216 423
1966	6 181 678	4 981 790	1 199 888
1967	6 268 056	5 082 108	1 185 948
1968	6 563 787	5 369 273	1 194 514
1969	6 947 074	5 774 545	1 173 529
1970	7 311 894	6 135 633	1 176 261
1971	8 064 092	6 798 146	1 265 948
1972	9 526 881	7 930 080	1 596 801
1973	10 858 491	9 165 094	1 693 397
1974	12 266 476	10 457 830	1 808 646
1975	14 629 517	12 595 514	2 034 003
1976	16 409 850	14 222 804	2 187 046
1977	17 045 079	14 675 284	2 369 795
1978	17 416 275	15 069 573	2 346 702
1979	17 262 408	15 053 332	2 209 076
1980	17 971 407	15 751 690	2 219 717
1981	17 929 550	15 825 064	2 104 486
1982	17 808 977	15 861 687	1 947 290
1983	18 509 562	16 617 485	1 892 067
1984	18 616 073	16 935 050	1 681 023
1985	19 600 849	17 789 582	1 811 267
1986	20 188 182	18 457 747	1 730 385
1987	21 634 757	19 837 424	1 797 333
1988	23 232 895	21 473 404	1 759 492
1989	22 629 343	21 025 887	1 603 456
1990	22 602 540	21 399 342	1 203 198
1991	23 034 516	21 932 426	1 102 090
1992	23 901 825	22 788 431	1 113 394
1993	24 236 095	23 144 396	1 091 699
1994	25 157 983	24 134 838	1 023 144
1995	27 565 000	26 501 000	1 064 157
1996	29 294 620	28 359 653	934 967
1997	31 919 001	30 436 295	1 482 706
1998	34 972 000	33 417 000	1 555 000
1999	36 928 000	35 236 000	1 692 000
2000	38 370 000	36 448 000	1 922 000
2001	42 901 000	40 506 000	2 395 000
2002	46 418 000	43 684 000	2 734 000

Note: Data from 1998 rounded to the nearest thousand.

Source: *Annual Reports*, various years.

Table 3.15	*Average Daily Patient and Member Load, VA Hospitals,*
Domiciliaries, and Nursing Homes, Fiscal Years 1931–2005[1]

Year	VA Hospital Average Daily Patient Load	VA Domiciliaries Average Daily Member Load	Nursing Homes Average Daily Patient Load
1931	32 949	19 523	
1932	42 606	24 388	
1933	42 129	17 205	
1934	36 583	14 547	
1935	41 333	14 566	
1936	43 524	16 741	
1937	44 879	15 296	
1938	48 973	19 136	
1939	52 763	21 687	
1940	56 251	22 926	
1941	58 423	22 662	
1942	57 927	20 101	
1943	56 147	15 328	
1944	61 332	13 852	
1945	68 260	13 161	
1946	78 566	15 190	
1947	98 248	18 637	
1948	105 882	20 552	
1949	106 985	22 000	
1950	108 038	24 307	
1951	104 391	24 564	
1952	105 110	24 792	
1953	104 482	25 035	
1954	108 944	25 291	
1955	110 733	25 774	
1956	113 458	25 786	
1957	114 325	25 846	
1958	114 581	25 991	
1959	114 103	26 518	
1960	114 356	26 274	
1961	114 321	26 197	
1962	113 764	25 435	
1963	112 593	25 173	
1964	112 881	24 575	
1965	111 782	23 526	208
1966	109 882	21 319	1475
1967	105 807	20 382	2748
1968	99 450	20 058	4000
1969	93 547	20 194	4000
1970	87 460	19 347	4002
1971	86 319	18 565	5052
1972	83 186	17 957	5819
1973	84 556	16 286	6508

Year	VA Hospital Average Daily Patient Load	VA Domiciliaries Average Daily Member Load	Nursing Homes Average Daily Patient Load
1974	83 534	15 584	6769
1975	82 253	15 030	7032
1976	80 519	14 652	7398
1977	77 617	14 214	7559
1978	75 390	13 957	7884
1979	71 983	13 744	8357
1980	70 251	12 786	8394
1981	68 479	11 925	8700
1982	66 582	11 580	9125
1983	66 634	11 341	9415
1984	64 586	10 637	9701
1985	60 756	10 314	10 399
1986	56 940	5767	11 317
1987	54 564	5837	11 741
1988	52 111	6061	12 145
1989	49 040	6315	12 402
1990	46 726	6526	12 925
1991	44 073	6575	13 592
1992	42 616	6440	14 561
1993	41 705	6197	14 790
1994	39 953	6051	14 887
1995	37 630	5711	15 029
1996	31 679	5504	15 336
1997	24 048	5462	15 098
1998	19 637	10 662	33 670
1999	18 336	10 496	32 204
2000	15 616	10 407	30 740
2001	15 110	10 697	31 941
2002	15 294	10 605	31 636
2003	13 089	10 619	33 408
2004e	12 727	10 046	33 069
2005e	12 473	10 844	31 579

Note: [1] Daily patient and member loads include patients in non-VA hospitals and domiciliary members in state homes.

Source: 1931–34: Administrator of Veterans' Affairs, *Annual Report, 1963* (Washington, DC: Government Printing Office, 1963): 194 (Table 4).
1934–68: Administrator of Veterans' Affairs, *Annual Report, 1968* (Washington, DC: Government Printing Office, 1969): 226–7 (Table 1).
1969–78: Administrator of Veterans' Affairs, *Annual Report, 1978* (Washington, DC: Government Printing Office, 1979):110–111 (Tables 4, 6).
1979–85: Administrator of Veterans' Affairs, *Annual Report, 1985* (Washington, DC: Government Printing Office, 1985): 164 (Tables 4, 6).
1986–97: Various Annual Reports.
Congressional Budget Office, *Budget of the United States*, 1997 through 2005.

Table 3.16 Average Obligations Per Patient Day, VA Hospitals and Nursing Homes, Fiscal Years 1977–2001 (dollars)

| Fiscal Year | VA Hospitals | | | | | Nursing Home Care Units |
	All Bed Sections	Medical Bed Sections	Surgical Bed Sections	Psychiatric Bed Sections	Intermediate Bed Sections	
1977	103.27	108.01	136.20	74.80		54.88
1978	119.10	124.43	159.29	85.46		62.15
1979	133.82	139.44	179.25	95.87		65.65
1980	154.00	159.10	208.65	111.03		75.39
1981	168.36	175.10	228.38	119.62		81.72
1982	190.36	236.46	267.21	131.03	106.87	91.17
1983	206.89	256.74	287.20	142.59	117.26	98.00
1984	220.49	273.21	314.41	150.51	122.33	107.84
1985	249.02	308.75	378.73	163.58	135.32	107.84
1986	255.16	316.91	415.43	165.56	136.92	118.24
1987	272.95	350.82	452.49	173.55	150.04	123.36
1988	289.27	365.91	525.19	184.32	156.43	128.74
1989	330.65	437.18	636.81	206.34	149.52	143.00

Fiscal Year					
1990	387.64	510.84	751.16	239.07	174.57	154.92
1991	438.29	558.06	834.63	279.49	207.70	169.98
1992	489.76	613.92	961.65	295.20	246.03	184.23
1993	526.73	662.09	1,057.27	312.20	256.83	196.51
1994	568.08	715.01	1,187.64	329.83	279.25	207.20
1995	624.61	785.68	1,361.21	353.44	304.72	222.38

Fiscal Year	Acute Hospital Care	Rehabilitative Care	Psychiatric Care	Nursing Home Care	Sub-Acute Care
1995	965.65	645.95	354.38	129.14	300.75
1996	1093.92	665.74	396.27	133.34	304.87
1997	1435.80	783.36	518.02	141.86	367.36
1998	1529.00	799.00	540.00	145.00	382.00
1999	1594.00	827.00	631.00	152.00	413.00
2000	1766.00	897.00	726.00	167.00	508.00
2001	1823.00	996.00	787.00	174.00	598.00

Notes: In fiscal year 1995, the Department of Veterans Affairs chose to alter the categories for which it reports data. In 1996 and subsequently, obligations per average patient day were broken down as in the lower part of the table (data refer to both VA and non-VA facilities).

Source: *Annual Reports*, various years.

The shift from inpatient to ambulatory care and an increase in chronic care needs in an aging population clearly undermine the reasons originally put forward for the government to operate a direct delivery health care system. The rationale for constructing this immense health care edifice was extremely weak to begin with but in light of the change in demand from acute to long-term treatment and from hospital to outpatient care, the arguments supporting a direct delivery system are practically non-existent. It is obviously impractical for the Veterans Health Administration (VHA) to duplicate the outpatient facilities available to non-veterans throughout the country and unless they were to attempt some such duplication, VHA outpatient facilities would of necessity remain geographically inaccessible to the majority of potential users. An aging and declining veteran population has led the governments of Australia, Canada, and the United Kingdom to close or convert their veterans' hospitals to other uses and to integrate the treatment of veterans into their general health care systems.[193] Surely this policy makes equal sense in the United States. At the very least, the Department of Veterans Affairs could subsidize the treatment of qualified veterans who consulted physicians or were hospitalized on a fee-for-service basis, as they do with respect to those covered by CHAMPVA. However, this policy is currently, except in very limited circumstances, against the law and is unlikely to be instituted inasmuch as most of the DVA's health care budget is spent on maintaining its direct delivery infrastructure.[194] 'Solutions' such as allowing veterans' dependents to use the VA's excess hospital capacity or converting acute-care hospitals into nursing homes undermine the whole purpose of the VA's medical programs and would pit government health care against private health care in direct competition. What direction these programs will eventually take remains an open question.

NOTES

1. For a brief history of federal efforts to provide domiciliary care for veterans, see Col. George E. Ijams, 'History of Medical and Domiciliary Care of Veterans', *The Military Surgeon* 76 (March 1935): 113–33, and *History of the National Home for Disabled Volunteer Soldiers* (Dayton, Ohio: United Brethren Printing Establishment, 1875): 17–50. Patrick J. Kelly, *Creating a National Home: Building the Veterans' Welfare State, 1860–1900* (Cambridge, MA: Harvard University Press, 1997) offers a sociological analysis of the role played by American soldiers' homes in creating a new form of citizenship, martial citizenship, at the point where the welfare state conjoined with a warfare state.
2. In reality a series of separate homes located in various parts of the country, the first of which was established in 1866 at Togus Spring, Maine and known as the Eastern Branch. This was followed by branches at Dayton, Ohio (1966), Milwaukee, Wisconsin (1967), and Hampton, Virginia (1870). William Pyrle Dillingham, *Federal Aid to Veterans, 1917–1941* (Gainesville, Fla.: University of Florida Press, 1952): 58, 111. Other than an initial appropriation of approximately $119 000 made by Congress in 1847, the Soldiers' Home and the Home for Disabled Volunteer Soldiers were financed by fines levied against soldiers who

had been court-marshaled and forfeitures on account of desertion. For a brief history of these homes see Col. George E. Ijams, 'History of the Medical and Domiciliary Care of Veterans', *The Military Surgeon* and *History of the National Home for Disabled Volunteer Soldiers*.

3. In addition, a number of states had established homes for indigent and disabled soldiers and sailors. It appears that the state homes and the National Home originally served as asylums for young, unmarried severely disabled veterans who remained there until their premature deaths. After 1884, however, the various branches of the National Home functioned primarily as old-age homes for disabled indigent veterans. See Theda Skocpol, *Protecting Soldiers and Mothers: The Political Origins of Social Policy in the United States* (Cambridge, MA: The Belknap Press of Harvard University Press, 1992): 140–41.

4. 23 Stat. L. 120, cited in Gustavus A. Weber and Laurence F. Schmeckebier, *The Veterans' Administration: Its History, Activities, and Organization* (Washington, DC: The Brookings Institution, 1934): 76.

5. Between 1884 and 1907, an additional six branches of the Home were established: those at Leavenworth, Kansas (1884), Sawtell, California (1888), Marion, Indiana (1890), Danville, Illinois (1898), Johnson City, Tennessee (1903), and Hot Springs, South Dakota (1907). In 1929, another home was established at Bath, New York, and in 1933, three additional homes were created at St Petersburg, Florida, Biloxi, Mississippi, and Roseburg, Oregon. These last three were absorbed by the Veterans Administration before they were completed. Weber and Schmeckebier, *The Veterans' Administration*, 75.

6. The total number of Union veterans assisted by the National Home for Disabled Volunteer Soldiers through June 1899 was only slightly over 97 000. Kelly, *Creating a National Home*, 204, n. 4.

7. Federal pensions awarded to Civil War veterans and their dependents were already among the most generous in the world, thanks to a series of prodigal Republican administrations. When, in 1887, Congress passed a bill that would have extended pensions to any person who had served at least three months in any war in which the United States had been engaged who were incapable of 'procuring subsistence by daily labor', President Grover Cleveland, a Democrat, in vetoing the bill, noted that the soldiers of the Civil War, in their pay, bounty, pension provisions, and preference for public employment, had 'received such compensation for military service as has never been received before since mankind first went to war'. *Congressional Record*, 49th Congress, 2d Session, vol. 18, Pt 2, p. 1638; quoted in Weber and Schmeckebier, *Veterans' Administration*, 42–3.

8. The number of Union veterans surviving the Civil War was close to 2 000 000 and they and their dependents represented a substantial block of voters to which the Republican Party was particularly attentive.

9. Pension expenditures, which had been substantial, increased markedly with enactment of the Arrears Act in 1879. Not only were settlements generous, but the terms of the Act completely politicized the amount and duration of payment. Despite the fact that the conditions of eligibility were ostensibly fixed by legislation, the statutes had, by 1879, reached a level of complexity such that Interior Department officials and Commissioners of Pensions were effectively granted broad discretionary powers not only in determining the status of applications and the speed with which they were processed, but in assessing entitlements. The politics of Civil War benefits are discussed at some length in Skocpol, *Protecting Soldiers and Mothers*, 102–51.

10. Richard Severo and Lewis Milford, *The Wages of War: When America's Soldiers Came Home – From Valley Forge to Vietnam* (New York: Simon & Schuster, 1989): 171.

11. The Grand Army of the Republic, the largest of the Civil War veterans' organizations, was founded in the spring of 1866 in Decatur, Illinois, as a 'national soldiers' mutual benefit society'. It soon developed into a Union-wide organization fiercely devoted to the Republican party and by the election of 1888 had a membership of over 370 000. Skocpol, *Protecting Soldiers and Mothers*, 127.

12. Even as late as the mid-1880s, the American electorate still comprised a substantial number of Union veterans, more than 10 percent. Skocpol, *Protecting Soldiers and Mothers*, 126.

13. Tanner was fully aware of the source of the money being paid out in pensions. Soon after the Civil War he settled in Brooklyn, New York, where he became, first, deputy tax collector and then tax collector for the city. In 1876 he was elected commander of the G.A.R.'s New York Department.

14. Donald L. McMurry, 'The Bureau of Pensions During the Administration of President Harrison', *Mississippi Valley Historical Review*, 13 (June 1926 to March 1927): 346. Not everyone regarded Tanner's appointment with equanimity. *The Nation* editorialized that Tanner's appointment did not bode well for the country and pointed out that pension expenditures had already reached $95 000 000 annually, 'a greater amount than the cost of the entire military establishment of Germany, under which the people of that nation groan so loudly'. 'The New Pension Building' (editorial), *The Nation*, 30 May 1889, pp. 438–9; quoted in Severo and Milford, *Wages of War*, 179.

15. Skocpol, *Protecting Soldiers*, 128.

16. Ibid., 128. The following table will give some idea of the increase in take-up rates for Civil War pensions:

	Union veterans in civil life	Disabled military pensioners	Percentage of veterans enrolled as pensioners
1865	1 830 000	35 880	1.96
1870	1 744 000	87 521	5.01
1875	1 654 000	107 114	6.48
1880	1 557 000	135 272	8.69
1885	1 449 000	244 201	16.85
1890	1 322 000	–	–
1891	–	520 158	39.34
1895	1 170 000	735 338	62.85
1900	1 000 000	741 259	74.13
1905	821 000	648 608	83.39
1910	624 000	562 615	90.16
1915	424 000	396 370	93.48

Source: Theda Skocpol, *Protecting Soldiers and Mothers: The Political Origins of Social Policy in the United States* (Cambridge, MA: Belknap Press of Harvard University Press, 1992): 109.

17. United States Bureau of Pensions, *Laws of the United States Governing the Granting of Army and Navy Pensions* (Washington, DC: Government Printing Office, 1925): 43, quoted in Skocpol, *Protecting Soldiers*, 129.

18. For a detailed history of war pensions, see Gustavus A. Weber, *The Bureau of Pensions: Its History, Activities and Organization* (Baltimore: Johns Hopkins Press, 1923). While the federal government bore none of the medical costs of those who had served in the military until 1917, it still managed to spend vast amounts of money on veterans. The following table gives some idea of the amounts expended in the form of pensions.

Fiscal Year	Paid as Pensions ($)	Costs, Maintenance and Expenses ($)	Total ($)	Number of Pensioners
1879	33 664 429	837 734	34 502 163	242 755
1880	50 689 229	935 027	51 624 256	250 802
1881	50 583 405	1 072 060	51 655 465	268 830
1882	54 313 172	1 466 236	55 779 408	285 697
1883	60 427 574	2 591 648	63 019 222	303 658

Fiscal Year	Paid as Pensions ($)	Costs, Maintenance and Expenses ($)	Total ($)	Number of Pensioners
1884	57 912 387	2 835 181	60 747 568	322 756
1885	65 171 937	3 392 576	68 564 513	345 125
1886	64 091 143	3 245 017	67 336 160	365 783
1887	73 752 997	3 753 401	77 506 398	406 007
1888	78 950 502	3 515 057	82 465 559	452 557
1889	88 842 721	3 466 968	92 309 689	489 725
1890	106 093 850	3 526 382	109 620 232	537 944
1891	117 312 691	4 700 636	122 013 326	676 160
1892	139 394 147	4 898 666	144 292 813	876 068
1893	156 906 638	4 867 734	161 774 372	966 012
1894	139 986 726	3 963 976	143 959 702	969 544
1895	139 812 295	4 338 020	144 159 315	970 524
1896	138 220 704	3 991 376	142 212 080	970 678
1897	139 949 717	3 987 783	143 937 500	976 014
1898	144 651 880	4 114 091	148 765 971	993 714
1899	138 355 053	4 147 518	142 502 571	991 519
1900	138 462 130	3 841 707	142 303 837	993 592
1901	138 531 484	3 868 795	142 400 279	997 735
1902	137 504 268	3 831 379	141 335 647	999 446
1903	137 759 654	3 993 217	141 752 871	996 545
1904	141 093 572	3 849 366	144 942 938	994 762
1905	141 142 861	3 721 833	144 864 694	998 441
1906	139 000 288	3 523 270	142 523 558	985 971
1907	138 155 413	3 309 110	141 464 523	967 371
1908	153 093 086	2 800 964	155 894 050	951 687
1909	161 973 704	2 852 584	164 826 288	946 194
1910	159 974 056	2 657 674	162 631 730	921 083
1911	157 325 160	2 517 127	159 842 287	892 098
1912	152 986 434	2 448 857	155 435 291	860 294
1913	174 171 661	2 543 247	176 714 908	820 200
1914	172 417 546	2 066 507	174 484 053	785 239
1915	165 518 266	1 779 860	167 298 126	748 147
1916	159 155 090	1 656 722	160 811 812	709 572
1917	160 895 054	1 562 855	162 457 909	673 111
1918	179 835 329	1 527 616	181 362 945	646 895
1919	222 159 293	1 433 192	223 592 485	624 427
1920	213 295 315	1 395 014	214 690 329	592 199
1921	258 715 843	1 389 922	260 105 765	566 053
Totals*	5 993 086 115	138 683 653	6 131 769 768	

Note: * Totals rounded.
Source: Weber, *The Bureau of Pensions*, 96.

19.   Julian Mack, who had been raised to the rank of Circuit Court judge in 1911, the highest judicial post attained by a Jew up to that time, was well-known for his work in social welfare and had been instrumental in lobbying the government's soldiers' insurance compensation legislation through Congress. McAdoo, one of Wilson's most loyal henchmen, was a central figure in the establishment of the Federal Reserve in 1913. During the war, he served simultaneously as Secretary of the Treasury, Chairman of the Federal Reserve, Chairman of the Federal Farm Loan Board, Chairman of the War Finance

Corporation, and, after they had been seized by the federal government, director general of the railroads.

20. President's Commission on Veterans' Benefits, *The Historical Development of Veterans' Benefits in the United States* (Washington, DC: Government Printing Office, 1956): 25–6.

21. Bess Furman, *A Profile of the United States Public Health Service, 1798–1948* (Washington, DC: Department of Health, Education, and Welfare, National Institutes of Health, National Library of Medicine, 1973): 319.

22. The Act of 4 March 1921, commonly known as the Langley Act, appropriated a total of $18 600 000 for the construction and remodeling of hospital facilities for veterans.

23. Its full title was the Committee to Investigate the Administration of the Law in Caring for the Crippled and Impaired Soldiers of the Late War.

24. The American Legion was chartered by Congress in September, 1919, and held its first convention in Minneapolis in November of that year, with the goal of advancing the interests of veterans. It quickly became the primary spokesman for those who had served in the military. Among its ongoing concerns was its inflexible opposition to any type of 'anti-Americanism', which the Legion associated with all manner of 'left-wing' causes, including opposition to higher military appropriations and to universal military service. It quickly set up a Committee on Americanism, still active, to root out 'Bolshevism', pacifism, and other 'alien' influences from American life. For a history of the Legion, see Thomas A. Rumer, *The American Legion: An Official History, 1919–1989* (New York; M. Evans & Co., 1990).

25. These were the Bureau of War Risk Insurance, responsible for life insurance, pensions, and disability compensation, the Federal Board for Vocational Education, which was charged with the rehabilitation and training of veterans, and the Public Health Service, which conducted the physical examinations that determined eligibility for government medical care and for providing the medical and hospital care itself.

26. Earlier that year, Dr Charles E. Sawyer, President Harding's personal physician from Marion, Ohio, had testified before the Senate Committee on Education and Labor, where he urged the creation of a cabinet-level agency, a Department of Social Welfare, to include the various federal agencies then involved in public education, public health, immigration, and veterans' benefits. Sawyer was joined in advocating this new Department by Senator William Kenyon of Iowa, one of Harding's close associates. Their support for the agency was encouraged by Harding, who had promised creation of the new cabinet post during the 1920 Presidential campaign.

27. On Forbes, see Severo and Milford, *Wages of War*, 247–57.

28. Rumer, *The American Legion*: 140.

29. Severo and Milford, *Wages of War*, 249.

30. Its predecessor agencies appear to have been little better. Late in 1919 the Federal Bureau of Vocational Rehabilitation reported that it had expended over $385 000 in salaries while at the same time it paid out only $140 000 in tuition for veterans. Severo and Milford, *Wages of War*, 249.

31. In mid-1921 there existed 65 hospitals devoted entirely or in part to caring for veterans, comprising over 19 000 beds. These were quickly transferred to the Veterans' Bureau and, in the following year, all dispensaries and outpatient clinics operated by the Public Health Service for the treatment of veterans were also transferred. Weber and Schmeckebier, *The Veterans' Administration*, 161–2.

32. See William Pyrle Dillingham, *Federal Aid to Veterans*, 14.

33. Dillingham, *Federal Aid to Veterans*, 15. The veterans' hospital built by Thompson-Black in Excelsior Springs, Missouri was constructed without any kitchen facilities. Severo and Milford, *Wages of War*, 251–2.

34. Ibid., 250.

35. Ibid., 251–3; US Senate, Select Committee on Investigation of Veterans' Bureau, *Investigation of Veterans' Bureau* (2 vols; Washington, DC: Government Printing Office, 1923): II: 974. The list of items sold covers over three pages of small type of the Senate subcommittee hearings (I: 769–72).

36. The subcommittee hearings detail a history of fraud on such a massive scale that even the reader accustomed to government misconduct is awed. Forbes' own testimony, in which he denies any wrongdoing whatever, covers over 300 pages (pp. 911–1224) and is a masterpiece of cant.

37. Severo and Milford, *Wages of War*, 257.

38. Dillingham, *Federal Aid to Veterans*, 62–3.

39. Ibid., 62.

40. One of the provisions of a statute enacted by Congress in 1922 permitted the extension of hospital facilities to all veterans, regardless of when they served, who were suffering from either neuropsychiatric or tubercular disorders. Weber and Schmeckebier, *Veterans' Administration*, 163.

41. A resolution calling on the government to extend veterans' medical coverage to all illnesses, regardless of where and how caused, was passed at each annual meeting of the Legion from its first convention in 1919, until Congress finally agreed to the change. See Dillingham, *Federal Aid to Veterans*, 68–9.

42. Louis M. Orr, 'To Socialized Medicine and Socialism by War of the Veterans Administration', *Journal of the American Medical Association*, 162 (27 October 1956): 861.

43. Dillingham, *Federal Aid to Veterans*, 69.

44. Orr, 'To Socialized Medicine', 861.

45. Dillingham, *Federal Aid to Veterans*, 70.

46. The federal government's receipts in 1932 were somewhat less than $2 billion, while expenditures were approximately $4.7 billion, thus increasing the total public debt in that year by 16.28 percent! These figures can be found in United States Department of Commerce, Bureau of the Census, *Historical Statistics of the United States, Colonial Times to 1970* (Washington, DC: Government Printing Office, 1975: 1104 (Series Y 335–8).

47. 47 Stat. L. 419, quoted in Weber and Schmeckebier, *Veterans' Administration*, 248.

48. 73rd Congress, House report, p. 166, quoted in Weber and Schmeckebier, *Veterans' Administration*, 250.

49. P.L. No. 2, 73rd Congress.

50. Dillingham, *Federal Aid to Veterans*, 107.

51. Weber and Schmeckebier, *Veterans' Administration*, 257.

52. Dillingham, *Federal Aid to Veterans*, 108.

53. Ibid., 108–9.

54. Weber and Schmeckebier, *Veterans' Administration*, 270.

55. Quoted in Louis M. Orr, 'To Socialized Medicine', p. 861.

56. William Shonick, *Government and Health Services: Government's Role in the Development of U.,S. Health Services, 1930–1980* (New York: Oxford University Press, 1995): 137.

57. All veterans' organizations, particularly the American Legion, aware that extra beds would go to veterans with non-service-connected problems, have engaged in an ongoing campaign for more hospital facilities.

58. Louis M. Orr, ' To Socialized Medicine', 861.

59. At a projected cost of $4000 per bed in construction costs, $400, in equipment costs, and $950 in annual operating costs, all, of course, in 1937 dollars. United States Veterans Administration, *Annual Report, 1937*, 3–4, cited in Dillingham, *Federal Aid to Veterans*, 109.

60. Veterans Administration, *Annual Report of the Administrator of Veterans' Affairs, 1944* (Washington, DC: Government Printing Office, 1944): 2.

61. The Hearst organization quickly assigned three full-time reporters to the project. Rumer, *The American Legion*, 245. Hearst was strongly opposed to Roosevelt's postwar international designs and apparently thought that if Congress could be persuaded to set up an elaborate benefits program for returning veterans, they would be less likely to appropriate funds for economic assistance to liberated countries. See Michael J. Bennett, *When Dreams Came True: The GI Bill and the Making of Modern America* (Washington, DC: Brassey's, 1996): 77.

62. According to one Gallup Poll, over 81 percent of Americans favored granting a bonus to returning veterans. Bennett, *When Dreams Came True*, 78.
63. In January 1942 the NRPB was ordered by President Roosevelt to prepare a document that would create new 'freedoms' applicable to all Americans to be added to the Bill of Rights, including the 'right' to fair pay, the 'right' to adequate food, a 'decent home', 'adequate medical care', to 'rest, recreation, and adventure', to 'adequate protection from the economic fears of old age, sickness, accident, and unemployment', and the right to a 'good' education. Otis L. Graham, Jr and Meghan Robinson Wander, eds, *Franklin D. Roosevelt: His Life and Times* (Boston, MA: G. K. Hall & Co., 1985): *s.v.* 'Planning'. The NRPB, with Roosevelt's help, did in fact draft such a document which Roosevelt later used in his 1944 State of the Union address, outlining a new economic Bill of Rights which was to be achieved through government. See Goodwin, *No Ordinary Time*, 485–6, and Frank Freidel, *Franklin D. Roosevelt: Rendezvous With Destiny* (Boston, MA: Little, Brown and Co., 1990): 500. In response to further prompting from the President, a yet more ambitious proposal was put forward by the NRPB in March 1943. Fearful of being outdone by Britain's Beveridge Report, the NRPB developed a comprehensive plan for extensive cradle-to-grave social security measures, most of which would be under the control of the federal government. Bennett, *When Dreams Came True*, 82–3, 87.
64. Radio broadcast of 28 July 1943, 'First Crack in the Axis', quoted in Bennett, *When Dreams Came True*, 88.
65. The original scheme provided that they be forced to remain in the military until they could be reabsorbed into civilian life. See Bennett, *When Dreams Came True*, 85–6.
66. The Hearst papers consistently placed passage of a veterans' bill alongside Roosevelt's international concerns, particularly the President's support for appropriations for the United Nations Relief and Rehabilitation Administration. Bennett describes one cartoon that ran in all the Hearst newspapers on 29 December 1943. 'Under the title "Merely Our Son" is shown a disabled veteran, with one foot gone, supporting himself on crutches and looking into a store window with a sign, "Ye New Deal Globaloney Shoppe: Goodies for Good Neighbors"'. *When Dreams Came True*, 101.
67. Indeed, the measure provided the most comprehensive package of benefits ever offered veterans of any country. Among its other provisions were the provision of medical and hospital care, readjustment allowances and compensation for temporary unemployment, home loan guarantees, vocational and on-the-job training, and loans for farming and small businesses.
68. 'National service', the President observed, 'has proven to be a unifying moral force – based on an equal and comprehensive legal obligation of all people in a nation at war'. 'Annual Address to Congress, January 11, 1944', in J.B.S. Hardman, *Rendezvous with Destiny* (New York: The Dryden Press, 1944): 230. The President's wife had been a longtime advocate of national service. In March 1942. after having attended a White House conference on manpower needs, she announced: 'I've come to one clear decision, namely that all of us – men in the services and women at home – should be drafted and told what is the job we are to do. So long as we are left to volunteer we are bound to waste our capacities and do things that are not necessary.' ' My Day' (Eleanor Roosevelt's daily newspaper column), 10 March 1942, quoted in Doris Kearns Goodwin, *No Ordinary Time: Franklin and Eleanor Roosevelt: The Home Front in World War II* (New York: Simon & Schuster, 1994): 331.
69. Perhaps nothing better reflects the totalitarian instincts shared by many during World War II than the fact that Roosevelt's proposals were embraced by a large number of educated Americans. Thus, the *New York Times* editorialized that a national service act was both fair and proper and 'in the spirit of democracy', 12 January 1944, p. 22.
70. Quoted in Bennett, *When Dreams Came True*, 148.
71. Even in an age of racism and open bigotry, Rankin stood out. He regarded communism as a creature of international Jewry and viewed blacks as subhuman and incapable of caring for themselves. One of the leading supporters of the House Un-American Activities Committee, Rankin responded to Walter Winchell's reservations about the work of the Committee by referring to Winchell as 'a little slime-mongering kike'. Rankin served 16

terms in Congress, representing the white population of his district in Mississippi. His distrust of government control of the means of production apparently did not extend to the generation and distribution of electric power inasmuch as he co-authored the bill creating the Tennessee Valley Authority.

72. Quoted in Bennett, *When Dreams Came True*, 150.

73. Ibid., 148.

74. Maisel's article was reprinted in the *Readers Digest* in April 1945. See Severo and Milford, *The Wages of War*, 304–5. Maisel's article was especially critical of the VA hospitals at Castle Point, New York, and Dayton, Ohio. The April 1945 of *Harpers* also ran a critical article, detailing the bureaucratic maze veterans just entering civilian life were forced to thread before receiving benefits.

75. Severo and Milford, *The Wages of War*, 306.

76. The Legion was concerned that placing veterans in private hospitals would become more common, thus 'diminishing the medical professionalism of the VA' and 'hindering the special medical and neuropsychological needs of veterans'. Rumer, *The American Legion*, 264.

77. See *The New York Times*, 2 February 1946. The statement is quoted in Rumer, *The American Legion*, 265. The acrimony between Bradley and Stelle was compounded by the fact that the VA had disregarded Stelle's suggestion that a new VA hospital be constructed in Decatur, Illinois, Stelle's hometown. Fearful that he had overstepped the bounds of legitimate criticism of the Veterans Administration and would lose support among his own legionnaires, Stelle later denied that his intent was to recommend that Bradley be replaced as Administrator.

78. Rumer, *The American Legion*, 268.

79. It was estimated that the number of living veterans, together with their dependents, amounted to almost 40 percent of the population of the United States.

80. This list of VA programs appears in Rumer, *The American Legion*, 310–11.

81. These data come from the Veterans Administration, *Annual Report, 1950* (Washington, DC: Government Printing Office, 1951): *passim*.

82. Within a few weeks of Japan's surrender in August 1945 members of the armed forces were being discharged at the rate of 100 000 per month. By the end of 1946, 9 million of the 12 million soldiers and sailors on active duty had been mustered out and by 1948 the army had been reduced from its high of 8 000 000 to 550 000. Bennett, *When Dreams Came True*, 5.

83. Supplement on 'Big Government: Can It Be Managed Efficiently? [A Digest of the Reports of the Commission on Organization of the Executive Branch of Government]' *Fortune* (May 1949): Supplement, 4.

84. Quoted in *Fortune*, Supplement, 2.

85. It should be underscored that the mandate of the Commission was not to recommend ways in which the federal government's powers could be curtailed but rather to deal exclusively with questions of organization and procedure. The sheer amount of government intrusion was not at issue and was scrupulously avoided by the Commission's membership.

86. 'Digest', *Fortune*, Supplement, 23.

87. 'Digest', *Fortune*, Supplement, 21.

88. Frank Gervasi, *Big Government: The Meaning and Purpose of the Hoover Commission Report* (Westport, Conn.: Greenwood Press, 1949): 177–8.

89. 'Digest', *Fortune*, Supplement, 22.

90. 'Digest', *Fortune*, Supplement, 22. Details of the proposed UMA can be found in Gervasi, *Big Government*, 176–90.

91. Ralph Godwin, who served on the National Executive Committee, quoted in Rumer, *The American Legion*, 313.

92. Rumer, *The American Legion*, 309.

93. In addition to recommending that the VA's medical functions be transferred to a new United Medical Administration, the Hoover Commission also proposed that a new government corporation be established to administer veterans' insurance.

94. Quoted in Rumer, *The American Legion*, 310.

95. The ostensible reason for this reduction was the fact that Congress had ordered a pay increase for federal employees but had failed to appropriate sufficient additional funds to the VA to offset these additional expenses.

96. Under the Reorganization Acts of 1945 and 1949, which granted to President Truman reorganizational authority for the executive branch, Truman submitted a series of Reorganization Plans to the House Committee on Expenditures, one of which – Number 27 – called for the creation of a cabinet-level agency, the Department of Health, Education, and Security, which would have taken over responsibility for veterans' affairs. The Legion feared that the creation of such an agency, whether or not the UMA was established, would almost certainly lead to a weakening of the Legion's influence and to a de-emphasis of the importance of veterans' benefits and their eventual loss.

97. Quoted in Rumer, *The American Legion*, 315.

98. Quoted in Rumer, *The American Legion*, 313.

99. The Hoover Commission Report noted that the 'VA has the advantage, from the viewpoint of the veterans' groups, of being deliberately designed to aid veterans as a special class'. Gervasi, *Big Government*, 181.

100. A Gallup poll taken in March 1950 found that only 31 percent of those polled were familiar with the details of the Hoover Report. Among those, however, more than 92 percent supported the recommendations. Even among the 69 percent who were uninformed about the Report's specific proposals, an overwhelming number supported the Commission's stated goals: to reduce the amount of waste and increase the efficiency of the federal government. Rumer, *The American Legion*, 315.

101. Herbert Hoover, 'The Reform of Government: The Burden Now Shifts from the Commission to the New Citizens Committee', *Fortune* (May 1949): 73.

102. Rumer, *The American Legion*, 318.

103. Ibid., 323.

104. Gervasi, *Big Government*, 186.

105. It had never been the case that veterans whose service was limited to peacetime received the same benefits as those who served in time of war. See *The Historical Development of Veterans' Benefits*, *passim*. This was to change when the draft officially ended on 31 December 1972, after which benefits were extended to all veterans by a series of Congressional acts.

106. The American Legion, in lobbying for an extension of benefits to veterans of the Korean conflict, had publicized several stories of Korean War veterans who had been refused hospital treatment at VA facilities for ailments that were service-related. One such case, reputed to have occurred on 9 May 1951, involved a 21-year-old Korean War veteran who sought to be admitted to the VA hospital in Tucson, Arizona, but was refused admission since he was regarded as 'a peacetime soldier', no formal declaration of war having been made by Congress. 'Under the present setup', the director of the Tucson hospital is reputed to have said, 'no returned veteran from Korea is eligible for hospital benefits unless he had been discharged from the service because of a duty disability'. The effect of such propaganda was quick passage of legislation extending benefits to Korean war veterans, which passed Congress on 11 May. Rumer, *The American Legion*, 347–8.

107. Quoted in Rumer, *The American Legion*, 350–51.

108. Rumer, *The American Legion*, 353.

109. Ibid., 355. The Legion had coined the term 'slide rule hospital care' to refer to the type of economic calculation of costs undertaken by the Hoover Commission and the Bureau of the Budget. Such calculations, they maintained, showed little appreciation for the 'human' side of the needs of disabled veterans.

110. Peri E. Arnold, *Making the Managerial Presidency: Comprehensive Reorganization Planning, 1905–1980* (Princeton, NJ: Princeton University Press, 1986): 167–8.

111. By this point in his career, Hoover's sense of self-importance had grown to the point where he demanded the kind of deference he had been denied since Roosevelt's election victory in 1932. He insisted that he be personally named as chairman by Eisenhower and he was given a crucial voice in recommending the other commissioners. Arnold, *Making the Managerial Presidency*, 169–70.

112. The Commission created a series of investigative committees, among them a Task Force on Medical Services, under the chairmanship of Dr Theodore G. Klumpp, president of Winthrop Laboratories, at the time one of the country's largest pharmaceutical firms. The task force was authorized to study the more than 60 federal agencies then operating in the medical and health areas and make appropriate recommendations.

113. Neil MacNeil and Harold W. Metz, *The Hoover Report, 1953–1955: What it Means to You as Citizen and Taxpayer* (New York: The Macmillan Co., 1956): 178–9.

114. MacNeil and Metz, *The Hoover Report*, 179.

115. This reached the extreme of 16.1 days in army hospitals. MacNeil and Metz, *The Hoover Report*, 180.

116. Commission on Organization of the Executive Branch of the Government, *Federal Medical Services*, A Report to the Congress, February, 1955 (Washington, DC: Government Printing Office, 1955): 19.

117. MacNeil and Metz, *The Hoover Report*, 183.

118. Ibid., 184.

119. Citizens Committee for the Hoover Report, *Digests and Analyses of the Nineteen Hoover Commission Reports* (Washington, DC: Citizens Committee for the Hoover Report, 1955): 24.

120. Citizens Committee for the Hoover Report, *Digests and Analyses*, 24.

121. MacNeil and Metz, *The Hoover Report*, 184–5.

122. Ibid., 192–3. The figures are impressive. In 1954, the federal government employed 10 percent of the nation's active physicians, 9 percent of its active dentists, and 6 percent of its active graduate nurses. Thirteen percent of all hospital beds were in federal hospitals, which admitted 7 percent of the nation's hospital patients. Citizens' Committee for the Hoover Report, *Digests and Analyses*, 22.

123. Citizens Committee for the Hoover Report, *Digests and Analyses*, 25.

124. MacNeil and Metz, *The Hoover Report*, 193.

125. Rumer, *The American Legion*, 377.

126. Arnold, *Making the Managerial Presidency*, 200.

127. Shonick, *Government and Health Services*, 148

128. Administrator of Veterans Affairs, *Annual Report, 1946* (Washington, DC: Government Printing Office, 1947): 3. This change in the status of the VA's professional employees, while welcomed by the medical profession, was criticized for not going far enough since it did not remove from the Civil Service system the host of auxiliary personnel, including clinical psychologists, dietitians, physical and occupational therapists, social workers, and laboratory and x-ray technicians of various types. See Roy R. Kracke, 'The Medical Care of the Veteran', *JAMA*, 143(15) (12 August 1950): 1323.

129. Administrator of Veterans Affairs, *Annual Report, 1969* (Washington, DC: Government Printing Office, 1970): 42–4. With particular regard to nursing, the number of nursing trainees increased from 6238 in 1966 to 14 191 in 1969, at which time the VA acted as a training ground for over 20 percent of all nurses enrolled full-time in graduate study.

130. House Committee on Veterans' Affairs, *Medical Care of Veterans* (90th Congress, 1st Session, Committee Print No. 4) (Washington, DC: Government Printing Office, 1967): 332.

131. The affiliation served the interests of both the VA and the nation's medical schools. The VA sought to acquire qualified physicians in order to deal with the major increase in its patient load as a consequence of World War II. The medical schools were equally desirous of expanding residency training to accommodate the increased postwar demand from the large number of physicians who had entered the military during the war without having had specialty training. Committee on Health-Care Resources in the Veterans' Administration, Assembly of Life Sciences, National Research Council, *Health Care for American Veterans* (Washington, DC: National Academy of Sciences, 1977): 242.

132. See, among others, 'Cranston Assails VA Hospitals' Lack of Care: Tragic Conditions Held Result of False Economy Measures by Government', *Los Angeles Times*, 10 January 1970; 'New VA Facilities' (editorial), *Los Angeles Times*, 26 January 1970; 'Improving Veterans' Medical Care' (editorial), *Los Angeles Times*, 29 August 1970; 'Two Doctors Hit Care at Veterans Hospital Here', *Los Angeles Times*, 29 August 1970.

133. 'VA Hospitals Provide Inadequate Care to Women, Study Says', *Washington Post*, 24 June 1993. There even exists a website, the Veterans' Alliance for Competent Medical Care, created by critical veterans, for the lodging of complaints against the health care treatment accorded by the VA. See http://www.vamc.com (accessed 21 July 1999).
134. National Research Council, *Health Care for American Veterans*, 271.
135. In February 1976, the VA was operating a total of 214 multipurpose outpatient clinics and most were in the VA's 171 hospitals. Only 32 hospitals had geographically separated multi-purpose satellite outpatient clinics. National Research Council, *Health Care for American Veterans*, 114.
136. National Research Council, *Health Care for American Veterans*, 115. The report goes on to note that 'Because most outpatient clinics are part of a hospital, and because average daily patient census is the prime 'workload' indicator used to determine a hospital's budget, there are strong indications that utilization of outpatient facilities is correlated with a hospital's inpatient admission and retention policies more closely than with the medical needs of the patients who apply for care' (p. 115).
137. Administrator of Veterans' Affairs, *Annual Report, 1974* (Washington, DC: Government Printing Office, 1974): 13.
138. P.L. 94-581, the Veterans' Omnibus Health Care Act of 1976. Administrator of Veterans' Affairs, *Annual Report, 1977* (Washington, DC: Government Printing Office, 1977): 7.
139. National Research Council, *Health Care for American Veterans*, 118. Approximately 69 percent of the outpatients were unemployed and only 21 percent were employed full-time.
140. National Research Council, *Health Care for American Veterans*, 116.
141. The number of outpatients treated increased by 4.48 percent between 1977 and 1982, while during the same period the number of patients admitted to VA hospitals increased by 5.45 percent.
142. Some years later, Dr Joseph McNinch, then the chief medical director of the VA, clearly overcome by the importance of dental care, was moved to note: 'The oral cavity, with its many functions, plays a very important part in a patient's physical, mental, and social well-being'. Quoted in Committee on Veterans Affairs, *Medical Care of Veterans*, 329.
143. Dillingham, *Federal Aid to Veterans*, 66.
144. Ibid., 66–7.
145. Administrator of Veterans Affairs, *Annual Report, 1943* (Washington, DC: Government Printing Office, 1944): 11.
146. Administrator of Veterans Affairs, *Annual Report, 1948* (Washington, DC: Government Printing Office, 1949): 19. Approximately $75 000 was spent for similar services in 1941.
147. P.L. 84-83, enacted on 16 June 1955.
148. Administrator of Veterans Affairs, *Annual Report, 1955* (Washington, DC: Government Printing Office, 1956): 58.
149. P.L. 87-583, enacted on 14 August 1962.
150. Committee on Veterans Affairs, *Medical Care of Veterans*, 331.
151. American Research Council, *Health Care for American Veterans*, 198–201. Pilot studies made in the 1960s indicated that approximately 50 percent of the newly hospitalized VA patients had not been treated by any dentist, government or private, for more than five years. The average patient examined required the extraction of more than three infected teeth. Committee on Veterans' Affairs, *Medical Care of Veterans*, 331.
152. Indeed, in 1979, as a result of new legislation (P.L. 96-22) some 35 000 veterans, those who had been prisoners of war for more than 180 days, were made eligible for VA dental treatment. See Administrator of Veterans Affairs, *Annual Report, 1980* (Washington, DC: Government Printing Office, 1980): 23.
153. Secretary of Veterans Affairs, *Annual Report, 1997* (Washington, DC: Government Printing Office, 1997): 70 (Table 8). Of these 247 477 were of inpatients, while 817 413 were outpatient visits.
154. The Report of the National Academy of Sciences' Committee on Health-Care Resources in the Veterans' Administration, prepared in 1977, concluded that 'about half the patients in acute medical beds, one-third of the patients in surgical beds, and well over half the

patients in psychiatric beds do not require – and are not receiving – the acute care services associated with these types of beds'. National Research Council, *Health Care for American Veterans*, 271.

155. P.L. 88-450. The President had earlier in 1964 called on the VA to develop a nursing-care program.

156. At the same time, the VA instituted a reimbursement program to State and private nursing homes for nursing bed care provided to eligible veterans. Administrator of Veterans Affairs, *Annual Report, 1965* (Washington, DC: Government Printing Office, 1966): 30–31.

157. According to the Committee on Health Care Resources, it was likely that at least 10 000 more patients who at the time were in VA general and psychiatric hospitals would have been more appropriately placed in nursing-home care beds. National Research Council, *Health Care for American Veterans*, 209. 'Long-term care beds' here include patients who were held in 'intermediate care' facilities, that is, facilities that accommodated patients who required more care than would be available in a nursing home but less than in an acute-care hospital.

158. National Research Council, *Health Care for American Veterans*, 216. According to the same study, the quality of care in the VA's intermediate care facilities was substantially worse, with 100 percent of the patients receiving inadequate care.

159. 'Medical and Dental Care Summary, Fiscal Year 1997', in Department of Veterans Affairs. *Summary of Medical Programs*, Table 1 (cited 4 August 1999), available from the World Wide Web at http://www.va.gov:80/sumedpr/fy97/f4s9701.htm

160. See Table 3.10.

161. These annual hospital censuses were based on a 20 percent sample of the VA hospital population. Administrator of Veterans Affairs, *Annual Report, 1974* (Washington, DC: Government Printing Office, 1975): 20.

162. P.L. 89-358: 3 March 1966.

163. Office of Public Affairs, Department of Veterans Affairs, *VA History in Brief* (Washington, DC: Office of Public Affairs, n.d.): 19.

164. The average age of American veterans, however, continued to increase. See Table 3.10.

165. Administrator of Veterans Affairs, *Annual Report, 1978* (Washington, DC: Government Printing Office, 1979): 13.

166. Nor did Medicare provide the costs of inpatient psychiatric care nor, at the time, any of the costs of prescription drugs. The effect was that a large proportion of Medicare-eligible veterans with lower incomes made use of VA facilities. See General Accounting Office, 'Veterans' Health Care: Use of VA Services by Medicare-Eligible Veterans', Report to the Chairman, Subcommittee on Oversight and Investigations, Committee on Veterans' Affairs, House of Representatives (October 1994) GAO/HEHS-95-13: 2.

167. 'Veterans' Health Care: Challenges for the Future', Statement of David P. Baine, Director, Health, Education, and Human Services Division, General Accounting Office: Testimony before the Subcommittee on Hospitals and Health Care, Committee on Veterans Affairs, House of Representatives (27 June 1996) GAO/T-HEHS-96-172: 1–2.

168. The increase in nursing-home patients and outpatient visits is shown in Tables 3.14 and 3.15. It appears that the VA was also treating a not insignificant number of people ineligible for VA medical care. In a study conducted by the Comptroller General for Senator William Proxmire's office it was found that during a 27-month period prior to January 1980 the Veterans Administration attempted to collect $15 000 000 from persons who had received medical treatment but who were ineligible for such benefits. Of this amount only $1 200 000 was in fact recovered and an additional $6 500 000 was written off as uncollectible. General Accounting Office, 'Cost of VA Medical Care to Ineligible Persons is High and Difficult to Recover', Report to the Honorable William Proxmire, United States Senate (2 July 1981) HRD-81-77.

169. P.L. 93-82 (September 1973).

170. The Department of Defense program, the Civilian Health and Medical Program, was known by its acronym CHAMPUS.

171. Administrator of Veterans Affairs, *Annual Report, 1975* (Washington, DC: Government Printing Office, 1976): 13.

172. See Thomas Rumer, *The American Legion, passim*, but esp. 504–35. Additionally, in the spring of 1987, the Legion was able to prevail on Congress and the President to enact a permanent GI Bill, the so-called Montgomery GI Bill, named after the Democratic representative from Mississippi, G.V. Montgomery, who had worked tirelessly for its passage, which granted to all veterans, whether or not they had volunteered for military service and whether they had served in combat or not, the benefits accorded the first beneficiaries of the GI Bill.
173. Thomas Rumer, *The American Legion*, 506–8.
174. P.L. 99-272.
175. Administrator of Veterans Affairs, *Annual Report, 1987* (Washington, DC: Government Printing Office, 1988): 16–17. Fiscal year 1987 was the first year in which means-test data were collected on all outpatients, inpatients, and applicants for medical care. VA statistics show that 95.5 percent of its medical workload consisted of Category A veterans, while Categories B and C each comprised 2.5 percent of the workload.
176. Quoted in Thomas Rumer, *The American Veterans*, 518.
177. Senate Committee on Governmental Affairs, *Proposals to Elevate the Veterans' Administration to Cabinet-Level Status*, 100th Congress, 1st and 2nd Sessions, 9 December 1987 and 15, 28 March 1988 (S. Hrg. 100-670): 9.
178. Senate Committee on Governmental Affairs, *Proposals to Elevate the Veterans Administration*, 105–9.
179. Quoted in Thomas Rumer, *The American Legion*, 526.
180. P.L. 100-527 (25 October 1988).
181. An additional 20 000 patients were admitted to other hospitals through the VA on a fee basis.
182. These data appear in Issue Briefs, 'VA Medical Care FY 2000 Funding', in Association of American Medical Colleges (cited 21 July 1999) available from the World Wide Web at http://www.aamc.org/advocacy/issues/approps/vacare00.htm. See also the House Committee on Appropriations, *Report on the Departments of Veterans Affairs and Housing and Urban Development, and Independent Agencies Appropriations Bill, 2000*, 106th Congress, 1st session (3 August 1999), Report No. 106-286: 4, 9–14.
183. The Secretary of Veterans Affairs, *Annual Report, 1997* (Washington, DC: Government Printing Office, 1998): 95–6 (Tables 22 and 23).
184. General Accounting Office, 'Veterans Health Care: Use of VA Services by Medicare-Eligible Veterans', 2.
185. John K. Inglehart, 'Reform of the Veterans Affairs Health Care System', *New England Journal of Medicine* (31 October 1996): 335(18): 2.
186. General Accounting Office, 'Substance Abuse Treatment: VA Programs Serve Psychologically and Economically Disadvantaged Veterans', Report to the Chairman, Committee on Veterans Affairs, United States Senate (5 November 1997) HEHS 97-6.
187. Department of Veterans Affairs, *Homelessness Among Veterans* (cited 22 August 1999), available from the World Wide Web at http://www.va.gov:80/health/homeless/index.htm. About 45 percent are estimated to be suffering from mental illness and (with considerable overlap) slightly more than 70 percent suffer from alcohol or other drug abuse problems. Roughly 56 percent are Black or Hispanic.
188. 'Special VA Homeless Assistance Programs and Initiatives', in Department of Veterans Affairs, *Homelessness Among Veterans* (cited 22 August 1999), available from the World Wide Web at http://www.va.gov:80/health/homeless/AssistProg.htm.
189. House Subcommittee on Health, Committee on Veterans Affairs, 'Statement of Thomas L. Garthwaite, M.D., Deputy Under Secretary for Health, Department of Veterans Affairs', in *VHA Capital Asset Management*, 106th Congress, 1st Session (10 March 1999).
190. The VHA's restructuring is discussed in great detail in Kenneth W. Kizer, *Vision for Change: A Plan to Restructure the Veterans Health Administration* (Washington, DC, March 1995).
191. These data are taken from the testimony of Thomas L. Garthwaite, Deputy Under Secretary for Health, Department of Veterans Health, before the House Subcommittee on Health, Committee on Veterans Affairs.

192. These include World War I and Mexican border veterans, veterans receiving care for disorders associated with exposure to toxic substances or environmental hazards while in service and compensable zero percent service-connected veterans.

193. General Accounting Office, 'Veterans' Health Care: Challenges for the Future', Testimony of David P. Baine, Director, Health Care Delivery and Quality Issues of the GAO to the Subcommittee on Hospitals and Health Care, House Committee on Veterans Affairs (27 June 1996), GAO/T-HEHS-96-172: 15–16.

194. General Accounting Office, 'Veterans Health Care: Challenges for the Future', 16.

4. The National Institutes of Health

One of the earliest goals of the American Public Health Association, formed in 1872 to advance the field of 'sanitary science' through extensive government regulation of all matters pertaining to the health and safety of Americans, was the creation of a cabinet-level department of public health. At the Association's first annual meeting in 1873, one speaker called for the establishment of a National Sanitary Bureau and this view was echoed at the 1875 annual meeting of the American Medical Association.[1] Its supporters regarded 'continuous scientific investigations' as a primary function of such a department and, toward this end, the forerunner of the Public Health Service, the Marine Hospital Service, formally established a Hygienic Laboratory for medical research in New York in August 1887.

In 1883 Congress had empowered the Marine Hospital Service (MHS), the forerunner of the Public Health Service, to quarantine foreign ships seeking entry into American ports if there was indication that any passenger harbored an infectious disease. As a consequence the MHS set up a bacteriological laboratory at the Marine Hospital on Staten Island and it was this research facility that served as the foundation of the Hygienic Laboratory established in Washington, DC four years later. As its first director, the Supervising Surgeon, John B. Hamilton, chose Dr Joseph J. Kinyoun, who had studied with Pasteur and Koch in Europe. In 1887 and 1888 Kinyoun isolated *Vibrio cholera* from immigrants at Ellis Island but the imposition of a strict quarantine appears to have prevented the entry of the disease into New York City.[2]

The ongoing struggle between officials of the Service, who argued for expansion of their bureau into a full-fledged cabinet department, and those who supported the establishment of a completely separate agency to oversee all health matters[3] contributed to delaying federal funding for medical research. However, the contributions of the Hygienic Laboratory to the war effort during the Spanish-American War led many Congressmen to view an expansion of the functions of the Marine Hospital Service far more favorably than they had earlier. During the conflict the Laboratory had been primarily employed to diagnose possible cases of infectious diseases, particularly typhoid fever, among American troops returning to the United States.[4] The Supervising Surgeon[5] was able to harness the goodwill the Service had built up in Congress to the point where, in 1901, Congress officially recognized the

Hygienic Laboratory by appropriating $35 000 for the construction of a laboratory in Washington, DC, and authorizing it to investigate the nature of infectious and contagious diseases.[6]

The Laboratory was given further recognition by Congress in the following year when the Marine Hospital Service was reorganized and its functions enlarged. One of the more powerful members of the Senate Committee on Public Health and National Quarantine, John C. Spooner of Wisconsin, dismayed that medical scientists disagreed on the causes and nature of certain diseases, seized on the suggestion of a prominent Washington physician that the Hygienic Laboratory assume the role of determining the orthodox official view on scientific matters having to do with medicine, thus doing away with conflicting and confusing claims.[7] Dr C. Lloyd Magruder, Dean of the Medical School at Georgetown University, advised Spooner: 'Let us have a clearing house; the hygienic laboratory should be the clearing house. We have some of the greatest scientists in the country connected with the Government today and if you make a clearing house of that hygienic laboratory, composed of the best scientists of the Government, with some men from outside, you will get something that can not be attacked.'[8] Spooner instructed Walter Wyman to draft new legislation reforming the Service as a whole and the Hygienic Laboratory in particular. As a result, the bill enacted in 1902 provided for a thorough reorganization of the Service and called for the creation of a new Division of Scientific Research, whose function was to coordinate all the Service's research activities.[9] Another provision of the Act, aimed at integrating the work of the Laboratory with medical research done elsewhere, established an eight-member Advisory Board, whose function was to bring the work undertaken by the Laboratory 'into scientific touch' with private research.

Doubtless Congress was encouraged to extend formal recognition to the Hygienic Laboratory because of the successes of European, particularly German, laboratories during the last decades of the nineteenth century in uncovering the microbial causes of a host of diseases, among them typhoid, malaria, tuberculosis, diphtheria, dysentery, tetanus, and cholera. Nor was the Hygienic Laboratory the first bacteriological laboratory established in the United States. In 1892 William H. Park had set up a microbiological laboratory in New York City which undertook work on the problems associated with a number of diseases and in 1888 public health laboratories were created in Providence, Rhode Island, and in Michigan.[10]

The 1902 statute created three new divisions within the Hygienic Laboratory alongside the existing Division of Pathology and Bacteriology, those of Chemistry, Pharmacology, and Zoology. When the Laboratory had initially been established in 1887, its sole full-time staff member was its Director, Dr Joseph Kinyoun, and this remained the case for the next decade.[11]

To staff these new Divisions, the 1902 Act empowered the Service to hire scientists who were not, like the Service's other staff, members of the PH-MHS Commissioned Officers Corps.[12] While it was proposed that Civil Service employees be provided with military ranks in time of war, the suggestion was rejected by Congress who wanted to avoid any implication that the Service would receive military status.

On the same day in 1902 that President Theodore Roosevelt had signed the legislation reorganizing the Marine Hospital Service, he signed a second act whose goal was 'to regulate the sale of viruses, serums, toxins, and analogous products in the District of Columbia' and 'to regulate the interstate traffic in such articles'.[13] Apparently there had been complaints from physicians that some biological preparations sold in the District were contaminated and these complaints had reached the ear of Zachariah T. Sowers, the personal physician to several political figures. Sowers was successful in gaining passage of the bill. Having passed the committees responsible for the District of Columbia, the 57th Congress was prevailed upon to enact the Biologic Control Act which granted to the Hygienic Laboratory authority to administer the new law. While the ostensible problem which the legislation addressed was a local one, Congress decided to extend the legislation to include interstate commerce in these items.[14]

The research undertaken by the Hygienic Laboratory following passage of the 1902 legislation was mainly in the areas of zoology and bacteriology. Wardell Stiles, who had been appointed director of the new Division of Zoology in August 1902, embarked on an ambitious program of identification and classification of insects, parasites, and protozoa that eventuated in the publication of the Laboratory's highly regarded *Index-Catalog of Medical and Veterinary Zoology*. The main focus of Laboratory research, however, was in the area of bacteriology, where efforts were concentrated on infectious diseases. Laboratory scientists were successful in identifying the bacteria responsible for tularemia and undulant fever and in advancing the study of typhoid fever.

During its first decade the Laboratory suffered under a number of constraints that limited its size and area of research. It was by law limited to investigating infectious and contagious diseases and its budget was not separated from that of the other Service's expenditures until 1907. In that year it was allocated $15 000.00 and had a total staff, including technicians, clerks, and laboratory aides, of 32.[15] These limitations prevented the Laboratory's staff from initiating open-ended research programs and undertaking major projects, especially those whose focus touched on areas outside those mandated by law.

Pressure to expand the activities of the Hygienic Laboratory was particularly great in the first decades of the new century, which was marked by a

Progressivist mentality that embraced government regulation and social planning on a massive scale and that distrusted private solutions to social problems. The Hygienic Laboratory had, as early as 1902, been authorized to regulate the interstate commerce of sera, vaccines, and toxins by the Biologic Control Act, thus making it one of the first federal regulatory agencies. The Laboratory's Division of Pathology and Bacteriology conducted regular inspections of laboratories manufacturing these products and issued licenses to firms that met the Laboratory's standards. This regulatory function soon involved the Laboratory in evaluating new products. The end result of these activities was that the Laboratory's researchers became engaged in a series of investigations which apparently went beyond the Act's authorization. In some areas which clearly went beyond what Congress intended, the Laboratory was encouraged by the American Medical Association (AMA). In some outbreaks of typhoid fever, for example, the Laboratory had determined that polluted water was at fault and this, in turn, led to a more extensive investigation of the nation's waterways. To this research the AMA lent its strongest support, calling on the Public Health Service to 'formulate and enforce necessary regulations to prevent pollution of the waterways'.[16]

In addition to being confronted with problems of this sort, the Public Health and Marine Hospital Service was, during this period, using its most strenuous efforts in lobbying Congress to change the Service into a cabinet-level national department of health. In this the Service was able to enlist the assistance of a large number of organizations and men distinguished in their field, including two prominent Yale University economists, J. Pease Norton and Irving Fisher. Both Norton and Fisher regarded the costs of illness and premature death as a wasteful drain on the economy that could easily be reversed through government intervention and called for creation of a central federal agency manned by experts to oversee the nation's health.[17] In 1906 the American Association for the Advancement of Science (AAAS) appointed a Committee of One Hundred on National Health[18] for the purpose of promoting legislation to that effect. Three years later the Committee's president, Irving Fisher, issued a report on the need for a national health department under which 'American vitality may reach its maximum development'. 'It is', he continued, 'both bad policy and bad economy to leave this work mainly to the weak and spasmodic efforts of charity, or to the philanthropy of physicians'.[19]

The Committee of One Hundred was able to assemble endorsements from both major political parties, including state governors and state and federal legislators. In addition, leaders of the Grange, of organizations representing labor and industry, and officials from the nation's boards of health, all supported the establishment of a new cabinet post. Indeed, so popular was the notion that it appeared almost certain that a federal Department of Health would shortly be created.[20] The Committee's proposal was enthusiastically endorsed by the Democrats and less intensely by the Republicans in the election of 1908 and was recommended by President Theodore Roosevelt in his last message to Congress.[21] However, forces supporting a Department were split over whether it should take the form of an entirely new bureaucratic entity or whether the Public Health and Marine Hospital Service should serve as the nucleus around which a larger department would be created. In addition, the proposal was not without opposition. The National League for Medical Freedom, representing practitioners and defenders of the various heterodox medical treatments,[22] rightly saw in a national Department of Health a threat to the recognition they had won from some states. The League claimed a membership of almost 70 000, including Clara Barton of the Red Cross, and was represented by John L. Bates, a former governor of Massachusetts. Irving Fisher was to accuse the League of being funded by patent medicine interests but it does not appear that this was ever proven.[23] In addition, the Anti-Vivisection League and the Christian Science Church strongly protested against any form of federal health reorganization.[24] Finally, the Service's Surgeon-General, Walter Wyman, fearful that raising the Service to cabinet level would dilute his own personal power and prestige within the Treasury Department, the home of the PH-MHS, opposed any change in status.[25]

It was soon apparent that the cabinet would not be expanded. During the second session of the 61st Congress, Senator Robert L. Owen, progressive Democrat of Oklahoma, introduced a bill to establish a Department of Public Health. Toward this end, a parade of distinguished public health officials and physicians representing a broad array of organizations were brought before Congress to support the measure during hearings on the bill in 1910. Among the arguments put forward against the bill was that the agency under consideration was delegated powers beyond those permitted to Congress by the Constitution.[26] And H. L. Gordon, another spokesman for the League, pointed to the invasion of privacy likely to follow upon passage of the measure, which, he feared, 'would open the door of every home in this country' and would authorize the new agency 'to investigate any personal disease or personal sickness, wherever it may be'.[27] In addition, the League encouraged those who embraced its views to bombard the relevant members of Congress with letters and telegrams opposing the new Department. The effect of all this was that the Owens bill was tabled in the House Committee on Interstate and Foreign Commerce in early 1911, where it died.[28]

In its place, Senator Duncan V. Fletcher (Democrat from Florida) and Representatives William Richardson (Democrat from Alabama) and William C. Adamson (Democrat from Georgia) introduced legislation expanding the Service and shortening its name to the Public Health Service to reflect the Service's main concern. The act further authorized the Service to publish information 'for the use of the public' and, most importantly, granted the

Service the authority to 'investigate the diseases of man and conditions influencing the propagation and spread thereof, including sanitation and sewage and the pollution either directly or indirectly of the navigable streams and lakes of the United States'.[29]

Passage of the 1912 law did not, however, put an end to attempts to create a Department of Health. Senator Owen, an indefatigable proponent of the new cabinet position, continued to introduce bills toward this end, with support from Senator Joseph E. Ransdell, Democrat of Louisiana, who was chairman of the Senate Committee on Public Health and National Quarantine. While conditions for passage were somewhat improved with the death of Surgeon General Wyman,[30] the Committee of One Hundred had become virtually moribund. In fact, in 1914, a second Committee of One Hundred was formed under the auspices of the American Association for the Advancement of Science, the membership of which included about 20 scholars whose field of expertise was biomedicine. However, the Committee had no real interest in the Public Health Service nor with its status within the federal bureaucracy.[31]

World War I required that the PHS and the Hygienic Laboratory redirect their attention to the concerns of the military, among them outbreaks of tetanus and anthrax among American troops. The causes of these infections were ultimately traced to the contaminated shaving brushes used by troops and to the 'bone points' that were employed to scarify the skin in preparation for administering smallpox vaccinations.[32] In 1918 Congress appropriated an additional $1 million to the Service for the purpose of combating the Spanish influenza pandemic that was eventually to cost the lives of some 40 million people worldwide, 600 000 in the United States. Despite the additional funds at the disposal of the PHS, however, little could be accomplished to reduce the severity of the epidemic. Influenza vaccines of any degree of effectiveness were not available until the 1930s and all Service resources were directed at caring for those who had succumbed to the illness. Even Hygienic Laboratory physicians with barely any experience as medical practitioners were dispatched to treat government workers in temporary hospitals established in the Washington, DC area.[33]

The War also added to the functions of the Public Health Service the authority to investigate the causes of venereal disease and to uncover the best methods for their control. Concern for the venereal status of American troops, especially those stationed along the Mexican border, led Congress in 1918 to enact legislation establishing a Division of Venereal Disease within the PHS. The Chamberlain-Kahn Act also called for the creation of an Interdepartmental Social Hygiene Board (ISHB), consisting of the secretaries of war, navy, and treasury, and the three surgeons-general to coordinate federal activities aimed at VD control. The ISHB was given authority to disburse $600 000 in four appropriations, two of $100 000, each of which was to be awarded as grants to university and other nongovernmental investigating bodies for scientific work on these diseases, $300 000 of which was to under-write sociological and psychological research, and an additional $100 000 to be used for any purpose mentioned in the Act.[34] These awards were among the earliest extra-mural grants conferred by the PHS and served as a crucial precedent for the National Institute of Health's future programs.

The PHS emerged from World War I considerably more powerful than it had been three years earlier. In early 1919, Congress designated the Service as the provider of medical and hospital services to discharged servicemen wounded in combat, thus substantially enlarging the Service's size. Although this function was removed in August 1921 when the Veterans' Bureau was created, the PHS continued to benefit from the goodwill it had acquired in Congress. In addition, progressive ideas about the need for greater government involvement in issues of personal health, including government-administered medical programs and more extensive biomedical research, encouraged legislators to greet proposals for the expansion of the Service sympathetically.

At the same time efforts were made to increase the efficiency of the federal bureaucracy and to cut back on the phenomenal growth in the size of govern-ment that had occurred during the war.[35] President Warren G. Harding had created a Bureau of the Budget in 1921, appointing Charles G. Dawes, McKinley's former Comptroller of the Currency and the chief purchasing agent for the United States during the War, as its first Director. Dawes resigned the position in the following year after having established the Bureau as the admin-istration's financial watchdog and Harding selected retired Brigadier General Herbert Mayhew Lord to replace him. Lord had been appointed the Army's Chief of Finance during the final days of World War I and was a strong propo-nent of cost-cutting in government. Lord was particularly unsympathetic to the Public Health Service, both because he was a Christian Scientist and because he regarded the Service's Commissioned Officer Corps as inappropriate for a civilian agency. This proved a particular sore point for the PHS since any legis-lation that carried an appropriation had to be approved by his Bureau.[36]

The Service's plans for expansion were severely hampered by its inability to enlarge its Commissioned Corps to include sanitary engineers, dentists, and pharmacists. In addition, the Service wished to establish a Nurses Corps. The only way to hire these specialists, however, was through the Civil Service, whose pay scales were woefully inadequate. To rectify this situation the Service sponsored several bills during the early 1920s creating a Nurses Corps and would have further authorized the President to transfer certain specialists from the PHS's Reserve Corps to its Commissioned Corps.[37] The bills, however, were blocked by those in Congress who shared the concerns of General Lord and the Bureau of the Budget.

Meanwhile, the Service found itself having to contend with the recommendations of a government commission that a new Department of Education and Public Welfare be established which would include the Public Health Service, the newly created Veterans' Bureau, and a number of smaller federal health, welfare, and educational agencies. Even prior to Harding's inauguration, the 66th Congress, in 1920, had enacted a joint resolution which created a Joint Committee to recommend changes in the executive bureaucracy that would provide greater coordination and efficiency. The Committee was chaired by Senator Reed Smoot, Republican of Utah, and Congressman Charles Frank Reavis, Republican of Nebraska, neither of whom was particularly friendly to the Public Health Service,[38] and among the Committee's recommendations was a scheme to establish the new department. While the PHS was in principle not opposed to greater coordination between agencies dealing with the public health, it did oppose the Smoot-Reavis recommendation on the grounds that the Service would be overshadowed by the much larger Veterans' Bureau. In the event, the PHS was temporarily spared the task of having to fight the creation of a new department when, on the death of President Harding in 1923, the recommendation was tabled.

The Service's reprieve, however, was short-lived. Harding's successor, Calvin Coolidge, had indicated that he supported establishment of a new Department, to be designated the Department of Education and Relief, along lines similar to the Smoot-Reavis recommendations. The bill was sponsored by Michigan Republican Carl Mapes in the House and, not surprisingly, by Reed Smoot in the Senate. And for similar reasons it was opposed by the PHS and a number of organizations sympathetic to the Service's mission. The *American Journal of Public Health* complained in an editorial that the Veterans' Bureau would constitute no less than 90 percent of the Department and 'would completely overshadow both education and public health'.[39] In fact so strong was the opposition from the medical profession that the bill was eventually defeated.

During the period following the war, the Hygienic Laboratory continued its research work, funded by an annual maintenance appropriation, occasionally supplemented by additional funding for special projects. Table 4.1, which indicates the level of funding and size of staff for the years prior to 1936, gives some indication of the level of funding for the period from 1907, when Congress began specifying the amounts earmarked for the Hygienic Laboratory, and 1937, by which time the Laboratory had been transformed into the National Institute of Health. The total size of staff and the number of scientists working for the Laboratory are also shown.

While most of the work undertaken at the Laboratory continued to be in infectious diseases, more projects involved investigation of the degenerative diseases, particularly of the cardiovascular system, and cancer. In 1922, J.W.

Table 4.1 *Hygienic Laboratory Appropriations and Staff, Fiscal Years 1907–1936*

Year	Appropriation ($)	Total Staff	Scientific Staff
1907	15 000.00	32	n/a
1908	15 000.00	n/a	n/a
1909	15 000.00	55	15
1910	15 000.00	52	15
1911	14 900.00	56	19
1912	14 900.00	56	17
1913	17 000.00	61	20
1914	20 000.00	71	28
1915	20 000.00	71	30
1916	20 000.00	69	27
1917	20 000.00	78	31
1918	20 000.00	92	43
1919	27 000.00	96	35
1920	36 000.00	101	32
1921	45 000.00	127	28
1922	50 000.00	128	41
1923	45 000.00	123	41
1924	45 000.00	113	43
1925	44 600.00	117	46
1926	43 400.00	114	45
1927	43 000.00	114	44
1928	43 000.00	118	45
1929	43 000.00	128	51
1930	43 000.00	129	51
1931	43 000.00	140	51
1932	48 000.00	153	57
1933	48.000.00	147	60
1934	54 775.00	149	62
1935	50 000.00	160	63
1936	64 000.00	177	73

Source: Victoria A. Harden, 'Toward a National Institute of Health: A Study in the Development of Federal Biomedical Research Policy, 1926–1930', unpublished Ph.D. Thesis, Emory University, 1983: 143.

Schereschewsky, the Director of the Laboratory, recommended that a Division of Physiology be added to the Laboratory although this was not acted upon. Indeed, the PHS's research activities were significantly decreased in 1924 when the House Appropriations Committee halted funds for the study of venereal disease, despite appeals from the new Surgeon General, Hugh Smith Cumming. While Cumming's own interests lay in the PHS's activities in sanitation and quarantine rather than in basic science,[40] he apparently made every effort, without success, to overcome Congressional opposition to the venereal disease program after the end of the World War.

It was evident that any further expansion of the Laboratory would require getting past the objections of the Director of the Bureau of the Budget. As a result, many supporters of greater government involvement in health care once again attempted to gain passage of legislation creating a new cabinet-level department comprising all federal health agencies. In this task, the Service was given substantial support by the newly created National Health Council. Members of the original Committee of One Hundred, now virtually defunct, were active in forming a National Health Council to which they invited all volunteer health agencies. In April 1913 the Council on Health and Public Instruction of the American Medical Association organized a conference of 39 health agencies, which in turn appointed Professor Selskar M. Gunn of the Massachusetts Institute of Technology to study the problems relating to the coordinating of these agencies. In 1915 Gunn reported that there were 24 national organizations whose major interest was in the health of Americans. Following the end of the World War, the American Public Health Association called another conference with a similar purpose, which eventuated in another study of the feasibility of an organization of health organizations, in this instance conducted by Donald B. Armstrong of the Metropolitan Life Insurance Company.[41]

Founded in 1920, the National Health Council chose Livingston Farrand, a former member of the Committee of One Hundred and the representative to the Council of the American Red Cross, as chairman and Donald Armstrong, author of the study that led to the Council's creation, as executive officer. Among the organizations holding membership were the American Red Cross, the Council on Health and Public Instruction of the American Medical Association, the American Public Health Association (APHA), the National Committee for Mental Hygiene, the National Organization for Public Health Nursing, and the National Child Health Council.[42] The Council immediately began its lobbying activities on issues relating to matters of health and began issuing bi-weekly reports on pending national health legislation. In addition, its Washington bureau under the direction of James Alner Tobey published regular newsletters regarding the current health activities of federal bureaus.

Tobey contributed a monthly column on public health law to the APHA's journal and had been intrigued by the recommendations of the Smoot-Reavis committee to establish a cabinet department for health. In his July 1924 column, Tobey wrote:

> It is about time that a practical plan for the centralization of federal health work, now widely scattered and uncoordinated, is proposed by a national organization with knowledge enough to understand the matter and energy enough to attempt to get it adopted. The National Health Council is undoubtedly the agency to do this.[43]

Partly as a result of his efforts, the APHA passed a resolution at its annual meeting in October 1925 calling for 'more effective centralization of federal health work under the direction of a competent, trained official who shall have the rank of at least an Assistant Secretary'.[44] While the resolution urged that the new department contain 'as many as practical of the bureaus engaged in public health and preventive medicine', it stipulated that the Veterans Administration be specifically excluded. In order to encourage the Administration to act promptly on the recommendation, the AHA struck a committee to lobby both the White House and Congress consisting of, among others, James A. Tobey, Lee K. Frankel, the Chairman of the National Health Council, William F. Snow, Director of the American Social Hygiene Association, and Milton Rosenau, professor of preventive medicine at Harvard University and at one time Director of the Hygienic Laboratory.

The Metropolitan Life Insurance Company had for some time been an active participant in preventive medicine programs and in lobbying governments at all levels to make such programs compulsory. In 1879, under the then president, Joseph F. Knapp, the company had decided to add 'industrial' or 'workingmen's' insurance policies to its range of offerings. In this it had followed the example of the British insurance companies, who had found the market for industrial insurance programs extremely lucrative. In order to sell these policies and collect workers' small weekly premiums, Metropolitan Life imported large numbers of British workers who were used to handling insurance sales door-to-door. Knapp's decision immediately proved successful and by 1880 the company was issuing over 700 new policies a day.

By 1909, Metropolitan Life had become the nation's largest insurer in terms of insurance in force. In the same year, the Company's Welfare Division, recently established by Lee Frankel, had instituted a visiting nurses program for its many industrial policyholders[45] and five years later it inaugurated free medical examinations to be conducted at the Life Extension Institute.[46] Both these programs were extremely effective and the mortality rate over the nine years following the program's introduction was reported to have declined by 20 percent. Not content with underwriting the costs of social programs itself, Metropolitan Life was tireless in its promotion of government activism in the area of public health. In fact, the funding for the National Health Council's campaign to centralize federal health care programs came largely from the company.[47]

Tobey worked unflaggingly to advance his proposal to centralize federal health programs. In 1926 the Institute for Government Research (forerunner of the Brookings Institution), funded by Robert S. Brookings, released Tobey's book-length study on the federal government and public health, in which Tobey pointed out how dispersed and uncoordinated were its health programs.[48] Tobey's proposed changes were clear: to consolidate the Public Health Service (in the Treasury Department), the Division of Vital Statistics (in the Commerce Department), the Children's Bureau (in the Labor Department), the Bureaus of Chemistry and Animal Industry (in the Department of Agriculture), and the Medical Division of the Office of Indian Affairs, St Elizabeths Hospital for the Insane, and the Freedman's Hospital (in the Interior Department) into one new Department of Health.[49] With specific reference to the Hygienic Laboratory, Tobey conceived of the Laboratory as an institute of applied science wherein practical solutions to the PHS's field problems would be devised and tested. He noted:

> The division of the Hygienic Laboratory, the chief medium for the research of the Public Health Service, should be utilized to provide agencies for the solution of public health problems, facilities for the coordination of research of health authorities and scientists engaged on special problems, and demonstration of sanitary methods and appliances. Such facilities should be extended for stated periods to health officers and scientists engaged in special investigations, and officers should be detailed to educational and research institutions for special studies of scientific problems and for the dissemination of information relating to the science of public health.[50]

A number of associations were quick to support Tobey's recommendations. Even before the annual meeting of the American Public Health Association in October 1925, two other organizations had enacted resolutions calling for the coordination of all federal public health activities. On 5 June 1925 the Conference of State and Provincial Health Authorities of North America, meeting in Montreal, urged that 'the now scattered health activities of the United States government should be more effectively coordinated and placed under the direction of a competent central authority'. And later that month the National Tuberculosis Association (which became the American Lung Association in 1973) similarly advocated that 'the now dispersed health activities of the Federal Government should be more effectively coordinated and placed under the central direction of a properly trained sanitarian'.[51]

These organizations were joined by a large number of eminent public figures, including Secretary of the Treasury Andrew Mellon and Secretary of the Interior Hubert Work,[52] and the recommendation for centralization even received the approval of President Calvin Coolidge. But despite this support, the proposal was to meet defeat, largely as a result of the opposition of several influential figures in the area of public health and, most importantly, in the Public Health Service itself. Among these was Dr William H. Welch, one of the most important and highly respected authorities in public health and a close associate of the PHS.[53] Named pathologist-in-chief at the Johns Hopkins hospital when it was founded in 1889, Welch was raised to the position of Dean of the Medical School at its establishment in 1893. He then helped organize the Johns Hopkins University School of Hygiene and Public Health in 1916 and became its first director. Welch was also a longtime member of the Hygienic Laboratory's Advisory Board. It was with some surprise, therefore, that Welch greeted the recommendations with a good deal of skepticism. In this, Welch had taken the lead from his professional colleague, Surgeon General Hugh S. Cumming. Cumming opposed centralization for reasons similar to those earlier offered by Surgeon General Wyman, that the appointment of an Assistant Secretary of Health would dilute the power of the PHS as the federal government's primary public health agency, with its militaristic characteristics and unique organizational structure. At the same time, the proposed changes would certainly compromise the close working relationship between the Surgeon General and his immediate superior, the Secretary of the Treasury.

In the place of Tobey's original proposal, Cumming directed the Assistant Surgeon General, John Kerr, to help him in drawing up a memorandum suggesting alternate legislation. Cumming's proposal in part read:

> First, maintain the present organization of the Public Health Service; second, provide for admission into the regular corps of scientific men other than those of the medical profession similar to the corps of the Foreign Service of our Government; third, enact legislation authorizing the head of the Public Health Service to detail personnel for public health duties in other Departments of the Government, thus solving the difficulty with reference to bureaus only partly devoted to medical subjects such as the Children's Bureau; fourth, provide for the transfer of the Division of Vital Statistics to the Public Health Service.[54]

Toby and his associates at the National Health Council and the American Public Health Association were so eager to gain passage of legislation that would advance the role of the federal government in public health that they were prepared to restructure their recommendations to meet Cumming's concerns. In addition to the suggestions put forward in Cumming's memorandum, it was suggested that the Hygienic Laboratory Advisory Board, created by the 1902 legislation, be transmuted into a National Advisory Health Council, with the power to make far-reaching recommendations regarding all biomedical research undertaken by the government. In March 1926 James S. Parker, Republican of New York and the Chairman of the House Committee on Interstate and Foreign Commerce, was prevailed upon to sponsor legislation along the lines suggested by Tobey's revised proposal.[55] Parker himself appears to have had little interest in the issue of public health and it seems clear that it was political obligations that motivated him to bring in the PHS measure.

The bill authorized the President or the Surgeon General to transfer PHS personnel to other federal agencies for the purpose of supervising matters relating to public health, thus empowering the Service with something like a supervisory role in such matters without the need to consolidate the government's various health agencies. Other sections of the bill provided that sanitary engineers, dental officers, and technical scientists could indeed become Commissioned Officers in the PHS, all of whom would henceforth be promoted at a rate comparable to that which existed in the Army's Medical Corps. In addition, a nurses' corps, operating under Civil Service rules, was created.

Several sections of the bill had particular reference to the Hygienic Laboratory. The Parker bill acknowledged the increasing complexity of medical research by permitting the Laboratory's medical and scientific personnel to be detailed to other research institutions, including universities 'for special studies of scientific problems relating to public health and for the dissemination of information relating to public health'.[56] At the same time the Hygienic Laboratories would be open to research personnel at other institutions when necessary. The greater coordination of PHS investigations with the broader area of biomedical studies throughout the country, Hygienic Laboratory scientists correctly concluded, would insure that governmental research remained at the forefront of medical studies and would assure its integration with non-governmental research. In addition, this provision would have the effect of extending the facilities of the Hygienic Laboratory to state and local health authorities.

The Parker bill further authorized the Secretary of the Treasury to establish additional divisions in the Hygienic Laboratory as he thought necessary, thus permitting the Laboratory to expand its research into any area it thought appropriate. Finally, the Advisory Board of the Hygienic Laboratory was to be renamed the National Advisory Health Council and its membership to be increased by five members.[57]

Despite the efforts of the Bureau and its numerous supporters, the Parker bill went no further than the House Committee on Interstate and Foreign Commerce, where it sat. Apparently, the Bureau of the Budget was firmly opposed to extending commissions in the PHS to non-physicians and to any pay increase whatever to commissioned officers. Even though the PHS had the approval of Secretary of the Treasury Andrew Mellon, Lord stood adamant. Tensions between the Service and the Bureau of the Budget continued to build over the course of the year when it appeared that the bill would remain locked in Committee, a tribute to the power of Herbert Lord, who was able to do battle both with a powerful and well-liked agency and with a public coalition of influential figures with whom the agency had allied itself.

Fortunately for the Hygienic Laboratory, paralleling the activities of the PHS and the national health movement was a second movement whose interests focused exclusively on the Hygienic Laboratory, one which sought to raise the agency to the foremost institution of health research in the world. Even before the Parker bill was introduced into Congress in 1926, Senator Joseph Ransdell, Democrat of Louisiana, had sponsored a bill seeking the creation of a National Institute of Health, where the 'fundamental problems' relating to the diseases of man would be studied. Having been convinced by the Assistant Surgeon General Dr Lewis R. Thompson, head of the Division of Scientific Research, that sponsoring such a measure would win him lasting national fame and honor,[58] Ransdell included in his bill an initial first-year appropriation of $15 000 000.00 to cover both capital construction and to underwrite the costs of research. America's experience in World War I, especially after the introduction of gas warfare, did much to motivate the government and others into believing that the nation was in dire need of a vast well-endowed institute of chemistry. Additionally, chemistry, particularly biochemistry, was commonly thought to be the most renowned science of the Progressive Era and basic scientific research in this area was considered the key to the medical advances of the next century, destined to lead the way to a healthier and more prosperous society.

With the outbreak of war in 1914, it became apparent that the United States had for years been relying on German pharmaceuticals, dyestuffs, and other products of German organic research. The 'need' for indigenous research and development became apparent to most men, especially to those fearful that the United States would remain a second- or third-class power in terms of basic scientific research. While the nation's largest firms, American Telephone and Telegraph, General Electric, Westinghouse, and Eastman all extended their research programs, creating substantial in-house research laboratories, these were regarded as insufficient. In 1916 The National Academy of Sciences [59] established the National Research Council (NRC) in order to bring the broader scientific and technological communities into closer touch with the Academy and help the Academy in its task of advising the federal government. The Council was the suggestion of George Ellery Hale of the Mt Wilson Observatory, California, who was concerned that the American scientific community was unprepared for the war ahead and who saw in the Council an institution that could coordinate research and bring together scientists from universities, industry, and government for the purpose of advising the government on issues of national defense.[60]

One of the very first tasks undertaken by the NRC, in cooperation with the American Chemical Society, was a census of American chemists. While the United States was still not an official combatant in early 1916, it was apparent to many that the nation had embarked on a course where intervention on Britain's side was inevitable, despite the Administration's protestations to the contrary. And, when, on 22 April 1915, the Germans had bombarded Allied lines at Ypres with chlorine gas, it became clear that chemists and pharmacologists would play a major role in the war effort. The census was directed by Charles Holmes Herty, the president of the American Chemical Society and a firm adherent of government-directed scientific research.

Herty was especially taken with team work, which he believed was far more effective than the individualistic methods so popular among scientists decades earlier. In its place Herty urged that research teams be organized and that their work be coordinated, that they collaborate on mastering a problem, even to the point where this required overcoming geographical hurdles to cooperation.[61] In actuality this method, in which researchers were broken down into teams, each assigned a specific aspect of a larger problem and encouraged to collaborate, had already supplanted research done in isolation.

In the summer of 1918 Herty conceived the idea of establishing a huge institute 'in which laboratory tests of all kinds would be made and to which, through the establishment of fellowships, manufacturing organizations could send well-trained young men for working out specific problems. Cooperation could be established between this institution and the organic laboratories of our universities, as well as with the hospitals of the country.' [62] The benefits of such a laboratory would be enormous, Herty believed. This was especially true with respect to chemical compounds that had the potential to become new medicinals. While research in dyestuffs and explosives seems to have progressed apace, pharmaceutical firms devoted less effort to basic research. The intense level of competition among drug manufacturers and the high costs involved in conducting basic research on the medicinal potential of various chemicals made these costs prohibitive.[63]

In the years prior to 1940 biomedical research was financed and conducted primarily by the major research universities and by industrial firms. In addition, research was undertaken by several nonprofit research institutions and, finally, a few government agencies. Immediately prior to World War II industry underwrote the costs of somewhat more than 50 percent of all biomedical research, while funds from universities and philanthropies were slightly less than 40 percent and federal government funds amounted to less than 7 percent.[64] By far the largest of these private medical research establishments at the turn of the century was the Rockefeller Institute for Medical Research.

At the urging of his pastor, the Rev Frederick T. Gates, and after speaking at some length with William H. Welch of Johns Hopkins University, John D. Rockefeller, Jr, was encouraged to contribute $1 000 000 in the form of a grant to underwrite a major medical research facility and as a consequence the Rockefeller Institute for Medical Research was founded in New York City in 1901.[65] In 1907 the Institute was presented with a permanent endowment of $2 620 000 and in 1920 Rockefeller raised this amount to $23 000 000. By 1928, Rockefeller's contribution had reached $65 000 000.[66] The Institute was not designed as a medical school and as a result its staff were freed from teaching and supplied with state-of-the-art equipment and the best technical assistance available. Nor did its physician-researchers engage in private practice. In 1910 a hospital was added to the Institute to advance the studies undertaken in the Institute's laboratories.[67]

Although by far the largest, the Rockefeller Institute was not the only research institute established during the period. Among the other more notable foundations were the Phipps Institute for the Study, Treatment, and Prevention of Tuberculosis founded in Philadelphia in 1910, the Otho S. A. Sprague Institute for Infectious Diseases (currently the Otho S. A. Sprague Memorial Institute), established in Chicago in 1911, and the John Rockefeller McCormick Memorial Institute for Infectious Diseases set up in Chicago in 1902.[68]

None of these private institutions appeared sufficiently large to satisfy Herty's notions of a massive laboratory complex that would accommodate the whole spectrum of biomedical and pharmacological research. Herty lobbied the most prominent people in the field, including Simon Flexner,[69] who had been appointed the director of the Rockefeller Institute, and William Welch of Johns Hopkins, both of whom eagerly supported a national center of the sort conceived by Herty. As editor of the *Journal of Industrial and Engineering Chemistry*, Herty wrote in September 1918 that what was needed was a privately endowed facility for drug research similar to the Mellon Institute for Industrial Research.[70] Herty originally appears to have supported a research institution that was a hybrid of university, government, and industry laboratories, but exactly what shape this would have taken is not at all clear.[71] Certainly it would have been difficult to fix upon a cooperative arrangement between academic pharmacologists, members of the American Society of Pharmacology and Therapeutics, and those who worked for pharmaceutical firms, who were deliberately excluded from membership of the Society. 'The lack of cooperation', noted one pharmacologist,

> which has existed between men in university chairs and manufacturing concerns has been due to many factors. The university man had to feel absolutely certain that his name and university connection would not be used in any way for advertising purposes.[72]

The *Philadelphia Public Ledger* responded warmly to Herty's editorial but put forward the alternative suggestion that the proposed laboratory be incorporated as part of the National Bureau of Standards,[73] which, the newspaper pointed out, already dealt with 'certain phases of chemistry'.[74] While the functions of the Bureau were clearly distinct and considerably more limited than were those envisioned by Herty, the *Ledger's* proposal did offer the federal government an alternative home for the new center, an option that was later to be taken far more seriously.

In order to encourage further interest and debate regarding his proposal, Herty set about structuring the November 1918 meeting of the New York Section of the American Chemical Society as a symposium on his institute, to which he invited the most prominent chemists and pharmacologists. In offering their views on the structure and purpose of the new laboratory, the various speakers naturally employed titles for the new entity that reflected their notions of its primary tasks. 'The National Institute for Drug Research', 'The Institute for Chemotherapy', 'The Institute for Research in Synthetic Organic Chemistry', 'The Therapo-chemical Institute', were all, at one point or another, suggested. But despite differences in emphasis, there appears to have been universal agreement on one issue, that the new institute, while acting in cooperation with government, should be under private auspices. With regard to the endowment needed to initiate the institute, the least suggested seems to have been about $1 000 000, although $5 000 000–$10 000 000 appeared more appropriate.

In March 1919 the committee that had emerged from the November meeting to put into practice Herty's scheme prepared a draft outline of the proposed institute, whose mission, they maintained, 'was the study of the fundamental problems connected with the living body (where every change is fundamentally a chemical change)'.[75] The institute's organization was to be divided into three major branches, chemistry, pharmacology, and experimental biology, and these in turn would be subdivided into seven subdivisions. It was projected that the salaries for each subdivision head would be $12 000.00, above whom would function the seven heads of each branch, a director, and an administrative support staff. Total annual operating costs were projected to be $420 000.00. At 5 percent, this would require an operating endowment of $8.4 million, to which an additional $2 million would have to be added for capital costs.[76]

The American Drug Manufacturers Association, doubtless convinced that the creation of such an institute would carry a sizeable portion of the basic research costs that the drug companies' own research facilities would otherwise have had to underwrite, quickly joined the chorus of those calling for a national laboratory. And in February of the following year, the Medical Science Division of the National Research Council, by this time one of the most prestigious scientific organizations in the country, associated itself with the movement. Even more significantly, it was as a consequence of Herty's efforts during this period that he was introduced to Francis P. Garvan, president of the Chemical Foundation.

The Chemical Foundation had been created by executive order of Woodrow Wilson in 1919 to administer captured German patents. In 1917, when the United States entered the war, Francis P. Garvan was serving in the office of the district attorney of New York City and at that point was appointed chief of the United States Bureau of Investigation and manager of the New York Office of the Alien Property Custodian. The office was charged with dismantling the German chemical companies operating in the United States, seizing their property, and licensing the patents they possessed to American chemical manufacturers. Garvan's immediate superior was A. Mitchell Palmer, who held the office of Alien Property Custodian, and both were apparently shocked by the arrangements made by the German companies to cartelize production of their compounds in America.[77] In their zeal to undo what they saw as the predatory behavior of the German companies, Garvan and Palmer sold the first German patents to American firms. It soon became apparent, however, that this policy simply transferred the monopoly returns previously captured by the German patent holders to an American company. As a consequence, when Palmer was elevated to Attorney-General and Garvan to Alien Property Custodian in 1919, they argued for the establishment of a corporation to administer the captured patents.

Organized as a private corporation whose stock was held by the American Dyes Institute, the American Manufacturing Chemists Association, and other groups involved in the chemical industry, the Foundation issued nonexclusive licenses for the use of captured German patents to US firms. The substantial income received was expended in a variety of ways including the publication of several American Chemical Society journals and a monograph series, prizes in chemistry, and a large number of research grants. The meeting between Herty and Garvan was thus particularly fateful since it added to Herty's efforts the substantial assets of the Chemical Foundation. So impressed was Garvan by Herty's projected institute that he agreed to use Chemical Foundation funds to promote the proposal.[78] Specifically, Garvan urged Herty to expand the notion of an 'Institute for Drug Research' into a broader 'Institute for Chemo-Medical Research' and to prepare a report on the glories that lay in wait once cooperative research under the umbrella of a giant research facility became possible. The report, entitled *The Future Independence and Progress of American Medicine in the Age of Chemistry*, was released in early 1921 and immediately attracted national interest,[79] in part, according to one historian, because Americans thought that the tremendous gains in efficiency brought about in the factory by Henry Ford could be replicated in the laboratory, once it was redesigned along scientific principles.[80]

Garvan saw to it that the report received the widest possible circulation. Over 1 million copies were printed at a cost of $80 000.00 and were mailed to all American physicians, in addition to prominent businessmen, educators, lawyers, authors, legislators, librarians, and the heads of agricultural, farmers', and women's organizations. The benefits that were projected as flowing from a national research institute were so enormous that it is no surprise that the proposal was enthusiastically received by most readers.

What was somewhat unexpected, however, was the large number of responses that suggested that the federal government act as sponsor for the institute.[81] The Report itself had made reference to the PHS's Hygienic Laboratory as 'the best adapted for development into a medium of cooperative research'.[82] Nevertheless, the reservations that had been expressed about making the institute a government entity, particularly the difficulties of holding prominent scientists on government salaries and the amount of red tape necessary to run a government bureau, were dismissed as of little consequence. *The Journal of the American Medical Association*, for example, thought a government institute no less than ideal and went so far as to suggest that it be located in the Public Health Service. 'Some twenty years ago,' the Journal noted,

> Congress, with rare vision, established the Hygienic Laboratory of the United States Public Health Service; the plan of organization was unsurpassed by that of any laboratory in the world. The staff included some of the foremost representatives of chemistry, pharmacology, bacteriology and medical zoology, the specialties most needed for a cooperative attack on the great problems of health, in the country. But subsequent congresses have failed to provide for any considerable growth of this laboratory; it stands virtually as it was two decades ago. Enlarged and with adequate support, this laboratory could give the United States the leading place in the world in this great scientific and humanitarian work.[83]

Support for a publicly funded institute was substantial enough that in 1924 Senator L. Heisler Ball, Republican of Delaware, himself a physician, introduced legislation that would establish a bureau of medical research very much along the lines suggested in the Chemical Foundation's report in the Department of the Interior. The reaction of the Public Health Service was, predictably, immediate. The PHS had jealously guarded its quasi-monopoly over issues of public health within the federal bureaucracy and was not about to remain passive while another department was awarded what would likely grow into a massive medical research establishment. Assistant Surgeon General Arthur M. Stimson was delegated the task of writing a memorandum on the Ball measure, S. 3239, in which he claimed that the creation of the laboratory in the Department of the Interior would result in 'unwarranted and extravagant expenditures in duplication of functions already assigned to the Public Health Service and in particular to the Hygienic Laboratory'.[84]

In the event, Senator Ball was unsuccessful in seeking renomination in 1924 and as a consequence his bill died. However, it did have the effect of accommodating PHS officials to the idea that were a public medical research institute established, its proper home was the Public Health Service. Additionally, the incapacity of Herty and the other authors of the report to find a private benefactor or, for that matter, to raise even a small portion of the massive sums needed to create the institute moved them closer to the idea of embracing public funding. As a consequence, both groups converged towards supporting a federal research agency.

By 1926 Herty had firmly committed himself to a research institute underwritten by government funds. In January and again in March he met with Senator Eugene Ransdell, who had earlier expressed great excitement over the idea of establishing a National Institute of Health.[85] Ransdell shared with Herty the fact that he was enormously impressed by *The Future Independence and Progress of American Medicine* and that he was prepared to draft a bill to create an institute and to speak in support of the measure. Partly as a result of his meetings with Herty, Ransdell drafted legislation that reflected many of the provisions of the Parker bill, promoted by the Public Health Service and introduced at approximately the same time. Ransdell's measure, however, while not as comprehensive as was the Parker bill, provided for a full-fledged National Institute of Health.

The Ransdell bill, S. 4540, reorganized, expanded, and redesignated the Hygienic Laboratory of the Public Health Service as the National Institute of Health. The bill carried an appropriation of $5 million for the choice of a site and the construction of necessary buildings. An additional $2 million per year for a five-year period was to be employed to enlarge the Hygienic Laboratory and to authorize a system of fellowships.[86] Ransdell regarded the primary function of the Institute as dedication to an attack on 'the fundamental diseases of man' through intensive and thorough investigation. The appropriation for the National Institute as it appeared in the first unrevised bill was similar to that projected in 1919 by the Committee on an Institute for Chemo-medical Research. While the Committee had established a total endowment of $10.4 million, Ransdell's bill provided for $15 million over five years. In addition, it exempted scientists from the Civil Service classification system, thus freeing their salaries from the Service's limitations.

Seemingly oblivious to the notion that basic science could be performed by the nation's private institutions, the *New York Times*, among others, was delighted with the bill. It reiterated Ransdell's argument that an appropriation of $20 000 000 per year to study the causes, prevention, and cure of disease was cheap when compared with annual expenditures of over $1 billion on the illnesses of Americans. To the argument that basic biomedical research could and should be undertaken by the several private institutes recently established, the *Times* put forward the standard response of the Institute's supporters. 'In most of these institutions comparatively little time is allowed for concentrated work on problems of major importance, or opportunity given for cooperative effort of the chemist, the biologist, the pharmacologist, the therapist and the physiologist.' [87] The editorial then went on to maintain:

Research service in the conservation of the health of the nation should not be left entirely to private interest, however generous, zealous, and intelligent. Particularly it is desirable that chemistry should be brought back in its highest development as a science, to the aid of the physician in the prevention of disease and the alleviation of suffering. It has turned its attention in recent decades mainly to the production of wealth in the industries. It has a higher ministry before it if it can be brought to cope with disease in time of peace as its aid was invoked by the Government during the war. We have gone further in our Federal departments in concern for the health of lower animals, and even of trees and plants, than we have for that of human beings.[88]

It soon became apparent to Francis Garvan of the Chemical Foundation that, despite the Foundation's earlier reservations regarding government direction of a national institute, the establishment of a public agency was far more likely than was the creation of a private laboratory. In fact, the American Chemical Society's Committee for an Institute on Chemo-medical Research, under Garvan's direction, now began to funnel large amounts of financial support toward this end. In 1926 Garvan hired Charles Herty as a full-time employee of the Foundation who was charged to work closely with Senator Ransdell to effect passage as soon as possible. At the same time the resources of the Foundation were placed at Herty's disposal.

One of Herty's first acts as an employee of the Chemical Foundation was to call for a national convention to be held in Washington, DC soon after the 70th Congress convened, whose purpose was to convey to the Administration the American people's enormous support for public health. The *New York Times* reported that Herty 'urged a national campaign sponsored and financed by the United States Government against disease'. Isolated instances of private philanthropy might prove helpful, Herty noted, but they 'could not meet the situation, which should be dealt with by the American taxpayers as a whole on their own initiative'. Having totally reversed himself on private medical research, Herty concluded that 'public health was no longer the province of the private practitioner. Men and women must be trained for the task and the community educated in prevention of disease and in the promotion of physical and mental health.'[89]

Garvan, Senator Ransdell, and other prominent advocates of a national institute were enthusiastic about proceeding with a convention to support the Ransdell bill but the reaction of the Surgeon General, Hugh Cumming, was lukewarm. Fearful that the Bureau of the Budget would bring to bear its not inconsiderable authority with both President Coolidge and with Congress against the measure, and with the Parker bill an added casualty, Cummings counseled that supporters of the Ransdell bill proceed cautiously. Both Cumming and the Assistant Surgeon General, John Kerr, had helped Ransdell's staff in drafting the bill and both favored increasing the PHS's research facilities but were somewhat apprehensive lest the Budget Bureau disapprove any increase at all.[90]

Meanwhile a somewhat revised Parker bill, under consideration by a subcommittee of the House Interstate and Commerce Committee, had run into difficulties over its provision to extend commissions to nonmedical personnel and to the creation of a nurses' corps. In addition, there was substantial opposition to the bill's provision that called for the transfer of other federal agencies dealing with health to the Public Health Service. Even though every effort was made to orchestrate testimony in favor of the measure, the members of the House subcommittee were reluctant to proceed in the face of opposition from the Bureau of the Budget. The result was that the 69th Congress adjourned in March 1927 without taking any action.

It was not until a presidential election had intervened in 1928 that the Ransdell and Parker bills were finally enacted by Congress. The election of Herbert Hoover as President presaged an administration particularly friendly to a significant expansion of the federal government, especially in those areas thought to contribute to the nation's efficiency. While Secretary of Commerce, Hoover had been struck by what he regarded as an imbalance between the applied research undertaken by the nation's industrial establishment and basic scientific research, which Hoover conceived of as one of the functions of government.[91] With particular reference to public health, Hoover had noted in his inaugural address:

> In public health the discoveries of science have opened a new era. Many sections of our country and many groups of our citizens suffer from diseases the eradication of which are mere matters of administration and moderate expenditure. Public health service should be as fully organized and as universally incorporated into our governmental system as is public education. The returns are a thousand fold in economic benefits, and infinitely more in reduction of suffering and promotion of human happiness.[92]

In addition, the winter of 1928–29 witnessed another serious influenza epidemic. In mid-December, the *New York Times* reported that the Public Health Service had estimated that there were over 700 000 cases in the United States and one month later it was calculated that, along with pneumonia, the epidemic was responsible for 28 000 deaths.[93] While in no way comparable to the pandemic of 1918–19, sickness was widespread,[94] as was the fear that the epidemic might well cause as much devastation as did the earlier outbreak.

Surgeon General Cumming was quick to point out that without the research aimed at uncovering a specific preventative, there existed no way to avert future epidemics. To these comments, Senator Royal S. Copeland of New York, a homeopathic physician who, in 1938, became the leading sponsor of the Pure Food, Drug, and Cosmetic Act, responded:

> There can be no more striking example of the need for enactment of your bill than the present situation regarding influenza. Considering the modern epidemics of this disease, we begin with the winter of '89 and '90. At that time we were absolutely ignorant of the causes of the disease and with no ideas whatever as to its control. In 1918 we felt the effect of the most terrific attack of modern times. We found ourselves without knowledge of the preventative agent. . . . Here we are at the end of ten years, having another epidemic, and to our amazement we find that no progress whatever has been made . . . since 1918, and practically no progress for a quarter of a century.[95]

The November election and the flu epidemic appear to have been of decisive importance in causing President Coolidge to change his mind. Early in the new year he withdrew his opposition to the Ransdell bill and in late January 1929 Secretary of the Treasury Andrew Mellon wrote the chairman of the Senate Commerce Committee indicating that the bill did not conflict with the President's financial program.[96] However, difficulties in the House and Senate, especially as a consequence of attempts to combine and then to once more separate the provisions of the Ransdell and Parker bills, led to both bills again being tabled in the 70th Congress.

Soon after the new 71st Congress convened, Herty urged that the Ransdell bill be considered by the House Committee on Interstate and Foreign Commerce as soon as possible, despite the fact that hearings were then being held on the Parker bill. At the same time, Herty was assured that the Senate Commerce Committee would proceed to consider the measure immediately upon completion of its hearings on the Smoot-Hawley tariff. When hearings were finally held, opposition in both the House and Senate committees was minimal. Indeed, the only group markedly hostile to the bill was the Citizen's Medical Reference Bureau, whose secretary, Harry B. Anderson, had testified against the Parker bill at the hearings held in 1928 and who was to testify against certain health provisions of the Social Security Act of 1935. The Bureau was founded in 1919 to 'oppose compulsory medication and the use of public funds for medical propaganda and on the strength of this propaganda seeking to make medical treatment compulsory'.[97] Despite the fact that Anderson's organization had the support of heterodox practitioners, his testimony was dismissed as worthless and did nothing to raise doubts about the value of a national laboratory.

Just as the 1928 influenza epidemic had aroused new interest in the idea of a National Institute, so an outbreak of psittacosis at the beginning of 1930 acted as a spur to passage of the enabling legislation. In October 1929 some nine people were reported to have died of 'parrot fever' in Buenos Aires and the disease was believed to have spread to Europe and the United States through parrots imported from the area. In January 1930 the Surgeon General, having been advised by the nation's health departments, reported 36 fatalities from the disease, ostensibly caused by a shipment of diseased parrots resold as Christmas gifts, recommended that the importation of all parrots be halted. Work conducted at the Hygienic Laboratory uncovered the fact that some 167 cases in the United States were caused by a filter-passing organism present in the sputum and organs of infected persons and in the organs and discharges of the infected birds.[98] Work on the disease at the Hygienic Laboratory was not without cost. One of the laboratory technicians died and both the chief investigator and one of his assistants contracted severe cases of psittacosis, as did the Laboratory's night watchman and a visiting bacteriologist. The result was that in April 1930 work on the disease was transferred to the Quarantine Station at Curtis Bay, in Baltimore.

That the Hygienic Laboratory's existing facilities could not easily accommodate research on viral diseases lent support to the arguments being put forward by supporters of the Parker and Ransdell bills, as did the claim that Laboratory researchers were daily risking their lives to advance the nation's health and were worthy of a new Institute. These considerations went some way to contributing to passage of the Parker bill, which came to the floor of the House in March 1930 and was passed by the Senate in early April. At that point, the PHS and its allies immediately turned their full attention to the Ransdell bill.

With the help of John H. Finley of the *New York Times*, who published an editorial praising the proposed National Institute on the day that hearings began in the House,[99] Herty, Cumming, and Ransdell orchestrated the testimony heard by a subcommittee chaired by Representative Carl E. Mapes of Michigan of the Committee on Interstate and Foreign Commerce charged with considering the measure. No one appeared in opposition to the bill and most of the testimony was laughably hyperbolic. Professor John Colt Bloodgood of the Johns Hopkins University Medical School noted that the measure constituted 'the greatest contribution to health that has ever been made in the world' and Senator Ransdell himself maintained that the bill was 'fraught with more potentialities for the benefit of mankind – for humanity in general – than any measure ever presented to the American Congress during the life of our Republic'.[100]

On 15 May the bill was reported favorably to the House and four days later passed with a two-thirds majority. Two days later, on 21 May, Ransdell moved that the amended bill receive assent from the Senate, which it did without opposition. Finally, on 26 May 1930 Herbert Hoover signed the measure into law as Public Law 71-251, with both Herty and Ransdell in attendance. The original legislation appropriated the sum of $750 000 for the construction of two buildings and authorized the new Institute to establish a system of fellowships. However, Congress was reluctant to be more generous at a moment when the country found itself in a Depression of historic proportions. In the elections of 1930, Ransdell was defeated in his attempt to regain his Senate seat by Huey Long and the Institute thus lost its greatest champion. However, before retiring Ransdell was pleased to announce the Institute's first donation to its fellowship program, from, unsurprisingly, the Chemical Foundation, which contributed $100 000 earmarked for fellowships in basic chemical research relating to public health.[101]

Few private donations followed. Efforts were made to encourage foundations and private individuals to contribute to the work of the NIH, despite the fact that Ransdell established a 'Conference Board of the National Institute' to solicit funds. Now unemployed, Ransdell assumed the position of executive director of the new organization and was able to raise some $20 000 per year for a two-year period to operate the Conference Board.[102] Despite Ransdell's attempts, however, he was totally unsuccessful in his attempts to solicit donations. In its first full year of operations, the Board managed to receive donations totaling $57.00![103] Unable to capitalize on his role in creating the National Institute of Health, Ransdell retired to his farm in Louisiana, where he lived in retirement until the age of 96. He had hoped to have one of the NIH buildings named in his honor but even in the face of repeated lobbying his efforts proved unsuccessful.

Despite initial plans to immediately expand the NIH, Congress saw fit in light of the Depression to keep appropriations for medical research at the same level as they had been in 1927.[104] However, the election of Franklin Roosevelt to the Presidency brought with it a new philosophy of government spending. New Deal thinking encouraged extensive expenditures and this fit in perfectly with the views of the new Assistant Surgeon General, Lewis Ryers 'Jimmy' Thompson, who was appointed director of the Division of Scientific Research at the PHS in 1930 and with those of Dr Thomas Parran, Jr. In 1932, upon assuming office, Roosevelt chose as his chief advisor on public health matters Dr Parran,[105] who had been the Public Health Service's director of its Division of Venereal Diseases until he was extended a leave of absence by President Hoover in 1930 at the urging of Roosevelt, at the time Governor of New York. Not only did Parran propose a substantial increase in the budget of the Public Health Service (and its component, the National Institute of Health) but he recommended an enormous expansion of the role of the federal government in health matters that was to include a compulsory national health insurance scheme and a consolidation of the various federal health agencies into one central organization.[106]

Parran's draft called for a Public Health Service comprised of three divisions, health protection, medical care, and the National Institute of Health. Not only would the Institute continue to conduct biomedical research, but it would be charged with the regulation of all biologic products. Parran's organizational plan was partially effected in 1939 with the creation of the Federal Security Agency, comprising the Public Health Service, the Bureau of Vital Statistics, the Food and Drug Administration, and the Children's Bureau. In 1953 these agencies in turn were transmuted into the 'Health' section of the Department of Health, Education, and Welfare.

The two buildings authorized by the original Ransdell Act, one a laboratory, the other an administrative center, were duly built in downtown Washington but in 1935 a plan was put forward by Assistant Surgeon General Thompson to rebuild the entire Institute on a 45 acre estate in Bethesda, Maryland.[107] The Congress, anxious to accommodate itself to the recommendations of the new President, approved the necessary funds for the campus, and construction was begun almost immediately. Not only did the Public Health Service lobby for more extensive facilities but the Service also sought authority to substantially expand the operations of the NIH. Soon after taking office, President Roosevelt had established a Science Advisory Board under the chairmanship of Karl T. Compton, physicist and president of the Massachusetts Institute of Technology. The Board whose membership was stacked with functionaries who were eager to extend the research operations of the federal government, set up a subcommittee charged with studying the state of medical research in the Public Health Service. Among the members of the subcommittee delegated to consider the PHS's request were the Surgeon General, Thomas Parran, Milton Rosenau, former director of the Hygienic Laboratory, and Simon Flexner, director of the Rockefeller Institute.

The findings of the subcommittee were predictable. Among its recommendations was that the NIH greatly increase its research in the area of chronic diseases and that funds marked for the scientific work of the Public Health Service be increased by $2 500 000 above the appropriation for 1934–35. In addition, the Surgeon General, with the approval of the National Advisory Health Council, was to be given discretion regarding where the funds would be used.[108] The PHS orchestrated a massive letter-writing campaign to win support for the committee's recommendations, which played a role in the passage of Title VI of the Social Security Act, passed in 1935, which authorized an expenditure of $2 000 000 per year on scientific research.[109]

Among the studies undertaken by the NIH was research into the causes of cancer, which had begun in 1922. The Public Health Service, in cooperation with the Department of Preventive Medicine and Hygiene of Harvard University, had established a Cancer Investigations Laboratory at Harvard which conducted experiments on the disease throughout the 1920s. The program undertook to investigate cancer along four major lines: (1) research into the nature of malignant cells and their response to radiation; (2) investigation of the nature and causes of resistance to malignancies; (3) examination of the causes of normal and malignant cell growth; and (4) research into the biochemistry of malignancies.

Despite a steady expansion in the Institute's cancer research over the course of the first six years of the 1930s, the Public Health Service continued to request ever larger appropriations for the study of the disease. Indeed, with the appointment of Thomas Parran as Surgeon General in 1936, emphasis on research on chronic illnesses such as cancer became intense.[110] Congress had shown a particular interest in the subject and several Congressmen had at one point or another proposed legislation that would have authorized the federal government to become more aggressive in dealing with the disease. In February 1927 Senator Matthew M. Neely, Democrat of West Virginia, put forward a bill that would have established a $5 000 000 award to the person responsible for a cure for cancer.[111] The only upshot of this inane plan, however, was that thousands of cures flooded the Senator's mail. Having come to the realization that his scheme was impractical, Neely then proposed legislation authorizing the National Academy of Sciences to undertake a study of how the federal government might play a leading role in cancer research. The bill passed the Senate but failed in the House and in 1928 Neely was defeated in his re-election bid to the Senate. Several other attempts were made to increase federal commitment to cancer research but by this point Congressional efforts were focused on the Ransdell bill and little attention was paid to the specific study of cancer.

In 1935, agitation once again began in support of federal involvement in cancer research. Numerous articles appeared in the press on how appalling the disease was and one respected national publication went so far as to suggest that its cure could be achieved through a federally funded research program.[112] Certainly the appointment of Thomas Parran as Surgeon General in 1936 played a decisive role in extending medical research done by the PHS to chronic diseases.[113] The organization of the National Cancer Institute (NCI) appears to have been the brainchild of Dr Dudley Jackson of San Antonio, who, in 1936, was successful in interesting his cousin Congressman Maury Maverick, Democrat of Texas, in sponsoring legislation leading to the creation of the NCI.[114]

At the same time, Senator Homer T. Bone and freshman Congressman Warren G. Magnuson, both Democrats from Washington, introduced identical bills in the Senate and the House on the same day calling for a substantial federal effort in cancer research. Bone's bill was unprecedented in having been co-sponsored by literally every member of the Senate and was immediately forwarded to the Committee on Commerce for consideration. The House

Committee on Interstate and Foreign Commerce, on the other hand, was confronted with two separate bills, those of Magnuson and Maverick, both having as their goal the creation of a national cancer laboratory. The reaction of Congress to both the Senate and House measures was extraordinary. Joint Senate–House hearings were held on all the proposed bills, in which virtually all testimony was favorable. The one dissenting voice was the American Medical Association, whose spokesman, Dr Olin West, was less than enthusiastic about centralizing research in a government laboratory. 'The dangers of putting the government in the dominant position in relation to medical research is apparent', the *Journal of the American Medical Association* warned.[115] Surgeon General Parran requested that Dudley Jackson, Charles C. Little, Director of the American Society for the Control of Cancer, and Lewis Thompson, the Assistant Surgeon General and Director of the NIH, proceed to draft a bill incorporating the most important features of the Bone-Magnuson and Maverick bills.[116] The result was the National Cancer Institute Bill, enacted on 23 July by unanimous vote in both houses. The measure was signed in law by President Roosevelt on 5 August 1937.

Passage of the National Cancer Institute Act proved to be of great historical moment in the history of the relation between government and biomedical research. The bill was passed with such haste that no executive branch reports relating to the Institute's proposed budgets were submitted to the congressional hearings.[117] More significantly, the establishment of an institute to investigate the nature and causes of cancer marked the fact that the federal government was now ready to undertake medical research in the whole spectrum of diseases. Senator Robert LaFollette, Progressive of Wisconsin, appears to have immediately embarked 'on measures designed to create institutes for other medical research problems'.[118] In fact, the NCI proved to be only the first of what are now no fewer than 18 separate institutes attached to the NIH, doing research in every area from diabetes to mental health.

The National Cancer Institute constituted a departure from the traditional research activities of the National Institute of Health in two important respects. First, the subject of investigation to which the NCI was dedicated was a noninfectious disease, thus granting, as one historian has put it, 'full recognition that health itself as a part of the public welfare was a proper subject of study by the federal government'.[119] Secondly, while the National Institute of Health and the Hygienic Laboratory that preceded it had concentrated on intramural research, that is, research conducted by its own scientists and carried on in the main in Public Health Service facilities, the National Cancer Institute began to expand the area of research conducted by non-PHS personnel. In fact, the NCI was authorized to embark on a trainee program whose goal was to improve the abilities of physicians to diagnose cancer. In addition, it was directed to institute a National Advisory Cancer Council to assist in the selection of grantees and trainees. As a result a good portion of the NCI's fairly extensive expenditures were used for extramural activities – its training for specialists, its fellowships, and its grants-in-aid – and were reported to have been responsible for establishing close ties with the medical schools and private investigators working on cancer.[120]

The National Advisory Cancer Council (NACC) authorized by the Act consisted of six members in addition to the Surgeon General who was its chairman *ex officio*. Among its functions was to pass on all research projects and programs submitted to it either by external applicants or NCI personnel and to review applications for grants-in-aid. It is worth underscoring that no agency of the federal government had previously supported research programs through grants-in-aid. The original members of the Advisory Council were somewhat reluctant to part with research funds, preferring to use them for intramural research and as a result at one of their first meetings they resolved to limit any such grants to 'projects closely connected with the work of the National Cancer Institute'.[121] The number of applications for grants-in-aid was not particularly large and remained small throughout the war years but with the end of hostilities this changed and in 1945 the NCI instituted a policy of supporting some grant-aided projects for periods longer than a year.[122]

A substantial proportion of the NCI's studies during World War II was related to the war effort, including, in the war's final years, those having to do with the atomic bomb. These dealt with, among other things, the effects of radiation on precipitating cancers and were undertaken by the Argonne National Laboratory at the University of Chicago and at Oak Ridge, Tennessee, under the aegis of and in cooperation with the National Cancer Institute. Despite the fact that there was a severe shortage of competent research staff, funding remained constant and while many of these funds were put to research that was almost purely war-related, a portion was set aside to maintain the major areas of peacetime research. Toward this end, the National Advisory Cancer Council voted in 1942 to give priority approval for the funding of extramural grants to what it regarded as the six major cancer research centers in the United States: the National Cancer Institute itself (!); Yale University; the Rockefeller Institute for Medical Research, New York; the Roscoe B. Jackson Laboratory at Bar Harbor, Maine; the University of Chicago; and the Memorial Hospital for the Treatment of Cancer (now the Memorial Sloan-Kettering Cancer Center) in New York City. Coincidentally, all six institutions were represented on the Council.[123]

With the introduction of extramural grants administered by the National Cancer Institute, it soon became apparent that the granting board was in danger of establishing an orthodoxy, or, at the least, a quasi-orthodoxy, regarding the issues to be investigated and would act accordingly in determining which investigators and which approaches to a problem were worth funding and which were not. This problem was to be compounded over time as the National Institutes of Health became responsible for an ever greater proportion of funding for research in biomedicine, the effect of which was to create a research bureaucracy responsible for vetting applications, thus placing in their hands the power to determine what would be regarded as acceptable approaches to a problem. With regard to the decisions of the National Cancer Institute at the beginning of World War II, acceptable approaches consisted in experiments that tended to replicate or extend those undertaken at the NCI itself. In 1942, its Council published the following policy:

> The Council desires to avoid undue competition and unnecessary duplication in cancer research, clinical as well as experimental, and will endeavor to initiate worthy projects with a view to organizing active cooperation in research with other suitable agencies. The Council, wishing to conserve the funds made available by Congress for the purpose of cancer research to the end that they may be employed to the best advantage of the country and having in mind the somewhat unsatisfactory experiences of other bodies in connection with the too wide-spread awarding of grants over a wide flung field, and further recognizing that many aspects of experimental cancer research cannot be distinguished from research in pure biology which may be outside the interest or responsibility of the Government; having in mind all these considerations the Council resolves that as a rule but without mandatory restrictions preference will be given to applications for aid of projects related to the general program of investigation being developed by the National Cancer Institute and Council.[124]

From the start of 1938 until January of 1943, the Director of the National Cancer Institute was Carl Voegtlin, who had been the Chief of the Division of Pharmacology at the NIH.[125] Voegtlin had determined that the staff of the NCI were to be kept insulated from the work done on cancer at other institutions and as a result Council sessions at which grant requests were considered were closed and their deliberations regarded as confidential. This policy of forced isolation extended to complete control over staff travel and a thorough review of all manuscripts and memoranda going beyond the Institute itself.[126] Apparently this sharp separation of the work of the Institute from that taking place at other research centers continued until the 1950s, when the intramural staff were invited to participate as project officers for the NCI's grants.

Following the end of the war, appropriations for Cancer Research took a quantum jump and continued to increase at a steady pace. The NACC had proposed that the NCI undertake research in new areas and that they expand their existing programs and these recommendations received a favorable reception from Congress and, to the surprise of many, from the Bureau of the Budget. As a consequence, the organizational structure of the NCI was redesigned into three branches, dealing with intramural cancer research, cancer research grants, and cancer control activities, each under its own administrative director. So successful was the public relations campaign conducted by the NIH and the American Cancer Society[127] in support of greater research that appropriations continued to increase, reaching over $100 000 000 in fiscal year 1961.

Table 4.2 indicates the obligations (appropriations and transfers) for the National Cancer Institute, covering extramural grants and internal operations, from its inception to 1971.

During the period 1941–45, the National Institute of Health, like all other government bureaus, had subordinated its other inquiries to research that would prove useful to the war effort. In 1941 President Roosevelt created the Office of Scientific Research and Development (OSRD) under the direction of Dr Vannevar Bush, the President's science advisor and, prior to that, president of the Carnegie Foundation. The OSRD was charged with overseeing all scientific research and development in support of the war. Directly under the OSRD was the Committee on Medical Research (CMR), established on 28 June 1941. It was charged with organizing and directing civilian personnel engaged in research on medical problems of military importance during the war, particularly problems concerning aviation medicine, antimalarial drugs, and penicillin. Its chairman was Dr Alfred N. Richards, professor of pharmacology at the University of Pennsylvania and among its regular participants was Dr Rolla Eugene Dyer, Director of the National Institute of Health. In the years between 1941 and 1947 the committee awarded no less than $25 million in contracts for work carried out in 135 universities, hospitals, research institutes, and industrial firms, involving approximately 1700 physicians and 3800 scientists.[128]

By far the greatest advance in medicine made during the war years was the discovery of the effectiveness of penicillin against infectious organisms by Ernst Chain and Sir Howard Florey of Oxford University. While research continued on the drug's efficacy, the major problems confronting medical technicians during the war were those associated with ongoing attempts to produce the antibiotic in massive quantities. American pharmaceutical firms were encouraged to produce as much penicillin as possible and by 1943, supplies of penicillin were such that it could be administered to all military casualties. During the war years, the NIH concentrated on problems associated with expanded use of the antibiotic and with its mass production, but it appears to have been unsuccessful in uncovering penicillin's molecular structure so that it could be synthesized, information that would be essential were the government to permit large-scale civilian use of the drug. As a result of the government's restrictions on civilian use of the drug, the Public Health Service's 1947 *Annual Report* noted that in 1946 there were 68 000 civilian deaths from influenza and pneumonia, almost 53 000 deaths from tuberculosis, and more than 500 000 new cases of syphilis and gonorrhea.[129]

Table 4.2　NCI: Total Obligations, Fiscal Years 1938–1971

Year	Amount ($ 000)
1938	400
1939	400
1940	570
1941	570
1942	565
1943	535
1944	530
1945	561
1946	549
1947	1821
1948	14 500
1949	14 000
1950	18 900
1951	20 086
1952	19 657
1953	17 887
1954	20 237
1955	21 737
1956	24 978
1957	48 432
1958	56 402
1959	75 268
1960	91 257
1961	111 000
1962	142 835
1963	155 742
1964	144 340
1965	150 011
1966	163 768
1967	175 656
1968	183 356
1969	185 150
1970	181 454
1971	233 160

Source:　Office of the Director, National Institutes of Health, *NIH Almanac 1997* (Washington, DC: Government Printing Office, 1999): 120.

The experience of directing the nation's medical research through the Committee on Medical Research of the Office of Scientific Research and Development induced the wartime medical administrators, among them the Surgeon General and the Director of the National Institute of Health, to attempt to extend the bureaucratic control placed in their hands beyond the end of the war. The large-scale extramural research program coordinated by the Committee, in which grants were made to medical schools, universities, and independent laboratories scattered across the nation to conduct research in their own facilities appeared to work smoothly and, more importantly, to achieve results sufficient to satisfy the Committee. As a consequence, Washington's research bureaucracy embraced the notion of establishing a federal scientific organization charged with coordinating and administering the whole spectrum of American medical research.

As early as 1943, Surgeon General Parran of the PHS established a committee of three, among whose members was Leonard Scheele, Parran's successor, to recommend changes in the legislation governing the Public Health Service in light of the war's not-too-distant termination. The outcome of this committee's deliberations was a legislative proposal that gave to the PHS authority similar to that assigned the CMR to underwrite the costs of extramural medical research. With the ardent endorsement of the Surgeon General and the Director of the NIH, Congress enacted a new Public Health Service Act in July 1944 which, among other things, gave the Surgeon General broad powers to conduct and support research into human diseases and disabilities, authorized the PHS to underwrite extramural projects and fellowships, and made the National Cancer Institute a division of the NIH. The result was a substantial extension of medical grants-in-aid which, up to that time, had been limited to the National Cancer Institute. In August 1944, the Director of the NIH wrote to Dr Richards suggesting that the Public Health Service now had the necessary credentials to continue to administer the Committee's wartime contracts should the Committee agree.[130] Immediately following passage of the new law, the PHS attempted to initiate a grants program but the Bureau of the Budget vetoed the proposal and continued to prevent the awarding of grants until the CMR ceased operations in December 1945.[131]

In November 1944 President Roosevelt, eager for an excuse to maintain the vast bureaucratic apparatus that had been established in Washington to direct the nation's scientific research once hostilities were terminated, requested that Dr Vannevar Bush prepare a report on the future of government involvement in this area. The result was Dr Bush's Report, entitled 'Science, The Endless Frontier', which he completed in July and which enthusiastically supported continuation of the OSRD, renamed the National Research Foundation, after the war. The government, Bush contended, was obligated to continue supervising the nation's research and underwriting its costs should private funding be unavailable since such research was vital to the nation's health and required coordination and direction from some central authority capable of assessing the nation's needs. The war against disease and advancing natural security, the public welfare, and 'the opening of new frontiers' all called for a central coordinating body which only the government could provide. Bush maintained:

> There should be a focal point within the Government for a concerted program of assisting scientific research conducted outside of Government. Such an agency should furnish the funds needed to support basic research in the colleges and universities, should coordinate where possible research programs on matters of utmost importance to the national welfare, should formulate a national policy for the Government toward science, should sponsor the interchange of scientific information among scientists and laboratories both in this country and abroad, and should ensure that the incentives to research in industry and the universities are maintained.[132]

President Roosevelt had died while Bush was preparing his Report and as a result it was submitted to President Truman, who took office in April. Truman appeared quite supportive and was prevailed upon to submit the proposal to Congress. However, Senator Claude Pepper of Florida, chairman of the wartime congressional Committee on Health and Education, preferred to see a separate foundation established solely for medical research. This had also been the recommendation of the subcommittee on medical research appointed by Bush in connection with his Report. Chaired by Dr Walter W. Palmer, later Director of the Public Health Research Institute, the subcommittee had proposed that 'the Federal agency concerned with medical research should be created *de novo* and be independent of all existing agencies'.[133] Despite these objections, Bush was able to prevail upon the Palmer subcommittee to acquiesce in his overall scheme.

The Bush proposal was immediately put before the Senate by Senator Warren Magnuson but, to the surprise of Truman, Bush, and a number of others, it met with surprising resistance. It appears that a number of Magnuson's colleagues feared that the NSF created under the Act would bring with it a government-funded elitist scientific establishment operated exclusively by and for researchers.[134] Additionally, not all scientists had embraced the view that a centralized government research bureaucracy was compatible with the freedom necessary for unfettered research. Bush had proposed that both military and civilian research be conducted under the umbrella of the proposed NSF, leading some scientists to fear that a cloak of government-mandated secrecy would be thrown over many of their inquiries. The effect was that the National Science Foundation was not created until 1950.[135] By that point the National Institute of Health had been substantially enlarged and the Public Health Service had greatly expanded its extramural grants program.

Having been empowered to award grants for medical research under the terms of the Public Health Service Act of 1944, the Surgeon General in 1946 established the Research Grants office to coordinate the rapidly flourishing program of extramural research. The speed with which the PHS-NIH sought to secure the remaining wartime contracts from the Committee on Medical Research guaranteed the agency its status as the federal government's preferred medical research arm, through which extramural funds would flow. Dr Dyer of the NIH was able to prevail on the CMR to transfer almost all its contracts for medical research that the army and the navy showed no interest in continuing to underwrite.[136] These transfers, in turn, were offered as evidence of the crucial role played by the NIH to reluctant officials at the Bureau of the Budget.[137] The budgets of the National Institute of Health in the two years prior to America's entry into the war, fiscal years 1940 and 1941, were slightly over $700 000 per year, with less than a third of that awarded in research grants.[138] By December 1947 the Public Health Service had awarded 1115 grants, for a total of $11 508 841.[139]

These transfers from the CMR to the NIH were crucial in establishing the NIH as the medical research arm of the federal government, which was to eventually take on such gigantic proportions. While the transformation from wartime contracts to civilian grants played such a critical role in the formation of the NIH, it went by relatively unnoticed by its opponents in both the Washington bureaucracy and the medical establishment. One historian has noted:

> The internal NIH documents that converted the procedures for a temporary transfer of contracts into policies for a permanent program of grants were, most likely, not read by anyone in Washington who opposed either the transfers or the use of grants as the mechanism to stimulate postwar medical research. As a result, PHS officials succeeded in transforming a wartime strategy to procure specific research products under sympathetic government scientific supervision into the program of investigator-initiated grants they had devised in 1943.[140]

The CMR contracts were originally administered by a small section of the Public Health Service but the number and complexity of these grants led, in early 1946, to the creation of an Office of Research Grants which was soon transformed into a Division of Research Grants (DRG), charged with administering the extramural programs of the NIH, the NCI, and the Division of Mental Hygiene. The Division soon found itself inundated by applications for grant money by the large number of investigators who were returning to civilian work and by the nationwide enthusiasm for science, which was credited with having won the war. Within a year of its establishment, the NIH had received more than 1000 requests for research money and by the end of 1946 21 study sections, charged with reviewing grant proposals, were created, in which more than 250 scientists from universities, medical schools, and research institutions served.[141] Between January 1946 and August 1947 the PHS-NIH had awarded over $10 000 000 to scientists conducting work in non-governmental institutions.

The efforts to expand the size and scope of government involvement in medical research were given considerable impetus by the wife of an advertising multimillionaire, Mrs Albert D. Lasker. Albert Lasker has been credited with establishing the principles of modern advertising, a field which amply rewarded him. His wife of 33 years having died in 1936, Lasker married Mary Woodard Reinhardt, an industrial designer from New York, in 1940 and it was she who encouraged her husband to establish the Albert and Mary Lasker Foundation for medical research in 1942.[142] While Albert Lasker had some interest in medical research, it was his wife who was at the forefront of the drive to enlarge the NIH.[143] Apparently, in 1944 Mary Lasker, tired of working with private voluntary organizations in the area of medical research, turned to government as a far more effective means to advance medicine.[144]

It was apparent by late 1944 that both the President and Congress intended to support a massive extension of peacetime scientific, and especially medical, research once the war ended. Following the 1944 elections, Senator Claude Pepper's Subcommittee on Wartime Health and Education held hearings on postwar medical research at which most of the witnesses, including several hand-picked by Mrs Lasker, supported an extensive government program of federal aid for medical research. Among the witnesses was Dr Dyer, the Director of the NIH, who put forward the idea that the NIH should act as the federal government's medical research institute, with supervisory powers over both intramural and extramural grants.

Dyer's testimony did not at first impress either Mrs Lasker or Senator Pepper, who was prepared to bring forward a bill proposing a National Medical Research Foundation. However, following the hearings, Mrs Lasker met Dr Leonard Scheele, who was to become Surgeon General in 1948, and Scheele was able to allay her doubts regarding the abilities of the PHS-NIH to administer a large-scale medical research program. As a result, when Congressman Percy Priest, Democrat of Tennessee, introduced a bill to establish a mental health division within the Public Health Service,[145] Mrs Lasker, who previously had reservations about the PHS, made strenuous efforts to see that it passed. Pepper was prevailed upon to introduce the measure in the Senate and Mrs Lasker underwrote the costs of a lobbyist to coordinate efforts to get the bill enacted.[146]

Just as had been the case following World War I, World War II sparked a renewed interest in psychiatry and in chemotherapeutic techniques for dealing with psychological problems. However, issues having to do with mental health and disease, to the extent that they involved state intervention, were regarded as the provenance of the State and not the federal government. Yet, the Public Health Service had, even prior to the War, cooperated with the American Psychiatric Association and the country's medical associations on the Mental Hospital Survey Committee, which prepared a series of studies of the nation's mental hospitals and this suggested that the PHS was prepared to extend its responsibilities to include mental health. Psychiatrists, of course, played a prominent role in the American war effort, from serving on induction boards where they purported to predict which prospective draftees were capable of managing the rigors of military life to operating in military hospitals and in the field, where they tended to soldiers with neuropsychiatric disorders.[147]

The fundamental presuppositions of psychiatry had altered considerably as a consequence of the war. While it had been thought by many that there was a clear demarcation between mental health and mental disease and that the preferred method of treatment was hospitalization, the wartime experience of military psychiatrists supported a more psychodynamic view of the mind in which health and disease were regarded as on a continuum and advocated that those suffering from neuropsychiatric disorders be treated on an outpatient basis.[148] In addition to bringing about a shift in these underlying assumptions, World War II thrust the psychiatric profession into far greater prominence than had been the case before American entry into the war. At the beginning of 1942, the Army Medical Corps had only 35 of its members assigned to neuropsychiatry. Two years later the field was raised to the level of a division in the Office of the Surgeon General of the Army, where it joined medicine and surgery, and by the end of the war approximately 2400 physicians were assigned to the field of psychiatry.[149]

Having been raised to such prominence, a number of psychiatrists proposed that psychiatry play an active role in shaping civilian life after the war. Since psychiatry was in a position to locate areas of mental stress in civilian as well as in military life, the directives issued by trained psychiatrists could insure the community's mental health. These directives went beyond claims relating to individual psychology to include programs relating to 'group mental health'. Thus, Dr William C. Menninger, who has been credited with being 'the most influential psychiatrist during the war and the immediate postwar period',[150] concluded that unemployment, prejudice, discrimination, substandard housing, and delinquency all had a destructive effect on mental health and every public effort should be made to abolish them.[151] This social activism became increasingly popular among younger psychiatrists, who regarded the more traditional view of the problems that psychiatry addressed as too confining. In the spring of 1946 Menninger led a group of psychiatrists in founding the Group for the Advancement of Psychiatry (GAP), whose function was to expand the role of psychiatry to include efforts to shape the social environment.[152] GAP's aims were clearly outlined in one of its periodical Reports, which declared that the group favored

> the most intensive study of the psycho-social factors influencing human welfare. We favor the application of psychiatric principles to all those problems which have to do with family welfare, child rearing, child and adult education, social and economic factors which influence the community status of individuals and families, inter-group tensions, civil rights and personal liberty.[153]

It was this new approach to psychiatry that energized the Public Health Service to expand into the area of mental health.

Even before the American entry into the war in 1941, Dr Lawrence D. Kolb, Director of the PHS's Division of Mental Hygiene and an expert on narcotics, had begun to agitate for the establishment of a National Neuropsychiatric Institute along the lines of the National Cancer Institute. Impressed by recent discoveries that suggested that vitamin deficiencies were linked to one's mental state and that blood sugar levels could affect mood, Kolb believed that much could be accomplished by a large-scale program to investigate the physiological basis of mental and nervous disorders.[154] While the psychiatric and psychological professions received Kolb's suggestion with enthusiasm, the war intervened and no action was taken by Congress. However, as soon as the war had concluded, the proposal was revived by Dr Robert H. Felix, who succeeded Kolb as Director of the Division in 1944. The Surgeon General, Thomas Parran, who hoped to take advantage of the enormous expansion in the size of the federal bureaucracy that occurred during the Depression and the war, approached Felix with the suggestion that Felix draft a proposal that would extend the authority of the existing Division of Mental Hygiene. Felix, eager to expand the government's role in the area of mental health, in turn, turned to Kolb's earlier recommendations as the basis for a radical reorganization of the Division. However, Felix's interests were not limited to medical research. One historian has summarized his intentions:

> A shrewd and knowledgeable individual completely familiar with organizational politics, Felix set to work to create a new bureaucratic structure within the federal government. In brief, his goal was to alter the entrenched tradition of state responsibility for mental illnesses, and use the prestige and resources of the national government to redirect mental health policies. Aware of pending changes in federal health policies generally, he was determined that mental health not be excluded.[155]

In this quest Felix was joined by the Surgeon General and by Oscar Ewing, the Administrator of the Federal Security Agency,[156] who both strongly supported Felix's suggestions. In addition, Felix had the able assistance of his colleague Mary Switzer, who helped in drafting legislation creating a National Neuropsychiatric Institute and in introducing him to Congressman J. Percy

Priest of Tennessee, who introduced the bill into the House in March 1945 and arranged hearings before his subcommittee of the Interstate and Foreign Commerce Committee. The proposal not only empowered the new agency to conduct research into questions relating to mental health but also authorized it to play a role in determining the education of professional personnel and in the availability of psychiatric services. In addition to financial and lobbying support from Mary Lasker, Felix was able to count on favorable endorsements for the measure in the Cox newspapers. Florence Mahoney, wife of Daniel Mahoney, the publisher of the *Miami Daily News*, who had family connections with the Cox newspaper chain, had joined Mary Lasker in her crusade to advance the role of government in the area of medical research. Mrs Mahoney had herself taken premedical courses while at college and fancied herself something of an expert on the economics of health care. Indeed, it appears that neither she nor Mary Lasker ever encountered a government program dealing with issues of health that they didn't fervently embrace.[157]

A few months after Representative Priest introduced the measure in the House, Senator Claude Pepper sponsored similar legislation in the Senate. Acting as co-sponsors of the bill were Senators Robert A. Taft of Ohio, George Aiken of Vermont, Robert La Follette of Wisconsin, Arthur Vandenberg of Michigan, and J. Lister Hill of Alabama. The testimony before Pepper's Health and Education Subcommittee of the Senate Committee on Education and Labor emphasized the social costs of mental illness and the paucity of research in psychiatry, besides underscoring how widespread neuropsychiatric problems were. In mid-March of 1946 the House passed the measure and two months later the Senate followed suit. On 3 July 1946 President Truman signed the National Mental Health Act, whose purpose was

> the improvement of the mental health of the people of the United States through the conducting of researches, investigations, experiments, and demonstrations, relating to the cause, diagnosis, and treatment of psychiatric disorders; assisting and fostering such research activities by public and private agencies, and promoting the coordination of all such researches and activities and the useful application of their results; training personnel in matters relating to mental health; and developing, and assisting States in the use of, the most effective methods of prevention, diagnosis, and treatment of psychiatric disorders.[158]

The new law authorized the establishment of the National Institute of Mental Health (NIMH) and the National Mental Health Advisory Council (NMHAC). The first meeting of the NMHAC was held on 15 August 1946; inasmuch as the Act did not carry with it any appropriations, the meeting was financed by a $15 000 grant from the Greentree Foundation of New York. In the following year, Congress did make an appropriation for the Institute and in April 1949 the NIMH was formally established with Robert Felix as its Director. At that point the Division of Mental Hygiene of the PHS was abolished and the NIMH became the third scientific institute of the NIH.

The creation of the NIMH went far beyond creating yet another research institute within the Public Health Service. For the first time, mental health professionals were able to rely on the Institute to lobby in their interests, thus spawning an array of programs and giving members of the profession a role in shaping policy. The effect was the formation of a mental health bureaucracy allied with an army of professional dependents who worked ceaselessly for an expansion of the role of the federal government in the area of mental hygiene.[159] This expansion was comparatively slow during the first few years after the NIMH was established; the Institute's budget in fiscal year 1949 was somewhat over \$9 000 000 and had risen to only \$14 000 000 by fiscal year 1955. However, in the next ten years increases in NIMH appropriations were nothing short of spectacular, increasing 15-fold in the next 11 years.

Table 4.3 shows the total obligations (appropriations and net transfers) for the National Institute of Mental Health from 1949 to 1966.

The powers granted to Dr Robert Felix as the Director of the NIMH to shape the nation's mental health policies were extremely far-reaching. Having developed a close relationship with the Congressional leadership responsible for legislation concerning health, Felix's testimony before the various Congressional committees was almost never questioned, nor were his budget requests. Most legislators had taken it as a given that research in the area of mental disease would soon uncover its underlying physiological causes which in turn would lead to effective treatment.[160] No longer was mental disease associated exclusively with hospitalization in distant custodial institutions. As Director of the NIMH from its inception until 1964, it was Felix more than anyone else who was responsible for legitimizing the notion that most Americans could profit from some form of professional psychological help and for encouraging the creation of community-based mental health clinics.[161] Beyond this, the research undertaken by neurochemists and physiologists at the NIMH held the promise that one day many of our undesirable mental states would be amenable to pharmacological manipulation and our earthly salvation might well rest with chemicals. This eclectic approach, in which both physiological and environmental factors were both regarded as crucial factors in the etiology of mental disease, marked the direction taken by the NIMH under Felix and his successors.

Despite Felix's reputation as the leading spokesman for psychiatric progress and for a mentally healthy population, however, he seems not to have been above using his position as Director of the NIMH to conduct experiments on those in his care in the interests of 'national security'. During the 1950s, at the height of the Cold War, the Central Intelligence Agency became obsessed in the pursuit of psycho-pharmacological agents that induce psychosis or that

Table 4.3 NIMH: Total Obligations, Fiscal Years 1948–1966

Year	Amount ($ 000)
1948	4250
1949	5821
1950	9234
1951	6970
1952	9813
1953	10 474
1954	11 741
1955	14 030
1956	18 052
1957	30 006
1958	38 457
1959	49 853
1960	67 470
1961	91 923
1962	107 711
1963	139 517
1964	170 990
1965	186 068[1]
1966	226 588

Notes: [1] Includes $35 000 000 for the construction of community mental health centers.

Source: Office of the Director, National Institutes of Health, *NIH Almanac 1997* (Washington, DC: Government Printing Office, 1999): 120.

would aid in interrogation. Soon after LSD came to the attention of the Agency in the early 1950s, it set up a grants program[162] to provide funds for testing the effects of the drug on both volunteers and unwitting recipients. The greatest number of involuntary subjects came from the NIMH's Addiction Research Center located at the Federal Narcotic Farm and Hospital in Lexington, Kentucky, where Dr Harris Isbell,[163] director of research at the prison, conducted a series of experiments with LSD, including a number which would have been impossible to undertake with voluntary subjects. These included one where he administered triple and quadruple doses to his subjects and another where he kept several patients on LSD for a period of 77 days![164] These experiments, performed upon inmates unaware of what was happening to them, were conducted with the full knowledge and consent of both the Director of the NIH, and Dr Felix of the NIMH.[165]

Having committed themselves to a large-scale effort in the area of medical research, the Administration and Congress were comparatively open to the creation of yet further research facilities. The Surgeon General and the Director of the National Institute of Health, eager to further expand their authority, recommended that further disease-oriented institutes be authorized and, indeed, two further research facilities were established by Congress in 1948, the National Heart Institute and the National Dental Research Institute. At the same time, the National Institute of Health was pluralized and the umbrella agency continued as the National Institutes of Health.

The NIH had, of course, been engaged in research on heart disease long before 1948. In 1938, soon after the Institute was established, Dr O. F. Hedley, a PHS commissioned officer who had been engaged in the investigation of heart disease at the field office in Philadelphia, had approached Surgeon General Thomas Parran about the creation of an Institute of Cardiovascular Diseases. While Parran was, of course, agreeable to the proposal, it appears that funding was not available and the idea was temporarily put aside. Soon after the end of World War II, however, Hedley's recommendations were revived, largely through the intercession of none other than Mary Lasker, the Godmother of government health programs.

Once again, Mrs Lasker approached Senator Claude Pepper, who had shown himself prepared to lend unlimited support and to appropriate unlimited tax monies to underwrite government biomedical research. However, the Congressional elections of 1946 had resulted in a Republican victory and as a result Senator Pepper had lost his committee chairmanships. Anxious to help, it struck both Mrs Lasker and Senator Pepper that Styles Bridges of New Hampshire, the new chairman of the Senate Appropriations Committee, had recently suffered a heart attack and might well support the creation of a facility devoted to heart research.[166] As predicted, Bridges held hearings in May on a deficiency appropriation for the NIH which would immediately make available funds for heart research, the witnesses for which were arranged by Mary Lasker. Leonard Scheele had replaced Thomas Parran as Surgeon General the previous month and this change encouraged Mrs Lasker to push for passage of the necessary legislation with even greater vigor.

It was Scheele who drafted the bill for establishing a heart institute, which, with two exceptions, he patterned after the Act creating the NCI. Unlike the National Cancer Institute Act, however, the new bill contained a provision which permitted the granting of funds for the construction of research facilities, which was of particular interest to universities, and another that allowed laymen to serve on the advisory councils of the National Institutes of Health. This was included with Mary Lasker in mind and, in point of fact, once legislation was enacted, Surgeon General Scheele immediately appointed Mrs Lasker to the Heart Institute's medical research advisory board. The bill was duly introduced into the Senate by Senator Bridges and co-sponsored by Senators Pepper, Irving M. Ives, Republican of New York, and James E. Murray, Democrat of Montana.

Hearings on the bill were held by the Subcommittee on Health of the Senate Committee on Labor and Public Welfare in April 1948, and by the House Committee on Interstate and Foreign Commerce in the following month. Testimony was predictable and all witnesses supported the creation of the new institute, among them representatives of a new organization, the National Heart Committee, created solely for the purpose of supporting the legislation. The Committee's membership included motion picture actors and directors, business leaders, industrial and labor leaders, writers and publishers, religious leaders, and several renowned heart specialists, and was clearly designed for its public relations value. Among the evidence presented by the Committee was a Fact Sheet containing statistics purportedly showing the horrendous cost to the nation of heart disease in terms of lost work days and the expense of treatment. In addition, the Fact Sheet referred to an opinion poll taken in January 1947 by Research Associates in which over 80 percent of the American public appeared to indicate that they were prepared to pay higher taxes for more research into tuberculosis and heart disease.[167]

As expected, both the Senate and House enacted the measure in short order. On 16 June 1948 President Truman signed the National Heart Act,[168] establishing the National Heart Institute (NHI). Dr Cassius J. VanSlyke, a PHS commissioned officer who had been Director of the National Institutes of Health Division of Research Grants, was named Director of the new NHI and Congress appropriated almost $3 000 000 in its first year of operation. During the late 1950s and early 1960s Congress was particularly generous to the Institute, having doubled its appropriation between 1957 to 1960 and doubled it again between 1960 and 1962. Table 4.4 shows the total obligations (appropriations and net transfers) for the National Heart Institute from 1949 to 1971.

1948 also witnessed the birth of the National Institute of Dental Research. The federal government had been involved in some measure with dental research as early as 1919, when the National Bureau of Standards established a dental research unit to investigate the question of dental fillings. Apparently the army had discovered that most of its recruits in World War I had been fitted with unsuitable fillings and the National Bureau was called upon to develop a set of specifications for dental amalgam. At the close of the World War and prior to the establishment of the Veterans' Bureau in 1921 the Public Health Service had been assigned the duty of providing hospital and medical care for veterans who were suffering from illnesses or injuries brought about by their military experience. A portion of the care provided these veterans was dental treatment and this, in turn, helped promote the notion that the PHS should undertake research into dental care. In addition, the American Dental

Table 4.4   NHI: Total Obligations, Fiscal Years 1949–1971

Year	Amount ($ 000)
1949	2835
1950	10 725
1951	14 200
1952	10 083
1953	12 000
1954	15 168
1955	15 688
1956	18 898
1957	33 396
1958	35 936
1959	45 613
1960	62 237
1961	86 900
1962	132 912
1963	147 398
1964	132 404
1965	124 824
1966	141 462
1967	164 770
1968	167 954
1969	166 926
1970	160 634
1971	194 925

Source: Office of the Director, National Institutes of Health, *NIH Almanac 1997* (Washington, DC: Government Printing Office, 1999): 120.

Association (ADA) was eager that the federal government carry on research in those areas it deemed pressing.

In May 1923 the Surgeon General appointed Dr Clinton T. Messner as chief of its dental services. Messner was a tireless advocate of extended dental research and he and the ADA were active in putting forward an ambitious plan of study at the 1928 Senate hearings on the creation of a National Institute of Health. The Ransdell bill creating the NIH was finally passed in May 1930 and Messner and the ADA were rewarded for their support of the legislation by the creation of a program of dental research at the Institute. In July 1931 Surgeon General Cumming, having appointed a committee of dental specialists to advise him as to which areas of research the Institute should concentrate on, ordered research to be undertaken in what were then regarded as the three most significant problems in dentistry: dental caries, dental infection, and mottled enamel.[169] At the same time, Dr Henry Treadway Dean was appointed the Institute's first dental scientist and was charged with conducting a national survey of mottled enamel.

When Dr Thomas Parran was appointed Surgeon General in 1936 he brought to the PHS ambitious plans for the Service's expansion. The establishment of the National Cancer Institute in 1937 was a model for the kind of research organization that Parran, Messner, and Dean hoped to create to carry on research in dentistry. However, the war intervened and the NIH's dental team devoted itself to dental problems that were particularly appropriate to American involvement in the war, in particular trench mouth. Their investigations indicated that the incidence of the disease could be substantially reduced by immediate scaling to remove tartar from the teeth and below the gum line and by brushing several times a day.

In 1939 the Public Health Service was moved from the Treasury Department to the newly created Federal Security Agency and, at the same time, the PHS and its subsidiary agency, the NIH, put forward plans to reorganize themselves. Encouraged by President Roosevelt's own schemes for reorganizing the executive branch, Dean and his fellow dental researchers proposed that a national dental institute be established. This suggestion was immediately taken up by Dr C. Willard Camalier, a Washington, DC dentist who was at one time President of the American Dental Association and prominent in Washington circles. Camalier was particularly friendly with Senator James E. Murray, Democrat from Montana, who had entered the Senate in 1933 and was assigned to the Committee on Education and Labor, which oversaw the Public Health Service. Murray was quickly won over to Camalier's suggestion and almost immediately introduced a bill into the Senate calling for the creation of a dental research facility. The measure failed but Congress did enact the Public Health Reorganization Act of 1944, whose provisions included the appointment of the PHS's chief dental officer as an Assistant Surgeon General and which upgraded the NIH's dental program.[170]

The establishment of the NIH in 1930 and the creation of the Office of Scientific Research and Development in 1941 proved to be a boon to propagandists hoping to expand the role of the federal government in scientific research following the end of hostilities. Not only was the atomic bomb credited to government research but the development of computers, advances in rocketry, and breakthroughs in the commercial preparation of penicillin, among countless others, were all proclaimed as examples of what could be accomplished by scientists working under the direction of a generous, beneficent bureaucracy with the nation's treasure at their disposal. It was against this backdrop that, in 1944, the American Dental Association's legislative committee prepared a new proposal to create a research institute, which they submitted to Senator Murray as the newly appointed Chairman of the Senate Committee on Education and Labor.[171]

Murray duly introduced the bill, S. 190, in January 1945. Among its provisions was the establishment of an institute to conduct research on the cause, prevention, and treatment of dental ailments and to provide extramural fellowships and grants-in-aid. In addition, the bill authorized a $1 million appropriation for a new building to house the research facility. Support for the bill among dental professionals was almost total.[172] In spring 1946 the Committee reported favorably on the measure and it was passed by the full Senate in June. The House, however, occupied with enacting new peacetime legislation, postponed consideration of the bill until the next Congress where it was once again considered in the following session. Both Democrats and Republicans in the Senate and the House introduced legislation calling for the establishment of a federal dental research institute. No fewer than six different measures were under consideration in 1947 and 1948.

The bill, as finally enacted by both the Senate and the House, provided for an appropriation of $2 million for a building and equipment and authorized the new institute not only to conduct research but to provide training and instruction on matters relating to dental diseases and conditions. In addition, a national Advisory Dental Research Council, composed of experts and laymen, was empowered to review dental research programs and support extramural dental research and training applications. On 24 June 1948 President Truman signed into law Public Law 755 and the Dental Research Section of the PHS was transformed into the National Institute of Dental Research (NIDR). In September Surgeon General Scheele appointed Dr Henry Treadway Dean as the Institute's first Director.

By far the most well-known of the NIDR's projects was that which led to the artificial fluoridation of America's water supply. Having studied the effects of natural instances of fluoridation on children's teeth, the Public Health Service had, in 1945, decided to launch an experiment in Grand Rapids, Michigan, the world's first artificial fluoridation project. The water supply of Grand Rapids was fluoridated while that of nearby Muskegon remained fluoride-free and the effects on the populations of the two towns were to be observed over the next 15 years. The experiment was inherited by the NIDR, who proceeded to examine the effect of fluoridated water on deciduous and permanent teeth and whether artificially fluoridated water was as effective as was naturally fluoridated water in inhibiting tooth decay. Despite the fact that the experiment's 15-year term was not yet over and no conclusive results had been arrived at, Dean and other dental scientists from the NIDR began to openly support fluoridation when the subject arose at professional meetings as early as 1949.[173]

The Director of Dental Health for the Wisconsin State Board of Health, Dr Francis A. Bull, had become no less than fanatical in his support for immediate fluoridation of the nation's water supply. In May 1950 Bull led a contingent of like-minded state dental health bureaucrats to Washington to demand that the NIDR swiftly endorse mass fluoridation. As a consequence, the chief dental scientist at the PHS issued a statement supporting the movement, and Dean, in his annual report for 1950, reported that the preliminary results of the Grand Rapids tests 'are sufficiently encouraging to indicate that this may prove to be one of the most feasible methods for controlling caries on a mass basis'.[174]

Table 4.5 indicates the total obligations (appropriations and net transfers) of the National Institute of Dental Research from 1949 until 2005. Its budget remained fairly constant from its inception until fiscal year 1956 when it shot up by over 250 percent. From that point on, appropriations followed the general pattern of those for the NIH's other institutes, almost doubling every five years.

Table 4.5   NIDR: Total Obligations, Fiscal Years 1949–2005

Year	Amount ($ 000)
1949	1733
1950	1780
1951	1955
1952	1618
1953	1650
1954	1740
1955	1990
1956	2176
1957	6026
1958	6430
1959	7420
1960	10 019
1961	15 500
1962	17 340
1963	21 199
1964	19 689
1965	20 083
1966	23 677
1967	28 308
1968	30 307
1969	29 984

Table 4.5 *(continued)*

Year	Amount ($ 000)
1970	28 754
1971	35 440
1972	43 388
1973	46 991
1974	43 959
1975	50 033
1976	51 291
1976TQ	7854
1977	55 573
1978	61 728
1979	65 213
1980	68 303
1981	71 114
1982	71 983
1983	79 292
1984	88 674
1985	100 688
1986	98 841
1987	117 945
1988	126 297
1989	130 709
1990	135 749
1991	148 918
1992	158 417
1993	161 301
1994	169 520
1995	162 430
1996	182 923
1997	195 825
1998	209 415
1999	234 183
2000	268 811
2001	306 211
2002	342 664
2003	371 636
2004	383 282
2005	391 829

Source: Office of the Director, National Institutes of Health, 'Appropriations', *NIH Almanac 2006* (Washington, DC, March, 2006).

Changes in the structure of the NIH that took place in 1948 and 1949, which witnessed the creation of the National Institute of Mental Health and the National Institute of Dental Research, encouraged the Director to reorganize several divisions within the National Institutes itself. Its core research departments, the Division of Tropical Diseases and the Division of Infectious Diseases, together with the Biologics Control Laboratory and the Rocky Mountain Laboratory, were brought together to form the National Microbiological Institute (NMI).[175] In 1955 the Biologics Control Laboratory was detached from the Institute and given division status in the NIH while the Institute itself was renamed the National Institute of Allergy and Infectious Diseases (NIAID) to reflect its growing interest in allergies and immunological disorders.

Among the ailments investigated by the NIAID were sexually transmitted diseases and in 1974 the Institute began establishing satellite centers dedicated to the multidisciplinary study of these infections. Accordingly, it was natural that the bulk of the AIDS studies later undertaken and supported by the NIH would occur through the facilities of the NIAID. In 1983 Congress enacted a supplemental appropriations bill for the PHS which included a provision for AIDS. This represented a landmark in NIH history since among the sums provided was $9 375 000 earmarked for the NIH, the first time that Congress appropriated monies for AIDS research. Table 4.6 gives some idea of the growth of the National Microbiological Institute and its successor, the NIAID, from its fiscal year 1952 to 1981.

Yet another institute was established at the same time as was the National Microbiological Institute. The Experimental Biology and Medicine Institute was the fourth constituent institute to be created in 1948 and lasted under that name for only two years. In 1950, with the passage of the Omnibus Medical Research Act, it was absorbed by the new National Institute of Arthritis and Metabolic Diseases (NIAMD). Indeed, under a variety of names changes,[176] the Institute's responsibilities and budget grew so rapidly that it was finally split in 1986 into the National Institute of Arthritis and Musculoskeletal and Skin Diseases and the National Institute of Diabetes and Digestive and Kidney Diseases.

Table 4.7 is indicative of this growth.

Thus, at the end of 1949, the National Institutes of Health comprised the following Institutes:

National Cancer Institute
National Institute of Mental Health
National Heart Institute
National Institute of Dental Research
National Microbiological Institute
Experimental Biology and Medical Institute

Table 4.6   NMI and NIAID: Total Obligations, Fiscal Years 1952–1981

Year	Amount ($ 000)
National Microbiological Institute	
1952	5501
1953	5534
1954	5738
National Institute of Allergy and Infectious Diseases	
1955	6180
1956	7775
1957	13 299
1958	17 400
1959	24 071
1960	34 054
1961	44 000
1962	56 091
1963	66 142
1964	68 723
1965	69 847
1966	77 987
1967	90 670
1968	94 422
1969	96 841
1970	97 342
1971	102 368
1972	109 117
1973	113 414
1974	111 089
1975	119 452
1976	126 852
1976TQ	27 638
1977	141 000
1978	162 341
1979	191 328
1980	215 364
1981	232 077

Source: Office of the Director, National Institutes of Health, *NIH Almanac 1997* (Washington, DC: Government Printing Office, 1999): 120.

Table 4.7   NIAMD, NIAMDD, and NIDDK Total Obligations, Fiscal Years 1952–2005

Year	Amount ($ 000)
National Institute of Arthritis and Metabolic Diseases (NIAMD)	
1952	4064
1953	4335
1954	7000
1955	8270
1956	10 840
1957	15 885
1958	20 385
1959	31 215
1960	46 862
1961	61 200
1962	81 831
1963	103 388
1964	113 679
1965	113 051
1966	123 203
1967	135 687
1968	143 954
1969	143 888
1970	131 761
1971	137 986
National Institutes of Arthritis, Metabolism, and Digestive Diseases (NIAMDD)	
1972	153 337
1973	167 316
1974	153 561
1975	173 514
1976	179 516
1976TQ	43 719
1977	219 600
1978	260 253
1979	302 767
1980	341 206
National Institute of Arthritis, Diabetes, and Digestive and Kidney Diseases (NIDDK)	
1981	368 191

Table 4.7 *(continued)*

Year	Amount ($ 000)
1982	368 188
1983	413 492
1984	464 026
1985	543 576
1986	544 858
1987	511 124
1988	534 733
1989	559 494
1990	581 477
1991	615 272
1992	658 925
1993	681 342
1994	716 054
1995	726 949
1996	770 582
1997	815 607
1998	900 860
1999	1 020 559
2000	1 168 476
2001	1 399 684
2002	1 562 144
2003	1 722 730
2004	1 821 803
2005	1 863 584

Source: Office of the Director, National Institutes of Health, *NIH Almanac 2006* (Washington, DC, March 2006.

Total NIH appropriations in fiscal year 1950 were $59 235 000, of which $43 823 000 was expended in the form of grants and the remaining $15 412 000, or about 26 percent, used for direct operations.

The NIH's expansion was facilitated by a Congress that was more than generous in its treatment of the agency. At the close of the war, it became apparent that medical research had become quite fashionable and Congress, now in the habit of appropriating huge amounts of tax dollars for favored projects, seemed prepared to treat the budget requests of the NIH similarly. The Republicans had taken control of Congress in the elections of 1946 and the NIH, encouraged by its friends, submitted a proposed budget of

$23 000 000 for fiscal year 1948, more than three times its budget for fiscal year 1947, when the Democrats were last in control. Not only did Congress approve this amount but it added $3 000 000 to its appropriation! Both Congressman Frank Keefe of Wisconsin and Senator Edward Thye of Minnesota, the chairmen of the appropriations subcommittees responsible for the NIH, were ardent supporters of an extensive government research program. Both these politicians saw in their chairmanships the opportunity to determine the scope and direction of medical research and how the American medical bureaucracy was structured.[177] In this respect, Keefe and Thye – and their Democratic counterparts – were in a particularly enviable position. The Public Health Act of 1944 had authorized the PHS to engage in research on a continuing basis, with no fixed ceiling on expenditures. Of course, Congress had still to annually determine how much it chose to make available to the agency but the task of securing annual authorizations and appropriations was removed. As a result, it was customary for the parent committees of the House and Senate to defer to the relevant subcommittee's decisions on the nature of the programs undertaken by the PHS-NIH and the proposed appropriations earmarked for its various projects. This placed the chairmen of these subcommittees in the position of effectively being able to determine the type and size of projects in which the NIH was engaged.[178]

When President Truman was re-elected in 1948, Congress once again reverted to Democratic control and John Fogarty of Rhode Island replaced Keefe as chairman of the House Labor-Federal Security Agency appropriations subcommittee. Despite this change, Keefe continued to exercise a good deal of authority in the House on matters of health and shaped Fogarty's approach to such expenditures. Among the lessons passed on were that the Bureau of the Budget must be deflected from reducing budget requests before they were considered by Congress and that such requests must never be allowed to become partisan political issues.[179] These lessons continued to guide Congressional leaders responsible for appropriations for biomedical research down to the present.

1950 was a particularly eventful year for Washington's research bureaucracy. In that year the National Science Foundation (NSF) was finally created, with the object of advancing fundamental research in science and engineering. While the NIH had effectively established itself as the government's primary agency for undertaking biomedical research, the NSF was also charged with addressing fundamental questions in biology, thus further expanding the role of the federal government in this area. In a less than convincing attempt to distinguish the goals of the NIH from the NSF's Medical Division, the Director of the NSF noted in 1960:

> The National Institutes of Health stresses research aimed at the care and cure of diseases, including basic research related to its mission ... The National Science

Foundation, on the other hand, supports basic research in this area primarily for the purpose of advancing our knowledge and understanding of biological and medical fields.[180]

In addition, Congress directed the Atomic Energy Commission to investigate the linkage between atomic research and cancer therapies and provided some $5 000 000 for this purpose in 1950. Finally, the Veterans Administration and the Defense Department at about this time began conducting research into medical problems that were related to military conditions.

Even more significant than these events was passage of the Omnibus Medical Research Act, which was signed by President Truman in May 1950. The Act authorized establishment of yet another research facility, the Institute of Neurological Diseases and Blindness, and the transmutation of the Experimental Biology and Medical Institute into a far larger Institute of Arthritis and Metabolic Diseases. In addition, the Act empowered the Surgeon General to create additional institutes as he determined the need for them and to 'conduct and support research and research training relating to other diseases and groups of diseases'.[181]

Over the course of the following half century the NIH continued to grow and its appropriations climbed steadily. Other than during the brief periods when the United States was involved in a major conflict, the NIH was treated most generously by Congress. This was especially true following the elections of 1954. In organizing the 84th Congress, the chairmanship of the Senate subcommittee charged with handling health appropriations would ordinarily have gone to Senator Denis Chavez of New Mexico. Chavez, however, chose to become chairman of the Defense Appropriations Subcommittee and as a result Senator J. Lister Hill took over as chairman of the subcommittee that oversaw appropriations in the area of health. Hill, the son of a physician,[182] a staunch supporter of government aid in all areas of health, was encouraged to take on the role of pre-eminent spokesman for federal support of medicine by Florence Mahoney, herself a tireless lobbyist for public health programs. In January 1955 Hill assumed the chairmanship of the Senate Subcommittee on Labor – (HEW) Health, Education, and Welfare and from then until his retirement he was the single most influential member of Congress in matters of health. During those 14 years no fewer than 60 measures relating to health were enacted under his sponsorship.[183]

While Hill was championing larger expenditures for medical research in the Senate, John Fogarty, Hill's opposite number in the House, was attempting the same thing in the lower chamber. Even in the face of somewhat more modest requests from the Secretary of Health, Education, and Welfare, the President, and the Bureau of the Budget, Fogarty's subcommittee regularly recommended higher appropriations.[184] Fogarty's philosophy was summed up in a statement he made before his subcommittee in response to an appeal by the Administration that Congress respect its wishes:

> I do not think we are going far enough. I think we should be doing more than we are doing . . . The Federal Government could do more than it is doing at the present time and accomplish results by spending money.[185]

Both Hill and Fogarty appear to have assumed that any medical condition that struck them or their colleagues as of some concern should be of concern to all taxpayers and taxed funds should be placed at the disposal of researchers to investigate the problem. Thus, Representative Fogarty, when questioning the Director of the National Institute of Mental Health during the 1958 hearings of his subcommittee, casually mentioned that he had read something on problem drinkers in American industry. As a result, a substantial appropriation was passed by Congress for research in this area and the NIMH initiated a huge research undertaking dealing with problem drinking that year. Similarly, Senator Hubert Humphrey approached Hill regarding a condition known as ulcerative colitis, from which the daughter of a friend was suffering. During questioning of Dr James A. Shannon, who had become Director of the NIH in 1955, Hill learned that the NIH was doing no research in this area; the result was that funds were immediately forthcoming to begin a research program centering on ulcerative colitis.[186]

In the 25 years between 1950 and 1975 the budget of the National Institutes of Health grew from $67 000 000 to almost $2 100 000 000. In addition, a number of new institutes were created to deal with more specialized areas of research. The following institutes were established during that period:

1955: National Institute of Allergy and Infectious Diseases (NIAID) (replacing the National Microbiological Institute, which had been created in 1948);

1963: National Institute of Child Health and Human Development (NICHD);

1963: National Institute of General Medical Sciences (NIGMS);

1968: National Institute of Neurological Diseases (NIND), (incorporating the Neurological Diseases Division of the National Institute of Neurological Diseases and Blindness, itself created in 1950). Later that year, renamed the National Institute of Neurological Diseases and Stroke (NINDS);

1968: National Eye Institute (NEI), (incorporating the blindness program of the National Institute of Neurological Diseases and Blindness, established in 1950);

1969: National Institute of Environmental Health Sciences (NIEHS);

1969: National Heart and Lung Institute (NHLI) (replacing the National Heart Institute, which was established in 1948);[187]

1970: National Institute of Alcohol Abuse and Alcoholism (NIAAA);

1972: National Institute of Arthritis, Metabolism, and Digestive Diseases (NIAMDD) (incorporating the National Institute of Arthritis and Metabolic Diseases, established in 1950);

1975: National Institute on Aging (NIA);

1975: National Institute of Neurological Diseases and Stroke once again underwent a name change to the National Institute of Neurological and Communicative Disorders and Stroke (NINCDS). When, in 1988, the National Institute of Deafness and Other Communication Disorders was severed from the parent institute, the NINCDS was renamed the National Institute of Neurological Disorders and Stroke (NINDS).

While support for all research and development in the United States from 1950 to 1975 increased tenfold, total support for biomedical research and development increased by a factor of 25 and the proportion funded by the federal government by a factor of 30. Tables 4.8 and 4.9 provide data on the growth of scientific research in general and of biomedical research in

Table 4.8 *Research and Development Expenditures, Selected Fiscal Years 1950–1995 ($ 000,000)*

	Total Nationwide	Medical Nationwide	Percent	All Federal Medical	Percent
1950	2900	161	5.6	73	45.3
1955	6279	261	4.2	139	53.3
1960	13 730	845	6.2	448	53.0
1965	20 439	1837	9.0	1174	63.9
1970	20 455	2731	10.3	1667	61.0
1971	27 336	3023	11.1	1877	62.9
1972	29 208	3354	11.5	2147	64.0
1973	30 100	3540	11.8	2225	62.4
1974	32 100	4291	13.3	2795	65.1
1995	183 013	25 202	13.8	11 407	45.3

Source: G. Burroughs Mider, 'The Federal Impact on Biomedical Research', in John Z. Bowers and Elizabeth F. Purchell, eds, *Advances in American Medicine: Essays at the Bicentennial* (2 vols, New York: Josiah Macy, Jr Foundation, 1976): 2: 851. Data for 1995: Kevin M. Murphy and Robert Topel, 'The Economic Value of Medical Research', September 1999 (gsbwww.uchicago.edu/fac/kevin.murphy/research/murphy&topel.pdf): Table 5.

Table 4.9   Federal Obligations for Health Research and Development by Agency, Selected Fiscal Years, 1950–1974[1]
($000,000)

Agency	1950	1955	1960	1965	1970	1971	1972	1973	1974
Total	73	139	448	1174	1667	1877	2147	2225	2796
Department of Health, Education, and Welfare	36	70	311	826	1177	1316	1584	1610	2076
National Institutes of Health	*28*	*60*	*281*	*715*	*873*	*1039*	*1271*	*1323*	*1738*
Atomic Energy Commission	18	29	50	85	104	105	103	111	127
Department of Defense	10	24	42	101	125	124	126	127	121
Department of Transportation	2	2	2	3	10	42	39	65	121
Veterans Administration	4	6	15	37	59	63	69	74	81
National Aeronautics and Space Administration	–	–	2	60	86	75	50	42	80
Department of Agriculture	5	9	15	41	50	60	67	61	60
National Science Foundation	–	2	12	20	28	34	37	46	47
Department of the Interior	2	2	2	2	4	23	34	33	33
Environmental Protection Agency	–	–	–	–	–	13	15	20	19
Other	0	0	3	1	24	22	23	36	31

Notes:
1   Data not strictly comparable from year to year.
2   Less than $ 1 000 000.

Source: John Z. Bowers and Elizabeth F. Purcell, eds, *Advances in American Medicine: Essays at the Bicentennial* (2 vols, New York: Josiah Macy Jr Foundation, 1976): 2: 852.

particular in the United States and the contribution of the National Institutes of Health to that growth.

It should be underscored that not all federal medical research is undertaken by the National Institutes of Health. For example, the Department of Agriculture is engaged in research relating to the diseases of domestic animals and to both animal and human nutrition, while the National Areonautics and Space Administration engages in research in the area of aerospace medicine. Table 4.9 breaks down the federal involvement in health research by agency.

While it has traditionally been assumed that President Eisenhower favored stringent economies in federal spending, he in fact supported fairly generous appropriations for health and welfare programs.[188] In this he both disappointed his first Director of the Bureau of the Budget, Joseph Dodge, and delighted his Secretary of Health, Education, and Welfare, Marion Folsom.[189] Indeed, Eisenhower actively supported Folsom's recommendations for larger

Table 4.10   Federal Obligations for Medical and Health Research and Development by Agency, 2005 and 2006 ($million)

	2005	2006
Department of Health and Human Services	29 023	28 981
National Institutes of Health	27 784	27 784
Department of Defense		
Medical Research	507	537
National Aeronautics and Space Administration		
Human Systems Research and Technology	925	791
Department of Energy		
Biological and Environmental Research	582	580
National Science Foundation		
Biological Sciences	577	582
Department of Homeland Security		
Biological Countermeasures	363	376
Radiological and Nuclear Countermeasures	123	210
Department of the Interior, US Geological Survey		
Biological Research	172	179
Department of Veterans Affairs		
Medical and Prosthetic Research	784	805
Total	33 056	34 041

Source: American Association for the Advancement of Science, R&D Funding Update, 4 January 2006: FY 2006 Final Appropriations (Part 2 of 2): Tables (http://www.aaas.org/spp/rd/upd1205tb.htm#tb2).

appropriations to the NIH budget in 1956 and 1957 and did not oppose the huge increases made by Congress in 1959 and 1960.[190] These massive increases were questioned by some and as a consequence it was decided to reassure the nation that these funds were well-spent by appointing a 'fact-finding' commission 'to determine whether the funds provided by the Government for research in dread diseases are sufficient and efficiently spent in the best interests of the research for which they were designated'.[191]

The Committee, chaired by Boisfeuillet Jones, the Vice President for Medical Affairs at Emory University, was a creature of the Senate Subcommittee on Health and was appointed by its chairman, Lister Hill. While Hill instructed Jones to engage in a thorough examination of federal spending on medical research and whether these funds were used wisely and constituted a proper proportion of the nation's resources, it was clear that the committee had been established for public relations purposes only. Its membership comprised an overwhelming number of supporters of government spending in the area, including Dr Michael DeBakey, the cardiac surgeon, Dr Sidney Farber, one of the nation's leading proponents of cancer research, Dr Harry Lyons of the American Dental Association (and later President of the American College of Dentists), Dr Cornelius Traeger, Medical Director of the National Multiple Sclerosis Society, Dr Cecil Wittson of the Menninger Clinic, and General David Sarnoff of RCA, a staunch supporter of government funding for biomedical research.

David Strickland, who has written exhaustively on the government's role in medical research, notes of this Committee:

> The opportunity which membership on the Committee of Consultants provided for those regular advisers to the Congress who had consistently urged rapid, solid expansion of the government's biomedical research effort was a rare one. Ordinarily, particular interest groups must take their chances with the rest of them, figuring out a way to gain access to the policy maker, competing for time to make their case, and often having to struggle against opposing interest groups. The medical research lobby not only had no opposite number, but the opportunity to present its case had already been elevated, guaranteed, institutionalized by the congressional committees that needed persuasion. They were high-class burglars, admitted Mike Gorman,[192] who walked right in the front door and were cordially welcomed by those holding the resources they were after. Now if the Jones Committee reached agreement on major points, that would be tantamount to passing approval on one's own grant.[193]

The report was predictable. The Committee, after having interviewed no fewer than '100 expert witnesses' and having consulted numerous documents, arrived at the unanimous conclusion that the funds that had been appropriated by Congress for medical research had been used 'with remarkable efficiency'. The NIH, it found, had maintained consistently high standards and had proved itself a model of how a grant-making institution should operate. If any complaint could be made about Congressional appropriations, it was that they were not sufficiently generous and thus the NIH was prevented from fully exploring new and promising areas of research that had opened up over the previous 15 years. In keeping with these findings, the Committee recommended hefty increases in future appropriations and even suggested areas that might well receive additional funds, increases, the Committee underscored, that should be viewed not as a maximum 'but as the floor from which further advances will be made in years to come'.[194]

These 'findings' formed the basis of many of the conclusions later reached by the Wooldridge Report of 1965, the most ambitious study yet made of the NIH. The Report had its origins in a request made by President John Kennedy that a study be conducted of the NIH's operations. Despite the fact that the Institutes' budgets had been growing rapidly and its activities were expanding at a substantial rate, it continued to request larger appropriations. Kennedy's first budget had called for an increase of $40 million, the largest dollar increase ever proposed for medical research by an Administration and the largest percentage increase since 1955. Yet even in the face of this request, Senator Hill and Congressman Fogarty were able to prevail on Congress to approve a final appropriation of $738 million, $110 million more than Kennedy had requested.[195]

Such differences between the President and Congress, coupled with an increasing number of complaints regarding the administration and management of the NIH, finally led Lawrence H. Fountain, Democrat from North Carolina and chairman of the Intergovernmental Relations Subcommittee of the House Government Operations Committee, to direct his committee to examine the operations of the NIH 'with a view to determining its economy and efficiency'. In point of fact the NIH had grown so large so quickly that it was inevitable that serious deficiencies in its grants program would be uncovered. The committee's first report was released in April 1961 and, having found that there were problems in the administration of the grants programs, the committee made a series of recommendations for improving the methods by which grant recipients were selected.

While Dr James Shannon, the Director of the NIH, was prepared to accept the committee's recommendations, he was alarmed and disturbed that the committee intended to continue its oversight activities. Everything beyond the task of choosing which scientists and which projects were to receive federal grants, Shannon contended, was trivial and need hardly be supervised by a Congressional committee. This attitude infuriated Representative Fountain and the other members of his subcommittee.[196] More importantly, the committee concluded:

It appears that Congress has been overzealous in appropriating money for health research. The conclusion is inescapable, from a study of NIH's loose administrative practices, that the pressure for spending increasingly large appropriations has kept NIH from giving adequate attention to basic management problems. The committee expects NIH to give high priority at this time to the task of correcting its management deficiencies and strengthening its capability for the effective and efficient operation of these vital health programs.[197]

These were the first strongly negative views put forward by either the Administration or Congress regarding the NIH and their effect was immediate. The NIH's fiscal 1964 appropriations were $15 million less than that recommended by the President, $7 million less than that for the previous year, and President Kennedy requested that a large-scale study be undertaken of the activities of the NIH, which, at the time, was responsible for 40 percent of the country's research in the area of health. The request was reaffirmed by President Lyndon Johnson immediately following Kennedy's assassination and in early 1964 a 13-member committee was set up to carry out the investigation.

Dr Dean E. Wooldridge, vice-president for research and development at Hughes Aircraft and co-founder of Ramos-Wooldridge Corporation, a firm established to provide science and engineering planning for the Defense Department's ballistic missile program, was chosen as chairman of the committee, to which were appointed seven university officials, a chairman of the board of a university, a foundation president, two business executives, and the Commissioner of Health of New York City. While for the most part favorably disposed toward government-sponsored research, the committee, unlike the members of the Jones Committee, were more objective in their weighing of the testimony and evidence presented to them, although the Wooldridge Committee's conclusions often reflected the same approving tone. Like the Jones Committee, the Wooldridge Committee – officially known as the NIH Study Committee – found 'that the activities of the National Institutes of Health are essentially sound and that its budget of approximately one billion dollars a year is, on the whole, being spent wisely and well in the public interest'.[198]

With respect to the overall management of the NIH, the Committee concluded that the NIH's central management lacked sufficient overall planning for allocating its funds in conformity with clearly established priorities. 'Central planning of the total program', the Report noted, 'needs more explicit attention . . . and the Director of the NIH should have more formal authority over the management of the program, and better-defined sources of advice as to how it should be managed'. And with particular regard to the Institutes' extramural grants, the Committee was displeased to find that the granting Institute's relationship with the faculty researcher was often such that it undermined the authority of the host institution to monitor the grantee. The Report's recommendations dealing with direct operations and intramural programs were somewhat more negative, reflecting 'lower scientific quality and . . . evidence of inadequate supervision'. All in all, however, the NIH Committee's differed very little from the conclusions earlier drawn by the Jones Committee.[199] So positive was the Report that the NIH's defenders immediately began to invoke it to support a further series of budget increases.

Dr Shannon was to run into some difficulties with Congress over the issue of technology transfers, that is, the appropriate balance between pure and applied research. What proportion of the NIH's efforts should be spent attempting to bring the discoveries of basic research to clinical medicine in the form of new drugs, devices, and medical and surgical procedures? Shannon was strongly opposed to targeting research at finding cures for specific health problems, which he regarded as a particularly wasteful approach to biomedical problems inasmuch as it tended to limit the benefits that came from broader investigations in science.[200] In refusing to encourage research that had specific short-term goals, Shannon was joined by Congressman Fogarty, who also believed that medical breakthroughs were likely to occur on a wide front. This view, however, was not shared by most members of Congress, who saw in the NIH an agency that would, over time, alleviate suffering from specific ailments. It was for this reason that Congress had insisted in the first instance on the categorical disease approach in the work done at the NIH's constituent institutes.

From time to time the Congressional committees responsible for the NIH's budget issued explicit directives that the NIH engage in certain clinical trials. In 1961, for example, a Senate directive urged the NIH to proceed with the development of 'categorical clinical research centers, specifically oriented towards major disease areas such as cancer, cardiovascular diseases, mental health, and neurological diseases' and ordered that 'the sums appropriated for strengthening clinical research resources will be used only for this purpose'.[201] The NIH, however, continued to approach the question of scientific research multicategorically, 'in a broad and free-ranging inquiry into all aspects of the phenomena of life'.[202] While the Congress and the medical profession were prepared to underwrite the substantial costs of basic research, they were not prepared to do so indefinitely, without short-term results that could be put to use in the prevention, diagnosis, and treatment of specific ailments. Finally, urged on by Mary Lasker,[203] who hoped to see the NIH translate some of its basic research into areas that would be of more immediate clinical benefit, President Johnson, in February 1964, called for the creation of a Commission on Heart Disease, Cancer, and Stroke. Its mandate was 'to recommend steps to reduce the incidence of these diseases through new knowledge, and more complete utilization of the medical knowledge we already have'.[204] As chairman of the Commission, Johnson, with the advice of

Mary Lasker, chose Dr Michael DeBakey, the nation's foremost cardiac surgeon and a loyal adherent of government-subsidized medical research. The Commission's membership included Dr Sidney Farber, who had sat on the Boisfeullet Jones Committee, Dr R. Lee Clark, one of the country's leading oncological surgeons and Director of the Texas Medical Center, Dr J. Willis Hurst of the Emory University Medical School and President Johnson's personal cardiologist, Mrs Harry Truman, who had known Mary Lasker since President Truman's tenure in the White House, Dr Frank Horsfall of the Sloan-Kettering Institute for Cancer Research, Emerson Foote, the prominent advertising executive, and none other than Mrs Florence Mahoney, whose connections with Mrs Lasker and the Cox newspaper chain have already been mentioned.

By 1964, when the Commission first met, the budget of the NIH had reached almost $800 000 000. Yet, despite these immense expenditures, little had been realized in terms of new methods of treatment for heart disease, cancer, and stroke. Nor was the onset of these serious diseases, associated with advancing age, appreciably delayed. The recommendations made in the DeBakey Report fell into two separate areas. Predictably, the Report recommended major increases in the funds available for ongoing research activities at the NIH. However, in addition to this, the Commission sought to tie the biomedical research being done at the NIH more closely to the medical care delivery system via an ambitious program of centers situated throughout the country whose functions would include clinical research, medical training, and the diagnosis and treatment of patients. At the apex of the recommended network were to be 25 heart disease centers, 20 cancer centers, and 15 stroke centers, all to be established within five years. Below these a massive number of diagnostic and treatment stations were to be set up, 150 for heart disease, 200 for cancer, and 100 for stroke. The estimated costs involved were $347 million in the first year, rising to $739 million in the fifth year, a total of almost $3 billion for the entire five-year period.

It is difficult to know what to make of these suggestions. It would have been obvious to even the most naive that the costs involved in implementing these recommendations made them politically worthless. To anyone with the least political sophistication it would have been immediately apparent that no one in Washington was in a position to seriously propose undertaking a project whose costs were the equivalent of between 15 and 20 percent of what was then spent on the police by all levels of government, local, state, and federal. What did emerge from the DeBakey Report was something far more modest than had been proposed. The Heart Disease, Cancer, and Stroke Amendments of 1965[205] established, instead of a series of regional centers, a few 'regional medical programs' (RMP) that combined research with patient care and affiliated with a postgraduate medical training facility. The Surgeon General, after much deliberation, assigned responsibility for these RMPs to the NIH, and Dr DeBakey was appointed chairman of the program's Advisory Council.

The 1965 legislation did not, however, solve the problem of technology transfers, as both Johnson and his unofficial advisor on such matters, Mary Lasker, observed. Again, she was able to prevail upon the President to act as she thought best by pushing the NIH into directing its research into areas that would be of immediate benefit to disease sufferers. The NIH had spent over $5 billion over the course of the previous ten years and yet little of their research had been translated into practical answers to therapeutic questions. As a result, on 27 June 1966 President Johnson invited the directors of the various Institutes of Health, together with the Surgeon General of the Public Health Service, and the Secretary of Health, Education, and Welfare, John W. Gardner,[206] to the White House for a discussion of the nature of research conducted at NIH. Johnson, referring to the group as his 'strategy council in the war against disease' inquired whether 'too much energy was being spent on basic research and not enough on translating laboratory findings into tangible benefits for the American people'.[207]

Johnson's question not only took the research establishment by surprise, but also caused great consternation among NIH administrators and the recipients of research grants at the many universities and laboratories throughout the country. It was feared that an unsophisticated Administration, untutored in the nature of scientific research, had been talked into abandoning support for basic research in favor of applied research and development.[208] This fear had reached such a pitch that Secretary Gardner felt compelled to meet with all NIH consultants in August to clarify the Administration's position. Having reassured the scientific community that basic research was still a priority, Gardner pointed to the new regional medical programs and the heart, cancer, and stroke centers as representing new opportunities to expand the amount of biomedical research underwritten by the federal government. In addition, early in the following year, the President spoke before the NIH at its Bethesda campus, where he congratulated them on their work. 'The government supports this creative exploration', he asserted, 'because we believe that all knowledge is precious; because we know that all progress would halt without it'. He then went on, to great applause, to refer to the NIH as 'a billion-dollar success story'.[209]

No sooner had the NIH been reassured that the President did not intend to shift the focus of NIH research than the Institute received a further blow in the form of a series of charges leveled against it by the Fountain Committee. In November 1967, just at the point where the House and Senate were preparing their conference committee report on NIH appropriations for the fiscal year 1968, the Fountain Committee accused the NIH of 'weak central management' and with having concentrated its grant-giving on a small group of institutions, thus widening the gap between rich and poor schools and exacerbating the disdain with which researchers at the better institutions regarded their colleagues at other colleges and universities. The Institutes were further charged with inept handling of reimbursements of the indirect costs associated with extramural research. More significantly, however, the Fountain Committee levied a long string of criticisms at the quality of the scientists and research projects that the NIH supported.[210]

The charges were regarded as so serious that coordination of the response was placed in the hands of the Department. It was Secretary Gardner who transmitted the NIH analysis of these charges to the Committee. While its reply was regarded as 'dignified and thoughtful', the NIH stood firmly behind those actions most criticized by the Committee. This was not sufficient, however, to prevent the House from paring $40 million from the NIH budget for the year following release of the Fountain Committee report. The agency had lost a staunch defender with the death of Congressman John Fogarty in January 1967 and Senator Hill was unable to exert sufficient pressure to do more than restore a portion of this amount to the final appropriation. As a result, the Congressional appropriation for the NIH was cut by $20 million, the largest budgetary decrease the agency had ever sustained, and 'the first time Congress had indicated genuine skepticism about medical research'.[211]

In the event this proved a temporary setback. The NIH had for several decades played an indispensable role in advancing the federal government's goal of supporting both health and science and the agency had become too large and too well-respected to be permanently harmed, even by the revelations of the Fountain Committee. Too much had been invested in the Institutes' good name to allow these charges to seriously undermine an institution as important as was the NIH which, in 1967, was supporting more than 67 000 senior research investigators at more than 2000 universities and medical schools. In fact, few politicians had any reservations about the work being done under NIH auspices, which was universally judged to be high. The agency continued to operate as it had in the past, emphasizing basic research while at the same time engaging in a few research projects that promised more immediate therapeutic benefit, including the regional medical programs established under the provisions of the Heart Disease, Cancer, and Stroke Amendments of 1965.

To those whose principal concern was cancer, however, NIH research into this disease was regarded as seriously deficient, especially in discovering new approaches to its early diagnosis and treatment. Particularly disappointing were the regional medical programs devoted to cancer, which received only 8 percent of the funds allocated for this project.[212] These complaints would eventually lead to passage of the National Cancer Act of 1971. This Act probably more than any other can be laid at the door of Mary Lasker and her doctor-allies,[213] who were able to galvanize the Congress, the executive branch, and the relevant professional community into supporting a major expansion of research in this area. Lasker, joined by a number of other critics of the NIH, had concluded that the agency was preoccupied with investigating the broader, underlying conditions of health and disease and was not devoting sufficient resources to studying new and potentially fruitful therapies. In addition, the Regional Medical Program, established in the wake of the DeBakey Report, appeared ineffective in bridging the gap between research and patient care. Impressed by the US space program, Lasker hoped that Congress could be convinced that a research effort of colossal proportions would bring the needed breakthroughs in the treatment of cancer.

Lasker first won the support of Senator Frank Yarborough, Democrat from Texas, who had assumed the Chairmanship of both the Senate Committee on Labor and Public Welfare and its subcommittee on health, following the retirement of Lister Hill. She then suggested that the Labor and Public Welfare Committee establish an outside citizen's committee to study the question of cancer research and advise the Committee of its conclusions regarding the best way to mobilize a major national cancer program.

Meanwhile in the House, again through Lasker's efforts, Representative John J. Rooney, Democrat of New York and a senior member of the Committee on Appropriations, introduced a Concurrent Resolution in March 1970, declaring:

> That it is the sense of the Congress that the conquest of cancer is a national crusade to be accomplished by 1976 as an appropriate commemoration of the two hundredth anniversary of the independence of our country; and
> That the Congress appropriate the funds necessary for a massive program of cancer research and for the buildings and equipment with which to conduct the research and for whatever other purposes are necessary to the crusade so that the citizens of this land and of all other lands may be delivered from the greatest scourge of history.[214]

The resolution, slightly amended, was unanimously adopted in the House in July and in the Senate in August.

The Panel of Consultants on the Conquest of Cancer (its official designation) was carefully chosen to include a mix of, on the one hand, medical and scientific members with proven credentials in favor of greater research expenditures, and lay members who were sympathetic to increased public spending to fight disease. Dr Sidney Farber and Benno C. Schmidt, a partner in the law firm of J.W. Whitney & Co. and a member of the board of the Sloan-Kettering Cancer Research Institute, were chosen as co-chairmen. Farber had served on both the Boisfeullet Jones Committee in 1960 and the DeBakey Commission in 1965, while Schmidt had been warmly recommended by Laurence

Rockefeller, to whom Lasker turned for help in selecting the panelists. The remainder of the panel was carefully selected to insure unreserved support for Rooney's Congressional Resolution.[215]

The Panel's Report, to no one's surprise, underscored the inadequacy of the funds spent on the second-leading cause of death in the United States. While it was true, the Report conceded, that the nature of cancer remained a mystery, the cure rate for those suffering from its many manifestations was generally improving. Fundamental advances in scientific knowledge had, in the previous decade, pointed the way to a host of promising areas for more intensive investigation. However, sufficient funds simply were not available to pursue these leads. 'A national program for the conquest of cancer', the Report stated, 'is now essential if we are to exploit effectively the great opportunities which are presented as a result of recent advances in our knowledge'.[216]

The Panel recommended that a new government agency – the National Cancer Authority – be established whose task would be 'the conquest of cancer at the earliest possible time'. The Authority would absorb the current functions of the National Cancer Institute and would be totally independent of the National Institutes of Health. Apparently this proposal emerged as a reaction to the bureaucracy and red tape which appeared to be a hallmark of the NCI. Mary Lasker had long been dismayed at the performance of the NIH in translating its research into therapeutic innovations and this disappointment was conveyed to the Panel of Consultants, who were also surprised at the numerous levels of bureaucracy under which researchers at the NCI worked. Recent changes in the organizational structure of the NIH created a Deputy Director for Science charged with responsibility for all extramural research grants and contracts as well as intramural research. This, in effect, placed in the hands of one person authority over all research undertaken at the NIH, regardless of area. It was therefore most unlikely that cancer research would be given priority by someone supervising the whole range of biomedical inquiry.

In addition, the Panel was impressed by the examples provided by agencies dedicated to specific goals, specifically the Manhattan Project and the space program. The notion that if one threw enough money at a problem it eventually got results appears to have been generally accepted in Washington and especially among the medical lobby. With respect to the level of expenditures necessary to bring about a positive outcome, the Report argued for an appropriation of $400 million in fiscal year 1972 and increasing thereafter at the rate of $100 to $150 million per year, reaching a level of $1 billion in 1976. Should this be thought of as too large, the Panel reminded its readers that these sums were quite small when compared to the national resources, human suffering, and economic loss attributable to cancer.[217]

Senator Yarborough was defeated for re-election to the 92nd Congress in

1970 and as a result Harrison Williams, Democrat of New Jersey, replaced Yarborough as Chairman of the Senate Committee on Labor and Public Welfare, while Senator Edward Kennedy, Democrat of Massachusetts, took over Yarborough's chairmanship of the subcommittee on health and assumed Yarborough's duty of seeing the National Cancer Act through to passage. That Kennedy would take up the measure was obvious to anyone familiar with Washington politics. Lasker had been a strong supporter of the late John Kennedy and had endorsed Robert Kennedy's bid for the Democratic nomination for President as soon as Johnson had announced that he would not run for the office. On 29 January 1971 Kennedy and Senator Jacob Javits, Republican of New York, introduced the Conquest of Cancer Act in the Senate.

The group most responsible for orchestrating passage of the bill, however, was Mary Lasker and her associates, who had proved extremely adept at manipulating the political process and in gaining the support of the public for an agency that promised a cure for this dreaded disease. Not only did they shape the political alternatives in such a way that both Democrats and Republicans were compelled to support the measure on pain of irreparable harm to their political careers, but they managed to win the approval of the Nixon Administration for a war on cancer.[218] Indeed, at one point, when it appeared that the measure might be jeopardized because of Congressional and medical opposition to removing the NCI from the authority of the National Institutes of Health, a large number of articles and stories about the horrors of cancer began appearing in the national press and in April 1971 Ann Landers devoted an entire column to urging support for the Senate bill. The effect of this column was that an avalanche of mail, numbering in the hundreds of thousands of letters, descended on the Senate.[219]

The National Cancer Act of 1971 was signed on 23 December 1971 in the State Dining Room of the White House.[220] While the Act, as passed, left the National Cancer Institute as a constituent agency of the National Institutes of Health, it did provide more autonomy for its Director. His position was elevated and expanded to include the authority to prepare and submit annual budget estimates directly to the President. In addition, the Director was to be appointed directly by the President. The measure initiated the National Cancer Program, whereby the Director, with the advice of a 23-member National Cancer Advisory Board, created by the Act, was to 'plan and develop an expanded, intensified, and coordinated cancer research program encompassing the programs of the National Cancer Institute, related programs of the other research institutes, and other Federal and non-Federal programs'. In addition, the Director of the NCI was authorized 'to coordinate all of the activities of the National Institutes of Health relating to cancer with the National Cancer Program'. The Act further established the International Cancer Research Data Bank (ICRDB), an information dissemination program, and a number of cancer control programs in cooperation with State and other health agencies. Finally, the first 15 research, training, and treatment cancer centers were authorized.

These changes in the status of cancer research at the NIH are reflected in the budgets of the NCI (see Table 4.11).

The National Heart Institute was so impressed with the success of the NCI in calling attention to and in enlarging its mission that it determined to copy the NCI's tactics.[221] The Director of the NHLI,[222] Dr Theodore Cooper, had convened a task force of scientists and physicians on arteriosclerosis and to report on the best means of combating the condition. The Task Force submitted its report in June 1971 and urged the creation of a 'national coordinated comprehensive program' that would apply the most recent basic and applied research to the problem. The Task Force complained that current studies tended to be fragmented into small programs taking place at a large number of universities and hospitals and suggested that several National Centers for the Prevention of Arteriosclerosis be established at several medical centers. In addition smaller Cardiovascular Disease Clinics should be created to screen those who might fall victim to the disease.

The Arteriosclerosis Task Force Report, coupled with pressure for new legislation, led to several bills being introduced into Congress including a couple, supported by Mary Lasker and her coterie, that would have removed the NHLI from the NIH and placed it directly under Presidential control. However, it was Ted Kennedy in the Senate and Paul Rogers in the House, the same two congressmen responsible for the National Cancer Act, who proved successful in gaining passage of the National Heart, Blood Vessel, Lung, and Blood Act of 1972. The Act called for the expansion and coordination of both basic and applied research in heart, blood vessel, lung, and blood diseases and the establishment of up to 30 National Research and Demonstration Centers for the study of heart and lung diseases. The NHLI's expanded interest in blood vessel and blood diseases resulted in the Institute's name being altered in 1976 to the National Heart, Blood and Lung Institute (NHBLI). Since that time the NHBLI has added genetic research and sleep disorders to its areas of concern.

The National Heart Institute was always regarded with special favor by American legislators, who traditionally operated on the assumption that the determination of which areas of research should receive most funding was a political and not a scientific question.[223] Even in the face of claims that the monies could be put to much better use were they applied to other projects, Congress has, for political reasons, directed that funds be spent conducting research into certain ailments.[224] While diseases of the heart had always been a particularly popular area of research, funding for the NHBI had come under pressure with passage of the National Cancer Act, which shifted funds to

Table 4.11   NCI: Total Obligations, Fiscal Years 1972–2005

Year	Amount ($ 000)
1972	376 794
1973	492 205
1974	527 486
1975	691 666
1976	761 727
1976TQ	152 901
1977	815 000
1978	872 388
1979	937 129
1980	999 869
1981	989 255
1982	986 717
1983	987 642
1984	1 081 581
1985	1 183 806
1986	1 203 369
1987	1 402 837
1988	1 469 327
1989	1 570 349
1990	1 634 332
1991	1 714 784
1992	1 962 587
1993	1 981 351
1994	2 082 267
1995	1 913 819
1996	2 254 940
1997	2 381 149
1998	2 547 314
1999	2 925 247
2000	3 314 554
2001	3 754 456
2002	4 181 233
2003	4 592 348
2004	4 739 255
2005	4 825 258

Source: Office of the Director, National Institutes of Health, *NIH Almanac 2006* (Washington, DC, March 2006).

cancer research and looked as if it might reduce the NHBI's traditional appropriation of about 15 percent of the NIH's total expenditures. However, the NHBI's investigations into blood diseases proved its salvation.

In his health message delivered before Congress on 18 February 1971, President Nixon, in anticipation of his 1972 Presidential campaign, announced that he supported a massive research effort into sickle cell anemia, a disease that affects Blacks almost exclusively. The Congress, not to be outdone, rushed to enact a bill, drawn up by the Congressional Black Caucus, that allocated $144 million over a three-year period to investigate the disease. The National Sickle Cell Anemia Control Act of 1972 was passed overwhelmingly in May 1972. Yet another blood disorder, Cooley's anemia, affected a disproportionate number of descendants of Greek and Italian immigrants. Despite the fact that the total number of sufferers from this condition numbered only about 5000 to 15 000,[225] it was regarded as politically expedient to include Cooley's anemia in the sickle cell anemia bill. The authors of that bill, however, did not want their efforts on behalf of Black voters to be watered down and, as a result, a completely new bill was enacted, with Senator Edward Kennedy of Massachusetts introducing Congressman Robert Giaimo's measure in the Senate in August. The National Cooley's Anemia Control Act, passed the day it was introduced, authorized expenditures of $11.1 million for a three-year program of research into the diagnosis and treatment of this condition.

Passage of these two measures assured that the annual budgets of the NHBI and its successor agency, the NHBLI, remained at traditional levels for the next 15 years. Table 4.12 indicates the total obligations of the Institute and its percentage of total NIH expenditures.

The National Heart, Blood Vessel, Lung, and Blood Act and the National Cancer Act were not the only Congressional measures that brought with them an important reorganization in the structure of the NIH during this period. In 1967 the National Institute of Mental Health was separated from the NIH and raised to bureau status within the Public Health Service.[226] This was the culmination of efforts by mental health bureaucrats within and outside the NIH to raise the level of social and behavioral 'disorders' to the level of physical diseases and to shift the locus of authority and responsibility for mental health policy from the states to the federal government.[227] In 1955, in deference to the demands of mental health researchers, Congress enacted the Mental Health Study Act, which authorized the establishment of the Joint Commission on Mental Illness and Health (JCMIH). The Commission was charged with conducting a five-year study of national mental health needs. Its mandate is best summarized in the testimony of Daniel Blain, the medical director of the American Psychiatric Association, who called for an exhaustive study

Table 4.12   NHBLI: Total Obligations, Fiscal Years 1972–2005

Year	Amount ($ 000)	NHBLI Obligations as Percentage of Total NIH Obligations
1972	232 577	15.4
1973	255 722	14.5
1974	327 270	18.3
1975	327 953	15.7
1976	368 648	16.0
1977	396 857	15.6
1978	447 968	15.8
1979	510 080	16.0
1980	527 248	15.4
1981	550 072	15.4
1982	559 800	15.4
1983	624 260	15.5
1984	705 064	15.7
1985	803 810	15.6
1986	821 901	15.6
1987	929 982	15.0
1988	965 283	14.5
1989	1 045 508	14.6
1990	1 070 683	14.1
1991	1 125 915	13.6
1992	1 190 070	13.3
1993	1 214 693	11.8
1994	1 277 852	11.7
1995	1 314 969	11.6
1996	1 351 422	11.3
1997	1 431 821	11.2
1998	1 526 276	11.2
1999	1 788 008	11.5
2000	2 027 286	12.7
2001	2 298 512	11.2
2002	2 572 667	11.0
2003	2 793 733	10.3
2004	2 878 691	10.3
2005	2 941 201	10.3

Source: Data for 1972 to 2000: National Heart, Lung and Blood Institute, *NHLBI FY 2000 Factbook* (Bethesda, Md.: National Institutes of Health, 2001): 65, and Table A7.
    Data for 2001 to 2005: Office of the Director, National Institutes of Health, 'Appropriations', *NIH Almanac, 2006* (Washington, DC, March 2006).

to reexamine our basic assumptions in the field, to see what actually takes place in hospitals with high discharge rates as compared to others with low discharge rates; to assist the factor [sic] which account for the tragic lag between the development of psychiatric knowledge and its application in the public mental hospitals; to determine the extent to which community services pay off in keeping people out of mental hospitals; to discover the most effective ways of utilizing present personnel; to find out more about the epidemiology of mental illness; to discover why it is that young professional students resist entering the field of mental illness; to find out exactly what our personnel needs are; to review our whole statistical system for gathering data on mental illness; to assess the contribution that psychiatry can make to the various social ills in which mental illness is a component, such as alcoholism, drug addiction, juvenile delinquency and crime, misfits in industry, accident proneness on the highways, suicides, and so on.[228]

The conclusions arrived at by the JCMIH were to have an immediate impact on the actions of Congress. In an interim report issued in 1959, the Commission emphasized the importance of clinical education and the need for improvement in the existing facilities. In light of the Commission's views, the NIMH's education and training budget was increased from $5 million to $25 million in the five years from 1955 to 1960. Similarly, in 1956 Congress, acknowledging the importance of psychopharmacology in the treatment of mental disorders, which had been emphasized by the Commission, appropriated $2 million for research in psychopharmacology at the NIMH. This expenditure led to the creation of the Early Clinical Drug Evaluation Unit Program, under which controlled testing of neuropsychopharmacological agents was carried out. In the same year, Congress included mental disorders in the Health Amendments Act of 1956, which authorized research in the diagnosis, treatment, and rehabilitation of the mentally ill.[229]

When it first convened the JCMIH had emphasized problems such as these that were pertinent to the severely mentally ill. However, over the course of its deliberations the distinction between those suffering from some form of acute mental illness and those confronting some psychological or personal problem was blurred as the Commission became more openly concerned with 'mental health', rather than with mental disease. No longer did the Commission concentrate on the issues associated with the hospitalization of the mentally ill but it sponsored a series of studies dealing with public attitudes and community responses (including schools and religious institutions) to mental health.[230] From this point forward, the NIMH has had two related but distinct goals. It seeks to improve the treatment of the mentally ill, which is the chief interest of Congress, and to expand the mission of the Institute to include the prevention of psychological disorders among the population and to promote a 'mentally healthy' community.

In March 1961 the Report of the JCMIH, *Action for Mental Health*,[231] was released, coinciding with the inauguration of John F. Kennedy as President.[232]

It attempted to lay bare the numerous shortcomings of the prevailing mental health establishment and suggested a series of improvements. These took the form of changes in several areas: (1) larger investments in basic research; (2) an expansion in the educational and research activities of the NIMH; and (3) federal funding for the creation of research centers throughout the country. The Commission estimated the cost of these improvements would require a doubling of total expenditures for public mental health services at all levels of government in five years and a tripling in ten. The overwhelming portion of this increase would, of course, have to be made by the federal government.

In December Kennedy set up a cabinet-level intra-agency committee, the Intra-Agency Task Force on Mental Health, nominally chaired by the Secretary of Health, Education, and Welfare, to examine these recommendations and to propose an appropriate federal response. At the same time the Administration made clear its strong interest in mental health. The Surgeon General met with state mental health authorities in January 1962 to discuss the Report and the HEW Secretary, Abraham Ribicoff, suggested that the Administration would support an expanded federal role by hastening the introduction of community programs and diminishing the role of large mental hospitals. One month later, William C. Menninger met privately with President Kennedy and concluded that the President was committed to the kinds of changes suggested in the Report. Finally, in February 1963, Kennedy forwarded a message to Congress on mental illness and mental retardation.

He proposed a 'bold new approach' to mental illness, in which the mentally ill would be 'quickly treated in their own communities and returned to a useful place in society'. Toward this end he called for a major expansion of clinical, laboratory, and field research into mental illness and mental retardation centering on comprehensive community health centers which would integrate 'diagnostic and evaluation services, emergency psychiatric units, outpatient services, inpatient services, day and night care, foster home care, rehabilitation, consultative services to other community agencies, and mental health information and education'. In addition, he urged Congress to authorize construction grants and short-term subsidies for staffing.[233] In response, Congress enacted the Mental Retardation and Community Mental Health Centers (CMHC) Construction Act of 1963, which authorized the construction of CMHCs across the country. The CMHC program, which rapidly grew, soon became a dominant component of the NIMH.

By the late 1960s the funds allocated to the NIMH had made it one of the largest of the NIH Institutes.[234] Its mission by that point had broadened to include not only the construction and staffing of community mental health centers but also clinical training. These programs occasionally placed the NIMH at odds with the rest of the NIH, whose concerns remained almost exclusively those associated with basic research. In point of fact, the mental health lobby had effectively achieved what it had originally sought, the creation of a massive federal bureaucracy whose concerns involved behavioral disorders and whose interests brought it directly into the community. The social environment, it was argued, constituted the pathogenic background within which personal disorders flourished and it was therefore the social environment itself that required study. The Administration and Congress, as well as a substantial proportion of the American public, were reassured to learn that unpopular behavior was often pathological behavior and that experts were at work searching for effective treatments for those suffering from even mild instances of psychopathic behavior.

Psychiatrists have traditionally passed judgement on a wide range of issues, claiming that their profession provided them with unique insights into social problems. Pretensions to a profound understanding of society, are, of course, common to a number of professions, but psychiatry has been particularly prone to this hubris inasmuch as its practitioners regularly assert that they have uncovered the arcana of social life. The social activism that follows from this assertion of professional omniscience was particularly acute during the decades of the 1960s and 1970s, when psychiatrists were prepared to make pronouncements on a host of social issues having only the vaguest connection with mental illness.[235] Dr Stanley F. Yolles, the Director of the NIMH from 1964 to 1970, was especially eager that psychiatrists take an active role in shaping the community and decried 'the professional isolation in the ivory tower of the private practice of yesterday'.[236] In this he was joined by President Johnson, who had pledged 'to apply science to solving societal ills'.[237]

This growing rift in the kinds of issues preoccupying the NIMH and the research being done at the NIH and the growing estrangement between these two agencies finally led, in 1967, to the NIMH being separated from the NIH and given bureau status within the Public Health Service. The intramural research program of the NIMH, however, remained in place, under the joint administration of the NIMH and the NIH. In the following year, the NIMH became the major component of the newly established Health Services and Mental Health Administration (HSMHA).

In 1970 Congress enacted the Comprehensive Alcohol Abuse and Alcoholism Prevention, Treatment and Rehabilitation Act,[238] which transferred the training and research programs associated with alcohol use to the newly created National Institute on Alcohol Abuse and Alcoholism (NIAAA). And in 1972, the programs relating to drug use were transferred to a new National Institute on Drug Abuse (NIDA).[239] The creation of these two new institutes marked a notable expansion of federal involvement in behavioral disorders. By this point it was clear that the notion of mental illness no longer referred solely to those patients needing hospitalization in mental hospitals but had been broadened to encompass people suffering from psychological problems of a severity insufficient to warrant their being committed. Indeed, under some definitions of mental illness that the NIMH and the HSMHA used, the notion had become so broad that it was possible to regard everyone as more or less mentally ill.

In 1973 President Nixon decided to abolish the HSMHA and in July the NIMH was temporarily moved back to the NIH until a more permanent home could be found for the agency. Finally, in 1974, Congress created the Alcohol, Drug Abuse, and Mental Heath Administration (ADAMHA), to house the NIMH, the NIAAA, and the NIDA. As these constituent agencies expanded, their responsibilities for both research and community-based treatment programs grew as well. Since these two functions were clearly disparate, it was suggested by some that their administration be separated. Consequently several studies commissioned by ADAMHA, the first conducted by the Lewin Group[240] and a second undertaken by the Institute of Medicine of the National Academy of Medicine, had concluded that there was no link between the two functions and that in fact research was often being damaged by its association with services.[241] As a result, the NIMH, the NIAAA, and the NIDA were again reorganized in 1992 when Congress passed the ADAMHA Reorganization Act. The Act abolished ADAMHA and transferred the research components of its constituent agencies to agencies in the NIH. The Institutes' services components were made part of a new Substance Abuse and Mental Health Services Administration (SAMHSA), charged with preventing and treating substance abuse and mental illness.

Certainly the most spectacular example of politically directed biomedical research currently undertaken by the NIH is that connected with Acquired Immune Deficiency Syndrome (AIDS). The condition was first reported in the United States in 1981 and has since reached immense proportions. It's estimated that about 900 000 Americans have been infected since the disease was first noted. In April 1984 it was announced that AIDS was caused by a virus, human immunodeficiency virus (HIV), which, by attacking a particular class of white blood cells known as 'helper T cells' that are crucial to the body's immune system, leaves the victim vulnerable to a whole range of parasites that are normally harmless. Many of these opportunistic infections are life-threatening and often fatal. While currently the largest number of sufferers are male homosexuals, the epidemic is growing most rapidly among Black and Hispanic males, especially intravenous drug users.[242] The current annual infection rate (2004) is 18.7 per 100 000 for adult and adolescent white males and 131.6 per 100 000 and 60.2 per 100 000 for Black and Hispanic males respectively.[243]

The earliest appropriation made by Congress for AIDS research was contained in a supplementary appropriations bill for the Public Health Service in July 1983, which included a provision explicitly allocating $9 375 000 to the NIH for that purpose. The amounts appropriated for AIDS research rapidly grew so that by fiscal year 1987, it had reached $70 000 000. This sum was increased by a factor of 3.5, to $247 700 000 in the following fiscal year and reached $448 000 000 in fiscal year 1988. The 1988 appropriation was accompanied by a requirement that any experimental drug developed for AIDS be tested as expeditiously as possible. In November 1988 under the terms of the Health Omnibus Programs Extension Act,[244] a coordinating office of AIDS research was established within the Office of the Director of the NIH. The National Institute of Allergies and Infectious Diseases (NIAID), which conducted research into sexually transmitted diseases and much of the earlier research into AIDS, was provided with yet additional authority to carry on its investigation of the disease.

Title II of the Health Omnibus Programs Extension Act, entitled 'Programs with Respect to Acquired Immune Deficiency Syndrome', was the first major law to explicitly address AIDS research and was massive in scope. Not only did it call for the creation of an Office of AIDS Research but it included provisions calling for the public dissemination of information on AIDS and funding for anonymous testing. The legislation provided for the establishment of a National Commission on AIDS to make recommendations on a consistent national AIDS policy and expedited the review process for AIDS-related grants. Requests for personnel and administrative support in connection with AIDS projects were to be given priority, the AIDS outpatient capacity at the NIH's Clinical Center was doubled, and community-based clinical trials of new therapies were authorized. Finally, under Title VI, titled the Health Professions Reauthorization Act, the federal government established a loan repayment for scientists who agreed to conduct AIDS research while employed by the NIH.

The Secretary of Health and Human Resources has declared AIDS the number one health priority of the Public Health Service and consequently huge amounts have been spent on attempting to fight the disease. The fiscal year 2000 budget allocated $8.2 billion dollars within the Department of Health and Human Services for this purpose,[245] a substantial portion of which was directed to the NIAID. Among its other researches, the NIAID was assigned the task of developing an effective vaccine against AIDS. Despite some doubts that such a vaccine can be designed, scientific evidence appears to be mounting that this is the only promising avenue that remains for destroying this unique pathogen. Since it is unlikely that the search to uncover a vaccine would be commercially viable, thus precluding the possibility that commercial firms would undertake a similar investigation, the NIH has taken on that role and has devoted a substantial amount of energy and effort to discovering a safe and affordable vaccine.

Table 4.13   NIAID: Total Obligations, Fiscal Years 1982–2005

Year	Amount ($ 000)
1982	235 695
1983	279 129
1984	319 596
1985	370 965
1986	366 964
1987	454 523
1988	638 800
1989	740 257
1990	832 977
1991	906 251
1992	959 082
1993	979 471
1994	1 065 583
1995	1 092 507
1996	1 168 483
1997	1 256 659
1998	1 351 655
1999	1 569 063
2000	1 778 038
2001	2 041 698
2002	2 342 313
2003	3 606 789
2004	4 155 447
2005	4 303 641

Source: Office of the Director, National Institutes of Health, 'Appropriations', *NIH Almanac 2006* (Washington, DC, March 2006).

The priority given to AIDS research is reflected in the larger budgets of each of the NIH's constituent institutes, but this is particularly true of the NIAID, the agency most directly involved in AIDS research. Table 4.13 shows the growth in the NIAID's budget from 1982 to 2005, in large measure because of funds allocated for this purpose.

In 1993, under the terms of the NIH Revitalization Act, Congress reaffirmed the authority of the Office of AIDS Research (OAR) within the NIH and expanded its authority to include the planning and coordinating of all AIDS research within the NIH. More significant, the OAR was authorized to

Table 4.14 **AIDS Appropriations to the National Institutes of Health, Fiscal Years 1995–2001 ($ 000)**

Year	Budget Estimate to Congress[1]	House Allowance	Senate Allowance	Appropriation
1995	1 379 052	1 337 606	1.337 606	1 335 421[2]
1995 (Rescission)				1 851
1996	1 407 824	[3]	1 382 861	[4]
1997	1 431 908	[3]	1 460 312	[4]
1998	1 540 765	[3]	[5]	[4]
1999	1 728 099[6]	[3]	[5]	[4]
2000	1 833 826	[3]	[5]	[4]
2001	2 111 224	[3]	[5]	[4]

Notes:
[1] Includes all amounts associated with the National Institutes of Health AIDS Research Program.
[2] Excludes procurement reform, rent, and salary and expense reductions of $2 185 000.
[3] The House did not provide separate funding for HIV/AIDS activities. The funds to support these activities are included in the appropriations of the Institutes and Centers.
[4] The Conferees did not provide separate funding for HIV/AIDS activities. The funds to support these activities are included in the appropriations of the Institutes and Centers.
[5] The Senate did not provide separate funding for HIV/AIDS activities. The funds to support these activities are included in the appropriations of the Institutes and Centers.
[6] Reflects a decrease of $2 697 000 for the budget amendment for bioterrorism.

Source: Department of Health and Human Services, *Annual Report, Fiscal Year 2001*, vol. V: National Institutes of Health (Washington, DC: Government Printing Office, 2001): Office of AIDS Research, OAR 39.

receive all NIH funds appropriated for HIV/AIDS research and to distribute these funds to the various constituent institutes as it determined. The effect of this change was to place the OAR in effective control over all federal AIDS studies and to have ultimate authority over a substantial portion of the NIH budget. Table 4.14 recounts the recent history of AIDS funds appropriated to the NIH.

These totals are reflected in the increased budgets of all of the constituent institutes. However, none was as much affected as was the National Institute of Allergy and Infectious Diseases, where, by fiscal year 2001, the AIDS distribution of its annual appropriation had reached 51 percent.[246]

Table 4.15 gives some idea of the amounts expended on AIDS by the NIH for research into the disease.

The history of NIH funding between 1976 and the present has mirrored the budgetary history of the previous 25 years. While the rate of growth has been significantly less spectacular when compared with the two decades following

Table 4.15 National Institutes of Health: Total Appropriations, AIDS Distributions, and Percentage Earmarked for AIDS, By Constituent Agency, 2005–2007 ($ 000)

Institute	Fiscal Year 2005			Fiscal Year 2006			Fiscal Year 2007		
	Total Appropriations	AIDS Distribution	AIDS Percent	Total Appropriations	AIDS Distribution	AIDS Percent	Total Appropriations	AIDS Distribution	AIDS Percent
NCI	4 828 000	265 907	5.5	4 793 000	253 666	5.3	4 754 000	244 104	5.1
NHLBI	2 941 000	74 690	2.5	2 922 000	67 351	2.3	2 901 000	65 094	2.2
NIDCR	392 000	24 985	6.4	389 000	19 688	5.1	386 000	18 601	4.8
NIDKK	1 864 000	31 151	1.7	1 855 000	30 898	1.7	1 844 000	30 674	1.7
NINDS	1 539 000	47 364	3.1	1 535 000	46 351	3.0	1 525 000	45 731	3.0
NIAID[1]	4 403 000	1 459 642	33.2	4 383 000	1 489 424	34.0	4 395 000	1 491 573	33.9
NIGMS	1 944 000	54 632	2.8	1 936 000	53 485	2.8	1 923 000	53 485	2.8
NICHD	1 270 000	132 992	10.5	1 265 000	133 555	10.6	1 257 000	133 435	10.6
NEI	669 000	12 562	1.9	667 000	10 585	1.6	661 000	9 451	1.4
NIEHS	645 000	8 702	1.4	641 000	7 513	1.2	637 000	7 235	1.1
NIA	1 052 000	5 459	0.5	1 047 000	5 389	0.5	1 040 000	5 294	0.5
NIAMS	511 000	6 697	1.3	508 000	4 866	1.0	505 000	4 652	0.9
NIDCD	394 000	1 734	0.4	393 000	1 412	0.4	392 000	1 412	0.4
NIMH	1 412 000	182 615	12.9	1 404 000	178 558	12.7	1 395 000	177 581	12.7
NIDA	1 006 000	313 137	31.1	1 000 000	300 073	30.0	995 000	299 266	30.1
NIAAA	438 000	27 166	6.2	436 000	26 942	6.2	433 000	26 942	6.2
NINR	138 000	12 236	8.9	137 000	12 114	8.8	137 000	12 114	8.8
NHGRI	489 000	6 862	1.4	486 000	6 835	1.4	483 000	6 835	1.4

NCRR	1 115 000	156 858	14.1	1 099 000	160 992	14.7	1 098 000	162 044	14.8
NCCAM	122 000	2 778	2.3	121 000	2 285	1.9	121 000	2 124	1.8
FIC	67 000	22 985	34.3	66 000	22 978	34.8	67 000	23 403	34.9
NLM	315 000	7 450	2.4	315 000	7 376	2.3	313 000	7 452	2.4
OD	405 000	60 899	15.0	528 000	60 290	11.4	668 000	59 290	8.9
B&F	110 000	0	0.0	81 000	0	0.0	81 000	0	0.0
TOTAL	**28 644 000**	**2 920 551**	**10.2**	**28 578 000**	**2 903 664**	**10.2**	**28 578 000**	**2 888 492**	**10.1**

Notes: *NCI*: National Cancer Institute; *NHLBI*: National Heart, Lung and Blood Institute; *NIDCR*: National Institute of Dental and Craniofacial Research; *NIDDK*: National Institute of Diabetes and Digestive and Kidney Diseases; *NINDS*: National Institute of Neurological Disorders and Stroke; *NIAID*: National Institute of Allergy and Infectious Diseases; *NIGMS*: National Institute of General Medical Sciences; *NICHD*: National Institute of Child Health and Human Development; *NEI*: National Eye Institute; *NIEHS*: National Institute of Environmental Health Sciences; *NIA*: National Institute on Aging; *NIAMS*: National Institute of Arthritis and Musculoskeletal and Skin Diseases; *NIDCD*: National Institute on Deafness and Other Communication Disorders; *NIMH*: National Institute of Mental Health; *NIDA*: National Institute on Drug Abuse; *NIAAA*: National Institute on Alcohol Abuse and Alcoholism; *NINR*: National Institute of Nursing Research; *NHGRI*: National Human Genome Research Institute; *NCRR*: National Center for Research Resources; *NCCAM*: National Center for Complementary and Alternative Medicine; *FIC*: John E. Fogarty International Center for Advanced Study in the Health Sciences; *NLM*: National Library of Medicine; *OD*: Office of the Director, National Institutes of Health; *B&F*: Buildings and Facilities.

[1] NIAID budget for FY 2006 includes $18 000 000 for Pandemic Influenza from the Public Health and Social Services Emergency Fund.

Source: National Institutes of Health, 'Summary Appropriations', *National Institutes of Health FY2007 President's Budget* (Washington, DC, 6 February 2006): 9; and Office of AIDS Research, 'Congressional Budget Justification, FY 2007', p. 23.

World War II, total appropriations have still managed to increase at a steady pace, from $2.3 billion in 1976 to $16 billion in the fiscal year 2000. Since 1980 the NIH continued to expand its areas of research and, sometimes in response to political pressure, established new institutes:

1981:   National Institute of Arthritis, Diabetes, and Digestive and Kidney Diseases (NIADDK) (replacing the National Institute of Arthritis, Metabolism and Digestive Diseases, which had been created in 1972);

1985:   National Institute of Diabetes, and Digestive and Kidney Disease (NIDDK) (replacing the National Institute of Arthritis, Diabetes, and Digestive and Kidney Disease, established in 1981);

1986:   Institute of Arthritis and Musculoskeletal and Skin Diseases (NIAMS) (incorporating the Division of Arthritis, Musculoskeletal and Skin Diseases of the NIADDK);

1988:   National Institute on Deafness and Other Communication Disorders (NIDCD);

1992:   National Institute on Drug Abuse (NIDA) (transferred from the Alcohol, Drug Abuse, and Mental Health Administration);

1993:   National Institute for Nursing Research (NINR);

1994:   National Human Genome Research Institute (NHGRI);

1995:   National Institute of Dental and Craniofacial Research (NIDCR) (replacing the National Dental Institute).

In 2001, yet another of the continually proliferating institutes of the NIH was established, the National Institute for Biomedical Imaging and Bioengineering (NIBIB), whose self-defined function is to encourage the development and application of biomedical technologies.

In 1991, some 15 scientific and professional societies whose members were involved with biomedical research formed the American Institute for Medical and Biological Engineering (AIMBE) and, some four years later, it was joined by the Academy of Radiology Research (ARR), an umbrella organization of groups concerned with medical imaging. One of the primary missions of these two organizations was to lobby for the creation of a new institute at the NIH devoted to this area of medical technology. Prior to this, the bulk of NIH research in the field of imaging was undertaken, first at the National Institutes of General Medical Sciences and, after 1978, at the National Cancer Institute, where the Cancer Imaging Program was established in 1995. These groups were successful in prevailing on Senator David F. Durenberger (Republican, Minnesota) to add a proviso to the NIH Revitalization Act of 1993 which directed the Department of Health and Human Services to report to Congress on the state of biomedical engineering research being undertaken at the NIH.

The report, *Support for Bioengineering Research*, was submitted by Secretary Donna Shalala to Congress in 1995 and, as could have been predicted, called for the creation of a new institute focusing on bioengineering.

It was this report that ultimately led Representative Richard M. Burr (Republican, North Carolina) to introduce legislation to establish a National Institute of Biomedical Engineering in the House in 1996. The bill, however, did not advance and further attempts, in subsequent sessions of Congress, stalled for one reason or another. Finally, in 2000, under pressure from the AIMBE and the ARR, a modified version of his earlier bill calling for the creation of a National Institute of Biomedical Imaging and Engineering was submitted to the House by Congressman Burr and a companion bill was introduced in the Senate by Trent Lott (Republican, Mississippi). What followed was an intense lobbying campaign by the bioimaging and bioengineering communities and the NIH, which proved successful. The bill passed the House in September and passed the Senate without debate in December. It was the last statute signed into law by President Clinton.

The NIH currently comprises 19 constituent Institutes and, in addition, supervises and coordinates the work of an additional eight centers. These are:

National Library of Medicine (NLM): Founded in 1836 as the Library of the Office of the Surgeon General of the Army and in 1922 renamed the Army Medical Library, the collection was transferred to the Public Health Service and redesignated the National Library of Medicine in 1956. In 1968 the NLM became a component of the NIH, the largest and, without question, the finest library of medicine in the world.

National Center for Research Resources (NCRR): Established in 1990 and incorporating the NIH's Division of Research Resources and its Division of Research Services, the NCRR was designed to provide the research infrastructure for all biomedical research undertaken by the NIH, including tools, technologies, and materials and to underwrite the costs of training.

NIH Clinical Center (CC): located in Bethesda, Maryland, the Clinical Center comprises the NIH's two clinical research hospitals, the Warren Grant Magnuson Clinical Center and the Mark O. Hatfield Clinical Research Center. The centers admit more than 7000 new inpatients and deal with over 100 000 outpatient visits a year, have some 1200 physicians, dentists, and Ph.Ds and 660 nurses on its staff and house more than 1600 laboratories. Construction of the Magnuson Center began in 1948 and the first patient was admitted in 1953. The Mark Hatfield Clinical Research Center, an inpatient research facility, was completed in 2004 and admits only those patients whose illnesses are precisely those of immediate interest to NIH researches.

National Center for Complementary and Alternative Medicine (NCCAM): The 1999 Omnibus Appropriations Bill, signed by President Bill Clinton in late 1998, authorized the Director of the NIH to raise the Office of Alternative Medicine to the level of a Center, whose task would be to facilitate and conduct medical research into complementary and alternative medical therapies. The Center's fiscal year 2001 budget request amounted to $72 392 000, as compared to an appropriation of $69 011 000 for fiscal year 2000.

Center for Information Technology (CIT): In 1998 the Division of Computer Research and Technology, the Office of Information Resources Management, and the Telecommunications Branch of the NIH were combined to create the CIT. The new unit's function is to provide, coordinate, and administer all information technology at the NIH, including its vast computer and telecommunications network.

John E. Fogarty International Center for Advanced Study in the Health Sciences (FIC): In 1967 Congress empowered the Director of the NIH to establish a center to support international biomedical research and scientific cooperation and to attempt to reduce international disparities in health. The Center's 2001 budget request was for $32 532 000, an increase of $3 600 000 over the previous year.

Center for Scientific Review (CSR): Located in the Office of the Director of the NIH, the CSR receives all research grant applications, determines which will be given further consideration and by which team of reviewers, and further determines which constituent institute or center will fund the application, if successful. In sum, the CSR has overall responsibility for the peer review of all requests for funds.

National Center on Minority Health and Health Disparities (NCMHD). Established in 1993 to investigate and promote health care among minorities and to eliminate health disparities. As with most other divisions of the NIH, the NCMHD conducts research and extends grants for the study of all aspects of minority health, including the medical infrastructure afforded minorities.

The peer review system lies at the heart of the whole NIH edifice and this warrants a few remarks before closing this chapter. In fiscal year 2002, NIH expenditures on biomedical research, either directly or through extramural grants, amounted to $22.8 billion, or 22 percent of total federal expenditures on research and development in all areas underwritten by the federal government, including defense research. The United States is the world's leader in such research, dwarfing the other major industrial nations.[247] Total expenditures on research and development in biomedicine in the United States amounts to approximately $100 billion per year, of which about one-third is underwritten by the federal government.[248] Of the remaining two-thirds, most of which is funded by industry, the overwhelming portion is devoted to development, not research. Thus, in the area of basic research the NIH dominates biomedicine, not only in the United States but throughout the world. The National Science Foundation provides detailed data on American research and development expenditures, both public and private, and their data show that in 2002 expenditures for research in the various fields encompassed by NIH grants[249] at American colleges and universities totaled $39 486 million and that of this amount $24 488 million, or 62 percent, was financed by the federal government.[250] That one granting agency should control such a large proportion of the nation's expenditures on biomedical research has raised serious concerns regarding the scope and direction of research. As is the case in other fields, there exists a prevailing orthodoxy regarding the basic principles of biomedical science, an orthodoxy embraced by its leading theoreticians and forming the core structural matrix of the discipline. This complex of basic assumptions gives shape to the presuppositions which lie behind all research and which are a crucial determinant of whether or not to underwrite certain research.

The problem with so much research being directed by one institution is that there exists an overwhelming likelihood that research that in some respects is incompatible with the prevailing paradigm will not receive financial support. Applications that are predicated on alternative non-traditional views of the body and disease have little chance of being supported through a system of peer review when the peers selected to undertake to assess the proposal are all chosen by the same institution. It is very unlikely that Louis Pasteur, had he applied for funds to support the experiments that led him to formulate the germ theory of disease, would have received financial aid from an agency comprising physicians who subscribed to the then prevailing paradigm of spontaneous generation.

Equally problematic are the difficulties researchers are likely to confront when seeking financial assistance to replicate prior experiments that had reached conclusions that called into question accepted scientific canon. An experiment's findings are valuable solely by virtue of their being replicable. However if its conclusions were at odds with orthodox opinion it is highly unlikely that funding would be granted to replicate the study that gave rise to them. From the standpoint of the granting organization, the best that could be hoped for should funds be awarded this kind of research would be that the original study erred. On the other hand, it would be less wasteful if these funds were put to use replicating a study whose conclusions looked 'more promising' (that is, whose conclusions fit the profession's preconceptions). This bias is compounded by the fact that a not insignificant amount of research is conducted in areas whose conclusions have political implications. Thus, given official pronouncements on the issue, if a series of experiments concluded that the ingestion of large quantities of marijuana does not cause long-term cognitive impairment it is far less likely that a grant to replicate this experiment would be made than had the experiment's conclusions been different.[251] Research into the effects of alcohol, illicit drugs, and almost anything having to do with race or human sexual activity, particularly intergenerational sexuality, are fraught with political implications and the findings of researchers who venture into these areas are extremely sensitive. Indeed, if the conclusions reached are such that they defy political orthodoxy, it is not unlikely that they will be dismissed. The effect, consciously or not, is to align one's findings to conform to official beliefs.

There is yet another area in which politics plays a significant role in shaping research and which can create serious problems when a substantial proportion of all research is concentrated in the same hands. This is the case with embryonic stem cell research, which is regarded by many as incompatible with a belief in the sanctity of human life, at least as that term is understood by certain religious groups. If one embraces the view that human life begins at conception then it follows that aborting a human fetus at whatever stage of development is murder. If, on the other hand, the fetus is regarded only as a 'potential' human being, then there occurs some point in its development when it does not possess all the rights accorded human beings. Other arguments may then be brought to bear regarding whether or not it may be aborted. As we are all aware, the issue is exceedingly complex and contentious and is not easily subject to compromise, despite the fact that the therapeutic potential of stem-cell research appears to be enormous.

Inasmuch as the NIH is an agency of government, it is subject to the policy guidelines set down by the Chief Executive. These guidelines, announced by President Bush in August 2001, stipulated that the agency could fund research using embryonic stem cells only if these cells were derived from an embryo that was created for reproductive purposes and only if the derivation process was initiated prior to August 2001. These requirements place severe limits on the amount of research that can be conducted using stem cells which are readily available.[252] And because of the peculiar position the NIH occupies in the world of biomedicine, the religious scruples of one man can determine the direction and quality of a huge proportion of all biomedical research.[253] These problems have been compounded since the 1998 decision to double the NIH's funding levels over the course of the following five years. In that year the Administration, with the eager support of both parties in Congress, announced its intention to double the appropriations of the NIH funding from its then level of $13.6 billion. This commitment was reiterated in February 2001 when President George W. Bush, who had recently been inaugurated, continued these efforts. As a consequence, the budget that was approved in fiscal year

2003 was $27.9 billion. Increases since then have dropped from about 15 percent annually to less than 3 percent, but this decrease in appropriations will almost certainly be temporary. Regardless of these reductions, the sums involved remain substantial and will only contribute to the problems brought about by the dominant position occupied by the NIH in biomedical research. Massive amounts of biomedical research might, in the end, prove a worthwhile investment[254] but we would do well to weigh the problems that follow when funding is concentrated in one agency lest much of this research prove destructive of good scholarship by advancing orthodox agendas at the expense of true science.

NOTES

1. Victoria A. Harden, *Inventing the NIH: Federal Biomedical Research Policy, 1887–1937* (Baltimore: Johns Hopkins University Press, 1986): 11. Harden's book offers an extensive history of the origins of federal biomedical research from the establishment of the Hygienic Laboratory of the Public Health Service in 1887 to the establishment of the second of the component institutes of the NIH, the National Cancer Institute, in 1937. Much of my discussion relies on Ms Harden's account.
2. W. E. van Heyningen and John R. Seal, *Cholera: The American Scientific Experience, 1947–1980* (Boulder, Colo.: Westview Press, 1983): 11.
3. This struggle, which pitted supporters of the American Public Health Association against the Marine Hospital Service, has been characterized by one historian of public health as a conflict between the new apostles of sanitary science in all of its ramifications and the older public health specialists who were primarily interested in quarantine control. See Richard Harrison Shryock, *The Development of Modern Medicine: An Interpretation of the Social and Scientific Factors Involved* (Madison, Wis.: University of Wisconsin Press, 1979): 240–41.
4. The Supervising Surgeon, Walter Wyman, noted the following in the Marine Hospital Service *Annual Report* for 1898: 'In closing this report, which is made at the close of a season notable by reason of the great apprehension which was felt at its beginning lest epidemic disaster should fall upon the country as a result of military and naval operations against Cuba, and notable, too, in the fact that no such results followed, I deem it proper to invite attention to the grave responsibilities and unusual exertions, continued throughout the summer and fall, which were imposed upon the Marine Hospital Service' (828, quoted in Harden, *Inventing the NIH*, 16).
5. Prior to passage of the 1902 statute reorganizing and renaming the Marine Hospital Service, the director of the Service was designated the Supervising Surgeon.
6. This constitutes the first legislative mention of the Hygienic Laboratory: 31 Stat. L. 1086.
7. Senator Spooner must have been prescient. Almost 100 years after passage of legislation reorganizing the Hygienic Laboratory, the National Institutes of Health, the Laboratory's successor, did exactly what Spooner had foreseen as one of the Laboratory's most worthwhile purposes: to adjudicate between conflicting scientific conclusions and to proclaim what would henceforth be the unequivocal orthodox view on a subject. In February 1997 the National Institute on Drug Abuse, a component of the National Institutes of Health, met to determine whether or not marijuana was the scourge of American youth, a hazardous and dangerous drug that had no real medicinal value and that should remain illegal. While the advisory panel charged with reviewing the evidence conceded that there was some support for the view that marijuana might prove useful in mitigating the noxious effects associated with chemotherapy, it was not prepared to issue a definitive ruling on this score. The

National Institute on Drug Abuse, as the only legal source of marijuana for research, continues to block any project seeking to investigate these benign properties. See 'Marijuana On Trial: Is Marijuana a Dangerous Drug or a Valuable Medicine?' *Science News*, 151 (22 March 1997): 178–81.

8. House Committee on Interstate and Foreign Commerce, *Hearings Before the Committee on Interstate and Foreign Commerce on Bills Relating to Health Activities of the General Government* (61st Congress, 2nd Session, and 61st Congress, 3rd Session, June 1920 and January 1911) (Washington, DC: Government Printing Office, 1911): 621.

9. At the time these consisted of the Hygienic Laboratory (which had been moved to Washington, DC in 1891), the Plague Laboratory in San Francisco, and the Rocky Mountain Spotted Fever Laboratory, which had been established to undertake research on yellow fever and Rocky Mountain spotted fever in cooperation with several universities.

10. George Rosen, *Preventive Medicine in the United States, 1900–1975* (New York: Prodist, 1977): 20–23. Rosen notes that 'within a few years almost every state and practically all large cities in the United States had established a diagnostic bacteriological laboratory. Through these laboratories, health departments to a considerable extent took over the task of diagnosing communicable diseases . . .' (24).

11. DeWitt Stetten, Jr, 'A Short History of the National Institutes of Health' (cited 23 July 2000), available from the World Wide Web at http://www.nih.gov/od/museum/exhibits/history/full-text.html.

12. To reflect the agency's wider concerns, the 1902 Act had altered the name of the Marine Hospital Service to the Public Health and Marine Hospital Service. In 1912, the name was changed to the Public Health Service. The Commissioned Officer's Corps was established in 1889 in order to lend an air of military efficiency and dedication to the Service's employees.

13. 32 Stat. L. 728.

14. G. Burroughs Mider, 'The Federal Impact on Biomedical Research', in John Z. Bowers and Elizabeth F. Purcell, eds, *Advances in American Medicine: Essays at the Bicentennial* (2 vols; New York: Josiah Macy, Jr Foundation, 1976); 2: 820.

15. Victoria H. Harden, 'Toward a National Institute of Health: The Development of Federal Biomedical Research Policy, 1900–1930', unpublished Ph.D. thesis, Emory University, 1983: 143.

16. Harden, *Inventing the NIH*, 30. Similarly, the Laboratory's research on pellagra, which was originally thought to be microbial in origin, came to an abrupt end when it was discovered to have a dietary origin.

17. Fisher had severe reservations regarding a *laissez-faire* economy and favored government action in a variety of areas including conservation, disease prevention, sanitation, and irrigation. He supported workmen's compensation laws and a government-administered compulsory health insurance scheme and was a firm adherent of the League of Nations. See Irving Fisher, 'Why Has the Doctrine of Laissez-Faire Been Abandoned', *Science* (4 January 1907): 24–5.

18. George Rosen, 'The Committee of One Hundred on National Health and the Campaign for a National Health Department, 1906–1912', *American Journal of Public Health*, 62 (1972): 261–3.

19. Irving Fisher, *Report on the National Vitality, its Wastes and Conservation* (Bulletin No. 30 of the Committee of One Hundred on National Health) (Washington, DC: Government Printing Office, 1909): 126.

20. A. Hunter Dupree, *Science in the Federal Government: A History of Policies and Activities to 1940* (Cambridge, MA: The Belknap Press of Harvard University Press, 1957): 269.

21. Victoria Harden has called attention to the fact that the Progressive Era campaign to place the management of the nation's health in the hands of a centralized bureaucracy owed much to the leadership fostered by President Roosevelt in support of extensive government programs to manage the nation's resources, both natural and human. *Inventing the NIH*, 32.

22. The leading heterodox (non-allopathic) therapies then current were homeopathy, eclecticism, and osteopathy. Homeopathy was developed into a system of medicine by Dr Samuel Hahnemann, who was born in Germany in 1755 and died in Paris in 1843. Disillusioned by

the therapeutic arsenal of orthodox medicine, which consisted in the main of administering large doses of mineral poisons, Hahnemann concluded on the basis of his experiments that medications – in extremely attenuated doses – that brought about the same symptoms as manifested by the disease – were the most efficacious. Eclecticism's roots also lay in its rejection of the 'heroic therapy' of allopathic medicine and relied primarily on the administration of natural herbs and other botanicals. Its most important practitioner and theoretician, Dr Samuel Thomson (1769–1843), believed that the function of therapy was to restore the body's vital energies and to rid it of its poisonous obstructions by the application of natural substances and steam baths. Osteopathy, developed by Dr Andrew T. Still, a Civil War Army physician, was predicated on a theory of medicine that placed primary emphasis on the structural integrity of the body. Most medical disorders, he maintained, were the result of the misalignment of the skeletal system and corresponding joints, muscles and ligaments, and in particular, the spinal system.

23. Harden, *Inventing the NIH*, 37.
24. Dupree, *Science in the Federal Government*, 270.
25. Mider, 'Federal Impact on Biomedical Research', 822.
26. To this President Taft replied:

> Now there is nothing in the Constitution especially about hogs or cattle or horses, and if out of the Public Treasury at Washington we can establish a department for that purpose, it does not seem to be a long step or a stretch of logic to say that we have the power to tell how we can develop good men and women. (Mider, 'Federal Impact on Biomedical Research', 823.)

27. Quoted in Harden, *Inventing the NIH*, 37.
28. While the United States did not establish a cabinet-level Department of Health until 1953, the movement to create a national administrative agency governing public health in Great Britain led to passage of the Ministry of Health Act in 1919, which abolished the Local Government Boards and created the Ministry of Health. The history of public health activity in Great Britain is dealt with in George Rosen, *A History of Public Health* (New York: MD Publications, Inc., 1958): 192–233, 467.
29. An Act to Change the Name of the Public Health and Marine Hospital Service, to Increase the Pay of Officers of Said Service, and for Other Purposes, 14 August 1912. 37 Stat. L. 309.
30. Wyman died suddenly in November 1911 in a diabetic coma and was replaced by Rupert Blue, who supported raising the PHS to cabinet level.
31. Mider, 'Federal Impact on Biomedical Research', 824. The Committee's primary concerns were the establishment of a central coordinating bureau for scientific research operating under the AAAS, the National Academy of Sciences, or the Smithsonian Institution, and the establishment of guidelines regarding scientific research in the nation's educational institutions and industrial laboratories.
32. Harden, 'National Institutes of Health: Celebrating 100 Years of Medical Progress', in *Encyclopedia Britannica: 1989 Medical and Health Annual* (Chicago: Encyclopedia Britannica, Inc., 1988): 162.
33. Harden, *Inventing the NIH*, 40–41.
34. Mider, 'Federal Impact on Biomedical Research', 828.
35. Federal expenditures were $713 000 000 in 1916 and $18 493 000 000 in 1919, an increase of almost 2600 percent. By 1920, expenditures had dropped to $6 358 000 000 and to $2 908 000 000 in 1924.
36. Harden, *Inventing the NIH*, 51. Under the terms of the Budget and Accounting Act of 1921 which created the Bureau of the Budget, all agencies were required to submit their budget proposals to the Bureau for approval.
37. Bills were introduced in 1921 and again in 1924.
38. Smoot appears to have particularly disliked the Public Health Service, whose functions, he thought, belonged to the states and not to the federal government. Smoot's career is dealt with somewhat glowingly in Milton R. Merrill, *Reed Smoot: Apostle in Politics* (Logan: Utah State University Press, 1990).

39.	'Federal Health Reorganization' (Editorial), *American Journal of Public Health*, 15 (February 1925): 143.
40.	Harden, 'Toward a National Institute of Health', 174.
41.	A brief history of the Metropolitan Life Insurance Company's public health program can be found in Metropolitan Life Insurance Company, *Twenty-five Years of Life Celebration* (New York: Metropolitan Life Insurance Company, 1934).
42.	Currently the National Health Council comprises 118 national health associations, 44 of which form the Council's core. One of the Council's explicit tasks is 'health related advocacy'.
43.	James Tobey, 'Public Health Legislation', *American Public Health Association Journal*, 14 (July 1924): 732.
44.	Resolution in favor of Correlation of Federal Health Activities adopted by the American Public Health Association at its 54th Annual Meeting, St Louis, Missouri, 19–22 October 1925, published in the *American Public Health Association Journal*, 15 (December 1925): 1102, quoted in James A. Tobey, *The National Government and Public Health* (Baltimore, Md.: Johns Hopkins Press, 1926); photo facsimile (New York: Anno Press, 1978): 405.
45.	The Company's visiting nurse program was to become truly gigantic. Between 1909 and 1934 the number of industrial policyholders increased from 7 000 000 to 17 000 000. During that period the Metropolitan's Nursing Service handled over 10 802 000 cases and made almost 65 000 000 visits! See Metropolitan Life, *Twenty-five Years of Life Conservation*, 20, 22.
46.	The Life Extension Institute was founded in 1913 by Frankel, the Yale economist Irving Fisher, and Eugene Lyman Fisk, medical director of the Provident Savings Life Association. It provided health examinations and education programs to its members, who were charged a $20.00 annual fee.
47.	Harden, *Inventing the NIH*, 59.
48.	Tobey, *The National Government and Public Health* (Baltimore, Md.: Johns Hopkins Press, 1926); photo facsimile (New York: Anno Press, 1978).
49.	Tobey, *National Government*, 384–7.
50.	Ibid., 398–9.
51.	The resolutions of both associations appear in ibid., 406.
52.	Ibid., 409.
53.	Harden, 'Toward a National Institute of Health', 185.
54.	Hugh S. Cumming, autobiography, 302; quoted in Harden, *Inventing the NIH*, 63
55.	H.R. 10125, introduced on 8 March 1926.
56.	The provision is quoted in Harden, *Inventing the NIH*, 66.
57.	Fearful of the reaction of the Bureau of the Budget, the PHS prepared two memoranda in which the costs of the new measure were calculated. According to PHS figures, the net effect of the bill would have been to add approximately $9500.00 per year to Public Health Service expenditures.
58.	Bess Furman, *A Profile of the United States Public Health Service, 1798–1948* (United States Department of Health, Education, and Welfare; Washington, DC: Government Printing Office, 1973): 374.
59.	Seeking to emulate the Royal Societies created by the various European states, Congress, at the urging of President Abraham Lincoln, in 1863 decided to charter a private, non-profit organization of distinguished scholars then engaged in scientific and technological research for the purpose of advising it on scientific matters.
60.	Hale prevailed upon the National Academy of Sciences to enact the following resolution at its 1916 meeting: 'That the President of the Academy be requested to inform the President of the United States that in the event of a break in diplomatic relations with any other country the academy desires to place itself at the disposal of the Government for any service within its scope'.
61.	Harden, *Inventing the NIH*, 74–7.
62.	The quotation appears in Herty's unsigned editorial 'War Chemistry in the Alleviation of Suffering', *Journal of Industrial and Engineering Chemistry* (10 September 1918): 673–4, and quoted in Harden, *Inventing the NIH*, 76.

63. Harden, *Inventing the NIH*, 76.
64. Eli Ginzberg and Anna B. Dutka, *The Financing of Biomedical Research* (Baltimore: Johns Hopkins University Press, 1989): 1–2.
65. The first hospital to establish its own laboratory was that of the University of Pennsylvania in 1894.
66. The Rockefeller University's budget (the Institute altered its name in 1965 following its decision to grant doctoral degrees) in fiscal year 2000 was $149.6 million. *Rockefeller University News and Notes*, 9 (4 June 1999): 1.
67. Richard Shryock, *American Medical Research*, 91–2.
68. The John Rockefeller McCormick Memorial Institute for Infectious Diseases was established by Harold McCormick, the heir to the agricultural machinery fortune, in memory of the death of his eldest son from scarlet fever. In was particularly fitting therefore that in 1925 the Institute, together with the Rush Medical College, and the Rush-Presbyterian-St Luke's Medical Center developed the first successful test to determine susceptibility to scarlet fever. American Association of Medical Colleges, 'U.S. Medical Schools and Teaching Hospitals – Innovations in Research and Medical Care', (cited 10 September 2000) World Wide Web at fever.http://www.kcom.edu/faculty/chamberlain/goodres.htm. Other medical research institutes established at the time included the Hooper Institute for Medical Research in San Francisco, the Harvey Cushing Institute in Cleveland, and the Trudeau's Tuberculosis Laboratory at Saranac, New York.
69. Unlike his brother Abraham Flexner, who undertook to survey and rate in all their particulars the medical schools operating in the United States and Canada without any background whatever in medicine or the sciences, Simon Flexner was a trained bacteriologist and thus had a legitimate claim to meeting the qualifications of director of the new Rockefeller Institute.
70. The Institute was established in 1913 on the campus of the University of Pittsburgh by Andrew W. and Richard B. Mellon as an institute whose goal would be new and better consumer products. This partnership between scientific research and industry was originally conceived by Dr Robert Kennedy Duncan of the University of Kansas. In 1927 the Institute was incorporated as a nonprofit research center.
71. It was purely fortuitous that the leading organizations that gave future shape to industrial research in the United States were private rather than, as in Great Britain, public. Indeed, the Department of Commerce was generally regarded as a natural focus for such activity, especially under the direction of its indefatigable Secretary, Herbert Hoover, who served in that capacity under both Presidents Harding and Coolidge. Hoover saw the Department not only as a potential center of scientific research but as a decisive instrument to eliminate inefficiency from the American economy. Dupree, *Science in the Federal Government*, 337–9.
72. A. S. Loevenhart, address before the New York section of the American Chemical Society, 8 November 1918, printed in 'An Institute for Cooperative Research as an Aid to the American Drug Industry', *Journal of Industrial and Engineering Chemistry*, 10 (December 1918): 10.
73. The National Bureau of Standards (since 1988 the National Institute of Standards and Technology) was established in 1901 within the Department of Commerce for the purpose of supplying industry standards and measurements.
74. 'A Central Laboratory of Research', *Philadelphia Public Ledger* (6 October 1918), quoted in Harden, *Inventing the NIH*, 78.
75. Committee report, 15 March 1919, Herty Papers, Box 102, folder 3; quoted in Harden, *Inventing the NIH*, 83.
76. The proposal's details appear in Harden, *Inventing the NIH*, 83–4.
77. They were appalled by the 'extent to which the American chemical industry and related industries . . . were controlled through the medium of international cartel manipulations and foreign owned American patents, the majority of which had been "shelved" to prevent production in America.' Arthur W. Hixson, 'Francis P. Garvan, 1875–1937', *Journal of Industrial and Engineering Chemistry* (News Edition): 15: 539; quoted in Harden, *Inventing the NIH*, 85–6.

78. Garvan offered Herty's committee $50 000.00 to draw up plans for an expanded institute and was instrumental in gaining the support of the American Chemical Society for the new proposal.
79. The report concluded: 'There is not a single organization whose purpose is a determined cooperative attack on the problems of disease and health, where intense chemical and physical research goes hand in hand with the medical and biological study of disease. The importance of chemistry and physics has been recognized, but the direction of research is still essentially in the hands of medical men. No one of the scientific groups alone should be entrusted with leadership. All are needed for coping successfully with the complex and formidable problems. Complete cooperation of a staff of experts, peers in every sense, each in his own field, with emphasis on the fundamental, chemical and physical character of the problems, has nowhere been accomplished. Consequently it is proposed that the attack be actually cooperative, from the selection of the problem and the formulation of the plan of work through the whole concentrated effort to grapple with Nature and ultimately to conquer outpost after outpost of the complex world of life.' Charles H. Herty, John Jacob Abel, and the American Chemical Society, *The Future Independence and Progress of American Medicine in the Age of Chemistry* (New York: Chemical Foundation, 1921): 80.
80. Fitzhugh Mullan, *Plagues and Politics: The Story of the United States Public Health Service* (New York: Basic Books: 1989): 89.
81. Harden, *Inventing the NIH*, 89.
82. Herty, *et al.*, *Future Independence and Progress*, 66
83. 'The Future Independence and Progress of American Medicine in the Age of Chemistry', *Journal of the American Medical Association*, 78 (18 March 1922): 807.
84. Quoted in Harden, *Inventing the NIH*, 90.
85. Ransdell appears to have been particularly concerned with legislation relating to health. As chairman of the Senate Committee on Public Health he spoke in 1916 on the topic 'Rural Health, the Nation's First Duty', in which he underscored two aspects of public health: that preventive medicine was far more economical than was therapeutic treatment (a notion popularized by Irving Fisher in his 1909 monograph *Report on National Vitality*) and 'since disease has absolutely no regard for state lines', that the federal government had primary responsibility for public health matters.
86. The bill also contained a provision which authorized the Secretary of the Treasury to accept private contributions to the Institute to be used 'for study, investigation, and research in pure science'. Any contribution larger than $500 000 would bear the name of the donor. These fellowships were apparently modeled after the industrial fellowship of the Mellon Institute.
87. It is worth pointing out that this argument, invented by the Institute's propagandists, had no merit whatever.
88. 'Chemistry and Disease', *New York Times* (7 July 1926): 24.
89. 'Wants Government to Lead Health Work', *New York Times* (Sunday, 26 September 1926): Part II, 2.
90. In fact, George W. McCoy, the Director of the Hygienic Laboratory, Rolla Eugene Dyer, the Laboratory's Assistant Director, and Arthur M. Dyer, Director of the Division of Scientific Research, were all apprehensive that the Hygienic Laboratory would find some difficulty in expending the funds that would come from quadrupling its research budget over night and supported the Laboratory's more gradual expansion. Harden, *Inventing the NIH*, 112.
91. Dupree, *Science in the Federal Government*, 340–41.
92. *Public Papers of the Presidents of the United States: Herbert Hoover* (Containing the Public Messages, Speeches, and Statements of the President, 4 March to 31 December 1929) (Washington, DC: Government Printing Office, 1974): 6. Hoover expressed similar sentiments in his State of the Union address of 3 December 1929: 'The advance in scientific discovery as to disease and health imposes new considerations upon us. The Nation as a whole is vitally interested in the health of the people; in protection from spread of contagious disease; in the relation of physical and mental disabilities to criminality; and in the economic and moral advancement which is fundamentally associated with sound body and

mind. The organization of preventive measures and health education in its personal application is the province of public health service. Such organization should be as universal as
public education. Its support is a proper burden upon the taxpayer. It can not be organized
with success, either in its sanitary or educational phases, except under public authority. It
should be based upon local and State responsibility, but I consider that the Federal
Government has an obligation of contribution to the establishment of such agencies.'
Public Papers, 427–8.

93. *New York Times* (20 December 1928): 15, col. 2; *New York Times* (12 January 1929): 28,
col. 4.
94. At its height, from mid-October to mid-November 1918, over 100 000 new cases were
reported in New York City alone. This compares with somewhat under 9000 new cases
from the last week of December 1928, to the last week of January 1929. 'Publicity Found
Influenza Weapon', *New York Times* (1 March 1929): 16. According to the Public Health
Service, more than one out of every four Americans living in the nation's cities had
contracted influenza, grippe, pneumonia, or severe colds. United States Public Health
Service, *Annual Report, 1928* (Washington, DC: Government Printing Office, 1928): 4.
95. Quoted in Harden, *Inventing the NIH*, 144.
96. Quoted in ibid., 145.
97. 'Statement of H. B. Anderson, of the Citizen's Medical Reference Bureau', in *Economic
Security Act* (Hearings Before the Committee on Ways and Means, House of
Representatives, 74th Congress, 1st Session on H.R. 4120) (Washington, DC: Government
Printing Office, 1935): 656.
98. Furman, *A Profile of the United States Public Health Service*, 382.
99. 'The Last Enemy', *New York Times*, 21 April 1930, 22.
100. *National Institute of Health* (Hearings Before the Committee on Interstate and Foreign
Commerce, House of Representatives, 71st Congress, 2nd Session on S. 1171, 21 April
1930) (Washington, DC: Government Printing Office, 1930): 7, 16, quoted in Harden,
Inventing the NIH, 156.
101. It was hoped that the Institute would receive a steady flow of substantial donations in
succeeding years.
102. Ransdell was quite open about his motives in establishing the Board. In a letter to President
Hoover, he noted that among the primary reasons for his setting up the Board was 'the
necessity of employment to earning a living after leaving Congress'. Quoted in Harden,
Inventing the NIH, 161. The $20 000 comprised two grants of $10 000 per year for two
years from the American Relief Association Children's Fund, a sum secured by President
Hoover, and a similar amount from the Chemical Foundation, secured through the intercession of Ransdell's old friend, Francis Garvan. Harden, *Inventing the NIH*, 161.
103. The largest of these was a donation of $25.00 from Senator Royal Copeland.
104. Indeed, expenditures for all research undertaken by the federal government started a head-
long decline in 1932 and did not reach their 1932 highs again until 1937. Dupree, *Science
in the Federal Government*, 344.
105. In deference to Surgeon General Cumming, Parran was not appointed Surgeon General
until Cumming's fourth term was completed in 1936.
106. In 1934 President Roosevelt appointed Parran to the Committee on Economic Security
which drafted the Social Security Act of 1935. Title 6 authorized millions of dollars for
public health departments and for biomedical research.
107. The estate was donated by Mr and Mrs Luke Wilson of the Wilson Sporting Goods
Company for the 'general benefit to the people of the United States'.
108. Donald S. Swain, 'The Rise of a Research Empire: NIH, 1930 to 1950', *Science*, 138 (14
December 1962): 1234. Swain notes that the National Academy of Sciences, already
annoyed that Roosevelt had created the Science Advisory Board without first consulting
the Academy, was especially outraged that Parran and Rosenau, neither of whom were
members of the Academy, were appointed to the Board. The result was to undermine the
effectiveness of the Board and it lapsed in 1935.
109. Section 603 provided that 'there is hereby authorized to be appropriated for each fiscal
year, beginning with the fiscal year ending June 30, 1936, the sum of $2 000 000 for

expenditure by the Public Health Service for investigation of disease and problems of sanitation . . . and for the pay and allowances and traveling expenses of personnel of the Public Health Service, including commissioned officers, engaged in such investigations'. Despite this provision, however, Congress refused to appropriate the maximum amount during the 1930s. However, $375 000 in additional funds were appropriated to the NIH in 1936, rising to $1.64 million in 1940. Swain, 'The Rise of a Research Empire', 1234.

110. Swain, 'The Rise of a Research Empire', 1234.
111. J. R. Heller, 'The National Cancer Institute: A Twenty-Year Retrospect', *Journal of the National Cancer Institute*, 19 (August 1957): 147.
112. 'The Great Darkness', *Fortune*, 15 (March 1937): 123–5, quoted in Nancy Carol Erdey, *Armor of Patience: The National Cancer Institute and the Development of Medical Research Policy in the United States, 1937–1971*, unpublished Ph.D. thesis; Case Western Reserve University, 1995: 44.
113. William S. Yaremchuk, 'The Origins of the National Cancer Institute', *Journal of the National Cancer Institute*, 34 (August 1977): 554.
114. Stephen P. Strickland, *Politics, Science, and Dread Disease: A Short History of United States Medical Research Policy* (Cambridge, MA: Harvard University Press, 1972): 11.
115. *Journal of the American Medical Association*, 109 (16 October 1937), quoted in Strickland, *Politics, Science, and Dread Disease*, 14. Organized medicine tended to regard government involvement in medical research as the opening wedge of government involvement in health care. A number of state medical societies had earlier opposed the opening of state cancer clinics by the American Association for the Control of Cancer. Erdey, *Armor of Patience*, 51.
116. Ibid., 48.
117. Strickland, *Politics, Science, and Dread Disease*, 13. Congress did honor President Roosevelt's wish that not more than $1 million per year be appropriated for cancer research. The annual appropriation made in its first year of operation was $700 000 (ibid., 13).
118. Quoted in ibid., 14.
119. Dupree, *Science in the Federal Government*, 366.
120. Ibid., 366. Between 1938 and 1940 the Institute made 33 grants totaling $220 000.
121. Quoted in Heller, 'The National Cancer Institute,' 154.
122. Ibid., 160.
123. Erdey, *Armor of Patience*, 72.
124. Proceedings of the National Advisory Cancer Council, 19 January 1942, quoted in Erdey, *Armor of Patience*, 72–3.
125. Some idea of Dr Voegtlin's pharmacological rigor can be garnered from his statements at an informal conference on Cannabis Sativa held at the Treasury Building in Washington, DC in January 1937, under the direction of Dr Harry Anslinger, US Commissioner of Narcotics. Anslinger, faced with smaller budgets, sought to criminalize marijuana and as a consequence made every effort to publicize the dangers of this killer drug. At the meeting Voegtlin maintained that 'it is an established fact that prolonged use [of marijuana] leads to insanity in certain cases, depending upon the amount taken, of course'. 'Conference on Cannabis Sativa L. [January 14, 1937]' in *Schaffer Library on Drug Policy* (cited 16 January 2001), available from the World Wide Web at http://www.druglibrary.org/schaffer/hemp/taxact/canncon.htm
126. Michael B. Shimkin, 'As Memory Serves – An Informal History of the National Cancer Institute, 1937–1957', *Journal of the National Cancer Institute*, 59(2) (Supplement): August 1977: 578.
127. The American Cancer Society was established in 1913 as the American Society for the Control of Cancer. Its primary activity in its early years was organizing public education campaigns about the disease and encouraging physicians to be alert for signs of cancer in their patients. It was not until the end of World War II that the organization, renamed the American Cancer Society (ACS) in 1943, began to underwrite research. This change was largely the work of Mary Lasker, a wealthy patron who had dedicated herself to increasing the amount of research being done in biomedicine. Mrs Lasker offered to pay for the ACS's

1945 national fund drive if one-quarter of the amount raised was earmarked for research. The drive was so successful that the ACS was able to raise almost $5 000 000 of which $1 000 000 was allocated for studies into the nature and causes of cancer. The early history of the ACS is touched on in Erdey, *Armor of Patience*, 117–34; Charles S. Cameron, 'The American Cancer Society: Its Development, Organization, and Fund Raising Methods', *Acta Unio Internationalis Contra Cancrum*, 14 (1958): 875–81; and, Richard A. Rettig, *Cancer Crusade: The Story of the National Cancer Act of 1971* (Princeton: Princeton University Press, 1977): 18–24.

128. Stephen P. Strickland, *The Story of the NIH Grants Programs* (Lanham, Md.: University Press of America, 1989): 15.
129. Administrator of the Federal Security Agency, *Annual Report, 1947*, Section III: US Public Health Service (Washington, DC: Government Printing Office, 1947): 263.
130. Strickland, *NIH Grants Programs*, 17.
131. Swain, 'The Rise of a Research Empire', 1233.
132. Vannevar Bush, *Science, the Endless Frontier* (A Report to the President by Vannevar Bush, Director of the Office of Scientific Research and Development, July 1945) (Washington, DC: Government Printing Office, 1945): 31.
133. Swain, 'The Rise of a Research Empire', 1236.
134. Strickland, *Politics, Science, and Dread Disease*, 20–21.
135. In 1948, President Truman addressed the American Association for the Advancement of Science on the occasion of its centenary. The President reiterated the recommendations of his Scientific Research Board whose Report, 'Science and Public Policy', proposed that the total amount, both public and private, spent on scientific research be doubled and that a National Science Foundation be created. It was this speech that served as the impetus for passage of the National Science Foundation Act of 1950. The speech appears in *Science*, 108 (24 September 1948): 313–14.
136. One of the reasons Dyer was able to convince the CMR that the nation's future was in some way dependent on the NIH assuming jurisdiction over these contracts was because he regarded it as likely that another war was imminent and that it was vital to America's military preparedness that the nation continue its medical research. Strickland, *Politics, Science, and Dread Disease*, 28.
137. Daniel M. Fox, 'The Politics of the NIH Extramural Program, 1937–1950', *Journal of the History of Medicine and Allied Sciences*, 41 (1987): 455.
138. Strickland, *Politics, Science, and Dread Disease*, 27. Strickland notes that in 1940 private foundations gave $4.7 million for research on medical problems.
139. Swain, 'The Rise of a Research Empire', 1236.
140. Fox, 'The Politics of the NIH Extramural Program', 457–8.
141. Strickland, *The Story of the NIH Grants Programs*, 25.
142. The Lasker Foundation annually selects the recipients of the Lasker awards in the medical and biological sciences, among the world's most prestigious awards in the field.
143. It is a curiosity of the Lasker fortune that a substantial part of Albert Lasker's fortune was made advertising Lucky Strike cigarettes. Mary Lasker's influence on national health policy is truly remarkable and without precedent in the history of American politics. She played a role, often a crucial role, in the history of every important piece of legislation relating to health between the end of World War II and her death in 1994. She and her allies in the health lobby are discussed in Elizabeth Brenner Drew, 'The Health Syndicate: Washington's Nobel Conspirators', *Atlantic* (Monthly), 220 (December 1967): 75–82.
144. One commentator maintains that 'Mrs. Lasker's own experience with private health-oriented organizations had convinced her that the private sector, alone, could never make sufficient headway against disease'. However, we are not told what factors associated with private health-oriented organizations would lead her to conclude that they were inadequate. Strickland, *Politics, Science, and Dread Disease*, 33.
145. The Division of Mental Hygiene of the Public Health Service, established in 1930, dealt exclusively with addiction to narcotics.
146. These events are recounted in Strickland, *Politics, Science, and Dread Disease*, 44–5. Mrs Lasker seems to have been an exceptionally shrewd woman, whose abilities to apply so

much leverage in shaping federal health care programs was in good part a function of her knack for knowing to whose election campaigns she should contribute to produce the optimal results.

147. During the war years there were 1.1 million admissions to hospitals for neuropsychiatric conditions (including duplicate admissions). Of these 15.8 percent were for neurological disorders, 6.1 percent for psychoses, 10.8 percent for character and behavior disorders, and 58.8 percent for psychoneuroses, while 8.5 percent were for other diagnoses. Somewhat over 61 percent of these admissions occurred in the United States. Gerald N. Grob, *From Asylum to Community: Mental Health Policy in Modern America* (Princeton: Princeton University Press, 1991): 13.

148. Ibid., 6–11.

149. Ibid., 16–17.

150. Grob, *From Asylum to Community*, 20. To those who regarded the intrusion of government into one's private life as unwelcome, Menninger was a particularly distasteful figure. He was the principal spokesman for 'social psychiatry', that is, the application of psychiatric findings to all human interrelationships, including those not concerned with mental disease. Indeed, Menninger would have designed and centrally directed all our social institutions in keeping with what he regarded as the principles of mental health. In these views he was joined by his brother, Dr Karl Menninger, who founded and directed the Menninger Clinic in Topeka, Kansas. See William Menninger, *A Psychiatrist for a Troubled World: Selected Papers of William C. Menninger* (New York: Viking Press, 1967), and Karl A. Menninger, *Man Against Himself* (San Diego: Harcourt Brace Jovanovich, 1985).

151. Grob, *From Asylum to Community*, 20.

152. Ibid., 28.

153. 'The Social Responsibility of Psychiatry: A Statement of Orientation', *GAP Report No. 13* (July 1950): 1–5; quoted in Grob, *From Asylum to Community*, 32.

154. Ibid., 46.

155. Ibid., 49.

156. The Federal Security Agency was created by President Roosevelt in 1939 and brought together the various government agencies responsible for health, education, and social security, including the Public Health Service. Its director between 1947 and 1953 was Oscar Ewing, an attorney who had been chief counsel for the Aluminum Company of America.

157. Both worked tirelessly for enactment of a national compulsory health insurance bill, which President Truman presented to Congress in September 1945. At the urging of the President's staff, the Laskers, the Mahoneys, Mrs Franklin D. Roosevelt, and the industrialist Henry Kaiser were among the group that formed the Committee on the Nation's Health to lobby for passage of a health-insurance scheme.

158. The National Mental Health Act, P.L. 79–487.

159. Gerald N. Grob, 'Creation of the National Institute of Mental Health', *Public Health Reports*, 111 (July/August, 1996): 380.

160. Grob, *From Asylum to Community*, 54.

161. See Robert H. Felix, 'Community Mental Health: A Great and Significant Movement', *American Journal of Psychiatry*, 122 (1966): 1056–7.

162. While funding for the work done at the Addiction Research Center was ostensibly paid for by the Navy and the NIMH, funds paid to academic and other research institutions were funneled through the Josiah Macy Jr Foundation and the Geschickter Fund for Medical Research of Washington, DC.

163. Dr Isbell had been a member of the Food and Drug Administration's Advisory Committee on the Abuse of Depressant and Stimulants Drugs and a long-time CIA researcher.

164. The CIA's involvement in covert LSD experimentation is recounted in John Marks, *The Search for the Manchurian Candidate: The CIA and Mind Control* (New York: Times Books, 1979).

165. Martin A. Lee and Bruce Schlain, *Acid Dreams: The Complete Social History of LSD: The CIA, the Sixties, and Beyond* (New York: Grove Press, 1985).

166.   Senator Pepper, in a 1984 interview, recalls that it was Mrs Lasker who suggested that Bridge's heart problem might make him agreeable to the creation of a heart institute. Pepper recounts that Lasker said 'I'll give you a little tip. Senator Bridges, Chairman of the Senate Appropriations Committee, has had a little heart trouble, and he might be interested in the subject if you mention it to him. If you get him to hold a hearing on an appropriation for a Heart Institute or some heart research money, I'll bring the outstanding experts down to testify before the committee at the hearing.' Quoted in Ernestine Taylor Lanahan, *A Salute to the Past: A History of the National Heart, Lung, and Blood Institute* (Bethesda, Md.: National Institutes of Health, 1987): 13.
167.   Lanahan, *A Salute to the Past*, 15.
168.   P.L. 80-655.
169.   These details are discussed at some length in Ruth Roy Harris, *Dental Science in a New Age: A History of the National Institute of Dental Research* (Rockville, Md.: Montrose Press, 1989): 17–41.
170.   Harris, *Dental Science in a New Age*, 77.
171.   Creation of the National Institute of Dental Research was further facilitated by a massive report on scientific research undertaken by the President's Scientific Research Board (PSRB) which, in 1946, had been ordered by President Truman 'to review current and proposed research and development (R&D) activities both within and outside of the Federal Government'. The Board was chaired by an economist, John R. Steelman, director of the Office of War Mobilization and Reconversion. The first volume of Steelman's report was entitled 'The Nation's Medical Research' and recommended an ambitious plan of government support for the whole range of scientific research, including medical and dental research. It proposed a doubling of total federal expenditures for basic scientific research to $2 000 000 000 by 1957, including biomedical research expenditures of $280 000 000.
172.   'Close to seventy organizations and individuals prominent in dentistry overwhelmingly supported the establishment of a federal dental research institute.' Harris, *Dental Science in a New Age*, 82.
173.   Ibid., 108.
174.   *Annual Report of the Federal Security Agency, Public Health Service 1950* (Washington, DC: Government Printing Office, 1951): 18.
175.   Both the Biologics Control Laboratory and the Rocky Mountain Laboratory dated back to 1902. The Rocky Mountain Laboratory was an outgrowth of the Public Health Service's facility, established in the foothills of the Bitterroot Range of the Rockies, to investigate the causes and possible treatment of Rocky Mountain spotted fever. The Biologics Control Laboratory had been established following passage of the Biologic Control Act, which authorized the Hygienic Laboratory to regulate the interstate commerce of vaccines and toxins.
176.   From May 1972 to June 1981: the National Institutes of Arthritis, Metabolism, and Digestive Diseases (NIAMDD); from June 1981 to April 1986: the National Institute of Arthritis, Diabetes, and Digestive and Kidney Diseases (NIDDK).
177.   Of Congressman Keefe's own concerns with respect to the government medical research program, one historian has noted that 'he simply wanted to retain supervisory direction over medical research within the subcommittee he chaired. Hence he could play, and did, a liberal role if the challenge to his position as "health research leader" came from the outside in the form of a restrictive executive budget; or he could, in the traditional fashion of earlier congressional friends of the Public Health Service, play a more conservative role if special promoters inside Congress or the committee tried to foist new activities on those directly in charge.' Strickland, *Politics, Science, and Dread Disease*, 77. It is worth noting that Keefe was a close friend of Mary Lasker, a native of Wisconsin with business interests in the state, on whose advice he appears to have relied.
178.   See Strickland, *Politics, Science, and Dread Disease*, 78–9.
179.   Ibid., 81.
180.   Alan T. Waterman, 'Preface', *Science: The Endless Frontier* (Washington, DC: National Science Foundation, 1960): xii.

181. P.L. 81-692.
182. Hill, who served in Congress from 1923 to 1969, was an unceasing champion of legislation bearing on the public health, which he regarded as his area of particular concern.
183. Strickland, *Politics, Science, and Dread Disease*, 93.
184. Despite the fact that President Eisenhower had requested $400 000 000 for the NIH for fiscal year 1961, Congress appropriated $547 000 000, almost 38 percent more!
185. *House Appropriations Hearings, 1955*, 84th Congress, 1st Session, 'Department of Health, Education, and Welfare' (Washington, DC: Government Printing Office, 1955): Part 1: 98. One analyst notes of Fogarty: '[He] seemed to have a new medical interest every year, often before it became the subject of popular concern. In 1958 he asked the Secretary of HEW, the Surgeon General, and the Director of the National Institute of Mental Health whether anything was being done about the origins of mental retardation. He wanted to know what NIH was doing about multiple sclerosis, Tay-Sachs disease, blindness, cystic fibrosis, retrolental fibroplasia.' Strickland, *Politics, Science, and Dread Disease*, 111.
186. Ibid., 112–14.
187. In June 1976, the National Heart and Lung Institute was renamed the National Heart, Lung, and Blood Institute (NHLBI).
188. Strickland, *Politics, Science, and Dread Disease*, 158.
189. Folsom, treasurer of the Eastman Kodak Corporation, had been a member of President Franklin Roosevelt's original Advisory Council on Economic Security which recommended creation of the Social Security program.
190. Congress appropriated 93 percent more for the NIH in fiscal year 1960 than it had in fiscal year 1958, from $172 000 000 in 1958 to $242 000 000 in 1959 to $332 000 000 in 1960.
191. US Congress, Senate Committee on Appropriations, *Federal Support of Medical Research* (Report of the Committee of Consultants on Medical Research to the Health Subcommittee), 86th Congress, 2nd Session, May 1960 (Washington, DC: Government Printing Office, 1960): xii; quoted in Strickland, *Politics, Science, and Dread Disease*, 160.
192. At the time Executive Director of the National Committee Against Mental Illness and an ardent member of the medical lobby.
193. Strickland, *Politics, Science, and Dread Disease*, 161.
194. US Congress, Senate, *Committee Report on Labor-HEW Appropriations, 1961*, 87th Congress, 1st Session (Washington, DC: Government Printing Office, 1960): 18; quoted in Strickland, *Politics, Science, and Dread Disease*, 162.
195. Ibid., 163.
196. In its June 1962 report on the NIH, the committee 'took strong exception to the view expressed by the NIH that all administrative actions subsequent to the selection of grant projects are "essentially trivial" in relation to the basic selection process. The selection process and grant management are essential and complementary parts of NIH research support. Excellence is required of both.' US Congress, House Committee on Government Operations, *The Administration of Grants by the National Institutes of Health: Re-examination of Management Deficiencies* (Fountain Committee Report), 87th Congress, 1st Session, June 1962 (Washington, DC: Government Printing Office, 1962): 25.
197. Fountain Committee Report, 26.
198. Department of Health, Education, and Welfare, NIH Study Committee, *Biomedical Science and its Administration: A Study of the National Institutes of Health* (Wooldridge Committee Report) (Washington, DC: Government Printing Office, 1965); 1.
199. 'In brief,' the Report concluded, 'we consider the NIH program to be sound and recommend its continued support. Its $1 billion budget is not high, when compared to the more than thirty billion dollars a year the American public pays for assorted health services; the money is on the whole competently and efficiently employed on a broad spectrum of health related research; lessons from the past history of science, supported by the current acceleration of medical discovery, strongly suggest a satisfactory future payoff. Furthermore, as discoveries are made in the life sciences, new opportunities will be created for health research, and these too should be exploited with the enthusiasm and vigor which has distinguished the NIH program during the past decade. We feel that the Congress in particular deserves considerable credit for its past support of this kind of farsighted program. We

suspect that there are few, if any, one billion dollar segments of the Federal budget that are buying more valuable services for the American people than that administered by the National Institutes of Health.' Wooldridge Committee Report, 7.

200. Strickland, *Politics, Science, and Dread Disease*, 189.

201. *Senate Committee Report for Labor-HEW Appropriations*, 1962, 87th Congress, 1st Session (Washington, DC: Government Printing Office, 1962): 27–8; quoted in Strickland, *Politics, Science, and Dread Disease*, 196.

202. James A. Shannon, 'The Advancement of Medical Research: A Twenty-year View of the NIH Role', Alan Gregg Memorial Lecture, San Francisco, 22 October 1966, p. 19; quoted in Strickland, *Politics, Science, and Dread Disease*, 189.

203. Mary Lasker had been a friend of Lyndon Johnson's from the time he served as Senate majority leader. Lady Bird Johnson had twice stayed at the Lasker home on the Côte d'Azur and Johnson had been invited to address the Lasker Awards luncheon while Vice-President, in 1961. In addition, Lasker was an ardent supporter of Lady Bird's beautification efforts. So close was the relationship between Mrs. Lasker and the President that she was the last person to see him before he left the White House for the hospital when he prepared for surgery in 1965. Strickland, *Politics, Science, and Dread Disease*, 206–7.

204. 'Special Message to the Congress on the Nation's Health', in *Public Papers of the President: Lyndon B. Johnson* (Containing the Public Messages, Speeches, and Statements of the President, 1963–64) (2 vols: Washington, DC: Government Printing Office, 1965): 282. Johnson later acknowledged that the commission was established 'at the insistence of the lovely lady, Mary Lasker'. Rettig, *Cancer Crusade*, 36.

205. P.L. 89-239.

206. Gardner's liberal credentials were impeccable. He had edited President Kennedy's book, *To Turn the Tide* and was President first of the Carnegie Corporation and then of the Carnegie Foundation for the Advancement of Education. He was later to serve as President of the National Urban Coalition and to receive the Presidential Medal of Freedom. In 1970 he founded and became head of Common Cause. While Secretary of HEW, from August 1965 to February 1968, he presided over the introduction of Medicare and Medicaid and helped shepherd the Older Americans Act through Congress.

207. *The New York Times*, 28 June 1966.

208. Strickland, *Politics, Science, and Dread Disease*, 207–8.

209. Elizabeth Brenner Drew, 'The Health Syndicate', 81.

210. Strickland, *Politics, Science, and Dread Disease*, 219.

211. Ibid., 222.

212. Rettig, *Cancer Crusade*, 40.

213. The press commonly referred to this group as her 'stable'. See Elizabeth Brenner Drew, 'The Health Syndicate', 75.

214. U.S. Congress, House, 91st Congress, 2nd Session, 1970, House Concurrent Resolution 526; quoted in Rettig, *Cancer Crusade*, 82. Despite the resolution's preposterous language, it is hard to imagine a member of Congress voting against it. Both for America and against disease, all in the same resolution!

215. The medical-scientific group included Dr R. Lee Clark, a personal friend of Yarborough's who, with Farber, had previously been on the DeBakey Commission, Dr Joseph Burchenal, vice-president of the Sloan-Kettering Cancer Institute, Dr James Holland of the Roswell Park Memorial Institute, Dr Jonathan E. Rhoads, President of the American Cancer Society, Dr Solomon Garb, author of *Cure for Cancer: A National Goal*; Dr Paul B. Cornely, President of the American Public Health Association, Dr William B. Hutchinson, a Settle surgeon and close friend of Senator Warren Magnuson, Lister Hill's successor on the Senate Appropriations Committee, Dr Mathilde Krim, a research associate at Sloan Kettering and the wife of the former treasurer of the Democratic National Committee, Dr Joshua Lederberg of Stanford University, Nobel laureate and strong supporter of increases in government spending on research, Dr Harry Kaplan, radiologist from Stanford University, Dr Wendell Scott, radiologist from Washington University, St Louis, and an activist in the American Cancer Society, and Dr Harold Rusch, professor of cancer research at the University of Wisconsin and well-known to the National Cancer Institute.

The lay members of the Panel were, in the main, close friends of either Mary Lasker or Senator Yarborough, or had been recommended to them by people they trusted. Among them was Emerson Foote, the advertising executive, Mrs Anna Rosenberg Hoffman, who had been assistant secretary of defense for manpower under President Truman and who had been an active medical lobbyist for decades, William McC. Blair, general director of the John F. Kennedy Center for the Performing Arts and Mary Lasker's host during her numerous Washington trips, Lewis Wasserman, president of the Music Corporation of America, Jubel R. Parten, a wealthy Houston philanthropist, Emil Mazey, secretary-treasurer of the United Automobile Workers, I. W. Abel, president of the United Steel Workers, Mary Wells Lawrence, chairman of the board of the advertising firm of Wells, Rich, and Greene, Inc., Michael J. O'Neill, managing editor of the *New York Daily News*, G. Keith Funston, chairman of the board of the Olin Mathieson Chemical Corporation, and Elmer Bobst, honorary chairman of the Warner-Lambert Pharmaceutical Co., and one of the primary forces behind the American Cancer Society's anti-smoking campaign.

In sum, the 25 panelists could all be relied on to recommend the kind of program envisaged by Mary Lasker.

216. US Congress, Senate Committee on Labor and Public Policy, *National Program for the Conquest of Cancer* (Report of the National Panel of Consultants on the Conquest of Cancer), Report 91-1402, 91st Congress, 2nd Session (Washington, DC: Government Printing Office, 1970): 3.

217. Report of the National Panel of Consultants, 7.

218. So popular had the issue of cancer research become that even the Administration took up the issue. In his State of the Union address before Congress in January 1971 President Nixon announced 'I will also ask for an appropriation of an extra $100 million to launch an intensive campaign to find a cure for cancer, and I will ask later for whatever additional funds can effectively be used. The time has come in America when the same kind of concentrated effort that split the atom and took man to the moon should be turned toward conquering this dread disease. Let us make a total national commitment to achieve this goal.' 'Annual Message to the Congress on the State of the Union' (22 January 1971) in *Public Papers of the President: Richard Nixon* (Containing the Public Messages, Speeches, and Statements of the President, 1971) (Washington, DC: Government Printing Office, 1972): 53

219. Rettig, *Cancer Crusade*, 175–7. See also Strickland, *Politics, Science, and Dread Disease*, 271.

220. P.L. 92–218.

221. Natalie Davis Springarn, *Heartbeat: The Politics of Health Research* (Washington and New York: Robert B. Luce, Inc., 1976): 53.

222. The Institute's name had been changed in November 1969 to the National Heart and Lung Institute to reflect its expanded functions.

223. In the five years following passage of the National Cancer Act in 1971 there were no fewer than 17 Congressional initiatives which had a major influence on NIH programming. Among the list of conditions targeted were sickle cell anemia, digestive diseases, Cooley's anemia, multiple sclerosis, sudden infant death syndrome, chronic exposure to sulfur oxides, diabetes, burns, and Huntington's chorea and epilepsy. Springarn, *Heartbeat*, 74.

224. This also held true for the creation of new institutes. Thus, following intense lobbying by organizations representing retired Americans, Congress, even in the face of a Presidential veto, enacted legislation in 1974 establishing the National Institute on Aging, thus moving all research on aging from the National Institute of Child Health and Human Development to the new Institute.

225. Not 200 000, as was claimed by the bill's sponsor, Congressman Robert N. Giaimo, Democrat of Connecticut.

226. P.L. 90-31.

227. See Grob, *From Asylum to Community*, 181–208.

228. Congress, US House of Representatives, *Mental Health Study Act of 1955* (Hearings before a subcommittee of the Committee on Interstate and Foreign Commerce) 84th Congress, 1st Session (Washington, DC: Government Printing Office, 1955): 70–71.

229. Lewis L. Judd, MD, 'Historical Highlights of the National Institute of Mental Health: From 1946 to the Present', *American Journal of Psychiatry*, 155 (September 1998): NIMH Special Supplement, 4.

230. Grob, *From Asylum to Community*, 196–8.

231. Joint Commission for Mental Illness and Health, *Action for Mental Health* (New York: Basic Books, 1961).

232. It appears that the Report could have been released some time earlier but it was feared that if it first appeared during the last days of the Eisenhower administration, its reception would have been seriously muted. Grob, *From Asylum to Community*, 203.

233. Quoted in ibid., 227.

234. In fiscal year 1965, in addition to its regular appropriation, the NIMH received $35 000 000 for the construction of community mental health centers. This amount was raised to $50 000 000 in fiscal year 1966.

235. See Grob, *From Asylum to Community*, 276.

236. Stanley F. Yolles, 'Past, Present and 1980: Trend Projections', *Progress in Community Mental Health* 1 (1969): 3–4, quoted in Grob, *From Asylum to Community*, 276.

237. Bertram S. Brown, MD, 'NIMH Before (1946–1970) and During the Tenure of Director Bertram S. Browne, M.D. (1970–1978): The Early Years and the Public Health Mission', *American Journal of Psychiatry*, 155 (September 1998): NIMH Special Supplement, 11.

238. P.L. 91–616.

239. The NIDA was created largely in response to the substantial increase in drug use that accompanied American involvement in the Vietnam War.

240. A health care research and consulting firm.

241. Frederick K. Goodwin, MD, 'NIMH During the Tenure of Director Frederick K. Goodwin, M.D. (1992–1994): The Return of the NIMH to NIH and the Fight for Parity', *American Journal of Psychiatry*, 155 (September 1998): NIMH Special Supplement: 33.

242. While approximately 84 percent of the Americans who've contracted AIDS have been male, the number of women is rising – from 6.6 percent in 1985 to 23.1 percent in the period January–June 1999. Of the 570 000 men who have been diagnosed as HIV positive, the number who appear to have contracted the condition from sexual activity with other men has dropped from 71.3 percent in 1985 to 43.8 percent in January–June 1999, while the number of men who have acquired AIDS from intravenous drug use has increased from 14.7 percent in 1985 to 19.4 percent during the first half of 1999. These figures do not include men who both had sexual contacts with other men and who also used drugs intravenously, which numbered 8.7 percent of all cases among males in 1985 and 5.0 percent in January–June 1999. National Center for Health Statistics, *Health, United States, 2000* (Hyattsville, Md.: National Center for Health Statistics, 2000): Table 54, pp. 224–5.

243. Centers for Disease Control and Prevention, 'Cases of HIV Infection and AIDS in the United States, 2004', Table 5b: Estimated number of cases and rates (per 100 000 population) of HIV/AIDS, by race/ethnicity, age category, and sex. 2004. http://www.cdc.gov/hiv/topics/surveillance/resources/reports/2004report/table5b.htm.

244. P.L. 100-607.

245. Anthony S. Fauci, MD, 'Statement Before the Subcommittee on Labor, HHS, and Education of the Senate Appropriations Committee', San Francisco, California, 9 July 1999, (cited 8 February 2001), available on the World Wide Web at www.naid.nih.gov/director/congress/1999/0709.htm.

246. In August 1990 Congress enacted the Ryan White AIDS Resources Emergency Act, a comprehensive measure providing financial relief to AIDS patients. The bill was passed after it came to the attention of Congress that a 13-year-old boy from Kokomo, Indiana, who was suffering from hemophilia had contracted AIDS through a transfusion of tainted blood and, as a result, had been denied access to his public school. The case became a national *cause célèbre* and White himself became a spokesman for government support of AIDS victims. The legislation's coverage was extensive and is administered through the HIV/AIDS Bureau of the Health Resources and Services Administration. The act consists of four sections: They are:

Title I: which provides funds for metropolitan areas with the largest number of reported cases of AIDS to meet emergency service needs;

Title II: which provides financial assistance to improve the quality, availability, and organization of health care and support services for individuals with HIV disease and their families. Services provided through this program include medical care, pharmaceuticals, dental care, rehabilitation, home health care, emergency housing, food and transportation;

Title III: which provides funding to support early intervention; and.

Title IV: which provides funds to support a series of specified provisions, including evaluation, reports, research, and services for pediatric patients.

Some six years after passage of the Ryan White Act, Congress legislated additional benefits for people with AIDS by enacting the Ryan White CARE Reauthorization Act, which extended the benefits offered in the 1990 Act for health care and support services. While the earlier Act had been limited to those with AIDS, all victims who were HIV-positive were eligible for the benefits outlined in the new Act. In addition, Title IV of the 1996 Act provided funds for pediatric HIV research and delineated added benefits for adolescent children with AIDS.

The following table gives some idea of the amounts expended on AIDS by the federal government.

Federal Expenditures in Connection with AIDS, Fiscal Years 2002–2004 (Millions of Dollars)

Agency and Program	2002	2003	2004
CDC: Prevention	787	794	788
Other Prevention[1]	136	147	145
HRSA: Ryan White: Total	1910	2018	2045
NIH: AIDS Research	2716	2850	
Other AIDS Research[2]	115	94	117
HUD: HOPWA	277	290	295
Medicaid Expenditures	4200	4800	5400
Medicare Expenditures	2100	2400	2600
Social Security Disability Insurance	987	1019	1050
Supplemental Security Income	385	395	415
Funding for the Minority HIV/AIDS Initiative[3]	391	411	404
Total: Domestic	**14 005**	**15 084**	**16 109**
Funding for International HIV/AIDS[4]	1031	1490	2250
Total	**15 036**	**16 574**	**18 359**

Notes:

[1]   Indian Health Service, Substance Abuse and Mental Health Services Administration, Health Resources and Services Administration, and the Departments of Justice, Defense, Veterans Affairs, and Justice.

[2]   Including the Food and Drug Administration and Department of Defense

[3]   Health Resources and Services Administration, Centers for Disease Control and Prevention, National Institutes of Health, Substance Abuse and Mental Health Services Administration, Office of Minority Health, DHHS, Office of Women's Health, DHHS, Office of the Secretary of HHS.

[4]   Includes totals for international research.

Agencies: *CDC*: Centers for Disease Control and Prevention; *HRSA*: The HIV/AIDS Bureau of the Health Resources and Services Administration; *NIH:* National Institutes of Health; *HOPWA*: Housing Opportunities for Persons With AIDS, an agency of the Department of Housing and Urban Development.

Source: Henry J. Kaiser Family Foundation, *Trends in U.S. Government Funding for HIV/AIDS, Fiscal Years 1981–2004* (Menlo Park, CA, March 2004).

247. United States expenditures on non-defense research and development is substantially larger than that of other nations. In 1998, the last year for which figures are available, it came close to equaling the combined total of expenditures from all the other G-7 countries. National Science Foundation, *Science and Engineering Indicators – 2002*. Chapter 4: 'U.S. and International Research and Development: Funds and Alliances'. Section 6: 'International Comparisons of National R&D Trends' (Arlington, Va.: National Science Foundation, April 2002): (http://www.nsf.gov/sbe/srs/seind02/c4/c4s4.htm).

248. Eva Ohlin, *The Structure and Financing of Medical Research in the United States: An Overview*, Swedish Institute for Growth Policy Studies, ITPS (Washington, DC: Embassy of Sweden, 2004): 7.

249. The life sciences, the biological sciences, and the medical sciences.

250. Only the Defense Department and the National Institutes of Health have substantial research and development budgets, which points to the fact that almost all the research in biomedicine is underwritten by the NIH.

251. See Rick Doblin, *Regulation of the Medical Use of Psychedelics and Marijuana*, unpublished Ph.D. dissertation: Kennedy School of Government, Harvard University, 2001.

252. Fertility clinics routinely permit potential mothers to choose what they wish to do with unused fertilized embryos. If they are prepared to donate them for research purposes, the likelihood is that more than enough such cells could be harvested to meet the demands of science.

253. Consider the following hypothetical. The President, a deeply religious man, believes that it is within God's design that sinners should suffer the consequences of their acts. Since such a high percentage of the HIV virus in the United States is transmitted either by homosexual activity (60 percent) or by injection drug use (25 percent), the President, with the consent of a passive Congress, issues an executive order that NIH funds are not to be used for basic research connected to ameliorating or curing AIDS. Thus, with a simple signature, most of the AIDS research currently undertaken would have to come to a halt and it is extremely unlikely, given the fact that so great a proportion of this research is done under NIH auspices, that private funding could replace it.

254. See Kevin M. Murphy and Robert Topel, 'The Economic Value of Medical Research', September 1999, available at gsbwww.uchicago.edu/fac/kevin.murphy/research/murphy&topel.pdf.

5. Medicare*

In June 1883, Otto von Bismarck, then Chancellor of a newly united Germany, was successful in gaining passage of a compulsory health insurance bill covering all factory and mine workers. This, together with a series of reform measures including accident insurance, disability insurance, and an old-age bill, formed the core of Bismarck's state socialist policy that was crafted both to outflank the entrepreneurial class and the liberal, *laissez-faire* party it supported and to detach labor from the social democratic left.[1] The original Act was later amended to include workers engaged in transportation and commerce and, in 1911, was extended to almost all employees, including agricultural and domestic workers, teachers, actors, and musicians.[2]

The motives that impelled the German government to enact a compulsory, state-run medical insurance law were not inconsistent with the views of most social reformers of the period, who regarded a powerful, centralized, bureaucratic state as capable of being a kind and beneficent institution. Bismarck's attempts to enact his social insurance bill did not, of course, go unopposed. A substantial portion of the imperial and Prussian bureaucracy held strong free-market views and resisted the Chancellor's attempts to introduce measures that so dramatically intruded into the marketplace. However, the opposition to Bismarck's program proved unsuccessful and his victory encouraged reformist elements in other countries to agitate for similar legislation. As a consequence, compulsory national health insurance was hailed throughout Europe as a model of progressive legislation and, over the course of the next 30 years, was emulated by a number of other nations.[3]

In Great Britain, David Lloyd George, Chancellor of the Exchequer from 1901 until 1914, was sufficiently animated by Bismarck's success to introduce a national health insurance scheme on the part of the Liberal government in 1911. Lloyd George, who had visited Germany in 1908 and had returned to Britain greatly excited by its social welfare legislation, hoped to introduce a similar series of measures at home. Indeed, he viewed compulsory health insurance as only the first installment in a far more ambitious plan of social

* This chapter on Medicare is reprinted with permission from the book *American Health Care: Government, Market Processes and the Public Interest*, edited by Roger D. Feldman, pp. 15–85 (New Brunswick, NJ: Transaction Publishers). © Copyright 2000, The Independent Institute, 100 Swan Way, Oakland, California 94621-1428; info@independent.org; www. independent.org.

reform.[4] The National Health Insurance Act that passed Parliament in 1911 provided for two types of benefits, a cash payment in the event of maternity or disability, and medical services, should the worker fall ill. All manual workers between the ages of 16 and 65, as well as nonmanual workers earning below a stipulated maximum, were required to contribute to and participate in the program;[5] in return, every participant was entitled to the services of a physician anywhere in Great Britain. Patients were free to select their doctor while doctors, who were compensated on a capitation basis, were free to refuse any individual seeking treatment.[6]

While at the outset there appears to have been some resistance by the medical profession to the introduction of health insurance legislation, opposition to the Act quickly disappeared as physicians' incomes increased under National Health. In addition, doctors, who felt their autonomy compromised by the restrictions imposed by the voluntary health insurance groups (known as Friendly Societies) that were replaced by the Act, no longer regarded themselves as constrained in determining the courses of treatment and the medications they prescribed to their patients.[7] Indeed, many hoped for a closer and more extended relationship with the government.

Early positive reports regarding the British compulsory health insurance program did much to encourage reformers in the United States in the belief that it would prove politically feasible to enact similar legislation here. In 1911, immediately after passage of the National Health Act in Britain, Louis D. Brandeis, who was later to be appointed to the Supreme Court but was at the time an attorney in private practice in New York, urged the National Conference on Charities and Corrections to vigorously support a national program of mandatory medical insurance.[8]

A compulsory system of health insurance soon became the subject of American Presidential politics. Affronted at having been denied the Republican nomination for President against the incumbent William Howard Taft, Theodore Roosevelt, in June 1912, decided to enter the Presidential race at the head of the Progressive, or Bull Moose, Party. On 6 August 1912, Roosevelt, after having learned that the Democrats had adopted a liberal platform and chosen Woodrow Wilson as their candidate, delivered what later came to be called his 'Confession of Faith', a long and somewhat tedious speech calling for, among a number of other paternalistic measures, a national compulsory health care scheme for all industrial workers.[9] He had been strongly influenced by a group of progressive economists from the university of Wisconsin, protégés of the labor economist John R. Commons, who taught at the university from 1904 to 1932.

Commons was a tireless and determined advocate of the welfare state and of economic planning. A staunch crusader for 'social justice', he regarded massive state intervention in the economic and social lives of Americans as absolutely essential to the nation's welfare.[10] In 1906, Commons, together with the other Progressive social scientists at Wisconsin, founded the American Association for Labor Legislation to lobby for reforms at both the state and federal level. Commons served as secretary of the new organization from 1908 to 1909 and was succeeded in this position by his former student John B. Andrews.

Roosevelt and other members of the Progressive Party were convinced, especially in the light of the recent passage of a national health program in Great Britain, that compulsory national health insurance would be heavily endorsed by working-class Americans. The American Association for Labor Legislation (AALL), regarded enactment of a bill along the lines of that passed in Great Britain as a priority. Indeed, the author of the health insurance plank in the 1912 Progressive Party platform was one of the leading members of the Association, Dr Isaac M. Rubinow,[11] who was in fact a member of the Socialist Party.[12]

Andrews' efforts to expand the membership of the AALL and to gain passage of the kinds of legislation the organization sought proved surprisingly successful. By 1913 he had managed to increase membership from a few hundred to more than 3000.[13] More important, in 1912, the AALL was awarded its first legislative victory when Congress voted to adopt an AALL-sponsored bill that prohibited the match industry from using phosphorus in its manufacturing process. This success appears to have 'catapulted the Association into a position of leadership in the movement for protective labor legislation and social insurance'.[14] Indeed, so prominent did the AALL become that it was able to attract a large number of academics and social workers to its ranks, some of great eminence. Among its earliest presidents were such notable academicians as Richard T. Ely of Wisconsin, Irving Fisher of Yale, Henry Seager of Columbia, and William F. Willoughby of Princeton.[15] (Willoughby, in fact, had authored a comprehensive report on European government health insurance schemes in 1898.)

The AALL next turned its attention to the question of a mandatory health insurance bill. Aware that terms such as 'mandatory' or 'compulsory' would almost certainly alienate prospective supporters and hoping to capitalize on the cooperative fellowship suggested by the term 'social', the Association adopted the term 'social insurance' in its place.[16] At its annual meeting in Boston in December 1912, the AALL established a Committee on Social Insurance to, among other things, 'prepare carefully for needed legislation'.[17] By 1914 the Committee had drafted a model bill, ostensibly a combination of the best elements in the German and British systems. It called for the mandatory enrollment of all workers earning less than $1200 per year, and voluntary enrollment of any self-employed person with incomes no higher than that amount. Premiums were ostensibly divided among employers, employees, and the government, with the government paying 20 percent and the employer paying a minimum, depending on the employee's earnings, of 40 percent.[18]

The AALL was naturally anxious to obtain the support of the American Medical Association in its campaign for enactment of a compulsory health insurance bill. Having limited its legislative lobbying to the state level prior to the turn of the century,[19] the AMA, following its reorganization in 1901, had discovered that it was equally possible to gain passage of federal legislation that would benefit its membership. Thus it had campaigned for pure food and drug legislation and, less successfully, for a cabinet-level Department of Health. There appeared every reason to believe that if it could be shown that the introduction of a mandatory national health insurance program would in fact profit physicians, then the AMA would throw its weight behind the proposed legislation. Toward this end, the AALL secured the aid of several prominent physicians in revising its draft bill, which was circulated to physicians' groups for possible further revision.[20]

As a consequence, the AMA established a Committee on Social Insurance in 1915 to study the issue and appointed Dr Alexander Lambert, physician to former President Roosevelt, a member of the AALL's Committee on Social Insurance, and chairman of the AMA's Judicial Council, as chairman. Doubtless Lambert's connections with the AALL account for his selecting Isaac Rubinow as the AMA committee's secretary. Lambert had earlier reported to the annual meeting of the AMA that the European experiment with national health insurance had proven good for both doctor and patient. Among other leading AMA figures who supported the AALL's program were George H. Simmons, who had been editor of the *Journal of the American Medical Association* (*JAMA*) since 1899, Abraham Jacobi, president of the AMA in 1912 and 1913, and, most important, Frederick R. Green, secretary of the AMA's Council on Health and Public Instruction.[21]

Green was a tireless campaigner for a national system of compulsory health insurance and had editorialized in the *JAMA* for its passage.[22] At one point he had written the secretary of the AALL that the Association's model bill and its plans to lobby for its enactment were 'exactly in line with the views that I have held for a long time regarding the methods which should be followed in securing public health legislation'.[23] Certainly one of the benefits that would accrue to medical practitioners, it was thought, was an increase in their incomes. The London correspondent for the *JAMA* reported in 1914 that the incomes of British doctors had risen substantially with the introduction of national health insurance, sometimes doubling in the case of physicians in the poorer industrial districts of the country and increasing by as much as 20 to 50 percent in the more prosperous areas.[24] Indeed, in the same year the secretary of the British Medical Association advised a visiting American physician that the incomes of general practitioners had in many instances quadrupled.[25]

With large numbers of physicians eager to reap the increased incomes that would likely follow in the wake of a health insurance plan in which payment of patients' charges would be underwritten by government, the AALL's model bill at first received little opposition from the medical profession. A commission appointed by the California legislature to consider the measure reported favorably on it, as did commissions in New Jersey and Ohio. It was introduced into the legislatures of Massachusetts and New Jersey and the New York Senate went so far as to pass the bill, although it was defeated in the Assembly.[26] Of greater significance, a few months prior to the 1916 elections Congress began holding a hearing on a national plan. What appears to have particularly buoyed the spirits of the measure's supporters was Woodrow Wilson's shift to a more 'liberal' position on social reform issues in preparation for his second election.[27] Certainly with passage of the War Risk Insurance Act of 1917 – which for the first time extended medical and hospital care to veterans – serving as a precedent, it would be unlikely that a universal health insurance plan would fail in Congress.

Despite these favorable signs, however, a compulsory government health insurance plan was not enacted, at either the state or national levels. The model bill put forward by the AALL apparently had one grievous flaw; it did not clearly stipulate whether physicians enrolled in the plan would be reimbursed on the basis of a capitation fee, as was the case in Great Britain, or fee-for-service, nor did it insure that medical practitioners be represented in ample numbers on the administrative boards to be established under the contemplated health insurance authority.[28] The effect of this was to seriously erode medical support for the bill.[29] In addition, insurance firms were bitterly opposed to the scheme. Not only did the model bill contain a provision for the payment of funeral benefits, thus competing directly with the coverage offered by private insurance companies but it also explicitly excluded private firms from acting as health insurance carriers.

Beyond physicians, who saw in the proposed legislation weaknesses that might lead to a substantial erosion in their incomes, and insurance companies, who objected to the bill's funeral insurance provisions, important members in organized labor regarded the proposal with suspicion. Samuel Gompers, the head of the American Federation of Labor, in particular, opposed a compulsory system of national health insurance on the grounds that its passage would deprive the labor movement of an extremely effective issue upon which to organize workers.[30] Finally, there appears to have been opposition on the part of some to covering the medical expenses of those whose illnesses were the product, not of work or accident, but of intemperate and wanton lives.[31]

With American entry into World War I, interest in passage of compulsory health insurance waned. The anti-German hysteria originally incited by government propaganda and so ably carried forward by more doltish

Americans proved an ally of those who opposed the measure. Its adversaries were not above stressing the German origins of mandatory medical insurance and referring to the AALL's bill as 'un-American'.[32] Indeed, the proposal's defenders were forced to imply that the scheme's origins were British rather than German and began referring to it as 'health insurance', its British designation, rather than the German 'sickness insurance'.[33] Even the president of the American Surgical Association, in speaking of the plan, warned that 'with a clear understanding of German methods in molding public sentiment and with utter detestation of that sinister thing – German Kultur – we should hesitate long before subscribing to a dictum or a doctrine emanating from such a source'.[34]

As opposition to the AALL bill became more organized and with the increasingly popular view that mandatory health insurance was in reality the product of a German conspiracy to impose Prussian values on America,[35] the movement to enact the measure disappeared until it again resurfaced during the New Deal era.[36] Renewed interest in mandatory health insurance emerged primarily as a consequence of the report of the Committee on Economic Security, a cabinet-level committee appointed by President Roosevelt in 1934. Eager to offer an alternative social welfare package to compete with those of Upton Sinclair,[37] Senator Huey Long of Louisiana[38] and Dr Francis E. Townsend,[39] whose popularity appeared to be increasing as the Depression worsened, Roosevelt's advisors, particularly the membership of the committee (Frances Perkins, the Secretary of Labor, Henry Morganthau, Jr, Secretary of the Treasury, Homer Cummings, Attorney-General, Henry Wallace, Secretary of Agriculture, and Harry Hopkins, Administrator of the Emergency Relief Administration),[40] advised the passage of a comprehensive social security system to include unemployment insurance, old-age security, and government-administered health-care insurance. Given the political biases of the committee, their recommendations can hardly be regarded as surprising.[41]

Support for a mandatory health insurance bill had earlier gained impetus with issuance of the final report of the Committee on the Costs of Medical Care in 1932. The Committee, organized four years earlier under the chairmanship of Dr Ray Lyman Wilbur, former Secretary of the Interior under President Hoover and former President of the AMA, had concluded that both the medical infrastructure and medical services in the United States were inadequate and recommended that physicians and other health-care personnel be organized around a hospital or clinic and that they be reimbursed through group payment financed either through insurance or taxes.[42] In addition, in 1935, the American Federation of Labor endorsed compulsory health insurance, thus reversing its earlier position.

But despite the favorable climate among social scientists, labor leaders, and politicians and the philosophical leanings of its members, the report of the

President's Committee on Economic Security did not include among its recommendations passage of a health insurance bill. While it did urge enactment of an unemployment insurance bill and of social security it failed to put forward a compulsory health insurance measure despite persistent pressure from Harry Hopkins, an indefatigable proponent of state medicine.[43] The reasons for this are clear. A substantial segment of the medical profession were adamantly opposed to any compulsory government-run health insurance program and made their views known, both in editorials in the major medical journals including the *JAMA*[44] and through a torrent of representations to members of Congress. While the President's committee wished to recommend a health insurance plan in addition to a comprehensive system of unemployment insurance and old-age security, the opposition of the AMA proved decisive and rather than jeopardize his other reforms the President advised that the issues be severed and that health insurance legislation be postponed until after passage of the social security bill.[45]

In an attempt to keep the subject of health insurance alive, Roosevelt established an Interdepartmental Committee to Coordinate Health and Welfare Activities immediately following passage of the Social Security Act and at the same time ordered his staff to keep the matter before the public. The result was that it became a major topic of public debate, both in speeches and in a host of articles in the nation's press; by 1938, no fewer than 15 books had been published on the subject.[46] At the same time, the federal government completed an extensive study of the nation's health which purported to show that 90 percent of the population was receiving inadequate medical care, the inescapable conclusion of which was that enactment of a national health care system was imperative.[47]

All this activity culminated in the convening of a National Health Conference under the auspices of the Interdepartmental Committee, which had earlier approved a report of its Technical Committee on Medical Care, predictably urging a huge extension of federal control over health matters. The conference, which took place in Washington in July 1938, opened with a statement by President Roosevelt which one report describes as marking 'the first definite affirmation by an American chief executive of the ultimate responsibility of the government for the health of its citizens'.[48] Among the conference's participants was the full complement of Roosevelt's closest advisors concerned with expanding the government's role in the area of medical care, together with numbers of social workers, public health officials, and representatives of women's and farmers' groups and labor unions, In addition, acting under instructions from its House of Delegates, the AMA sent several representatives including its president, Dr Irvin Abell, and the editor of the *JAMA*, Dr Fishbein.[49]

The Conference, acting on the advice of its 'technical committee', ultimately recommended that the federal government enact legislation in several areas including (1) an expansion of the public health and maternal and child health programs included in the original Social Security Act; (2) a system of grants to the various states for direct medical care programs; (3) federal grants for hospital construction; (4) a disability insurance scheme that would insure against loss of wages during illness; and (5) grants to the states for the purpose of financing compulsory statewide health insurance programs.[50] The total cost of these programs was estimated at about $850 000 000 a year.[51]

While the Conference had proposed legislation that would provide for a tax-funded system of compulsory health care insurance, it had urged adoption of these programs at the state level in an attempt to placate the majority of medical practitioners. It was thought that the reason why physicians so adamantly opposed such programs, especially at the national level, was that they feared that, at best, they were unlikely to have much say in their administration and, at worst, that physicians would eventually become salaried employees of the government.[52] This was, of course, less likely to be the case, were the plans managed by the various states.[53] However, it was clear to all, including the membership of the AMA, that any legislation introduced in Congress aimed at putting into effect the Conference's recommendations would call for a national program of health insurance. And indeed this is precisely what occurred. When, in 1943, Senator Robert Wagner of New York,[54] together with Senator James Murray of Montana and Representative John Dingell of Michigan, introduced a bill reflecting the recommendations of the National Health Conference, it called for, among other things, a compulsory national health insurance program. The bill was exceedingly ambitious. Not only did it provide for mandatory health insurance, but also for a federal system of unemployment insurance, broader coverage and extended benefits for old-age insurance, temporary and permanent disability payments underwritten by the federal government, unemployment benefits for veterans attempting to re-enter civilian life, a federal employment service, and a restructuring of grants-in-aid to the states for public assistance.[55]

Although Roosevelt had no objections to the Wagner-Murray-Dingell bill,[56] he was not yet prepared to endorse a measure quite so sweeping and, as a consequence, the bill died in committee. There is evidence that he once again wished to reserve the issue of national health care for the next Presidential campaign in 1944 and for his fourth term, when he could personally sponsor the measure. During the campaign he called for an 'Economic Bill of Rights', which included 'the right to adequate medical care and the opportunity to achieve and enjoy good health' and 'the right to adequate protection from the economic fears of old age, sickness, accident, and unemployment' and in his budget message of January 1945 he announced his intention of extending social security to include medical care.[57]

The idea of a government-administered health insurance scheme appears to have been received with so much popularity in some areas of the country that it was even taken up by some prominent Republican politicians in an effort to curry favor with the voters. In 1945, Governor Earl Warren of California, who was to become the Republican Vice-Presidential nominee in 1948, proposed passage of a compulsory health insurance bill to the California legislature. The California Medical Association expended substantial resources to defeat the measure but the events in California had brought the issue to national prominence.[58]

With Roosevelt's death in April 1945, Harry Truman took over the Presidency committed to most of the same domestic policies as his predecessor. Truman was determined to carry through with Roosevelt's intentions respecting national health insurance and he made it a crucial part of his 'Fair Deal' program. A few weeks after Japan's surrender in October 1945, Truman submitted a health message to Congress, accompanied by a slightly reworked version of the Wagner-Murray-Dingell bill for its consideration.[59] However, the revised bill was unable to obtain hearings in the House Ways and Means Committee prior to the elections of 1946, at which point the Republicans, for the first time since 1932, held majorities in both the Senate and the House of Representatives. Nevertheless one title of the Wagner-Murray-Dingell bill, relating to federal grants for hospital construction, was enacted into law in 1946. The Hill-Burton Hospital Survey and Construction Act was to have an enormous impact on the shape, direction, and extent of American hospital care for the next 25 years.

The 1948 election, in which Truman was re-elected and which returned control of Congress to the Democrats, revived the hopes of those supporting national health insurance. This was especially true since the Democratic Party had called for passage of a health insurance bill in their platform and Truman had made Congressional inaction on the proposal a major campaign issue. However, a coalition of Republicans and conservative Democrats was able to block yet another revision of the Wagner-Murray-Dingell bill once again. The AMA's unyielding opposition to any form of federal control of the nation's health delivery system, coupled with waning support from the labor unions, who had switched their efforts to trying to obtain private health insurance coverage from employers, certainly made this decision more politically palatable.[60]

Attempts to enact a health insurance bill during the Truman era came to a definitive end with the election of 1950. A number of prominent proponents of the measure in Congress, including Senators Elbert D. Thomas of Utah and Glen H. Taylor of Idaho, were defeated, in large measure because of a vigorous and costly campaign by the American Medical Association. The AMA, as the pre-eminent lobbyist against compulsory health insurance, had succeeded in associating Truman's plan in the mind of the public with notions of socialism, now in disrepute thanks to the Cold War mentality Truman himself had so energetically encouraged. By mid-1951 the Association was confident enough that it had made impossible any serious attempt to reintroduce the measure that it began reducing the scale of its propaganda operations.[61] Nor was the issue raised in President Truman's State of the Union address in 1952.

Despite these setbacks, there remained substantial support, among both politicians and the public, for some form of government-administered compulsory health insurance. While Truman's closest advisors agreed that there was little chance of enacting legislation of the sort called for in the Wagner-Murray-Dingell bill, whose provisions would have universal applicability, two officials in the Federal Security Agency,[62] Wilbur J. Cohen – instrumental in drafting the original Social Security Act of 1935 and later to become Secretary of Health, Education, and Welfare – and I.S. Falk, conceived of resurrecting a health insurance scheme by limiting its coverage to social security beneficiaries.[63] The proposal was enthusiastically received by Oscar Ewing, the director of the Federal Security Agency and, according to one analyst, 'shaped the entire strategy of health insurance advocates in the period after 1951'.[64] The idea of restricting coverage to the elderly was politically brilliant. Among the principal criticisms leveled against a general compulsory health insurance plan were that it did not distinguish between the deserving and undeserving poor and that it covered those who were well off as well as those in need. Since it appeared intuitively obvious that the elderly as a group were less likely to afford, while at the same time more apt to have need of, medical care, no means test would be necessary to determine which recipients required assistance.[65] In addition, Americans had been gulled into accepting the notion that social security was in fact a funded program in principle no different from any other savings plan, thus depriving it of much of the onus of a welfare measure. Finally, in order to assuage the fears of physicians that a government-administered health insurance plan would eventually lead to control of the medical system by a health-care bureaucracy, the new plan's coverage excluded physicians' services.[66]

In 1952, the Social Security Administration's annual report recommended enactment of health insurance for social security beneficiaries and this recommendation was echoed by the President's Commission on the Health Needs of the Nation later that year. The issue was to become moot, however, since General Eisenhower, who was to take office as President, had made clear his opposition to government health insurance. Yet, despite the Eisenhower administration's antipathy to an extension of government involvement in medical care, a series of occurrences in 1956 once again brought the issue of health insurance to public prominence. In that year Congress enacted a permanent program of health-care coverage for the dependents of servicemen (what has been described as a military 'medicare' program) and at the same time began to debate adding to the Social Security Act cash benefits to totally and permanently disabled persons over the age of 50. Inasmuch as the proposed legislation required some government supervision of those private physicians who would be making the determination of medical disability, the AMA opposed the amendment. The battle between those supporting and opposing this extension of the social security program was viewed by many as a test of strength between physicians and health reformers and when the measure passed, supporters of government health insurance were elated.[67] Buoyed by passage of a disability insurance measure, a Democratic member of the House Ways and Means Committee, Aimé J. Forand, introduced a medicare bill just prior to adjournment of the House in late 1957.

The public hearings on the bill, held in June 1958 before the House Ways and Means Committee, proved inconclusive. By this point, a number of national groups had lined up on either side of the issue. Supporting the bill were the AFL-CIO, the National Farmers' Union, the Group Health Association of America, the American Nurses Association, The American Public Welfare Association, and the National Association of Social Workers. Those opposed included the National Chamber of Commerce, the National Association of Manufacturers, the Pharmaceutical Manufacturers' Association, the American Farm Bureau Association, the Health Insurance Association of America, and, of course, the American Medical Association.[68]

The National Insurance Association of America had been recently formed and represented some 264 insurance companies. These firms had good reason to be fearful that a further extension of government insurance would again cut into their sales,[69] as had been the case with government life insurance for servicemen during World Wars I and II and, most dramatically, with the passage of social security and its extensions. Its spokesman at the Forand bill hearings in 1958 estimated that the costs of the measure would exceed $2 billion per year, not the $850 million predicted by its proponents.[70] In the event, of course, this proved a colossal underestimate.

Given the controversial nature of the Forand bill and the President's opposition, the outcome of the proposal was inevitable and the measure died in committee. Hearings were again held in 1959, but with the same result. Finally, in March 1960 Forand was able to obtain a vote on the bill in the Committee, where it was defeated by a vote of 17 to 8. Yet, in spite of its defeat, momentum in support of the proposal seemed to be increasing. Both the House Speaker, Sam Rayburn, and the Senate Majority Leader, Lyndon Johnson, spoke in favor of the measure, and lobbying on behalf of the bill increased substantially.[71]

Confronted with what appeared to be increasing popularity for a government-administered health insurance plan for the elderly, the Chairman of the

Ways and Means Committee, Wilbur Mills, introduced a bill that would provide medical assistance – through the states – to a new class of recipients, the 'medically indigent', to comprise the elderly who might not otherwise quality for state welfare payments but who required help with their medical bills.[72] The proposal had the advantage of having been approved by the AMA, who saw no reason to oppose government-sponsored medical benefits if they were limited to those who were unlikely to seek medical help in the absence of a subsidy. In addition, Mills' proposal met the complaints of those who objected to instituting a tax-supported measure that would benefit the well-to-do and had the further advantage of being a Democratic bill. The bill was quickly approved by the Ways and Means Committee and by the full House and sent to the Senate. In the Senate, the measure was somewhat modified, renamed the Kerr-Mills bill after its Senate sponsor, Senator Robert Kerr of Oklahoma, and, in August 1960, passed by a vote of 91 to 2.[73]

Passage of Kerr-Mills by no means ended the agitation for a comprehensive health insurance program for the elderly and the defeat of the Forand bill provided a ready-made campaign issue for the Democratic Presidential candidate, John F. Kennedy. Kennedy, together with Clinton P. Anderson of New Mexico, had introduced a measure similar to the Forand bill in the Senate that summer and although the Kennedy-Anderson proposal was defeated in favor of Kerr-Mills, the 1960 Democratic platform contained a provision supporting an extensive hospital insurance scheme for the aged. Indeed, to the surprise of both candidates, so much public interest appears to have been generated by the proposal that Kennedy made it a subject of his speeches far more often than he had originally intended.[74] Even prior to the new Administration's taking office, a White House Conference on Aging again brought the issue of government health insurance to prominence and its advocates were encouraged by the fact that Eisenhower's Secretary of Health, Education, and Welfare, among several other prominent Republicans, joined them in supporting enactment of a comprehensive measure.[75]

On 9 February 1961, almost immediately following his inauguration, President Kennedy sent a message to Congress calling for the extension of social security benefits to cover hospital and nursing home costs. Sponsored by Senator Anderson and Representative Cecil King of California, the bill would have covered 14 million recipients of social security over the age of 65 and provided for 90 days of hospital care, outpatient diagnostic services, and 180 days of nursing home care. Curiously, the measure did not include the costs of medical or surgical treatment.[76] The annual costs of the program were estimated to be approximately a billion and a half dollars. However, in light of Kennedy's thin margin of victory in November and the fact that the Democrats had lost 20 seats in the House, it was deemed expedient not to press for passage of the measure until the following year.

The reaction of the American Medical Association was swift and vigorous. In April 1961, the Association had placed a seven-column advertisement in 31 newspapers, attacking the King-Anderson bill. And one month later, its Board of Trustees gave formal approval to the creation of a political action committee, the American Medical Political Action Committee (AMPAC).[77] Joining in opposition to the bill were the commercial health insurance carriers and Blue Cross-Blue Shield,[78] who questioned the cost estimates put forward by the Kennedy Administration. Over the course of 1961, the AMA distributed millions of pamphlets and advertised extensively on radio and TV against government health insurance. Posters attacking the King-Anderson bill were sent to all members for display in their offices and physicians were encouraged to send leaflets containing the same text to all their patients. There seems little doubt that what particularly exercised the Association was that the measure included a fee schedule for hospitals, nursing homes, and nurses which could serve as a precedent should government insurance be expanded to include physicians' services.[79]

Despite strong support for a Social Security-supported plan of limited hospital care for the elderly both within the Administration and among Democrats in Congress, the King-Anderson bill faced strong opposition from the powerful House Ways and Means Committee, the majority of whose members were either Republicans or Southern Democrats who opposed the measure.[80] Unable to bring direct pressure on the membership of the Committee, the Kennedy Administration decided to demonize the American Medical Association's opposition in the hope that the bill's critics would fear being branded as equally mean-spirited. The AMA was accused of thwarting the public will in the interests of lining the pockets of its membership and of employing the worst scare tactics against a government whose only concern was to extend to the aged and infirm needed medical benefits which otherwise would be denied them.

Supporting the efforts of the Administration were organized labor, which lobbied extensively in favor of the measure, and several new organizations whose creation was in large part aided by the White House and the Democratic National Committee. Among them was the Physicians' Committee for Health Care Through Social Security, whose formation was in part an outgrowth of the support extended King-Anderson by the American Public Health Association. The organization's chairman was Dr Caldwell Esselstyn, former personal physician to Eleanor Roosevelt and President of the Group Health Association of America, and boasted among its members several well-known physicians including Drs Benjamin Spock, Michael E. DeBakey, and Arthur Kornberg and Dickinson W. Richards, both Nobel laureates.[81]

In July 1961 organizers for the AFL-CIO aided in establishing the National Council of Senior Citizens, an outgrowth of the earlier Senior Citizens for

Kennedy, once again chaired by retired Congressman Aimé Forand. With a nucleus of union retiree organizations[82] as its base, the Council soon attracted other associations of seniors, among them a number of union and church groups, whose affiliation brought the Council's membership to more than 1 million people. The size of its membership and the fact that older voters had played a decisive role in Kennedy's victory in a number of key districts led to the Council receiving financial support from the Democratic National Committee. The Council's agitation culminated in a rally in Madison Square Garden in May 1962 at which President Kennedy himself spoke. Before 20 000 enthusiastic supporters of the administration's health-care bill and a TV audience estimated at more than 20 million people, the President proceeded to deliver one of the worst speeches of his political career. Not only did it fail to rouse the general public in support of the King-Anderson bill, but it left the impression in the minds of many that the President's own support for the measure was at best luke-warm.[83]

Meanwhile, during the spring of 1962, there appears to have been some small movement in favor of some form of health-care bill in the House Ways and Means Committee. Hearings before the Ways and Means Committee the previous year had proved inconclusive; the testimony reflected the same divisions as had existed earlier and in the late summer of 1961 the House Speaker reported that 15 Congressmen opposed King-Anderson, while only ten supported it.[84] However, a proposal to limit coverage to instances where the elderly were faced with 'catastrophic' charges appears to have won the tentative support of three Representatives who would otherwise have voted against the bill, changing the tally to 13 in favor, with 12 against. In return for their support, the Committee members involved demanded that the Kerr-Mills program be repealed and that the elderly who had earlier retired be required to contribute premiums in order to qualify for benefits, conditions the White House was not prepared to concede.[85] As a consequence, no compromise was in the end reached. After three weeks of executive sessions on King-Anderson in the late spring of 1962, Committee support and opposition to King-Anderson remained exactly as before.

The Congressional stalemate continued following the Congressional elections of 1962. While the Democrats maintained control of Congress, the King-Anderson bill, by now commonly referred to as Medicare, still did not command a majority in the House.[86] Both opponents and supporters of the measure had made determined efforts to influence the electorate but foreign policy appears to have been of far greater importance in the minds of most voters in November 1962 than was the government's health insurance plan. Indeed, the AMA's campaign against those candidates who had supported Medicare was a failure and not one seat in either the Senate or the House was lost by a candidate who had endorsed the bill.[87]

In the wake of the assassination of President Kennedy in November 1963 Congressional support for Kennedy's legislative program swelled. Large numbers of politicians rushed to embrace many of the proposals Kennedy had put forward as if by doing so they could more clearly distance themselves from the actions of his murderer. President Johnson, a longtime master of legislative manipulation, was able to play upon these simple-minded sentiments to push for enactment of a host of reform measures, among them Medicare. In one of his earliest speeches to Congress, Johnson referred to Medicare as 'one of his top priorities'[88] and in March 1964 the *Wall Street Journal* predicted that the measure was 'a good bet to come out of Congress this year'.[89] Under intense pressure from President Johnson, the Senate Finance Committee finally agreed to hold public hearings on the King-Anderson bill in August 1964. And, although the measure again failed in committee, its supporters were able to bring it to the floor of the Senate without committee sanction as an amendment to a bill authorizing increased social security benefits. On 2 September 1964 the full Senate passed the amendment by a vote of 49 to 44, thus putting the Senate on record as approving a mandatory federal health insurance scheme for the elderly.[90] The vote was a particularly bitter defeat for the Republican Presidential candidate, Barry Goldwater, who had flown back from Arizona solely for the purpose of casting his vote against the measure.

Meanwhile, support for Medicare was gaining headway on the House Ways and Means Committee. By 1964 two Democratic seats on the Committee previously held by anti-Medicare Southerners had opened up as a consequence of retirement. These were filled by Representatives who ultimately pledged themselves to support a Medicare bill, thus narrowing the division against mandatory health insurance for the elderly to 12 votes for as opposed to 13 against.[91] In light of the actions of the Senate in September, however, the Johnson administration conceived the notion of bypassing the Committee entirely. Since Senate passage of Medicare had taken the form of a rider to a previously enacted House bill, the differences between the two measures would have to be reconciled by a Senate–House conference committee. Were the House to pass a resolution instructing its conferees on the Senate–House committee to vote for the Medicare provisions earlier enacted by the Senate, a vote in the Ways and Means Committee would no longer be necessary before presenting the reconciled bill to the full House for a vote. This would, of course, have meant that the Ways and Means Committee would have lost control over the content of any Medicare bill finally enacted by the House. Anticipating this, Wilbur Mills, Ways and Means' chairman, was able to prevail upon the pro-Medicare Democrats on the Committee to reject the rider in return for his promise that a Medicare bill would 'be the first order of business' in the following year.[92]

The November election proved decisive in the history of Medicare.

President Johnson's campaign underscored the central importance of extending social security benefits to cover health-care costs, while Barry Goldwater was adamantly opposed to the plan. It became a central issue in the campaigns of many congressional candidates who supported the measure while at the same time organized medicine devoted substantial sums either directly or through political action committees in an attempt to defeat Medicare's chief defenders.[93] In the event, the election proved a disaster for Medicare's opponents. In the House, the Democrats gained 38 seats while the pro-Medicare majority appears to have increased by 44 seats.[94] In almost every instance, organized medicine had been unsuccessful in defeating those candidates who had made passage of a Medicare bill a key aspect of their campaign. Of the 14 physicians who ran for Congress in the election 11 lost, and of the three that were elected one was a Medicare supporter.[95] More important, as a consequence of the election and of changes to House rules brought in by the new Congress, the composition of the Ways and Means Committee was altered from 15 Democrats and ten Republicans to 17 Democrats and eight Republicans.[96]

There seems little question that the electoral outcome was due in large part to the strong support given pro-Medicare candidates by older voters. It has been estimated that approximately 22 percent of Americans who voted in the 1964 election were over the age of 60 and that 2 million of these had switched from voting Republican to voting Democratic. In addition, all ten states with the highest percentage of elderly voters, seven of which were traditionally Republican, voted Democratic.[97] The prominence given the prospective passage of a Medicare bill during the campaign led to its being given pride-of-place in the 89th Congress. The King-Anderson bill was the first bill introduced into each chamber (H.R. 1 and S. 1) when Congress convened on 4 January 1965. Three days later, the President, in a Special Message to Congress, urged swift passage of the measure. The bill thus brought before Congress at the beginning of 1965 was, in almost every important respect, similar to the measure earlier introduced by Representative King and Senator Anderson in 1963 and approved by the Senate in 1964.[98] The measure was thus a hospital insurance scheme only and did not cover physicians' services, although apparently most voters believed that physicians' fees were included among the bill's benefits.[99]

Since it now appeared inevitable that Congress and the Administration would proceed to enact a bill mandating compulsory health insurance for the elderly, the American Medical Association was confronted with the option of either acceding to the provisions of King-Anderson or of trying to amend the measure so that its shape was more to organized medicine's liking. As a consequence, in early January 1965 the AMA proposed an alternative, which it called 'Eldercare', that would have expanded the Medical Assistance for the

Aged program established under the Kerr-Mills Act.[100] The Eldercare bill would have allowed MAA funds to be used for either partial or full payment of the premium costs of private health insurance while at the same time substantially easing the means-test requirements imposed by Kerr-Mills. On 27 January two members of the Ways and Means Committee, Thomas B. Curtis (Republican, Missouri) and A. Sydney Herlong (Democrat, Florida), introduced legislation along these lines, underscoring the fact that King-Anderson limited benefits to hospital services while their proposal provided far more sweeping coverage.

The AMA's campaign in support of Eldercare,[101] which concentrated on the comprehensive coverage afforded by the bill, appears to have struck a sympathetic chord among the electorate. In a survey financed by the AMA during January and February 1965, it was found that about 72 percent of respondents agreed that any government health insurance plan should cover physicians' fees.[102] Far from weakening support for King-Anderson, however, the survey served to encourage the bill's more ardent adherents to expand its provisions to include a whole range of medical services. Most Congressional backers of a government health insurance plan were in fact secretly delighted with the results of the AMA poll since it signaled widespread popular support for extending the coverage offered by King-Anderson.

To further complicate matters yet a third bill was introduced in the Ways and Means Committee by its ranking Republican member, John Byrnes of Wisconsin. Fearful of being deprived of any credit for a health insurance law, the Republicans on the Committee proposed what amounted to an extension of the private health insurance plan then offered by the Aetna Life Insurance Company to federal employees. The plan called for the creation of a government-administered insurance scheme for the elderly that covered not only hospital expenses but both physicians' services and the costs of drugs and permitted older Americans to either opt out of the scheme or not, as they saw fit.

Rather than choose between these various alternatives, Wilbur Mills, the Committee's Chairman, hit upon the idea of combining the most ambitious components of all three bills into a new proposal. Mills' suggestion was quickly embraced by the Administration, who regarded it as insurance against any Republican attack.[103] On 23 March 1965 the Ways and Means Committee voted 17 to eight to substitute Mills' bill for King-Anderson and on the following day the bill was introduced on the House floor. Finally, on 8 April, after only one day of floor debate, the Mills bill was passed without amendment by a vote of 313 to 115. The features of the new bill were incorporated into two amendments to the Social Security Act, which provided in Title 18 for a universal hospital insurance program for the elderly and for optional coverage of physicians' services while Title 19 (since known as Medicaid) expanded the Kerr-Mills program of medical coverage for the needy.

The Mills bill was then referred to the Senate for its consideration. There was no question that the more liberal Senate would enact some form of health insurance but exactly what its shape would be remained uncertain. The Finance Committee, chaired by Russell Long of Louisiana, held public hearings on the bill during late April and early May and met in executive session to consider the measure during the following month. The Mills bill was eventually reported out of committee on 24 June by a vote of 12 to five, having been amended no fewer than 75 times.[104] The full Senate, having considered a further 250 amendments, passed the measure on 9 July by a 68 to 21 vote and the bill, as amended, was then sent to a Senate–House conference committee whose task it was to resolve the over 500 differences between the two chambers.[105]

On 27 July the House passed the bill as finally revised, officially part of the Social Security Amendments of 1965, by a vote of 307 in favor with 116 opposed and the next day the Senate approved the measure by a vote of 70 to 24. Finally, on 30 July 1965 President Johnson, having flown to Independence, Missouri, to append his signature to the Medicare bill in the presence of former President Truman, signed the measure into law.

The main provisions of the 1965 legislation were as follows:[106]

Title XVIII, Part A   Hospital Insurance (HI) provides that all persons over the age of 65 otherwise entitled to benefits under the Social Security or Railroad Retirement Acts were eligible and were automatically covered. Benefits were to be measured in 60-day periods, each period ending 60 days following discharge from a hospital or extended-care facility. During each benefit period subscribers were entitled to up to 90 days in a hospital, 100 days in an extended-care facility, and home-care benefits for up to one year after the most recent discharge from either a hospital or extended-care facility. (In 1967, Congress amended this provision to add to each beneficiary's coverage an additional lifetime reserve period of 60 days of hospital care.) Care in either a psychiatric or tuberculosis hospital was limited to a lifetime amount of 190 days, provided the patient was certified by a physician as being 'reasonably expected to improve'. Subscribers were required to impose a 'front-end' deductible for each hospital stay of up to 90 days (initially $40, by 1997 this amount had risen to $760 for the first 60 days and an additional $190 for days 61–90). No front-end deductibles were imposed for the use of extended-care facilities for the first 20 days but after that point a daily co-payment was levied (in 1997 this amount was $95.00). The program was financed by earmarked payroll taxes levied on employers and employees and disbursements were made from this fund either directly to providers or through an intermediary insurance company who then reimbursed the provider. The rate of reimbursement was ostensibly based on 'reasonable costs'.

Title XVIII, Part B   Supplementary Medical Insurance (SMI). All persons over 65 were eligible for participation in this program on a voluntary basis, without the requirement that they had earlier paid into the Social Security program. Benefits included physicians' services at any location and home health services of up to 100 visits per year. Coverage also included the costs of diagnostic tests, radiotherapy, ambulance services, and various medical supplies and appliances certified as necessary by the patient's physician. Subscribers were at first required to pay one-half the monthly premium, with the federal government underwriting the other half. After July 1973, premium increases levied on subscribers were limited to 'the percentage by which Social Security cash benefits [had] been increased since the last . . . premium adjustment'. Each enrollee was subject to a front-end deductible ($50 per year originally; $100 in 1997). After having met this payment, patients were responsible for a co-insurance of 20 percent of the remaining 'reasonable' charges. Limits were set on the amount of psychiatric care and routine physical examinations. Among the exclusions were eye refraction and other preventive services, such as immunizations and hearing aids. The cost of drugs was totally excluded. Similar financing arrangements as prevailed for Part A coverage were put in place for Part B for the payment of benefits. Premium payments were placed in a trust fund, which made disbursements to private insurance companies – carriers – who reimbursed providers on a 'reasonable cost' or, in the case of physicians, 'reasonable charge' basis. Physicians were permitted to 'extra bill' patients if they regarded the fee schedule established by the carriers as insufficient payment.

Title XIX   Medicaid. The 1965 legislation provided states with a number of options regarding their level of participation in Medicaid, ranging from opting out of the program entirely to including all covered services for all eligible classes of persons. The federal government provided matching funds for two of the three groups stipulated in the legislation (the 'categorically needy' and those 'categorically linked', while in the case of the third group ('not categorically linked but medically indigent') only administrative funds (and no medical expenses) were matched. Each state was required to include members of the first group, the categorically needy, in a medical care program acceptable to the Department of Health, Education, and Welfare, while inclusion of the other groups was optional. Eligibility standards varied (and continue to vary) from state to state, depending on state legislation.[107] The three groups were:

(1)   The Categorically Needy. This group included all persons receiving federally matching public welfare assistance, including Families with Dependent Children, the permanently and totally disabled, the blind, and

the elderly whose resources fell below welfare-stipulated levels. The federal government matched state expenditures from 50 to 80 percent, depending on the state's per capita income.

(2) The Categorically Linked. This class included persons who fell into one of the four federally assisted categories whose resources exceeded the ceiling for cash assistance. Should the state designate members of this class as medically indigent, benefits had to be extended to all four subgroups. The amount of federal matching funds was determined by the same formula as was used for the Categorically Needy.

(3) Not Categorically Linked but Medically Indigent. Members of this group could include those eligible for statewide general assistance and those between the ages of 21 and 65 deemed medically indigent. State operating expenses were not matched by the federal government, who confined their grants to matching the costs of administering the program if the benefits extended to members of this group were comparable to those provided to other groups.

Among the benefits that the various states were required to provide recipients were (1) inpatient hospital care (other than in an institution for tuberculosis or mental disease), (2) outpatient hospital services, (3) laboratory and x-ray services, (4) nursing facility services for those over the ages of 21 (and, after 1 July 1970, to home health services), and (5) physicians' services, regardless of location of treatment. In addition, states could underwrite a host of other services, including physical therapy, dental care, diagnostic, preventive, and rehabilitative services, and the cost of prescribed drugs, dentures, prosthetic devices, and eyeglasses. The elderly insured by Medicare who were also eligible by virtue of their incomes for Medicaid had their hospital deductibles and co-payments paid by Medicaid.[108]

In 1967, the Johnson Administration proposed amendments to the Social Security program that included extending Medicare benefits to the disabled who were otherwise eligible for cash payments. To pay for this extension, a higher earnings base on which Medicare taxes would be levied was recommended. From the then current $6600, the amount was to rise to $7800 in 1968, $9000 in 1971, and $10 800 in 1974 and thereafter. Despite strong support from the Administration, the House Ways and Means Committee voted to defer consideration of the extension in light of the substantial costs associated with the amendment. While it had been the Administration's contention that medical costs per disabled beneficiary would prove to be about the same as those associated with Medicare recipients over the age of 65, a study released while the bill was before the committee indicated that in fact these costs would be about two and a half to three times as high.[109]

It was clear following the first full year of operation of the Hospital

Table 5.1   *Comparison of Estimates (E) with Actual Costs (A) of Hospital Insurance and Supplementary Medical Insurance, Calendar Years 1966–1967[1] (in millions of dollars)*

| | Hospital Insurance | | | | Supplementary Medical Insurance | | | |
| | 1966 | | 1967 | | 1966 | | 1967 | |
	(E)	(A)	(E)	(A)	(E)	(A)	(E)	(A)
Benefit payments	1023	891	2477	3353	324	128	1124	1197
Administrative expenses	54	107	77	77	87	74	97	110
Total	1077	998	2554	3430	411	202	1221	1307

Note: [1] Cost estimates are intermediate and are determined by averaging low-cost and high-cost estimates.

Source: Robert J. Myers, *Medicare* (Bryn Mawr, Pa.: McCahan Foundation, 1970): Tables 11–16 and 11–17 (pp. 253–4).

Insurance program that its costs significantly exceeded the estimates put forward by the program's proponents.[110] The main purpose of enacting a national health insurance bill had been, after all, to encourage greater use of health-care facilities by the elderly. It was therefore not surprising that with the measure's passage there should have been an increased demand for hospital and medical services. However, not only was there greater utilization of medical facilities on the part of those covered by the Medicare program, but there followed a far higher increase in the prices of covered services than had been expected. Table 5.1 gives some idea of the disparity between the original estimates for hospital insurance and supplementary medical insurance programs and their actual costs for 1966 and 1967.

In light of these data, Congress increased the contribution schedule along the lines suggested by the administration despite its not having incorporated the disabled among the program's beneficiaries.

By 1972, the costs associated with Medicare had increased at such a rate that even the administration and Congress were expressing concern.[111] As a consequence a number of studies were undertaken to examine whether the cause of this rise was attributable primarily to the increased use of medical facilities or to the higher prices that followed in the wake of increased demand.[112] Among the conclusions reached was that hospital service charges rose much faster than the Consumer Price Index and additionally faster than the medical care component of that index. Further, over the course of the first five years of Medicare that ended in 1971, physicians' charges rose 39 percent, compared with a 15 percent rise in the five years before the advent of Medicare. While this increase was not as great as was the overall increase in the Consumer Price Index, it reflected a substantial rise in the average annual charge per patient (that is, collected physician income per patient), which rose from $66 in 1965 to $95 in 1967. Equally important, the proportion of total health-care expenditures of the elderly that originated in public sources rose far more sharply than had been expected prior to Medicare's passage. In fiscal year 1966, government programs provided 31 percent of the total expended on health care for the elderly. Just one year later this proportion had risen to 59 percent and Medicare alone accounted for 35 cents of every dollar spent on health services by or for those over the age of 65.

Even more dramatic increases occurred in the Medicaid program during its first few years. The wording of Title XIX provided that the federal government had an open-ended obligation to help underwrite the costs of medical care for a wide range of services to a large number of possible recipients, depending on state legislation. There was therefore no accurate way of predicting the ultimate costs of the program. In 1965, the House Ways and Means Committee had estimated that if all the states were to take full advantage of the program – that is, if each state were to include all the services for which each possible beneficiary could receive assistance and if all categories of possible beneficiaries were included at the highest level of eligibility – the additional federal cost of medical assistance (beyond that already provided by previously existing programs) would amount to $238 000 000. However, In fiscal year 1967, total Medicaid payments amounted to $1 944 000 000, about half of which were federal funds, in a program that was operating in only 28 states. It is true that with the introduction of Medicaid, federal funding for other programs (for example, Medical Assistance for the Aged) sharply declined. Yet even if the drop in expenditures for these other programs is factored in, federal outlays increased dramatically. By the end of the calendar year 1968, 41 states had opted into the Medicaid program and total expenditures (of which about 50.1 percent were federal) amounted to $3 783 000 000. (As a point of comparison, total federal outlays for all medical assistance programs in fiscal year 1965, prior to the introduction of Medicare and Medicaid, amounted to $1 239 000 000.)

In 1971, the House Ways and Means Committee, still under the chairmanship of Wilbur Mills, began hearings on a new H.R. 1, whose goal was to contain the spiraling costs of Medicare and Medicaid. Among the large number of individuals and organizations that testified before the committee were members of the Nixon Administration who suggested a whole series of cost-control measures, among them that new legislation promote a system of capitation payments to health maintenance organizations (HMOs) and that Medicaid introduce cost-sharing while Medicare expand its own cost-sharing policies.[113] Many of these recommendations eventually found their way into the final bill to reform these programs, which became law in October 1972. Among the changes to the Medicare program was (1) the inclusion of the totally disabled as eligible for Medicare benefits. Workers of any age, and widows and disabled dependent widowers over the age of 50 were eligible to receive Medicare benefits after having received APTD (Aid to Permanently and Totally Disabled) assistance for 24 months. This added approximately 1 700 000 beneficiaries to the Medicare rolls and was the first instance of any group under the age of 65 being made eligible for benefits. Additionally, (2) beneficiaries of Part B (Supplementary Medical Insurance) who otherwise were ineligible for Part A (Hospital Insurance) by virtue of not qualifying for Social Security coverage could now voluntarily enroll in Part A by paying a monthly premium, and (3) provision was made for capitation payments to HMOs, and certain limits were placed on the items that a health-care facility could include in calculating its cost.

Perhaps the most significant change to the Medicaid program contained in the 1972 amendments was the repeal of a provision contained in the 1965 legislation that made it mandatory that each state expand its Medicaid program each year until it offered comprehensive coverage for all the medically needy by 1977. When Medicare and Medicaid were first introduced, Congress had hoped to establish a universal hospital and medical insurance scheme for the needy using Medicaid as its foundation but largely as a result of the swelling costs of the program, this design was abandoned in 1972.[114]

A further provision of the 1972 legislation was the establishment of Professional Standards Review Organizations (PSROs), whose function it was to assume responsibility for monitoring the costs, degree of utilization, and quality of care of medical services offered under Medicare and Medicaid. It was hoped that these PSROs would compel hospitals to act more efficiently.[115] In keeping with this goal, in 1974 a reimbursement cap was instituted that limited hospitals from charging more than 120 percent of the mean of routine costs in effect in similar facilities, a limit later reduced to 112 percent.[116] Despite these attempts at holding down costs, they continued to escalate inasmuch as hospitals were still reimbursed on the basis of their expenses and the caps that were instituted applied only to room and board and not to ancillary services, which remained unregulated.[117] Table 5.2 gives some idea of the costs associated with the Medicare program from its inception to the mid-1980s.

It had been surmised by some analysts during the 1970s that escalating hospital expenditures could be largely accounted for by increases in input prices that exceeded the general increase in consumer prices and that price controls on hospital expenditures might prove effective in limiting Medicare costs. This theory, that an inflation in the price of hospital input prices was the driving force behind rising Medicare costs, was tested by, among others, John Virts and George Wilson,[118] who concluded that somewhat less than half the change in hospital expenditures between 1965 and 1972 could be attributed to

Table 5.2 Medicare Benefit Payments and Annual Percentage Change,
1966–1984

Year	Total ($ billions)	Hospital Insurance ($ billions)	Supplementary Medical Insurance ($ billions)	Annual Change (%)
1966	1.0	0.9	0.1	–
1967	4.6	3.4	1.2	346.5
1968	5.7	4.2	1.5	25.2
1969	6.6	4.7	1.9	15.9
1970	7.1	5.1	2.0	7.5
1971	7.9	5.8	2.1	10.8
1972	8.6	6.3	2.3	9.9
1973	9.6	7.1	2.5	10.9
1974	12.4	9.1	3.3	29.6
1975	15.6	11.3	4.3	25.5
1976	18.4	13.3	5.1	18.2
1977	21.8	15.7	6.0	18.2
1978	24.9	17.7	7.3	14.5
1979	29.3	20.6	8.7	17.6
1980	35.7	25.1	10.6	21.7
1981	43.5	30.3	13.1	21.7
1982	51.1	35.6	15.5	17.6
1983	57.4	39.3	18.1	12.4
1984	62.9	43.3	19.7	9.5
ACRG[1]	16.6%	16.1%	17.9%	
ACRRG[2]	9.1%	8.6%	10.3%	

Notes:
[1] Annual compound rate of growth.
[2] 1967 to 1984: Annual compound rate of real growth (that is, the rate of growth adjusted for changes in the Consumer Price Index, 1967–1984).

Source: Marian Gornick, Jay N. Greenberg, Paul W. Eggers et al., 'Twenty Years of Medicare and Medicaid: Covered Populations, Use of Benefits, and Program Expenditures', *Health Care Financing Review, 1985, Annual Supplement*, 43.

changes in price, while over 40 percent was attributable to changes in utilization. Table 5.3 summarizes their findings.

Virts and Wilson further found that of the $57.2 billion in increased hospital expenditures that could be attributed to price changes during the 10 years from 1972 to 1981 no more than $7.1 billion (somewhat less than 10 percent of the total increase in hospital expenditures) could be ascribed to inflationary

Table 5.3   Sources of Change in Hospital Expenditures, 1965–1981

	1965–1981		1965–1972		1972–1981	
	$ billions	%	$ billions	%	$ billions	%
Change in prices	67.3	64.6	10.1	48.1	57.2	68.8
Change in utilization	28.2	27.1	9.2	43.8	19.0	22.9
Change in population	8.6	8.3	1.7	8.1	6.9	8.3
Total	104.1	100.0	21.0	100.0	83.1	100.0

Source: Jack A. Meyer, *Passing the Health Care Buck: Who Pays the Hidden Cost?* (Washington, DC: American Enterprise Institute for Public Policy Research, 1983): 48.

rises peculiar to the health-care sector. The implications of the Virts-Wilson study are clear: beyond a general increase in all prices, increased utilization was the single most important factor responsible for the unrelenting rise in Medicare hospital costs.

In 1974 new legislation was enacted whose goal was to reduce the construction of new hospitals in the hope that this would diminish overall utilization of hospital facilities and thus lessen the rate of increase in Medicare-Medicaid expenditures. The National Health Planning and Resource Development Act mandated that certificate-of-need (CON) programs be instituted in each of the states to regulate the construction of new health-care facilities. Since little could be done to limit the demand for medical services that were effectively underwritten by the government, it was hoped that limiting the supply of these services might act as a brake on rising costs.[119] This program too was of limited value despite its huge costs, having had little impact on new hospital construction.[120]

With the election of Ronald Reagan some attempt was made to cut Medicare and Medicaid funding. Toward this end the PSRO program, which had proved a disaster, was all but abolished and, with passage of the Omnibus Budget Reconciliation Act (OBRA) of 1981, limits were placed on reimbursements for a large number of inpatient and outpatient services. The main thrust of OBRA, however, was not Medicare but Medicaid. Under the Act's provisions, federal transfers to the states were to be reduced over the course of three years and the states themselves were empowered to limit the services extended to beneficiaries. The Tax Equity and Fiscal Responsibility Act (TEFRA), enacted in 1982, introduced a flat payment per hospital patient based on the historic average cost of care and instituted a ceiling on increases in hospital revenue. This Act also permitted states to require co-payments from most Medicaid recipients, altered the terms under which HMOs entered into risk-sharing contracts to make them more attractive, and made Medicare the secondary, rather than the primary, insurer in the case of workers under the age of 70 covered by a company health insurance plan.[121]

The combined effect of the OBRA and TEFRA reforms was to introduce hospital budget caps for Medicare patients. These caps, which reimbursed medical facilities on the basis of average cost without regard to variations in severity of illness, were regarded as unworkable by the nation's hospitals, who lobbied for some change in these provisions. Denied any flexibility by TEFRA, hospitals were left with no room to benefit from any increases in efficiency they might introduce. As a consequence, most hospitals in 1982 regarded almost any change in Medicare's method of payment as preferable to the existing arrangements and it was this that appears to have eased the way for radical payment reform. The result of their lobbying was the Social Security amendments of 1983, which substituted Medicare's cost-based system of reimbursement for hospitals (which in 1983 accounted for more than 68 percent of total Medicare expenditures) with a Prospective Payment System (PPS), under which the program currently operates.

Henceforth hospitals were to be paid a prospectively determined rate per patient per stay, based on a diagnosis of each Medicare patient's illness. Upon discharge each patient is categorized as having fallen into a Diagnosis-Related Group (DRG)[122] which in turn determines the amount of reimbursement Medicare is prepared to make. Payments to hospitals are adjusted for the average wage rate in the community in which the hospital is located, whether the facility is situated in an urban, large urban, or rural area, and whether it is a teaching hospital.[123] Given that fairly large regional differences existed in hospital expenses and fearful that what amounted to national pricing for hospital care might result in substantial transfers of federal dollars from high to low-income areas, these national rates were to be phased in over a period of four years. Under this new system of payment, hospitals would no longer have an incentive to encourage long hospital stays and to perform unnecessary tests and medical procedures, as seems to have been the case when they were reimbursed retrospectively on the basis of their costs. Rather, these facilities would now be able to garner any rewards for increases in efficiency in the delivery of medical care or for reducing the costs per patient while he was undergoing treatment.

The most effective way of cutting costs is, of course, to limit the length of a patient's hospital stay for any particular illness. While the length of stay had been decreasing for Medicare beneficiaries (and for the population as a whole) for several years, this trend accelerated following the introduction of PPS; from 1983 to 1985 the average hospital stay for Medicare patients declined from 9.7 days to 8.7 days.[124] In 1985 there were 22.8 million fewer hospital days as compared with 1983,[125] no doubt in part in response to the incentives generated by Medicare's new method of calculating payments to health care facilities. Despite this decline, however, Medicare expenditures continued to increase. This appears to have largely resulted from shifting some procedures that had been routinely performed on an inpatient basis to the outpatient departments of hospitals and to doctors' offices. Thus, certain tests and some surgery (for example, cataract surgery) are now conducted almost exclusively on an outpatient basis and it is the policy of most hospitals to 'unbundle' tests performed on Medicare patients either immediately before their admission or immediately after their discharge from a hospital.[126]

The PPS reforms did not address the question of Medicare's physician reimbursement costs under Supplementary Medical Insurance, which had been increasing substantially. In fact, over the course of the 1980s, the growth in physician payments had actually outpaced the growth in hospital costs, which had been moderating in response to the Prospective Payment System. Between 1975 and 1982, the number of physicians' services employed by the average Medicare beneficiary increased by 6 percent per year.[127] In 1970, Medicare spent $1.8 billion on physicians' services; by 1983 this amount had reached $14 billion. Indeed, during this period, expenditures for physicians' services were growing more rapidly than any other component of the Medicare program or, in fact, any other program in the federal domestic budget. Between 1970 and 1983, Medicare payments to doctors grew at a rate of over 17 percent.[128] As a consequence of this dramatic increase, a freeze was put on the 'prevailing charge' – the absolute cap on physicians' charges allowed by Medicare. However, in the wake of intense lobbying by physicians' groups, this freeze was lifted in 1986. Not only did the Administration support reform in Medicare's payment structure for physicians, but a large number of practitioners supported some reform because of the system's perceived inequities. For example, physicians were paid far more for high-technology services than for basic care and, more important, practitioners in rural areas were compensated at substantially lower rates than those practicing in cities, thereby encouraging physicians to congregate in urban areas.

Agitation for reform led Congress in 1986 to establish a Physician Payment Review Commission, whose function was to recommend to Congress and the Reagan Administration how the payment system should be altered. Among the Commission's recommendations was a resource-based, relative value scale that was later to form the basis of the fee schedule passed into law in 1989. Under the terms of the relevant provisions of the Budget Reconciliation Act of 1989, payments for surgical interventions and other expensive procedures were reduced while reimbursements for office visits were substantially increased. The legislation called for these reforms to be phased in starting in January 1992, and to be fully in place by 1996. The new fee schedule is based on an incredibly complex system of 'relative value units' awarded to each procedure on the basis of the time and complexity (and desirability) of the

Table 5.4   Impact of Medicare Fee Schedule by Physician Speciality

Speciality	Change in Payments per Service (%)
Family practice	28
General practice	27
Cardiology	–17
Internal medicine	5
Gastroenterology	–18
Neurology	–4
Psychiatry	3
Urology	–8
Radiology	–22
Anesthesiology	–27
Pathology	–20
General surgery	–13
Ophthalmology	–21
Orthopedic surgery	–11
Thoracic surgery	–27
All specialities	–6

Source: Marilyn Moon, *Medicare Now and in the Future* (Washington, DC: The Urban Institute Press, 1993), Table 3.5 (p. 70).

service performed.[129] Beyond establishing the fee schedule, the 1989 legislation further limited physicians' ability to extra-bill Medicare patients. Physicians who decline to 'accept assignment'[130] may bill their Medicare patients no more than 10 percent above the fee schedule. While the new fee schedule is far from simple (it contains over 7000 codes and 233 geographic areas and occupies 317 pages in the *Federal Register*), the Health Care Financing Administration has attempted to calculate its impact on various medical specialties when compared with the method of payment in place prior to 1992.

As had been the case with the introduction of a PPS method of reimbursement for hospital care, the effect of these reforms in payments to physicians appears to have been to moderate the increase in the costs of physicians' services and to decrease disbursements to physicians as a percentage of total Medicare costs. However, payments to physicians continued to increase and were projected to reach $104 billion by the year 2000.[131]

In light of the Reagan Administration's ostensible concern with reintroducing market forces into the various government programs affecting hospital and

Table 5.5   Medicare Expenditures for Physicians' Services, Selected Years

Year	Amount (billions)	Percent of Total Supplementary Insurance Expenditures
1970	1.8	90.6
1975	3.4	79.9
1983	14.1	77.7
1984	15.4	78.5
1985	17.3	75.4
1986	19.2	73.2
1987	22.6	73.4
1988	24.4	71.7
1989	27.1	70.7
1990	29.6	69.6
1991	32.3	68.3
1992	32.4	65.7
1993	35.3	65.4
1994	38.1	n/a
1995 (FY est.)	40.0	n/a
1996 (FY est.)	45.6	n/a

Source: 1970 to 1993: Health Care Financing Administration, *Health Care Financing Review*, Medicare and Medicaid Statistical Supplement, 1995: Table 55 (pp. 280–81); 1994: Katharine R. Levit et al., 'National Health Expenditures, 1994', *Health Care Financing Review*, 17(3) (Spring 1996): Table 17 (pp. 239–40); 1995 and 1996: 'National Health Care Expenditures: Medicare Benefit Outlays', Washington, DC, October 1996 (http://www.hcfa. gov/stats/nhce96.htm).

medical services and in the face of the spectacular growth in Medicare and Medicaid costs, it is almost beyond comprehension that the largest expansion of the Medicare program since its inception occurred under Reagan's presidency.[132] In June 1988, Congress enacted the Medicare Catastrophic Coverage Act, which was signed amid the usual pageantry in the Rose Garden on 1 July. The Act was the product of recommendations put forward by the Bowen Commission, which had earlier been empaneled by the President. The Commission, chaired by a former Secretary of Health and Human Services, Otis Bowen, was charged with the task of studying the issue of catastrophic health costs, including both acute and long-term care. This problem appears to have been particularly severe in the case of the elderly, who, by 1987, were spending about the same proportion of their incomes on health care as had obtained before the advent of Medicare.[133] The Bowen Commission released its final report in the fall of 1986 and limited itself to recommendations respecting acute care for Medicare beneficiaries, which it regarded as most amenable to a solution. The Report proposed expanding Medicare by placing an annual $2000 limit on beneficiaries' out-of-pocket expenses for hospital and physician charges. Any expenditures above that amount would be absorbed by Medicare. The program would be financed by increasing Medicare's existing Part B premium by $59 per year.

The Reagan Administration agreed to support the recommendations of the Commission since it regarded this extension of the Medicare program as revenue-neutral. It was thought that projected additional annual costs of $2 billion would be made up by the $59 annual charge levied on beneficiaries and it was only on that condition that the Administration agreed to support the proposal. The House Ways and Means Committee, however, insisted on adding further benefits to the package. These additions at first were somewhat modest (that is, improved home health care and skilled nursing home care coverage) but were soon extended to include further benefits to the Medicaid program[134] and the addition of prescription drugs to Medicare's coverage. While the Senate Finance Committee's recommendations were not quite as ambitious as were these, they did end up reporting out a scaled-down version of the House bill, minus the drug benefit. In July 1987, the Congressional Budget Office reassessed the cost of the original Bowen proposal at $78 per Medicare enrollee and $226 per enrollee should the House version be enacted. In addition, the House version called for the payment of an additional graduated premium based on income, rising to $580 annually for those with adjusted gross incomes of more than $14 166. The 'premium' – Congress was insistent that this was not an increase in taxes – was to be collected by the IRS and was mandatory.

The Act as finally passed in June 1988 contained several adjustments to Part A of the Medicare program, including a reduction in the liability of Medicare beneficiaries for hospital care to one deductible per year. In addition, hospital benefits were calculated for the full year, without regard to 60-day blocks, and provided for unlimited inpatient care while eliminating all co-payments and deductibles except for the one annual amount. The skilled nursing facility benefit was extended to 150 days per year and required no prior hospital stay, as in the past. A co-insurance payment was limited to the first eight days per year, at 20 percent of the average daily cost. Hospice and home health benefits were expanded and requirements for participation eased. With respect to Part B, the new legislation placed a limit on deductibles and co-payments for physicians' services, including payments to surgeons. Additionally, Medicare reimbursements were extended to cover outpatient prescription drugs above a $600 deductible, which were to be phased in over a period of several years with decreasing co-payments by the beneficiary. Finally, Part B coverage was expanded to biennial mammography screening. Changes to Medicaid were much along the lines recommended by the House

Ways and Means Committee, including exempting low-income Medicare beneficiaries from deductibles and co-payments and protecting the assets of spouses of nursing home residents. In sum, according to the Congressional Budget Office, the changes brought about by the Medicare Catastrophic Coverage Act would have increased Medicare benefits for each beneficiary by about 7 percent. Catastrophic benefits would have added an average of approximately $194 to the $2801 in benefits per enrollee under the old law.[135]

These extensions of Medicare and Medicaid coverage were to be financed by a flat premium levied on all beneficiaries except Medicaid recipients plus an income-related supplement, to be paid by all enrollees with an income tax liability of $150 or more at the rate of $22.50 per $150 of tax liability (or 15 percent). The maximum liability was set at $800 per person. The surtax rate was scheduled to increase over time to a maximum of 28 percent by 1993. As in the House version, 'premiums' were mandatory and collected by the IRS.

While the American Association of Retired Persons was pleased with the legislation, a number of groups had serious reservations about one or another of its provisions. The Pharmaceutical Manufacturers Association was fearful that the inclusion of coverage for prescription drugs would eventually lead to cost controls on pharmaceuticals, and the National Committee to Protect Social Security and Medicare was strongly opposed to the supplemental premium as an additional tax on the elderly. Indeed, since many of the benefits of the new legislation were to be phased in over a period of several years while premiums were set to begin immediately, critics of the new legislation could with some justification claim that the Act was in reality aimed at reducing the deficit at the expense of the elderly. This conclusion seemed to be supported by the Treasury, who reported in the spring of 1989 that collections of the supplemental premium would be higher than anticipated and would generate a substantial increase in the Catastrophic Coverage Trust Fund.[136] On the heels of this report, the Congressional Budget Office released figures showing that the costs of some benefits under the 1988 legislation had been seriously underestimated. This was particularly true of the costs associated with skilled nursing facilities, where average stays increased from 27 to 34 days between 1988 and 1989, while the number of persons covered rose from 392 000 to 591 000 during the same period. The cost of the prescription drug benefit was also revised upward, to more than double the original estimates. These new figures now suggested that not only would the Trust Fund not show a surplus, but that a huge shortfall would likely occur. These data served the Act's opponents well, who were able to capitalize on the legislation's profound shortcomings. For some reason, the media appear to have been somewhat skeptical about the value of this extension of Medicare and this added to the general discontent about the increase in taxes (that is, 'mandatory premiums') by which the Act was funded.

There followed a period of vigorous lobbying in Congress by interest groups representing the elderly to amend the Catastrophic Coverage provisions in such a way that the benefits contained in the Act would be retained while the supplemental premium was eliminated. However, in the face of the federal government's huge deficit, this 'compromise' was not politically feasible and there appeared no option but to repeal the Act. In October 1989, the House of Representatives voted to repeal all but the Medicaid provisions of the Medicare Catastrophic Coverage Act and in the following month the Senate followed suit. This appears to be the first instance in the legislative history of national health-care insurance when Congress was forced to confront the realities of the program's increasingly heavy expenditures.

Independent of its abortive catastrophic coverage provisions, the costs of Medicare continued to increase at a spectacular pace. These increases alarmed a number of organizations, among them the American Medical Association, the American Association of Retired Persons, and the American Hospital Association. Fearful that the government would be unable to underwrite the costs of coverage very much longer and that as a result benefits would be sharply reduced, these organizations and a number of others agitated for reforms in the program. In 1997, Congress enacted the Medicare Advantage (formerly Medicare+Choice) program, whose goal was to reduce the costs of Medicare by encouraging Medicare recipients to receive their health-care coverage through private insurance companies.[137] It was hoped that, by creating a new segment of coverage – known as Part C – the costs of Part B of the benefits package, that is, that portion of Medicare that extended coverage to include supplementary medical insurance beyond the costs of hospitalization, would drop.

The legislation was to prove a failure and by 2004 over 40 percent of those eligible for these coordinated private plans were unable to receive them since private insurance companies found it unprofitable to cover Medicare recipients with the level of service mandated by the government. Indeed, between 1998 and 2003 the number of private plans associated with the program dropped from 346 to 188.[138] As a consequence of this decline in availability the 2003 Medicare Drug Act, whose main focus was the addition of a prescription drug benefit, provided for increased payments to insurance companies associated with the Medicare Advantage program. The effect has been a slight increase in availability; however, one-third of Medicare recipients remain unable to take advantage of these private plans. More significant, a study conducted by the General Accounting Office in 2000 uncovered the fact that Medicare Advantage, introduced as a cost-cutting measure, had actually increased the costs to the government.[139]

By far the most significant change in the Medicare program occurred in 2003, when Congress, at the urging of President George W. Bush, enacted the Medicare Prescription Drug, Improvement and Modernization Act, the most substantial enlargement of Medicare since its original passage in 1965. In the President's message to Congress exhorting them to pass the bill, he noted that the drug provisions were calculated to cost approximately $405 billion over the period from 2004 to 2013,[140] despite his knowing that the Medicare chief actuary had put the figure at $535 billion.[141] The difference, apparently, was crucial to enactment of the bill inasmuch as it was passed by only the narrowest of margins and some Congressmen were likely to have refused to approve the measure had its projected costs been higher. It was only one month after the bill was passed that President Bush conceded that the $535 billion figure was a more accurate one. The prescription drug provision went into effect at the start of 2006, at which point estimates of its costs had risen to over $700 billion.

The formula for calculating benefits under the program is itself sufficiently complex that it appears beyond the abilities of a large number of older Americans to determine whether enrollment in the plan is to their advantage. Those covered by a Medicare drug plan are required to pay a monthly premium to a private insurance company, each of which is in competition with the others. Most plans do not cover the first $250.00 of drug costs. Between annual drug expenditures of $250 and total out-of-pocket drug costs (including the cost of the plan itself) of $2250.00, 75 percent of the cost of prescription medications will be covered by the plan, but only up to $3600.00. At that point, enrollees must pay all drug costs up to an annual cost of $5100.00. Ninety-five percent of the costs above that amount are covered by the insurer. The total cost to the enrollee will vary from plan to plan, depending on the monthly premium, which drugs the insurer is prepared to cover, the amount of the co-payment, and which pharmacies are associated with the particular insurer. This allows for so much variation that the prospective buyer tends to be overwhelmed by the calculations needed to determine whether paying the monthly premium is worthwhile.

Despite its limitations, the Medicare drug subsidy program will cost the government about $720 billion through 2015; and as pressure is brought to bear by the increasing number of older Americans who become eligible for Medicare's benefits, Congress is likely to expand the program, increasing Medicare's deficit still more.[142] In fact, projections regarding the deficit for the whole Medicare program are massive. The Office of the Chief Actuary of Medicare has estimated that just to bring the Hospital Insurance portion of the program (Part A) into actuarial balance would require either an immediate 107 percent increase in income or a 48 percent reduction in outlays! While Medicare as a whole currently spends 3.3 percent of GDP, projections by the Medicare trustees project expenditures of 13.6 percent of GDP by 2079.[143]

For a number of decades Medicare spending has increased at a pace far outstripping the growth in national income.[144] Currently, although Medicare beneficiaries constitute only 15 percent of the population, they account for over 37 percent of all national health-care expenditures. Nor are these expenditures distributed fairly evenly among Medicare's 41 million recipients. The top 5 percent of beneficiaries – ranked by spending – account for over half of all fee-for-service spending, while the top 25 percent account for about 90 percent. The program thus constitutes a substantial transfer of funds from the younger segment of the population to its oldest members. The Financial Management Service of the US Treasury estimates that the current value of net future expenditures (the program's unfunded liability) is a staggering $29 899 billion.[145] Beside having created a lien on the incomes of future taxpayers, Medicare has created a sizeable addition to the federal government's entitlements, which increased from 32 percent of the budget in 1962 to 60 percent in 2002, leaving that much less for discretionary spending.

While both Congress and the various administrations have in the past made modest attempts to moderate the growth in Medicare and Medicaid spending that have marked these programs since their birth, the lure of votes has been far stronger. There seems little doubt that the majority of Americans want far more health care than they are individually willing to pay for and socializing the costs associated with health care is an excellent way of disguising its real costs. That this brings in its wake further dislocations in the economy as costs are shifted is of no interest or concern to most politicians. Indeed, even the attempts that have been made to set rates in the form of a Prospective Payment System for hospitals and a Medical Fee Schedule for physicians simply disguise the true costs of Medicare programs by shifting and masking them. There is evidence that one of the effects of placing effective caps on hospital charges below what they would otherwise have been is that hospitals subsidize Medicare beneficiaries at the expense of their other patients and their insurance companies. The same thing, of course, holds for physicians' services. Nor is increasing Medicare premiums the solution since its effect is to raise business costs and lower real incomes for workers. In 1966, the maximum Medicare tax imposed on employees and the self-employed was $23.10; by 1993, this amount had increased to $1957.50 and double that, $3915.00, for self-employed workers. In 1993, employees with earnings of $26 382, the annual average pay, had $382.25 withheld from their paychecks while their employers contributed another $382.25 on their behalf, a total of $764.50. Yet, despite these increases in Medicare taxes (which have since again been raised), Hospital Insurance (Part A) expenditures exceeded the Hospital Insurance Trust Fund's annual income in 2004. The Fund's income was estimated to meet only 79 percent of expenditures in 2020 and 27 percent in 2080.[146]

The lessons of Medicare seem clear. The program is spending far more than it receives in premiums and payroll taxes and this shortfall is increasing; indeed, at current rates of growth, expenditures on hospital insurance alone will exhaust the Hospital Insurance Trust Fund by the year 2020.[147] The nation can ill afford a health insurance program that constitutes such a drain on the nation's resources and distorts individual costs such that there is simply no incentive to economize on health care. Nor are we encouraged to economize. We are enjoined to consult a physician for almost every possible ailment or in connection with even the most minor decisions affecting our health. And physicians themselves, eager to recommend the best care money can buy, often recommend expensive diagnostic procedures and elaborate surgical interventions even for the extremely old. It is now theoretically possible to keep the bodily organism functioning almost interminably, although often at huge cost. We are naturally reluctant to call an end to our own lives and those of the people we love. But the truth is that we simply cannot afford unlimited health-care coverage under a program that draws no distinction in terms of out-of-pocket expenses between the most comprehensive options and a more modest level of care. It is unfortunate that politicians, whose horizons rarely extend beyond the next election, are so little concerned with these problems. Limiting oneself to making the occasional judicious-sounding statement about the need to restructure the government's health programs to halt waste and increase efficiency will not solve Medicare's deficiencies nor will an infinite amount of tinkering with the program's details, inasmuch as a government-operated mandatory national health insurance scheme is fatally flawed. Nothing better misrepresents the actual effects of government control over the health-care system than the following claim:

> The more services are made free to the patient at time of receipt of service, and the more the system is planned and regulated by the state in the public interest, the better is the quality of service, the better the health of the people – and the less it costs.[148]

Such sentiments are a recipe for disaster and display an appalling ignorance of both the most rudimentary conclusions of economics and the empirical data on government health-care programs. Only the market allows consumers to make these tradeoffs, in which we can weigh the benefits of elaborate medical procedures against their cost. Medicare masks these costs and distorts our choices while packaging the program in a massive regulatory system subject to the decisions of bureaucrats rather than consumers.

Table 5.6   Medicare: Tax Rates and Maximum Tax Bases

Year	Maximum Tax Base ($)	Tax Rate (Percent of Taxable Earnings) Employee and employer, each	Self-employed	Maximum Tax Employee portion ($)	Self-employed ($)
1966	6600	0.35	0.35	23.10	23.10
1967	6600	0.50	0.50	33.00	33.00
1968	7800	0.60	0.60	46.80	46.80
1969	7800	0.60	0.60	46.80	46.80
1970	7800	0.60	0.60	46.80	46.80
1971	7800	0.60	0.60	46.80	46.80
1972	9000	0.60	0.60	54.00	54.00
1973	10 800	1.00	1.00	108.00	108.00
1974	13 200	0.90	0.90	118.80	118.80
1975	14 100	0.90	0.90	126.90	126.90
1976	15 300	0.90	0.90	137.70	137.70
1977	16 500	0.90	0.90	148.50	148.50
1978	17 700	1.00	1.00	177.00	177.00
1979	22 900	1.05	1.05	240.45	240.45
1980	25 900	1.05	1.05	271.95	271.95
1981	29 700	1.30	1.30	386.10	386.10
1982	32 400	1.30	1.30	421.20	421.20
1983	35 700	1.30	1.30	464.10	464.10
1984	37 800	1.30	2.60	491.40	982.80
1985	39 600	1.35	2.70	534.60	1 069.20
1986	42 000	1.45	2.90	609.00	1 218.00
1987	43 800	1.45	2.90	635.10	1 270.20
1988	45 000	1.45	2.90	652.50	1 305.00
1989	48 000	1.45	2.90	696.00	1 392.00
1990	51 300	1.45	2.90	743.85	1 487.70
1991	125 000	1.45	2.90	1 812.50	3 625.00
1992	130 200	1.45	2.90	1 887.90	3 775.80
1993	135 000	1.45	2.90	1 957.50	3 915.00
1994	no limit	1.45	2.90	no limit	
1995	no limit	1.45	2.90	no limit	
1996	no limit	1.45	2.90	no limit	
1997	no limit	1.45	2.90	no limit	
1998	no limit	1.45	2.90	no limit	
1999	no limit	1.45	2.90	no limit	
2000	no limit	1.45	2.90	no limit	

Source: Board of Trustees, Federal Hospital Insurance Trust Fund, *1999 Annual Report* (Washington, DC: 1999): Table II.B1 (p. 20).

Table 5.7 Number of Enrollees in the Medicare Hospital and/or Supplementary Medical Insurance Programs, by Type of Coverage and Type of Entitlement, Calendar Years 1966–1998 (in thousands)

Year	Hospital Insurance and/or Supplementary Medical Insurance			Hospital Insurance			Supplementary Medical Insurance		
	Total	Aged Enrollees	Disabled Enrollees	Total	Aged Enrollees	Disabled Enrollees	Total	Aged Enrollees	Disabled Enrollees
1966	19 109	19 101	–	19 082	19 082	–	17 736	17 736	–
1967	19 521	19 521	–	19 494	19 494	–	17 893	17 893	–
1968	19 821	19 821	–	19 770	19 770	–	18 805	18 805	–
1969	20 103	20 103	–	20 014	20 014	–	19 195	19 195	–
1970	20 491	20 491	–	20 361	20 361	–	19 584	19 584	–
1971	20 915	20 195	–	20 742	20 742	–	19 975	19 975	–
1972	21 332	21 332	–	21 115	21 115	–	20 351	20 351	–
1973	23 545	21 815	1731	23 301	21 571	1731	22 491	20 921	1570
1974	24 201	22 273	1928	23 924	21 996	1928	23 167	21 421	1745
1975	24 959	22 790	2168	24 640	22 472	2168	23 905	21 945	1959
1976	25 663	23 371	2392	25 313	22 920	2392	24 614	22 446	2168
1977	26 458	23 838	2619	26 094	23 474	2619	25 363	22 991	2373
1978	27 164	24 371	2793	26 777	23 984	2793	26 074	23 531	2543
1979	27 859	24 948	2911	27 459	24 548	2911	26 757	24 098	2659

Year									
1980	28 478	25 515	2963	28 067	25 104	2963	27 400	24 680	2719
1981	29 010	26 011	2999	28 590	25 591	2999	27 949	25 182	2759
1982	29 494	26 540	2954	29 069	26 115	2954	28 412	25 707	2705
1983	30 026	27 109	2918	29 587	26 670	2918	28 975	26 292	2682
1984	30 455	27 571	2884	29 996	27 112	2884	29 415	26 764	2651
1985	31 083	28 176	2907	30 589	27 683	2907	29 989	27 311	2678
1986	31 750	28 791	2959	31 216	28 257	2959	30 590	27 863	2727
1987	32 411	29 380	3031	31 853	28 822	3031	31 170	28 382	2788
1988	32 980	29 879	3102	32 413	29 312	3101	31 617	28 780	2837
1989	33 579	30 409	3171	33 040	29 869	3171	32 099	29 216	2883
1990	34 213	30 961	3252	33 731	30 479	3252	32 636	29 691	2945
1991	34 870	31 485	3385	34 429	31 043	3385	33 237	30 185	3052
1992	35 598	32 019	3579	35 159	31 581	3578	33 956	30 722	3234
1993	36 339	32 477	3863	35 924	32 063	3862	34 643	31 162	3480
1994	36 935	32 801	4135	36 543	32 409	4135	35 167	31 447	3720
1995	37 535	33 142	4393	37 135	32 742	4393	35 685	31 742	3942
1996	38 064	33 424	4640	37 662	33 022	4640	36 140	31 984	4155
1997	38 445	33 630	4815	38 052	33 237	4815	36 460	32 164	4296
1998	38 825	33 802	5023	38 432	33 410	5023	36 781	32 308	4472

Source: 1966–3: Medicare and Medicaid Statistical Supplement, 1995, *Health Care Financing Review* (1995): Table 5 (p. 161). 1994–8: Medicare Enrollment Trends, 1966–1998, 'Medicare Aged and Disabled Enrollees by Type of Coverage' (Cited 8 October 1998), available from the World Wide Web at http://www.hcfa.gov/stats/enrltrnd.htm

Table 5.8 Medicaid Users, by Eligibility Group, Fiscal Years 1975–1997 (thousands)

Year	Total	Low-income Children	Low-income Adult	Low-income Aged	Low income Disabled	Other
1975	22 007	9598	4529	3615	2464	1801
1976	22 815	9924	4773	3612	2669	1837
1977	22 862	9651	4785	3636	2802	1958
1978	21 965	9376	4643	3376	2718	1852
1979	21 520	9106	4570	3364	2753	1727
1980	21 605	9333	4877	3440	2911	1044
1981	21 980	9581	5187	3367	3079	766
1982	21 603	9563	5356	3240	2891	553
1983	21 554	9535	5592	3372	2921	134
1984	21 607	9684	5600	3238	2913	172
1985	21 814	9757	5518	3061	3012	466
1986	22 515	10 029	5647	3140	3182	517
1987	23 109	10 168	5599	3224	3381	737
1988	22 907	10 037	5503	3159	3487	721
1989	23 511	10 318	5717	3132	3590	754
1990	25 255	11 220	6010	3202	3718	1105
1991	27 967	12 855	6703	3341	4033	1035
1992	31 150	15 200	7040	3749	4487	674
1993	33 432	16 285	7505	3863	5016	763
1995	36 200	17 600	7800	4200	6000	600
1996	37 500	18 200	8000	4400	6300	600
1997	38 700	18 700	8300	4600	6600	500

Source: Data for 1975 through 1993: Medicare and Medicaid Statistical Supplement, 1995 *Health Care Financing Review* (1995): Table 105 (p. 359). Data for 1995 through 1997: Medicaid recipients, HCFA Statistics: *Populations*, Table 11, available from the World Wide Web at http://www. hcfa.gov/stats/hstats96/blustats.htm.

Table 5.9 Operations of the Hospital Insurance Trust Fund, Calendar Years 1970–2008 (millions)

Year	Income				Disbursements			Balance at end of Year
	Payroll Taxes	Reimbursement for Uninsured Persons	Interest and other income[1]	Total	Benefit Payments[2]	Administrative Expenses	Total	
Historical Data:								
1970	4881	863	235	5979	5124	157	5281	3202
1975	11 502	621	857	12 980	11 315	266	11 581	10 517
1980	23 848	697	1552	26 097	25 064	512	25 577	13 749
1985	47 576	766	3055	51 397	47 580	834	48 414	20 499
1986	54 583	566	4117	59 267	49 738	664	50 422	39 957
1987	58 648	447	4969	64 064	49 496	793	50 289	53 732
1988	62 449	475	6315	69 239	52 517	815	53 331	69 640
1989	68 369	515	7837	76 721	60 011	792	60 803	85 558
1990	72 013	413	7946	80 372	66 239	758	66 997	98 933
1991	77 851	605	10 383	88 839	71 549	1021	72 570	115 202
1992	81 745	621	11 469	93 836	83 895	1121	85 015	124 022
1993	84 133	367	13 687	98 187	93 487	904	94 391	127 818
1994	95 280	506	13 784	109 570	103 282	1263	104 545	132 844
1995	98 421	462	16 144	115 368	116 368	1236	117 604	130 267
1996	110 585	419	13 598	124 603	128 632	1297	129 929	124 942
1997	114 670	481	15 003	130 154	137 762	1690	139 452	115 643
1998	124 317	34	16 196	140 547	133 990	1782	135 771	120 419

Table 5.9 (continued)

Year	Income				Disbursements			Balance at end of Year
	Payroll Taxes	Reimbursement for Uninsured Persons	Interest and other income[1]	Total	Benefit Payments[2]	Administrative Expenses	Total	
Intermediate Estimates:								
1999	128 880	652	16 134	145 666	143 140	2051	145 191	120 894
2000	133 464	470	16 835	150 769	140 238	2223	142 461	129 202
2001	139 172	202	17 944	157 318	148 215	2344	150 559	135 962
2002	145 134	170	18 576	163 880	154 759	2451	157 210	142 632
2003	151 571	158	19 223	170 952	163 082	2553	165 635	147 949
2004	158 636	156	19 851	178 643	171 821	2606	174 427	152 165
2005	166 685	161	20 488	187 334	181 949	2667	184 616	154 883
2006	174 808	168	21 117	196 093	193 252	2737	195 989	154 987
2007	183 966	175	21 746	205 887	205 309	2816	208 125	152 749
2008	193 100	179	22 411	215 690	217 910	2901	220 811	147 628

Notes:
[1] Other income includes railroad retirement account transfers, premiums from voluntary enrollees, payments for military wage credits and, beginning in 1994, the income from the taxation of benefits.
[2] For the period 1998 to 2008, benefit payments include monies transferred to the Supplementary Medical Insurance Trust Fund for home health agency costs, as provided for in Public Law 105–33.

Source: Board of Trustees, Federal Hospital Insurance Trust Fund, *1999 Annual Report* (Washington, DC, June, 1999): Table II.D2 (pp. 34–5).

*Table 5.10   Total Benefits Under the Supplementary Medical Insurance
Program, Calendar Years 1967–2008*

	Aggregate Benefits (millions) (%)	Percent Change	Per Capita Benefits ($)[1]	Percent Change	SMI Benefits as a Percent of GDP
Historical Data:					
1967	1197	–	66.97	–	0.14
1968	1518	26.8	82.27	22.8	0.17
1969	1865	22.9	97.86	19.0	0.19
1970	1975	5.9	101.30	3.5	0.19
1971	2117	7.2	106.68	5.3	0.19
1972	2325	9.8	114.91	7.7	0.19
1973	2526	8.6	122.02	6.2	0.18
1974	3318	31.4	144.47	18.4	0.22
1975	4273	28.8	179.96	24.6	0.26
1976	5080	18.9	207.39	15.2	0.28
1977	6038	18.9	239.27	15.4	0.30
1978	7252	20.1	279.58	16.8	0.32
1979	8708	20.1	326.86	16.9	0.34
1980	10 635	22.1	389.87	19.3	0.38
1981	13 113	23.3	471.15	20.8	0.42
1982	15 455	17.9	545.55	15.8	0.48
1983	18 106	17.2	627.79	15.1	0.52
1984	19 661	8.6	670.77	6.8	0.50
1985	22 947	16.7	768.25	14.5	0.55
1986	26 239	14.3	861.37	12.1	0.59
1987	30 820	17.5	992.69	15.2	0.68
1988	33 970	10.2	1076.64	8.5	0.67
1989	38 294	12.7	1195.42	11.0	0.70
1990	42 468	10.9	1305.14	9.2	0.74
1991	47 336	11.5	1426.90	9.3	0.80
1992	49 260	4.1	1454.81	2.0	0.79
1993	53 979	9.6	1562.66	7.4	0.82
1994	58 618	8.6	1670.03	6.9	0.85
1995	64 972	10.8	1824.03	9.2	0.90
1996	68 599	5.6	1901.88	4.3	0.90
1997	72 756	6.1	1998.68	5.1	0.90
1998	76 125	4.6	2074.65	3.9	0.89
Intermediate Estimates:					
1999	83 403	9.6	2258.03	8.8	0.94
2000	95 666	14.7	2567.11	13.7	1.04
2001	101 539	6.1	2669.46	5.2	1.06
2002	110 098	8.4	2899.25	7.4	1.10
2003	119 448	8.5	3111.05	7.3	1.14
2004	128 035	7.2	3294.56	5.9	1.16
2005	136 799	6.8	3475.22	5.5	1.18
2006	147 169	7.6	3686.45	6.1	1.21
2007	158 882	8.0	3914.20	6.2	1.24
2008	172 071	8.3	4156.51	6.2	1.28

Notes: [1] All Part B enrollees.

Source: Data for 1967 through 1984: Board of Trustees, Federal Supplementary Medical Insurance Trust Fund, *1996 Annual Report* (Washington, DC, June 1996): Table II:D3 (pp. 34–5).
Data for 1985 through 2008: Board of Trustees, Federal Supplementary Medical Insurance Trust Fund, *1999 Annual Report* (Washington, DC: June 1999): Table II:D3 (p. 31).

Table 5.11   Operations of the Supplementary Medical Insurance Trust Fund, Calendar Years 1970–2008 (millions)

	Income				Disbursement			Balance at end of Year
Year	Premiums from enrollees	Government Contributions[1]	Interest and other income	Total	Benefit Payments[2]	Administrative Expenses	Total	
Historical Data:								
1970	1096	1093	12	2201	1975	237	2212	188
1975	1918	2648	107	4673	4279	462	4735	1444
1980	3011	7455	408	10 874	10 635	610	11 245	4530
1985	5613	18 250	1243	25 106	22 947	933	23 880	10 924
1986	5722	17 802	1141	24 665	26 239	1060	27 299	8291
1987	7409	23 560	875	31 844	30 820	920	31 740	8394
1988	8761	26 203	861	35 825	33 970	1260	35 230	8990
1989	12 263	30 852	1234	44 349	38 294	1489	39 783	13 556
1990	11 320	33 035	1558	45 913	42 468	1519	43 987	15 482
1991	11 934	37 602	1688	51 224	47 336	1541	48 877	17 828
1992	14 077	41 359	1801	57 237	49 260	1570	50 830	24 235
1993	14 193	41 465	2021	57 679	55 780	2000	57 784	24 131
1994	17 386	36 203	2018	55 607	58 618	1699	60 317	19 422
1995	19 717	39 007	1582	60 306	64 972	1627	65 599	13 130
1996	18 763	65 035	1811	85 609	68 598	1810	70 408	28 332
1997	19 289	60 171	2464	81 924	72 757	1368	74 124	36 131
1998	20 933	64 068	2711	87 711	76 125	1505	77 630	46 212

Intermediate Estimates:

1999	18 655	58 096	2821	79 572	83 403	1549	84 953	40 832
2000	21 689	70 009	2779	94 477	95 666	1596	97 261	38 047
2001	23 607	76 056	2686	102 348	101 539	1650	103 188	37 207
2002	25 747	83 236	2668	111 650	110 098	1708	111 805	37 052
2003	28 335	91 426	2677	122 438	119 448	1771	121 219	38 272
2004	30 919	96 831	2730	130 480	128 035	1840	129 875	38 877
2005	33 019	103 627	2773	139 419	136 799	1915	138 715	39 581
2006	35 834	112 247	2854	150 934	147 169	1994	149 163	41 452
2007	38 968	122 086	3018	164 071	158 882	2078	160 960	44 464
2008	42 226	132 242	3250	177 719	172 071	2167	174 238	47 944

Notes:
[1] Government contributions constitute transfers from the general fund of the Treasury and are determined by calculating the expected cost per beneficiary less expected premium collections, following a formula set down by statute.
[2] Benefit payments less monies transferred from the Hospital Insurance Trust Fund for home agency costs, as provided by the Balanced Budget Act of 1997.

Source: Board of Trustees, Federal Supplementary Medical Insurance Trust Fund, *1996 Annual Report* (Washington, DC, June 1996): Table II.D2 (p. 28).

Table 5.12 *Comparative Growth Rates of Medicare, Private Health Insurance, and National Health Expenditures, 2000–2014*

Calendar year	Incurred outlays minus dedicated revenues (%)	Incurred Medicare outlays (%)	Average Annual Growth Rate in:		
			GDP (%)	National health expenditures (%)	Private health insurance (%)
2000	-6.9	5.8	5.9	7.2	8.9
2001	29.3	10.2	3.2	8.9	10.2
2002	22.6	7.4	3.5	9.3	10.6
2003	23.6	6.4	4.9	7.7	9.3
2004	14.3	9.0	6.7	7.5	7.7
2005	6.0	7.8	5.3	7.3	6.7
2006	57.7	30.3	5.4	7.3	4.6
2007	7.0	6.4	5.3	7.5	7.4
2008	8.2	6.7	5.2	7.5	7.6
2009	6.6	6.3	5.1	7.3	7.4
2010	9.1	6.6	5.0	7.0	6.9
2011	6.6	6.6	5.0	6.9	6.8
2012	10.4	8.2	4.9	6.9	6.4
2013	11.9	8.9	4.8	6.8	6.3
2014	11.6	8.8	4.7	6.7	5.9
2015–2029	10.0	8.1	4.5		
2030–2054	6.6	6.0	4.4		
2055–2079	6.0	5.7	4.3		

Source: Board of Trusteees, Federal Hospital Insurance and Federal Supplementary Medical Insurance Trust Funds, *2005 Annual Report* (Washington, DC: June 2005): Table III.A5 (p. 34).

488

NOTES

1. The details of this state-socialist program and the motives that impelled Bismarck to craft these measures can be found in Otto Pflanze, *Bismarck and the Development of Germany*, vol. III: *The Period of Fortification: 1880–1898* (Princeton, NJ: Princeton University Press, 1990): 145–84. Bismarck's sentiments in placing this legislation before the Reichstag were best expressed in his *Motive* that accompanied the first accident insurance bill: 'That the state should assist its needy citizens to a greater degree than before is not only a Christian and humanitarian duty, of which the state apparatus should be fully conscious; it is also a task to be undertaken for the preservation of the state itself. The goal of this task is to nurture among the unpropertied classes of the population, which are the most numerous as well as least informed, the view that the state is not only a necessary but also a beneficent institution.' Quoted in Pflanze, *Bismarck*, III: 159.

2. For a detailed examination of the provisions of the health insurance bill and its amendments by one of its chief admirers, see William Harbutt Dawson, *Social Insurance in Germany, 1883–1911* (London: T. Fisher Unwin, 1912). In writing of Bismarck's policies, Dawson, at his most repellent, notes of German politics, 'long before the era of constitutional government and Parliamentary systems, wise rulers and far-seeing Ministers were always ready, when social evils became acute and new conditions and needs arose, to take occasion by the hand and readjust discordant relationships even in the absence of the active pressure of popular demand' (p. 2). Dawson's book contains not one word of criticism of Bismarck's policies and the chapter that is devoted to the 'attitudes of employers and workpeople' towards the social insurance act is an unrelieved litany of praise.

3. Austria enacted similar legislation in 1888; Hungary, in 1891; Luxembourg, in 1901; Norway, in 1909, Serbia, in 1910; Great Britain, in 1911; Russia, in 1912; and Romania, in 1913. Ronald Numbers, *Almost Persuaded: American Physicians and Compulsory Health Insurance, 1912–1920* (Baltimore: Johns Hopkins University Press, 1978): 10.

4. Daniel M. Fox, *Health Policies, Health Politics: The British and American Experience, 1911–1965* (Princeton, NJ: Princeton University Press, 1986): 5

5. The Act covered about one-third of the population of Great Britain. J. Rogers Hollingsworth, *A Political Economy of Medicine: Great Britain and the United States* (Baltimore: Johns Hopkins University Press, 1986): 24.

6. Details of the original program are contained in Hollingsworth, *Political Economy of Medicine*, 19–25.

7. Fox, *Health Policies, Health Politics*, 8.

8. Richard Harris, *A Sacred Trust* (Baltimore, Md.: Penguin Books Inc., 1966): 4. In fact, a compulsory government-administered health insurance scheme had a long history. In 1798 Congress enacted legislation that provided hospital care for merchant seamen, the cost of which was originally underwritten by compulsory monthly contributions from those covered. The 'care' to which they were entitled was provided by the Marine Hospital Service, forerunner of the United States Public Health Service. The plan as originally conceived, proved unworkable and eventually degenerated into hospital care for indigent seamen, financed out of general revenues (Herman Miles Somers and Anne Ramsay Somers, *Medicare and the Hospitals: Issues and Prospects* (Washington, DC: The Brookings Institution, 1967): 1–2).

9. Henry F. Pringle, *Theodore Roosevelt* (New York: Harcourt, Brace, 1956): 396–7.

10. See Lafayette G. Harter, *John R. Commons: His Assault on Laissez-Faire* (Corvallis, Oregon: Oregon State University Press, 1962). From his base at the University of Wisconsin, Commons was able to successfully lobby for three of Wisconsin's pathbreaking reforms: (1) the regulation of the state's public utilities by an administrative commission; (2) the creation of the Wisconsin Industrial Commission to regulate safety in the workplace and to administer a workmen's compensation program; and (3) the institution of unemployment compensation. Harter argues that Commons' 'greatest contribution to government was his share in the development of the administrative commission' (p. 4). Indeed, Commons was one of the originators of the regulatory and administrative agency

which would be possessed of sufficient flexibility to determine the outcome of specific cases that came before it on an ad hoc basis, a flexibility ordinarily denied the courts. See Edward Berkowitz and Kim McQuaid, *Creating the Welfare State: The Political Economy of Twentieth-Century Reform* (2nd edn, rev.; New York: Praeger, 1988): 47.

11.	James G. Burrow, *Organized Medicine in the Progressive Era: The Move Toward Monopoly* (Baltimore: Johns Hopkins University Press 1977): 140.

12.	The Socialist Party had called for the establishment of a national system of health insurance in 1904.

13.	Numbers, *Almost Persuaded*, 15–16.

14.	Lloyd F. Pierce, 'The Activities of the American Association for Labor Legislation in Behalf of Social Security and Protective Labor Legislation', Ph.D. dissertation, University of Wisconsin, 1953, quoted in Numbers, *Almost Persuaded*, 16.

15.	Numbers, *Almost Persuaded*, 15.

16.	The term was understood to incorporate a whole series of government-administered compulsory insurance schemes, including accident insurance, unemployment insurance, old-age insurance, disability insurance, and, of course, medical insurance.

17.	Numbers, *Almost Persuaded*, 16. Among the Committee's members were Edward Devine, Director of the New York School of Philanthropy, Henry R. Seager, Professor of Economics at Columbia University, and Isaac M. Rubinow.

18.	Robert J. Myers, *Medicare* (Bryn Mawr, Pa.: McCahan Foundation, 1970): 4–7.

19.	See Ronald Hamowy, 'The Early Development of Medical Licensing Laws in the United States, 1875–1900', *Journal of Libertarian Studies*, 3 (Spring 1979): 73–119.

20.	Burrow, *Organized Medicine in the Progressive Era*, 142.

21.	Numbers, *Almost Persuaded*, 33. In mid-1917 the Committee on Social Insurance admonished those in the medical profession who opposed any compulsory government-administered health insurance scheme in the following words: 'To work out these problems [that might arise with such a plan] is a most difficult task. The time to work them out, however, is when the laws are molding, as now, and the time is present when the profession should surely study earnestly to solve the questions of medical care that will arise under various forms of social insurance. Blind opposition, indignant repudiation, bitter denunciation of these laws is worse than useless; it leads nowhere and it leaves the profession in a position of helplessness as the rising tide of social development sweeps over it' (*JAMA*, 68 (9 June 1917): 1755).

22.	'A Model Bill for Health Insurance', *JAMA*, 65 (20 November 1915): 1824.

23.	Quoted in Numbers, *Almost Persuaded*, 34.

24.	London Correspondent, 'Mr. Lloyd-George on the Insurance Act', *JAMA*, 62 (1914): 789, and 'Medical Remuneration under the Insurance Act', *JAMA*, 62 (1914): 945, quoted in Numbers, *Almost Persuaded*, 32.

25.	*Journal of the South Carolina Medical Association*, 12 (1916): 260, quoted in Numbers, *Almost Persuaded*, 125, n. 28.

26.	James Rorty, *American Medicine Mobilizes* (New York: W. W. Norton & Co., Inc., 1939): 74–5.

27.	Peter A. Corning, *The Evolution of Medicare . . . from Idea to Law* (Washington, DC: US Department of Health, Education, and Welfare, Social Security Administration, Office of Research and Statistics, 1970): 9.

28.	Substantial representation on such boards was, of course, crucial since the prospective health authority was empowered to draw up the fee schedules determining physician compensation.

29.	The response of the medical profession to the proposal to institute a national compulsory health insurance plan, both favorable and unfavorable, is discussed in some detail in Numbers, *Almost Persuaded*, *passim*, and Burrow, *Organized Medicine in the Progressive Era*, 133–53.

30.	Howard Wolinsky and Tom Brune, *The Serpent on the Staff: The Unhealthy Politics of the American Medical Association* (New York: G. P. Putman's Sons, 1994): 18.

31.	These views were apparently voiced by, among others, George MacAdams, 'Do We Want to Pay the Health Insurance Bill?', *New York Times Magazine*, 11 March 1917, p. 11, quoted in Burrow, *Organized Medicine in the Progressive Era*, 153.

32. Numbers, *Almost Persuaded*, 77.
33. Ibid., 76.
34. Thomas W. Huntington, 'Address of the President', American Surgical Association, *Transactions*, 36 (1918): 5–6, quoted in Numbers, *Almost Persuaded*, 77.
35. That the campaign to institute a mandatory national system of medical insurance proved unsuccessful in large part because Americans still embraced free market and Social Darwinist views has no historical warrant. See Peter A. Corning, *The Evolution of Medicare*, 12–13.
36. It is worth noting that the costs of physicians' services for most American workers was not prohibitively high prior to the 1920s. A substantial number of proprietary medical schools graduated an abundance of practitioners until release of the Flexner Report in 1910 encouraged the various state licensing boards to set their criteria for acceptable medical education at a level that most of these schools were unable to meet. Nor indeed was medical care itself particularly efficacious for most ailments before the late 1930s, when the sulfonamide drugs came into common use, while it was only in World War II that penicillin was introduced as a therapeutic agent. And what held for physicians' services was equally true for hospital care, which most Americans regarded as necessary only in cases of surgery or tuberculosis. Finally, to the extent that private health insurance policies were available, most offered benefits in terms of cash payments for disability or illness rather than medical services. For a comprehensive discussion of the financing of medical care in the United States prior to the introduction of Medicare, see Herman Miles Somers and Anne Ramsay Somers, *Doctors, Patients, and Health Insurance: The Organization and Financing of Medical Care* (Washington, DC: The Brookings Institution, 1961).
37. The socialist muckraker and author Upton Sinclair won the Democratic nomination for governor of California in 1933 on a platform which he called End Poverty in California (EPIC). His supporters, organized into the End Poverty League, embraced Sinclair's plan to have the state of California institute a state-wide system of production and exchange, in which the state would set up land colonies in which farmers would live and produce the state's food while at the same time the state would employ all the urban unemployed in government factories and 'great productive units'. Sinclair was defeated for the governorship, largely through the defection of manufacturers and other businessmen who would otherwise have supported the party. Excerpts from Sinclair's plan appear in Edward H. Merrill, *Responses to Economic Collapse: The Great Depression of the 1930's* (Boston, MA: D. C. Heath and Co., 1964): 101–4.
38. With an eye to running for the Presidency in 1936, Long, in 1934, set out an economic program for the country which he called the Share Our Wealth Plan. It called for the confiscation of all large fortunes and the redistribution of this wealth to all those in need (that is, those with an estate worth less than $5000). Each family would be guaranteed a 'household estate' of $5000 (sufficient to provide each recipient with a house, an automobile, a radio, and other 'necessities'), together with a guaranteed annual income of $2500 per year. Share Our Wealth Clubs became extremely popular, especially in the South and West, and Long's slogan 'Every man a king, but no one wears a crown' became a rallying cry for hundreds of thousands of American workers and farmers. See Alan Brinkley, *Voices of Protest: Huey Long, Father Coughlin, and the Great Depression* (New York: Alfred A. Knopf, 1982): *passim*.
39. Townsend's Old Age Revolving Pension Plan was based on the crackpot program earlier put forward by Major C. H. Douglas, founder of the Social Credit movement. Townsend's plan called for the federal government to pay every unemployed American over the age of 60 a pension of $200 per month (estimates put this amount at approximately twice the average income of workers). Pensioners were required to spend the full amount each month in order to be eligible for the next month's payment. Payments were to be financed by a 2 percent federal sales tax. The proposal was received with such enthusiasm that thousands of Townsend clubs were established, not only in Townsend's home state of California, but throughout the country. A bill to enact Townsend's scheme was actually put before the House of Representatives in 1939 and received 101 votes! See Edward Merrill, *Responses to Economic Collapse*, 97–100.

40. The committee's executive director was Edwin E. Witte, chairman of the economics department of the University of Wisconsin. Witte, like Hopkins and Wallace and, indeed, like the President himself, all embraced a 'purchasing-power' thesis respecting the cause of the Depression: that what lay at its root was an inequitable distribution of purchasing power which, in turn, led to consumptive capacity lagging behind productive capacity. The result was overproduction and unemployment. Recovery, it was thought, rested on increasing total purchasing power and this required that a larger share of the national income go to wages rather than profits. For a discussion of this 'explanation' and its adherents, see Theodore Rosenof, *Dogma, Depression, and the New Deal: The Debate of Political Leaders over Economic Recovery* (Port Washington, NY: Kennikat Press, 1975): 39–43.

41. Fearful that a national mandatory social security system would be struck down by the Supreme Court, Frances Perkins is reported to have asked Justice Harlan F. Stone, then on the Court, whether he thought the program might fail, to which Stone is reputed to have replied 'The taxing power of the federal government, my dear; the taxing power is sufficient for everything you want and need'. Frances Perkins, *The Roosevelt I Knew* (New York: Viking Press, 1946): 286. As a result, the legislation eventually enacted by Congress provided that unemployment insurance be based on a tax placed on employers and that old-age pensions be ostensibly paid for through payroll taxes levied on both employer and employee. Lewis E. Weeks and Howard J. Berman, eds, *Shapers of American Health Care Policy: An Oral History* (Ann Arbor: Health Administration Press, 1985): 53.

42. For brief discussions of the Committee's work, see James G. Burrow, *AMA: Voice of American Medicine* (Baltimore: Johns Hopkins Press, 1963): 180–83; and James Rorty, *American Medicine Mobilizes* (New York: W.W. Norton, 1939) *passim*.

43. Hopkins had at one time directed the New Orleans Red Cross and had been the director of the New York Tuberculosis and Health Association before being appointed to head the Federal Emergency Relief Administration.

44. The campaign against enactment of a compulsory health-insurance bill was led by the *JAMA*'s editor, Dr Morris Fishbein, probably the most powerful medical lobbyist in the country. Not only was Fishbein considered the leading spokesman on questions relating to the medical profession and its relation to government policy but, as the editor of the *JAMA* from 1924 to 1949, his views came to dominate the meetings of the AMA's Board of Trustees.

45. The decisive issue for Roosevelt appears to have been the 1936 presidential election. He apparently felt it essential to get a social security bill enacted prior to the campaign and was advised that it was unlikely to be passed expeditiously if health insurance were included as a part of the legislation. Weeks and Berman, eds, *Shapers of American Medical Policy*, 53, The social security bill did in fact pass Congress in August 1935.

46. Corning, *The Evolution of Medicare*, 44.

47. Among the findings of the *National Health Survey* of 1935–36 were: (1) those with incomes below $1000 per year suffered from 47 percent more acute illnesses and 87 percent more chronic illnesses than did those with incomes above $3000 per year; (2) the duration of illness for those on relief was 63 percent longer than for the rest of the population; (3) 30 percent of those on relief were not receiving medical care for disabling illnesses lasting a week or longer (versus 17 percent for those with an income above $3000 per year); (4) annual mortality rates from accidents and infant mortality rates exceeded that of any other industrialized nation; (5) 40 percent of the nation's counties, containing 18 000 000 people, possessed no registered general hospital; and, finally, (6) a substantial portion of the American population simply could not afford the costs of medical care. The Survey concluded that it would cost approximately $850 000 000 a year to provide adequate medical coverage for the lowest income groups. Excerpts from the Survey's conclusions are quoted in Rorty, *American Medicine Mobilizes*, 22–4.

48. Ibid., 21.

49. Burrow, *AMA: Voice of American Medicine*, 216.

50. The recommendations are printed in full in Rorty, *American Medicine Mobilizes*, 312–19.

51. This amount would have increased the federal government's expenditures on health by a factor of 17! In 1940, federal expenditures on health, exclusive of the Veterans Administration, amounted to approximately $55 000 000.

52. See Burrow, *AMA: Voice of American Medicine*, 205–27. The AMA's representatives at the Conference apparently had no objection to the other four recommendations and a delegation of AMA leaders, meeting with the members of the Interdepartmental Committee to Coordinate Health and Welfare Activities, offered to support the other recommendations if the government were prepared to drop its insistence on passage of a compulsory health-insurance scheme. Corning, *The Evolution of Medicare*, 48.

53. In 1935 the California legislature had established a committee to study the creation of a state-wide compulsory health insurance plan and the California Medical Association had agreed to cooperate with the committee in drafting an acceptable program. The plan that was eventually recommended provided for compulsory medical insurance for all employees (including agricultural and domestic workers) earning less than $3000 per year while allowing voluntary enrollment to those earning over that amount. Employers who provided suitable alternative medical-care plans were permitted to opt out of the government program. The plan's medical care coverage was extensive and included almost all hospitalization and prescription drug costs. There was even provision to allow for the inclusion of dental care, should sufficient funds be available. The plan was to be financed by contributions of 1.5 percent of income from the employer and 3.5 percent from each employee, with persons voluntarily covered paying the full 5 percent, up to a $3000 annual maximum. The proposal, which called for no regulation of physicians' fees, was considered by the California State Assembly in 1939 and, despite the fact that the state medical association had played a role in its drafting, was decisively defeated. Myers, *Medicare*, 16–17.

54. Senator Wagner had introduced similar legislation in 1939 and in fact had arranged for hearings on the bill that April but the attempt to gain support for its passage failed, in large part because Roosevelt hoped to make national health insurance a campaign issue when the President came up for re-election in 1940. Corning, *The Evolution of Medicare*, 48–9. It thus seems clear that Roosevelt had determined to run for a third term as early as 1938.

55. It appears that by 1943 most Americans, influenced by a decade of government propaganda, believed that market forces were responsible for the economic ills that the nation had suffered in the 1930s and that government intervention alone was able to provide a social safety net to protect the great mass of people from the horrors of an unrestrained capitalist system. As a consequence, public opinion shifted in favor of a compulsory national health insurance program. While in 1938 only 53 percent of the public supported health insurance of any kind, either public *or* private, by 1942 no fewer than 74 percent favored national health insurance. See Corning, *The Evolution of Medicare*, 48 n., and Monte Poen, *Harry S. Truman Versus the Medical Lobby: The Genesis of Medicare* (Columbia, Mo.: University of Missouri Press, 1979): 30.

56. In 1942 the Social Security Board announced its support for a comprehensive system of social insurance, including health benefits, and in fact was instrumental in drafting the Wagner-Murray-Dingell bill.

57. See Corning, The *Evolution of Medicare*, 56. Roosevelt appears to have been outraged that Sir William Beveridge was being credited with having authored the blueprint for the modern welfare state. When the Beveridge Report (under the title *Social Insurance and Allied Services*) was released in November 1942, Roosevelt is reported to have whined to his Secretary of Labor, Frances Perkins, 'Why does Beveridge get his name on this? Why does he get credit for this? You know that I have been talking about cradle to grave insurance ever since we first thought of it. It is my idea. It is not the Beveridge plan. It is the Roosevelt plan.' Frances Perkins, *The Roosevelt I Knew*, 144.

58. Somers and Somers, *Medicare and the Hospitals*, 4.

59. The provisions respecting veterans' benefits were eliminated inasmuch as the GI Bill had been enacted in the meantime.

60. Apparently the public were less enthusiastic about a compulsory national insurance scheme than had been the case earlier. A Gallup poll taken in late 1949 showed only 51 percent supported the measure. Corning, *The Evolution of Medicare*, 67. In the same year all the major welfare organizations of the Catholic church opposed the notion of government insurance, as did the General Federation of Women and the National Medical Association, both earlier supporters. Poen, *Harry S. Truman Versus the Medical Lobby*, 161–2.

61. Burrow, *AMA: Voice of American Medicine*, 374.
62. The Federal Security Agency was created in 1939 to bring together most of the health, welfare, and education services of the federal government and, in turn, became the core component of the Department of Health, Education, and Welfare when it was established in 1953.
63. See Theodore R. Marmor, *The Politics of Medicare* (London: Routledge & Kegan Paul, 1970): 13–14.
64. Marmor, *The Politics of Medicare*, 14.
65. The health commission established by President Truman in 1952 had concluded that Americans over 65 were indeed poorer and in greater need of medical care for which they lacked insurance than was the average American and these data were often cited in support of linking hospital insurance to social security. However, as one analyst has observed: 'Proof that the aged were the most needy was based on calculation for *all* persons over 65. Yet social security financing would in 1952 have restricted Medicare benefits to seven million pensioners out of the twelve and one-half million persons over 65. This would have meant not insuring five and one-half million aged whose medical and financial circumstances had been used to establish the "need" for a Medicare program in the first place'. Marmor, *The Politics of Medicare*, 22.
66. The political implications of this new approach to government health insurance are discussed at length in Marmor, *The Politics of Medicare*, 13–28.
67. Corning, *The Evolution of Medicare*, 75.
68. Ibid., 80–81.
69. Private health insurance had witnessed a spectacular growth during the postwar years. The Secretary of Health, Education, and Welfare, Marion B. Folsom, testified before hearings on the Forand bill that between 1952 and 1958 the number of people covered by hospitalization policies had increased from 91 million to 121 million; those covered by surgical insurance had risen from 73 million to 109 million; and those covered by medical insurance had doubled, from 36 million to 72 million.

Percent of Individuals with Health Insurance Prior to the Introduction of Medicare By Type of Coverage

Type of Coverage	1953 (%)	1958 (%)	1963 (%)
Hospital	57	65	68
Surgical-medical	48	61	66
Outpatient doctor visits[1]	2	2	35
Major medical	2	2	22
Outpatient drugs[3]	2	2	26
Dental	2	2	2

Notes:
[1] Includes first dollar doctor visit coverage as written by prepaid group practice plans, unions, and certain other insurers, and all major medical policies whether or not connected with a base plan.
[2] Not available.
[3] Includes first dollar drug coverage as written by some prepaid group practices, unions, and certain other insurers, and major medical policies.

Source: US Department of Health, Education, and Welfare, Public Health Service, Health Resources Administration, National Center for Health Statistics, *Health: United States 1975* (Washington, DC, 1976): Table A-3 (p. 51).

70. Richard Harris, *A Sacred Trust* (Baltimore: Penguin Books, Inc., 1966): 78. Apparently the Eisenhower Administration's own estimates showed that the bill would cost less than

$1 billion a year and that there was little likelihood of its unbalancing the social security budget (p. 78).

71. Corning, *The Evolution of Medicare*, 84. It appears that when, in the spring of 1960, Walter Reuther, the President of the United Auto Workers and one of the leading proponents of a national health insurance bill, urged Lyndon Johnson to publicly endorse the Forand bill, Johnson agreed to do so only on condition that Reuther support Johnson's bid for the Presidential nomination. Despite the fact that Reuther is reported to have been unwilling to commit himself, Johnson did speak in favor of the proposal. Harris, *A Sacred Trust*, 108.

72. Congress appeared deadlocked between Democrat-sponsored measures that sought to extend hospital insurance to all the elderly, and the approach favored by Republicans (and embodied in a bill proposed by Senator Jacob Javits of New York) that limited federal grants for medical care to the lower-income elderly only. One analyst has charted the distinctions between the two approaches in the following way:

	Forand Social Security Approach	*Welfare Approach*
Beneficiaries:	Only the aged who were covered under social security	Anyone over 65 whose resources were insufficient to meet his medical expenses
Benefits:	Hospitalization, nursing, home and in-hospital surgical insurance (Medicare bills introduced after 1959 specified hospitals and nursing home insurance only).	Comprehensive benefits for physicians' services, dental care, hospitalization, prescribed drugs, and nursing care.
Source of financing:	Regressive social security taxes	Progressive federal income tax revenues, plus state matching funds
Administration and Setting of Standards:	Uniform national standards administered by the Social Security Administration.	Standards varying by state, administered by state and local officials

Theodore R. Marmor, *The Politics of Medicare* (London: Routledge, Kegan Paul, 1970): 38. Marmor points to the irony of the two approaches. While the Forand backers wished to extend benefits to all social security beneficiaries, it proposed limiting benefits to hospital and surgical insurance, to be paid for by a regressive social security tax. The more conservative welfare advocates, on the other hand, proposed a broader package of benefits for a smaller group, to be financed by progressive federal tax revenues (p. 37).

73. Only Senators Barry Goldwater of Arizona and Strom Thurmond of South Carolina opposed the measure.

74. Harris, *A Sacred Trust*, 117. A group known as Senior Citizens for Kennedy, headed by none other than newly retired Congressman Aimé Forand, was formed to keep the issue before the public (Corning, *The Evolution of Medicare*, 87).

75. Ibid., 87.

76. Certainly such a provision would have won the immediate enmity of the medical profession which remained adamantly opposed to any government determination of the fees paid doctors. In any case this appears to have made no difference since physicians regarded the King-Anderson proposal as a first step towards a completely socialized medical system.

77. Frank D. Campion, *The AMA and U.S. Health Policy Since 1940* (Chicago: Chicago Review Press, 1984): 216. No political action committee existed prior to the creation of AMPAC except the Committee on Political Education (COPE) of the AFL-CIO, formed in 1943 for the purpose of achieving organized labor's political objectives.

78. Blue Cross had its origins in the Depression, when hospitals hit upon the scheme of instituting prepayment plans for hospital care as a cure for the large number of empty beds with

which they were faced. The movement, which started at the Baylor University Hospital in Dallas, Texas, in 1929, soon spread to other cities and expanded into community-wide programs. In 1934 the American College of Surgeons formally endorsed such prepayment plans for medical and surgical services and four years later the American Medical Association approved them. In 1940 there were over 6 000 000 enrollees in Blue Cross plans covering hospitalization and 370 000 enrollees in Blue Shield plans covering surgical expenses. By 1958 these numbers had grown to 52 000 000 and 40 400 00 respectively and there is every reason to believe that both plans would have continued to sign up new members at the same rate. If one were to add all those covered by commercial medical insurance, the totals in 1958 show that approximately 128 000 000 people, or about 72 percent of the civilian population, had some form of hospital insurance. This figure probably includes a 5 to 6 percent overlap while of those covered about 75 to 80 percent held group rather than individual coverage. However, in the early 1950s insurance companies had started offering benefits programs that covered all major medical expenses whether the enrollee were part of a group or not and by the close of the decade both Blue Cross-Blue Shield and the commercial carriers began designing programs to provide comprehensive medical coverage for the elderly (Somers and Somers, *Doctors, Patients, and Health Insurance*, 364). The history of private attempts to provide medical insurance to the public belies Wilbur Cohen's self-serving claim that 'the political threat of Federal legislative action on health insurance in the 1930's and early 1940's and the economic impact of wage and price controls during World War II and the Korean War [were what] stimulated private and commercial health insurance plans to expand their coverage' (Wilbur J. Cohen, 'Policy Planning for National Health Insurance', in US Department of Health, Education, and Welfare, *Health in America: 1776–1976* (DHEW Pub. No. (HRA) 76-616) (Washington, DC: 1976): 175). It is true that the introduction of wage and price controls and the absence of controls on corporate profits during World War II encouraged firms to increase wages in the form of fringe benefits including health insurance, but this is hardly sufficient to account for the spectacular growth in medical prepayment plans after 1945.

79. Harris, *A Sacred Trust*, 125.
80. For an extended discussion of the composition of this committee in the context of the Anderson-King bill, see Marmor, *The Politics of Medicare*, 44–53.
81. Corning, *The Evolution of Medicare*, 91; Harris, *A Sacred Trust*, 132–3. The Committee hardly represented the wishes of most physicians. In the spring of 1961 the *Medical Tribune* reported that no fewer than 81 percent of American physicians were opposed to the King-Anderson bill (Harris, *A Sacred Trust*, 130).
82. Including the United Auto Workers, the United Steel Workers, and the International Ladies Garment Workers Union (Corning, *The Evolution of Medicare*, 91).
83. Harris, *A Sacred Trust*, 142.
84. Corning, *The Evolution of Medicare*, 92–3.
85. Ibid., 95–6.
86. HEW's congressional liaison staff estimated in 1961 that the House breakdown on Medicare was about 23 votes short of the 218-seat majority (Marmor, *The Politics of Medicare*, 58).
87. Harris, *A Sacred Trust*, 149.
88. Corning, *The Evolution of Medicare*, 107.
89. *Wall Street Journal*, 25 March 1964, quoted in Harris, *A Sacred Trust*, 162.
90. Corning, *The Evolution of Medicare*, 108.
91. Ibid., 104.
92. Marmor, *The Politics of Medicare*, 60. Wilbur Mills' role during the conference committee's deliberations are recounted in Harris, *A Sacred Trust*, 167–71.
93. The American Medical Association was not above suggesting in some of its election propaganda that supporters of Medicare were playing into the hands of the world communist conspiracy. There is, however, no evidence to support the contention that 'as many as a third of the members of the A.M.A.'s House of Delegates [were] also members of the John Birch Society'. Harris, *A Sacred Trust*, 172.

94. Somers and Somers, *Medicare and the Hospitals*, 12.
95. Harris, *A Sacred Trust*. 174.
96. Marmor, *The Politics of Medicare*, 63.
97. Harris, *A Sacred Trust*, 174.
98. For a detailed discussion of the provisions of the various health insurance proposals and modifications introduced into Congress between 1961 and 1964, see Myers, *Medicare*, 42–50.
99. Marmor, *The Politics of Medicare*, 64.
100. Besides increasing federal matching grants to the states for medical vendor payments, Kerr-Mills also provided for public assistance with medical bills for the medically indigent. Medical Assistance for the Aged (MAA) was extended to those whose incomes and assets might be sufficient to cover their normal living expenses but who were unable to meet the substantial costs of medical care. Federal financing was available to help with the costs of the full range of medical services, including hospitals, nursing homes, physicians, dentists, nurses, physical therapists, laboratory work, prescribed drugs, home health care, and so on.
101. Total costs to the AMA of their campaign to promote Eldercare during 1965 amounted to $1 669 0000 (Campion, *The AMA and U.S. Health Policy*, 274).
102. Marmor, *The Politics of Medicare*, 65.
103. Ibid., 68.
104. The most significant event that occurred during these sessions was a series of surprise amendments put forward by Senator Long to eliminate time limits on the use of hospitals and nursing homes. To underwrite the increased costs associated with this change Long's revisions called for a sliding scale of deductibles, to be paid by the patients themselves based on their incomes. These changes were approved by the Committee – in part because of Long's misuse of a proxy earlier provided to him by Senator J. William Fulbright – but the Administration eventually prevailed on those who had supported the Long amendments and the Committee reversed itself some days later. See Harris, *A Scared Trust*, 196–205,
105. Theodore Marmor (*The Politics of Medicare*, 77–8) has ably summarized the decisions of the Senate-House conference committee as follows:

> *Benefit duration* – House provided 60 days of hospital care after a deductible of $40. Senate provided unlimited duration but with $10 co-insurance payments for each day in excess of 60. *Conference* provided 60 days with the $40 House deductible, and an additional 30 days with the Senate's $10 co-insurance provision.
> *Posthospital extended care (skilled nursing home)* – House provided 20 days of such care with 2 additional days for each unused hospital day, but a maximum of 100 days. Senate provided 100 days but imposed a $5 a day co-insurance for each day in excess of 20. *Conference* adopted Senate version.
> *Posthospital home-health visits* – House authorized 100 visits after hospitalization. Senate increased the number of visits to 175, and deleted requirements of hospitalization. *Conference* adopted House version.
> *Outpatient diagnostic services* – House imposed a $20 deductible with this amount credited against an inpatient hospital deductible imposed at the same hospital within 20 days. Senate imposed a 20 percent co-insurance on such services, removed the credit against the inpatient hospital deductible but allowed a credit for the deductible as an incurred expense under the voluntary supplementary program (for deductible and reimbursement purposes). *Conference* adopted Senate version.
> *Psychiatric facilities* – House provided for 60 days of hospital care with a 180 day lifetime limit in the voluntary supplementary program. Senate moved these services over into basic hospital insurance and increased the lifetime limit to 210 days. *Conference* accepted the Senate version but reduced the lifetime limit to 190 days.

106. An extended summary of the law's provisions appears in William Shonick, *Government and Health Services: Government's Role in the Development of U.S. Health Services,*

1930–1980 (New York: Oxford University Press, 1995): 285–91, from which this account is taken.

107. The following data give some idea of the variation in Medicaid eligibility in a selection of states.

Medicaid Eligibility Requirements: Family of Four, 1986

	Eligibility Standard ($)	Eligibility as a Percentage of the Federal Poverty Level (%)
Alabama	1764	16
California	11 208	100
Indiana	4356	39
New York	8484	76
Texas	3612	32
Average of all 50 states	5665	51
Federal Poverty Level, Family of Four	11 203	100

Source: Ullrich K. Hoffmeyer and Thomas R. McCarthy, eds, *Financing Health Care* (2 vols: Dordrecht: Kluwer Academic Publishers, 1994): Table 15.1 (II:1194).

108. By March 1971 all states except Alaska and Arizona had joined the Medicaid program. The participation of 25 of the 48 states receiving matching grants from the federal government was limited to offering the minimal required five services – and perhaps a few others – solely to the obligatory group of public assistance recipients. In the remaining jurisdictions Medicaid coverage was extended to the categorically linked medically needy as well. Shonick, *Government and Health Services*, 296.

109. Myers, *Medicare*, 64–5.

110. Estimates of income and expenditures for the Hospital Insurance Trust Fund and the Supplementary Medical Insurance Trust Fund under the original 1965 Act are shown in the tables below. These estimates should be compared with the actual data as shown in Tables 5.9 and 5.11.

Original Estimates of the Hospital Insurance Trust Fund, 1965 Act Intermediate Cost Estimates (in millions)

Year	Contributions	Benefit Payments	Administrative Expenses	Interest on Fund	Balance in Fund at End of Year
1966	1617	987	50	18	618
1967	2756	2 210	66	25	1 123
1968	3018	2 406	72	46	1 709
1969	3123	2 623	79	66	2 196
1970	3229	2 860	86	82	2 561
1971	3329	3 077	92	91	2 812
1972	3433	3 303	99	95	2 938
1973	3891	3 540	106	100	3 283
1974	4096	3 788	114	108	3 585
1975	4260	4 047	121	112	3 789
1980	6113	5 307	159	166	5 790
1985	7026	6 860	206	259	8 341
1990	9015	8 797	264	323	10 426

Original Estimates of the Supplementary Medical Insurance Trust Fund, 1965 Act High Cost Estimates (95 Percent Participation) (in millions)

Year	Premiums from Participants	Government Contributions	Benefit Payments	Administrative Expenses	Interest on Fund	Balance at End of Year
1966	325	325	410	100	5	145
1967	665	665	1260	110	5	110

Source: Robert J. Myers, *Medicare* (Bryn Mawr, Pa.: McCahan Foundation, 1970): Tables 10-4 and 10-6 (pp. 200–203).

111.   Shonick, *Government and Health Services*, 291.
112.   A number of these studies appeared in the *Social Security Bulletin*. See especially Regina Loewenstein, 'Early Effects of Medicare on the Health Care of the Aged', *Social Security Bulletin*, 34(4) (April 1971): 3–20; Howard West, 'Five Years of Medicare – A Statistical Review', *Social Security Bulletin*, 34(12) (December 1971): 17–27; Loucele A. Horowitz, 'Medical Care Price Changes in Medicare's First Five Years', *Social Security Bulletin*, 35(3) (March 1972): 16–29; Barbara S. Cooper, 'Medical Care Spending for Three Age Groups: 1966–1971' *Social Security Bulletin*, 35(5) (May, 1972): 3–16; and, Julian H. Pettengill, 'Trends in Hospital Use by the Aged', *Social Security Bulletin*, 35(7) (July 1972): 3–15. A summary of these authors' findings appears in Shonick, *Government and Health Services*, 292–4, to which this account is indebted.
113.   Shonick, *Government and Health Services*, 299. Inasmuch as HMOs are paid in advance to provide a range of medical benefits to their subscribers, there is a strong incentive for them to conserve on the delivery of services, either by increasing preventive care, avoiding unnecessary duplication and overutilization of services, substituting less costly for more expensive forms of health care, and, finally, by simply not providing certain services that would otherwise be available in the marketplace.
114.   William Shonick's discussion of the 1972 legislation forms the basis of this account. See Shonick, *Government and Health Services*, 300–303.
115.   The PSRO program proved to be worse than useless. According to a Congressional Budget Office analysis undertaken in 1980, the program operated at a net loss of between 30 and 60 cents for each dollar it spent (US Congressional Budget Office, *The Impact of PSROs on Health Care Costs: 1980 Update of the CBO Evaluation*, Staff Draft Analysis, 2 May 1980 (Washington, DC: Congressional Budget Office, 1980)).
116.   These came to be known as Section 223 limits, named after the Social Security statute.
117.   Marilyn Moon, *Medicare Now and in the Future* (Washington, DC: The Urban Institute, 1993): 48.
118.   John R. Virts and George W. Wilson, 'Inflation and the Behavior of Sectoral Prices', *Business Economics*, 18(3) (May 1983): 45–54. Their findings are summarized in Jack A. Meyer, *Passing the Health Care Buck: Who Pays the Hidden Cost?* (Washington, DC: American Enterprise Institute for Public Policy Research, 1983): 47–9. The conclusions reached by Virts and Wilson confirmed the findings arrived at as early as 1976. See Martin Feldstein and Amy Talor, *The Rapid Rise of Hospital Costs* (Washington, DC: Council on Wage and Price Stability, January 1977): 20.
119.   Excess demand would thus be translated into queues. This appears to be the method of choice for limiting expenditures on health care in Canada, where long waits in doctors' offices and for 'non-emergency' diagnostic and surgical procedures are the norm.
120.   Judith Bentkover, Philip Caper, Mark Schleslinger, and Joel Suldan, 'Medicare's Payments of Hospitals', in David Blumenthal, Mark Schlesinger, and Pamela Brown Drumheller, *Renewing the Promise: Medicare and Its Reform* (New York: Oxford University Press, 1988): 93.
121.   Shonick, *Government and Health Services*, 328–9.

500 *Government and public health in America*

122. At the outset there were 468 different categories of diagnosis, covering all possible discharge diagnoses listed in the International Classification of Diseases. The number of DRGs has since been somewhat reduced by the Health Care Financing Administration.
123. A number of facilities were either partially or completely exempted from the PPS provisions, including psychiatric hospitals, children's hospitals, and sole community hospitals.
124. National Center for Health Statistics, *Health, United States, 1990* (Hyattsville, Md.: US Public Health Service, 1991).
125. Joe Feingold and James J. Holloway, 'The Initial Impact of the Medicare Prospective Payment System on U.S. Health Care', *Medical Care Review*, 48 (Spring 1991), quoted in Moon, *Medicare Now and in the Future*, 92. There is evidence to suggest that this reduction in average length of hospital stay has, in some cases, been at the expense of the health of some Medicare recipients. A study conducted by the Rand Corporation in 1990 concluded that of the four health conditions studied, hospital readmissions, while falling for the other three, increased for those with myocardial infarctions. Additionally, the proportion of beneficiaries discharged in an unstable condition increased by 22 percent after PPS was initiated. Of those patients discharged home, as opposed to some institution, the discharge rate for unstable patients rose to 43 percent. Katherine Kahn, Lisa V. Rubenstein, David Draper et al., 'The Effects of the DRG-Based Prospective Payment System on Quality of Care for Hospitalized Medicare Patients', *Journal of the American Medical Association*, 264(15) (1990): 1953–55, quoted in Moon, *Medicare Now and in the Future*, 93–4.
126. Moon, *Medicare Now and in the Future*, 95.
127. United States Congress, Senate, Special Committee on Aging, *Medicare: Paying the Physician – History, Issues, and Options*, quoted in David Blumenthal and William Hsiao, 'Payment of Physicians Under Medicare', in Blumenthal et al., *Renewing the Promise*, 116.
128. *Health Care Financing Review*, Medicare and Medicaid Statistical Supplement: 1995, 280–81 (Table 55). During the five-year period 1979 and 1984 the increase in these expenditures had accelerated to an annual rate of 21 percent! Blumenthal and Hsiao, 'Payment of Physicians Under Medicare', 116.
129. Other factors considered in calculating the 'relative values' of various physicians' services were the physician's expenses and whether use of the particular procedure had grown at an undesirable rate. It should be underscored that the 'relative values' of each procedure are determined not by the consumers of physicians' services but by academics and bureaucrats and that these values are not subject to quick and simple change, as are market prices.
130. That is, those physicians who agree to bill Medicare directly rather than billing their patients.
131. Sally T. Burner, Daniel R. Waldo, and David R. McKusick, 'National Health Expenditures Projections Through 2030', *Health Care Financing Review*, 14(1) (Fall 1992): Table 10 (pp. 26–7). Projections of Medicare expenditures on physicians' services into the 21st century are truly mind-numbing. They are projected to reach $324.3 billion in 2010, $733.9 billion in 2020, and $1533.5 billion in 2030, in part because the first of the baby-boomer generation will have reached 65 years of age by 2015 and by 2030 will have entered their seventies and eighties. At that point it is estimated that those over the age of 65 will account for slightly more than 20 percent of the population, with those over 75 accounting for 9 percent.
132. The account which follows relies heavily on that contained in Moon, *Medicare Now and in the Future*, 107–37.
133. A sizeable proportion of these costs were associated with the increased deductible and co-insurance payments under the Medicare program in addition to increased fees for those services not covered by Medicare (nursing home care, prescription drugs, dental and vision care, and home services). It has been estimated that the average annual liability of Medicare beneficiaries, not including out-of-pocket expenses associated with the Medicare program, was $1278 in 1987. Moon, *Medicare Now and in the Future*, 108.
134. Among them, that Medicaid pay all co-insurance, deductible, and premium costs for all Medicare beneficiaries whose incomes were below federal poverty levels – which tended to be substantially higher than state Medicaid eligibility requirements – and raising the

income and asset maximums of the spouses of nursing home residents below which these residents could receive Medicaid support. Attempts by Congressman Claude Pepper to add a comprehensive home care package to the bill, however, failed.

135. Congressional Budget Office, 'The Medicare Catastrophic Coverage Act of 1988', Staff Working Paper (Washington, DC, 1 August 1988), quoted in Moon, *Medicare Now and in the Future*, 119–20.

136. Moon, *Medicare Now and in the Future*, 124.

137. The same Act authorized the Health Care Financing Administration (HCFA), which had been created in 1977 to administer Medicare, Medicaid, and Child Health Insurance, to enlarge the number of medical services that would be subject to a system of prospective payments, and provided for set rates for specific services. HCFA's name was altered in 2001 to the Centers for Medicare and Medicaid Services (CMS).

138. These data appear in the Medicare Advisory Commission's *Report to Congress, March, 2004: Medicare Payment Policy* (Washington, DC, 2004): 208 (Table 4-1).

139. United States General Accounting Office, *Medicare+Choice: Payments Exceed Cost of Fee-for-Service Benefits, Adding Billions to Spending* (Washington, DC, August 2000): 6. 'Medicare+Choice, like its predecessor managed care program, has not been successful in achieving Medicare savings. ... In 1998 we estimate that the program spent about $3.2 billion, or 13.2 percent, more on health-plan enrollees than if they had received services through traditional FFS [fee-for-service] Medicare'.

140. Congressional Budget Office, Cost Estimate of H.R. 1 and S. 1: Medicare Prescription Drug and Modernization Act of 2003 (23 July 2003): 4.

141. The chief actuary, Richard Foster, was threatened with dismissal by the Administrator of the Centers for Medicare and Medicaid Services, Thomas Scully, if he disclosed the real figure. See Amy Goldstein, 'Foster: White House Had Role in Witholding Medicare Data', *Washington Post*, 19 March 2004: p. A02.

142. Several Democratic Congressmen have already indicated their willingness to expand the drug program that, if enacted, would increase federal outlays by $1 trillion over a ten-year period. Joseph Antos and Jagadeesh Gokhale, 'Medicare Prescription Drugs: Medical Necessity Meets Fiscal Insanity', Cato Institute Briefing Paper No. 91 (9 February 2005): 3.

143. *2005 Annual Report of the Board of Trustees of the Federal Hospital Insurance and Federal Supplementary Medical Insurance Trust Funds* (Washington, DC, 23 March 2005): 28.

144. See the Medicare Payment Advisory Commission, *Report to Congress, March, 2005: Medicare Payment Policy* (Washington, DC, 2005): 5–7.

145. Financial Management Service, *Financial Report of the United States Government, 2005* (Washington, DC, 2005): 42. The current value of net future expenditures (net future expenditures less net future revenues) is the current amount of funds needed to cover the program's projected shortfalls over the next 75 years. The total reflects the current value of net future expenditures for Medicare, Part A (Federal Hospital Insurance): $8829 billion; Medicare, Part B (Supplementary Medical Insurance): $12 384 billion; and Medicare, Part D (the prescription drug benefit): $8686 billion.

146. Board of Trustees of the Federal Hospital Insurance and Federal Supplementary Insurance Trust Funds, *2005 Annual Report* (Washington, DC, March 2005): 9.

147. Federal Hospital Insurance Trust Fund, *2005 Annual Report*, 2.

148. Gordon H. Hatcher, Peter R. Hatcher, and Eleanor C. Hatcher, 'Health Services in Canada', *Comparative Health Systems: Descriptive Analyses of Fourteen National Health Systems* (University Park, Pa.: Pennsylvania State University Press, 1984): 90. While this claim reflects a startling degree of ignorance and dishonesty, the general sentiment is, alas, shared by most social planners.

Index

AAAS (American Association for the
    Advancement of Science) 27, 345
AALL (American Association for Labor
    Legislation) 446–8, 449
Abbott, Grace 39, 40
abortion, Satcher and 78
academic research, grants-in-aid for
    48–9
Academy of Managed Care Pharmacy
    232–3
Accum, Fredrick 106, 107
acetanilid, patent medicine labelling and
    138–9
aconite, nineteenth-century medical
    treatment and 109
ACT UP (AIDS Coalition to Unleash
    Power) 228
ADA (American Dental Association)
    383–4, 385, 386
ADAMHA (Alcohol, Drug Abuse, and
    Mental Health Administration)
    (formerly NIAAA/National
    Institute of Alcohol Abuse and
    Alcoholism; NIDA/National
    Institute on Drug Abuse; NIMH/
    National Institute of Mental
    Health) (later SAMHSA/
    Substance Abuse and Mental
    Health Services Administration)
    66, 416
Adams, John 1
Adams, Samuel Hopkins 125, 126, 132
Adamson, William C. 132, 344
Addiction Research Center (NIMH) 381
additives see food additives
Administration of the Law in Caring for
    the Crippled and Impaired
    Soldiers of the Late War,
    Committee to Investigate the
    273
ADRs (adverse drug reactions) see
    drugs, ADRs

adulteration see drug adulteration; food
    adulteration
advertising
    FDA and 160–61, 164, 166, 202, 222
    FTC and 162–3, 165, 166–7, 171
    see also labelling
AFL–CIO (American Federation of
    Labor and the Congress of
    Industrial Organizations) 189–90,
    456
Aging, White House Conference on 455
Agriculture and Forestry, Senate
    Committee on 126, 150–51
Agriculture Department
    Copeland's third bill and 172, 173
    corn syrup and 134
    food standards and 145–6
    insecticides and 146
    meat inspection and 127, 128–30
    medical research and 398
    sulfanilamide and 170
    Tugwell bill and 152, 153, 156
    see also Animal Industry Bureau;
        Chemistry Bureau
AHA (American Hospital Association)
    50, 350
AHRQ (Agency for Healthcare Research
    and Quality) 80
AIDS (Acquired Immune Deficiency
    Syndrome)
    FDA and 228–9
    federal government expenditure on
        441–2
    NIAID research 417, 418, 419
    NIH and 389, 416–17, 418–19,
        420–21
    PHS and 74–5, 389, 416–17
AIDS, National Commission on 417
AIMBE (American Institute for Medical
    and Biological Engineering) 422,
    423
Alaskan natives 57–8

alcohol
  abuse 310, 395
  food and drug adulteration and,
      nineteenth century 111
  labelling, Heyburn bill and 130–31
  medical treatment and, nineteenth-
      century 7, 109
  patent medicine labelling and 138–9,
      143–4
  PHS and 74, 77
  whiskey, labelling of 'blended' 134–5
  wine adulteration, nineteenth century
      106
  see also drugs; patent medicines
Aldrich, Nelson W. 130
Allen, William V. 123
almonds, nineteenth-century food
    adulteration and 106
Alsberg, Carl L. 147
Alvarez, Walter 152
AMA (American Medical Association)
  cancer research and 368
  child and maternal health and 39
  Copeland's second bill and 159
  Copeland's third bill and 164, 170
  eclectic and homeopathic
      practitioners and 4
  Eldercare and 459–60
  Flexner Report and 5
  food adulteration and 125–6, 131
  food standards and 178
  FSA reorganization and 56
  health care and, call for more
      government intervention 25
  health department proposals and 349
  health insurance and 447, 450, 452–3
  hospitals post WWII and 51
  Hygienic Laboratory and 343
  John Knowles and 66
  King-Anderson bill and 456, 457
  medical education and 5–6
  Mills bill and 455
  National Department of Public Health
      and 25
  National Sanitary Bureau and 340
  patent medicines and 138
  PHS expansion and 34
  practitioner numbers curtailed by 6–7
  Pure Food and Drugs Act and 133
  self-medication and 198

  Sheppard-Towner opposition 39
  Social Security Act amendment and
      454
  sulfanilamide and 167–8
Ambruster, Howard K. 150
American Indians 57–8
American Legion
  benefits and 280–81, 282, 283, 289,
      290
  civilian establishment and 284–6
  Commission on Organization of the
      Executive Branch investigation
      and 288
  Dawes Commission and 273
  federal government medical services
      merger and 290–91
  Hoover Commission and 293–4
  PHS reform and 33
  universal medical care for veterans
      and 276, 279
  VA hospital programs and 275
  VA medical programs and 283,
      307–8
  Veterans' Bureau founding and 33–4
aminotriazole, cranberries and 213–14
AMPAC (American Medical Political
    Action Committee) 456
amphetamines, FDA and 217–18
ANDA (Abbreviated New Drug
    Application) *see* drugs, ANDA
Anderson, Clinton P. 455, 459
Anderson, Harry B. 363
Anderson, Oscar E. 119
Andrews, John B. 446
anemia research 411,
anesthesia, nineteenth-century surgery
    and 8, 9
Angell, George Thorndike 115–16, 118
Animal Industry Bureau (Agriculture
    Department) 127, 129
annatto, nineteenth-century food
    adulteration and 106
anthrax, Hygienic Laboratory and 345
Anti-Saloon League 135
Anti-Vivisection League 344
antibiotics, off-label usage 212
antimony, nineteenth-century medical
    treatment and 108
antisepsis, nineteenth-century surgery
    and 8, 9

AOAC (Association of Official
Agricultural Chemists) 122, 123
AphA (American Pharmaceutical
Association)
Copeland's third bill and 158–9, 170
founding 104
prescription-only drugs and 194,
196
Pure Food and Drugs Act and 133
APHA (American Public Health
Association) 25, 26, 349–50, 456
'apple cider vinegar', food labelling and
145
apples *see* fruit, apples and pears
appropriations
FDA (1960–70) 214
Hygienic Laboratory (1907–36) 348
NCI (1938–71) 372
NIAID (1952–81) 390
NIH (National Institutes of Health)
61, 392, 399
PHS (1933–44) 47
see also budget; costs
Appropriations Committee, House 349
Argonne National Laboratory 369
Armour, Ogden 129
Armour, Philip 118
Armstrong, Donald B. 349
Army Medical Museum and Library
(later NLM/National Library of
Medicine) 58
ARR (Academy of Radiology Research)
422, 423
arsenic 108, 148, 172
Arteriosclerosis Task Force 409
Arthur, Chester 121
asepsis *see* antisepsis
aspirin 8, 10, 212
ASSA (American Social Science
Association) 116
Assistant Chief Medical Director for
Extended Care Office 305
Assistant Secretary for Health (formerly
Assistant Secretary for Health and
Scientific Affairs) 66
Assistant Secretary for Health and
Scientific Affairs (later Assistant
Secretary for Health) 65
Associated Grocery Manufacturers of
America 157

Association of American Medical
Colleges 5
Association of Manufacturers and
Distributors of Food Products
124–5
ATDSR (Agency for Toxic Substances
and Disease Registry) 81–2
Atomic Energy Commission 394

Babcock, Joseph W. 124
Bachmeyer, Arthur C. 50
bacteriology 7, 25, 324
Baehr, George 47
Bailey, Josiah 159, 165
Bailey, M.J. 103
Ball, L. Heisler 359, 360
Banting, Frederick 179
barbiturates 181, 217–18
Barton, Clara 344
Bates, John L. 344
Beale, Richard Lee 116
bean meal, nineteenth-century food
adulteration and 105
Behring, Emil von 7
benefits
Medicare 467, 485
state, under Medicare 463, 467
see also pensions
Benson, James 224
benzoic acid, cranberries and 138
Best, Charles 179
Beveridge, Albert J. 129, 30
Billings, John Shaw 58
biological products, sale regulation
120–21, 342, 366
biological research *see* medical research,
biological
Biological Safety Laboratory (later
Biological Standards Division)
(FDA) 56–7
Biological Standards Division (formerly
Biological Safety Laboratory)
(FDA) 57
biomedical engineering, NIH (National
Institutes of Health) and 422, 423
biomedical research
growth in 396–9
NIH 12, 366, 368, 370, 393
see also medical research
biotechnology, hospital costs and 10
see also technology

bioterrorism, FDA and 233–6
Bishop resolution 50
Bismark, Otto von 444
Black, Loring M. 157
blacks (as ethnic group) 21, 30, 411
Blain, Daniel 411, 413
Blair, Frank 153
Bliley, Tom 190
blistering, nineteenth-century medical
      treatment and 108
Bloodgood, John Colt 364
bloodletting, nineteenth-century medical
      treatment and 108, 109
Blue, Rupert 33
BNDD (Bureau of Narcotics and
      Dangerous Drugs) (Justice
      Department) 219
   see also Narcotics Bureau
Bok, Edward William 126
Boland, Patrick J. 157, 158
Bone, Homer T. 367
Bothell, George 24
Bowen, Otis 76, 472
Bowen Commission 472–3
Bradley, Omar N. 283, 284, 294
Brady, Mildred Edy 192
Brandeis, Louis D. 445
Brandt, Edward 73
bread, nineteenth-century food
      adulteration and 105
Bridges, Styles 382, 383
Brookings, Robert S. 351
Brosius, Marriott 122, 123, 125
Brown, Clarence 291
Bryan, William Jennings 34, 143
budget
   FDA 173–4, 237–8
   NCI (1972–2005) 410
   NIH (National Institutes of Health)
      (1950–75) 395
   NIMH (1950s) 413
   see also appropriations; costs
Budget Bureau
   biomedical research funding and 393
   cancer research funding and 370
   founding 346
   Hygienic Laboratory and 349
   NIH and 361–2
   PHS and 60, 62, 65, 353–4, 373
   VA and 291

Bull, Francis A. 387
Burney, Leroy E. 62
Burton, Harold H. 51
Bush, George 77
Bush, George W. 426, 476
Bush, Vannevar 49, 371, 373–4
Butler, Matthew C. 118
Byrnes, John 460
Byrns, J.W. 163

caffeine, as poisonous additive 140–41
Califano, Joseph 71
California Medical Association 452
Camalier, C. Willard 385
Campbell, Tom 229
Campbell, Walter G.
   Chemistry Bureau director (1921)
      147
   Copeland bills and 160, 163, 169,
      170
   FDA expansion efforts and 149, 150
   prescription only drugs and 177
   self-medication, on 175
cancer
   drug treatments, FDA and 203–4
   food additives and 186–9
   patent medicines and 142
   research 366–7, 371, 405–6, 407, 409
Cancer, International Union Against 187
Cancer, Panel of Consultants on the
      Conquest of 406–7
Cancer Advisory Board, National 408
Cancer Investigations Laboratory 366–7
Cancer Program, National 408
Cancer Society, American 371
Candler, Asa Griggs 140
cannabis, nineteenth-century food and
      drug adulteration and 111
Cannon, Joseph 130
carbolic acid, nineteenth-century
      antisepsis and 8
Carmona, Richard 79
Carnegie Foundation for the
      Advancement of Teaching 5, 6
Carter, Jimmy 67, 71
Catastrophic Coverage Trust Fund 474
CC (NIH Clinical Center) 417, 423
CDC (Center for Disease Control) 66, 71
CDC (Centers for Disease Control)
      (formerly MCWA) 53–4, 68, 74,
      225

CDC (Centers for Disease Control and Prevention) 80–81
Census Bureau 33, 55
Chain, Ernst 371
Chain Drug Stores, National Association of 220
CHAMPVA (Civilian Health and Medical Program of the Veterans' Administration) 307, 326
Chapman, Virgil 159–60, 164, 166, 167, 170
Charities and Corrections, National Conference on 445
Chase, Salmon P. 23
Chavez, Denis 394
cheese *see* dairy products
Chemical Foundation 37, 358–9, 361, 365
Chemical Society, American 355, 357, 360, 361
Chemistry Bureau (later Chemistry and Soils Bureau; Food, Drug and Insecticide Administration) (Agriculture Department)
  alcohol content of medicines and 144
  Babcock bill and 124
  Brosius bill and 123
  budget 146–7
  Coca-Cola case 140–41
  enforcement powers 149
  expansion under McKinley administration 122
  food additives and 137–8
  food adulteration and 121, 131
  food standards and 145–6
  glucose and 134
  insecticide residues in food and 147–8
  Johnson case 141–2
  Lexington Mill and Elevator Company case 142–3
  narcotic content of medicines and 143
  Paddock bill and
  patent medicines and 138–9
  product description and 145
  Pure Food and Drugs Act and 11–12, 133–4
  research and regulatory functions separated 146

  self-medication and 198
  whiskey and 134–5
  see also Wiley, Harvey Washington
Chemistry and Soils Bureau (formerly Chemistry Bureau) (Agriculture Department) 146
Chief Actuary of Medicare, Office of the 476
Child Health and Protection 1930, White House Conference on 39–40
Children's Bureau (in 1939 FSA; in 1950 HEW) (Labor Department) 38–40, 42–3, 366
children's health services *see* health services, children's
chiropractice, nineteenth-century 6, 21
chloral hydrate 109, 111
chloroform, nineteenth-century anesthesia and 8
Christian Science Church 344
CIA (Central Intelligence Agency) 380–81
CIT (Center for Information Technology) 424
Citizens' Advisory Committee 199
Citizens' Committee for the Reorganization of the Executive Branch 289
Citizen's Medical Reference Bureau 363
Civilian Defense Office 46, 47–8
Clark, Bennett Champ 280
Cleveland, Grover 118–19, 122, 272
Clinton, Bill
  FDA legislation signed by 190, 225
  Medicare and 77
  NIH legislation signed by 423
  saccharin warning label removed by 189
  Surgeon General vacancy and 78
  Tuskegee syphilis study apology by 30
Clinton, Hillary Rodham 77
CMHCs (Community Mental Health Centers) 414
CMR (Committee on Medical Research) (OSRD) 371, 373, 375
Coast Guard 46, 93
Coca-Cola 140–41
cocaine 7, 34, 109–10, 111
coffee 105–6, 187

Cohen, Wilbur 64, 65, 453
Colwell, A.P. 5
Commerce Committee, Senate 363, 367
Commissioned Corps
    FDA and 68
    NIH (National Institutes of Health)
        and 68
    PHS and 48, 67–8, 69, 76–7, 78–9
Commons, John R. 445–6
Communicable Disease Center
        (formerly MCWA program) 54, 65
Community Health Centers (formerly
        Neighborhood Health Centers) 72
Community Nursing Home Care 205
Compton, Karl T. 366
Congressional Black Caucus 411
Congressional Budget Office 473, 474
Consultants Committee 399–400
consumer protection 114–15, 239
Consumers' Research Organization 150,
        151, 152, 156–7, 160
control *see* regulation
Coolidge, Calvin
    Hoover compared 39
    narcotics legislation signed by 35
    NIH founding and 362, 363
    PHS expansion vetoed by 34
    Ransdell bill and 37
    Smoot-Reavis recommendations and
        347
    Tobey recommendations and 351
Cooper, Theodore 205, 409
Cooper Committee 205
Copeland, Royal
    first (Tugwell) bill and 152, 153
    NIH founding and 363
    second bill and 156, 157
    Senate Agriculture and Forestry
        Committee and 150–51
    third bill and 158, 163, 164, 165–6,
        170
Corliss, John B. 124
Corn Products Refining Company 134
corruption, MHS and 23–4
costs
    health care (1929–2003) 13–19
    hospital, Medicare (1965–81) 468
    hospital, modern biotechnology and
        10
    Medicaid 465–6, 473–4

Medicare 463–8, 472–3, 477–8
    physician reimbursement, Medicare
        470–72
    see also appropriations; budget
Costs of Medical Care, Commission on
        the 449
Covington, James 142
CPEHS (Consumer Protection and
        Environmental Health Service)
        65, 66
CPSC (Consumer Product Safety
        Commission) 217
cranberries *see* fruit, cranberries
Criminal Investigations Office (FDA)
        221
Crump, Edward Hull 162
CSR (Center for Scientific Review) 424
Cuforhedake Brane-Fude 138–9
Cullom, Shelby M. 124
Culp, Oveta *see* Hobby, Oveta Culp
Cumming, Hugh Smith
    federal grants and 39
    influenza epidemic 1928–29 and 363
    NIH dental research and 384–5
    PHS reorganization proposals and 36,
        352
    Ransdell bill and 361–2, 364
    venereal disease research funding and
        349
Cummings, Martin 59
Curtis, Thomas B. 460
Customs Service 103

dairy products, nineteenth-century food
        adulteration and 105, 106
    see also oleomargarine
Daniel, Price 217
Davis, Ewin L. 162–3
Dawes, Charles G. 273, 346
Dean, Henry Treadway 385, 386, 387
DeBakey, Michael 403, 404
Defense, Council of National 46
Defense Department 397, 394
Delaney, James T. 185, 186, 187
Delano, Frederic A. 280
Democratic National Committee 456,
        457
dental research
    NIH (National Institute of Health)
        and 385

PHS and 385
see also NIDR
dental program, VA 299–301, 302
dental treatment, PHS and 383
Dental Research Council, National
Advisory 386
Derwinski, Edward J. 309
DESI (Drug Efficacy Study
Implementation) 202
DeWitt, John L. 46
dietary supplements *see* food additives,
dietary supplements
Dietary Supplements Taskforce (FDA)
224
diethylene glycol, sulfanilamide and
167–9
digitalis, nineteenth-century medical
treatment and 7–8, 10
Dingell, John 220, 229, 451
diphtheria antitoxin 10, 120–21
disabled servicemen *see* veterans,
disabled
Disabled Veterans of America 282
Disabled Volunteer Soldiers, National
Home for 271
disease
chronic, NIH (National Institute of
Health) research 366
contagious, PHS research 28
eclecticism and 3, 4, 8, 108
germ theory 2
heart, NIH (National Institute of
Health) research 382
'heroic' therapy and 2–3
homeopathy and 3–4
infectious 28, 342
microbial cause of, Hygienic
Laboratory founding and 341
orphan, FDA and 225–7
Reich's heretical theory of 191–4
study and investigation of, PHS and
28
see also sexually transmitted diseases
Disease Prevention and Health
Promotion Office 72–3
dispensaries *see* pharmacies
Dodge, Joseph 398
Douglas, Paul 204
DRG (Division of Research Grants) 375
drug abuse 217–19, 310

Drug Abuse, White House Conference
on (1962) 218
Drug Abuse Control Bureau (FDA) 219
drug addiction, Kolb's research 35–6
drug adulteration 103–4, 111–14, 167–9,
173, 181
Drug Development, Tufts Center for the
Study of 210–11, 226, 230
Drug Evaluation Unit Program, Early
Clinical 413
Drug Manufacturers Association,
American 158, 164, 357
drug safety 170, 200–203
Drug Trade Conference, National 157
drug trade regulation 26, 219–21
druggists *see* pharmacists
drugs
ADRs (adverse drug reactions), FDA
responsibility for 232–3
ANDA (Abbreviated New Drug
Application) 202–3
cancer-treating, FDA and 203–4
control of, by FDA 174–5, 179
development times 230–31
efficacy, FDA and 211–12
Elders and 77
'ethical' 110, 158
FDA approval process 207–9,
229–30, 232
generic, new and 227–8
labelling, FDA and 176–8, 181–3,
211–13
medical devices as 205
NDAs (new drug approvals) *see*
NDAs
new 209–11, 227–8, 233
off-label usage 212–13
over-the-counter 195–6
orphan, FDA and 225, 226, 227
prescription only 176–7, 219, 234–5
prescription-only and FDA 194–6,
199, 200, 202–3
production and distribution 108, 200
recreational 110–11, 218
sale and distribution of, nineteenth-
century 11
subsidy program, Medicare 476–7
therapeutic effectiveness, FDA and
198–9
user fees 229–30, 231, 232
see also alcohol; morphine; narcotics

Dunbar, Paul B. 151, 185, 194
Dunn, Charles Wesley 153, 157, 195
Durenberger, David F. 422
Durham, Carl 194
Durovic, Marko 204
Durovic, Stevan 203, 204
Durrett, J.J. 171
Dyer, Eugene 49
Dyer, Rolla Eugene 371, 375, 376

Eastland, James 201
eclecticism 3, 4, 8, 108
Economic Opportunity Office 72
Economic Security, Committee on 449,
    450
Eddy, Bernice 56
Education and Labor, Senate Committee
    on 379
Edwards, Thomas Owen 103, 104
Egeberg, Roger 66–7
EHS (Environmental Health Service) 66
EIS (Epidemic Intelligence Service)
    59–60
Eisenhower, Dwight D.
    color additives in foods and 189
    health insurance and 453–4
    Kefauver and 199
    NIH budget and 398–9
    PHS and 56, 57
    VA and 291
Elders, Jocelin 77
electrocardiograph, first use 9
Eliot, Charles 5
Elixir Sulfanilamide *see* sulfanilamide
Emergency Medical Service 46
EMS (Eosinophilia-Myalgia Syndrome),
    L-tryptophan and 223
Energy and Commerce, House
    Committee on 220, 225
EPA (Environmental Protection Agency)
    64, 66, 69, 189
epidemiological studies 34, 59–60
Esselstyn, Caldwell 456
ether 8, 10
Evans, Samuel 167
Ewing, Oscar R. 55, 194, 378, 453
Executive Branch, Commission on
    Organization of the (Hoover
    Commission) 56, 60, 62, 286,
    291

Executive Departments, House
    Committee on Expenditures in the
    290
expenditure *see* appropriations; budget;
    costs
Experimental Biology and Medicine
    Institute (later National Institute
    of Arthritis and Metabolic
    Diseases; National Institute of
    Arthritis and Musculoskeletal and
    Skin Diseases; National Institute
    of Arthritis, Diabetes, and
    Digestive and Kidney Diseases)
    389, 394

Falk, I.S. 453
Farber, Sydney 406
Farrand, Livingston 349
Fauci, Anthony 228
FDA (Food and Drug Administration)
    (formerly FDIA) FDA (in 1939
    FSA; in 1953 HEW)
    advertising and 162, 166, 174
    AIDs and 228, 229
    aminotriazole on cranberries and
        213–14
    appropriations and personnel
        (1960–70) 214
    barbiturates and amphetamines and
        217–18
    NDAs (new drug approvals) *see*
        NDAs
    bioterrorism and 233–6
    budget 173–4, 237–8
    Commissioned Corps and 68
    consumer protection agency, as 239
    Copeland's second bill and 158–9,
        160–61, 163–4
    Copeland's third bill and 164–5,
        170–72, 173
    CPEHS and 66
    dietary supplements and 221–2, 223,
        224–5
    Dotterweich decision and 181
    drug abuse and 218–19
    drug labelling and 176–8, 181–3,
        211–13
    drug safety and 200–203
    drug trade regulation and 174–5, 179,
        219–20, 221

drug user fees and 229–30
expansion (1960s) 213
Federal Security Agency, moved to
    180
food additives and 184–6, 188–9, 190
food standards and 178–9
food substitutes and 148–9
founding 11–12, 146
hazardous household substance
    labelling and 214–15
health food advertising and 222
HEW, functions transferred to 65
insulin and 179–80
Krebiozen and 203–4
Mucorhicin and 203
off-label drug usage and 212–13
oleomargarine and 183, 184
orphan drugs and 225, 226, 227
penicillin and 180
powers, increase in 149–52
prescription-only drugs and 194–6,
    199, 200, 202–3
product safety and 216–17
public health promotion and
    protection and 236–9
publicity campaign for Tugwell bill
    154–6
reform (1997) 231–2
'refusal to file' policy 230
regulatory decisions 174
Reich's orgone boxes and 191–3
responsibilities 103
self-medication and 175–6, 180–81,
    198–9, 203
sulfanilamide and 168–70, 177
summary 82
thalidomide and 196–8
therapeutic devices and 190–91, 205,
    206–8
Tugwell bill (Copeland's first bill)
    and 152–4, 156–8
Wilhelm Reich and 191–4
see also Biological Standards
    Division
FDIA (Food, Drug and Insecticide
    Administration) (later FDA) 146,
    147
Felix, Robert 54, 55, 378, 379, 380
Ferguson, Homer 291
FIC (John E. Fogarty International

Center for Advanced Study in the
    Health Sciences) 424
Finance Committee, Senate 458, 461,
    473
Financial Management Service
    (Treasury) 477
Finch, Robert 66, 67
Finley, John H. 364
Fisher, Irving 27, 343, 344
Flemming, Arthur S. 189, 199, 21
Fletcher, Duncan V. 344
Fletcher, Robert 58
Flexner, Abraham 5
Flexner, Simon 5, 356
Flexner Report 5–6
Florey, Sir Howard 371
fluoridation, NIDR and 386–7
Fogarty, John 393, 394–5, 400, 402,
    405
Folsom, Marion 398
Food, Nutrition and Health 1969, White
    House Conference on 179
food additives
    dietary supplements 178–9, 221–2,
        223–5
    FDA and 184–6, 188–9, 190
    food adulteration and, nineteenth
        century 105–6
    food safety and 184–5, 186–8,
        189–90
food adulteration 104–8, 115–16, 125–6,
    173
food safety 184 – 8.189–90
food standards 145–6, 178–9
foods
    artificial 115–19, 148–9
    preservatives 133–4, 137–8
    purification, measures introduced in
        Congress 119–20, 124, 245–6
Foods, Pesticides and Product Safety
    Bureau (FDA) 216
Forand, Aimé J. 454, 457
Forbes, Charles R. 33, 34, 274–5, 299
Ford, Gerald 71, 206
Fountain, Lawrence H. 400
Fountain Committee 404–5
Frankel, Lee 350
fruit
    apples and pears 148
    cranberries 138, 213–14

FSA (Federal Security Agency) (later
    HEW) 45, 56, 180, 366, 453
FTC (Federal Trade Commission)
    food, drugs and cosmetics advertising
        and 163, 165, 166–7
    founding 161–2
    health food advertising and 222–3
    prescription drug advertising and 202

Galbraith, Frederick 273
GAP (Group for the Advancement of
    Psychiatry) 377–8
Gardner, John W. 404, 405
Garvan, Francis P. 358, 359, 361
Gates, Frederick T. 355
GBS (Gillian-Barer Syndrome) 71
General Accounting Office
    alcohol and drug abuse amongst
        veterans and 310
    Commissioned Corps and 76
    Medicare Advantage program and
        475
    Personal Care Home Program (VA)
        and 305
    VA hospitals and 292, 293, 296–7
germ theory of disease 2
GFWC (General Federation of Women's
    Clubs) 113–14
Giaimo, Robert 411
Glenn, John 308, 309
glucose 115, 116–17, 134
Goldwater, Barry 189, 458, 459
Gompers, Samuel 448
Gordon, H.L. 344
Government Operations Committee,
    House 400–401
Government Reform, House Committee
    on 79
Government Research, Institute for 351
Governmental Affairs, Senate Committee
    on 308–9
Grand Army of the Republic 272
Granger, Walter P. 184
grants
    NLM 59
    PHS 48
grants-in-aid
    academic research 48–9
    children's health services 38–9, 40,
        42–3

state and local health departments 40,
    41, 44
venereal disease control 29, 30, 44
Gray, Carl Raymond Jr. 289
GRECC (Geriatric Research, Education
    and Clinical Centers program) 305
Green, Frederick R. 447
Griffith, Paul H. 284
Gunn, Selskar M. 349

Hahnemann, Samuel 3–4, 108, 109
Hale, George Ellery 354
Hamilton, John B. 26, 340
Hansborough, Henry Clay 123, 125
Harding, Warren
    Budget Bureau and 346
    Forbes and 274
    PHS and 33
    Sawyer and 273
    Veterans' Bureau and 34
Harper, Robert N. 138, 139
Harris, Oren 52, 189, 201
Harrison, Benjamin (President) 127, 22
Harrison, Walter T. 46
Hart, Ronald 187
Hassall, Arthur Hill 107
Hatch, Orrin 223, 224, 225
Haugen, Gilbert Nelson 144
Hayes, Rutherford B. 271
HCMI (Homeless Chronically Mentally
    Ill) sites 311
health, diet and, FDA regulation of
    advertisements and 222–3
Health, International Conference (1946)
    55
Health, National Board of 25, 26
Health and Human Services Department
    78, 79, 228, 417, 422
Health and Welfare Activities,
    Interdepartmental Committee to
    Coordinate 450
health care
    expenditures (1929–2003) 13–19
    federal involvement in 1, 2, 12
    PHS and (1946–71) 52
    practitioner number curtailment and,
        early twentieth-century 6–7
    see also mental health; public health
Health Care Through Social Security,
    Physicians' Committee for 456

Health Council, National Advisory 366
health insurance
    AALL and 446–7, 448, 449
    AMA and 447, 452–3, 456
    Clinton administration and 77
    Forand bill and 454
    Germany 444
    Great Britain 444–5
    introduction of 12
    Kerr-Mills bill and 455
    King-Anderson bill and 455–6, 457
    military 'medicare' program and
       453–4
    Mills bill and 455
    National Council of Senior Citizens
       and 456–7
    National Health Conference 1938 and
       450–51
    New Deal era and 449–50
    Parran and 45
    private, prior to Medicare
       introduction 494
    WWI and 448–9
    see also Medicaid; Medicare
Health Maintenance Organization
    Service *see* HMOs
Health Manpower Bureau 65
Health Needs of the Nation, Commission
    on the 453
Health Resources Administration (later
    HRSA) 66, 68, 71
health services, children's 38–40, 42–3
Health Services Administration (later
    HRSA) 66, 72
Hearst, William Randolph 280
Heart Disease, Cancer, and Stroke
    Commission 402–3
Hedley, O.F. 382
Hepburn, Willam P. 124, 125, 131–2
heretical theory of disease, Reich 191–4
Herlong, A. Sydney 460
'heroic therapy' 2– 3, 108, 109
heroin 34, 143–4
Herty, Charles Holmes
    census of American chemists and 355
    Chemical Foundation and 358, 361
    drug research facility and 356, 357,
       360
    Ransdell bill and 37, 363, 364, 365
HEW (Health, Education and Welfare

Department) (formerly FSA)
    FDA functions transferred to 65
    founding 56–7
    Medicaid and 462
    narcotic drugs and marijuana and 218
    NIH (National Institutes of Health)
       and 38
    PHS functions transferred to 65
    product safety and 216
    reorganization (1968 and 1970s) 66,
       67
    water pollution control and 64
Heyburn, Weldon 130
HI (hospital insurance), Medicare and
    461, 463–4, 498
Hill, Lister
    color additives in food and 189
    Hill-Burton bill and 51
    Hill-Harris Amendments and 52
    medical research funding and 399,
       400
    NIH appropriations and 405
    NLM and 59
    political influence 394
Hines, Frank T. 276, 283, 299
HMOs (health maintenance
    organizations) 70–71, 465, 466,
    468
Hoard, William D. 124
Hobby, Oveta Culp 56, 57, 199
Hoffmann, Felix 8
Hoge, James F. 176
Hoge, Vane M. 50
Hollis, Mark D. 54
homeopathy 3–4, 108–9
Hoover, Herbert
    government-by-experts ethos 39
    NIH founding and 364
    Parker bill and 36
    public health, on 362
    Ransdell bill and 37–8
    VA budget cut recommendations 278
Hoover Commission *see* Executive
    Branch, Commission on
    Organization of the
Hopkins, Harry 450
Hospital Care Commission 50
Hospital Division (PHS) 34, 55–6
Hospital Insurance Trust Fund 477–8,
    483–4

Hospitalization Board 279
hospitals
    costs 10, 468
    Hill-Burton Construction 53
    marine 23, 55–6, 75–6
    Medicare costs and 466–70
    'narcotics' 35–6
    origins of 9–10
    PHS, closed (1981) 75–6
    PHS construction program,
        corruption and 274
    PHS expansion (1917–21) and 31, 32
    PHS undoing and 62
    post WWII 50–53
    prison 35, 36, 41
    see also MHS
HRSA (Health Resources and Services
    Administration) (formerly Health
    Resources Administration; Health
    Services Administration) 76, 82–3
HSMHA (Health Services and Mental
    Health Administration) (up to
    1968 NIMH/National Institute of
    Mental Health) 65, 66, 71, 415,
    416
Humphrey, Hubert H. 194, 395
Hundley Report 62
Hygiene and Heredity Department 111
Hygienic Laboratory of the Public
    Health Service (later National
    Institute of Health)
    anthrax and tetanus in WWI and 345
    appropriations and staff (1907–36)
        348
    cancer research and 367
    Chemical Foundation report and 37,
        359
    founding 340–43
    health department proposals and 349,
        351, 352, 353–4
    influenza pandemic 1918 and 345
    Kolb and 35
    Parker bill and 36
    psittacosis and 364
    research post WWI 347–9

ICRDB (International Cancer Research
    Data Bank) 408
IHS (Indian Health Service) 57–8, 83
Indian Affairs Bureau (Interior
    Department) 57

Industrial Hygiene and Sanitation Office
    (PHS) 70
Industrial Research, Mellon Institute for
    356
Infantile Paralysis, National Foundation
    for 56
infectious diseases *see* disease,
    infectious
Infectious Diseases, John Rockefeller
    McCormick Memorial Institute
    for 356
Infectious Diseases, Otho S.A. Sprague
    Institute for 356
influenza 33, 71, 345, 362–3
insecticides *see* pesticides
insulin, FDA and 179–80
Interior Department 25, 64, 359
Interstate and Foreign Commerce, House
    Committee on
    cancer research and 368
    heart disease research and 383
    Heyburn bill and 131–2
    mental health and 379
    Owen bill and 344
    Parker bill and 353, 362
    prescription drugs and 194
    pure food bill hearings 124
    Ransdell bill and 363, 364
Inventive Products 207
Iowa Grain Dealers' Association 134
IRS (Internal Revenue Service) 473, 474
Isbell, Harris 381
ISHB (Interdepartmenal Social Hygiene
    Board) 29, 345–6
Ivy, Andrew 203–4

Jackson, Dudley 367
Japanese-Americans 46
Javits, Jacob 408
JCMIH (Joint Commission on Mental
    Illness and Health) 411, 413–14
Jeffords, James 231
Jenkes, Virginia 157
Johnson, Lyndon
    BNDD and 219
    Commission on Heart Disease,
        Cancer and Stroke and 402–3
    health insurance and 12, 454
    Heart Disease, Cancer and Stroke
        Amendments 1965 and 404

Medical Device Safety Act 1966 and 205
Medicare and, 458, 459, 461, 463
mental health and 415
NIH appropriations and 401
Johnson, Robert L. 289
Jones, Boisfeullet 399
Justice Department 218, 219

Kallett, Arthur 151, 152, 157, 160
Kebler, Lyman 138, 139
Keefe, Frank B. 185, 393
Kefauver, Estes 199, 200, 201
Kefauver Commission 199
Kelsey, Frances Oldham 197, 198
Kennedy, Edward 224, 408, 409, 411
Kennedy, John F.
    consumer protection and 200
    cranberries and 213
    drug abuse and 218
    drug bill 201
    health insurance and 455, 457, 458
    medical devices and 205
    mental health and 413, 414
    NIH appropriations and 400, 401
Kerr, John 352, 362
Kerr, Robert 455
Kessler, David 190, 224
King, Cecil 455, 459
Kinyoun, Joseph J. 340, 341
Kitasato, Shibasaburo 7
Knapp, Joseph F. 350
Knowles, John 66
Koch, Robert 7
Kolb, Lawrence 35, 54, 378
Koop, Everett 73–4, 75, 76, 77, 79
Krebiozen, FDA and 203–4
Krebiozen Research Foundation 204
Kyros, Peter 222

L-tryptophan, EMS and 223
labelling
    alcohol, Heyburn bill and 130–31
    'blended' whiskey 134–5
    drugs 174–5, 176–8, 181–3, 211–13
    hazardous household substance, FDA
        and 214–15
    patent medicine 138–9, 143–4
    see also advertising
Labor, American Federation of 448, 449

Labor and Human Resources, Senate
    Committee on 224
Labor and Public Welfare, Senate
    Committee on 383, 406, 408
LaFollette, Robert M. 115, 368
LaGuardia, Fiorello 4
Lamb, Ruth deForest 160–61
Lambert, Alexander 447
Landers, Ann 408
Landon, Alf 166
Langmuir, Alexander 59–60
Larrick, George 195, 217–18
Lasker, Albert D. 376
Lasker, Mary
    background 376
    Commission on Heart Disease,
        Cancer and Stroke and 402,
        403
    Conquest of Cancer Act and 408
    government health programs and 379,
        382
    Heart Disease, Cancer and Stroke
        Amendments 1965 and 404
    National Cancer Act 1971 and 405,
        406
    NCI and 407
    NHLI and 409
Lea, Clarence 166, 171
lead 106, 108
Leavitt, Michael 79
legislation
    Act for the Relief of Sick and
        Disabled Seamen 1798 85
    ADAMHA Reorganization Act 1992
        416
    Adulteration of Food Act 1860 (Great
        Britain) 107
    Agricultural Appropriations Act 133
    Arrears Act 1879 271
    Biologic Control Act 1902 342, 343
    Bioterrorism Act 2002 233
    Budget Reconciliation Act 1989 470
    Chamberlain-Kahn Act 1918 345
    Child Protection Act 1966 215
    Child Protection and Toy Safety Act
        1969 215
    Comprehensive Alcohol Abuse and
        Alcoholism Prevention,
        Treatment and Rehabilitation
        Act 1970 415

Comprehensive Drug Abuse and Control Act 1970 219
Consumer Product Safety Act 1972 217
Deficiency Appropriations Act 170
Dependent Pension Act 1890
Dietary Supplement Act 1992 224
Dietary Supplement Health and Education Act 1994 225
Drug Price Competition and Patent Restoration Act 1984 (Hatch-Waxman Act) 227
Economy Act 1933 278
Federal Trade Commission Act 223
Food, Drug and Cosmetic Act 1938 149, 173, 221
Food and Drug Administration Modernization Act 1997 (FDAMA) 213, 231, 232
Food Quality Protection Act 1996 190
Harrison Narcotic Act 1914 34–5, 143, 250
Hazardous Substances Labelling Act 1960 214
Health Amendments Act 1956 413
Health Maintenance Organization Act 1973 70–71
Health Omnibus Programs Extension Act 1988 417
Hill-Burton Hospital Survey and Construction Act 1946 452
Indian Self-Determination Act 1975 58
Insecticide Act 1910 146
Meat Inspection Act 1890 127
Meat Inspection Act 1910 11
Medical Device Safety Act 1966 205
Medical Library Assistance Act 1965
Medicare Catastrophic Coverage Act 1988 472, 474, 475
Medicare Drug Act 475
Medicare Prescription Drug, Improvement and Modernization Act 2003 476
Mental Health Study Act 411
Mental Retardation and Community Mental Health Centers (CMHC) Construction Act 1963 414

National Cancer Act 1971 405, 408, 409, 411
National Cancer Institute Act 1937 368
National Cooley's Anemia Control Act 1972
National Health Insurance Act 1911 (Great Britain) 445
National Health Planning and Resources Development Act 1974 52, 468
National Heart Act 1948 55, 383
National Heart, Blood Vessel, Lung and Blood Act 1972 409, 411
National Industrial Recovery Act (NIRA) 162
National Library of Medicine Act 1956 59
National Mental Health Act 1946 54, 379
National Sickle Cell Anemia Control Act 1972 411
National Venereal Disease Control Act 1938 44
NIH Revitalization Act 1993 418, 422
Nurse Training Act 1943
Nutrition Labeling and Education Act 1990 (NLEA) 223, 224
Omnibus Budget Reconciliation Act 1981 (OBRA) 75, 76, 468, 469
Omnibus Medical Research Act 1950 389, 394
Orphan Drug Act 1983 226
Parker Act 1930 36, 41
Prescription Drug Marketing Act 1988 219, 220, 221
Prescription Drug User Fee Act 1992 (PDUFA) 229, 230, 231, 232
Public Health Reorganization Act 1944 385
Public Health Service Act 1902 28
Public Health Service Act 1944 40, 48, 373, 375, 393
Public Health Service Act 1946 (Hill-Burton Act) 51–2
Pure Food and Drugs Act 1906 25, 108, 111, 121, 133
Pure Food and Drugs Act 1910 11
Ransdell Act 1930 37–8

Ryan White AIDS Resources
    Emergency Act 1990 441–2
Servicemen's Readjustment Act 1944
    282
Sheppard-Towner Act 1921 38, 39,
    40
Social Security Act 1935 *see* Social
    Security Act 1935
Sweet Act 1921 34
Tariff Act 1842 104
Tax Equity and Fiscal Responsibility
    Act 1982 (TEFRA) 468, 469
Transfer Act 1954 57
Veterans' Health Care Expansion Act
    1973 307
Veterans Readjustment Benefits Act
    1966 305
Volstead Act 1919 144
War Risk Insurance Act 1917 272–3,
    448
World War Veterans' Act 1924 276,
    278
leprosy, PHS and 56
Lewis, John L. 273
Lincoln, Abraham 23
liquor *see* alcohol
Lister, Joseph 2, 8
Lloyd George, David 444
Long, Huey 449
Long, Russell 461
Lord, Herbert Mayhew 34, 37, 346, 353,
    354
Lorimer, William 129
Loring, George 121
Lott, Trent 423
LSD (lysergic acid diethylamide),
    experiments on prisoners 381
Lugar, Richard 190

Mack, Julian W, 272
Magnuson, Warren G. 68, 216, 367, 369,
    374
Magruder, C. Lloyd 341
Mahoney, Florence 379, 394
Maisel, Albert Q. 283
malaria, PHS and 53–4
Mann, James R. 124
Manufactures, Senate Committee on
    124
Mapes, Carl 347, 364

Mason, William E. 123–4
Massachusetts Society for the Prevention
    of Cruelty to Animals 115
Massengill, S.E. 169
Maternity and Infant Hygiene Board 38,
    39
Maverick, Maury 367, 368
May, Andrew Jackson 280
McAdoo, William G. 272
McCarren, Pat 157
McClellan, John 200
McCormack, John W. 280, 288–9
McCumber, Porter J. 124, 130
McGinnis, J. Michael 72, 73
McKellar, Kenneth D. 162
McKeown, Thomas 10
McKinley, William 122, 123
McNary, Charles 150
MCWA (Malaria Control in War Areas
    program) (later Communicable
    Disease Center) 54
meat-packaging industry
    Beveridge bill and 129–30
    Sinclair's *The Jungle* and 127–9
Medicaid
    costs 465–6, 473–4
    debate 64
    eligibility requirements 498
    funding cuts attempts 70, 468, 477
    Medicare legislation provisions for
        462–3
    Mills bill 460–61
    PHS reorganization (1970s) and 66
    users, by eligibility group (1975–97)
        482
    see also health insurance
Medical Care, Technical Committee on
    450
medical devices *see* therapeutic devices
medical education 4–6, 68
medical error, preventable deaths due to
    22
Medical Freedom, National League for
    27–8, 344
Medical Quackery, Congress on (1961)
    198, 199
medical research
    biological, PHS and 28
    grants for, first 26
    Mental Hygiene Division 35

NIH (National Institute of Health)
and 375–6, 371
see also biomedical research; cancer,
research
Medical Research, Rockefeller Institute
for 355–6
Medical Services Bureau (PHS) 63
Medical Society of the District of
Columbia 120–21
Medicare (formerly King-Anderson
bill)
1965 legislation main provisions
461–3
1988 adjustments 473–5
Advantage program 475
AMA and 459–60
benefit payments 467, 485
'cost containment' schemes and 70
costs 463–8, 472–3, 477–8
coverage extended 473–5
debate 64
disabled and 463–4
drug subsidy program 476–7
enlargement (2003) 476
funding cuts 468–70
growth rates (2000–2014), private
health insurance and national
health expenditures compared
486
hospital costs (1965–81) 468
Hospital and/or Supplementary
Medical Insurance programs,
enrollee numbers 480–81
lessons from 478
PHS reorganization (1970s) and 66
PHS undoing and 60
Mills bill and 460–61
physician reimbursement costs
470–72
PPS reforms 469–70, 471
state benefits under 463, 467
tax rates and maximum tax bases 479
veterans and 303, 306, 310
Ways and Means Committee support
for 458
see also health insurance
medicine
preventive, PHS and 73–4
primitive nature of, nineteenth
century 108

state of, turn of twentieth-century
10–11
see also patent medicines
Medicine and Surgery Department 294,
296
Medicine Manufacturers, Institute of 161
MEDLARS (Medical Literature Analysis
and Retrieval System/NLM) 59
Mège-Mouriés, Hippolyte 117
Mellon, Andrew 351, 353, 363
Menninger, William C. 377, 414
mental health
1999 report 78
Mental Hygiene Division research
35, 54
PHS reorganization and 65
see also health
Mental Health, Intra-Agency Task Force
on 414
Mental Health Council, National
Advisory 55
Mental Hospital Survey Committee 377
Mental Hygiene Division (formerly
Narcotics Division) (PHS) 35, 54,
375, 378
mercury, nineteenth-century medical
treatment and 108, 109
Messner, Clinton T. 384
Metropolitan Life Insurance Company
350–51
Metzenbaum, Howard 223
MHS (Marine Hospital Service) (later
PHS)
corruption and 23–4
founding 1–2
health department proposals and 343,
344
Hygienic Laboratory and 340, 341
name change 1902, consequences 11,
342
National Board of Health and 26
progressivism and 24
quarantine regulations and 26
reorganization (1870) 24
see also hospitals
Miles, Nelson A. 123
Military Affairs Committee, House 280
milk *see* dairy products
Miller, A.L. 185
Miller, William Jennings 182

Mills, Wilbur 455, 458, 460, 465
Mines Bureau 70
mitomycin, off-label usage 212
Moakley, John 223
Money, Hernando DeSoto 131
morphine
    Harrison Narcotic Act 1914 and 34
    medical treatment and, nineteenth-
        century 7, 10, 109
    sale regulation, nineteenth century
        110
    see also drugs; patent medicines
Moss, John E. 216
Mountin, Joseph 54
Mucorhicin, FDA and 203
Murphy, Justice 181
Murray, James E. 385, 386, 451

NACC (National Advisory Cancer
    Council) 368–9, 370
Narcotic and Drug Abuse, Advisory
    Commission on (Prettyman
    Commission) 218
narcotics
    patent medicine labelling and 143–4
    prescription drugs, as 35
    see also drugs; opium
Narcotics Bureau (Treasury Department)
    217, 218, 219
    see also BNDD
Narcotics Department 111
Narcotics Division (later Mental
    Hygiene Division) (PHS) 35
NAS (National Academy of Sciences)
    cancer research proposals and 367
    DESI 202
    glucose investigation 117
    NRC and 354
    VA nursing-care study 303
    VA outpatient care survey 297–9
NASA (National Aeronautics and Space
    Administration) 398
National Health Conference (1938) 45,
    450–51
National Health Council 36, 349
National Health Service Corps 68, 72
National Insurance Association of
    America 454
NCCAM (National Center for
    Complementary and Alternative
    Medicine) 424

NCI (National Cancer Institute)
    budget (1972–2005) 410
    founding 367
    history (1937–71) 368–71
    imaging and 422
    fiber consumption/cancer link and
        222
    Krebiozen and 204
    National Cancer Act 1971 and 408
    obligations (appropriations and
        transfers) (1938–1971) 372
    Panel of Consultants on the Conquest
        of Cancer and 407
NCMHD (National Center on Minority
    Health and Health Disparities)
    424
NCRR (National Center for Research
    Resources) 423
NDAs (new drug approvals)
    accelerated 229
    adverse drug reactions 232
    cost 210–11
    Critical Path Initiative 233
    Hatch-Waxman Act and 227
    IND (investigational new drugs)
        209–10
    processing times 207–8
    see also drugs; FDA
Neely, Matthew M. 367
NEI (National Eye Institute) 395
Neighborhood Health Centers (later
    Community Health Centers)
    72
Neill, Charles P. 129
nervous diseases *see* mental disorders
Neurological Diseases and Blindness,
    Institute of 394
New Deal *see* Roosevelt, Franklin D.
NHBLI (National Heart, Blood and
    Lung Institute) (formerly NHLI/
    National Heart and Lung
    Institute) 409–11, 412
NHGRI (National Human Genome
    Research Institute) 422
NHI (National Heart Institute) (later
    NHLI/National Heart and Lung
    Institute) 55, 382, 383,
    384, 409
NHLI (National Heart and Lung
    Institute) (formerly NHI/National

Heart Institute; later NHBLI/
National Heart, Blood and Lung
Institute) 396, 409–11
NIA (National Institute of Aging) 396
NIAAA (National Institute of Alcohol
Abuse and Alcoholism) (later
ADAMHA/Alcohol, Drug Abuse,
and Mental Health
Administration; NIDA/National
Institute on Drug Abuse) 396,
415, 416
NIADDK (National Institute of Arthritis,
Diabetes, and Digestive and
Kidney Diseases) (formerly
NIAMD/National Institute of
Arthritis and Metabolic Diseases)
(later NIDDK/National Institute of
Diabetes, and Digestive and
Kidney Disease) 422
NIAID (National Institute of Allergy and
Infectious Diseases) (formerly
NMI/National Microbiological
Institute)
AIDS research 417, 418, 419
founding 389, 395
obligations (1952–1981) 390
NIAMD (National Institute of Arthritis
and Metabolic Diseases) (formerly
Experimental Biology and
Medicine Institute) (later
NIADDK/National Institute of
Arthritis, and Digestive and
Kidney Diseases) 389, 391–2, 394
NIAMDD (National Institutes of
Arthritis, Metabolism and
Digestive Diseases) 391, 396
NIAMS (National Institute of Arthritis
and Muskuloskeletal and Skin
Disease) (formerly Experimental
Biology and Medicine Institute;
NIADDK/National Institute of
Arthritis, Diabetes, and Digestive
and Kidney Diseases) 395, 422
NIBIB (National Institute for Biomedical
Imaging and Bioengineering) 422
NICHD (National Institute of Child
Health and Human Development)
395
NIDA (National Institute on Drug
Abuse) (formerly NIAAA/
National Institute of Alcohol

Abuse and Alcoholism; later
ADAMHA/Alcohol, Drug Abuse,
and Mental Health
Administration; 1992 transferred
to NIH) 415, 416, 422
NIDCD (National Institute on Deafness
and Other Communication
Disorders) 422
NIDCR (National Institute of Dental and
Craniofacial Research) (formerly
National Dental Institute) 422
NIDDK (National Institute of Diabetes,
and Digestive and Kidney
Disease) (formerly Experimental
Biology and Medicine Institute;
NIADDK/National Institute of
Arthritis, Diabetes, and Digestive
and Kidney Diseases) 389, 391,
422
NIDR (National Institute of Dental
Research) 55, 382, 383, 384–5,
386–8
NIEHS (National Institute of
Environmental Health Sciences)
395
NIGMS (National Institute of General
Medical Sciences) 395, 422
NIH (National Institute of Health) (up to
1937 Hygienic Laboratory of the
Public Health Service; 1948
onwards National Institutes of
Health)
cancer research and 366–7, 371
dental research and 385
enlargement 374
founding 37–8, 364–5
growth 50
heart disease research 382
medical research contracts 375–6
NCI and 373
original proposals for (1926) 354,
360
OSRD and 49
Parran proposals for 365–6
penicillin and 371
PHS reorganization and 65, 66
rebuilding proposals 366
research in chronic diseases and 366
research useful to WWII and 371
NIH (National Institutes of Health) (up

to 1948 National Institute of
Health)
ADAMHA and 416
administrative weakness 400–402,
404–5
AIDS and 389, 416, 417, 418, 419,
420–21
appropriations 61, 392, 399
biomedical engineering and 422, 423
biomedical research 370, 393, 396–8,
403–5, 424–7
budget increase (1950–75) 395
cancer research 405–6, 407, 409
Commissioned Corps and 68
composition (1949) 389
composition, current 423–4
expansion 392–4, 395–6, 422
heart disease research 402–3
independence of, potential for 60
medical research funding and
399–400
NIMH and 414, 415
poliomyelitis vaccine and 56
PHS reorganization 1968–70 and 67
research authority, as 28
structural reorganization (1967) 411
summary 83–4
technology transfers and 402, 404
see also CC (NIH Clinical Center)
NIMH (National Institute of Mental
Health) (later ADAMHA/
Alcohol, Drug Abuse, and
Mental Health Administration;
HSMHA/Health Services and
Mental Health Administration)
1999 joint report 78
alcohol abuse research 395
budget increases (1950s) 413
Felix as Director 380–81
founding 55, 379–80, 389
JCMIH report and 414
NIH rift 414–15
mental illness definition 416
PHS, transfer from NIH to (1967)
411, 415
NIND (National Institute of
Neurological Diseases) (later
NINDS/National Institute of
Neurological Diseases and Stroke;
NINCDS/National Institute of

Neurological and Communicative
Disorders and Stroke) 395
NINDS (National Institute of
Neurological Diseases and Stroke)
(for a time NINCDS/National
Institute of Neurological and
Communicative Disorders and
Stroke) 396
NINR (National Institute for Nursing
Research) 422
nitrites, food additives and 142–3
nitrous oxide, nineteenth-century
anesthesia and 8
Nixon, Richard
'cost containment' schemes and 70
cranberries and 213
federal spending increases and 68–9
Food, Nutrition and Health, White
House Conference on 179
HEW reorganization and 66
Hill-Burton bill and 52
National Cancer Act 1971 and 408
NIMH and 416
sickle cell anemia research endorsed
by 411
NLM (National Library of Medicine)
(formerly Army Medical Museum
and Library) 59, 65, 423
NMHAC (National Mental Health
Advisory Council) 379
NMI (National Microbiological Institute)
(later NIAID/National Institute of
Allergy and Infectious Diseases)
389, 390
NORD (National Organization of Rare
Disorders) 226
Norton, J. Pease 27, 343
NOSH (National Institute of
Occupational Safety and Health)
70
Novello, Antonia 77
NRC (National Research Council) 190,
354–5, 357–8
NRPB (National Resources Planning
Board) 280–81
NSF (National Science Foundation) 374,
393–4, 425
Nurse Education Division (PHS) 48
nurse training 46–8, 68
nursing profession, emergence of 9

nutrients *see* dietary supplements
nutrition, nineteenth-century mortality
　　reduction and 10

OAR (Office of AIDS Research) 417
　　418–19
obesity, Koop and 74
obligations *see* appropriations
Obstetricians, Gynecologists and
　　Abdominal Surgeons, American
　　Association of 150
occupational safety and health, PHS and
　　70
oleomargarine
　　artificial foods debate and, nineteenth
　　　　century 115, 116, 117–19
　　post Food, Drug and Cosmetic Act
　　　　1938 183–4
OMB (Office of Management and
　　Budget) 73, 76
OPHS (Office of Public Health and
　　Science) 78, 84–5
opium
　　food and drug adulteration and,
　　　　nineteenth century 111
　　Harrison Narcotic Act 1914 and 34
　　medical treatment and, nineteenth
　　　　century 109
　　patent medicine labelling and 143–4
　　sale regulation, nineteenth century
　　　　109–10
　　recreational drug, as, nineteenth
　　　　century 110–11
　　see also narcotics; patent medicines
Orgone Institute 192, 193
orphan diseases *see* disease, orphan
orphan drugs *see* drugs, orphan
Orphan Products Development Office
　　(FDA) 227
OSHA (Occupational Safety and Health
　　Administration) (Labor
　　Department) 69, 70
OSRD (Office of Scientific Research
　　and Development) (later National
　　Research Foundation) 48–9, 371,
　　373, 385
osteopathy, nineteenth-century 6, 21
Owen, Robert L. 344, 345

Paddock, Algernon Sidney 120, 126

Palmer, Bissell 160
parasitology, nineteenth-century public
　　health and 25
Parker, James S. 36
Parran, Thomas
　　cancer research and 367
　　CDC and 54
　　Commissioned Corps and 48
　　Council of National Defense and 46
　　dental research and 385
　　grants-in-aid and 41, 373
　　hospitals and 50–51
　　Mental Hygiene Division and 378
　　NIH and 365, 366, 382
　　Nurse Education Division created by
　　　　48
　　PHS expansion during tenure of 44–5
　　PHS post-WWII aims set out by
　　　　49–50
　　venereal disease and 44
　　WHO and 55
　　see also PHS
Palmer, A. Mitchell 358
Palmer, Walter W. 374
Park, William H. 341
Parker, James S. 352 –3
Pasteur, Louis 2
patent medicines
　　advertising and 164
　　Copeland and 158, 159
　　FDA powers increase and 152–3
　　Harrison Narcotic Act 1914 and
　　　　143–4
　　labelling 138–9, 143–4
　　nineteenth century 110–11
　　Pure Food and Drugs Act and
　　　　138–42
　　twentieth century 125–6
　　see also alcohol; drugs; medicine;
　　　　morphine; opium
Patent Trademark Office 227
Pathology and Bacteriology Division
　　(Hygienic Laboratory) 341, 343
pears *see* fruit
Peltzman, Sam 211
Pemberton, John Styth 140
penicillin 71, 180, 371
pensions, veterans 271–2, 328–9
　　see also benefits
Pensions Bureau 271, 272, 275

pepper, nineteenth-century food
adulteration and 105
Pepper, Claude 374, 376, 379, 382
Perkins, John A. 67
Personal Care Home Program (later
Residential Care Program) 305
personnel
FDA (1960–70) 214
Hygienic Laboratory (1907–36) 348
pesticides 148, 172, 185–7, 189–90
Pharmaceutical Manufacturers
Association 157, 158, 220, 474
Pharmaceutical Research and
Manufacturers Association
209–10
pharmaceutists *see* pharmacists
pharmacies, PHS expansion (1917–21)
and 31, 32
pharmacists
adulterated drugs and, nineteenth
century 103, 104
FDA campaign against self-
medication and 180–81
licensing 236
nineteenth-century 11
patent medicines and, nineteenth
century 111
prescription only drugs and 181–2,
199
prescription refills and 194
Progressive Era 11
Philips, M.C. 160
PHS (Public Health Service) (formerly
MHS) (in 1939 FSA; in 1950
HEW)
AIDS and 389, 416–17
aims (post WWII) 49–50
American Indians and Alaskan
natives and 57
anthrax and tetanus in WWI and
345
appropriations (1933–44) 47
biological products applicable to
human disease, sale regulation
of 120, 121
Budget Bureau and 346
Census Bureau Vital Statistics
Division transferred to 55
child and maternal health and 38, 39
CMR and 373

Commissioned Corps 48, 67–8, 69,
76–7, 78–9
composition, current 79–85
constitution, WHO constitution
modeled on 55
dental research and 385
dental treatment and 383
enlargement (1919) 346
environmental health and 62–3
expansion 30–31, 32, 34, 38
fluoridation project and 386, 387
founding 1, 11, 23, 26, 28
functions 60–62, 65, 75–6, 93
grants and 48–9, 373, 374, 375
health department proposals and 343,
344, 351, 352–3, 354
health insurance and 45
heart disease research and 382
hospitals post WWII and 51
Hygienic Laboratory and 343
influence declines (1950s and 60s)
63–4
influenza epidemic 1928–29 and
362–3
influenza pandemic 1918 and 33, 345
inter-agency coordination proposals
and 347
malaria control work 53–4
marine hospitals and 55–6
medical library and 58, 59
medical research contracts and 375–6
medical research institution proposals
and 359, 360, 366
Medicare and Medicaid debate and
64
mental health and 78, 376, 377
mortality and disability reduction,
1979 report 72
narcotics and 34–5
national health program and 41–4
Neighborhood Health Centers and 72
NIMH and 415
Nurses Corps proposals 346
Parran proposals for 365–6
penicillin and 371
personal medical care and 45
preventive medicine and 73–4
prisons and 41
program cuts (Reagan administration)
75–6

public health report (1979) 72–3
reform, Harding administration 33–4
reorganization (1920s) 36–7
reorganization (1943) 48
reorganization (1960s) 98, 411
reorganization (1968–70s) 64–7
reorganization (1996) 78–9
research expenditure and 366, 367, 393
revival 72
sanitation and 41
scientific research and 34
sexually transmitted diseases and 44
state and local health department funding and 40, 41
Surgeon General's status changed 64–5
tuberculosis and 57
undoing 60, 62
venereal disease and 345, 349
veterans and 31, 33–4, 273, 383
WWI military forces, as part of 28–9
WWII and 45–8
see also Hospital Division; Hygienic Laboratory; IHS; MHS; Mental Hygiene Division; Narcotics Division; NIH (National Institute of Health); Parran, Thomas; Tuberculosis Division; Venereal Diseases Division; Veterans' Bureau; War Risk Insurance Bureau
Physician Payment Review Commission 470
physicians
drug prescription and 35
health insurance and 448
HMOs and 70
nineteenth-century 11
patent medicines and 110, 111, 126
PHS and 26–7
prescription only drugs and 194–5, 199
Progressive Era 11
reimbursement costs, Medicare and 470–72
Platt, Laurence 68
pneumonia, alcohol as treatment for, nineteenth century 109

poliomyelitis immunization, HEW and 56–7
Political and Social Science, American Academy of 158
pollution 26, 64
see also EPA
practitioners see pharmacists; physicians; surgeons
Prettyman Commission see Narcotic and Drug Abuse, Advisory Commission on
Priest, Percy 376, 379
prisoners
hospitals for 35, 36, 41
LSD experiments on 381
medical services for 35, 41
Prisoners, Medical Center for Federal 41
Prisons Bureau (Justice Department) 41
product safety, FDA and 215–17
Product Safety, National Commission on 216
Product Safety Bureau (FDA) 216
Proprietary Association 144, 156, 172, 176
proprietary medicines see patent medicines
Project Head Start 72
Protestantism, nineteenth-century food and drug adulteration and 112–13, 114
Proxmire, William 222
psittacosis, NIH founding and 363–4
PSROs (Professional Standards Review Organizations) program 466, 468
Psychiatric Association, American 377
Psychoanalytic Association, American 193
Public Citizen 188, 190, 232
public education, PHS, sexually transmitted diseases and 29, 30
public health
FDA and 236–9
federal government and 25
MHS and 26
nineteenth-century medical advances and 25
PHS and 72–3
Roosevelt (Theodore) administration and 11–12
see also health

Public Health, proposed National
    Department of 25, 33
Public Health Department 27–8
Public Health Service, Study Group on
    the Mission and Organization of
    the 62
Public Information Division (FDA) 199
Pure Food and Drug Congress 1898,
    National 122–3

quarantine
    Hygienic Laboratory founding and
        340
    MHS and 26
    National Board of Health and 25, 26
quinine, nineteenth-century medical
    treatment and 8, 10, 109

rabies immunization, nineteenth-century
    medical treatment and 10, 22
Rankin, John E. 280, 282, 283–4, 291
Ransdell, Joseph Eugene
    NIH and 37, 354, 360, 361, 364–5
    support for Owen 345
Raum, Green B. 272
Rayburn, Sam 159, 163, 280, 454
Reagan, Ronald
    AIDS and 75
    Medicare and Medicaid and 73, 468,
        470, 471–2, 473
    pharmaceutical industry and 220
    PHS and 73
    VA elevation to cabinet status and
        308, 309
Reavis, Charles Frank 347
Reece, Carroll 170
regulation
    biological products sales 120–21,
        342, 366
    dietary supplements industry, FDA
        221–2, 223–5
    drug abuse, FDA 218–19
    drug trade 26, 219–21
    drugs, by FDA 174–5, 179
    quarantine 25, 26
    venereal disease, grant-in-aid for 29,
        30, 44
    water pollution, by HEW 64
Reich, Wilhelm 191–4
Research Institute, National 202

Resources Defence Council, National
    189
Retail Druggists, National Association of
    194, 220
Retail Grocers, National Association of
    125
Retired Persons, American Association
    of 474
Reynolds, James B. 129
Ribicoff, Abraham 201, 414
Richards, Alfred N. 371
Richardson, Elliot 67
Richardson, William 344
Richmond, Julius 67, 71–2, 79
RMP (Regional Medical Program) 403,
    406
Rockefeller, John D. Jr. 356
Rockefeller, Laurence 407
Rogers, Frank Bradway 59
Rogers, Paul 67, 205, 409
Rooney, John J. 406
Roosevelt, Eleanor 155, 165
Roosevelt, Franklin Delano
    Bush report and 373
    Copeland bills and 163, 165, 173
    Council of National Defense and 46
    executive structure, on 286
    FDA expansion and 149, 150
    FTC and 162
    health insurance and 449, 450, 451
    'Health Inventory' and 41
    'Health Security' and 45
    Hoover's influence on 39
    National Cancer Institute Act 1937
        and 368
    NIH expansion and 365, 366
    OSRD founding and 371
    Reorganization Plan No.2 55
    VA hospital construction program and
        280
    veterans' benefits cuts and 278, 279
    veterans' vocational training and 281
Roosevelt, James 171
Roosevelt, Theodore
    ambitions of, federal government in
        public interest and 11
    Biologic Control Act 1902 and 121,
        342
    'Confession of Faith' speech 445
    Harper case interference 139

Health Department proposals
endorsed by 344
health insurance and 12, 446
meat-packing industry study 129
pure food and drug act and 130, 133
Sinclair's *The Jungle* and 127, 128
Rorty, James 160
Rosenwald Fund 30
Rubinow, Isaac M. 446, 447
Rusby, Henry Hurd 150
Rusk, Jeremiah 126, 127

saccharin, food safety and 188–9
safety *see* drug safety; food safety;
occupational safety and health;
product safety
sailors *see* veterans
Salk, Jonas 56
SAMHSA (Substance Abuse and Mental
Health Services Administration)
(formerly ADAMHA/Alcohol,
Drug Abuse, and Mental Health
Administration) 78, 84, 416
sanitation
food adulteration and, nineteenth
century 107, 108
mortality reduction and, nineteenth-
century 10
PHS and 28, 29, 41, 46
Satcher, David 78
Sawyer, Charles E. 273
Scheele, Leonard 55, 373, 376, 382,
386
Schereschewsky, J.W. 349
Schlink, F.J. 151, 152, 157, 158, 160
Schmidt, Benno C. 406
Schweiker, Richard 73
Science Advisory Board 366
Science and Health, American Council
on 258–9
Science in the Public Interest, Center for
188, 225, 259
Scientific Instruction Department 111
scientific research, PHS and 34
Scientific Research Division (PHS) 341,
365
self-medication, FDA and 175–6,
180–81, 198–9, 203
Senior Citizens, National Council of
456–7

septicaemia, nineteenth-century surgery
and 8, 9
sex education, PHS and 77
sexually transmitted diseases
NIAID and 389
Parran and 44
PHS and 29
syphilis 30, 71
see also disease; venereal diseases
Shalala, Donna 423
Shannon, James A. 395, 400, 402
Sherley, J. Swagar 142
Sherman, William Tecumseh 24
sickle cell anemia *see* anemia
Silvert, Michael 193
Simpson, Alan 309
Sinclair, Upton 125, 126, 127–8, 132,
449
smallpox immunization 10, 22, 29
SMI (supplementary medical insurance),
Medicare and 462, 464, 470, 499
Smith, Adolphe 128
Smith, William 186
smoking, PHS and 62, 63, 73–4, 77
see also tobacco
Smoking and Health, Advisory
Committee on 63
Smoking and Health, Joint Report of the
Study Group on 62
Smoot, Reed 36, 347
Social and Rehabilitation Service 66
Social Insurance, AALL Committee on
446
Social Insurance, AMA Committee on
447
Social Security Act 1935
health insurance and 450, 451, 454
Medicaid and 460
PHS expansion and 38
Title V 49
Title VI 40, 41, 44, 366
see also legislation
Social Security Administration 60, 66,
453
Social Security and Medicare, National
Committee to Protect 474
software, as medical devices 207
soldiers *see* veterans
Sorovich, William 155
Sowers, Zachariah T. 342

Sparkman, John 51
Spooner, John C. 341
Springer, William 216
staff *see* personnel
Staggers, Harley 216
Standards Bureau 357, 383
starch, nineteenth-century food
    adulteration and 105
State and Provincial Health Authorities
    of North America, Conference of
    351
State Services Bureau (PHS) 62, 63
Steinfeld, Jesse 67
Stelle, John 283, 284
Stevenson, Adlai 199
Stiles, Wardell 342
Stimson, Arthur M. 359
Strickland, David 399
sulfa drugs, self-medication and 181,
    182
sulfanilamide 167–70, 177
sulphonal, nineteenth-century medical
    treatment and 109
Supplementary Medical Insurance Trust
    Fund 486–7
Surgeons, American College of 296
surgery, nineteenth century 8–9
Sweet, Burton Erwin 34
Swift, Gustavus 118
'swine flu' *see* influenza
Switzer, Mary 378
syphilis *see* sexually transmitted diseases

Taft, William Howard 28, 135, 142
Tanner, James 272
Tax Foundation 289–90
taxation, Medicare and 479
Taylor, Glen H. 452
tea, nineteenth-century food adulteration
    105
technology, nineteenth-century medical
    treatment and 9
    see also biotechnology
Technology Assessment Office 210
Temin, Peter 175–6, 176–7, 195–6, 211
temperance movement, nineteenth-
    century food and drug adulteration
    and 111–12
Templeton, Clista 192–3
Terry, Luther L. 63

tetanus 120, 345
thalidomide 196–8, 201–2
therapeutic devices, FDA and 190–91,
    204–8
Thomas, Elbert D. 452
Thomas, John R. 118
Thompson, Lewis R. 354, 365, 366
Thompson, Tommy 79
Thomson, Samuel 3, 108
Thurmond, Strom 309
Thye, Edward 393
tobacco, nineteenth-century food and
    drug adulteration and 111
    see also smoking
Tobey, James Alner 349–50, 350–51,
    352, 353
Townsend, Francis E. 449
Toxicological Research, National Center
    for 187
Treadway, Walter L. 54
Treasury Department 23–4, 26, 45,
    218
Truman, Harry S.
    Bush report and 374
    health insurance and 452–3
    Hill-Burton bill and 51
    National Heart Act 1948 and 383
    National Mental Health Act 1946 and
        54, 379
    NIDR and 386
    oleomargarine and 184
    Omnibus Medical Research Act 1950
        and 394
    Parran not re-appointed Surgeon
        General by 55
    VA and 283, 289, 290
tuberculosis 7, 21, 56, 57–8
Tuberculosis, Phipps Institute for the
    Study, Treatment and Prevention
    of 356
Tuberculosis Association, National 351
Tuberculosis Division (PHS) 60
Tugwell, Rexford 149–50, 157, 160, 172
tularemia, Hygienic Laboratory research
    and 342
typhoid
    alcohol as treatment for, nineteenth
        century 109
    Hygienic Laboratory research and
        342, 343
    immunization, PHS and 29

typhus, MCWA and 54

ulcerative colitis, NIH research 395
UMA (United Medical Administration)
    288, 289, 290
undulant fever, Hygienic Laboratory
    research and 342
United Medicine Manufacturers of
    America 161
United States Soldiers' Home 271
users
    drug, fees for 229–30, 231, 232
    Medicaid, by eligibility group
        (1975–97) 482

VA (Veterans Administration) (later
        Veterans Affairs Department)
    alcohol and drug dependence and 310
    American Legion and 281, 283–4
    annual enrolment system and 312
    benefits cuts and 278–9
    dental program 299–301, 302
    expansion 284–5
    founding 275–6
    health care and 306
    homelessness and 310–311
    Hoover Commission and 286–8, 289
    hospital benefits 276–7, 305
    hospital care costs 306
    hospital care standards 296–7
    hospital program 279–80, 290,
        292–3, 326
    inpatient statistics 322–5
    medical care eligibility and 307–8
    medical expenses statistics 316–19
    medical program 282–3, 284, 292–3,
        301–3, 305
    medical research and 394
    medical schools and 294–6
    medical services 309–10
    nursing care program 303
    outpatient care and 297–9, 320–21
    resources waste and 286–8, 291–2,
        297, 301–3
    supplies and prosthetic devices and
        278
VanSlyke, Cassius J. 383
Venereal Disease Control, National
        Conference on (1936) 44
venereal diseases 29, 30, 44, 345–6, 349
    see also sexually transmitted diseases

Venereal Diseases Division (PHS) 29,
        30, 60, 345
veratrum, nineteenth-century medical
        treatment and 109
veterans
    average age of, changes in 303–5
    benefit cuts 278–9
    disabled, PHS and 31
    homelessness and 310–11
    medical and hospital care for, WWI
        272–3
    Medicare and 303, 306, 310
    numbers and average age
        (1969–2005) 313
    pensions 271–2, 328–9
    PHS and 34
    sailors, MHS medical services
        increased for 26
    vocational training 280–81
    see also MHS
Veterans Affairs Department (formerly
        VA) 308–9, 310, 311, 326
Veterans' Bureau
    corruption in 273–5
    dental services 299
    founding 12, 33, 34, 309
VHA (Veterans Health Administration)
        309, 311–12, 314–15, 326
Virts, John 466–8
VISNs (Veterans Integrated Service
        Networks) 311
Vital Statistics Bureau (in 1939 FSA; in
        1950 HEW) 366
vitamins *see* dietary supplements
Voegtlin, Carl 370

Wadsworth, James W. 129, 130
Wagner, Robert 45, 451
Wakley, Thomas 107
Walgreen, Charles 153
Walker, Robert J. 104
Wallace, Henry 163, 171, 172
War Production Board 180
War Risk Insurance Bureau 33
Ward, Michael 209
Wardell, William 208
Warren, Earl 452
Washington Legal Foundation 213
water
    fluoridation, NIDR and 386–7
    pollution 64

Water Pollution Control Administration
64
Watkins, Harold Cole 167, 169
Waxman, Henry 223, 225–6
Ways and Means Committee, House
    King-Anderson bill and 456, 457,
        460
    Medicaid and 465, 473–4
    Medicare and 458, 459, 463, 473
    Oleomargarine Tax Law and 118
WCTU (Woman's Christian Temperance
    Union)
    Heyburn bill and 131
    National Pure Food and Drug
        Congress 1898 and 123
    patent medicines and 126
    pure food and drug act and 111
    social objectives 112–13
    whiskey and 135
Wedderburn, Alexander 122
Weinberger, Casper 66, 67
Wells, Marguerite 173
Welch, William H. 352, 356
West, Olin 368
Wheeler, Burton K. 150, 166
whiskey *see* alcohol
WHO (World Health Organization) 55
Wholesale Liquor Dealers' Association,
    National 131, 134
Wilbur, Ray Lyman 449
Wiley, Harvey Washington
    ambitions 136–7
    Babcock bill and 124
    Coca-Cola and 140–41
    FDA powers and 150
    food safety and 134
    Hepburn bill and 125, 132
    Heyburn bill and 131
    Paddock bill and 120
    patent medicine labelling and 138–9
    post-1906 Act 136–8
    Pure Food and Drugs Act 1906 and
        121, 133, 135–6

    temperance movement and 112
    whiskey and 134–5
    see also Chemistry Bureau
Willard, Frances 113
Williams, Harrison 408
Williams, Louis L. Jr 54
Wilson, George 466–8
Wilson, James 128, 129, 136
Wilson, Woodrow 28, 161, 272, 358,
    448
wine *see* alcohol
Wittenmyer, Annie 112, 113
women
    Copeland's third bill and 164–5
    food and drug adulteration and,
        nineteenth century 112–14
    medical education and, nineteenth-
        century 21
    Pure Food and Drugs Act 1906
        reform and 155–6
Women Voters, National League of 38,
    173
Wood, Charles 192–3
Woodward, William C. 34
Woodworth, John Maynard 24, 25
Wooldridge, Dean E. 401
Wooldridge Report 400, 401–2
Work, Hubert 351
worker safety *see* occupational safety
    and health
Wyman, Walter 28, 38–9, 70, 341,
    344

X-rays, discovery of 9

Yarborough, Frank 406, 407, 408
yellow fever, 1879 New Orleans
    epidemic 25
Yolles, Stanley F. 415
Young, Hiram Casey 116–17

Zoology Division (Hygienic Laboratory)
    341, 342